D0847924

Corporate Governance and Initial Public Offerings

Initial Public Offerings (IPOs) are unique economic and governance events as privately held firms issue common stocks or shares to the public for the first time. The governance issues surrounding IPOs are relatively unexamined compared to more established, and usually larger, firms. As such, they provide a unique context to study corporate governance and its development around the world. Based on a collaborative international research project, this book analyses the corporate governance of IPOs in twenty-one countries, each of which is characterized by different governance environments and different levels of IPO activity. The end result is a broad and deep assessment of governance practices and IPO activity for an array of economies that represent roughly 80 percent of the global economy. These chapters collectively provide new insights into what a global theory of corporate governance might look like, and offer guidance to policy makers and academics regarding national governance configurations.

ALESSANDRO ZATTONI is Professor of Management at Parthenope University of Naples. He is also Professor of Corporate Governance at Bocconi University and Director of the Strategic and Entrepreneurial Management Department of SDA Bocconi School of Management. He is one of two screening editors for *Corporate Governance: An International Review*.

WILLIAM JUDGE is Professor of Strategic Management and the E.V. Williams Chair of Strategic Leadership at Old Dominion University (ODU). He is Editor-in-Chief of *Corporate Governance: An International Review*, the premier scholarly journal in corporate governance.

Corporate Governance and Initial Public Offerings

An International Perspective

Edited by

ALESSANDRO ZATTONI
*Parthenope University and SDA Bocconi School of Management
Milan, Italy*

and

WILLIAM JUDGE
*Old Dominion University
Norfolk, Virginia, USA*

CAMBRIDGE UNIVERSITY PRESS
Cambridge, New York, Melbourne, Madrid, Cape Town,
Singapore, São Paulo, Delhi, Mexico City

Cambridge University Press
The Edinburgh Building, Cambridge CB2 8RU, UK

Published in the United States of America by
Cambridge University Press, New York

www.cambridge.org
Information on this title: www.cambridge.org/9781107016866

First published 2012

Printed in the United Kingdom at the University Press, Cambridge

A catalogue record for this publication is available from the British Library

Library of Congress Cataloging-in-Publication Data
Corporate governance and initial public offerings : an international perspective / edited
by Alessandro Zattoni & William Judge.
    p.   cm.
ISBN 978-1-107-01686-6 (Hardback)
    1. Corporate governance.   2. Going public (Securities).   3. Corporations–Investor
relations.   I. Zattoni, Alessandro.   II. Judge, William
    HD2741.C774917 2012
    658.15′224–dc23
                                                                          2011034025

ISBN 978-1-107-01686-6 Hardback

Contents

Figures

Tables

Contributors

EMMANUEL AFOLABI ADEGBITE is a lecturer in the Accounting, Governance and Disclosure subject group at Newcastle Business School, Northumbria University. Emmanuel's research interests include comparative corporate governance systems; institutional configurations of corporate governance in varieties of capitalism; corporate governance in developing countries; corporate governance regulation; corporate social responsibility; and business ethics. He has notable publications in books and academic journals as well as numerous paper presentations at leading national and international conferences. Before joining Newcastle Business School, Emmanuel held a visiting appointment at Cass Business School, London, where he also received his PhD.

R. GREG BELL is currently serving as an assistant professor in the Graduate School of Management, University of Dallas. He received his PhD in Strategic Management from the University of Texas at Arlington, and teaches courses in international business strategy and corporate sustainability. His research has been published in the *Journal of Business Venturing, Entrepreneurship Theory & Practice* and the *Journal of Small Business Management.* He has also presented his papers at various national and international conferences.

JEAN JINGHAN CHEN currently serves as Chair in Financial Management at the University of Surrey. She obtained her PhD in Economics from Lancaster University. Her research interests include financial economics, corporate governance, corporate finance and international accounting. She has published widely in books and leading academic journals and has been a plenary session and keynote speaker on corporate governance issues at several international conferences. She is an associate editor for Emerald academic journal *Nankai Business Review International.* She also serves on the editorial board for the academic journals *Corporate Governance: An International Review* and *Accounting Research in China* (published by Chinese Accounting Society). Dr. Chen has substantial international consultancy experience for professionals, academics and public organizations, such as the British government authorities (DFID and DTI), the EU, the Chinese Ministry of Education and private companies.

IGNACIO DANVILA DEL VALLE is Professor of Human Resources Management and Business Administration and Organizational Theory at the Complutense University of Madrid, Villanueva University and European Business School. He holds a PhD in Business Administration, and a BA in economics. He was a professor in the Royal University College, El Escorial. He was Chief of Studies of Segur Ibérica's Training Department. He has published several books and different articles in specialized journals on human resources such as *The International Entrepreneurship and Management Journal, International Journal of Manpower, Contaduria y Administracion, Revista de Economica y Empresa* and *Forum Empresarial*. In addition, he has taken part in numerous international Congresses.

BENGI ERTUNA is Associate Professor of Finance at Bogazici University. She has obtained her PhD in finance from Bogazici University. Her primary research interests include initial public offerings, corporate governance and corporate social responsibility. She has published articles on initial public offerings and ownership structure in Turkey. She has received teaching awards and worked in consultancy projects and executive training programs for leading multinational corporations in Turkey.

STAV FAINSHMIDT is a PhD student in strategic management at Old Dominion University. His primary research interests are international listings, top management team and board of directors' demographic diversity, and cross-national institutional environments. Stav obtained his BA in economics and business administration from the Ariel University Center (Israel) and his MBA in finance and financial management from The College of Management (Israel). He is also an Israeli CPA. Prior to his PhD studies, Stav worked at Deloitte (ISR) as a senior auditor. His experience includes, in addition to providing auditing and tax services, participation in due diligence and IPO processes of companies in various industries.

YVES FASSIN is a part-time professor in the Faculty of Economics and Business Administration, Ghent University, and Research Fellow at Vlerick Leuven Gent Management School. He has an MSc in engineering from Ghent University and a Vlerick Masters in general management. His recently completed PhD in applied economics was awarded the 2008 Emerald/EFMD Outstanding Doctoral Research Award in the category Management and Governance. Yves combines his academic interests with an entrepreneurial career. He has been managing director of a small company since 1993, is a board member or advisor of a few other SMEs and has also actively participated in a few business start-ups. He has completed the Executive Program at Stanford Business School. He is a member of the SME Committee of the Federation of Belgian Industries. He was also a member of the 'Comité Consultatif des Actionnaires' of Suez. His research interests include corporate responsibility, business ethics, stakeholder management and corporate governance, and ethical issues in the fields of innovation and entrepreneurship. He has published about twenty international articles in among others the *Journal of Business Ethics*, *Corporate Governance: An International Review* and *Business Ethics: A European Review*.

JONAS GABRIELSSON is Associate Professor in Entrepreneurship at CIRCLE, Lund University. Prior to joining CIRCLE, he served as an associate professor at the Department of Innovation and Economic Organization, Norwegian School of Management BI. He has also previously served as a lecturer in business administration at the School of Business and Engineering, Halmstad University. He obtained his PhD from the School of Economics and Management, Lund University. His research on corporate governance has primarily been conducted from an entrepreneurial and strategic management perspective, with a particular interest in actual board behavior and how board members contribute to innovation and firm-level entrepreneurship in small, privately held firms. For this work he has received the Annual Award to Young Entrepreneurship Researchers granted by the Swedish Foundation for Small Business Research (FSF) and Swedish Agency for Economic and Regional Growth (NUTEK). His research on boards and corporate governance has appeared in journals such as *Corporate Governance: An International Review*, *Entrepreneurship and Regional Development*, *Entrepreneurship: Theory and Practice*, *International Small Business Journal*, *International Studies of*

Management and Organization and *Venture Capital: An International Journal of Entrepreneurial Finance*.

DIMITRIOS G. GEORGAKAKIS is a PhD candidate in strategic management at the University of St. Gallen. He is employed as a research assistant at the Research Institute for International Management at the University of St. Gallen. Before joining St. Gallen University he worked as a business consultant and received his MSc in management from Brunel University (UK) with distinction. His primary research interests are in the areas of corporate governance, top management team diversity, executive selection, compensation and turnover.

STEPHEN X.H. GONG is Assistant Professor of Finance in the School of Accounting and Finance of the Hong Kong Polytechnic University. His main areas of expertise are finance, corporate governance and transportation economics and his current research focusses on examining the stock market effects of media coverage, corporate disclosures, and information quality. His research has appeared in a range of books, academic journals and the business press. He is currently on the Editorial Advisory Board of *Banking and Finance Review* and has consulted for international as well as local organizations.

WILLIAM JUDGE is Professor of Strategic Management and the E.V. Williams Chair of Strategic Leadership at Old Dominion University (ODU). He obtained his MBA and PhD degrees from the University of North Carolina at Chapel Hill. Bill is Editor-in-Chief of *Corporate Governance: An International Review*, the premier scholarly journal in corporate governance. He has also served as the program coordinator for the strategic management doctoral program at ODU since 2006. He has held and currently holds various administrative duties within the Academy of Management and the Strategic Management Society. In 2010, Bill co-authored a simulation with Linda Hill on change management which was published by Harvard Business Publishing. In 2001, Bill served as a Fulbright Scholar at MGIMO University in Moscow, Russia. In the 1990s, he served as a trustee for a non-profit health services system for nine years. Dr. Judge's primary research interests are strategic leadership, organizational change and corporate governance. He has published nearly fifty peer-reviewed articles in these areas. He has earned teaching awards on five separate occasions, and has taught executives in ten different countries.

NISHA KOHLI is Associate Professor of Accounting and Finance at GD Goenka World Institute. She has over eight years of teaching experience along with working in an MNC. Prior to joining GDGWI she worked at Pearl School of Business. She has handled several consulting assignments in valuations and price determination and has also conducted a number of management development programs in finance for private- as well as public-sector undertakings. She has authored a number of papers on corporate governance. She was awarded a scholarship in the year 2008 from International Corporate Governance Network for her outstanding research in corporate governance. Her current research interests are in corporate governance, IPOs, risk management and valuations.

ABIGAIL LEVRAU currently serves as Doctor Assistant and a member of the Management Committee of GUBERNA (the Belgian Governance Institute). She is also affiliated as a research fellow to the Vlerick Leuven Ghent Management School. She is responsible for different corporate governance research projects both in the private and public sector. She holds a PhD in economics from Ghent University. Her thesis focused on the determinants of board effectiveness and it was one of the few dissertations in corporate governance at the Faculty of Economics and Business Administration at that time. She is also actively involved in board evaluations and acts as a lecturer in training programs on governance (mainly for executives and directors). Dr. Levrau's primary research interest is corporate governance, with a focus on boards of directors. She has published several articles in Belgian and international journals and is the author of several book chapters. She is a member of the Benchmarking and Information Committee of ecoDa (European Confederation of Directors' Associations) and the European Council on Corporate Governance – The Conference Board.

KRISTA LEWELLYN is a research assistant and PhD student in strategic management at Old Dominion University and is managing editor of *Corporate Governance: An International Review*. She was formerly a division manager of a Fortune 500 company. She has an MS in chemical engineering from the Institute of Paper Science and Technology and an MBA from Robert Gordon University. Her primary research interests include corporate governance, executive compensation, and the role of power in executive decision making.

FÉLIX J. LÓPEZ-ITURRIAGA is Associate Professor of Financial Economics at the University of Valladolid. He has been visiting scholar at Boston College, Johns Hopkins University and Columbia University. He has taught finance courses at the University of Exeter (UK), the Innsbruck Universität (Austria), the Université de Mons (Belgium), the Université de Rennes I (France), Skövde University (Sweden), Lüneburg Universität (Germany), Budapest Business School (Hungary) and Vilnius University (Lithuania). He has earned teaching awards on three occasions and a number of research awards from the European Investment Bank, the Spanish Centre for Financial Studies, and the Foundation for Financial Studies. He has published several books, and many papers in international journals such as *Applied Economics, Applied Financial Economics, Corporate Governance: An International Review, Emerging Markets Finance and Trade, Research Policy, International Business Review* and *Journal of Management and Governance*. His main research topics are related to auditing, corporate finance and corporate governance.

TEYE MARRA is Assistant Professor of Financial Accounting in the Faculty of Economics and Business of the University of Groningen. He obtained his PhD from Tilburg University and has been a visiting scholar at the University of Michigan Business School. He was a lecturer in the Finance Department and a member of the CentER Accounting Research Group at Tilburg University. His research interests are in the areas of empirical corporate finance, corporate governance and financial accounting.

DANIEL J. MCCARTHY is the Alan S. McKim and Richard A. D'Amore Distinguished Professor of Global Management and Innovation at Northeastern University, Boston. He is also a fellow at the Davis Center for Russian Studies at Harvard University. He obtained his DBA from Harvard University and AB and MBA degrees from Dartmouth College. Dr. McCarthy has more than 100 publications, including four editions of *Business Policy and Strategy*, as well as *Business and Management in Russia, The Russian Capitalist Experiment* and *Corporate Governance in Russia*. He is also the lead director of Clean Harbors, Inc., an NYSE-listed company, and has consulted in the US and Europe for more than forty companies. He ranks as the number one most published author (tied) in the *Journal of World Business* from 1993 to 2003, and has been ranked in the top 5 percent of all authors worldwide who published in the leading international business journals from 1996 to 2005, according to a Michigan State University study. He is also one of the top three scholars internationally in business and management in Russia and Central and Eastern Europe, based on a *Journal of International Business Studies* article analyzing publications in thirteen leading journals from 1986 to 2003.

CHIARA MOSCA is resident fellow for the Paolo Baffi Centre in Central Banking and Financial Regulation, and Assistant Professor at the Angelo Sraffa Department of Law, Università Bocconi. She teaches several courses whose main focus is corporate governance and regulation of financial markets. She joined the Department of Law after a PhD in internal and international commercial law, Università Cattolica, Milan, and an MSc in law-related topics at the London School of Economics. She has published several articles in law reviews and books, dealing with takeover regulation, board structure and financial information.

WILLIAM PACZKOWSKI is a doctoral student in management at the Lally School of Management and Technology, Rensselaer Polytechnic Institute. He earned his Juris Doctorate (JD) from Albany Law School and his MBA from Union Graduate College. Mr. Paczkowski has taught graduate and undergraduate college courses in management principles, business law and corporate taxation. His research interests are focused on the business and managerial applications of strategy and leadership in corporations and knowledge-intensive service industries. Mr. Paczkowski was a captain in the United States Army Judge Advocate General's (JAG) Corps for thirteen years.

SHEILA M. PUFFER is the Walsh Research Professor and Cherry Family Senior Fellow of International Business at Northeastern University, Boston, USA. She is also a fellow at the Davis Center for Russian Studies at Harvard University. She obtained her PhD in business administration from the University of California, Berkeley, and her BA (Slavic studies) and MBA degrees from the University of Ottawa, Canada. She also earned a degree from the executive management program at the Plekhanov Institute of the National Economy in Moscow. Dr. Puffer has more than 140 publications. She has been recognized as the number one scholar internationally in business and management in Russia, the former Soviet Union, and Eastern Europe (2005 *Journal of International Business Studies* article analyzing thirteen leading academic journals from 1986 to 2003). She also ranks as the number one most published author (tied) in the *Journal of World Business* from 1993 to 2003. She has been ranked in the top 5 percent of authors worldwide who published in the leading international business journals from 1996 to 2005 (Michigan State University study). She was also ranked among the top 100 authors who published in *Administrative Science Quarterly* from 1981 to 2001. She has served as the editor of *The Academy of Management Executive.*

MAJDI QUTTAINAH is a fourth year PhD candidate specializing in Strategic Management and Corporate Governance at the Lally School of Management and Technology, Rensselaer Polytechnic Institute. He obtained his MBA with merits from the University of Newcastle-Upon-Tyne, UK. Mr. Quttainah's primary research interest covers strategic management of distinct organizations and corporate governance, with a special focus on boards of directors and codes of governance and their effects on firms' strategies and performance.

JOSE LUIS RIVAS is Associate Professor of Management at ITAM's business school where he teaches leadership and development of managerial capabilities both at the undergraduate and graduate levels. He earned his MBA from the Kellogg School of Management and his PhD in management from Instituto de Empresa in Madrid. He served in different corporate roles at Grupo ADO in Mexico before switching to academia; lived in Chiapas and Oaxaca managing their regional businesses; co-founded their luxury bus business unit; and was Chief Quality Officer. He also served as a board member for eight years. His research interests focus on board and TMT composition and its relationship to firm internationalization. Jose has forthcoming papers in *International Business Review* and the *International Journal of Human Resource Management.* One of his dissertation papers was published in the Academy of Management Best Paper proceedings in Chicago and was runner up for best paper in *International Business Strategy*. He received a teaching award in 2010. Jose is also visiting professor at Tulane University.

WINFRIED RUIGROK is Professor of International Management and Dean of the Executive School of Management Technology and Law (ES-HSG), University of St. Gallen, Switzerland. His research focuses on corporate governance, the internationalization of top management teams and boards as well as internationalization and restructuring strategy. Prior to his professorship at the University of St. Gallen, he held positions at Warwick Business School (UK), Erasmus University/ Rotterdam School of Management (NL), the University of Amsterdam (NL) and the European Commission (B), among others.

HIDEAKI SAKAWA is Assistant Professor of Finance in the Graduate School of Economics, Nagoya City University, Japan. Prior to joining Nagoya City University, he worked as a post-doctoral fellow at the Institute of Social and Economic Research, Osaka University. His main areas of expertise are corporate governance and corporate finance, especially in respect to the empirical analysis of Japanese economy and business environment. His most recent publication, in the *Asian Economic Journal* (2008), was empirical analysis of executive compensation and corporate governance mechanisms in Japan. His two research papers received awards from Osaka Banker Association in both 2008 and 2011.

DHIRENDRA SHUKLA is an associate professor and Dr. J. Herbert Smith/ACOA Chair in Technology Management and Entrepreneurship in the Faculty of Engineering at the University of New Brunswick (Canada). He did his BEng in chemical engineering and Msc in computing and performance engineering at the University of Bradford (UK). He worked for several years in the telecom sector for Nortel Networks (Canada) in various roles and prior to joining Nortel Networks he worked for Croda International (UK). He also obtained his MBA from the Telfer School of Management at the University of Ottawa (Canada) and completed his PhD in entrepreneurial finance at the University of London, UK (King's College London). His current research interests are in venture capital, syndication, entrepreneurship, corporate finance, performance, governance, top management teams and boards of directors. He has taught entrepreneurial finance, strategy, technology management, entrepreneurship and international business.

TILL TALAULICAR is Professor of Organization and Management at the University of Erfurt. He obtained his doctoral degree and his *venia legendi* in business administration from the Technical University of Berlin and has been a visiting scholar at the Fuqua School of Business at Duke University. Moreover, he is Associate Editor of *Corporate Governance: An International Review* and a member of the Editorial Review Board of *Organization Science*. His main research and teaching expertise is in the areas of corporate governance, business ethics and organization design. He has published widely in these areas in German and international journals. His dissertation thesis on corporate codes of ethics has been granted a research award by the Plansecur Foundation for best research in the field of business ethics.

MONICA GUO-SZE TAN is Lecturer in Finance at the RMIT University in Melbourne. Prior to joining RMIT, she had taught in the field of economics at Deakin University, Australia, and undertaken a postdoctoral research fellowship at Monash University, from where she also obtained her PhD. Monica has extensive corporate experience as Client Manager in Risk and Governance at Deloitte Touche Tohmatsu, Melbourne, specializing in corporate governance, compliance and enterprise risk management. She also has professional experience in the reinsurance industry and as an industry and market analyst. Her primary research interest focuses on board of directors' composition and structure, corporate ownership structure, business networks and affiliations and fund governance. She has published in numerous journals, industry publications and conferences.

LUTGART VAN DEN BERGHE is Executive Director of GUBERNA (Belgian Governance Institute) and Extra-Ordinary Professor at the University of Ghent (B). She is also a partner of the Vlerick Leuven Gent Management School. In the school, she served for many years as Chairman of the Competence Center "Entrepreneurship, Governance and Strategy," where she founded the MBA Financial Services and Insurance as well as the Impulse Centre Business in Society. For the last two decades, her main domain of interest has been corporate governance, a field in which she has published numerous books and articles. She also has extensive governance experience gained as a member of the Belgian Commission for Corporate Governance and non-executive director in several international companies, such as SHV (NL), Electrabel (B) and Belgacom (B). At EcoDA (European Confederation of Directors' Association), she is a member of the management and chairwoman of its policy committee. Formerly she served as a non-executive director of the ING Group (NL, 1991–2003), KLM (NL, 2001–2004), Solvay (NL, 2003–2007), CSM (NL, 1998–2010), Capco NV (B, 2000–2003) and DVV (B, 1995–1997), member of the Audit Committee of the Flemish Government (B, 2000–2004) and Chairman of the Proximus Foundation (until 2005). She was also a member of the Advisory Board of Lazard (Benelux, 2007–2010). Lutgart Van den Berghe is doctor in business economics of the University of Ghent (B).

HANS VAN EES is Professor of Corporate Governance and Institutions at the Faculty of Economics and Business of the University of Groningen, the Netherlands. His research deals with corporate governance, theory of business groups, board of directors, sustainable corporate performance and building trust within and between organizations. He is screening editor of *Corporate Governance: An International Review* and vice-president of the *European Academy of management (EURAM)*. As director of the *Corporate Governance Insights Centre* of the University of Groningen, he is involved in executive teaching, training, consultancy and contract research for private companies and the Dutch government on issues related to good governance and industrial democracy.

NAOKI WATANABEL is Assistant Professor of Finance in the Faculty of Business Administration, Toyo University. Prior to joining Toyo University, he worked as research fellow at Osaka School of International Public Policy (OSIPP). His main areas of expertise are corporate governance and financial accounting, especially in respect to the empirical analysis of the Japanese economy and business environment.

HELEN WEI HU (PhD Monash University) is Lecturer of International Business at the Department of Management and Marketing, University of Melbourne, Australia. She has taught in the field of corporate governance, business ethics and business in China. Helen obtained her PhD from Monash University, Australia, where she was also an honorary research fellow from 2007 to 2009. Her primary research interests are corporate governance, with a focus on ownership structure, board process and internationalization. She has published chapters in books, and articles in leading journals and conferences. She has earned the Dean's Certificate for Excellent Teaching at the University of Melbourne, and she has also taught in universities in Singapore and China.

MICHAEL A. WITT is Professor of Asian Business and Comparative Management at INSEAD and Associate in Research at the Reischauer Institute at Harvard University. He earned his PhD at Harvard University and his AB at Stanford University. The focus of his work is on exploring variation in the cultural and institutional underpinnings of different types of capitalism, especially in the Asian and Western European context, and on the attendant implications for firm strategy and performance. Among his publications are two books, *Changing Japanese Capitalism* (Cambridge University Press) and *The Future of Chinese Capitalism* (with Gordon Redding).

SIBEL YAMAK is Professor of Management at Galatasaray University. She has a doctorate in organization theory from Bogazici University. She has been visiting scholar at many different universities such as the Panthéon Sorbonne University, Strasbourg Louis Pasteur University and Manchester University, among others. Her publications focus on business elites, top management teams, governance and corporate social performance. In 2007, she received an Emerald Literati Network award. She is a member of the editorial board of *British Journal of Management* and *Society and Business Review*. She is a co-editor of a special issue on top management teams in *International Studies of Management and Organization*.

ALESSANDRO ZATTONI is Professor of Management at Parthenope University of Naples. He is also Professor of Corporate Governance at Bocconi University and Director of the Strategic and Entrepreneurial Management Department of SDA Bocconi School of Management. He is screening editor of *Corporate Governance: An International Review* and a member of the Editorial Review Board of *Journal of*

Management & Governance. He has earned teaching awards for masters courses on three separate occasions. His primary research interest is corporate governance, with a focus on board of directors, codes of good governance, business groups, and executive compensation. He has published several books, and many articles in Italian and international journals. He has earned best paper awards from *Corporate Governance: An International Review* and *Economia & Management*.

Preface

The birth of the research project

This book results from a large, collaborative international research project aimed at exploring IPOs and corporate governance around the world. Other outputs of the project include several working papers submitted to academic conferences, and multiple peer-reviewed management publications. In this preface, we want to describe the rationale and approach behind this collaborative research as it may encourage other scholars to conduct their own collaborative research.

Our particular research project started at the end of 2008. William (Bill) Judge was interested in exploring corporate governance phenomena across a wide variety of countries that went beyond the limitations of archival data sources. He was convinced that one of the problems in doing international corporate governance research was the lack of reliable and valid data that span multiple governance environments. Following the example of the GLOBE project (House, Javidan, Hanges et al., 2002), he believed that there was an opportunity to fill this void by forming a team of corporate governance experts from a wide variety of nations.[1]

To achieve this he asked three colleagues – who were working with him in the editorial team of *Corporate Governance: An International Review* – if they were available to join him in developing and leading the research project. All three scholars enthusiastically accepted the invitation, and a group of four core team members of different

---

[1] Project GLOBE stands for "Global Leadership and Organizational Behavior Effectiveness." Nearly 150 social scientists from sixty-one nations participated in this huge project as they collaboratively sought to understand the relationship between national culture and leadership behavior throughout the global economy. Specifically, nine dimensions of national social culture and six dimensions of leadership behavior were collected for sixty countries at two time periods (House, Javidan, Hanges et al., 2002).

nationalities was established. It consisted of Bill Judge, Igor Filatotchev, Till Talaulicar, and Alessandro Zattoni.

The first Professional Development Workshop at the Academy of Management meeting

We started to design the research project in January 2009. The first objective was to develop a Professional Development Workshop (PDW) proposal to be submitted to the Academy of Management meeting to be held in Chicago in August 2009. As the deadline was fast approaching, we did our best to share ideas and to develop a common view of the project in just a few short weeks. The central idea was to build a research team in similar range and scope to Project GLOBE, while focusing on corporate governance variables and various firm- and national-level outcome variables. The original and central research question which we intended to explore was this: what is the relationship between corporate governance effectiveness and firm- and/or national-level outcomes?

Specifically, we planned to pursue three objectives with the workshop: (1) to design a data dictionary that addresses important gaps in corporate governance research; (2) to assign responsibility to national representatives for the collection of data (consistent with the data dictionary) for their particular country; and (3) to enable the project team to perform systematic international, comparative corporate governance research after the database has been assembled. We submitted the proposal to both the International Management and the Business Policy and Strategy Division hoping that it might be accepted for the annual meeting. To our great delight, the PDW proposal was accepted. The acceptance represented both an incentive for the core team to further refine and develop the project, and an opportunity to organize a meeting where we could present the project and meet potential team members.

Once we received the email of acceptance from the organizers, we invested more energy in the development of our research project. In the following months, we started to recruit national corporate governance experts using our personal networks. We wanted to both explore their interest in joining the project, and to raise awareness of the research project before the Academy of Management annual meeting. We had already included an initial listing of national representatives from fifteen countries in the PDW proposal. In the following weeks, we contacted all of them plus other well respected governance scholars in order to secure a base of trustworthy colleagues covering the main countries for GDP. Beyond taking advantage of our personal networks, we planned to find new colleagues interested in the project at the PDW session.

Till Talaulicar created a wikispace so that the four project leaders could assemble correspondence and documentation, which was quickly accumulating. We uploaded to the wikispace different files illustrating both the overall proposal for the PDW, and four individual research project proposals (including the research question, the motivation of the study, the theoretical framework, the research design, and the key references). After some discussion, we decided to merge the four individual proposals into three sub-projects: one led by Igor, one by Bill, and one jointly by Till and Alessandro. We realized later that the wikispace was probably excessive for our purposes, as we did not need all of the capabilities it provided for interaction. In any case, it was useful as it allowed us to develop the research project to present at the PDW.

Just before the Academy of Management meeting, we made some key decisions. First, we decided on the specific sample of companies to analyze. We explored a number of criteria, such as listing, size, industry, etc. In the end, we decided to investigate companies entering the public markets for the first time, since initial public offerings (IPOs) raise some important governance challenges and these same firms were of growing importance to the global economy. Furthermore, it is also a relatively less investigated phenomenon by management and governance scholars in countries outside of the United States and the United Kingdom. In order to limit the number of IPOs to collect in countries with a large number of IPOs per year, we initially decided to focus on a five-year study period, 2004–8.

Second, we had to decide which data to collect for companies in each country. In order to leverage the variety of proposals within our team, we decided to split the research project and the data collection into two parts: one part aimed at exploring the relationship between corporate governance and firm performance, and the second part aimed at analyzing the relationship between top management teams' decision-making processes and firm performance. We then decided to develop two templates for the collection of data: one for archival data related to all companies listed in the study period, and the second one for primary data collected through questionnaire surveys sent to two randomly selected firms which went public during the study period. We enriched the templates by taking advantage of the different experiences and interests we had, and we developed two templates to present at the PDW.

Finally, before the PDW at the Academy of Management, Bill Judge called David Ralston in order to get his first-hand experience of managing research projects with a number of scholars from forty-one different countries (e.g., Ralston, Egri, de la Garza-Carranza et al., 2009). David was very helpful in explaining how he structured the project, and helpfully discussed the unique challenges and some solutions to managing a multi-country research project. After the call, Bill shared with the core team a short report summarizing the insights derived from their discussion.

Two crucial points of the conversation were the selection of scholars and the structure of incentives. The selection of scholars is very important as it can have a major impact on the quality of data and the adherence to deadlines. The best option was to choose scholars we already knew and with a strong interest in the project. However, as we would not have been able to cover all countries with this particular group, we had also to invite scholars who were not known to us. In this case, we decided to choose scholars with a strong knowledge of the local language and of the corporate governance of the country, as these competences were crucial in collecting good quality data.

The incentive structure of the project is also very important as it can affect the commitment and motivation of participants. After some discussion, we decided to offer each participant who collected national data of good quality and within the deadlines co-authorship of one of the three sub-projects and guaranteed authorship of the national chapter of the edited book describing corporate governance and IPOs around the world (i.e., this book).

On August 8, 2009 we presented the research project proposal to those colleagues who registered for the PDW. The objectives of the meeting were (i) to provide an overview of the project, (ii) to sort out individual project commitments, and (iii) to establish some governance principles for managing the project itself. Before the meeting, we identified nineteen scholars with a potential interest in the project. At the meeting, we attempted to discern if these scholars were really interested in joining the project. At the same time, we were looking for scholars covering major countries not already assigned to someone else. Ten out of nineteen scholars in our initial list decided to join the project; the others declined our invitation as they either did not have a clear interest in the project or had previous commitments that conflicted with our deadlines. However, at the meeting a number of new colleagues showed a sincere interest in the project, and for a few countries we were able to choose between two or more candidates.

The issue that provoked most discussion during the meeting was the governance of the project, and particularly the incentives or the payoff for each team member. This was not surprising, as academic scholars are always involved in a number of competing activities and research projects, and they join a new project only if they are sufficiently interested in it and if the payoff is large enough. The key issues raised by participants were the workload required to complete the data collection in each country, the possibility of participating in more than one sub-project, and the opportunity to develop other articles using the dataset. All questions were pertinent and we took a few weeks to think about it. We promised to send, by the end of August, a more detailed overview of the project to all scholars who had shown an interest in the project. At the conclusion of the Academy meetings, twenty-nine scholars from as many countries committed to the project. While we knew that not everyone would deliver, we were encouraged with this level of response.

After the Professional Development Workshop

In the weeks after the PDW, Greg Bell joined the core team as Igor was forced to step down due to too many previous and competing commitments. In the meantime, the core team started to develop a Word file of one page with an overview of the project to send to all potential team members. Following the discussions at the Academy of Management meeting, we changed some aspects of the research project. In particular, we decided: (1) to focus on a shorter study period (2006–8) as we realized that we only needed to cover both "hot" (i.e., 2006) and "cold" (i.e., 2008) years, and that the workload to collect data in some countries (such as the US or the UK) could be excessive; (2) to allow team members collecting complete and reliable data by the deadlines to be eligible to author a chapter on the national governance explored, and to serve as co-authors for all scholarly articles emanating from the collaborative database; and (3) to allow any team member to propose an additional scholarly research study which should be approved by the core team, after the initial sub-projects have been submitted to journals.

In exchange for this richer payoff and reduced workload, we asked all potential team members to do their best to respect three milestones over the data collection period. First, they should communicate their formal participation in the project by September 15, 2009. Second, they should provide an Excel spreadsheet with the requisite archival data for each IPO for the country for which the team member was responsible by December 31, 2009. Third, they should complete an Excel spreadsheet with the primary data collected for two IPO firms selected for their country by February 28, 2010.

In the following months, we agreed upon the final team of scholars involved in the project, and we revised and finalized the template for data collection after a few comments and requests for clarification coming from team members. Then, all team members started to collect archival data for their specific country. In this phase, we introduced a second tool of coordination: regular Skype meetings. In particular, the core team decided to have monthly conference calls to discuss the fulfillment of milestones, the issues raised by team members, and any other relevant facts related to the project. These meetings were very effective as they pushed us to develop activities related to each sub-project, and to encourage team members to respect deadlines. They were also important as they contributed to the development of a personal relationship between the participants and a reciprocal commitment to fulfilling the project's goals. The creation of relationships of trust and friendship among the core team members and among all team members are key elements for the success of such research projects. Trust and mutual respect are crucial ingredients for stimulating commitment to the project in peers with so many conflicting activities.

In this phase of the project, we were able, with regular reminders, to maintain a high level of commitment from team members to the project. The majority of team members completed the archival data collection on time, and only a few asked for an extension of a few weeks or a month. The workload to collect archival data differed substantially across countries. For some countries, such as Switzerland and the Netherlands, the archival data collection was relatively easy as there were fewer than a dozen IPOs and the prospectuses were readily available and contained all data necessary to fill the template. For other countries, such as the UK and the US, the prospectuses were available and contained all information, but there were hundreds of IPOs and so the workload to complete the data collection was enormous. In order to reduce the workload and the weight on the global sample, we decided that the scholars collecting data in countries with more than 100 IPOs (i.e., China, India, UK, and US) were only required to collect 75 percent of the eligible IPOs. Finally, in some cases, such as Russia and Saudi Arabia, it was very difficult to find archival data as prospectuses seemed to be incomplete or difficult to find. Fortunately, these countries only had a limited number of IPOs to code. Due to these decisions, twenty governance scholars delivered on their promises (of the overall twenty-nine original members).

The second PDW at the Academy of Management meeting

Once the data collection for archival data was completed, the core group merged the data into one single dataset, and then produced some descriptive statistics. Moreover, we decided to submit a proposal for a second PDW to the Academy of Management in 2010. The objective of the second PDW was: (1) to present the preliminary empirical results of the research project; (2) to start planning the publication process of the main outputs of the project; (3) to share the lessons learned during the IPO project; and (4) to explore the launch of a new international research project building on the experience of the first year. Once again, we were successful in getting our proposal accepted.

In the meantime, all team members started to contact IPO companies in their countries to explore their availability to provide primary data on decision-making processes. This second phase of data collection seemed immediately more difficult than the previous one as many IPO companies refused to disclose private information to team members. Due to these difficulties, we decided to extend the deadline for primary data collection in order to give team members the opportunity to collect a sufficient number of IPOs. However, even after the extension of the deadline, team members experienced large difficulties in obtaining the data, and these problems were insurmountable in some countries.

The second PDW took place at the Academy of Management annual meeting in August 2010. More than thirty scholars registered for this meeting. While we were delighted with the strong turnout, we were somewhat surprised that the majority of attendees were new to the project. During the meeting, we presented an update of all sub-projects and the book, collected comments and suggestions from team members, and decided the milestones for the publication process. It was also nice to see how many governance scholars – involved or not involved in the research project – were inspired to develop a second large international project building on the team members' network. Our hope is, in fact, that this network of scholars will continue to work and to develop joint international governance projects. There will be slight differences in the composition of participants across projects as some team members may decide to step down and some new scholars may join the project; there will be different team leaders taking the responsibility for developing and managing the project; there will also be new research questions, theories, or methods. However, we believe that the network of governance scholars involved in this project represents an important resource for the future development of the discipline. We are, in fact, convinced that governance phenomena will be more widely explored at international level in projects such as this.

Overview of the book

This book consists of twenty-two chapters. The first chapter provides an overview of the book and begins to explore the notion of "national governance bundles." Then, there are twenty-one chapters presenting corporate governance in a given national setting. Each national chapter presents several topics related to corporate governance mechanisms and IPO activity in each country. The chapters are listed alphabetically by governance environment. Typical topics covered in each chapter include corporate law, code of good governance, governance of listed companies, regulation of IPOs, characteristics of IPOs in 2006–8, and an in-depth description of an IPO that occurred during the study period in the country of interest. It is our hope that governance and/or IPO scholars with a particular interest in a particular economy can benefit from this book, or scholars interested in collaborative international research will be inspired to launch a project of their own. We certainly learned a lot about the process of collaborative international research, and are pleased with the outcome of this collaboration. Like most worthwhile endeavors, it was much more work than we anticipated but it also was much more satisfying.

Acknowledgments

Before concluding, we want to thank a few people who helped us in realizing this ambitious project. First, we want to thank Till Talaulicar and Greg Bell because they shared with us the responsibility for making many decisions on the project, and took leadership of some key activities. We also want to thank Krista Lewellyn who joined our project after it began, but who provided an effective contribution in merging all of the data into a unique dataset and in developing the first set of analyses. We want to thank Igor Filatotchev for being an active and participative member of this project in its formative phase. We are sorry he was forced to leave this project due to other competing commitments, and we hope there will be an opportunity for joint research projects in the future.

Second, we want to thank all of the team members involved in the project as they provided an effective contribution to its success. We apologize if we have been over-zealous in chasing project deadlines and if we have pushed you to take a more active role for its success. It has been great working with all of you and we hope there will be opportunities for collaboration in the future.

Finally, we are grateful to Cambridge University Press for their professional contribution in publishing this book. We particularly want to thank Paula Parish because her competence and kindness pushed us to choose Cambridge as a partner in this nice adventure. In addition, we also want to take the opportunity to thank Philip Good and Sarah Roberts for their help in managing all the small issues that we encountered in writing and editing the book.

A.Z. & W.J.
Milan and Norfolk, December 2011

References

House, Robert, Javidan, Mansour, Hanges, Paul et al. 2002. Understanding cultures and implicit theories of leadership across the globe: An introduction to Project GLOBE, *Journal of World Business*, 37: 3–10.

Ralston, David A., Egri, Carolyn P., de la Garza-Carranza, Maria Teresa et al. 2009. Ethical preferences for influencing superiors: A 41-society study, *Journal of International Business Studies*, 40(6): 1022–45.

1 | *Introduction*

WILLIAM JUDGE AND ALESSANDRO
ZATTONI

This edited volume reports the results of a major international collaborative research study on corporate governance and initial public offerings (IPOs) in twenty-one countries. We wrote this book for scholars interested in comparative corporate governance, IPOs, or both fields of study. This is not the first study on comparative corporate governance, and it will not be the last one as governance policies are rising in importance due to globalization pressures and because governance practices within and across nations are in a state of continuous flux and evolution (Aguilera and Jackson, 2003). However, this book provides a relatively comprehensive, novel, and detailed perspective on these issues as the study departs from previous works with respect to both theoretical and methodological approaches.

The comparative study of IPOs is even less explored than that of corporate governance. The vast majority of studies of IPOs are conducted in the United States (e.g., Aggarwal, Krigman and Womack, 2002; Arikan and Capron, 2010; Certo, Daily and Dalton, 2001; Heeley, Matusik and Jain, 2007; Higgins and Gulati, 2006; Howton, Howton and Olson, 2001; Pollock, Porac and Wade, 2004; Wang, Winton and Yu, 2010) or the United Kingdom (e.g., Bruton, Chahine and Filatotchev, 2009; Filatotchev and Bishop, 2002). While there are some empirical studies on IPOs in multiple countries, most of them focus on only two or three variables (e.g., Boulton, Smart and Zutter, 2009; Foley and Greenwood, 2009; Lim, Morse, Mitchell et al., 2010) or are entirely descriptive in nature (e.g., Bancel and Mittoo, 2009; Brau and Fawcett, 2006; Lipman, 2009).

To our knowledge, the only previous comprehensive international perspective on corporate governance and IPOs was an edited volume produced by a diverse collection of finance scholars (Gregoriou, 2006). While it was an informative and relatively comprehensive examination of a number of financial considerations associated with

IPOs in a dozen (mostly developed) countries, it did not systematically consider the corporate governance context in which the IPO firms arose nor did it consider non-financial corporate governance mechanisms. Furthermore, it limited its perspective to the agency theoretical perspective, which has dubious relevance to nations other than the United States (Gordon and Roe, 2004; Lubatkin, Lane, Collin et al., 2005).

As such, there are a number of unique features associated with this book. First, our study extends the variety of countries considered by previous studies as it includes both developed and emerging economies, many of which have not been considered before in the literature. The new countries are both large and fast growing economies such as Russia, China, and India, and also small and relatively unique countries such as Nigeria, Saudi Arabia, and Israel. Thanks to the inclusion of these relatively unexplored countries, the book provides a more complete picture of corporate governance practices around the world. As can be seen in Table 1.1, we examine twenty-one national economies in this study and collectively they represented 73 percent of the global economic output in 2008.

Second, the study systematically explores the national characteristics of a variety of internal and external governance mechanisms utilizing country experts from each economy. This relatively broad perspective on corporate governance is pursued with the conviction that governance mechanisms are complementary and partially substitute in addressing the potential negative consequences coming from the separation of ownership and control (Aguilera, Filatotchev, Gospell et al., 2008; Rediker and Seth, 1995; Ward, Brown and Rodriguez, 2009). In other words, they are formal and informal collections or "bundles" of governance mechanisms that should be explored with a conceptually sound framework.

Third, our study systematically examines multiple IPO outcomes within a national economy. In contrast, the majority of empirical works has typically analyzed just one IPO outcome (e.g., IPO underpricing) and considered one or two corporate governance mechanisms (e.g., board composition or legal system) within a single nation or a few nations. To have a broad and deep knowledge of corporate governance phenomena at the country level, each national chapter has been written by a country expert having an intimate knowledge of the current national context, practices, and policies.

Table 1.1 *Listing of national economies examined in this comparative study*

Number	Country	2008 GDP (billions USD)	Global GDP	GDP rank
1	Australia	1,039.4	2%	14
2	Belgium	505.4	1%	20
3	Canada	1,499.1	2%	11
4	China	4,521.8	7%	3
5	Germany	3,634.5	6%	4
6	India	1,214.2	2%	12
7	Israel	202.1	<1%	41
8	Italy	2,296.6	4%	7
9	Japan	4,887.0	8%	2
10	Kingdom of Saudi Arabia	475.1	1%	23
11	Mexico	1,089.9	2%	13
12	Netherlands	872.9	1%	16
13	Nigeria	207.1	<1%	39
14	Russia	1,667.0	3%	9
15	Singapore	193.3	<1%	43
16	Spain	1,594.5	3%	10
17	Sweden	487.6	1%	22
18	Switzerland	502.5	1%	21
19	Turkey	730.3	1%	17
20	United Kingdom	2,662.7	4%	6
21	United States	14,369.1	23%	1
	Total	44,652.0	73%	

Source: World Bank (2010b)

Fourth, this book examines corporate governance and IPO activity over a three-year study period from 2006 until 2008. As can be seen from Table 1.2, our twenty-one nations collectively represented roughly 80 percent of the global marketplace, with a low of 78 percent in 2007 and a high of 81 percent in 2006. Clearly, 2008 was an unusual year in the financial markets, and the global market capitalization dropped from 66.4 trillion USD to 34.4 trillion USD due to the global financial crisis. As might be expected, IPO activity dropped considerably in 2008 as well due to high uncertainty in the financial markets (see Table 1.3). Previous research has shown that IPO

Table 1.2 *Market capitalization for economies in this comparative study (billions USD)*

Country	2006	%	2007	%	2008	%
Australia	1,095.5	2%	1,298.1	2%	675.6	2%
Belgium	396.3	1%	386.6	1%	167.8	0%
Canada	3,608.2	7%	2,185.9	3%	1,002.9	3%
China	1,141.8	2%	6,205.5	9%	2,785.5	8%
Germany	1,640.2	3%	2,110.7	3%	1,101.3	3%
India	819.2	2%	1,819.6	3%	645.9	2%
Israel	173.3	0%	236.9	<1%	134.4	0%
Italy	1,026.7	2%	1,072.9	2%	521.3	2%
Japan	4,835.0	9%	4,823.2	7%	3,220.5	9%
Kingdom of Saudi Arabia	327.0	1%	515.0	1%	246.6	1%
Mexico	348.7	1%	397.9	1%	232.1	1%
Netherlands	779.4	1%	956.5	1%	387.6	1%
Nigeria	32.8	0%	86.3	<1%	49.7	0%
Russia	1,057.3	2%	1,502.5	2%	396.7	1%
Singapore	276.4	1%	353.5	1%	180.0	1%
Spain	1,323.7	2%	1,799.6	3%	945.5	3%
Sweden	573.1	1%	612.4	1%	252.6	1%
Switzerland	1,212.4	2%	1,274.6	2%	866.2	3%
Turkey	162.5	0%	286.7	0%	117.8	0%
United Kingdom	3,793.3	7%	3,859.9	6%	1,853.2	5%
United States	19,430.8	36%	20,024.0	30%	11,739.6	34%
Total 21 countries	44,053.4	81%	51,807.7	78%	36,980.0	80%
Global economy	54,448.2	100%	66,389.7	100%	34,356.3	100%

Source: World Bank (2010a)

dynamics are different in "cold" and in "hot" markets (Gulati and Higgins, 2003; Wang, Winton and Yu, 2010). Our study covers a three-year period including 2006 representing a "hot" market, 2007 a "lukewarm" market, and 2008 a "cold" market. In sum, our study considers three different market conditions for examining governance dynamics.

Finally, this book focuses on small-, medium-, and large-sized IPO firms using both archival and primary data. Most comparative corporate governance and IPO research only considers large, publicly held firms using archival data. Initial public offerings provide a unique

Table 1.3 *IPO activity across twenty-one economies in this comparative study**

Country	2006	2007	2008	3 year total	Average age (yrs)	Average size (employees)
Australia	2	1	46	49	9	46
Belgium	7	6	1	14	10	160
Canada	4	31	10	45	6	353
China	17	24	6	47	5	11,108
Germany	22	19	2	43	20	1,695
India	39	47	30	116	15	937
Israel	37	56	1	94	8	414
Italy	17	25	4	46	36	1,037
Japan	176	116	42	334	22	593
Kingdom of Saudi Arabia	14	15	12	41	19	1,267
Mexico	3	4	2	9	25	2,207
Netherlands	10	5	1	16	16	2,872
Nigeria	4	4	5	13	15	807
Russia	12	12	2	26	11	17,522
Singapore	0	30	22	52	10	888
Spain	10	11	2	23	24	1,600
Sweden	28	31	6	65	12	267
Switzerland	6	8	2	16	10	1,089
Turkey	9	7	0	16	15	2,131
United Kingdom	141	91	11	243	3	439
United States	109	100	19	228	8	1,720
Total 21 economies	667	643	226	1,536	13	1,460

Source: EurIPO (2006, 2007, 2008)
* For some countries characterized by an intense IPO activity (e.g., India, Japan, UK, and USA), our study collected and analyzed data on a sample made by about 75 percent of the total IPOs in the period.

context to study corporate governance as they are privately held firms that entered a publicly traded stock market for the first time (Certo, Holcomb and Holmes, 2009). IPOs have to adopt governance systems that meet their specific needs to collect funds from the financial community, and to balance the interests of both inside and outside shareholders. This "genesis" of corporate governance from private to public companies is rarely explored.

In sum, the main objective of this introductory chapter is to present the theoretical framework and the main results of the empirical study that aimed to explore corporate governance mechanisms at national and cross-national levels. In particular, we start with an overview of the inter-disciplinary field of corporate governance. Next, we discuss the initial public offering event by way of background for the remainder of the book. In addition, we discuss how internal and external corporate governance mechanisms act and interact to influence the IPO event. Finally, we conclude with our cluster analysis of the twenty-one economies along prominent corporate governance mechanisms in order to begin to think about how national economies are similar and different as they seek to reconcile the many economic and social interests associated with the initial public offering event.

Overview of the field of corporate governance

Corporations possess enormous economic power, and with that economic power comes political power. Corporate governance is concerned with how that power is directed – for the welfare of society or for the welfare of a few individuals, corporations, or an industry to the exclusion of others. In essence corporate governance addresses both efficiency and economic equity issues. From a relatively narrow view, corporate governance focuses on the design of board of directors and/or a protection of ownership rights in order to guarantee the shareholder value maximization, or to assure investors a return on their investments (Shleifer and Vishny, 1997). From a broader perspective, it encompasses the whole set of legal, cultural, and institutional mechanisms that determine who controls companies, how that control is exercised, and how risk and returns are allocated (Blair, 1995). In this book, we take a relatively broad perspective on the role, function, and impact of corporate governance on initial public offerings.

Regardless of the breadth of perspective, corporate governance plays a key role in all companies (e.g., industrial and financial, small and large, listed and unlisted, profit and non-profit) as in any company the misappropriation of corporate funds and low value creation are relevant issues (Monks and Minow, 2004). However, it is of particular importance in listed companies as the separation between ownership and control both serve to emphasize the risk of misappropriation and of an incompetent decision-making process (Berle and Means, 1932).

The first issue (i.e., the potential abuse of managers at the expense of shareholders) is considered the most important governance problem. This risk is particularly relevant when there is a dispersion of share capital among a large number of small investors. The dispersion of shareholdings favors, in fact, the separation between ownership and control, i.e., shareholders tend to delegate decision-making rights to top managers. Moreover, the small fraction of voting and cash flow rights shareholders own can reduce incentives to exercise an effective monitoring of top managers' behavior. In sum, when ownership is dispersed, managers are able to make decisions that can ignore the rights of minority shareholders (Berle and Means, 1932; Jensen and Meckling, 1976).

The value creation process is particularly important as companies can fail or produce lower results due to poor managerial decision making. Managerial greed and opportunism may lead to the misappropriation of corporate resources. Negative firm consequences may also result from managerial incompetence (Hendry, 2005). For example, an incompetent top management team may make a disastrous acquisition or a number of small business decisions leading the company to a slow decline (Charkham, 2005). Governance mechanisms should address these issues by selecting talented managers, monitoring managers' decisions, providing them with proper incentives, and firing incompetent executives.

The most common theoretical approach to analyze and provide solutions to corporate governance issues is agency theory. According to this view, the relationship between shareholders and top managers in a widely held company – or one with controlling and minority shareholders in a company with concentrated ownership – represents an agency relationship (Jensen and Meckling, 1976). In an agency relationship, the principal delegates the agent to fulfill some activities in his interest, but he loses control of the final performance that is based on the unobservable effects of the agent and on chance. The asymmetry of information among subjects, and the uncertainty in the task, allow the agent to deviate from the principal's expected outcome, and give rise to agency costs. These costs include the monitoring costs of the agent's behavior, the costs of reassurance of the principal, and any other loss of wealth originated in the relationship (Jensen and Meckling, 1976).

Recent formulations of agency theory consider conflicts that arise from multiple agents (e.g., Arthurs, Hoskisson, Busenitz et al., 2008) and multiple principals (e.g., Young, Peng, Ahlstrom et al., 2008). Classical corporate governance mechanisms that stem from the agency perspective are monitoring of agents through such practices or mechanisms as independent boards, dominant shareholders, and the market for corporate control, as well as incentive alignment mechanisms that offer ownership stakes to the agents as well as legal mechanisms which punish opportunistic behavior (Denis and McConnell, 2003).

More recently, other theoretical perspectives are emerging to challenge the agency theoretic perspective in describing and explaining the antecedents and effects of corporate governance. For example, the institutional perspective argues that corporations seek legitimacy above shareholder value creation, and it points to the role of institutions in guiding and constraining the misuse of corporate power (Scott, 2001; Suchman, 1995). Stewardship theory argues that managers are, in general, all trying to be good stewards of the resources for which they have been entrusted, in direct contrast with the behavioral assumptions underlying agency theory (Davis, Schoorman and Donaldson, 1997). And resource dependency theory argues that social actors and social systems are simply trying to avoid being controlled by others and seeking to gain control over resources that guarantee the future survival of the firm (Hillman and Dalziel, 2003).

In sum, the field of comparative corporate governance is in considerable flux currently, particularly as the depth and breadth of economies are considered. In this study, we collect and analyze data from multiple theoretical perspectives in order to provide the broadest review of corporation governance dynamics surrounding IPO firms throughout the world.

Overview of the initial public offering event

Changing from a private to a public firm is a major milestone in the life of a company. The first step in going public typically involves drafting the registration statement to be filed with the securities regulator for the country in which the firm aspires to be listed. Drafting a registration statement is a group activity combining the efforts of the company's executives, the underwriters, the outside counsels, and the auditors. In some countries, a preliminary prospectus is prepared for distribution to potential investors. This prospectus includes all relevant information about the offering except the initial price of the stock and the number of shares to be offered. Filing a registration statement with the regulatory authority typically triggers a "quiet period," in which the members of the firm are not permitted to grant interviews or otherwise promote the company in any way.

The company is permitted, however, to conduct "road shows" around the country, in which the underwriters and top management team meet with prospective investors, analysts, and potential members of the underwriting syndicate. The corporation is usually prohibited in these meetings from presenting information not included in the prospectus, but it may clarify issues raised in the prospectus and respond to audience questions (Pollock, Porac and Wade, 2004).

During this registration period, the underwriter must determine the offering price of the stock. The underwriter first contacts prospective investors and determines the number of shares these investors are willing to purchase at various price levels. The underwriter then uses this information to assess how the market initially values the company and to identify potential investors for the public offering. Once the regulatory authority is satisfied that all relevant information about the company has been presented in a clear and accurate way, the company is permitted to file a final pricing amendment that includes the stock's price, the number of shares to be sold, the underwriter's commission, and the effective date on which the company has a right to offer its stock to the public. Representatives of the company sign the underwriting agreement with its investment bank and then set the offering price. The company's stock is offered to the public shortly after the IPO goes effective (Pollock, Porac and Wade, 2004).

After the firm goes public, there typically is a "lockup period" in which the members of the top management team are prevented from selling their shares in the firm. In the United States, this lockup period is often 180 days. In other countries, the lockup period is quite different or non-existent. If the market is "efficient," the market price of the stock will balance supply of shares with the demand for shares at a market clearing stock price. However, much is unknown about privately held firms, so this can lead to market inefficiencies. For example, in a review of the IPO literature in the United States, most IPOs are underpriced after the first day of the offering and most IPOs' stock underperforms their industry peers during their first year of being public (Brau and Fawcett, 2006; Ritter, 1991).

Depending on the national governance environment, the corporate structure of the corporation often changes just before or just after the firm goes public. Importantly, the shares of the firm often become less concentrated, though this dilution of share ownership varies considerably from country to country. For example, in a study of 2,700 firms in thirty-four countries, Foley and Greenwood (2009) showed that IPOs in countries with relatively strong investor protections are more likely to experience significant decreases in shareholder concentration than IPOs in countries with relatively weak investor protections.

Typically, the proceeds from the public offering are used to reward investors who gambled on the firm while it was privately held, as well as invest in the business to grow it more aggressively. For example, many IPOs often make acquisitions of other companies with this additional capital (Arikan and Capron, 2010). Alternatively, some IPO firms venture overseas for the first time (Lim, Morse, Mitchell et al., 2010). Still other IPO firms embark on aggressive development of an expensive technology, such as biotechnology firms (Higgins and Gulati, 2006).

Corporate governance of IPOs throughout the world

Ultimately, the global economy needs a global theory of corporate governance that can adequately describe and explain the antecedents and effects of corporate governance throughout the world. This is an ambitious task, since business practices in general, and corporate governance practices in particular, vary so much throughout the world. For example, financial accounting standards are converging slowly toward a common set of standards, but there remain important differences in structure and practice (Judge, Li and Pinsker, 2010). While some have argued that the global economy needs to converge towards the Anglo-American system of governance, increasing numbers of policy-makers and practitioners are pioneering new models (Gordon and Roe, 2004). To simplify our task somewhat, we begin with a discussion of the primary corporate governance mechanisms that confront firms which enter the public financial markets for the first time.

While there is no comprehensive typology of corporate governance mechanisms, the field generally distinguishes between two types: internal and external mechanisms. Internal corporate governance mechanisms primarily focus on governance levers that operate within the firm's boundaries. External corporate governance mechanisms focus on governance levers that primarily operate outside of the firm. Recent literature has begun to recognize that these mechanisms substitute and complement each other, but the ways in which they interact is still unclear (Aguilera et al., 2005; Rediker and Seth, 1995; Ward, Brown and Rodriguez, 2009).

Internal corporate governance mechanisms

In this international study, we considered five internal corporate governance mechanisms. The five mechanisms are: (1) board composition, (2) CEO duality, (3) executive compensation, (4) shareholder dispersion, and (5) dominant shareholder type. In the following paragraphs, we will describe and explain each of these mechanisms.

Board composition

This mechanism arises from agency theory, and it assumes that by assembling a board of directors that is sufficiently independent of top management, the board will monitor management adequately and protect the shareholders' and/or society's interests. The primary prescription explored for this mechanism is to make sure that the board is composed of a majority of outside, or non-executive, directors. While the empirical results behind this prescription are equivocal at best (Dalton, Daily, Ellstrand et al., 1998), boards throughout the world are often dominated by non-executive directors and it is generally seen as a global best practice by the OECD (2004) and the Cadbury Committee (1992).

Corporate law and governance codes are encouraging boards to increase the number of non-executive independent directors, in the conviction that they may play an invaluable role in the accountability process. There are at least two good reasons why the primary focus of governance reforms has been placed on independent directors. First, almost all the other potential sources of accountability (such as the market for corporate control or the courts) come into play only after allegations of management misconduct have been made, while independent directors may act in a preventative capacity to avoid bad or illegal decisions being made in the first instance. Second, independent directors, by keeping informed and ensuring that the disclosure process is functioning properly, may guarantee the efficiency of other governance mechanisms based on public information (Zattoni and Cuomo, 2010).

Directors' independence is seen primarily as a necessary prerequisite for unbiased board oversight of management (e.g., Judge and Zeithaml, 1992). Independent directors play an important role also as members of the nomination, audit, and remuneration committees. However, independence may have a second effect that is also relevant in the accountability process. Independence implies the ability of non-executive directors to see things differently (e.g., Roberts, McNulty and Stiles, 2005). Non-executive directors should bring to the board their past experience which, together with their distance from the day-to-day running of the company, allows them to offer different perspectives from executives on strategic decisions (Roberts, McNulty and Stiles, 2005). The interplay of a variety of skills and perspectives amongst different board members increases the likelihood of creative and innovative solutions to problems and improves the quality of the strategic decision process (Roberts, McNulty and Stiles, 2005).

CEO *duality*

Perhaps the second most common prescription that emanates from agency theory is that the roles of the CEO and board chairperson must be separated. When they are separate, the board is said to operate with a "dual" leadership structure. When they are not separate, the board is said to operate with a "unitary" structure. From an agency perspective, dual leadership structures are always preferred. However, from a resource dependency perspective, unitary leadership structures might be more optimal (Hillman and Dalziel, 2003).

Boards in the United States have predominantly unitary leadership structures with the reasoning that unity of command permits faster and more unified strategic behavior. However, in other Anglo-American governance environments, such as in the United Kingdom or in Australia, dual boards are required or highly recommended (Judge, Gaur and Muller-Kahle, 2010). As a result, there has been a trend toward designating a "lead director" amongst the outside directors within boards where there are unitary leadership structures so that the board has a mechanism to deal with concerns associated with the CEO and his or her strategic direction chosen (Penbera, 2009).

Executive compensation

Past studies have brought to light the dissimilarities in the pay packages of managers in Anglo-Saxon countries as compared to other nations. In the United Kingdom and the United States, remuneration encompasses a variety of components, and short- and long-term variable pay carries more weight than elsewhere. In other countries, however, fixed wages have always been the main ingredient in top managers' pay schemes. Over time, variable short-term pay has become more substantial, and the impact of fringe benefits has gradually grown. Notwithstanding, incentives linked to reaching medium- to long-term company goals have never been widely used outside the United States and the United Kingdom (Zattoni and Minichilli, 2009).

In recent years, however, pay packages of managers have undergone an appreciable change as variable pay has increased considerably, even outside Anglo-Saxon countries. In particular, managers in most countries have experienced an increase in the variable pay related to long-term goals. Within the context of this general trend toward medium- and long-term incentives, there is a pronounced tendency to adopt plans involving stocks or stock options (Towers Perrin, 2000 and 2005). Particularly important triggers of the convergence towards the US pay paradigm are both market-oriented drivers such as the evolving share ownership patterns or the internationalization of the labor market, and law-oriented drivers such as corporate or tax regulation. Driven by these changes in the institutional and market environment, we observe a global trend toward the "Americanization of international pay practices," characterized by high incentives and very lucrative compensation mechanisms (Cheffins and Thomas, 2004).

Ironically, the spread of the US pay paradigm around the world happens when it is hotly debated at home. In particular, the critics concern both the level of executive compensation packages, and the use of equity incentive plans (Cheffins and Thomas, 2004). Critics stressed that US top managers, and particularly the CEOs, receive very lucrative compensation packages. The 1980s and 1990s saw an increasing disparity between CEOs' pay and that of rank-and-file workers. Thanks to this effect, their direct compensation has become a hundred times that of an average employee. The main determinants of the increasing level of CEOs' and executives' compensation are annual bonuses and, above all, stock option grants. Stock option plans have recently been criticized by scholars and public opinion because their characteristics are too generous and symptomatic of a managerial extraction of the firm's value (Bebchuk and Fried, 2006).

Shareholder concentration

This is a key internal governance mechanism as small shareholders have little incentive to monitor management. A shareholder owning a significant fraction of the share capital has, instead, both an incentive to monitor managers, and the possibility to take actions in case of underperformance. The large shareholders can, in fact, elect their own representatives in the board of directors, and vote in annual assembly meetings to influence the final decision. As shareholders influence corporate decision making mostly through their votes, shareholders can discipline top managers more easily in countries with higher investors' rights (Hart, 1995).

The presence of a large investor does not completely solve or resolve agency problems. For instance, a large shareholder may not adequately fulfill the monitoring activity as he or she receives only a fraction of all benefits that are proportional to his or her fraction of cash-flow rights. Moreover, a dominant shareholder may use his or her voting power to influence decisions in his or her interests, or even become the chief executive to further private benefits. Finally, if the large shareholder is an industrial or financial company, there is a second agency level to consider as managers of these companies can deviate from their shareholders' interests (Hart, 1995).

Dominant shareholder type

Disclosure of details associated with details on the dominant shareholder(s) for a particular corporation differs considerably across governance environments. In some countries, typically the Anglo-Saxon ones, the shareholder structure is widely dispersed and there are typically no dominant shareholders. In these countries, the shareholding is traditionally fragmented among a number of households, but more recently there has been an increase in the incidence of institutional investors becoming large blockholders of listed companies. The institutional investors have been traditionally passive investors, as they penalized underperforming companies by selling their shares (i.e., the "Wall Street walk"). Since the 1990s, they have become much more active shareholders as their indexing strategies (buy the index) and the increasing amount of shares owned in each company reduced the possibility to use the exit option. As a result, they have started to more actively monitor companies' decisions and governance structures. The activism takes different forms including voting in assembly meetings, engaging with company management, and public blacklisting of companies underperforming (Charkham, 2005). Large institutional investors are today influential watchdogs of corporate managers. However, it is not clear how much the mutual fund managers are accountable to the people on whose behalf they invest.

In other countries, banks and other companies are typically large shareholders of industrial companies. In Germany and Japan, there has historically been a strict relationship between banks and industrial companies due to the development of the main bank model. Main banks (in Germany called Hausbanks) were involved in the governance of industrial companies as they played multiple roles as shareholders, lenders, and advisors. This multiple involvement can produce large benefits in terms of managing the convergence of conflicting interests, but it may also generate tensions and conflicts among stakeholders. More recently, however, the internationalization process of the banking system directed the attention of bank managers towards the expansion in their industry. Consequently, in the last decades, the influence of banks on industrial companies has largely diminished (Charkham, 2005).

Despite the recent privatization process, which has led to a diminished role of the state in a number of countries, the government is still an important shareholder in many countries. This is in some way surprising as state-owned companies are characterized by high managerial discretion and non-profit maximization due to the high separation between ownership and control. On the one hand, the ultimate owners are citizens who hold much dispersed cash-flow rights, and for this reason have low incentives to monitor top managers. On the other hand, the control is exercised directly by top managers, and indirectly by political parties without cash-flow rights. Both subjects do not have cash-flow rights in the company, and are free to pursue goals that diverge from the maximization of firm performance. Accordingly, most empirical studies find state involvement is negatively related to firm profitability (Gugler, 2001).

In general, the most common dominant shareholders of large companies are wealthy families or individuals (La Porta, Lopez-de-Silanes and Shleifer, 1999). Families or individuals maintain the control of large groups thanks to the use of some legal devices aimed at separating control rights – i.e., voting rights – from cash-flow rights – i.e., residual income rights. The most common mechanisms used to this purpose are: (1) pyramidal groups, (2) dual class shares, and (3) syndicate agreements (La Porta, Lopez-de-Silanes and Shleifer 1999). Family firms are typically managed by family members or by professional managers without equity ownership. In any case, whoever manages the firm is accountable to large shareholders and not to minority shareholders. In family firms there is a tension between controlling and minority shareholders as the first ones are ideal monitors of management, but at the same time they have the power – and sometimes also the interest – to expropriate minority shareholders.

External corporate governance mechanisms

External governance mechanisms are levers working at the industry, societal, and/or market level that operate outside of the firm's boundaries. They include such mechanisms as (1) legal system, (2) market for corporate control, (3) business groups, and (4) social norms.

Legal system

La Porta and associates (1997, 1998) emphasize the role of laws and legal enforcement in the governance of companies, the development of the financial markets, and overall economic growth. They reason and provide empirical support for the notion that a firm's ability to raise external capital and grow is limited by the extent to which control can be effectively separated from ownership without increasing the risk that investors are expropriated by management. In essence, better legal protection for investors reduces the risk of expropriation, allows more separation between ownership and control, and increases growth. La Porta et al. (1998, 1999) also predict that companies in countries with lower investor protection and civil law are characterized by greater ownership concentration than companies in countries with common law and higher investor protection. The essential insight underlying the law and finance approach is that, in an unregulated environment, there is a real danger that insiders (i.e., controlling shareholders or senior executives) will cheat outside investors.

By comparing legal rules across forty-nine countries, La Porta et al. (1997) showed that legal rules from different legal traditions differ significantly. With respect to protection against expropriation by insiders, common law countries protect both shareholders and creditors the most, and French civil law countries the least. German and Scandinavian civil law countries are somewhere in the middle of these two extremes.

La Porta, Lopez-de-Silanes and Shleifer (1999) show also that legal origin and investor protection affect ownership concentration and the financial markets. In common law countries the legal system regulates quite closely opportunistic conduct by insiders and in this sort of protective environment minority shareholders feel comfortable. Such confidence means that investors are willing to pay full value for shares available for sale, which in turn lowers the cost of capital for firms that choose to sell equity in financial markets. Moreover, most controlling shareholders will be content to unwind their holdings since the law will largely preclude them from exploiting their position. The conditions therefore are well suited for a widely dispersed pattern of share ownership (Cheffins, 2003).

In civil law countries where the legal system offers little protection against cheating by insiders, potential investors, fearing exploitation, will shy away from buying shares. Insiders will decide not to sell equity to the public and will opt instead to retain the private benefit of control and to rely on different sources of finance, even if they have to forego pursuing potentially profitable opportunities in doing so. In these countries dispersed ownership structure will therefore not become dominant (Cheffins, 2003).

Market for corporate control

This external governance mechanism relies on market forces to govern corporate behavior and discipline underperforming managers. In order to be effective, the market for corporate control needs that some prerequisites are satisfied. First, it is important that the financial market is efficient, i.e., the value of shares should reflect the future perspectives of the company. To reach this purpose, it is necessary that the firm information flow allows external stakeholders – and particularly minority shareholders – to correctly appreciate the company's value. Second, the firm control should be contestable, i.e., the shareholding should be widely held and no shareholder should own the majority or a large fraction of a company's shares. These two characteristics are not so common in a number of countries, even if there is a trend in this direction (Charkham, 2005).

Different financial tactics may be used to change the control of a company. The most common tactics are proxy fights, friendly takeovers, or hostile takeovers. With proxy fights, a dissident shareholder – unsatisfied by company performance – proposes a list of candidates to stand against management's candidates, and tries to persuade other shareholders to vote for its list. Proxy fights are not a common method to reallocate a company's control for several reasons. First, they involve a significant free-rider problem as the dissident shareholder bears all costs of both analyzing companies' performance, and launching a proxy fight. In contrast, the dissident can only gain a small fraction (i.e., equal to his fraction of cash-flow rights) of the benefits of improved management in the form of a higher share price. Second, minority shareholders typically do not vote since their vote is unlikely to make a difference for the final decision, and when they vote they tend to support incumbent managers. Finally, national company law can allow managers to use companies' funds to promote their self-interest (Hart, 1995).

Takeovers consist in the launch of an offer to buy all or a large fraction of shares of the target company. They are friendly or hostile depending if there is an agreement or not between the bidder and incumbent managers. Takeovers are also not very common. On the one hand, they are much more powerful mechanisms than proxy fights as they allow an investor identifying an underperforming company to gain a large reward from his action. With the launch of a public offer the raider can, in fact, obtain a fraction of benefits from improved management equal to his shareholding after the takeover. On the other hand, they are very expensive and generally seen as too radical a mechanism for disciplining managers. Moreover, in order to gain the control of the target company, the corporate raider will have to overcome several obstacles. First, minority shareholders can think their decision cannot affect the success of the bid or may prefer to gain a small fraction of the benefits coming from the change of control. Second, the raider may face some competition from other bidders that think the company is undervalued, or that the managers invite and favor in order to avoid the hostile takeover (white squire). In any case, the benefit in the form of capital gains may not be realized because of competitive dynamics. Finally, as in the case of proxy fights, the bidder may face strong opposition from incumbent managers. This opposition may take various forms such as restructuring plans to increase shareholders' value or the use of anti-takeover provisions such as super-majority amendments, staggered boards, or poison pills (Hart, 1995).

In sum, the market for corporate control is an external mechanism of governance that disciplines top managers. Changes of control are a rare event as the dissident shareholder or the bidder will need to overcome many obstacles that may limit both the probability of success and the gain from the operation. However, the effectiveness of the market for corporate control as a mechanism to safeguard minority shareholders' interests should not be minimized as its simple existence and the menace of its intervention can be enough to discipline managers.

Business groups

A business group is a collection of legally independent firms that are linked together through multiple ties, which can include cross-ownership, strict market exchanges, and social relationships (such as those among influential actors, such as owners or managers). Group-affiliated firms are coordinated through these ties in order to achieve common goals. This definition captures two particular features of business groups – the presence of multiple ties holding group firms together and the existence of coordinated actions enabled by those ties (Khanna and Rivkin, 2001).

These two features differentiate business groups from other organizational forms, such as independent firms or strategic networks, in several ways (Zattoni, Pedersen and Kumar, 2009). First, group-affiliated firms are bound together by various overlapping ties, such as cross-ownership, interlocking directorates, market transactions, intercompany loans, and social relationships. The social and organizational relationships among actors (such as shareholders and managers) that tie member firms together do not exist among independent firms. Second, a core entity (e.g., the founding owner, a financial institution, or a state-owned enterprise) inside business groups usually offers administrative control or managerial coordination to affiliated firms. Strategic networks do not have a core entity coordinating the operations of member firms.

Business groups are far from uniform across countries. The labels used to define business groups differ. For example, Japanese groups are called "keiretsu," Latin American groups are known as "grupos economicos," and South Korean groups are called "chaebols" (Granovetter, 1994). Furthermore, the characteristics of business groups differ across countries. Business groups vary along many dimensions, such as the types of ties among affiliated firms (i.e., cross-shareholdings, personal relationships, market exchanges), and in terms of the intensity of coordination inside the group. Due to these differences, the definitions and characteristics of business groups are highly contingent on the institutional contexts in which they operate.

Theoretical contributions and empirical evidence suggest that group-affiliated firms may show superior performance in emerging economies. The rationale is that labor and product markets are characterized by larger imperfections, and that the internalization of market transactions may lead to superior performance. Some recent research highlights the possibility that the group effect may decrease over time as markets become more efficient (Zattoni, Pedersen and Kumar, 2009).

Social norms

Social norms are rooted in the national culture, i.e., the complex set of meanings, symbols, and assumptions about what is good or bad and legitimate or illegitimate in a country (Hofstede, 1985; Licht, Goldschmidt and Schwartz, 2005). A national culture affects corporate governance practices in a more informal way than legal systems, the market for corporate control, or through business groups. However, some argue that this informal influence may be the most powerful means by which corporations are governed in certain countries, such as Scandinavia (Minichilli, Zattoni, Nielsen et al., 2011).

There is growing evidence that social culture may affect corporate governance of companies. The culture of a country determines whether the welfare of shareholders is the focus of governance mechanisms as in the Anglo-Saxon model, or if other stakeholders (mainly employees and suppliers) take an important role as in the German model (Charkham, 2005). Moreover, there is evidence of the existence of a large national variation in the social norms about trust and cooperation of the average individual (Dore, 2005).

One social norm that has considerable influence on the governance practices within a nation is the degree to which corruption is considered an acceptable practice. Corruption is defined as the abuse of public power to the unfair benefit of certain individuals, firms, or industries in the private sector. Clearly, when corruption is frowned upon within a society by its social culture, corporations function more efficiently and equitably. However, when corruption becomes the norm within a social culture, corporate governance is degraded (Judge, McNatt and Xu, 2011). In essence, the degree to which corruption is considered "normal" is a reflection of the trust that operates within a society as a whole.

Another social norm that has considerable influence on the governance practices within a nation is the extent to which institutional collectivism operates. Project GLOBE conceptualizes institutional collectivism as the degree to which the group's or organization's goals are emphasized at the expense of individual goals (House, Hanges, Javidan et al., 2004). Institutional collectivism has been shown to influence leadership practices, organizational culture, and other important social phenomena. Overall, social norms such as corruption perceptions and institutional collectivism interact to influence many informal governance norms such as information disclosure, stakeholder versus stockholder primacy, and voluntary versus mandatory corporate governance codes.

Internal and external corporate governance bundles for IPOs in twenty-one economies

Table 1.4 contains the typical state of the international corporate governance mechanisms for the twenty-one economies in this study. Clearly, there are some interesting similarities and differences across the economies considered. For example, most economies now require that publicly held firms be composed of boards that contain a majority of outside, non-executive, and independent directors. However, there are some notable exceptions to this general rule, such as China, India, Japan, and Mexico. As such, this suggests that other mechanisms are operating to assure that corporations are operating properly in these nations.

Table 1.4 *Internal corporate governance mechanisms for IPOs in twenty-one economies*

Country	Typical board composition	CEO duality norms	Executive compensation	Shareholder dispersion	Dominant shareholding type
Australia	Mostly outsiders	Dual	10x–25x	Dispersed	Institutional
Belgium	Mostly outsiders	Dual	10x–25x	Concentrated	Family
Canada	Mostly outsiders	Unitary	>25x	Dispersed	Institutional
China	Mostly insiders	Dual	<10x	Concentrated	State
Germany	Only outsiders	Dual	10x–25x	Concentrated	Family and business groups
India	Mostly insiders	Dual	>25x	Concentrated	Family
Israel	Mostly outsiders	Unitary	10x–25x	Concentrated	Family
Italy	Mostly outsiders	Dual	10x–25x	Concentrated	Family
Japan	Mostly insiders	Dual	<10x	Concentrated	Family and business groups
Kingdom of Saudi Arabia	Mostly outsiders	Dual and unitary	>25x	Concentrated	Family
Mexico	Mostly insiders	Unitary	<10x	Concentrated	Family
Netherlands	Only outsiders	Dual	10x–25x	Concentrated	Institutional
Nigeria	Mostly outsiders	Unitary	<10x	Concentrated	Family
Russia	Mostly outsiders	Dual	10x–25x	Concentrated	Family and business groups
Singapore	Mostly outsiders	Dual	10x–25x	Concentrated	Family
Spain	Mostly outsiders	Unitary	10x–25x	Concentrated	Family
Sweden	Mostly outsiders	Dual	10x–25x	Concentrated	Family or institutions
Switzerland	Mostly outsiders	Dual and unitary	10x–25x	Concentrated	Family or institutions
Turkey	Only outsiders	Dual	10x–25x	Concentrated	Family
United Kingdom	Mostly outsiders	Dual	>25x	Dispersed	Institutional
United States	Mostly outsiders	Unitary	>25x	Dispersed	Institutional

Regarding board leadership structures, most of the economies studied in this research project operated with "dual" structures whereby different persons occupy the CEO and chairperson's roles. However, there are some notable exceptions here as well, which include Canada, Israel, Mexico, Nigeria, and the United States. Interestingly, some economies have a rough balance between dual and unitary structures such as Saudi Arabia and Switzerland.

As discussed previously, executive compensation varies considerably throughout the world. The fourth column of Table 1.4 contains the typical compensation multiples for the highest paid executive compared to the average worker in a firm. Based on data from Weller and Burton (2008) supplemented by data on individual countries, we observe that relatively low executive compensation is less than ten times the average worker; moderate compensation is ten to twenty-five times; and relatively high compensation is greater than twenty-five times the average worker. As can be seen in the table, the highest-paid executives appear to operate in Canada, India, Saudi Arabia, the United Kingdom, and the United States; while the lowest paid executives appear to operate in China, Japan, Mexico, and Nigeria.

As La Porta et al. (1997, 1998) noted, most economies operated with concentrated ownership structures whereby majority owners oversee and control the corporation. However, market-based economies such as Australia, Canada, the United Kingdom, and the United States are notable exceptions to this norm. As a result, these market-based economies must rely on other governance mechanisms besides a majority shareholder to govern the corporation.

A fifth and final internal corporate governance mechanism examined in this study is the dominant shareholder type. This mechanism suggests that the nature of the dominant shareholder has important governance interests. For example, when the dominant shareholder is a family member or members (e.g., India, Israel, and Italy), the assumption is that family interests will predominate. However, other economies rely heavily on the state (e.g., China) or business groups (e.g., Japan) to provide checks and balances on corporate power. Still other economies operate where institutional shareholders, such as pensions, mutual funds, and hedge funds, predominate (e.g., Australia, the United Kingdom, and the United States). Since each entity has different interests, leverage points, and legal constraints, it is assumed that each entity will govern differently.

Table 1.5 *External corporate governance mechanisms for IPOs in twenty-one economies*

Country	Legal system	Market for corporate control	Business groups	Prevalence of corruption	Institutional collectivism
Australia	Common law	Active	No	Low	Moderate
Belgium	Civil law	Inactive	Yes	Moderate	Moderate
Canada	Common and civil law (Quebec)	Active	Yes	Low	Moderate
China	Civil law	Inactive	Yes	High	High
Germany	Civil law	Inactive	Yes	Moderate	Low
India	Common law	Inactive	Yes	High	Moderate
Israel	Common law	Inactive	Yes	Moderate	Moderate
Italy	Civil law	Inactive	Yes	High	Low
Japan	Civil law	Inactive	Yes	Moderate	High
Kingdom of Saudi Arabia	Civil law	Inactive	Yes	High	Moderate
Mexico	Civil law	Inactive	Yes	High	Moderate
Netherlands	Civil law	Inactive	No	Low	Moderate
Nigeria	Common law	Inactive	Yes	High	Moderate
Russia	Civil law	Inactive	Yes	High	Moderate
Singapore	Common law	Inactive	Yes	Low	High
Spain	Civil law	Inactive	Yes	Moderate	Low
Sweden	Civil law	Inactive	Yes	Low	High
Switzerland	Civil law	Inactive	No	Low	Moderate
Turkey	Civil law	Inactive	Yes	High	Moderate
United Kingdom	Common law	Active	No	Moderate	Moderate
United States	Common law	Active	No	Moderate	Moderate

Table 1.5 contains a summary of the five dimensions of external corporate governance mechanisms for the twenty-one economies within our study. The first dimension is the legal system, and most of the legal systems in this study operate within a civil law code whereby the states' well-being is emphasized over individuals' well-being. Nonetheless, our study contains several common law countries, which include Australia, Canada, India, Israel, Nigeria, Singapore, the United Kingdom, and the United States. Previous research by La Porta et al. (1997, 1998) has shown that property rights and minority

shareholders are better protected in common law legal systems, so we can expect that these legal systems all emphasize individual rights.

The second dimension of external corporate governance considered in this study was the market for corporate control. Technically, the market for corporate control exists for each and every economy. However, some economies possess much more active markets while other economies possess much less active markets. As shown in Table 1.5, the majority of economies in our study do not possess an active market for corporate control.

The third external corporate governance mechanism considered in this study was the prevalence of business groups. In those countries where the individual or property rights are not adjudicated in the legal system or in the marketplace, business groups sometimes substitute here. Interestingly, for many of the economies with inactive markets for corporate control, business groups are often common (and vice versa).

Our fourth dimension of external governance is the prevalence of corruption. In this case, we utilized the Corruption Perceptions Index (CPI) for 2008 put forth by Transparency International (2010). The CPI is an annual survey measure of individuals who are very familiar with business transactions for a particular economy. Transparency International is a non-governmental organization based in Germany that collects, analyzes, and reports this data on an annual basis. The index ranges from 1.0 to 10.0 with "low" levels of corruption indicated by relatively high index values (greater than 8.0), "moderate" levels indicated by medium index values (5.0 to 8.0), and "high" levels indicated by relatively low index values (under 5.0). For our study, six countries operated with relatively low levels of perceived corruption, seven countries operated with moderate levels of perceived corruption, and eight economies operated with relatively high levels of perceived corruption.

Our fifth and final dimension of external governance was the perceived level of institutional collectivism. According to project GLOBE, institutional collectivism is defined as "the degree to which organizational and societal institutional practices encourage and reward collective distribution of resources and collective action" (House et al., 2004, p. 30). In societies with relatively high institutional collectivism, organizational members assume that they are highly interdependent within the organization, the society's economic system tends to emphasize the collective well-being of its members, and rewards are driven with seniority, personal needs, or within-group equity. In contrast, low institutional collectivist societies have just the opposite tendencies. Clearly, this cultural milieu can have major contextual implications for the governance of firms in general, and IPOs in particular.

National governance bundles of corporate governance mechanisms

Previous scholarly research has attempted to distill governance environments into a reduced set of configurations of internal or external governance mechanisms, or both. For example, Weimer and Pape (1999) argued for "Market-oriented" and "Network-oriented" governance bundles. Next, Hall and Soskice (2001) argued that developed economies basically reduced to two types of national governance bundles – "Liberal Market Economies" and "Coordinated Market Economies." Somewhat later, Millar, Eldomiaty, Choi and Hilton (2005) recognized that emerging markets need to be considered due to their increasingly important role in the global economy. Accordingly, they arrived at three national governance bundles: "Anglo-American," "Communitarian," and "Emerging Market." While all three studies greatly contributed to the field of corporate governance, none has paid sufficient attention to differences within emerging markets, all three took a conceptual approach, and typically external governance mechanisms were emphasized over internal mechanisms.

In this book, we take a much more balanced, systematic, and empirical approach to understanding governance environments surrounding IPOs. While Tables 1.4 and 1.5 give a complex and multi-dimensional perspective on how corporate governance mechanisms operate throughout the global economy, it can be useful to attempt to distill that information into a simpler form of national governance bundles. To do so, we conducted a cluster analysis of the various states across the ten dimensions of corporate governance throughout the world for the twenty-one economies in this particular study. Cluster analysis is a multi-variate statistical technique for grouping cases (Ketchen and Shook, 1996), in this situation economies, into similar and dissimilar clusters. In essence, it is a computerized technique for

Table 1.6 *Cluster analysis of corporate governance mechanisms in twenty-one economies*

Cluster no.	Cluster name	Nations within cluster
1	Emerging relations	China, Mexico, Nigeria
2	Developed oriental	Japan
3	Developed market	Australia, Canada, Netherlands, United Kingdom, United States
4	Developed niche	Belgium, Israel, Singapore, Sweden
5	Developed relations	Germany, Italy, Switzerland
6	Emerging owners	India, Russia
7	Patriarchal family	Kingdom of Saudi Arabia, Spain, Turkey

grouping economies in ten dimensional space according to similarity. In essence, what we are doing here is quite similar to what Solis and Tseng (2006) did in clustering national production functions throughout the world.

Table 1.6 contains the results of our cluster analysis for the twenty-one economies. Overall, our analysis revealed seven distinct clusters of governance mechanisms. The cluster analysis revealed which economies clustered together, but we had to assign names which summarized the overall cluster. Cluster 1 contained China, Mexico, and Nigeria, and we called this cluster our "Emerging Relations" governance bundle. All three countries are developing economies that utilize relatively low executive compensation, concentrated shareholding structures, and interconnected business groups, and must contend with relatively pervasive corruption that escapes the rule of law. In China's case, the state provides the glue that holds everything together through its ownership stakes and intimate relationships with all major businesses. For Mexico and Nigeria, family members are often the dominant shareholding type. All three governance environments benefit from above average levels of institutional collectivism which can serve as an informal governance mechanism that curbs excessive opportunism.

Cluster 2 consists of only a single economy, namely Japan. We call this cluster our "Developed Oriental" governance bundle. Other observers have noted that Japan is quite unique in its business and governance practices, and some argue that this is due to the relatively homogeneous, densely populated nation operating on an island (Oguchi, 2000). As the second largest economy (in 2008), Japan is a highly developed economy and is relatively unique in its governance environment characteristics. Corporations are governed by insiders with a high sense of loyalty to the firm and to the overall nation. Ownership is concentrated, and interconnected business groups provide checks and balances to corporate behavior. Executives are paid at a relatively low level, but the high institutional collectivism helps to guide human behavior. Decision making is highly consensual, and the fortunes of the firm and/or the nation are often put ahead of the individual (Tung, 1984).

Cluster 3 is our largest cluster of governance environments and it consists of Australia, Canada, the Netherlands, the United Kingdom, and the United States. We call this cluster the "Developed Market" governance bundle. All of these economies are highly developed from an economic perspective with relatively wealthy citizens. Except for the Netherlands, all economies in this governance bundle are "common law" nations which emphasize property rights protections and the rights of the individual. All five nations have relatively transparent information disclosure systems in order to facilitate the proper operation of their markets, and all compensate their executives at moderate or relatively high levels compared to the average worker. Business groups are rare or non-existent in these economies, and institutional collectivism is moderate in each economy. All five economies mandate that the board of directors is composed of a majority or exclusively of non-executive directors to assure that an independent board can oversee management. In essence, market mechanisms and board of director responsiveness to the market is the key driver for this governance bundle.

Cluster 4 consists of Belgium, Israel, Singapore, and Sweden. All four of these economies are developed, but relatively small. Because of these two facts, we called this cluster the "Developed Niche" governance bundle. All four economies rely on families and/or business group relationships to govern their corporations. Shareholding is usually concentrated around a few individuals or firms. All four economies are civil law legal systems, and their corporate governance codes are all "comply or explain" in nature, which permits flexibility. Singapore and Sweden rely on their relatively "clean" and transparent business dealings as well as their relatively high levels of institutional collectivism to govern their corporations, while Belgium and Israel rely more on familial skill and reputations to govern their corporations.

Cluster 5 consists of Germany, Italy, and Switzerland, and we call this cluster the "Developed Relations" governance bundle. All three are highly developed economies with a history of heavy reliance on family and/or bank relationships to govern their corporations. In recent years, all three economies have been moving toward more market-based governance mechanisms, but progress has been slow and history and culture mitigate against this progress. All three economies pay their executives at a moderate level compared to the average worker; however, they all vary in terms of how much they rely on their social norms to guide corporations. Both Germany and Italy possess relatively low levels of institutional collectivism, but Germany allows moderate levels of corruption while Italy must contend with relatively high levels of corruption. In contrast, Switzerland benefits from relatively little corruption while operating with a moderate level of institutional collectivism. In sum, this governance bundle relies on highly refined and tested relationships to govern their firms within a developed economy.

Cluster 6 consists of India and Russia, and we have named this cluster as the "Emerging Owners" governance bundle. Both economies are developing rapidly, possess a moderate level of institutional collectivism, and suffer from relatively high levels of corruption. Furthermore, both governance environments rely heavily on concentrated dominant shareholders through family members and/or business groups to govern the corporation.

Cluster 7 consists of Saudi Arabia, Spain, and Turkey. These three economies all operate on the coast of the Mediterranean Sea. Due to the predominance of the family patriarch and his ownership and control stake in the corporation in these civil law countries with concentrated ownership, we call this our "Patriarchal Family" governance bundle. For these countries, allegiance to the family and/or "tribe" is the paramount governance driver.

Conclusion

After this introduction, the book contains national chapters written by the country experts to describe and explain how corporate governance mechanisms provide a context within which entrepreneurial threshold firms enter the public markets in their particular national economy. In each chapter, extensive details are provided on the governance context and general IPO activity for each nation. Each chapter concludes with an in-depth case study of an individual IPO event during our study period of 2006–8. Additional conclusions and insights are provided for individuals just interested in that governance environment, as well as scholars interested in comparing and contrasting these IPO practices and outcomes.

IPO firms are an especially attractive research context for studying investor reactions to corporate governance dynamics (Certo et al., 2009). Most empirical IPO research relies on publicly available data (Brau and Fawcett, 2006). This edited book is unique in that it considers both financial and managerial issues associated with initial public offerings and their governance context using both public archival data and privately collected primary data to describe and explain these interactions in a wide array of economies.

IPOs are "entrepreneurial threshold firms" that are shifting their ownership structure, entering the public markets, and are subject to much more scrutiny and disclosure requirements in many economies. Research has shown that this transition can be aided by effective firm-level corporate governance mechanisms and practices (Zahra and Filatotchev, 2004), but not much is known from a comparative international perspective. Since previous governance research suggests that national context has a dominant if not overwhelming impact on governance practices and organizational outcomes at the firm level (Doidge, Karolyi and Stultz, 2007), this suggests that we need a more global perspective on corporate governance and IPOs.

Capitalist economies are constantly evolving as they seek to balance economic efficiency concerns with social welfare of a society. Each society uses economic and political institutions to govern corporations, and the state of these institutions influences what governance mechanisms are emphasized or ignored (Gomez and Korine, 2008; Hall and Soskice, 2001). As such, we predict that institutional perspectives on corporate governance will eventually replace agency explanations for governance phenomena over time.

We believe that academics as well as policy-makers will benefit by gaining access to this systematically collected and reported data and findings. In addition, executives within privately held firms might be interested in reading this book since there is a growing number of firms that are either cross listed in their home country as well as in another foreign country, or they choose to forego their home country listing and focus exclusively on a foreign country listing (Lipman, 2009).

References

Aggarwal, Rajesh, Laurie Krigman and Kent Womack. 2002. Strategic IPO underpricing, information momentum, and lockup expiration selling. *Journal of Financial Economics*, 66: 105–37.

Aguilera, Ruth and Gregory Jackson. 2003. The cross-national diversity of corporate governance: Dimensions and determinants. *Academy of Management Review*, 28(3): 447–65.

Aguilera, Ruth, Igor Filatotchev, Howard Gospel and Gregory Jackson. 2008. An organizational approach to comparative corporate governance: Costs, contingencies, and complementarities. *Organization Science*, 19: 475–92.

Arikan, Alsi and Laurence Capron. 2010. Do newly public acquirers benefit or suffer from the pre-IPO affiliations with underwriters and VCs? *Strategic Management Journal*, 31: 1257–89.

Arthurs, Jonathan, Robert Hoskisson, Lowell Busenitz and Robert Johnson. 2008. Managerial agents watching other agents: Multiple agency conflicts regarding underpricing in IPO firms. *Academy of Management Journal*, 51: 277–94.

Bancel, Frank and Usha Mittoo. 2009. Why do European firms go public? *European Financial Management*, 15: 844–84.

Bebchuk, Lucian and James Fried. 2006. Pay without performance: Overview of the issues. *Academy Management Perspectives*, 1: 5–24.

Berle, Adolf and Gardiner Means. 1932. *The Modern Corporation and Private Property*, New York, Macmillan.

Blair, Margaret. 1995. *Ownership and Control – Rethinking Corporate Governance for the Twenty-first Century*, Washington, The Brookings Institution.

Boulton, Thomas, Scott Smart and Chad Zutter. 2009. IPO underpricing and international corporate governance. *Journal of International Business Studies*, 41: 206–22.

Brau, James and Stanley Fawcett. 2006. Initial public offerings: An analysis of theory and practice. *Journal of Finance*, 61: 399–436.

Bruton, Garry, Salim Chahine and Igor Filatotchev. 2009. Founders, private equity investors, and underpricing in entrepreneurial IPOs. *Entrepreneurship Theory and Practice*, 25: 909–28.

Cadbury Committee. 1992. *The Financial Aspects of Corporate Governance*, London, Gee and Co.

Certo, S. Trevis, Catherine Daily and Dan Dalton. 2001. Signaling firm value through board structure: An investigation of initial public offerings. *Entrepreneurship Theory and Practice*, 25: 33–50.

Certo, S. Trevis, Tim R. Holcomb and R. Michael Holmes Jr. 2009. IPO research in management and entrepreneurship: Moving the agenda forward. *Journal of Management*, 35(6): 1340–78.

Charkham, Jonathan P. 2005. *Keeping Better Company: Corporate Governance Ten Years On*, Oxford University Press.

Cheffins, Brian. 2003. Law as bedrock: The foundation of an economy dominated by widely held public companies. *Oxford Journal of Legal Studies*, 23(1): 1–23.

Cheffins, Brian and Randall Thomas. 2004. The globalization (Americanization?) of executive pay. *Berkeley Business Law Journal*, Fall: 233–89.

Dalton, Dan, Catherine Daily, Alan Ellstrand and Jonathan Johnson. 1998. Meta-analytic reviews of board composition, leadership structure and financial performance. *Strategic Management Journal*, 19: 269–90.

Davis, James, F. David Schoorman and Lex Donaldson. 1997. Toward a stewardship theory of management. *Academy of Management Review*, 22: 20–47.

Denis, Diane and John McConnell. 2003. International corporate governance. *Journal of Finance and Quantitative Analysis*, 38: 1–36.

Doidge, Craig, G. Andrew Karolyi and Rene Stultz. 2007. Why do countries matter so much for corporate governance? *Journal of Financial Economics*, 86: 1–39.

Dore, Ronald. 2005. Deviant or different? Corporate governance in Japan and Germany. *Corporate Governance: An International Review*, 13(3): 437–46.

Filatotchev, Igor and Kate Bishop. 2002. Board composition, share ownership, and underpricing of UK IPO firms. *Strategic Management Journal*, 23: 941–55.

Foley, C. Fritz and Robin Greenwood. 2009. The evolution of corporate ownership after IPO: The impact of investor protection. *Review of Financial Studies*, 23: 1231–60.

Gomez, Pierre-Yues and Harry Korine. 2008. *Entrepreneurs and Democracy: A Political Theory of Corporate Governance*, New York, Cambridge University Press.

Gordon, Jeffrey N. and Mark J. Roe (eds.). 2004. *Convergence and Persistence in Corporate Governance*, Cambridge University Press.

Granovetter, Mark. 1994. 'Business groups' in Neil J. Smelser and Richard Swedberg (eds.) *The Handbook of Economic Sociology*, Princeton University Press.

Gregoriou, Greg (ed.). 2006. *Initial Public Offerings: An International Perspective*, New York, Butterworth Heinemann.

Gugler, Klaus (ed.). 2001. *Corporate Governance and Economic Performance*, Oxford University Press.

Gulati, Ranjay and Monica Higgins. 2003. Which ties matters when? The contingent effects of interorganizational partnerships on IPO success. *Strategic Management Journal*, 24: 127–44.

Hall, Peter A. and David Soskice (eds.). 2001. *Varieties of Capitalism – The Institutional Foundations of Comparative Advantage*, Oxford University Press.

Hart, Oliver. 1995. Corporate governance: Some theory and implications. *The Economic Journal*, 105: 678–89.

Heeley, Michael, Sharon Matusik and Neelan Jain. 2007. Innovation, appropriability, and the underpricing of initial public offerings. *Academy of Management Journal*, 50: 209–25.

Hendry, John. 2005. Beyond self-interest: Agency theory and the board in a satisficing world. *British Journal of Management*, 16: 55–63.

Higgins, Monica and Ranjay Gulati. 2006. Stacking the deck: The effects of top management backgrounds on investor decisions. *Strategic Management Journal*, 27: 1–25.

Hillman, Amy and Thomas Dalziel. 2003. Boards of directors and firm performance: Integrating agency and resource dependence perspectives. *Academy of Management Review*, 28: 383–96.

Hofstede, Geert. 1985. The interaction between national and organizational value systems. *Journal of Management Studies*, 22(4): 347–57.

House, Robert, Paul Hanges, Mansour Javidan, Peter Dorfman and Vipin Gupta. 2004. *Culture, Leadership and Organizations: The GLOBE Study of 62 Societies*, Thousand Oaks, CA, Sage Publications.

Howton, Shawn, Shelly Howton and Gerard Olson. 2001. Board ownership and IPO returns. *Journal of Economics and Finance*, 25: 100–14.

Jensen, Michael and William Meckling. 1976. Theory of the firm: Managerial behavior, agency costs, and capital structure. *Journal of Financial Economics*, 3: 305–60.

Judge, William and Carl Zeithaml. 1992. Institutional and strategic choice perspectives on board involvement in the strategic decision making process. *Academy of Management Journal*, 35: 766–94.

Judge, William, Ajai Gaur and Maureen Muller-Kahle. 2010. Antecedents of shareholder activism target firms: A multi-country study. *Corporate Governance: An International Review*, 18: 258–273.

Judge, William, Shaomin Li and Robert Pinsker. 2010. National adoption of international accounting standards: An institutional perspective. *Corporate Governance: An International Review*, 18: 161–74.

Judge, William, D. Brian McNatt and Weichu Xu. 2011. The antecedents and effects of national corruption: A meta-analysis. *Journal of World Business*, 46: 93–103.

Ketchen, David and Chris Shook. 1996. The application of cluster analysis in strategic management research: An analysis and critique. *Strategic Management Journal*, 17: 441–58.

Khanna, Tarun and Jan W. Rivkin. 2001. Estimating the performance effects of business groups in emerging markets. *Strategic Management Journal*, 22(1): 45–74.

La Porta, Rafael, Florencio Lopez-de-Silanes and Andrei Shleifer. 1999. Corporate ownership around the world. *Journal of Finance*, 54: 471–517.

La Porta, Rafael, Florencio Lopez-de-Silanes, Andrei Shleifer and Robert Vishny. 1997. Legal determinants of external finance. *Journal of Finance*, 52(3): 1131–50.

La Porta, Rafael, Florencio Lopez-de-Silanes, Andrei Shleifer and Robert Vishny. 1998. Law and finance. *Journal of Political Economy*, 106: 1113–55.

Licht, Amir N., Chanan Goldschmidt and Shalom H. Schwartz. 2005. Culture, law, and corporate governance. *International Review of Law and Economics*, 25(2): 229–55.

Lim, Dominic, Eric Morse, Ronald Mitchell and Kristie Seawright. 2010. Institutional environment and entrepreneurial cognitions: A comparative business systems perspective. *Entrepreneurship Theory and Practice*, 34: 491–516.

Lipman, Frederick. 2009. *International and U.S. IPO Planning: A Business Strategy Guide*, Hoboken, NJ, Wiley.

Lubatkin, Michael, Peter Lane, Sven-Olaf Collin et al. 2005. Origins of corporate governance in the USA, Sweden and France. *Organization Studies*, 26: 867–88.

Millar, Carla C.J.M., Tarek Eldomiaty, Chong Ju Choi et al. 2005. Corporate governance and institutional transparency in emerging markets. *Journal of Business Ethics*, 59(1/2): 163–74.

Minichilli, Alessandro, Alessandro Zattoni, Sabina Nielsen and Morten Huse. 2011. Board task performance: An exploration of micro- and macro-level determinants of board effectiveness. *Journal of Organizational Behavior*, forthcoming.

Monks, Robert and Nell Minow. 2004. *Corporate Governance*, Cambridge, Basil Blackwell.

OECD. 2004. Principles of corporate governance. URL: http://www.oecd.org/document/49/0,3343,en_2649_34813_31530865_1_1_1_1,00.html. Accessed March 18, 2011.

Oguchi, Takashi. 2000. Geomorphology and GIS in Japan: Background and characteristics. *GeoJournal*, 52: 195–202.

Penbera, Joseph. 2009. What lead directors do. *Sloan Management Review*, 50: 15–24.

Pollock, Timothy, Joseph Porac and James Wade. 2004. Constructing deal networks: Brokers as network architects in the U.S. IPO market and other examples. *Academy of Management Review*, 29: 50–72.

Rediker, Kenneth and Anju Seth. 1995. Boards of directors and substitution effects of alternative governance mechanisms. *Strategic Management Journal*, 16: 85–99.

Ritter, Jay. 1991. The long-run performance of initial public offerings. *Journal of Finance*, 46: 3–27.

Roberts, John, Terry McNulty and Philip Stiles. 2005. Beyond agency conceptions of the work of the non-executive director: Creating accountability in the boardroom. *British Journal of Management*, 16: 5–26.

Scott, W. Richard. 2001. *Institutions and Organizations*, 2nd edn., Thousand Oaks, CA, Sage Publications.

Shleifer, Andrei and Robert Vishny. 1997. A survey of corporate governance. *Journal of Finance*, 52: 737–83.

Solis, Rafael and K.C. Tseng. 2006. Cluster analysis as a reprocessor for fitting aggregate production functions. *Journal of Global Business*, 17: 33–53.

Suchman, Mark. 1995. Managing legitimacy: Institutional and strategic approaches. *Academy of Management Review*, 20: 571–610.

Towers Perrin. 2000. Worldwide total remuneration study.

Towers Perrin. 2005. Equity incentives around the world.

Transparency International. 2011. URL: http://www.transparency.org/. Accessed January 14, 2011.

Tricker, Robert I. (ed.). 2000. *Corporate Governance*, Aldershot, Dartmouth Publishing.

Tung, Rosalie. 1984. Human resource planning in Japanese multinationals: A model for U.S. firms? *Journal of International Business Studies*, 15: 139–49.

Wang, Tracy, Andrew Winton and Xiaoyun Yu. 2010. Corporate fraud and business conditions: Evidence from IPOs. *Journal of Finance*, 45: 2255–92.

Ward, Andrew, Jill Brown and Dan Rodriguez. 2009. Governance bundles, firm performance, and the substitutability and complementarity of governance mechanisms. *Corporate Governance: An International Review*, 17(5): 646–60.

Weimer, Jeroen and Joost Pape. 1999. A taxonomy of systems of corporate governance. *Corporate Governance: An International Review*, 7(2): 152–66.

Weller, C. and J. Burton. 2005. CEO pay soars, while middle class struggles. URL: http://www.americanprogress.org/issues/2005/04/b504723.html. Accessed January 14, 2011.

World Bank. 2010a. Market capitalization statistics, 2006–08. URL: http://data. worldbank.org/indicator/CM.MKT.LCAP.GD.ZS. Accessed November 8, 2010.

World Bank. 2010b. Gross domestic product statistics, 2006–08. URL: http:// data.worldbank.org/indicator/NY.GDP.MKTP.CD. Accessed November 8, 2010.

Young, Michael, Michael Peng, David Ahlstrom, Garry Bruton and Yi Jiang. 2008. Corporate governance in emerging economies: A principal–principal perspective. *Journal of Management Studies*, 45: 196–220.

Zahra, Shaker and Igor Filatotchev. 2004. Governance of the entrepreneurial threshold firm: A knowledge-based perspective. *Journal of Management Studies*, 41: 885–97.

Zattoni, Alessandro and Francesca Cuomo. 2010. How independent, competent and incentivized should non-executive directors be? An empirical investigation of good governance codes. *British Journal of Management*, 21(1): 63–79.

Zattoni, Alessandro and Alessandro Minichilli. 2009. The diffusion of equity incentive plans in Italian listed companies: What is the trigger? *Corporate Governance: An International Review*, 17(2): 224–37.

Zattoni, Alessandro, Torben Pedersen and Vikas Kumar. 2009. The performance of business group affiliated firms during institutional transition: A longitudinal study of Indian firms. *Corporate Governance: An International Review*, 17(4): 510–23.

2 | Corporate governance and initial public offerings in Australia

HELEN WEI HU AND MONICA GUO-SZE TAN

Corporate governance mechanisms

The Australian continent was inhabited by the Aboriginal and Torres Strait Islander people before the European settlement began in the late 1700s. Since then, Australia has continued to receive waves of migrants, which sees its population grow in size and diversity. A federation of six states formed the Commonwealth of Australia in 1901 under a single constitution. The Australian legal system originates from the common law system of the UK. The Australian rule of law is based on judicial precedents. Hence, the rules for company conducts are based on common law principles including segregation of powers, fairness and integrity. Corporate ownership in Australia is relatively concentrated, though principal–agent is still the main governance issue present in the corporate sector. Therefore, companies and managers are constantly under the scrutiny of an active takeover market. Investor protection is well defined and enforced because corporate governance principles are explicitly expressed and implemented in the country.

Corporate ownership is moderately concentrated among the largest companies listed on the Australian Securities Exchange (ASX). Relative to the US and UK, the Australian corporate ownership is more concentrated. For example, half of the banking companies had an owner with a shareholding greater than 50 percent (Shehzad et al., 2010). Although financial institutions are the dominant shareholder group in Australia, it is common that many of them are acting as the nominees for local or overseas investors (Chaikin, 2005), which can conceal the true extent of corporate ownership. Other investors such as family and individual shareholders are also present. Australian companies follow a non-prescriptive set of corporate governance principles, which are based on enhancing integrity, transparency, accountability, fairness and performance, drafted by the ASX Corporate

Governance Council. Companies adopt the "comply or explain" approach when implementing these principles.

Current regulatory framework

All companies in Australia are governed by a comprehensive legal framework. The Corporations Act 2001 outlines regulations related to private and publicly listed company registration and operations in Australia at the federal and interstate levels. It addresses a vast array of topics related to corporate governance, including the duties and powers of officers, the appointment and termination of directors, secretaries and auditors, the relationships and interactions between shareholders, debt holders and boards of directors, conflicts of interest and related party transactions, financial reporting, and accounting and auditing standards. The Australian Securities and Investments Commission Act 2001 establishes the administrative power and functions of the Australian Securities and Investments Commission (ASIC) as a regulator of corporations and financial markets. Furthermore, it establishes other regulatory and advisory bodies, including the Takeovers Panel, the Companies Auditors and Liquidators Disciplinary Board, the Financial Reporting Council, the Australian Accounting Standards Board, the Auditing and Assurance Standards Board, the Financial Reporting Panel, and the Parliamentary Joint Committee on Corporations and Financial Services. These committees have specific functions and provide expert advisory services in their respective fields. Public companies trading on ASX are subject to the ASIC Market Integrity Rules 2010. In August 2010, ASIC assumed the task of market supervision, which had previously been the responsibility of ASX; ASX Compliance, a subsidiary of ASX, retained a supervisory role with regard to compliance. This change occurred after a long debate regarding potential conflicts of interest that might arise as long as ASX was both a market watchdog and a listed company on the ASX stock exchange. Financial institutions including banks, insurance companies, funds, building societies and credit unions operating in Australia are subject to additional prudential supervision by the Australian Prudential Regulation Authority. To keep abreast of ongoing market changes and company needs, the Australian federal government set up the Corporate Law Economic Reform Program to review and re-draft Australian business regulations on an

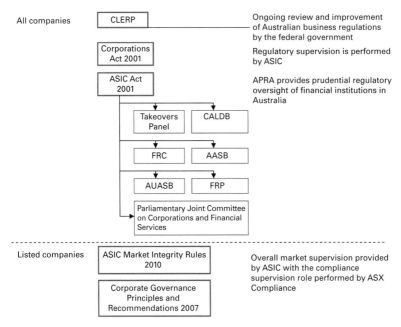

Notes: Corporate Law Economic Reform Program (CLERP); Companies Auditors and Liquidators Disciplinary Board (CALDB); Financial Reporting Council (FRC); Australian Accounting Standards Board (AASB); Auditing and Assurance Standards Board (AUASB); and Financial Reporting Panel (FRP).

Figure 2.1 Overview of the regulatory framework of Australian companies

ongoing basis. A summary of the Australian regulatory framework is depicted in Figure 2.1.

Principles of good corporate governance

The ASX Corporate Governance Council was formed in August 2002 and consisted of representatives from key industry groups, regulatory and advisory bodies and the top 100 Australian publicly listed companies. It has drawn up corporate governance guidelines, the first version of which was released on March 31, 2003 and the revised revision presented on August 2, 2007, to promote better governance practices in Australia. The latest version, known as the *Corporate Governance Principles and Recommendations* [hereafter the "*Principles*" (ASX, 2007)], reduced ten principles to a more concise set of eight principles in which the remaining two were embedded. The underlying principles, which are based on integrity, transparency, accountability, effective governance structure, risk management, and proper remuneration, have not changed. Australia has adopted the "comply or explain" (i.e., "if not, why not") approach to corporate governance to recognize the diverse needs and natures of companies.

In terms of board structure, Australian companies have a single-tier or unitary board of directors composed of both executive and non-executive directors (including independent directors). According to the *Principles*, the board of directors is responsible for (1) overseeing the company, including its control and accountability systems; (2) appointing and removing the chief executive officer (CEO) or equivalent; (3) where appropriate, ratifying the appointment and the removal of senior executives; (4) providing input into and final approval for corporate strategy and performance objectives developed by company management teams; (5) reviewing, ratifying and monitoring systems of risk management and internal control, codes of conduct and legal compliance systems; (6) monitoring senior executives' performance and strategy implementation; (7) ensuring that appropriate resources are available to senior executives; (8) approving and monitoring the progress of major capital expenditure, capital management, and acquisitions and divestitures; and (9) approving and monitoring financial and other reporting (ASX, 2007: 13).

With the aim of ensuring that the board effectively performs these functions, the *Principles* emphasize the independence of the board of directors. These guidelines require a board to have mainly independent directors who are not substantial shareholders, are not employed by the company and are not closely related to the company or its management through significant business, family or other ties (ASX, 2007: 17). An independent chair or lead director is also required and it is recommended that the chair and CEO be different individuals. This requirement was established because when the CEO is also the board chair, the CEO is often very powerful whereas the board is relatively weak (Daily and Dalton, 1993; Pearce and Zahra, 1991). Moreover, some of the benefits derived from the influence of the board chair position, including mentoring and consulting, are diminished under a combined leadership structure (Stewart, 1991). In general, the *Principles'* emphasis on strong independent directors and an independent chair on a single-tier board are comparable to that of many corporate governance codes and guidelines around the world.

In addition, it is strongly recommended that Australian listed companies establish sub-committees; this allows the board of directors to assign specific tasks to a sub-committee, which, with independence and diligence, can improve the overall standard of corporate governance and help to ensure that board duties are rigorously discharged (Higgs Review, 2003). According to the *Principles*, three sub-committees are particularly important for their roles in corporate governance: the audit committee, the nomination committee and the remuneration committee (called the "compensation committee" in the US). The key roles and functions of each committee are different. For example, the audit committee is responsible for examining companies' internal audit mechanisms as well as their external auditing to ensure the integrity of their final reporting, the nomination committee is responsible for selecting the right candidates for directorships and CEO positions, and the remuneration committee is responsible for determining the level of remuneration for directors, the company CEO and senior executives. To reduce potential conflicts of interest in this context, the *Principles* require these committees to be composed mainly of independent directors and to be chaired by an independent director.

In June 2010, the ASX Corporate Governance Council made some new amendments to the *Principles* that put a greater emphasis on diversity, remuneration, trading policies and briefings (ASX, 2010b). These new changes are expected to take effect on January 1, 2011. Overall, the presence of a strong business regulatory framework and a national stock exchange provides uniform investor protection.

Stock exchange and corporate ownership

The Australian Stock Exchange Limited was established in 1987 and listed on October 14, 1998. In July 2006, the Australian Securities Exchange (ASX) was created as a result of the merger between the Australian Stock Exchange and the Sydney Futures Exchange. On August 1, 2010, a group structure (the ASX group) was established to replace the ASX. The latter continues to manage the primary, secondary and derivative market services. Today, ASX is one of the world's top ten listed exchange groups in terms of market capitalization.

In Australia, the existing capital is concentrated within the largest listed companies on the ASX. The S&P/ASX 300 index is comprised of the 300 largest Australian listed companies, which held 91 percent of market capitalization in the overall equity market in 2009–10; the top 50 companies contribute 72 percent, and the top 100 companies contribute 81 percent, of market capitalization (Standard & Poor's, 2010). According to ASX, as of June 2010, domestic market capitalization is valued at approximately USD1.67 trillion, with 2,192 listed companies on the stock exchange (see www.asx.com.au). The three largest sectors on the stock exchange in terms of market capitalization are Resources (Metals and Mining) (30.93 percent), Financials (14.69 percent) and Resources (Energy and Utilities) (13.84 percent). Given the high concentration of capital within the largest companies on the ASX, it is crucial to determine to what degree shareholding and control are concentrated among particular actors, as these actors have a strong influence on domestic corporate governance practices.

Australia is often compared with the other Anglo-American countries, which are dominated by dispersed ownership. La Porta et al. (1999) showed that though ownership was quite fragmented among the twenty largest publicly listed companies in Australia at the end of 1995, it became more concentrated as companies got smaller. In fact, 70 percent of medium-sized companies had an owner with a >20 percent ownership stake. Likewise, research by Shehzad et al. (2010) found that Australian banking companies were closely held for the 2005–7 period: 43 percent of the Australian sample firms in the study had an owner with a 10–25 percent ownership stake, and half of them had an owner with an ownership stake greater than 50 percent.

An examination of the ownership structure of the 100 largest companies – S&P/ASX 100 companies – listed on the stock exchange for the year 2009 is conducted in this study, and the descriptive statistics are shown in Table 2.1. Table 2.1 shows ownership is quite concentrated in the hands of the top twenty shareholders. The combined holdings of the top twenty shareholders in S&P/ASX 100 companies average 69.06 percent, with a minimum of 34.68 percent and a maximum of 99 percent. The average stake owned by the largest shareholder is 22.31 percent, with a minimum of 5.67 percent and a maximum of 87.87 percent. Correspondingly, the average stake owned by the second-largest shareholder is 12.80 percent, though

Table 2.1 *Descriptive statistics for the top one, top two and top twenty shareholders of S&P/ASX 100 companies in 2009*

	N	Average	Min	Max	Std. deviation
First shareholder ownership (%)	100	22.31	5.67	87.87	12.99
Second shareholder ownership (%)	100	12.80	3.95	23.81	3.84
Top twenty shareholders ownership (%)	100	69.06	34.68	99.00	14.15

the range is smaller: between 3.95 and 23.81 percent. This indicates that corporate ownership in Australian firms is relatively concentrated, contrary to the common belief that Australia is similar to many Anglo-American countries with a dispersed ownership structure.

In Australia, institutional ownership is less important than is the case globally, and it is found mostly among large listed companies. For instance, in a recent cross-country study for the years 2004–8, Aggarwal et al. (2011) showed that the average total institutional ownership of firms was low (with the highest level being 14.3 percent in 2007), although it is increasing over time. Of institutional owners, the majority (78 percent) were foreign investors domiciled in the common law country (85 percent). In contrast, Henry's (2010) study of 300 ASX-listed companies over the 1992–2002 period found that the average proportion of institutional ownership was approximately 23 percent. However, the latter study acknowledges that the inclusion of nominees obscured the true extent of institutional ownership (Henry, 2010).

This study investigates ownership type for the largest shareholder, the second-largest shareholder and the top twenty shareholders in S&P/ASX 100 companies; the results are shown in Table 2.2. This table suggests that the top shareholder with the highest level of ownership was a non-financial corporation; the average ownership stake was 33.94 percent, and the maximum ownership stake was 87.87 percent, suggesting a rather concentrated ownership structure. The most common ownership type was nominee and custody companies, which had an average 18.17 percent ownership stake. There was only one financial institution that was the top shareholder in an S&P/ASX 100 company, with a 21.64 percent ownership stake. No trusts or individuals were found to be the top shareholders. This suggests that individual

Table 2.2 Ownership type for the top one, top two and top twenty shareholders of S&P/ASX 100 companies in 2009

Ownership type	Average ownership (%) of the first shareholder				Average ownership (%) of the second shareholder				Average ownership (%) of the top twenty shareholders			
	N	Owned	Min	Max	N	Owned	Min	Max	N	Owned	Min	Max
Financial institutions	1	21.64	21.64	21.64	2	6.95	5.99	7.90	439	1.01	0.06	21.64
Nominee and custody	73	18.17	5.67	33.47	84	13.20	4.65	23.81	1,256	4.01	0.01	33.47
Trusts	0	0	0	0	1	3.95	3.95	3.95	36	0.78	0.13	3.95
Non-financial corporations	26	33.94	8.14	87.87	13	11.86	5.70	18.36	184	7.11	0.02	87.87
Individuals	0	0	0	0	0	0	0	0	85	1.15	0.01	9.00
Total (N)	100				100				2,000			

and family ownership are not prevalent in the largest Australian companies. Furthermore, nominee and custody companies were the most likely second-largest shareholders, with an average ownership stake of 13.20 percent. Next were non-financial corporations, with an average 11.86 percent ownership stake. Two financial institutions were the second-largest shareholders of S&P/ASX 100 companies, with an average 6.95 percent ownership stake. Finally, there was one trust in the second-largest shareholder category, with a 3.95 percent ownership stake. This again indicates that ownership is relatively concentrated and that the second-largest shareholders are important actors in the largest publicly listed companies in Australia.

Table 2.2 also shows that many of the top twenty shareholders are nominee and custody companies, whose ownership stake averages 4.01 percent. The nominee and custody companies mainly represent institutional, family and individual owners, who are non-substantial (<5 percent ownership) shareholders of the listed companies. Through the nominee or custody companies, the true identity of these institutional, family and individual owners remains anonymous to the public. According to ASIC Regulatory Guide 149, the nominee and custody service companies offer help to their clients in administering accounts and maintaining effective communication and reporting as related to their securities, without offering any investment advice or opportunities. In Table 2.2, financial institutions comprise the second-largest ownership group; they include banks, insurance companies, and investment and managed fund companies. This group of shareholders enjoys an average 1.01 percent ownership stake. The third-largest group of shareholders in the top twenty is composed of non-financial corporations, including holding companies, which have average holdings of 7.11 percent shares. Next come individual shareholders, with average holdings of 1.15 percent, and trusts, with average holdings of 0.78 percent of shares. Overall, more than half of the top twenty shareholders in S&P/ASX 100 companies are registered under a nominee company. On average, companies on the S&P/ASX 100 have approximately thirteen nominee companies registered on their list of top twenty shareholders. This shows the full extent of nominee ownership in the Australian equity market. Although banks do not appear to be large shareholders on the list, many nominee companies are subsidiaries of banks, for example ANZ Nominees Ltd., HSBC Custody Nominees (Australia) Ltd., Citicorp Nominees Ltd. and

National Nominees Ltd. Nevertheless, the nominee and custody companies also include various other types of owners, including banks, corporations, individuals, families, governments and managed funds, all of which can choose to hold shares indirectly via a nominee account instead of disclosing their true identity to shareholders.

The results in Table 2.2 are of considerable concern, as they clearly show that measuring ownership concentration by ownership type may not yield accurate results given the great presence of nominee and custody companies in Australia. In some studies, researchers may treat nominees as institutional investors (Hsu and Koh, 2005). This is because, on paper, Australian ownership appears concentrated in the hands of financial institutions when nominee companies are considered as institutional shareholders. It is difficult (if not impossible) to isolate institutional, individual and family shareholders within the more general category of nominee and custody companies. This may result in a serious underestimation of the influence of wealthy individuals or families that are large shareholders. In addition, it is difficult to identify whether a shareholder behind a nominee company is domestic or foreign, and this distinction can have a substantial influence on the corporate governance of listed companies. For instance, Aggarwal et al. (2011) argue that foreign institutional investors originating from a strong institutional market are more likely to improve governance practices in domestic firms. Moreover, it has been found that institutional investors that do not have business relationships with the firms in which they invest are likely to positively influence governance practices at those firms. Therefore, without adequate disclosure regarding the true identities of those shareholders and their holding companies via nominee ownership, it is challenging to fully understand the efficacy and effectiveness of different types of shareholders with regard to the governance of Australian firms (Craswell et al., 1997; Henry, 2010).

Board of directors

Using the yearly board composition study conducted by the Australian Council of Superannuation Investors (ACSI), a summary of the board structure and its independence of the S&P/ASX 100 companies is presented in Table 2.3. Table 2.3 shows that, for almost a decade, the average board size has been consistent at around nine

Table 2.3 *Board structure and independence in S&P/ASX 100 companies during the 2001–9 period (numbers are based on average values)*

	2001	2006	2007	2008	2009
Board structure					
Board size	8.7	8.4	8.5	8.8	8.5
Executive directors (%)	22.9	19.8	18.8	18.2	17.1
Non-executive directors (%)	77.1	80.2	81.2	81.8	82.9
Independent non-executive directors (%)	–	64.5	65.4	65.5	69.1
CEO/chair role duality (%)	3.8	3.3	1.1	2.3	2
Independent non-executive chair (%)	36.7	78.7	76.4	74.7	82
Independence at sub-committee level					
All three committees (%)	47	79.7	78.4	77.3	85.9[1]
Audit committee (%)	54.2	82.4	81.3	80.4	60
Nomination committee (%)	54.6	76.4	74.1	72.9	70.6
Remuneration committee (%)	46.7	79.7	78.9	79.5	80

Source: ACSI (2003, 2007, 2008, 2009, 2010)

[1] Starting in 2009, ACSI changed its research criteria for "independence at the sub-committee level". The new research criteria used investigate the level of compliance of S&P/ASX 100 companies with the ACSI Corporate Governance Guidelines (2005).

members. In 2009, Rio Tinto (a dual-listed company) had the largest board on the S&P/ASX 100 list, with sixteen members. However, the level of independence of S&P/ASX 100 boards has increased gradually over the past nine years. In 2001, 77 percent of board members were non-executive directors, but that proportion increased to 80 percent in 2006 and 83 percent in 2009. Since 2003, when the previous version of the *Principles* presented the first prescriptive definition of "independent directors", the percentage of independent directors on boards has increased consistently. In fact, on average, 60 percent of board members at S&P/ASX 100 companies over the past four years were independent, and 69 percent were independent in 2009; this certainly shows companies' compliance with the *Principles*. At S&P/ASX 100 companies the roles of chair and CEO are distinctly separate and very few companies feature a combined leadership structure. That this corporate governance practice is so common among Australian companies can be attributed to related recommendations made in the Bosch Report, released in 1991.

Furthermore, as Table 2.3 shows, there have been two notable improvements in corporate governance in recent years. First, the number of independent chairpersons has increased significantly. About 37 percent of S&P/ASX 100 companies had an independent chair in 2001, but in 2009, nearly 82 percent of the companies had boards chaired by an independent director. Secondly, at the sub-committee level, the number of independent directors has also increased substantially. For instance, the percentage for all three types of committees was 47 percent in 2001 and it increased to 77 percent in 2008. On audit committees, only half (54 percent) of the committee members were independent in 2001, but by 2008 a super-majority of committee members (80 percent) was independent. Similar trends were also observed on nomination and remuneration committees.

However, the ACSI changed its research approach in 2009 such that the data for 2009 onwards are calculated based on different criteria. Instead of examining the level of independence of sub-committees, ACSI investigated the number of S&P/ASX 100 companies that had complied with the ACSI Corporate Governance Guidelines (2005). Although most of the recommendations in the ACSI guidelines for independence at the committee level are similar to those in the *Principles*, there is a clear distinction between them in terms of the level of independence prescribed for audit committees. Unlike the *Principles*, the ACSI guidelines require the audit committee to be composed solely of independent directors. This requirement is certainly more stringent than that of the *Principles*. As a result, in 2009, about 60 percent of S&P/ASX 100 companies met the ACSI's governance standards for audit committee, whereas the other 40 percent had not met the standards for various reasons; for instance, related committees had not been established, or the companies had not met the audit committee composition requirements. In contrast, the two sets of standards have similar composition requirements for the nomination and remuneration committees; the compliance levels for these two committees are high according to ACSI standards: 71 percent and 80 percent, respectively. Overall, 86 percent of S&P/ASX 100 companies complied with the governance requirements presented by both the ACSI guidelines and the *Principles* in 2009, which suggests a strong emphasis on and engagement in sound governance practices at the board level (see ACSI, 2003, 2007, 2008, 2009, 2010).

IPO activity between 2006 and 2008

The regulation of IPOs

The ASIC and ASX are the two main governing bodies for IPO applications, with the former supervising the Corporations Act and the latter regulating the Listing Rules. In essence, ASX manages the securities market in Australia. Its Listing Rules can be traced back to 1987, when the stock exchange was established. ASX released its first set of Listing Rules on April 1, 1987 and has continuously developed the Listing Rules over time. According to ASX, its "Listing Rules govern the admission of entities to the official list, quotation of securities, suspension of securities from quotation and removal of entities from the official list. They also govern disclosure and some aspects of a listed entity's conduct. Compliance with the Listing Rules is a requirement for admission to the official list" (ASX, 2010a: 1). Furthermore, the Listing Rules are enforced by the Corporations Act, and any listed entities that breach such rules can face a variety of sanctions. To be listed on the ASX, companies have to comply with the requirements presented in the ASX Listing Rules.

The IPO process specifically requires a couple of steps that privately owned companies need to undertake in order to become publicly listed companies that can raise capital from the equity market. These steps consist of reviewing the corporate governance structure of the company such as ownership structure, board composition and executives' and managers' remuneration packages, detailing the assets and businesses that the company intends to offer for the IPO, and finalizing the proper legal and financial structure for the IPO. In particular, these processes include (1) appointing professional advisers such as lawyers, accountants and underwriters to work on the IPO process, (2) conducting discussions with ASX to indicate the company's interest in undertaking the IPO process, (3) preparing a prospectus and conducting due diligence, (4) lodging the prospectus with ASIC and the listing application at ASX, (5) offering shares to the public after the lodgement of the prospectus, (6) receiving admission to the official list from ASX after the completion of the IPO capital raising, and (7) starting trading on ASX (Hardie, 2009). In general, the timeline for an IPO can vary from three months to two years depending on the complexity and amount of the

Table 2.4 *Key criteria for listing on the ASX*

Admission criteria	General requirement
Number of shareholders	Minimum 500 investors @ USD2,000
	or
	Minimum 400 investors @ USD2,000 and
	25 percent held by unrelated parties
Company size	USD1 million net profit during previous 3 years +
(a) Profits test	USD400,000 net profit during previous 12 months
	or
(b) Assets test	USD2 million net tangible assets
	or
	USD10 million market capitalization

Source: www.asx.com.au

transaction, though it usually takes approximately six months for companies to be listed.

In addition, there is a set of basic admissions criteria that companies need to meet to be qualified for listing. These criteria are related to shareholder number and company size (i.e. satisfying either the profits test or the assets test). According to ASX, to be listed on the stock exchange, a company must have a minimum of 500 shareholders, each with at least USD2,000 in investments. Alternatively, it can have just 400 shareholders with at least USD2,000 in investments each if unrelated parties hold 25 percent of the company shares. In terms of company size, either net profits of USD1 million over the previous three years along with net profits of USD400,000 during the previous twelve months are sufficient for a company to be listed in Australia; or the company needs to have USD2 million in net tangible assets or USD10 million market capitalization to be listed on the ASX. The details of the admission criteria and general requirements are summarized in Table 2.4, and further financial and business-related requirements are explained in Table 2.5. Once listed, companies need to comply with the ASX Listing Rules for corporate governance compliance and information disclosure; they must also meet ongoing requirements and provide required documentation (see ASX, 2010a).

Table 2.5 *Other requirements for listing on the ASX*

Requirement	Profit test	Assets test
Working capital	No minimum requirement.	The company must have working capital of at least USD1.5 million (which may include budgeted revenue for the first full financial year after listing). The prospectus must state that the company has enough working capital to carry out its stated objectives, or the company must give ASX such a statement from an independent expert.
Form of assets	No minimum requirement.	Either: • less than 50 percent of the company's total tangible assets (after any fundraising) must be cash or in a form readily convertible to cash; or • the company must have commitments consistent with its business objectives to spend at least 50 percent of its cash and assets in a form readily convertible to cash.
Business	The company must be: • a going concern or a successor of a going concern; and • must have conducted the same business activity during the last 3 full financial years.	The company's business objectives must be clearly stated in the prospectus and include an expenditure program.
Accounts	The company must give ASX: • audited financial statements for the last 3 full financial years together with unqualified audit reports; and	The company must give ASX: • financial statements for the last 3 full financial years together with any audit reports or reviews, if available; and

Table 2.5 (*cont.*)

Requirement	Profit test	Assets test
	• a reviewed pro forma balance sheet, reflecting the effect of the IPO, together with the review conducted by an auditor or independent accountant.	• a reviewed pro forma balance sheet, reflecting the effect of the IPO, together with the review conducted by an auditor or independent accountant.

Source: Baker & McKenzie (2007: 8)

IPOs between 2006 and 2008

This section examines companies that went public on the ASX during the period from 2006 to 2008. When cross-listed firms are excluded, there were sixty "true IPOs" found during this period. However, four companies were also excluded (APAC Coal, Eastern Iron, Ivanhoe Australia and White Canyon Uranium) because they were spin-offs, three companies (Aluminex Resources, Soil Sub Technologies and The Rewards Factory) that were delisted after an IPO, two companies (Handini Resources and Zeehan Zinc) that were suspended after an IPO, one company (United Overseas Australia) that was listed on the ASX in 1992 but whose name changed, and one company (Austofix Group) for which data were missing. Thus, the final sample included forty-nine companies. By focusing on four areas, namely IPO year and the industry category, firm size and performance, ownership structure and board structure, the results of these companies are shown in Tables 2.6 to 2.9.

Table 2.6 shows that nearly all companies in the sample went public in 2008 (forty-six companies), whereas only two went public in 2006 and one went public in 2007. Because Australia is one of the largest natural resource-producing countries in the world, thirty-two of forty-nine IPOs were in the basic materials industry, which includes companies in the basic resources area such as industrial metals and mining. The other large IPO industries were industrials (eight companies) and oil and gas (three companies).

Because the IPO admission requirements with regard to company size (i.e. profits/assets test) are relatively easy to meet, recent IPO companies have typically been young and small. Table 2.7 shows that most IPO

Table 2.6 *IPO year and industry classification*

	2006	2007	2008	Total
Consumer goods	0	0	2	2
Basic materials	1	1	30	32
Financials	0	0	1	1
Healthcare	0	0	2	2
Industrials	1	0	7	8
Oil and gas	0	0	3	3
Technology	0	0	1	1
Total	**2**	**1**	**46**	**49**

companies are under five years old, whereas only two were established more than ten decades ago (Anaeco in 1905 and Greenpower in 1899); overall, these firms have been in existence for an average of nine years and the companies are generally small. On average, they have 46 employees, with USD3 million in revenues and USD11 million in assets. The largest company is Runge, which is a computer services technology company that was established in 1977. It has 346 employees and had net revenues of USD60 million at the time of its initial listing. In terms of assets, the largest company is China Steel Australia, which had net revenues of USD21 million and total assets of USD66 million at the time of its initial listing. China Steel Australia was listed on the ASX on February 29, 2008, and its main regional offices are in China and Singapore. Although IPO companies in Australia are relatively small and most are unprofitable, these companies show strong sales growth. For instance, they are generally not profitable, with a negative average ROA (−19 percent) and negative average ROE (−27 percent), but their sales growth over the past three years was 3,303,823 percent. This is because most of these companies are in the resource industry, which has extremely high growth potential. Given the continuously increasing prices of commodities for national resources on the market, the sales growth of Australian IPOs has remained very positive, along with their projected future profitability.

In terms of ownership structure, the government and banks clearly have not played a significant role in these IPOs for both pre- and post-IPO periods, as shown in Table 2.8. This is because unlike S&P/ASX 100 companies, the companies in question are relatively young and

Table 2.7 *IPO size and performance*

	Age	Employees	Size		Performance		
			Revenues (USD)	Assets (USD)	ROA	ROE	Sales growth
Min	2	1	11,410	2,086,727	−113%	−248%	−56%
1st quartile	3	6	94,476	4,351,634	−21%	−27%	222%
2nd quartile	3	12	161,974	6,894,572	−11%	−12%	1,907%
3rd quartile	5	27	557,626	10,375,894	−4%	−5%	17,549%
Max	111	346	60,379,296	66,019,829	21%	56%	48,569,000%
Average	9	46	2,820,722	10,827,275	−19%	−27%	3,303,823%

Table 2.8 *IPO ownership structure (data in percent)*

	Family		Bank		Govt.		VC		Angels		Top 1		Top 3	
	pre	post	pre	post	pre	post	pre	post	pre	post	pre	post	pre	post
Min	0	0	0	0	0	0	0	0	0	0	0	5	0	12
1st quartile	0	5	0	0	0	0	0	0	0	2	4	8	11	19
2nd quartile	5	12	0	2	0	0	0	0	1	5	11	15	24	33
3rd quartile	16	26	3	5	0	0	0	0	5	9	22	26	38	44
Max	48	46	22	25	0	0	2	2	19	35	65	82	67	94
Average	10	16	3	4	0	0	0	0	3	7	15	20	25	35
No. of cases	31	42	16	34	0	0	1	1	22	32	49	49	49	49

Table 2.9 *IPO boards of directors*

	Size	Executive directors	Non-executive directors	Independent directors	Engineering, operations, R&D	Marketing, sales	Finance, accounting, law
Min	3	0	1	0	0	0	0
1st quartile	3	1	2	1	1	0	1
2nd quartile	4	1	3	1	2	0	2
3rd quartile	4	2	3	2	3	1	3
Max	6	2	6	6	4	2	4
Average	3.9	1.4	2.5	1.5	1.9	0.6	1.9

small; thus, family ownership is still most typical among these companies. Indeed, the average family ownership percentage is about 10 percent for the pre-IPO period and 16 percent for the post-IPO period, with many found to be in the mining companies. Given that family ownership consistently links with how much the business capital is tied to private wealth, the level of control becomes more demanding compared to other ownership types. Between 2006 and 2008, Interstaff Recruitment and Phosphate Australia had the highest pre-IPO family ownership rates, 48 percent and 44 percent respectively. After the IPO process, Pacific Environment and Interstaff Recruitment had the highest post-IPO family ownership percentages (46 percent and 45 percent respectively). In contrast, angel investors and banks are the second and third largest shareholder groups, but their pre- and post-IPO ownership figures are much smaller than those of family shareholders. Consistent with the results of our earlier study on S&P/ASX 100 companies, new IPO companies had a relatively concentrated ownership structure; the top shareholder tends to hold about 15 percent of the pre-IPO shares and 20 percent of the post-IPO shares on average, and these figures are 25 percent (pre-IPO) and 35 percent (post-IPO) for the top three shareholders' combined ownership. Of the forty-nine companies, Advanced Share Registry had the most concentrated pre-IPO ownership (ownership stakes of 65 percent for the top shareholder and 67 percent for the top three). The largest shareholder for Energy & Minerals Australia had the highest post-IPO ownership share (82 percent), and the top three shareholders for China Steel Australia have the highest combined post-IPO ownership share (94 percent).

Because IPO companies are relatively small in size, they have relatively small boards as well. Table 2.9 shows that, on average, there are four members on a board: one executive director and three non-executive directors, of whom two are independent directors. Female directors are very rare in Australia during the study period. Therefore, the recent ASX Listing Rules have focused on diversity in the boardroom. IPO boards have a strong preference for directors in both throughput functions (such as engineering, operations and research and development) and peripheral functions (such as finance, accounting and law), but there are not many in the area of output functions (such as marketing or sales). Furthermore, more than half of the IPO companies have an audit committee (twenty-nine companies) with an average committee size of two members, and some have a nomination committee (thirteen companies) and a remuneration committee (seventeen companies). Among the IPO companies, there were only ten companies that had established every type of sub-committee required by the *Principles*. This may be because the corporate governance requirements presented in the *Principles* are built on the "comply or explain" model.

Description of an IPO: Genera Biosystems Limited

The firm before the IPO

Genera Biosystems was founded in 2001, and at that time, it was named Geneflow Pty Limited. Initially, several scientists from the Walter and Eliza Hall Institute, the Australian Genome Research Facility and the University of Melbourne formed the company to commercialize a portfolio of technologies. In 2002, the company changed its name to Genera Biosystems Pty Limited, and it became a publicly listed company in 2008. According to the Prospectus (Genera Biosystems, 2008b), Genera Biosystems is a single corporate entity without any related subsidiaries or holding companies, and it is in the healthcare industry – biotechnology sector. In particular, Genera Biosystems develops and commercializes multiplexed molecular diagnostic tests, which is a fast growing area with a current market value of approximately USD2.6 billion.

The ownership structure of the firm at the time of its IPO would be considered dispersed. Among the 470 shareholders at that time, the largest shareholder was one of the company's major partners: the Walter and Eliza Hall Institute of Medical Research Ltd., with direct shares of 5.47 percent. Another major business partner, Sonic Healthcare Ltd., maintained a 3.91 percent share in the company. Both partners were closely involved with the company in different forms, with the former receiving stock because of the original IP, whereas the latter received stock in exchange for clinical development support services (Genera Biosystems, 2010). At the time of the IPO, there were three directors sitting on the board, with one executive director – Dr. Karl Poetter, who is the chief scientific officer (CSO) of the company – and two non-executive directors, one of which was the chair. Due to the nature of its business, the company has established two scientific advisory boards and an audit and risk committee. The Clinical Development Advisory Board (CDAB) specifically provides advice related to near-market opportunities, addressing issues such as clinical trial design and Food and Drug Administration (FDA) consultation. The second advisory board, the Scientific Advisory Board (SAB), provides advice to the company in the area of emergent technology. This includes its QSand^{TM} platform (Genera Biosystems, 2008b: 21). The company's SAB invited well-known scientists to sit on its board, including the inventor of the HPV vaccine and 2006 Australian of the Year, Professor Ian Frazer. The two non-executive directors are both members of the audit and risk committee. At the time of the IPO, all three board members held shares in the company. Two non-executive directors held combined shares of 185,000 together with another 800,000 share options. Under the company's executive scheme option plan, the CEO would receive 1,689,326 share options after the allotment of shares stated on the prospectus. In contrast, Dr. Karl Poetter, who is the CSO and the executive director, did not receive any share options but he held 723,000 company shares at the time of the IPO (Genera Biosystems, 2008b).

The offer

Genera Biosystems started its IPO process in May 2008. The company particularly targets the market of molecular diagnosis of women's conditions and it made 10 million shares out of a total 41 million available before its IPO. The new shares offered by the company during the IPO comprised 19.5 percent of the total share capital. After the IPO, the company's shares were estimated to number over 52 million. The company raised around USD6.83 million prior to its IPO in June 2008 at prices ranging from USD0.07 to USD0.55 (Genera Biosystems, 2010). During the IPO, the shares were offered at a fixed price at USD0.35 per share, and the firm raised USD3.5 million as a result. After the IPO, the company's overall market capitalization increased to USD17.66 million (Genera Biosystems, 2008b).

The firm after the IPO

Although there was no merger and acquisition activity after the IPO, the ownership structure of the company exhibited slight changes.

The two business partners and shareholders via institutional nominee and custody accounts increased their shareholdings and continued to be the long-term supporters of the stock. Employee shareholding also shifted toward key personnel, particularly to the non-executive directors. The combined shares of four non-executive directors reached 3.49 million (i.e., about 6 percent of the company issued shares) with another 1.35 million share options. One non-executive director, Mr. Bill Tapp, holds 2.67 million shares, which accounts for 4.55 percent of company shares (Genera Biosystems, 2009). Whereas the proportion of shares in the possession of management was small before the IPO, that had slightly increased after the IPO, with the CEO, CSO and company secretary holding 30,000, 815,798 and 4,000 shares, respectively.

To ensure compliance with the ASX's *Principles*, the board of Genera Biosystems has taken several actions, including (1) implementing formal policy and procedures regarding board governance (the Board Charter governs the board's conduct); (2) appointing more experienced directors to the board (i.e., appointed another two non-executive directors in 2009 and 2010), which increased the board size to five, four of whom are non-executive directors; (3) conducting regular (typically monthly) board meetings to discuss current events and issues that are relevant to the company's operations and performance; and (4) establishing two more committees in addition to the audit and risk committee (the nomination and remuneration committees, as recommended by the *Principles* (Genera Biosystems, 2008a, 2009)). According to the company itself, it will "utilize its platform DNA analysis technologies to exploit the potentially lucrative molecular diagnostics market", and the capital obtained from its IPO will be used to further develop and commercialize existing technologies (Genera Biosystems, 2008b: 12).

In short, Genera Biosystems is a typical Australian firm, which was listed during the period 2006–8, and which is a relatively small, young and fast-growing company. Its corporate ownership is shared among business entities, institutional investors and key company personnel. It has implemented a proper governance structure such as the board being dominated by non-executive directors, separation of the CEO and board chair roles with the latter being a non-executive director, establishment of sub-committees to perform specific committee tasks, and implementation of an appropriate executive pay scheme that emphasizes both fixed and variable pay components. Even though mandatory corporate governance compliance is not required in Australia, Genera Biosystems has engaged in good governance practices.

Conclusion

Australian regulators such as ASX, ASIC, Financial Reporting Council, Australian Prudential Regulation Authority and ACSI continuously develop and promote their corporate governance standards through internal and external governance mechanisms. For instance, they actively promote various internal governance mechanisms by encouraging ownership representation, shareholder activism and institutional investor involvement, recommending stronger independence and diversity at the board and sub-committee levels, and encouraging transparent and timely information disclosure to strengthen the protection of shareholder value. External governance mechanisms such as those regulating the takeover market and business regulations are also found to be closely associated with the development of financial markets and investor protection. La Porta et al. (2000) point out that advanced economies with more mature financial markets are more capable of providing effective investor protection. Therefore, the presence of a well-built regulatory framework and a competent national stock exchange are essential in providing support for the development of corporate governance in Australia and identifying the governance mechanisms that best suit the needs of the corporate sector.

References

ACSI. 2003. *Board composition and non-executive director pay in the top 100 companies: 2002.* Melbourne: Australian Council of Super Investors Inc.

—— 2005. *Corporate governance guidelines: A guide for superannuation trustees to monitor listed Australian companies.* Melbourne: Australian Council of Super Investors Inc.

—— 2007. *Board composition and non-executive director pay in the top 100 companies: 2006.* Melbourne: Australian Council of Super Investors Inc.

—— 2008. *Board composition and non-executive director pay in the top 100 companies: 2007.* Melbourne: Australian Council of Super Investors Inc.

—— 2009. *Board composition and non-executive director pay in the top 100 companies: 2008.* Melbourne: Australian Council of Super Investors Inc.

2010. *Board composition and non-executive director pay in the top 100 companies: 2009.* Melbourne: Australian Council of Super Investors Inc.

Aggarwal, Reena, Isil Erel, Miguel Ferreira and Pedro Matos. 2011. 'Does governance travel around the world? Evidence from institutional investors', *Journal of Financial Economics*, 100, 1, 154–81.

ASX. 2007. *Corporate governance principles and recommendations.* Sydney: ASX Corporate Governance Council.

2010a. *ASX listing rules: Introduction.* Sydney: Australian Securities Exchange.

2010b. *Corporate governance principles and recommendations with 2010 amendments.* Sydney: ASX Corporate Governance Council.

Baker & McKenzie. 2007. *IPO guide: Floating a company on ASX.* Sydney: Baker & McKenzie International.

Chaikin, David. 2005. 'Nominee shareholders: Legal, commercial and risk aspects', *Australian Journal of Corporate Law*, 18, 3, 288–303.

Craswell, Allen T., Stephen L. Taylor and Richard A. Saywell. 1997. 'Ownership structure and corporate performance: Australian evidence', *Pacific-Basin Finance Journal*, 5, 3, 301–23.

Daily, Catherine M. and Dan R. Dalton. 1993. 'Board of directors leadership and structure: Control and performance implications', *Entrepreneurship Theory and Practice*, 17, 3, 65–81.

Genera Biosystems. 2008a. *Annual report: 2008.* Scoresby: Genera Biosystems Ltd.

2008b. *Prospectus.* Scoresby: Genera Biosystems Ltd.

2009. *Annual report: 2009.* Scoresby: Genera Biosystems Ltd.

2010. *Intersuisse: 2010 (November).* Scoresby: Genera Biosystems Ltd.

Hardie, Paul. 2009. *The IPO process in Australia.* Perth: Hardies Lawyer.

Henry, Darren. 2010. 'Agency costs, ownership structure and corporate governance compliance: A private contracting perspective', *Pacific-Basin Finance Journal*, 18, 1, 24–46.

Higgs Review. 2003. *Review of the role and effectiveness of non-executive directors.* London: The Department of Trade and Industry.

Hsu, Grace C.-M. and Ping-Sheng Koh. 2005. 'Does the presence of institutional investors influence accruals management? Evidence from Australia', *Corporate Governance: An International Review*, 13, 6, 809–23.

La Porta, Rafael, Florencio Lopez-de-Silanes and Andrei Shleifer. 1999. 'Corporate ownership around the world', *Journal of Finance*, 54, 2, 471–517.

La Porta, Rafael, Florencio Lopez-de-Silanes, Andrei Shleifer and Robert Vishny. 2000. 'Investor protection and corporate governance', *Journal of Financial Economics*, 58, 1–2, 3–27.

Pearce, John A. and Shaker A. Zahra. 1991. 'The relative power of CEOs and boards of directors: Associations with corporate performance', *Strategic Management Journal*, 12, 2, 135–53.

Shehzad, Choudhry Tanveer, Jakob de Haan and Bert Scholtens. 2010. 'The impact of bank ownership concentration on impaired loans and capital adequacy', *Journal of Banking and Finance*, 34, 2, 399–408.

Standard & Poor's. 2010. *The S&P/ASX map of the market*. Standard & Poor's.

Stewart, R. 1991. 'Chairmen and chief executives: An exploration of their relationship', *Journal of Management Studies*, 28, 5, 511–27.

3 | Corporate governance and initial public offerings in Belgium

YVES FASSIN, ABIGAIL LEVRAU AND
LUTGART VAN DEN BERGHE

Corporate governance mechanisms

Belgium has a number of characteristics which are worthwhile mentioning as a reference frame. From a political perspective, Belgium is a rather complex country with several 'internal' political layers (federal, regional, communities, provinces and municipalities) combined with an increasing impact of the European level. Belgium is a founding member of the European Union and hosts its headquarters and other international organizations as well, such as NATO. From a socio-economic perspective, Belgium has a tradition of large industries, but under international competitive pressure more attention has been given by public as well as private forces to diversifying into new start-ups, spin-offs. The role of the government in the economy has been important to foster such transition and supports the consensus model of collective labor agreements and social cohesion. Employees benefit from an advanced social system.

The Belgian economy can be characterized as a very open economy, depending upon export as well as direct foreign investments of numerous international groups. Besides the impact of important holding and investment companies, family businesses form the backbone of many small, medium-sized but also larger companies. Numerous listed companies are controlled either by holding or investment companies or by families. In contrast, institutional investors are not prevalent and shareholder activism is rarely witnessed. As a result, the market for corporate control is relatively inactive.

As to the regulatory environment, Belgium has inherited a civil law legal system based on the 'Code Napoléon'. Although French-civil-law countries are considered to afford less legal protection to shareholders, Belgian law foresees several mechanisms that are protective of minority shareholders.

Moreover, information disclosure has been improved over the years due to many driving forces. Increasing legal requirements for disclosure of listed companies are complemented by more detailed recommendations in the corporate governance codes (Corporate Governance Committee, 2009). The code for listed companies and its comply-or-explain approach has recently been embedded into law, whereas the code for non-listed companies is totally voluntary.

The Belgian corporate law also attaches quite some importance to good stakeholder relations. Directors have to foster the corporate interest first, even when such interest might diverge from the (short-term) interest of shareholders.

Corporate boards are always single-tier in nature and composed of mostly outside, non-executive directors. In addition, a separation of roles of the CEO and chairman of the board is nowadays common practice. Executive remuneration packages are quite different in larger listed versus small-cap companies. The median fixed remuneration package (in 2007/8) varied between 37 (Bel-20), 50 (Bel-Mid) and 72 percent (Bel-Small), the remainder being variable bonus (respect-ively 26, 38, 23 percent) and share options (mainly for Bel-20 companies – 30 percent). The variable bonus is mainly based on financial indicators, such as EBIT or EBITA.

The governance environment in Belgium is influenced by various legal and self-regulatory initiatives. Similar to many other European countries, the Belgian corporate world has been hit by the financial crisis, with trust in corporations drastically degrading in the last couple of years. In particular, the effectiveness of corporate govern-ance reforms has been put into question. With the aim of rebuilding trust, Belgian politicians have been strengthening corporate govern-ance legislation as well as financial regulations.

Corporate law

An important milestone that has changed the legal context in Belgium is the 2002 Corporate Governance Act. This regulatory reform has introduced some basic governance principles into the Belgian Com-pany Code.

Under Belgian law, companies are headed by a unitary board of directors. This implies that the board of directors has the extensive powers to manage the company and perform all acts necessary to achieve the company's objectives. The board of directors may appoint one or more persons to carry out the daily management of the company. In this respect, two particularities in the Company Code receive special attention.

First, the Company Code foresees a modified one-tier board structure by introducing the possibility to install a management committee (*directiecomité/comité de direction*) (Van der Elst, 2004). This management committee is composed of executives who may (but not necessarily) sit on the board. In fact, the powers, composition, remuneration and organization of the management committee are determined by the board of directors. In the extreme case the board of directors may transfer all its powers to the management committee except for the determination of the overall company policy and powers explicitly vested in the board of directors. The main purpose of this provision is to provide current business practices a legal foundation as the notion of 'daily management' is being interpreted by jurisprudence in a very restrictive way. At the end of 2009 only twenty-four listed companies had an active management committee in accordance with the legal prescriptions. An average management committee consists of five members, of whom one or two are also serving on the board as executive directors.

Second, the Company Code allows public limited companies to opt for a two-tier board structure if they accommodate the Statute for a European Company (Societas Europaea (SE)). Although this new corporate vehicle enables companies a greater flexibility with respect to their governance structures, the SE is far from being a success in Belgian practice. Until today, not a single company in Belgium has opted for the format of an SE.

Given the specific governance challenges of the Belgian listed companies, with controlling shareholders, the 2002 Corporate Governance Act also introduced more stringent regulations on conflicts of interest. In particular, Article 524 of this Act foresees in a detailed governance process if controlling shareholders undertake transactions with related parties. In this context the role of an ad hoc committee of minimum three independent directors is crucial to evaluate the strategic and financial relevance of such transactions. Also the workers' council will have to give its opinion on the deal at hand. Moreover, strict regulations on the transparency of these evaluations (in the annual report) form the third cornerstone of this governance mechanism that has been installed to protect the rights of minority shareholders.

Following the reform of 2002, a new wave of adaptations to the Company Code has recently been introduced, transposing the provisions of various European Directives into Belgian law. A first new law (8 January 2009, transposing the European Directive 2006/46/EC) obliges listed companies to establish an audit committee within their statutory governance body. In its Article 526ter, this law also includes a legal definition of 'independent directors' (replacing the previous definition included in Article 524 of the 2002 Corporate Governance Act). A second legal initiative aims at enhancing shareholders' rights in listed companies. On 5 March 2010 the bill on the exercise of certain rights of shareholders in listed companies was adopted at the Council of Ministers. The bill foresees the transposition of the European Directive 2007/36/EC.

A third initiative, referred to as the Corporate Governance Act of 6 April 2010, imposes several new governance rules. First, all companies listed on a regulated market are obliged to adopt a corporate governance code. By Royal Decree of 6 June 2010, the Belgian Corporate Governance Code (see below) has been designated as the reference code for Belgian listed companies. Another new binding rule, included in the 2010 governance law, refers to directors' and top executives' remuneration in listed companies, including tougher disclosure requirements and the obligation to install a remuneration committee. It is clear that most of these initiatives are aimed at reinforcing corporate governance in listed companies in the aftermath of the financial crisis.

Codes of good governance

It must be noted, the debate on corporate governance in Belgium started some years before regulatory reforms took place. For many European continental countries, including Belgium, the initial impetus was given by the Cadbury Code (1992) in the UK. However, the concern of the business world was the danger of gratuitously copying Anglo-American corporate governance recommendations without taking into account the particularities of the Belgian corporate governance environment (e.g., an overwhelming impact of controlling shareholders). At the same time, there was a growing awareness that

Belgian companies would have to live up to high corporate governance standards in order to compete in a globalizing capital market (Van den Berghe and Levrau, 1998).

Listed companies

The first codes on corporate governance for listed companies appeared at the end of the 1990s. Next, in January 2004, the Banking, Finance and Insurance Commission, the Federation of Enterprises in Belgium and Euronext Brussels took the joint initiative to establish the Corporate Governance Committee.[1] Its original purpose was to draft a single reference code for Belgian listed companies and the Belgian Corporate Governance Code was published in due course on 9 December 2004. In the mean time, the Code has been revised, and a new edition was published on 12 March 2009.[2] The Code is based on nine principles, which are viewed as the pillars of good governance (see Table 3.1).

The focus of the Code is essentially on the functioning of the board of directors and its relationship with management. In addition some attention is paid to the relationship with shareholders and stakeholders. Vital for the Code is the flexibility it allows in adapting the recommendations to the company's size, needs and commercial realities. This flexibility is strengthened by two key elements: the comply-or-explain approach and transparency. Regularly, the application of the Code is assessed (Guberna, 2009) and, up till 2009, the Belgian Corporate Governance Code was merely voluntary. The latter has changed by the Corporate Governance Act of 6 April 2010 and the adjunct Royal Decree, which impose the Belgian Corporate Governance Code as the reference code for listed companies. This implies that listed companies are legally required to declare publicly which recommendations they adopt as well as to provide an explanation for non-compliance. Although listed companies are faced with stricter requirements on corporate governance, it is still too early to assess the

---

[1] In May 2007, the Committee adopted the more permanent legal form of a private foundation. The aim of the foundation is to contribute to the development of corporate governance among listed companies by regularly monitoring enforcement of the Code, submitting suggestions for amendments, amending the Code or issuing positions on any regulatory initiative or other initiative pertaining to corporate governance.

[2] For more information see www.corporategovernancecommittee.be.

Table 3.1 *Nine principles of the Belgian Corporate Governance Code*

PRINCIPLE 1	The company shall adopt a clear governance structure
PRINCIPLE 2	The company shall have an effective and efficient board that takes decisions in the corporate interest
PRINCIPLE 3	All directors shall demonstrate integrity and commitment
PRINCIPLE 4	The company shall have a rigorous and transparent procedure for the appointment and evaluation of the board and its members
PRINCIPLE 5	The board shall set up specialized committees
PRINCIPLE 6	The company shall define a clear executive management structure
PRINCIPLE 7	The company shall remunerate directors and executive managers fairly and responsibly
PRINCIPLE 8	The company shall enter into a dialogue with shareholders and potential shareholders based on a mutual understanding of objectives and concerns
PRINCIPLE 9	The company shall ensure adequate disclosure of its corporate governance

effectiveness of this evolution. Table 3.2 provides a brief overview of the characteristics of the boards of directors of Belgian listed companies.

Non-listed companies: Code Buysse

Parallel with the developments for listed companies, a separate commission was formed, chaired by Baron Buysse, in order to develop a set of tailor-made governance recommendations for non-listed companies (Commissie 'Corporate governance voor niet-beursgenoteerde ondernemingen', 2005, referred to as the 'Code Buysse'). The rationale behind this initiative is a strong belief that appropriate governance mechanisms can act as an efficient tool in promoting the growth and sustainability of non-listed companies. After all, they are key providers of current and future employment and substantially contribute to a nation's economic growth. The challenge for the initiators was huge since the diversity within the universe of non-listed companies is far more pronounced compared to listed companies. The interpretation of the set of recommendations should therefore offer great flexibility to guarantee not to stifle the entrepreneurial dynamic.

Table 3.2 *The characteristics of the board of directors of Belgian listed companies*

Variables	Characteristics of Belgian listed companies
Sample	*94 listed companies (BEL-20, BEL-MID, BEL-SMALL)*
Mix between executive and non-executive directors	*Average size of BoD = 9.8; average number of executive directors = 1.8; average number of non-executive directors = 8; average number of independent directors = 4.1*
Nationality of members	*In total 34 percent non-national directors; average number of foreigners on a BoD = 3.9*
Gender diversity	*In total 7 percent women; average number of women on a BoD = 0.7*
Number of meetings	*Average number of board meetings = 7.4*
Presence at the meetings	*Average attendance record at board meetings = 89.6 percent*
Executive committee	*88 companies have an 'executive committee' including 24 companies with a management committee in accordance with the legal provision; on average an 'executive committee' has 5.8 members*
Audit committee	*88 companies have installed an audit committee[1]*
Remuneration committee	*21 companies have installed a separate remuneration committee; 64 have installed a joint remuneration and nomination committee*
Nomination committee	*15 companies have installed a separate remuneration committee; 64 have installed a joint remuneration and nomination committee*
Compensation of board of directors	*Annual remuneration of the chairman: 60,000 € (median!) (~80,000 USD); annual remuneration of a non-executive director: 20,000 € (median!) (~27,000 USD)*

Source: Monitoring Study, 2009, GUBERNA

[1] The legal requirement to install an audit committee was not yet in force at the time of the study.

Table 3.3 *The four phases in the Code Buysse*

Phase 1: Sound entrepreneurship

This is the phase in which entrepreneurs have not yet legally structured their business as a firm. For them, as for that matter for all enterprises throughout their existence, sound entrepreneurship is important.

Phase 2: The advisory council

In this phase an entrepreneur uses an advisory council for support, which gives him a sounding council regarding his management style.

Phase 3: The active board of directors

In this phase the board of directors is activated by frequent meetings and dealing with important and strategic matters. The functioning of the board of directors is optimized when non-executive, or outside, directors are added to it.

Phase 4: The continued expansion of the instruments of governance

Larger or faster-growing enterprises will need to continue to develop their corporate governance with special attention to committees.

Source: www.codebuysse.be

In fact, they should be implemented in a spirit of proportionality as companies grow in terms of size and complexity while avoiding additional bureaucracy and costs. In this respect, the revised version of the Code Buysse[3] has adopted a phased approach (see Table 3.3). In addition, it also includes a chapter with specific recommendations for family enterprises.

Besides, the initiators also face the challenge of enforcement. In contrast to listed companies, external monitoring or pressure from the market does not exist and a legal grounding is also lacking. It is clear that the driver for enforcement mainly comes from within the company. Put differently, the Code contains recommendations to which companies should adhere on a voluntary basis and appeals to the individual responsibility to do so.

The Code, first published in 2005 and revised in 2009, was unique in the world. In the meantime similar initiatives were taken in other European countries such as Spain and Finland. In the beginning of 2010, the European Confederation of Directors' Associations (ecoDa) published Corporate Governance Guidance and Principles

---

[3] For more information see www.codebuysse.be.

for Unlisted Companies in Europe which represents a pioneer initiative to provide practical tools to board directors in Europe.[4]

Stock exchange and listed companies

The relevance of the Belgian stock exchange in the national economy

The capital market plays a relatively limited role in the Belgian economy and the attraction of the stock exchange has decreased over the years. As shown in Table 3.4, the number of listed companies gradually dropped with respect to both domestic and foreign firms. This downswing is also reflected in the evolution of the stock market capitalization (see Table 3.5). In particular from 1999 onwards, Belgium has lost an important part of its market capitalization due to the fact that a number of large listed companies were delisted after being taken over by foreign owners.[5] This decreased market capitalization

Table 3.4 *The number of companies listed on the Belgian stock exchange (1972–2009)*

	Stock exchange		Free market	Alternext	Total
	Companies		Companies	Companies	Companies
Year	*Domestic*	*Foreign*			
1972	*338*	*131*	–	–	*469*
1975	*289*	*149*	–	–	*438*
1980	*225*	*152*	–	–	*377*
1985	*192*	*144*	–	–	*336*
1990	*182*	*159*	–	–	*341*
1995	*143*	*138*	–	–	*281*
2000	*144*	*110*	–	–	*254*
2009	*128*	*37*	27	11	*203*

Source: Euronext Brussels, yearly reports

[4] For more information see www.ecoda.org.
[5] Examples are BBL, Royale Belge, Generale Maatschappij, Petrofina, Tractebel, CBR, Cockerill-Sambre, Cobepa, GIB, Electrabel and Fortis.

Table 3.5 *Evolution of stock market capitalization as percent of GDP* (*1913–2008*)

	1913	1929	1960	1970	1975	1980	1985
Belgium	99	131	32	23	15	8	26
	1990	1998	1999	2000	2005	2008	
Belgium	33	98	75	79	81	35	

Sources: Becht (2010), Van der Elst (2001), Levrau (2010)

Table 3.6 *Evolution of stocks traded, total value as percent of GDP[1]* (*1990–2009*)

	1990	1995	2000	2005	2007	2009
Belgium	3.2	5.4	16.4	33.4	55.8	27.3

Source: Worldbank, yearly reports
[1] Stocks traded refer to the total value of shares traded during the period. This indicator complements the market capitalization ratio by showing whether market size is matched by trading.

could not be compensated for by a number of initial public offerings (IPOs) of smaller and mid-sized firms, principally on the NYSE Euronext free market in Brussels created in 2004, and on the NYSE Alternext created in 2005 to meet the needs of small and mid-sized companies. In addition, the consequences of the financial crisis on market capitalization are also apparent.

In contrast, the shares of listed companies have increasingly been traded on the stock exchange, as can be deduced from the statistics reported in Table 3.6, indicating that the liquidity/velocity of the shares increased until the start of the financial crisis.

Some factors explain why Belgian companies may still be reluctant to go public: (1) companies might refrain from (further) opening up their capital because they fear the consequence of having to share control with (minority) shareholders or of losing control, (2) the tougher disclosure and governance requirements may have a deterrent effect, (3) the costs of going public may be perceived as disproportionate for small and medium-sized companies while (4) the financial crisis has shown the vulnerability of the capital markets.

Table 3.7 *Shareholder structure of Belgian listed companies*

	Average percent	Median percent	Min. percent	Max. percent
Largest shareholder (N=80)	43.48	44.10	3.55	83.89
Second largest shareholder (N=68)	10.55	9.10	1.04	42.80
Third largest shareholder (N=45)	6.68	4.97	0.47	23.92
Fourth largest shareholder (N=28)	3.69	3.61	0.15	11
Fifth largest shareholder (N=16)	2.76	1.65	0.12	10

Source: Levrau (2007)

The ownership structure of Belgian listed companies

Listed companies in most continental European countries show a remarkably high level of ownership concentration (Barca and Becht, 2001). This evidence also applies to Belgium. With respect to Belgian listed companies, the largest shareholder possesses on average 43.5 percent of share capital and the stake of the second largest shareholders is on average 10.5 percent. Table 3.7 provides an overview of the average shareholder structure of Belgian listed companies.

The concentration of ownership can also be studied from a different angle, namely the analysis of control (Becht and Mayer, 2001). More specifically, it is possible to provide insight into the number of listed companies that are controlled by a single shareholder or a group of shareholders, acting in concert. Control can be measured in different ways. From a legal point of view, a single shareholder controls a company when he holds at least 50 percent of the shares.[6] However, a single shareholder can obtain control even with a direct stake less than 50 percent. This is the case when single shareholders, holding small stakes, form coalitions through voting pacts and similar arrangements (Becht and Mayer, 2001; Van Der Elst, 2001). The findings for Belgium are the following (Levrau, 2007): 43 percent of Belgian listed companies are controlled by a single shareholder holding at least 50 percent of the shares. Moreover, a small number of listed companies (6 percent) have a dominant shareholder with a minimum stake of 75 percent. At 37 percent of the listed companies in Belgium,

---

[6] It must be noted that the principle of 'one share–one vote' is in force in Belgium. This implies that a shareholder who holds at least 50 percent of the shares obtains at least 50 percent of the votes.

a major shareholder could be found with a participation in share capital between 25 percent and 50 percent. Taken together, 80 percent of Belgian listed companies have a 'controlling' shareholder. In this context, ownership by non-financial companies and families is particularly striking.

The concentration of ownership of Belgian listed companies is also reflected in a limited free float on the Brussels Stock Exchange. In 2009 the average free float on the Euronext Stock Market (Brussels) was 49.65 percent, ranging from minimum 6.95 percent to maximum 100 percent.

The characteristics of the Belgian capital market have important governance implications. First, the market for corporate control is less prominent in Belgium. An active take-over market is considered as an important governance mechanism (Walsh and Seward, 1990; Shleifer and Vishny, 1997). In particular it acts as a discipline on firms, allowing control to be transferred from inefficient to efficient management teams and encouraging a convergence of interests between corporate management and shareholders. Second, the presence of institutional investors as shareholders in Belgian listed companies is rather limited. From a corporate governance point of view, the role and power of institutional investors cannot be underestimated. They are viewed to be important actors in ensuring that best practices as set out in the Codes are being implemented. The 'shareholder activism' phenomenon is a key element in the Anglo-American capital markets. Although some large institutional investors have expanded their operational territory and started to influence the continental European corporate governance scenery, Belgian listed companies have not frequently caught sight of shareholder activists. Third, in contrast to the Anglo-American governance environment, the issue at stake in Belgium is not the (agency) conflict relationship between owners and managers (Fama and Jensen, 1983), but the conflicts of interest that may occur between the dominant shareholder and minority shareholders (La Porta et al., 1998). In a context where shareholders hold a large fraction of equity, the problem of managerial control per se is not as severe as it is in a context of dispersed ownership.

However, ownership by outside blockholders is not an unequivocally positive force from the perspective of the other shareholders because holders of large blocks of shares are in a position to engage in activities that benefit them at the expense of minority shareholders

(La Porta et al., 2000). The exploitation of the control position by a major shareholder to derive special benefits is referred to as 'private benefits' (Van den Berghe et al., 2002). While dispersed ownership creates weak shareholders and strong managers, ownership concentration creates strong majority shareholders, weak managers and weak minority shareholders (Gugler, 2001). In both cases there exists an unbalanced power position, providing the potential for misuse of corporate resources and the occurrence of conflicts of interest. In this perspective, boards of directors are assumed to be important monitoring governance devices. They are also considered to be instrumental for protecting a company's interest in general, and the interests of minority shareholders in particular.

IPO activity between 2006 and 2008

The regulation of IPOs

Table 3.8 gives an overview of the listing requirements that prevail for admission to the stock exchange as well as those required on an ongoing basis. Classic admission documents and prospectuses are requisites for admission. A minimum of 25 percent of free float is required, or 5 percent if more than 5 M € (~6.6 M USD) share value is quoted. Yearly financial statements and half yearly reports are demanded and disclosure of sensitive information is required.

The IPOs between 2006 and 2008

During the period 2006–8, forty-two Belgian companies went public, seventeen in 2006, seventeen in 2007, and eight in 2008. Thirteen companies were listed on the Eurolist of Euronext, five on the Alternext market of Euronext, and one company (Hansen Transmissions) on the Official List of the London Stock Exchange. The majority of these issues, twenty-three companies, were listed on the Free Market (Marché Libre/Vrije Markt) – Euronext. In addition, a few companies were listed on two markets (Brussels and Paris or Brussels and Prague).

In this section only the fourteen companies that decided to go public in the Eurolist and Alternext market of the Euronext were analyzed, as the average funds raised on the Free Market IPOs amounted only to around 1.5 M € (around 2 M USD) and did not have much trading after the IPO.

Table 3.8 *Main admission to listing requirements and ongoing obligations for the Belgian regulated market Euronext Brussels*

Admission requirements

Free float	*Minimum 25 percent of share capital or minimum of 5 percent if > 5 M € (~6.6 M USD) – see Rule 6702/1*
Market cap	*At least € 10 M € (~13 M USD), lower for Alternext and Free Market*
Age	*3 years certified financial statements (but exemptions possible – see Rule 6702/2)*
Sponsor	*Listing Agent required* (a legal person assisting the Issuer by which it is appointed for the admission to listing of Securities on a Euronext Securities Market) – *see Rules 6201 and 6204 and the Notice 6–01*
Admission documents	*Application form to be filled + documents required in it to be provided – form provided by Euronext Brussels to the Applicant on its request*
Prospectus	*Prospectus approved by CBFA required to be published by law for the admission to listing on a regulated market*

Ongoing requirements

Price-sensitive information	*YES, linked to market abuse prohibition (required by law + by Rule 61005 of the Euronext Rule Book)*
Minimum free float	*NO, but delisting possible if less than 5 percent, provided accompanying measures approved by CBFA (Rule 6905/1(ii), (c))*
Financial statements	*YES* (annual statement, annual report, half-yearly report, interim management report or quarterly report) + *IFRS required for consolidated accounts (required by law + by Rule 61005 of the Euronext Rule Book)*
Transactions of significant persons	*YES, falls under* Transparency requirements *(required by law + by Rule 61005 of the Euronext Rule Book)*

Sources: www.euronext.com/tools/documentation/wide/documents-2397-EN.html (Euronext Rule Book + Information Vade Mecum) + www.cbfa.be

Table 3.9 *IPO year and industry classification*

	2006	2007	2008	Total
Consumer goods	0	0	0	0
Consumer services	1	1	0	2
Financials	0	1	0	1
Biotech	0	2	0	2
Healthcare	2	0	0	2
Industrials	2	1	0	3
Information technology	2	0	0	2
Oil and gas	0	0	1	1
Technology	0	1	0	1
Total	7	6	1	14

Three companies (Nyrstar, Arseus and Punch Telematix) that were spin-offs of existing listed companies were excluded, even if Nyrstar was – at the launch – one of the highest capitalizations in Belgium. Also one company in real estate in Tchechia was excluded, and BgB, a computer services company, where no IPO information could be found. The study will thus focus on the five companies listed on Alternext and the nine on the Eurolist of Euronext.

Most of the fourteen companies in the sample went public in 2006 (seven companies) and 2007 (six companies); only one company went public in 2008, before the financial crisis.

As Table 3.9 illustrates, Belgian IPOs are focused in biotech and healthcare, in industrials and in information technology.

The average firm age of the fourteen Belgian IPOs was somewhat more than ten years. Half of the Belgian companies, going public, are young entrepreneurial and high growth companies, with less than seven years of existence. Two of them had only three years of existence: the biotech company Oncomethylome and 4Energy in fuel. Four companies had fifteen to twenty-two years of experience.

Belgian companies going public in this period were small companies with up to 200 employees; only two companies have around 300 employees and one amounts to 750.

Due to the sectors, average revenues were low and amounted to around 20 M USD and average assets were equal to 6 M USD (see Table 3.10), but with huge differences.

Table 3.10 *IPO size and performance*

	Size			Performance		
	Employees	Revenues (USD)	Assets (USD)	ROA percent	ROE percent	ROS percent
Min	21	554	243	−91	−115	0
1st quartile	43	6,430	1,210	−2	−15	0
2nd quartile	80	20,273	3,969	3	10	1
3rd quartile	181	37,799	7,576	5	24	5
Max	743	56,109	33,033	105	115	6
Average	160	20,154	5,901	−1.68	2.31	3.22

The smallest companies – in terms of employees and revenues – were Emakina (service activity in media, specializing in branding) and De Rouck Geo, a company founded in 1926, commercializing active geographic maps. The largest ones are Banimmo, a real estate company, and two industrial companies, Transics – a producer of fleet management solutions – and Metris – a producer of metrological solutions.

About the performance, companies going public have low profitability ratios on assets, net capital and revenues (see Table 3.10); one-third of the fourteen companies in the sample have a negative profitability in the year preceding the IPO. These are three biotech companies, Tigenix (university spin-off that focuses on innovative local treatments for damaged and osteoarthritic joints), Oncomethylome (advanced molecular diagnostic tests for personalized cancer treatment) and Ablynx (discovery and development of Nanobodies), all with three to seven years of existence. The company with the highest profitability is the fourth pharmaceutical biotech company, Thrombogenics, active for fifteen years in the development of novel therapeutics in a number of important diseases related to the back of the eye, bloodvessels and cancer.

About the ownership structure, illustrated in Table 3.11, IPOs present similar characteristics to high tech companies. The largest shareholder of a company that goes public is typically (seven out of fourteen cases) represented by a venture capital company or a bank (five cases) through their VC (venture capital) department; in eight of the fourteen companies, the family or the founder was shareholder,

Table 3.11 *IPO ownership structure (data in percent)*

	Family		Bank		Govt.		VC		Angels		Top 1		Top 3	
	pre	post	pre	post	pre	post	pre	post	pre	post	pre	post	pre	post
Min	5	1	11	2	0	0	13	3	0	0	23	19	45	33
1st quartile	5	2	13	7	0	0	24	14	0	0	39	28	57	34
2nd quartile	11	5	28	16	0	0	66	46	0	0	54	40	78	61
3rd quartile	24	7	28	17	0	0	76	50	0	0	83	58	97	91
Max	74	7	35	17	0	7	91	67	0	0	90	76	100	100
Average	18	4	23	12	0	7	48	33	0	0	56	44	73	54
No. of cases	8	8	5	5	1	1	7	7	0	0	14	14	14	14

but only for 18 percent on average. The government was present in one of the companies.

Moreover, even if companies going public show a decrease of the share capital owned by the first shareholder, the major shareholder prefers to retain the control of the company after the IPO, often in consortium. The top three shareholders maintain a majority in most cases, while the major shareholder maintains a blocking share.

After going public, VCs and banks maintain an average of respectively 33 percent and 12 percent of the shares. Belgian IPOs tend to be dominated by the major shareholders.

In these IPOs, the absence of business angels in the share capital of companies before and after the IPO is noted; this is probably to be explained by the sectors (biotech and industrial companies), a longer existence or by the fact that business angels may have been bought out in previous rounds of financing.

Due to the importance of the sector of biotech and technology in Belgian IPOs, venture capital and private equity funds play a large role in supporting IPOs.

Most Belgian companies that launched an IPO are majority owned by national subjects.

Boards of directors of IPO companies have on average seven directors: two executive directors and five non-executive directors, three of those non-executives being independent directors[7] (see Table 3.12).

---

[7] This number of three fits into the legal obligation on the management of conflicts of interests as prescribed in Article 524 of the 2002 Corporate Governance Act (for more information see p. 65).

Table 3.12 *IPO board of directors*

	Size	Executive directors	Non-executive directors	Independent directors	Engineering, operations, R&D	Marketing, sales	Finance, accounting, law
Min	4	0	2	1	0	0	2
1st quartile	6	1	4	3	1	1	4
2nd quartile	7	2	6	3	2	2	6
3rd quartile	8	3	7	3	5	2	6
Max	10	4	9	4	5	5	7
Average	7.4	1.8	5.6	2.8	2.4	1.8	5.1

Only four boards have female directors. Nine of the fourteen boards have international directors. There are no employee representatives on the board as the law does not require them.

In terms of functional background, IPOs' boards have a majority of members with a functional background in peripheral functions (such as finance and law), 30 percent of directors have a background in throughput functions (such as engineering, operations and research and development), and less than two directors have a background in output functions (such as marketing or sales).

In line with the traditional structure of Belgian listed companies, more than half (nine) of the IPO companies created an audit committee before the IPO and a remuneration committee (nine); the latter committee is often combined with a nomination committee. Most companies will create such committees after the IPO, as suggested by the code of corporate governance (and now made legally obligatory by the laws of 2009 and 2010). No company created separate governance or technology committees (foreseen neither by the Code, nor by law).

The post-IPO evolution

Two companies were acquired and delisted in 2009: Porthus in information technology and the industrial company Metris by Nikon. At the end of 2010, De Rouck was the first stock quoted company to file for the new law on the 'continuity of the corporation', the Belgian variant of Chapter 11. Thrombogenics issued a capital increase in the winter of 2010, while Banimmo is also preparing a new capital round.

The description of an IPO: nv Ablynx

The firm before the IPO

Ablynx was established in November 2002 as a spin-off of VIB (Flemish Institute of Biotechnology) and the Free University of Brussels (VUB) with seed financing of 2 M € (~3 M USD) provided by venture capital company GIMV. Additional financing rounds with Sofinnova and Gilde in 2002 and with Alta Partners and Abingworth in 2004 brought an additional 5.5 M € (~7 M USD). Ablynx signed collaboration agreements in the discovery and development of novel Nanobody-based therapeutics against disease targets that are difficult to address with conventional antibodies with different pharmaceutical companies such as Procter and Gamble Pharmaceuticals (2004), Novartis (2006) and Centocor (Johnson and Johnson).

Ablynx succeeded in one of the largest finance rounds in Europe during 2006 to raise 40 M € (~50 M USD) led by KBC, and SR One, the venture capital arm of GSK. Ablynx moved into brand new facilities on the Technology Park near Ghent, with 3,000 m² for 200 people. After a few additional exclusive worldwide research and licensing agreements, Boehringer Ingelheim and Ablynx announced a major global strategic alliance to discover, develop and commercialize up to ten different Nanobody therapeutics across multiple areas including immunology, oncology and respiratory disease.

The ownership structure of the company at the time of the IPO, at the end of 2007, consisted of institutional shareholders, GIMV (14 percent), the VC that launched the company with the VIB vzw (6 percent) and Biotech Vlaanderen (10 percent), and the other VCs that joined at successive financing rounds: Sofinnova (20 percent), Abingworth Bioventures (16 percent), ACP (13 percent), KBC (7 percent) and SR One (2 percent).

The board of directors of Ablynx consists of seven members, one executive director (CEO) and six non-executive directors, including three independent directors. The chairman combines the function of CEO, and the three non-executive directors represent the major shareholders, three VCs. The board of directors has set up an audit committee and a nomination and remuneration committee. Both committees are composed of three members, who are exclusively non-executive directors; two of them are independent directors. The executive committee consists of four members, the CEO, the CFO, the chief business officer and the chief medical officer, an international team with large experience in life sciences and pharmaceuticals; the latter two members are women. The CEO, Edwin Moses, has been chairman of the board since 2004 and has been asked for the function of CEO in 2006, the year before the IPO.

Before the IPO a warrant plan had been approved for about 6.4 percent of the share capital. The beneficiaries of the plan are the CEO (1.6 percent), the other members of the executive management team (1.9 percent), the personnel (1.6 percent) and other former personnel and consultants (1.3 percent).

The offer

The cash from the offer varied between 56 and 73 M € (~81 and 106 M USD) for a total market capitalization of the firm after the IPO varying between 225 and 295 M € (~325 and 425 M USD). The price per share ranged from a minimum of 6.50 € to a maximum of 8.50 € (~8.6 to 11 USD).

Ablynx successfully completed its initial public offering (IPO) and was listed on Eurolist by Euronext Brussels on 7 November 2007 under the symbol 'ABLX'. The IPO was priced at 7.00 € per share (~10 USD). Pursuant to the offering, 10,714,285 new shares, equivalent to 75 M € (~97 M USD), were issued by Ablynx. From the 23.9 percent of the newly issued shares, Boehringer Ingelheim could make use of its subscription rights to acquire 4.2 percent. The over-allotment option amounted to 3.6 percent and allowed Ablynx to raise an additional 10.2 M € (~13 M USD) for 1,607,142 shares. Ablynx raised a total gross amount of 85.2 M € (~110 M USD) in its initial public offering.

The total amount of the remuneration of top management was 1.2 M € (~1.5 M USD) in 2006 and was foreseen to rise to 1.6 M € (~2 M USD) in 2007, the year of the IPO. The individual remuneration of the CEO has not been disclosed, but he was awarded 1.5 percent stock options, on a total of 4.1 percent for the executive committee. The independent directors had a yearly remuneration of 20,000 € (~25,000 USD), which is situated at the higher end of the IPOs studied, and around the median for the stock exchange in Brussels, which includes the more traditional and larger companies.

The firm after the IPO

As no existing shares were sold at the IPO, the ownership structure of the firm after the IPO saw an almost proportional decreasing of the shares owned by the shareholders, i.e., 23.9 percent and 27.5 percent in case of over-allotment. After the exercise of the warrants and the IPO, the VCs' shares declined from 99.1 percent to 69.6 percent; while Boehringer Ingelheim acquired 4.2 percent of Ablynx through its subscription rights.

The cash was planned to further develop the research investments in Nanobody®, a new generation of therapeutic antibodies. Ablynx continued to advance its own Nanobody® research and development programs with the goal to build a unique proprietary pipeline. Ablynx selectively chose to partner with companies that had therapeutic expertise in relevant disease areas and a significant commitment to development and commercialization of biologics. Partnering opportunities ranged from early-stage leads to clinical-stage licensing opportunities.

After several important milestones and successes in technology developments, Ablynx succeeded in raising 50 M € (~65 M USD) with a Secondary Public Offering in March 2010. The 6,666,667 new shares were priced at 7.5 € (~10 USD) per share. Ablynx moved into new R&D facilities in Zwijnaarde and won the European Mediscience Award for 'Best Technology' for the second year in a row.

Like most IPO introductions in this period, Ablynx complies with the Belgian Code. The major exception is the combination of the functions of chairman and CEO.

Conclusion

Corporate governance in Belgium has evolved considerably in the last decades thanks to both new legislation and the introduction (and revision) of the corporate governance code for listed companies. With the code of conduct for non-quoted companies, Belgium had a document unique in the world.

Gradually, most listed companies have adopted the recommendations of the Belgian corporate governance codes while at the same time making use of the flexibility offered by the 'comply-or-explain' approach. Due to the growing alignment between corporate governance codes, the characteristics of the Belgian board of directors are increasingly similar to the best practices at international level. However, the impact of insider shareholders on the board of directors remains a specific characteristic of many Belgian as well as continental European boards of listed companies. Indeed, despite the evolution of corporate law and corporate governance towards more European harmonization, the ownership structure of Belgian listed companies is still very concentrated, as is the case in numerous other continental European companies. Combined with an absence of active and independent institutional investors, the board is selected by the major shareholder or the controlling shareholders (acting in concert). With the exception of a few companies with a more widespread share capital, the assembly meetings are more of a formality than a real open discussion platform.

The Belgian stock exchange plays a role in the national economy, although this role has been declining since the globalization of the economy. A number of growing Belgian companies, including family businesses, started to make use of the stock market in the 1980s and 1990s, but this tendency has (drastically) decreased over the last two decades. As in many European countries, the large diffusion of family businesses, and the smaller size of companies, explain a certain reluctance of national entrepreneurs to go public and to share control with third parties. The administrative burden and costs of a public listing have also led to an increasing number of delistings in the last decade. Other larger companies have been acquired by international groups, and have been delisted (although sometimes, the group is then itself traded on Euronext Brussels).

Over the last couple of years, only a small number of companies have gone public, despite the initiatives to favor their access to the financial market with more accessible formats such as the Alternext market and the Free Market of Euronext. The reasons for this are the reluctance to share control, other constraints as explained before and the limited liquidity in trading of these very small caps.

In the three years of investigation of this study from 2006 to 2008, only forty-two companies decided to go public. The largest number are small operations under 1 or 2 M €, on the Free Market. As there is hardly any transaction on this market, after the IPO, this study focused on the fourteen more important IPOs.

They operate in a variety of sectors (i.e., industrial, consumer goods and services). However, a number of important IPOs have taken place in the biotech sector, a result of the spearhead sector of the Belgian universities and governmental initiatives, allied to industrial and financial partners. Venture capital (or VC arms of banks) and private equity have played a role in many of these high tech IPOs, and still play an important role after the IPO. For more traditional sectors, the ownership structure, even after the IPO, is still relatively concentrated and often a family is the major shareholder.

The board of directors has an average of seven directors, two executives and five non-executives, with a majority with a background in finance. Due to the prescriptions of the law, nearly all IPOs adopted the rule of minimum three independent directors.

In the years following the study, the global financial crisis led to very limited IPO activity. At the end of 2010 some new introductions or capital increase operations in the biotechnology and real estate may lead the way to new listings in a more favorable economic climate.

References

Barca, Fabrizio and Marco Becht (eds.), 2001. *The Control of Corporate Europe*, Oxford University Press.

Becht, Marco, 2010. 'Corporate governance: a historic European perspective', Belgian Corporate Lawyer Day, 18 November 2010.

Becht, Marco and Colin Mayer, 2001. 'Introduction' in Barca and Becht (eds.), *The Control of Corporate Europe*, Oxford University Press, pp. 1–45.

Cadbury, Adrian, 1992. *The code of best practice*, report of the Committee on the Financial Aspects of Corporate Governance, London, Gee and Co. Ltd.

Commissie 'Corporate governance voor niet-beursgenoteerde ondernemingen', 2005. *Buysse Code II: Corporate Governance – Recommendations for non-listed enterprises*, www.codebuysse.be/en/default.aspx.

Corporate Governance Committee, 2009. *The 2009 Belgian Corporate Governance Code*, www.corporategovernancecommittee.be/en/2009_code/latest_edition/default.aspx.

Fama, Eugene and Michael Jensen, 1983. 'Separation of ownership and control', *Journal of Law and Economics*, 26(2), 327–49.

GUBERNA, 2009. *Naleving van de Belgische Corporate Governance Code door de Belgische beursgenoteerde ondernemingen ('monitoring study')*, unpublished report in collaboration with the Federation of Enterprises in Belgium.

Gugler, Klaus, 2001. 'Corporate governance and performance: the research questions' in K. Gugler (ed.), *Corporate Governance and Economic Performance*, Oxford University Press, pp. 1–59.

La Porta, Rafael, Florencio Lopez-de-Silanes, Andrei Shleifer and Robert Vishny, 1998. 'Corporate ownership around the world', *Journal of Finance*, 54(2), 471–517.

2000. 'Agency problems and dividend policies around the world', *Journal of Finance*, 55(1), 1–33.

Levrau, Abigail, 2007. *Corporate governance and the board of directors: a qualitative-oriented inquiry into the determinants of board effectiveness*, unpublished PhD thesis, Ghent University.

Shleifer, Andrei and Robert Vishny, 1997. 'A survey of corporate governance', *Journal of Finance*, 52(2), 737–83.

Van den Berghe, Lutgart and Abigail Levrau (eds.), 1998. *Corporate Governance – Het Belgisch Perspectief*, Het Instituut voor Bestuurders, Intersentia.

Van den Berghe, Lutgart, Abigail Levrau, Steve Carchon and Christoph Van der Elst, 2002. *Corporate Governance in a Globalising World: Convergence or Divergence? A European Perspective*, Boston, Kluwer Academic Publishers.

Van der Elst, Christoph, 2001. *Aandeelhoudersstructuren, aandeelhoudersconcentratie en controle van beursgenoteerde ondernemingen?*, unpublished PhD thesis, Ghent University.

2004. 'Corporate Governance: een wettelijke (r)evolutie. De gevolgen van de wet "Corporate Governance" op de organisatie van genoteerde vennootschappen', *TRV*, 70–6.

Walsh, James and James Seward, 1990.'On the efficiency of internal and external corporate control mechanisms', *Academy of Management Review*, 15(3), 421–58.

4 | Corporate governance and initial public offerings in Canada

DHIRENDRA SHUKLA

Corporate governance mechanisms

Canada is a nation of immigrants, whose most distinctive cultural feature is a highly individualistic social culture. The legal system is based on English common law, except in the province of Quebec, where a civil law system is used, based on French law.

The corporate ownership in most firms is not fragmented, as it is relatively common for an individual or family to hold more than 20 percent of the firm's shares. An interesting trend has emerged in Canada, where the growth of foreign ownership of Canadian companies has dramatically increased. Currently, the dominant ownership groups are foreign investors, followed by individual and family blockholders of the companies. The rights of minority shareholders are protected by law. The boards of corporations are single-tier and CEO duality is not common (where the CEO is also the chairman of the board). The boards of corporations are composed of mostly outside independent non-executive directors. Executive compensation, and the CEO compensation in general, is non-egalitarian in nature, where their compensation levels are well above that of the average workers.

In the Canadian principles-based system, with the exception of mandatory rules related to audit committees, companies are required to publicly disclose the extent of their compliance with the suggested best practices and, where a firm's practices depart from such guidelines, to describe the procedures implemented to meet the same corporate governance objectives (Broshko and Li, 2006). Therefore, the Canadian approach is a principles-based approach that relies on comply or explain norms. This is an approach that is similar to that taken by the UK, Europe and Australia. In the US it is different, as they use the rules-based approach, which is oriented toward mandatory compliance with legislation and stock exchange requirements, with a much greater emphasis on regulatory enforcement, rather than voluntary compliance (Broshko and Li, 2006). Corporate information disclosure in Canada is relatively transparent and corporate controls are generally robust.

Canada is the second largest country in land mass, after Russia, and has a population of 34 million people. Canada is divided into ten provinces and three territories and became a self-governing country in 1867, while still retaining ties to the British Crown (as the current head of state is Queen Elizabeth II). It has two official languages; English is spoken by 59 percent of the people and French is spoken by 20 percent, based on the 2006 Census report.

Economically and technologically, Canada has developed in parallel to its neighbor, the US. As a natural resource-based country, it has had impressive growth of the manufacturing, mining and service sectors, which has transformed the nation from a largely rural economy into one that is primarily industrial and urban. The global economic crisis resulted in the economy dropping into a sharp recession in 2008, and the country posted its first fiscal deficit in 2009, after twelve years of surplus. Canada's major banks, however, emerged from the financial crisis of 2008 among the strongest in the world, owing to the financial sector's tradition of conservative lending practices and strong capitalization.

The corporate governance of Canadian public companies is regulated by corporate law and securities law. Canadian companies may be incorporated under the federal Canada Business Corporations Act, or one of the similar provincial or territorial corporate statutes. These statutes regulate ordinary and extraordinary corporate transactions. Securities regulation is the responsibility of the provincial and territorial governments, each of which has its own legislation and securities regulatory authority. The provinces of Ontario and Quebec have additional rules that are designed to ensure fair treatment of minority shareholders, in connection with certain types of transactions involving related parties. The provincial and territorial securities regulatory authorities coordinate their activities through the Canadian Securities Administrators (CSA), which is a forum for developing a harmonized approach to securities regulation across the country. In recent years, the CSA has developed a system of mutual reliance, which designates one securities regulator as the lead agency when it comes to reviewing applications, or disclosure documents, from Canadian public companies. The largest Canadian public companies are listed on the Toronto Stock Exchange (TSX); therefore, the Ontario Securities Commission is generally regarded as the lead securities regulatory authority in Canada.

The board of directors' structure is one tier. Public companies must hold a general shareholders' meeting every fifteen months to elect directors and to appoint auditors and authorize their remuneration (McDermott and Farrell, 2004). They are also required to hold a special shareholders' meeting to approve other ordinary and extraordinary corporate transactions. Shareholders holding at least 5 percent of the shares may convene a special shareholders' meeting for any purpose.

Canadian public companies follow a "monistic" system, where the company management normally nominates director candidates on the recommendation of the board of directors and, where applicable, the nomination committee. Shareholders holding at least 5 percent of the shares may nominate director candidates before a shareholders' meeting. Any shareholder may nominate director candidates at a shareholders' meeting. Since management controls the solicitation of proxies for shareholders' meetings, and because of the concentration of share ownership in Canada, management's nominees are usually elected. Battles for proxies are unusual and shareholders are entitled to obtain lists of shareholders, in order to solicit proxies at shareholders' meetings. Typically, directors are elected for a one-year term. Staggered, multiple-year terms of up to three years are permitted.

Code of good governance

The Canadian Coalition for Good Governance (issued in March 2010) provides guidelines for "Building High Performance Boards", which provides the following guidelines: (1) facilitate shareholder democracy; (2) separate the roles of chair and chief executive officer; (3) ensure that directors are competent and knowledgeable; (4) establish reasonable compensation and share ownership guidelines for directors; (5) evaluate board, committee and individual director performance; and (6) oversee strategic planning, risk management and the hiring and evaluation of management.

(1) Facilitate shareholder democracy

The shareholders have the fundamental right to vote their shares, and every shareholder has a duty to responsibly exercise that right. Every public company must have a voting system that supports shareholder democracy and should communicate the results of voting promptly and completely. Expected best practices are that all of the directors are up for election each year and a majority vote policy is adopted. Moreover, at least two-thirds of every board should be independent of management, to ensure directors are aligned with shareholders and not with management. "Independence" means that a director is not beholden to management, does not have a material relationship with the company and, except for director fees and share ownership, does not financially benefit from the company. A material relationship is any relationship that could interfere with a director's ability to exercise independent judgment, or inhibit his or her ability to make difficult decisions about management and the business. For example, employees of a company, its service providers and relatives or close friends of a senior executive all have a material relationship with the company.

As much as possible, directors should also be independent of each other. For example, boards should have policies to limit interlocking board relationships of all kinds, including: (1) board interlocks – when two directors of Company A sit on the board of Company B; and (2) committee interlocks – when two directors sit together on another board, and are also members of the same board committee.

(2) Separate the roles of chair and chief executive officer

The board chair and CEO have different responsibilities and a different focus. The chair is responsible for leading the board and making sure it acts in the long-term best interests of the corporation, as it oversees management and the company's growth. The CEO is responsible for leading management, developing and implementing the company's business strategy and reporting to the board. Separating the roles resolves inherent conflicts of interest and clarifies accountability – the chair to the shareholders and the CEO to the board. During a transition, companies may consider appointing an independent lead director for a short period of time.

(3) Ensure that directors are competent and knowledgeable

As the character and effectiveness of a board is driven by its directors, the single most important corporate governance requirement is to have directors of quality, both individually and as a whole. "Quality" is subjective and has no legislative or regulatory definition, but by definition a director of quality is someone with integrity, competence, knowledge, business and industry experience and the motivation to carry out his or her fiduciary duties in the long-term best interests of the company and all of its shareholders. It is expected that boards are diverse. A high quality board will have directors with a wide variety of experiences, views and backgrounds. A number of directors should have direct experience in the industry or industries that the company operates in, to make sure the board asks for the right information from management, asks knowledgeable and insightful questions and has the background it needs to take appropriate positions in response to management and their recommendations. While some directors will know the industry more deeply than others, all directors should, at a minimum, have a reasonable level of familiarity with the company and its business. Directors must be curious. They must be willing to ask the questions of management that will give them a fuller understanding of the risks and rewards of any proposed plan of action and how it will affect the long-term viability of the corporation. Every director must also clearly understand the legal requirements of the role. It is also believed that director education creates boards with ever-increasing professionalism and enhances the effectiveness of directors, boards and board committees. At a minimum, a director education program should include an initial orientation and ongoing educational programs and guidelines, such as formal education courses, in-house sessions and conferences.

The guidelines further provide for ensuring that the goal of every director is to make integrity the hallmark of the company. To have integrity is to be principled, moral, honest and responsible; it is to be above reproach in all things. A public company's reputation for integrity is fundamental in creating value for shareholders and other stakeholders. Every director on the board should be a person with demonstrated integrity, and the importance of integrity should be at the forefront in the boardroom and in every board committee discussion. The board also must make every effort to ensure that the CEO and other senior officers are people of integrity and are creating, or continuing to build on, a culture of integrity throughout the organization. Moreover, the boards should establish mandates for board committees and ensure committee independence. Board committees do a large part of the work of the board and then present their recommendations to the entire board for final approval, so conflicts of interest between management and shareholders are most likely to arise at the committee level first. It is therefore important that most, if not all, board committees be composed only of independent directors. It is poor governance to allow directors who are not independent to approve policies, procedures and appointments recommended by management. The audit committee, for example, reviews and approves the financial statements, risk management programs and internal controls developed by management. The compensation committee reviews and approves the performance and compensation of the CEO and other senior executives. The nominating/governance committee selects and recommends board candidates to oversee management. The independence of these committees is critical. In some cases, it may be appropriate for a controlling shareholder (who controls the company through equity ownership) to appoint representatives to a particular committee. The board should form a conflict of interest committee in this situation, made up entirely of independent directors, to provide an independent point of view on all related party transactions.

(4) Establish reasonable compensation and share ownership guidelines for directors

The directors should be paid fees for their services, set at a level that is reasonable and will attract qualified and experienced candidates. Director compensation should not, however, be so high or structured in such a way that it interferes with a director's ability to be independent, forthright in his or her views, or willing to challenge the status quo. Directors will usually represent the company more effectively if they are also shareholders in the company. Boards should decide on the level of share ownership that directors should maintain during their tenure (often expressed as a multiple of annual director fees), and should include a reasonable phase-in period for new directors. Director compensation should not be incentive-based. Stock options are not an appropriate form of compensation for the directors of large, established public issuers. Directors with stock options have no capital at risk, so their financial interests are not aligned with the interests of shareholders. Stock options can be granted when share prices decline and exercised when share prices rise, so they focus attention on short-term share performance instead of on the company's long-term sustainability. Most large Canadian companies have abolished stock options for directors. Directors can receive forms of compensation other than cash. For example, shares can be issued at market value (generally taxable at the time of grant), or compensation can be paid in deferred share units (DSUs), which are equivalent in value to a common share, often with the dividend rights of a common share. DSUs have valuable tax deferral benefits for the director, because they are generally taxable at the time of exercise as ordinary income. Directors should be required to hold their DSUs until they retire from the board.

(5) Evaluate board, committee and individual director performance

A board needs processes in place to evaluate and improve its performance, the performance of its committees and the performance of individual directors. These processes are often managed by the nominating/governance committee. To assess the need for change to structures or processes, many boards confidentially survey directors once a year and have the nominating/governance committee review the results. Annual performance reviews help directors assess their personal strengths and weaknesses, make decisions about the need for further education and decide when it might be appropriate to step down. These decisions should be based on each candidate's ability to make an effective contribution – and not on the time he or she may already have served on the board.

(6) Oversee strategic planning, risk management and the hiring and evaluation of management

Directors are responsible for setting the overall vision and long-term direction of the corporation (including expectations for risk and return and non-financial goals). The board hires senior management and delegates the management of the business of the corporation to them, evaluates their progress and oversees the process of evaluating and managing business risks. Management's primary job is to develop and implement an appropriate business strategy that will help the company achieve its vision, while managing the risks of the business, following the board's direction. The board reviews, questions, discusses and ultimately approves management's recommended strategy. The board then oversees management's decisions to make sure they are consistent with the approved vision, objectives, goals and parameters, and that they follow the approved approach to risk management.

Additionally, the board assesses the CEO and plans for succession. The board is responsible for hiring, and the decision to continue to employ, the CEO, reviewing his or her performance every year and establishing a succession plan. They develop and oversee executive compensation plans. Senior executives should be compensated fairly and competitively, with a large component of compensation being performance-based. Executives should also be significant shareholders in the company to more closely align their interests with those of shareholders. Further, executives report governance policies and initiatives to shareholders. Boards need to make every effort to help shareholders understand the board's governance policies and how it will fulfill its management oversight and control responsibilities.

The board should communicate with shareholders through multiple channels, including print, the company website, webcasts, the Annual General Meeting (where questions should be encouraged), and one-on-one or group meetings. All written communication with shareholders should be in plain language. The Canadian Coalition for Good Governance believes that shareholders should be allowed to have regular, constructive engagement with the boards of companies they invest in, in order to create open relationships, to have the opportunity to explain their perspectives on governance, compensation and disclosure practices, and to provide detailed comments on the company's practices. When these meetings are about compensation, or other matters related to management, they should normally be held without management or advisers.

In general, McDermott and Farrell (2004) point out that the Canadian approach to corporate governance is influenced by the following: (1) the relatively small size of the Canadian capital markets; (2) the large number of small-cap Canadian public companies (more than twice as many companies are listed on the TSX Venture Exchange than on the TSX); (3) the concentration of share ownership (over 25 percent of the largest 300 companies listed on the TSX have a controlling shareholder, while an even larger number have a significant shareholder); and (4) the privileged access that eligible Canadian public companies have to the US capital markets. Several Canadian companies can avail themselves of the Canada–US Multi-jurisdictional Disclosure System, a unique regime that allows eligible Canadian public companies to access the US public markets using Canadian disclosure documents (which are subject to review only by Canadian securities regulators), and without becoming subject to the US domestic registration and reporting system. In many cases, Canadian continuous reporting documents can also be used to satisfy US continuous reporting obligations.

Corporate legal system

Canadian corporate governance is currently undergoing significant reform, influenced by recent US initiatives, such as the Sarbanes-Oxley Act, and the desire of Canadian securities regulators to maintain investor confidence in the Canadian regulatory system and preserve Canada's privileged access to the US public markets. The CSA recently introduced a series of national instruments and policies, which affect the corporate governance of Canadian public companies (the CSA Rules). The CSA Rules closely follow Sarbanes-Oxley and the consequential rules and guidelines established by the US Securities and Exchange Commission (SEC) and US stock exchanges. The rules deal with the following issues (McDermott and Farrell, 2004): (1) oversight of external auditors, including pre-approval of audit and non-audit services, prohibited services, audit partner and audit review partner rotation, and cooling-off periods for hiring employees of external auditors; (2) chief executive officer (CEO) and chief financial officer (CFO) certification with respect to the accuracy of public disclosure and filings (e.g., annual and interim financial statements, and related management discussion and analysis (MD&A)), disclosure controls and procedures, and internal control over financial reporting; (3) composition, authority and responsibilities of audit committees, including the requirements that public companies have an audit committee composed of at least three directors, all of whom are independent and financially literate, and an audit committee charter giving the audit committee responsibility for things like appointing the external auditors, setting their compensation, overseeing the work of the external auditors, reviewing all public disclosure of financial information, and establishing procedures for dealing with complaints with respect to accounting or auditing matters, and for whistle blowing; (4) continuous disclosure obligations, including earlier filing of interim and annual financial statements and related MD&A, and expanded interim and annual MD&A; and (5) disclosure of corporate governance practices, including disclosure of whether (and if not, why not) public companies have adopted the non-prescriptive corporate governance best practices recommended by the CSA. Best practices include having a majority of independent directors, appointing a chair who is an independent director or, where this is not possible, a "lead" director who is an independent director, adopting a charter setting out the responsibilities and operating procedures of the board of directors, adopting a written code of business conduct and ethics, and establishing nomination and remuneration committees composed entirely of independent directors.

Under the CSA rules, a director is considered "independent" if he is independent of management or any other direct or indirect material business, or other relationship with the company and its subsidiaries that could reasonably interfere with the exercise of his objective, unfettered or independent judgment, or his ability to act in the company's best interests. He is considered "financially literate" if he has the ability to read and understand a set of financial statements, presenting a breadth and level of complexity of accounting issues, which are generally comparable to the breadth and complexity of the accounting issues that can reasonably be expected to be raised by the financial statements of the company. Public companies listed on the TSX Venture Exchange are exempt from some of the CSA Rules.

In addition to the CSA Rules, the Ontario government intends to amend Ontario's securities laws to make public companies and their directors statutorily liable for misrepresentations contained in their continuous disclosure documents. Currently, public companies and their directors are liable only for misrepresentations contained in prospectuses and other offering documents. The Ontario government has also amended Ontario's securities laws to increase the maximum penalties for securities law offenses.

Meanwhile, the federal government has amended the Canada Criminal Code to (1) prohibit, and impose criminal penalties for, insider trading (which is also regulated under provincial securities laws); (2) prohibit, and impose criminal penalties for, threatening or retaliating against whistleblowers; and (3) to increase the penalties for public market-related offenses and establish aggravating factors to assist courts in imposing penalties that reflect the seriousness of the crime.

A recent report, the Board Index published by Spencer Stuart Canada (2010), shows the following (see Table 4.1): (1) a good mix between executive and non-executive directors; (2) a sufficient number of independent directors; (3) the high presence of board members at the meetings; and (4) the large diffusion of internal control and remuneration committees.

Issues include: (1) the low presence of foreign and women directors; (2) the low number of meetings per year; (3) the high number of positions in governance bodies of a significant number of board members; and (4) the lack of compensation details.

The ownership structure of Canadian listed companies

The ownership data was collected from the Financial Post Top 500 database. The method used by Claessens et al. (2002) was used to divide firms into five categories, based on a 20 percent control threshold: firms were classified by whether they were controlled by an individual/family, government entity, non-financial corporation or financial institution. The firms that were classified as widely held were the ones where no shareholder owned more than 20 percent of the voting rights. Table 4.2 shows that in 2010, using 300 companies, Canada had fewer widely held firms (36 percent), with more ownership by individual/family (24 percent), and by foreign investors (39 percent). The current study is compared to King and Santor's (2008) study, using 1998 data, and shows that widely held firms have gone down from 55 percent to 36 percent and the firms that had 20 percent controlled shareholder ownership went from 45 percent to 64 percent, while individual investors/family firms decreased from 70 percent to 24 percent and financials also went down from 24 percent to 7 percent. The overall increase was due to the raise in control by corporations that went up from 6 percent to 12 percent, state-owned went up from 0 percent to 18 percent and foreign investors went from 0 percent to 39 percent.

In Canada, the market capitalization, as well as the number of listed firms, has fluctuated during the 2003–10 period (Table 4.3), due to the

Table 4.1 *The characteristics of the board of Canadian listed companies in 2010*

Variables	Characteristics of Canadian listed companies
Sample	100 listed companies (TSX 100)
Mix between executive and non-executive directors	On average, 80% of the directors are considered to be independent
Duality	85% of companies separated the role of board chair and CEO
Nationality of members	Foreign directors represent 30% of the directors in the sample
Gender of directors	Women directors represent 14% of the directors in the sample
Number of meetings	9 meetings
Number of committee meetings	5 meetings
Audit committee	100%
Nominating/governance committee	99%
Compensation and human resources committee	98%
Additional committees	Environment, health and safety committee 37%; pension/investment committee 18%; executive committee 13%; risk committee 6%; finance committee 9%; conduct committee 8%; social responsibility/public policy committee 5%; strategy/planning committee 3%
Board evaluations	100% of the companies review the performance of their individual directors, committees and the board overall; 85% of the companies' boards evaluated their board chairs and 48% were led by the governance committee; 52% of surveyed companies had a formal evaluation process for their committee chairs, in addition to the regular director evaluation; 48% of the companies used the peer evaluation method of assessing director performance; one in every two director evaluations was supplemented by a one-on-one review with the board chair
Compensation of board of directors	$119,500 is the all-inclusive average total compensation for non-employee directors, with equity accounting for 34%, cash fees 66%

Source: Board Index 2010

Table 4.2 *Ownership concentration of Canadian listed companies (2010)*

	Current study		King and Santor (2008)	
	Value	Percentage	Value	Percentage
Widely held	107	36%	55.4	55%
Controlled at 20% threshold	193	64%	44.6	45%
Of which:				
Individual investors/family	46	24%	31.2	70%
Corporation	24	12%	2.6	6%
Financial	14	7%	10.8	24%
State-owned	34	18%	0	0%
Foreign investors	75	39%	0	0%

Table 4.3 *Market capitalization of Canada stock exchanges 2003–10*

Number of companies listed		Market capitalization (December 31st)
Exchange	TSX	(USD)
2003	3,616	910
2004	3,630	1,178
2005	3,758	1,482
2006	3,842	1,701
2007	3,951	2,187
2008	3,841	1,033
2009	3,700	1,677
2010	3,714	2,170

Source: World Federation of Exchanges Annual Statistics, www.world-exchanges.org

global recession. At the end of 2010, there were 3,714 companies listed on the TSX, with the total listings having a market capitalization of $2.2 trillion (World Federation of Exchanges, 2010).

Corporate governance and IPOs in Canada

The regulation of IPOs

In Canada, when private companies become public companies, they are required to meet the TSX requirements, or the TSX Venture rules, based on their industry sector. The initial listing requirements for industrial, mining and oil and gas companies are broken down into profitable companies, companies forecasting profitability, technology companies, and companies focused on research and development. It is clear that these companies require varying operating structures to be successful and this is demonstrated by the varied listing criteria. The criteria set out by the TSX are used to ensure that companies are adequately poised to be successful traders in their particular industry. For instance, companies that are profitable, or forecasting profitability, must demonstrate substantial net tangible assets. In comparison, companies that are based on research and development, as well as technological-based growth, require no set assets, but do require proper planning and financial reserves to meet the development criteria for at least one year. The TSX utilizes the listing requirements to allow the flexibility of various markets to go public and be competitive.

Canada is home to many natural resources, which is of great benefit to the economy and is evident by the large quantity of mining and oil and gas companies. The TSX has made special criteria for these resource-based companies. As with the differences between companies producing a profit and technological companies, there are just as many and perhaps even more differences between mining companies in production and exploration stages, as well as producing oil companies.

Mining companies in production require the highest level of net tangible assets at $4 million, while those in exploration and development require only $3 million. For resource-based companies, it is not as much about the current profit, but proven profitable reserves. For an exploration and development stage mining company, they must have demonstrated a work program for exploration and development, with the recommendation of an independently qualified person, such as a professional geologist. Finally, in terms of producing oil and gas companies, a proven developed reserve base of $3 million is required, as well as a capital structure and the necessary funds to help reasonably increase reserves. The TSX utilizes flexibility in its listing criteria to maximize the potential market and ability for companies to reach IPO and be successful on a broad base.

Tier 2 is considered the lower level in the TSX Venture. The differences between Tier 1 and Tier 2 issuers are that Tier 1 has fewer filing requirements. The majority of traders of the TSX Venture can be found to be in Tier 2.

As with the regular TSX, the Venture is set up such that it distributes companies based on industry, so as to increase flexibility of the market. It also has similar, but not identical, listing requirements, as compared to the TSX. In terms of resource-based companies, there are no requirements for net tangible assets, but the companies do require significant interest and ability to utilize the properties, based on geological recommendations. Oil and gas companies are divided inside Tier 2, into exploration and reserves. Exploration is set up so that companies have the opportunity to pursue reservoirs that are unproven and possible prospectus offerings. Reserves are set up so that companies with proven reservoirs can go public, based on the total value of such reserves. All resource-based companies require legal documentation from a professional geologist registered in that province.

Industrial and technological-based companies, as well as real estate and investment companies, are also separated in the Venture. A variety of financing measures can allow these companies to go IPO. Net tangible assets of $750,000, or $500,000 in revenue, or even $2 million in arms-length financing, can be utilized to go IPO. It is clear that Canadian companies are provided with numerous avenues to maximize their potential IPO status.

Similar to the Tier 2 TSX Venture and overall TSX, Tier 1 separates the industries into four segments: mining; oil and gas; industrial/technology/life sciences; and real estate/investment. The noticeable difference is the higher value required to achieve the Tier 1 listing. For example, in mining, net tangible assets are not required for Tier 2, but are $2 million for Tier 1. This can also be applied to property reserves, such as oil and gas exploration, where a minimum of $3 million in reserves must be established and $1 million worth must be proven.

Table 4.4 shows the requirements of the TSX Venture for companies to continue to be listed, based on the industry segments for Tier 2 and Tier 1 issuers. Tier 2 requires the listed companies to have at least 10 percent of their shares floated to the public and this should not be less than 500,000 shares. The exchange requires the companies to have sufficient financial resources that are greater than $50,000 and to have the ability to maintain operations and cover general and administrative expenses for six months.

Table 4.4 *Listing and ongoing requirements in the TSX Venture*

Tier 2 continued listing requirements				
Standards	Industry			
	Mining	Oil and gas (exploration or reserves)	Industrial or technology or life sciences	Real estate or investment
Public distribution and market capitalization	(i) no less than 500,000 listed shares in the public float (ii) 10% of listed shares must be in public float (iii) listed shares in public float must have minimum market capitalization of $100,000 (iv) at least 150 public shareholders holding at least one board lot each, free of resale restrictions			
Working capital	Adequate working capital or financial resources of the greater of (i) $50,000 and (ii) an amount required in order to maintain operations and cover general and administrative expenses for a period of 6 months			
Assets and operations	No requirements generally, although the Exchange retains discretion to declare that an issuer no longer meets Tier 2 continued listing requirements if, in the Exchange's opinion, the issuer or its principal operating subsidiary substantially reduces or impairs its principal operating assets, ceases or discontinues a substantial portion of its operations or business for any reason, or seeks protection, or is placed under the protection of any insolvency or bankruptcy laws, or is placed into receivership			
Activity	Either A or B below: A) For the issuer's most recently completed financial year: i) positive cash flow; ii) significant operating revenue; or iii) $50,000 of exploration or		Either A or B below: A) For the issuer's most recently completed financial year: i) positive cash flow; ii) $150,000 of operating revenues; or iii) $150,000 of expenditures directly related to	

Table 4.4 (*cont.*)

Tier 2 continued listing requirements	
development expenditures	development of its assets or business
B) In aggregate, for the issuer's two most recently completed financial years, $100,000 of exploration or development expenditures	B) In aggregate, for the issuer's two most recently completed financial years, either: i) $300,000 of operating revenues; or ii) $300,000 of expenditures directly related to the development of its assets or business

Tier 1 continued listing requirements			
Mining	Oil and gas (exploration or reserves)	Industrial or technology or life sciences	Real estate or investment

Tier 1 issuer is considered to meet continued listing requirements for Tier 1 if, after listing, the Tier 1 issuer continues to meet initial listing requirements

Source: TSX Venture Continued Listing Criteria

The IPO process is complicated in Canada, and as a result, it is an expensive process and this ensures that companies are not just rushing to get listed. Coupled with the listing requirements, as well as the requirements to stay listed, there is shareholder protection. In general, shareholders are entitled to one vote per share. Some Canadian public companies have a dual-class share structure, with one class having multiple voting rights, which gives the holders of those shares voting control. In most cases, shareholders holding the other class of shares have "coat-tail" rights in the event of a takeover bid or similar transaction.

Shareholder approvals and protections are important and the ordinary corporate transactions require majority approval of the shareholders (over 50 percent of the votes cast). Extraordinary corporate transactions require special approval of the shareholders (66.6 percent of the votes cast). Most corporate statutes give shareholders the right to dissent with respect to extraordinary corporate transactions and demand fair value for the shares held by them. The provinces of Ontario and Quebec have securities rules (including approval by a majority of the minority shareholders and independent valuation of the subject matter of the transaction), which apply in certain circumstances, and which are designed to ensure fair treatment of minority shareholders in connection with certain types of transactions involving related parties. Canadian courts have broad remedial powers under Canadian corporate statutes to intervene in transactions that are determined to be oppressive or unfairly prejudicial to shareholders, or which unfairly disregard the interests of shareholders. They also have broad powers to permit shareholders to commence an action on behalf of a Canadian public company, or intervene in an action involving a Canadian public company for the purpose of prosecuting, defending or discontinuing the action on behalf of the company. The Canadian courts additionally have broad powers with respect to the conduct and enforcement of these derivative actions.

Institutional investors as shareholders, which own approximately 50 percent of the shares of Canadian public companies, have recently become more active with respect to corporate governance matters, and have shown an increased willingness to use the courts and regulatory authorities to challenge board decisions and processes.

The ownership and governance model of Canadian companies

La Porta et al. (1998) and Baums (1996) showed that the Canadian model is different from the American and British models. Half of the top firms in Canada, and most large firms elsewhere in the world, have controlling shareholders – wealthy families, other firms or large financial institutions. These controlling shareholders usually dominate the board and so are entrusted by their countries with the governance of those firms. The study by Morck et al. (2005) showed that the figures for Canada fluctuated through the twentieth century, but that a high level of family control characterized most years since the 1960s. Morck and Yeung (2006) suggest that "Canada should follow Israel in moving towards the Anglo-American model and away from the Italo-Latin American model" (page 20). They further add that the Canadian model was more like the

Chilean variety and less like the Anglo-American variety than Canadians are comfortable admitting. Embarrassing as this may be, the fact needs to be acknowledged in our corporate governance debates. Dual-class shares, like pyramiding, were commonplace in the United States in the early 20th century, and may have served an economic purpose similar to pyramiding, though no evidence supports this. Perhaps families with reputations for fair dealing might reassure public shareholders of their continued stewardship, by holding super-voting shares even as their firms raise ever more capital through equity issues. (page 21)

In the 1997 study by Rafael La Porta, Florencio Lopez-de-Silanes, Andrei Shleifer and Robert Vishny, they classified Canada as a common law jurisdiction, but Canada actually stands out as unique in the world financial markets, as one of the few countries with both common and civil law traditions (Puri, 2009). In Canada, the federal government and twelve of the thirteen provinces and territories operate under the common law system. Quebec operates under a civil law system, within the larger Canadian common law framework.

The study by Puri (2009) shows that the Canadian context matters when looking at the laws related to investor protection within a country. Puri further adds that in Canada, as in many other jurisdictions, securities laws and securities structure have an impact on investor protection. The debate in Canada on having a common securities regulator has focused on improving investor protection and improving enforcement. Furthermore, banking laws and the banking framework play an important role in investor protection.

In Canada, investor protection is reflected in the conservative nature of the Canadian banking system, which allowed Canadian financial institutions to escape relatively unscathed from the recent financial crisis. Finally, the Canadian system is structured, and has evolved in such a way that investor protections are fairly consistent between the common law and civil law provinces, even when the civil law statute does not necessarily mimic the common law statute. This is because of various unifying bodies, such as the Canadian Securities Administrators for provincial securities laws, and the unifying role of the Supreme Court of Canada for corporate law principles across the country.

Table 4.5 *IPO year and industry classification*

	2006	2007	2008	Total
Oil and gas	1	6	0	7
Basic materials	1	12	5	18
Industrials	0	3	2	5
Consumer services	1	1	1	3
Healthcare	0	2	0	2
Financials	0	1	2	3
Information technology	1	5	0	6
Telecommunication	0	1	0	1
Total	4	31	10	45

The IPOs between 2006 and 2008

From 2006 to 2008, 45 companies went public and, since 2007, there has been a considerable drop from 31 to 10. Table 4.5 captures the IPOs, based on the different industry sectors, for the period 2006 to 2008. Most of the companies in the sample went public in 2007 (31 companies). Only 10 went public in 2008, due to the global financial crisis. Moreover, as Table 4.5 shows, IPOs are focused in basic materials (18), oil and gas (7), and information technology (6).

Canadian companies going IPO, as shown in Table 4.6, on average had 355 employees, revenue of $27 million and assets equal to $66 million. The Canadian companies going public were entrepreneurial companies that were on average 6 years old, but the mix does contain companies that were 10, 42 and 109 years old. The smallest companies, in terms of employees, were Ithaca Energy and Strategic Resources, both with 7 employees. The largest company, in terms of employees, was Heavy Construction with 2,750 employees. In terms of performance, on average ROA was 0 percent, while ROE was 15 percent and ROS was 92 percent.

Ithaca Energy is a Canadian oil and gas exploration company, which focuses its exploration and development in the North Sea, in the United Kingdom region. The company possesses four major reservoirs along the North Sea. Ithaca produced 38.5 billion barrels of oil equivalents by the end of 2008, and is looking to continue its acquisition and production of North Sea wells. Ithaca is currently traded on

Table 4.6 *IPO size and performance*

	Size			Performance		
	Employees	Revenues	Assets	ROA	ROE	ROS
Min	7	0	2,688,567	−139%	−164%	0%
1st quartile	59	249,304	18,701,455	−10%	−10%	0%
2nd quartile	110	12,691,690	29,251,302	−1%	0%	0%
3rd quartile	380	31,217,000	76,113,714	2%	14%	0%
Max	2,750	303,976,221	450,945,375	408%	791%	900%
Average	355	26,819,417	66,256,781	0%	15%	92%

the AIM (in the UK) and TSXV. The company boasted a third-quarter net profit of $13.5 million in 2010, in comparison to a net loss of $1.1 million in the third quarter ending September 30, 2009.

Strategic Resources (SR) is a Saskatchewan-based IPO. The company focuses on rare earth, vanadium, lithium and uranium exploration and production. Strategic Resources is a young company with four projects currently in the works. SR is a forward-thinking company looking to future energy sources as well as ulterior sources of strategically important minerals for technological growth and innovation. SR's current operations are found in America (New Mexico and Oregon). The company is listed on the TSX Venture. Currently, Strategic Resources has no revenue, with projected six-month losses in 2010 of $168,062 and $495,451 in 2009.

The ownership structure of thirty-seven Canadian IPO companies, before going public, was that the family owned 2 percent of the share capital, and the venture capitalists owned 1 percent (Table 4.7). Families, venture capitalists and the government after the IPO on average own 1 and 2 percent of the shares. There was an absence of banks, government and business angels in the share capital of companies, before and after the IPO.

The composition of boards of directors of IPO companies, as shown in Table 4.8, on average is made up of ten directors: five executive, one non-executive and four independent. The functional background of the directors in the areas of finance, accounting and law was on average 52 percent; in marketing and sales it was 32 percent; and in engineering, operations and R&D it was 53 percent.

Table 4.7 *IPO ownership structure (data in percent)*

	Family		Bank		Government		VC		Angels		Top 1		Top 3	
	Pre	Post	Pre	Post	Pre	Post	Pre	Post	Pre	Post	Pre	Post	Pre	Post
Min	5	0	0	0	0	0	0	0	0	0	80	0	52	0
1st quartile	0	0	0	0	0	0	0	0	0	0	15	0	0	0
2nd quartile	0	0	0	0	0	0	0	0	0	0	6	17	0	0
3rd quartile	1	1	0	0	0	0	0	0	0	0	0	46	16	33
Max	17	8	3	10	0	0	22	24	8	7	26	100	99	74
Average	2	1	0	0	0	0	1	2	0	0	10	27	12	16

Table 4.8 *IPO board of directors*

	Size	Executive directors	Non-executive directors	Independent directors	Engineering, operations, R&D (%)	Markets, sales (%)	Finance, accounting, law (%)
Min	4	0.00	0.00	0.00	0.00	0.00	0.00
1st quartile	8	4.00	0.00	3.00	41.50	19.25	39.00
2nd quartile	10	5.00	0.00	4.00	57.00	31.50	50.00
3rd quartile	12	6.00	1.00	5.00	63.00	46.25	63.00
Max	19	12.00	4.00	9.50	100.00	64.00	100.00
Average	9.8	5.00	0.96	3.85	52.82	32.27	51.89

The description of an IPO: Bridgewater

The firm before the IPO

Bridgewater was founded in 1997 by Russ Freen and Doug Somers. The company provides mobile personalization products and services, which enable global service providers to manage and profit from mobile data services, content and commerce. The growth of Bridgewater has been due to mobile Internet, which has accelerated during 2009 and 2010. In 2007, before the company went public, the three major shareholders were Alcatel–Lucent (23.31 percent), VenGrowth Investment Fund Inc. (15.12 percent) and Wesley Clover Corporation (11.30 percent).

One of the founders, Russ Freen, continues to serve as a director on the board, while Doug Somers is now the co-president and CEO of Cassidy Bay Group Inc., which specializes in individual executive coaching, team building, leadership training and achieving organizational alignment. The Wesley Clover Corporation was an initial investor in Bridgewater, and founder and chairman of Wesley Clover, Sir Terence Matthews, continues to be involved in the company as the chairman of the board.

The current president and CEO of Bridgewater Systems is Ed Ogonek. The board of directors of Bridgewater includes ten directors, and has a chairman, four vice presidents, one CFO, a founder and two independent directors, and the CEO. The company had the following committees: Audit Committee (three members), Compensation Committee (three members) and Nominating and Governance Committee (two members).

The offer

The firm's shares grew to 22,727,689. The net proceeds from the IPO were expected to be $17,300,000. The cash from the offer varied between 10 and 15 percent to expand professional services capability, approximately 20–25 percent to increase product portfolio, which would in turn create new products and services, and approximately 15–20 percent to expand sales and move into new markets. The price range per share varied from a minimum of $1.15 to a maximum of $4.40 in 2006, with an offering price of $5.50.

The price of the shares opened on the TSX at $5.40, went as high as $5.50, and as low as $5.00, and finally ended up closing at $5.10. The number of shares traded on that day was 568,194, which was one of the highest trading days for the company.

The firm after the IPO

The cash coming from the IPO has been used to enhance Bridgewater's future. The financial crisis did not alter the growth of the company, whose revenues reached $22.4 million in 2009. Bridgewater Systems continues to maintain its headquarters in Ottawa, Canada. Bridge-water is a global company with regional offices in the UK, Australia, Hong Kong and the USA. Bridgewater Systems focuses on intelligent broadband controls and solutions, which can be integrated with mobile networks, optimizing connections and other subsequent mobile technologies.

The total market capitalization of the firm is $206.06 million, and the number of shares outstanding is 24.89 million. The revenue increased by 51 percent to $66.7 million for 2009, compared with $44.2 million for 2008. The net earnings for 2009 were $11.2 million, or $0.44 per share fully diluted, versus $2.8 million, or $0.11 per share fully diluted, in 2008. Bridgewater ended the year with a strong balance sheet, with cash and short-term investments of $67.3 million and no debt. Bridgewater is listed on the TSX and has experienced substantial growth in a short period of time, with net earnings of $11,203,821 in 2009 to $22,995,396 in 2010.

Conclusion

Corporate governance in Canada continues to evolve, particularly as the Canadian securities regulators try to follow the Sarbanes-Oxley Act, as well as the rules and guidelines established by the US SEC. Corporate law and the code of good governance are in place to protect the shareholders' rights and maintain investor confidence in the public market.

The capital market in Canada is relatively small, the number of women directors is limited, and there is very low government involvement, as shown from the recent IPOs. In the three years studied, the number of companies that went IPO decreased, and they have the following characteristics: (1) they are resource-based companies (basic materials and oil and gas); (2) their average age is six years old; and (3) their board of directors has an average of ten directors, five executive and one non-executive, the majority of whom have a background in engineering, operations and R&D.

In Canada, there is a much higher level of wealthy individuals and families as controlling shareholders, particularly when compared to the US and UK. The interesting trend in recent years, when looking at publicly traded companies, is the concentration of foreign ownership. It is not common for corporations to have CEO duality, and the boards are made up of mostly outside independent directors.

Several governance experts have been very critical of corporate governance in Canada, calling for faster reform and pushing for it to move closer to the Anglo-American model. Other researchers, like La Porta et al. (1997), failed to acknowledge Canada as having both a common law system as well as civil law. Nonetheless, during the financial crisis,

Canada provided a considerable amount of leadership and guidance. The study by Puri (2009) points out that more effort is required to understand that Canadian context, as it has played a key role in protecting investors from the current financial crisis.

References

Baums, Theodor. 1996. 'Universal banks and investment companies in Germany', in Anthony Saunders and Ingo Walter (eds.), *Universal Banking: Financial System Design Reconsidered*. Chicago: Irwin, 124–60.

Broshko, Erinn B. and Kai Li. 2006. 'Playing by the rules: Comparing principles-based and rules-based corporate governance in Canada and the U.S.', *Canadian Investment Review*, 19(4), 18–24.

Canadian Coalition for Good Governance: www.ccgg.ca/site/ccgg/assets/pdf/CCGG_Building_High_Performance_Boards_Final_March_2010.pdf. Retrieved February 15, 2011.

Claessens, Stijn, Simeon Djankov, Joseph P.H. Fan and Larry H.P. Lang. 2002. 'Disentangling the incentive and entrenchment effects of large shareholdings', *Journal of Finance*, 57(6), 2741–71.

King, Michael R. and Eric Santor. 2008. 'Family values: Ownership structure, performance and capital structure of Canadian firms', *Journal of Banking & Finance*, 32(11), 2423–32.

La Porta, Rafael, Florencio Lopez-de-Silanes, Andrei Shleifer and Robert W. Vishny. 1997. 'Legal determinants of external finance', *Journal of Finance*, 52(6), 1131–50.

  1998. 'Law and finance', *Journal of Political Economy*, 106(6), 1113–55.

McDermott, Robert and Sean Farrell. 2004. *Corporate Governance in Canada. Global Corporate Governance Guide 2004: Best Practice in the Boardroom*. London: Globe White Page.

Morck, Randall and Bernard Yeung. 2006. *Some Obstacles to Good Corporate Governance in Canada and How to Overcome Them*. Study commissioned by the Task Force to Modernize Securities Legislation in Canada.

Morck, Randall K., Michael Percy, Gloria Tian and Bernard Yeung. 2005. 'The rise and fall of the widely held firm: A history of corporate ownership in Canada', in Randall K. Morck (ed.), *A History of Corporate Governance around the World: Family Business Groups to Professional Managers*. University of Chicago Press.

Puri, Poonam. 2009. 'Legal origins, investor protection, and Canada', CLPE – Working Paper No. 03/2010.

Spencer Stuart Canada. 2010. 'Board index – Canada 2010'.

TSX Listing Criteria: http://tmx.complinet.com/en/display/display_viewall. html?rbid=2072&element_id=9&record_id=9. Retrieved February 15, 2011.

TSX Venture Listing Criteria: www.tmx.com/en/listings/venture_issuer_ resources/finance_manual.html. Retrieved February 15, 2011.

World Federation of Exchanges: www.world-exchanges.org/statistics. Retrieved March 1, 2011.

5 Corporate governance and initial public offerings in China

JEAN JINGHAN CHEN AND STEPHEN X.H. GONG

Corporate governance mechanisms

Governed by a powerful Communist government, the People's Republic of China (PRC) is a country with strong state central control and whose most distinctive cultural feature is its highly homogeneous social culture. Hence, it is very socially cohesive. After the establishment of the PRC in 1949, a civil law system has been built up gradually and improved considerably during the 1990s in the sense of supporting the market-oriented economic reforms which encourage the market to play a fundamental role in allocating economic resources. Meanwhile, maintaining the control of critical and strategic resources throughout the country, including large state-owned enterprises (SOEs), has been emphasized. During that period, a number of those large SOEs were restructured into joint stock companies and then floated on the two domestic stock markets in Shanghai and Shenzhen, forming the majority of China's listed companies. However, the market for corporate control is inactive for firms that underperform in their industries since many of those activities still need to be approved by the government. Information disclosure is opaque in the sense that information is manipulated, delayed, and even falsified in some cases. Nevertheless, things improved a lot after the thirty-nine new accounting principles released in 2006, which indicates the moving towards convergence with International Financial Reporting Standards (IFRS). Corporate governance codes are mandatory, which means that the regulatory authority may instruct companies to correct their inappropriate governance practices to comply with the codes. The business group is the common form of corporate governance which is dominated by the state.

Corporate ownership in most of the listed firms is highly concentrated as the state still keeps more than 50 percent of the majority of listed firms' shares. Accordingly, the state (including the central

115

government and local governments) is generally the dominant share-holder, but individual and family blockholders exist in some firms as well and the number has been increasing in recent years. Minority shareholders have little legal protection for their rights and their interests are often ignored and even appropriated by major shareholders. Institutional shareholders have emerged significantly since the 1990s, but the institutional environment for them to exercise shareholder activism has not been developed. Corporate boards are two-tier in nature with board of directors (which is an executive board of management) and board of supervisors in place at the same time. CEO duality is less common whereby the CEO chairs the board after the publication of the Corporate Governance Code in 2002. Corporate boards consist of at least one-third outside, non-executive directors playing a role of independent monitoring specified by the Corporate Governance Code. Executive compensation is egalitarian in nature. The CEO and top management team are mainly compensated with cash compensation, and only a few of them are rewarded with variable compensation that is usually tied to the financial performance of the firm. Such linking of compensation to performance is required by the Corporate Governance Code, but may not necessarily be the case in practice.

Corporate law

China's legal framework for securities markets and listed companies took shape in the early 1990s. Current major laws include the Securities Law, the Company Law, the Securities Investment Fund Law, and the Criminal Law (Huang, 2010). The Company Law, which regulates the organization and behavior of a company, was promulgated in 1993 and was subsequently amended in 1999 and more recently in 2005. It was the most important source of corporate governance rules prior to 2002. According to the 1993 Company Law, listed companies are required to form three corporate governing bodies: (1) the shareholders, acting as a body at the general meeting; (2) the board of directors; and (3) the board of supervisors. In addition, the Company Law introduced two new statutory corporate positions – the Chairman of the board of directors and the Chief Executive Officer (CEO). In 1998, another important statute for China's securities markets, the Securities Law, was promulgated, which greatly promoted the development and the regulation of the market (Huang, 2010). The new Chinese Bankruptcy Law also went into effect on June 1, 2007.

The China Securities Regulatory Commission (CSRC), the national regulator charged with enforcing listing and delisting rules, maintaining order, and generally protecting investors, has adopted an administrative governance approach to regulate China's stock market. Under this approach, CSRC uses accounting numbers (e.g., return on equity) amongst others to decide whether to list or delist a company (or designate it as Special Treatment, essentially an indication of poor performance and/or financial distress of a listed firm), and to approve a listed company's application for a rights issue. Such a regulatory approach provides the listed companies with strong incentives to engage in "financial packaging" prior to the public listing, and to manage reported earnings in order to maintain their listing status (Aharony et al., 2000; Liu and Lu, 2007).

A major problem with corporate governance practices in China in the pre-2002 years was that no independent directors were appointed to the board of directors. In recent years, CSRC has initiated a series of mandatory structural reforms to boost the quality of listed companies, to protect investors' rights and interests, and to promote the sustained development of capital markets. These include the Code of Corporate Governance for Listed Companies in China 2002; Opinions on Upgrading the Quality of Listed Companies 2005; and Administrative Measures on the Securities Investor Protection Fund 2005 (Huang, 2010).

China currently adopts a two-tier board structure which is similar to that used in the continental European countries (e.g., Germany, the Netherlands). Shareholders appoint the members of the supervisory board, whilst the supervisory board appoints the members of the management board (i.e., the board of directors). The supervisory board is charged with overseeing the firm, while the board of directors focuses on the daily operations of the firm. Even after the share-split reform (which started in 2005 and was essentially completed in 2007) under which previously large blocks of non-tradable shares primarily held by the state were converted into tradable shares, the state remains as the majority shareholder in the vast majority of listed companies, and the participation of institutional investors is limited. To date the state continues to exert significant influence in major corporate decision-making, ranging from securities issuance to the appointment

Table 5.1 *Summary of key characteristics influencing Chinese corporate governance*

Feature	Key characteristic
Main business form	State-owned enterprise, joint stock companies
Predominant ownership structure	State
Legal system	Civil Law
Board structure	Two-tier board model
Other important aspects	Influence of Communist Party

Source: Mallin (2010)

of directors and determination of executive compensation. Mallin (2010) categorizes the key factors that influence the development of Chinese corporate governance into several aspects, including the business form, ownership structure, legal system, and board structure, among others (Table 5.1).

Code of good governance

Recent corporate scandals, such as Guangxia (Yinchuan) Industry Co. Ltd, Lantian Co. Ltd, and Sanju Pharmaceutical Co. Ltd, etc., have helped fuel the drive for corporate governance reforms in China. Specifically, in January 2002, CSRC issued the Code of Corporate Governance for Listed Companies in China (hereafter the Code) (CSRC, 2002) which is broadly based on the *OECD Principles of Corporate Governance* (2004). The main objectives of the Code are to address "the protection of investors' interests and rights, the essential behavior rules and moral standards for directors, supervisors, managers and other senior management members of listed companies" (CSRC, 2002: Preface). The Code is seen as the yardstick by which a company is able to measure its corporate governance; if there are deficiencies in the corporate governance of a company, the securities supervision and regulatory authorities may instruct the company to correct its corporate governance to comply with the Code. The Code contains seven main chapters and the key provisions in each chapter are discussed below, along with related research findings.

Shareholders and shareholders' meetings

The Code states that "the corporate governance structure of a company shall ensure fair treatment towards all shareholders, especially minority shareholders. All shareholders are to enjoy equal rights and bear the corresponding duties based on the shares they hold" (CSRC, 2002: Section 1.2). Shareholders should have equal rights and, if their rights are infringed, then they could have redress through legal action.

The Code also requires that companies establish communication channels with shareholders and that shareholders be informed of significant matters that affect the company (CSRC, 2002: Section 2.5). Shareholders should be notified in good time of a shareholders' meeting and agenda items should be given an appropriate amount of time in the meeting.

Listed company and its controlling shareholders

This section of the Code deals with a protocol for how the controlling shareholders should behave when an enterprise is being restructured or reorganized prior to listing. Certain aspects of the enterprise, such as its non-operational institutions and welfare institutions, are normally not transferred to the listed company, but may continue to provide services to the listed company in the capacity of a separate company based on commercial principles. The controlling shareholders should not act in a way detrimental to the listed company's or shareholders' legal rights and interests by adversely restructuring assets or otherwise taking advantage of their position (CSRC, 2002: Sections 2.20 and 2.21). The controlling shareholders initially nominate the candidates for directors and supervisors on the basis of their professional skills, knowledge, and experience. The shareholders' meeting or the board of directors will then approve the appointments as appropriate (CSRC, 2002: Section 2.20). The listed company should be able to act independently from the controlling shareholders, including its personnel, and also the financial and accounting management systems of the listed company should be independent from the controlling shareholders (CSRC, 2002: Sections 2.23, 2.24, and 2.25). In reality, however, a growing body of research suggests that controlling shareholders (in most cases, the central or local government or their various agencies) of listed companies in China exert strong influence on the listed companies, both in terms of the appointments of senior officers and in terms of major corporate decision-making (e.g., Fan et al., 2007; Firth et al., 2007).

Earnings management has been found as a common practice in most listed companies in Chinese stock exchanges (e.g., Aharony et al., 2000). In addition to accrual-based earnings management practices, recent literature reveals that related party transactions (RPTs) (defined as any transaction between a firm or any of its subsidiaries and a connected party, e.g., the directors, the chief executive and their associates or any firms holding substantial shares of the listed firm) are widespread among Chinese listed companies. The disclosure of RPTs was originally governed by the 15 January 1997 CSRC Circular on Content and Format Standards of Information Disclosure for Securities Issuing Companies No. 7 – Announcement on Related Party Transactions (Cheung et al., 2009). The Code further requires that RPTs should, in principle, be at market value (CSRC, 2002: Sections 2.12, 2.13, and 2.14). Recent research finds that RPTs are often made at non-market prices (Chan and Lo, 2004) and are widespread among Chinese listed companies. They are often used as a means of transferring value out of the listed company to the controlling shareholders or as a means of propping up poorly performing companies (Cheung et al., 2009; Jiang et al., 2010; Lo et al., 2010; Peng et al., 2010).

Directors and board of directors

China has adopted a two-tier board system of corporate governance, with a board of directors and a board of supervisors in place at the same time.

The board of directors is accountable to shareholders, shall treat all shareholders equally, and be concerned with the interests of stakeholders (CSRC, 2002: Section 3.43). The directors should faithfully, honestly, and diligently perform their duties for the best interests of the company and all shareholders, and they should also devote adequate time and energy to their role as director and attend board meetings (CSRC, 2002: Sections 3.33, 3.34, and 3.35). The board of directors should meet periodically and have a pre-set agenda, with timely and clear information about the agenda items being sent to all the directors. If two or more independent directors feel that the information is unclear or inadequate, they may apply to postpone the meeting or the discussion of the relevant agenda item.

According to Section 3.49 of the Code, a listed company shall introduce independent directors to its board of directors in accordance with relevant regulations. Independent directors shall be independent from the listed company that employs them and the company's major shareholders. An independent director may not hold any other position apart from independent directorship in the listed company. The independent directors shall bear the duties of good faith and due diligence and care towards the listed company, and shall be especially concerned with protecting the interests of minority shareholders from being infringed (CSRC, 2002: Section 3.50). In addition, the CSRC issued the Guidelines for Introducing Independent Directors to the Board of Directors of Listed Companies in the summer of 2001. The guidelines mandate all domestically listed companies to amend their articles as necessary to comply with the guidelines and to appoint at least one-third of the board as independent directors.

The Code also recommends that various committees of the board be established, such as a corporate strategy committee, a remuneration and appraisal committee, an audit committee, and a nominations committee (CSRC, 2002: Section 3.52). Independent directors should be in a majority on these committees. At least one independent director from the audit committee shall be an accounting professional. The importance of having an independent board and of having directors with financial expertise in China is underscored in a few recent studies. For example, Liu and Lu (2007) find that earnings management among China's listed companies is negatively associated with the percentage of outside directors. Firth et al. (2010) find that the proclivity of listed companies in China to falsify financial statements and thus have to restate in subsequent years is tempered by a high percentage of directors with financial expertise.

Supervisors and board of supervisors

The supervisory board is accountable to shareholders, and its duties include supervising corporate finance and the directors' and managers' performance, and protecting the company's and shareholders' legal rights and interests. It should comprise individuals with professional knowledge or working experience in such areas as law and accounting. The supervisory board's members should be provided with appropriate information to enable them to do their job effectively, and the supervisory board's meeting should be minuted (CSRC, 2002: Sections 4.59,

4.60, 4.61, and 4.66). However, in practice, Chen (2005) suggests that supervisory boards in China's listed firms are weak and ineffective. More research, however, is required to better understand the relationship between composition of the supervisory board (as well as the professional experience of members of the supervisory board) and corporate governance and performance.

Performance assessments and incentive and disciplinary systems

Directors', supervisors', and management's performance should be assessed through a fair and transparent procedure, with directors and management being evaluated by the board of directors or by the remuneration and appraisal committee (CSRC, 2002: Sections 5.69 and 5.70). Independent directors and supervisors should be evaluated by a combination of self-assessment and peer review. The performance and compensation of the directors and supervisors should be reported to the shareholders' meeting (CSRC, 2002: Sections 5.70 and 5.71).

There is much demand from employees in Chinese companies, particularly at the higher levels where an awareness of the Western practices is more apparent, to link compensation with performance. The Code recommends that the compensation for management personnel be linked to both the company's performance and the individual's work performance (CSRC, 2002: Sections 5.77 and 5.78). However, Chen et al. (2010) suggest that supervisory boards in China's listed firms are weak and exert little influence on executive pay. Furthermore, the state exerts considerable influence on top management pay. Firth et al. (2006) find that firms that have a state agency as the major shareholder do not appear to use performance-related pay; in contrast, firms that have private blockholders as their major shareholders relate the CEO's pay to increases in stockholders' wealth or increases in profitability. Pay disparity between top executives and workers in China, whilst rising in recent years, is nowhere comparable to the levels observed for US firms (Kim and Lu, 2009). In recent years, there has also been a tendency for the Chinese government to try to narrow the pay gap between top executives and workers in order to maintain social equality (Firth et al., 2010). In contrast to the pay setting in Western countries, compensation in the form of stock options is not commonly used in China. This is a major difference between the components of executive compensation in China and those in the US and the UK. Another notable feature of executive compensation in China is that compensation for managers often takes the form of non-cash compensation, including various allowances (e.g., entertainment, traveling, meeting expenses) and political promotion (Firth et al., 2010).

Stakeholders

The Code states that "while maintaining the listed company's development and maximizing the benefits of shareholders, the company shall be concerned with the welfare, environmental protection and public interests of the community in which it resides, and shall pay attention to the company's social responsibilities" (CSRC, 2002: Section 6.86). In addition, the Code also mentions that the company should respect the legal rights of the various stakeholder groups and provide them with information as appropriate (CSRC, 2002: Sections 6.81 and 6.84). In particular, employees are encouraged to provide feedback on various issues that might affect them by direct communication with the board of directors, the supervisory board, and management personnel (CSRC, 2002: Section 6.85). There is currently a lack of studies related to the extent to which China's listed companies fulfill corporate social responsibility.

Information disclosure and transparency

The quality of financial reporting lies at the heart of the Code. The Code recommends that a listed company shall establish sound financial and accounting management systems in accordance with laws and regulations and shall conduct independent business accounting. In regard to information disclosure, the Code stipulates that information disclosure is a continuing responsibility of listed companies. A listed company shall truthfully, accurately, completely, and timely disclose information as required by laws, regulations, and the company's articles of association. Furthermore, a listed company shall also voluntarily and timely disclose all other information that may have a material effect on the decisions of shareholders and stakeholders, and shall ensure equal access to information for all shareholders (CSRC, 2002: Section 7.89). Anecdotal as well as empirical evidence suggests, however, that there is much to be desired with respect to the quality and reliability of financial disclosures among China's listed companies. A large number of studies show that listed companies in China manipulate their financial figures/statements in order to meet regulatory requirements or to defraud or mislead investors, either before the IPO process and/or after the IPO process (Aharony et al., 2000; Liu and Lu, 2007; Aharony et al., 2010; Firth et al., 2010). Cheung, Jiang and Tan (2010) find a positive relation between company transparency and market valuation in China, and hence regulatory reforms aimed at enhancing transparency and disclosures are called for and will benefit the listed companies as well as investors.

Stock exchange and listed companies

The Chinese stock market was initially organized by the government to partially privatize its state-owned enterprises (SOEs) in an effort to relieve the government of its funding burdens and to improve the operating performance of the SOEs (Chen, 2005). Usually the profitable operating units of an SOE were listed, and the non-operating and non-profitable units were retained by the SOE. Since its inception in 1990/1991, the Chinese stock market (Shanghai Stock Exchange and Shenzhen Stock Exchange) has grown rapidly along with its fast-growing economy. By the end of 2009, there were more than 1,500 listed companies in China with a market capitalization of US$3.21 trillion, making it one of the largest in the world in terms of market capitalization.

The Chinese domestic capital market is segmented into A-share, B-share, and H-share markets. A-shares (denominated in RMB) are open to Chinese domestic investors only. Originally, B-shares (denominated in US dollars on the Shanghai Stock Exchange and in Hong Kong dollars on the Shenzhen Stock Exchange) were open to foreign investors only, but they became accessible to individual domestic investors in 2001 provided they had foreign currencies. H-shares, listed on the Stock Exchange of Hong Kong, are available to any investor.

These listed companies are governed by listing and delisting rules set by CSRC, which was set up in 1992 and is the equivalent of the Securities and Exchange Commission in the US. The two stock exchanges essentially implement these rules.

Traditionally China implements a quota system under which companies seeking a public listing must seek approval from the CSRC.

Quotas are usually allocated to ministries and provinces. Typically strategic (or "protected") industries and companies with strong political connections (i.e., key SOEs under the central or local governments) are accorded higher priority for public listing (Aharony et al., 2000). Starting from 1993, an increasing number of companies whose ultimate ownership may be traced to mainland China have sought a listing in overseas markets including the US, Hong Kong, Singapore, and the UK. Research has identified a few reasons for choosing an overseas listing, including access to a larger and more mature investor base, pursuit of long-term growth, and lower transaction costs in a more efficient institutional and information environment amongst other factors (Yang and Lau, 2006; Ding et al., 2010).

Table 5.2 shows the number of IPO companies over time and by stock exchange. As of 31 December 2009, there are a total of 1,875 listed companies in the Shanghai Stock Exchange and the Shenzhen Stock Exchange (including the main board, the Small and Medium Enterprises Board, and the ChiNext market).[1] In terms of number of newly listed firms, the peak occurred in 1997. It is noteworthy that a public listing in China's stock markets has always been a hot commodity. A number of reasons may be responsible for the keen competition for a public listing. First, the cost of external equity financing is relatively low – in fact, a survey found that the cost of debt for Chinese companies was 35.5 percent higher than the cost of public equity in 2004 (Ding et al., 2010). In part, this may be because the debt market in China is underdeveloped, and it is usually difficult to get a large bank loan. Second, many listed

---

[1] The Small and Medium Enterprises Board (SME Board), launched in May 2004, and ChiNext, launched in October 2009, were new additions to China's multi-tier capital market system. The SME Board is a segment of the Shenzhen Stock Exchange's main board. The listing standards for the SME Board are the same as those for the main board. Smaller companies satisfying main board listing standards are exclusively traded on the SME Board following an independent trading system. ChiNext, as an independent market on the Shenzhen Stock Exchange, offers a capital platform tailor-made for the needs of enterprises engaged in independent innovation and other growing venture enterprises. The difference between ChiNext and the main board lies in its mechanisms of financing, investment, and risk management for issuers at various stages of development, rather than simply the size. Further details are available from the Shenzhen Stock Exchange website: www.szse.cn/.

Table 5.2 *Distribution of China IPO companies over time and by stock exchange*

| Year | Shanghai | | Shenzhen | | | |
	A-shares	B-shares	A-shares	B-shares	ChiNext	Total
1990	7	0	1	0	0	8
1991	0	0	5	0	0	5
1992	22	9	18	9	0	58
1993	72	13	52	10	0	147
1994	69	12	42	5	0	128
1995	15	2	9	10	0	36
1996	103	6	100	9	0	218
1997	85	8	121	8	0	222
1998	53	2	53	3	0	111
1999	46	2	52	0	0	100
2000	87	1	49	5	0	142
2001	78	0	1	0	0	79
2002	70	0	1	0	0	71
2003	67	0	0	0	0	67
2004	61	0	39	0	0	100
2005	3	0	12	0	0	15
2006	14	0	52	0	0	66
2007	25	0	101	0	0	126
2008	6	0	71	0	0	77
2009	9	0	54	0	36	99
Total	892	55	833	59	36	1,875

Source: Wind database

companies do not pay dividends, or just pay very low dividends. Third, the highly concentrated ownership structure among China's listed companies (with the state controlling, either directly or indirectly, more than 80 percent of the voting shares on average) means they do not need to fear losing control due to the dilution of ownership when they issue new shares. The entry barrier to the stock market, and hence the need to maintain the public listing status, have given rise to certain phenomena that are unique to China, including the incentives to manipulate earnings both prior to the IPO and after the IPO (Aharony et al., 2000; Aharony et al., 2010).

The ownership structure of Chinese listed companies

Table 5.3 shows the ownership structure of Chinese listed companies by type of shares. Depending on whether or not the shares are freely tradable on the stock exchange, shares in China may be divided into tradable (private-owned) and non-tradable shares (state-owned). When the two Chinese stock exchanges were first established, over 90 percent of the listed companies were owned by the state. It is apparent from Table 5.3 that state shares, which are non-tradable, represent the single largest category, averaging over 40 percent. Before the share-split reform in 2005, non-tradable shares (including state and legal person shares) represented over 60 percent of the shares issued. The percentage of non-tradable shares started to decline in 2005 and reached only 31 percent by 2009. The percentage of state shares has also declined steadily. In addition, an increasing number of Chinese companies have sought a public listing in the Hong Kong Stock Exchange, with the percentage of H-shares rising from 0 in 1992 to 15 percent in 2009.

Table 5.3 *Ownership structure by type of shares (data in percent)*

	1992	1995	1999	2001	2003	2005	2006	2007	2008	2009
State shares	41	39	36	41	49	46	53	55	49	25
Other non-tradable shares	28	25	29	20	15	16	13	8	7	6
Sub-total of non-tradable shares	69	64	65	61	64	62	66	63	56	31
A-shares	16	21	26	32	27	30	21	21	27	53
B-shares	15	7	5	2	3	3	2	1	1	1
H-shares	0	8	4	5	6	5	14	15	16	15
Sub-total of tradable shares	31	36	35	39	36	38	37	37	44	69
Total	100	100	100	100	100	100	100	100	100	100

Source: Wind database

Board of directors

To study the composition and operation of boards of directors in China's listed companies, we apply a stratified random sampling method to the population of Chinese listed companies during 2006–9 and select 200 companies for a closer examination of their corporate governance characteristics. Among the sample firms, 120 are from the manufacturing sector (reflecting the dominance of this sector) and the rest are from other sectors (ranging from 3 to 8 firms per sector). As reported in Table 5.4, the average number of directors in China's listed companies is 11.57. Among these, there is an average of 2.8 executive directors (or 24.20 percent of the board of directors), an average of 4.71

Table 5.4 *Characteristics of the board of directors (mean values)*

	2006	2007	2008	2009
Number of members	11.45	11.15	11.65	12.01
Number of executive directors	2.68	2.97	2.91	2.64
Percentage of executive directors	23.40	26.60	25.00	22.00
Number of non-executive directors	4.87	4.31	4.67	5.00
Percentage of non-executive directors	42.50	38.70	40.10	41.60
Number of independent non-executive directors	3.90	3.87	4.07	4.37
Percentage of independent non-executive directors	34.10	34.70	34.90	36.40
Number of directors representing employees	n/a	0.06	0.08	0.08
Percentage of directors representing employees	n/a	0.50	0.70	0.70
Number of board meetings	7.99	9.48	10.52	10.52
Attendance rate at board meetings (%)	88.00	87.67	82.86	92.27
Number of sub-committees	3.41	3.43	3.70	3.84
Number of members in the audit committee	4.04	3.98	3.74	3.87
Number of members in the remunerations committee	4.47	4.24	3.89	3.85
Number of members in the nominations committee	4.92	4.32	2.85	2.78
Total number of meetings convened by the sub-committees	6.93	9.19	10.00	10.35
Number of training sessions for board of directors	n/a	0.03	0.14	0.25

Source: Wind database

non-executive directors (or 40.73 percent of the board of directors), and an average of 4.05 independent directors (or 35 percent of the board of directors). The number of directors representing employees averages 0.07 (or 0.7 percent of the board of directors). On average there are 3.60 sub-committees under the board. The average number of members is 3.90 for the audit committee, 4.06 for the remuneration committee, and 3.72 in the nominations committee. The various committees have an average of 9.12 meetings per year, and on average the board of directors participates in 0.14 training sessions per year.

Board of supervisors

Table 5.5 reports the basic characteristics of the board of supervisors in China's listed companies. There is an average of 5.15 members in the board of supervisors. Among these, supervisors from outside the firm average 1.82 persons (or 35.24 percent of the board of supervisors), and those representing employees average 1.9 (or 36.89 percent of the board of supervisors). The board of supervisors on average meets 4.41 times per year, and the average attendance rate is 87.58 percent. While the percentage of outside supervisors shows an upward trend, the attendance rate at meetings has shown a steady decline. The noted decline in attendance rates at meetings of the board of

Table 5.5 *Characteristics of the board of supervisors (mean values)*

	2006	2007	2008	2009
Number of members of board of supervisors	4.87	4.95	5.41	5.36
Number of outside supervisors	0.09	1.97	2.58	2.62
Percentage of outside supervisors	1.86	39.80	47.69	48.88
Number of supervisors representing employees	1.76	1.83	1.94	1.93
Percentage of supervisors representing employees	36.14	36.97	35.86	36.01
Number of board of supervisors' meetings	3.52	4.37	4.69	5.04
Attendance rate at board of supervisors' meetings (%)	89.88	89.22	87.11	84.09
Number of training sessions for supervisors	n/a	0.03	0.08	0.11

Source: Wind database

supervisors raises the concern whether the board of supervisors (in particular outside supervisors) is informed about the company's situation in a timely manner.

Executive compensation

Table 5.6 reports the summary statistics for executive compensation in China's listed companies. The executives (including executive directors) suffered a sharp decline in their compensation in 2009, most probably due to the global financial crisis. In contrast, non-executive directors and independent directors (and to a lesser extent, members of the supervisory board) have experienced an increase in their pay, although the rate of increase slowed down in 2009 (with the exception of independent directors, whose pay has actually shown a steady increase over time). Although the Chinese Corporate Governance Code recommends that executive compensation should be linked to firm performance, Chen et al. (2010) find that, in China, the compensation committees' decisions on executive pay level are largely influenced by the global peer group's pay level, rather than linking it to

Table 5.6 *Executive compensation (in RMB10,000)*

	2007	2008	2009
Number of executives (persons)	19.16	22.73	23.87
Total executive compensation	714.89	1,510.09	1,201.85
Per capita executive compensation	37.31	58.39	47.16
Total compensation for board of directors	357.86	702.87	601.57
Per capita compensation for board of directors	35.15	46.92	37.02
Total compensation for executive directors	222.40	518.60	363.51
Per capita compensation for executive directors	74.88	178.21	137.69
Total compensation for non-executive directors	100.20	139.70	175.50
Per capita compensation for non-executive directors	23.25	29.91	35.10
Total compensation for independent directors	35.26	44.57	62.38
Per capita compensation for independent directors	9.89	10.95	14.27
Total compensation for supervisory board	102.28	159.53	167.35
Per capita compensation for supervisory board	20.66	29.49	30.65

Source: Wind database

firm performance. The Chinese compensation committees target the global pay levels for setting their executives' pay in order to attract talents; therefore, they tend to award generous pay packages to their executives, especially in foreign invested firms.

IPO activity between 2006 and 2009

The IPO process

In preparing for an IPO, Chinese SOEs typically undergo a significant restructuring of ownership. In most cases, a new company limited by shares is established as a wholly owned subsidiary of the SOE of which it was originally a part. Usually, profit-generating units would be carved out from the original SOE and transferred into the new company, while social welfare functions, such as schools and hospitals, and any other less-profitable business assets, would be kept in the original SOE, which becomes the parent company after listing. The incorporated company then makes new equity offerings to the public and raises funds from the market (Green, 2003).

The regulation of IPOs

To qualify for an IPO on the main board in China's stock exchanges, a company must meet a number of requirements with respect to trading record, profitability, and other criteria. According to the listing requirements, firms with equity capital over RMB30 million are eligible for listing on the Shanghai and Shenzhen stock exchanges. The detailed regulations are summarized in Table 5.7.

In addition to the regulations summarized in Table 5.7, the share allocation method has been changed several times, but broadly in two phases. Before 1996, the allocation of IPO shares to investors was made via application forms by computer system. After 1996, the allocation was carried out through a lottery mechanism. There was an important regulatory reform implemented in May 2002, during the second phase, when the lottery mechanism was changed in favor of an allocation based on the market value of investors' tradable shareholdings. After May 2002, investors were able to subscribe to new issues only if they already owned tradable shares, while the amount of the new shares subscription was determined by the quantity of their

Table 5.7 *Regulations relating to IPOs in China*

Criteria for share issuance	Specific requirements
The applicant	A lawfully incorporated joint stock company
Years in operation	A trading record of not less than 3 financial years
Profitability requirements	(1) A net profit for each of the most recent 3 years, and an aggregate net profit of over RMB30 million during the most recent 3 years;
	(2) An aggregate amount of net cash flows from operations not less than RMB50 million, or an aggregate amount of revenues exceeding RMB300 million in the most recent 3 financial years; and
	(3) No reported loss in the most recent financial year
Assets requirement	Intangible assets as a percentage of net assets in the most recent year must not exceed 20% (excluding land use rights and rights of mining etc.)
Equity requirement	Pre-issue equity value must be not less than RMB30 million
Requirement in respect of main business	There have not been any significant changes in the nature of its main business in the most recent 3 years
Board of directors and management team	No significant changes in the most recent 3 years
Ultimate controlling shareholder	No change in the ultimate controlling shareholder in the most recent 3 years
Within-industry competition	The issuing company must not compete for business with the majority shareholder or the ultimate controlling shareholder or any other enterprises that they own or control
Related party transactions	Related party transactions must be on an equitable basis and be at market prices; there should not be manipulation of earnings through related party transactions
Use of proceeds	Use of the proceeds must be clearly specified; in principle the proceeds are to be used in the company's main business

Table 5.7 (*cont.*)

Criteria for share issuance	Specific requirements
Restrictions	Restrictions on share issuance are imposed:
	(1) If significant changes have occurred or will occur in respect of the issuer's business model and type of products or services and such changes will have significant adverse effects on the issuer's continued profitability;
	(2) If the industry position of the issuer or the environment of the industry in which the issuer operates has changed or will change in a significant way and such changes will have significant adverse effects on the issuer's continued profitability;
	(3) If the issuer's operating income or net profit in the most recent financial year heavily relies on a related party or a customer about whom there exists substantial uncertainty;
	(4) If the issuer's net profits in the most recent year are mainly derived from investments outside what is covered under the consolidated financial statement;
	(5) If the issuer is exposed to risks of significant adverse changes to its key assets or technologies, including trademarks, patents, proprietary technologies, and franchises it currently holds or will need to procure; or
	(6) If there exist any other circumstances which may have significant adverse effects on the issuer's continued profitability
Illegal acts	Any unauthorized public issuance (either outright or under disguise) of securities in the most recent 36 months, or continuation of such acts which might have begun over 36 months ago

Sources: CSRC (2008) and China Securities Law

tradable shareholdings – the more the existing shareholding, the higher the probability of winning the IPO "lottery." Before the May 2002 policy reform the odds of winning the "lottery" depended on the money spent on the subscription. There was considerable debate on

Table 5.8 *Distribution of IPOs by year and industry during 2006–9*

	2006	2007	2008	2009	Total
Public utilities	0	1	0	2	3
Finance and insurance	4	9	0	2	15
Power generation and gas	1	0	0	1	2
Machinery and equipment	1	1	2	2	6
Construction	0	1	1	2	4
Transportation and logistics	6	3	0	1	10
Mining	3	5	3	0	11
Media and cultural	0	1	0	0	1
Real estate	2	0	0	0	2
Ferrous and non-ferrous	0	3	0	0	3
Total	17	24	6	10	57

Source: Wind database

this regulation change. On one side, it was argued that the reform is beneficial to small investors and helps the stability of the market; on the other, it was criticized for its failure to motivate institutional investors.

The IPOs between 2006 and 2009

There were a total of fifty-seven IPOs in China on the main boards of the country's two stock exchanges during 2006–9. Among these, fifty-six were listed in the Shanghai Stock Exchange, and only one was listed in the Shenzhen Stock Exchange (the others are listed in the SME Board and the ChiNext market). In terms of geographical distribution, twenty-three of the newly listed firms are from Beijing, seven are from Shanghai, and five are from Guangdong, with the rest spreading over a dozen other provinces or municipalities directly administrated by the central government. In terms of sectors, fifteen newly listed companies are from the finance and insurance sectors, ten are from the transportation sector, and eleven are from the mining and exploration sectors. Such sectoral distribution reflects the rapid rise of these sectors during 2006–9. However, as can be seen from Table 5.8, the number of IPO companies during this period exhibited a steady decline compared to the pre-2006 period. Also, most of the IPOs took place in 2006–7 and there were only sixteen IPOs during 2008–9. This may be due to deteriorating business conditions and market sentiment after the global financial crisis.

Another feature of the IPOs during 2006–9 is that most of the newly listed companies are large SOEs. These large SOEs sought a public listing after the share-split reform started in 2005, but they still have the Chinese government as their majority shareholder (the state has retained an ownership stake of over 50 percent in each of these companies). Indeed, on average, the state retains a direct shareholding of 41.68 percent after the SOEs go public. In terms of indirect shareholdings, the state on average retains 71.35 percent even after the IPO. Thus the state has absolute control over large SOEs both before and after they go public. In contrast, Chinese banks play a minor role in the public-listed companies. They had an average shareholding of 2.56 percent in only three of the newly listed firms during 2006–9. Similarly, venture capital (VC) and angel capital have played almost no role in the IPOs.

The board of directors of the sample IPO companies has an average of 9.25 members, aged 48.33 on average. The average percentage of independent directors (non-executive directors) is 35.64 percent (36.23 percent). In 35.83 percent of the IPO companies, the chairperson of the board is also the CEO. This is a higher percentage than that observed in Western listed companies. The average tenure of directors is 2.93 years, with the shortest being 1 year and the longest being 7 years. Some 39.33 percent of the IPO companies have an audit sub-committee, staffed by an average of 2.84 members. Approximately 33 percent (38.20 percent) of the IPO companies have a nomination committee (a remuneration committee), with an average of 2.80 (2.90) members. None of the IPO companies has a corporate governance committee or a technical committee. Among the sample firms, the board of director on average meets 7.51 times a year, with the maximum being 22 times and the minimum being 3 times. Thus there is substantial variation in the number of board meetings among Chinese listed companies.

Before the IPO, members of the board of directors on average hold 19.08 percent of the shares. This drops to 11.18 percent after the IPO. The corresponding figures for non-executive directors are 8.30 percent before the IPO and 6.02 percent after the IPO. Chairs of the board on average hold 12.64 percent of the shares before the IPO, and 7.33 percent after the IPO. All the IPO shares experience positive initial day returns, with the largest increase being RMB4.24 and the smallest being

RMB0.03; the average is RMB1.10. 80 percent of the IPO shares experience a price rise during the first year post-IPO, with the largest percentage increase being 464 percent (the average price rise is 89.65 percent). Slightly less than 20 percent of the IPO shares perform poorly during the first year after going public; the worst performance is a fall of 54 percent.

Description of an IPO: China Haisum Engineering Company Limited (China Haisum)

The firm before the IPO

China Haisum Engineering Company Limited (China Haisum) is the largest light industry engineering consultancy company in China which provides civil engineering consultation, design, supervision, and EPC including procurement, construction, training, trial run, etc. The company was established as a joint stock company with limited liability under the Chinese Company Law on 2 December 2002. China Haisum was set by privatizing a state-owned entity, Shanghai Design Institute of Light Industry of China (SDILI). Under the restructuring and listing plan, China Haisum International Engineering Investment Institute Company Limited (CHIEII), which belongs to China Light Industry Group, restructured its subsidiary SDILI and transferred all the assets and liabilities of SDILI to establish a joint stock company, China Haisum, as the main initiator. The company was listed on the Shenzhen Stock Exchange on 15 February 2007 and issued a total of 29,000 A-shares. After the public offering, CHIEII has possessed about 56 percent of China Haisum's total shares as the controlling shareholder.

There are twelve members of China Haisum's board of directors; all of them are Chinese citizens. There are two executive directors (one of whom serves as both the vice chairman of the board and the CEO of the company) and ten non-executive directors (four of whom are independent non-executive directors). The board of directors has three sub-committees (established in 2007 after the public offering), which are the Investment and Development Committee, the Audit Committee, and the Evaluation and Remuneration Committee. The Audit Committee has three non-executive directors; among these, two are independent non-executive directors (one serves as chief member, responsible for the leadership of the Committee) and at least one possesses the expertise in accounting and finance. The Audit Committee holds two regular meetings a year. The

Evaluation and Remuneration Committee consists of three directors, two of whom are non-executive directors (one serves as chief member, responsible for the leadership of the Committee), and it holds regular meetings twice a year. The Investment and Development Committee consists of three directors, two of whom are non-executive directors, and the Committee holds two regular meetings a year. The board of supervisors consists of five members; among these, two are employees' representatives and three are shareholders' representatives. The supervisors have tenure of three years and may be re-elected. China Haisum has a total of eight senior management members, including a president, four vice presidents, one CFO, one chief engineer, and one secretary.

The offer

In this public offering of A-shares, China Haisum targeted domestic investors (including natural persons, legal persons, and other eligible entities) and sold a total of 29,000 A-shares, representing 25.44 percent of its shares outstanding after the offering. The IPO was sponsored by CHIEII, its controlling shareholder. The offer price was RMB6.88 per share, and through the offer the company aimed to raise a total amount of RMB199.52 million. The net proceeds were estimated at RMB182.72 million. After the offer, the Company had an estimated earnings-per-share of RMB0.23, and a price-earnings ratio of 29.91. The net-asset-value per share was RMB1.90 before the offer, and was to be RMB3.02 after the issue.

The firm after the IPO

China Haisum still remains under state control after the IPO. The state controlling shareholder, CHIEII, retains approximately 56 percent of its shares. Since its establishment, China Haisum has set up and improved its corporate governance structure, in accordance with the Chinese Corporate Governance Code, the Company Law, and the Mandatory Provisions for the articles of association. According to China Haisum's annual reports and website, the shareholders' meeting, the board of directors, and the board of supervisors of the company operate independently and effectively in line with the articles of association. The company has won recognition in the capital market for its good corporate governance and profitability since the IPO.

Conclusion

China's economic reform is characterized as a "one-third privatized" reform (Green, 2003), because Chinese SOEs usually sell only about one-third of their equity to public investors during their IPOs, with the state retaining majority control in most cases. Such partial privatizations have left Chinese listed companies with some unique features, including concentrated ownership (usually state ownership) and hence political interference. One consequence of continuing state control is generally poor performance after the IPO. For instance, Sun and Tong (2003) find that state shares are negatively associated with a listed firm's performance, and suggest that the partial privatization program in China has had only limited success. Similarly, Chen et al. (2006) find a decline in the performance (measured by profitability, asset utilization, etc.) of privatized firms in China in the five years after privatization. They attribute the overall poor performance of privatized firms in China to the "half-hearted" nature of the enterprise reforms, and suggest that the state needs to relinquish ownership control of the listed firms so that economic efficiency and financial performance can be improved. Another consequence of concentrated state control post-IPO is expropriation of minority shareholders; for example, in the form of related party transactions, which benefit the controlling shareholder (e.g., Liu and Lu, 2007; Jiang et al., 2010). It may be fair to suggest that, unless China further reforms its administrative governance model of the stock market and improves the ownership structure and corporate governance of its listed companies, the ultimate goal of improving the efficiency and performance of the SOEs by way of subjecting them to market discipline may remain to be a difficult, if not impossible, mission.

References

Aharony, Joseph, Chi-Wen Jevons Lee and Tak Jun Wong. 2000. 'Financial packaging of IPO firms in China', *Journal of Accounting Research*, 38, 1, 103–26.

Aharony, Joseph, Jiwei Wang and Hongqi Yuan. 2010. 'Tunneling as an incentive for earnings management during the IPO process in China', *Journal of Accounting and Public Policy*, 29, 1–26.

Chan, K. Hung and Agnes W.Y. Lo. 2004. 'The influence of management perception of environmental variables on the choice of international transfer pricing methods', *The International Journal of Accounting*, 39, 93–110.

Chen, Gongmeng, Michael Firth and Oliver Rui. 2006. 'Have China's enterprise reforms led to improved efficiency and profitability?', *Emerging Markets Review*, 7, 82–109.

Chen, Jean Jinghan. 2005. 'Corporate governance of former Chinese SOEs', in A. Brown and A. MacBean (eds.) *Challenges for China's Development: An Enterprise Perspective*, London: Routledge Curzon, 58–71.

Chen, Jean Jinghan, Xuguang Liu and Weian Li. 2010. 'The effect of insider control and global benchmarks on Chinese executive compensation', *Corporate Governance: An International Review*, 18, 2, 107–23.

Cheung, Yan-Leung, Ping Jiang and Weiqiang Tan. 2010. 'A transparency disclosure index measuring disclosures: Chinese listed companies', *Journal of Accounting and Public Policy*, 29, 259–80.

Cheung, Yan-Leung, Lihua Jing, Tong Lu, P. Raghavendra Rau and Aris Stouraitis. 2009. 'Tunneling and propping up: an analysis of related party transactions by Chinese listed companies', *Pacific-Basin Finance Journal*, 17, 372–93.

CSRC. 2002. *Code of Corporate Governance for Listed Companies in China*, File: Zhengjiafa [2002], No.1, 7 Jan. 2002, available at: www.csrc.gov.cn/en/homepage/index_en.jsp.

   2008. *China Capital Markets Development Report*, Beijing: China Finance Publishing House.

Ding, Yuan, Eric Nowak and Hua Zhang. 2010. 'Foreign vs. domestic listing: an entrepreneurial decision', *Journal of Business Venturing*, 25, 175–91.

Fan, Joseph P.H., Tak Jun Wong and Tianyu Zhang. 2007. 'Politically connected CEOs, corporate governance, and post-IPO performance of China's newly partially privatized firms', *Journal of Financial Economics*, 84, 330–57.

Firth, Michael, Peter M.Y. Fung and Oliver M. Rui. 2006. 'Corporate performance and CEO compensation in China', *Journal of Corporate Finance*, 12, 4, 693–714.

   2007. 'How ownership and corporate governance influence Chief Executive pay in China', *Journal of Business Research*, 60, 776–85.

   2010. 'Justifying top management pay in a transitional economy', *Journal of Empirical Finance*, 17, 852–66.

Green, Stephen P. 2003. *China's Stockmarket: A Guide to Its Progress, Players and Prospects*, London: The Economist in association with Profile Books.

Huang, Xiao. 2010. 'Modernizing the Chinese capital market: old problems and new legal responses', *International Company and Commercial Law Review*, 21, 1, 26–39.

Jiang, Guohua, Charles M.C. Lee and Heng Yue. 2010. 'Tunneling through interoperate loans: the China experience', *Journal of Financial Economics*, 98, 1, 1–20.

Kim, Han and Yao Lu. 2009. *Compensation dispersion, work interdependence, and performance*, University of Michigan working paper.

Liu, Qiao and Zhou (Joe) Lu. 2007. 'Corporate governance and earnings management in the Chinese listed companies: a tunneling perspective', *Journal of Corporate Finance*, 13, 881–906.

Lo, Agnes W.Y., Raymond M.K. Wong and Michael Firth. 2010. 'Can corporate governance deter management from manipulating earnings? Evidence from related-party sales transactions in China', *Journal of Corporate Finance*, 16, 225–35.

Mallin, Christine A. 2010. *Corporate Governance*, 3rd edition, Oxford University Press.

OECD. 2004. *OECD Principles of Corporate Governance*, available at: www.oecd.org/dataoecd/32/18/31557724.pdf.

Peng, Winnie Q., K.C. John Wei and Zhishu Yang. 2010. 'Tunneling or propping: evidence from connected party transactions in China', *Journal of Corporate Finance*, 17, 306–25.

Sun, Qian and Wilson H.S. Tong. 2003. 'China share issue privatization: the extent of its success', *Journal of Financial Economics*, 70, 183–222.

Yang, Ting and Sie Ting Lau. 2006. 'Choice of foreign listing location: experience of Chinese firms', *Pacific-Basin Finance Journal*, 14, 311–26.

6 | Corporate governance and initial public offerings in Germany

TILL TALAULICAR

Corporate governance mechanisms

Corporate governance in Germany has witnessed some important changes during the last fifteen years. These changes include the further development of the stock market, some unwinding of ownership and supervision network structures, and a modified role of the banking sector that has reduced its influence on corporate Germany. Nonetheless, some peculiarities of the German system remain, particularly in comparison to the Anglo-American one. In general, German corporate governance appears to be less focused on shareholders since various stakeholders are considered as corporate constituencies. Germany has a civil law legal system. The German stock corporation has to be managed in the interest of the enterprise and to take into account the interests of its shareholders, employees and other stakeholders, with the objective of sustainable creation of value. Transparency requirements have been strengthened, in particular for listed companies, by means of domestic regulations as well as transposed directives by the European Union (EU). Due to the development of the stock market, unsolicited tender offers have become more frequent. However, the market for corporate control appears to be still less pronounced than, for instance, in the United States. A code of corporate governance was established in 2002. The Code follows the comply-or-explain principle and has a legal basis as listed firms are stipulated to disclose an annual statement of conformity.

Corporate ownership is in most firms still relatively concentrated, although it has become more dispersed during the last decade due to corresponding promotions by the tax reform of 2000. Whereas the stakes of institutional owners tend to increase, family and company blockholders remain the dominant ownership group. The legal regime protects minority ownership rights. However, asserting these rights can sometimes be burdensome due to required quorums and litigation costs. The stock corporation has always had a two-tier board. There-fore, the supervisory boards are solely composed of non-executive directors. Executive compensation has grown significantly, particu-larly due to an increase of variable compensation components. In major listed companies, the compensation system can hardly be char-acterized as egalitarian.

General regulatory framework: corporate law and the code

Empirical prevalence of the German stock corporation
German company law offers several alternative legal structures that founders, or founded companies, can choose from. Incorporated firms include the limited liability, or private limited, company (*Gesellschaft mit beschränkter Haftung, GmbH*), the stock corporation (*Aktienge-sellschaft, AG*), the joint-stock corporation (*Kommanditgesellschaft auf Aktien, KGaA*) and, most recently, the European company (*Socie-tas Europaea, SE*). Only the stock corporation, the joint-stock corpor-ation and the European company can issue shares that are listed and traded at a stock exchange.

While there were about 900,000 GmbH registered in Germany in 2007, the number of AG amounted to a much lower figure of 13,510 in November 2009 (Deutsche Bundesbank, 2010). Nonetheless, the number of AG has increased significantly during the last decade (from 3,527 in 1994 to 16,002 in 2004). This increase is caused, inter alia, by the Small Stock Corporations and Deregulating Stock Corporation Law Act (*Gesetz für kleine Aktiengesellschaften und zur Deregulier-ung des Aktienrechts*), which became effective on August 10, 1994. This law was intended to facilitate the going public of medium-sized companies and to strengthen the capital market. In particular, this law released small and newly founded stock corporations from some regulations and codetermination, which were previously mandatory without exception for this legal form and considered to be a barrier against choosing this corporate form and also, consequently, against going public.

Since the end of 2004, companies can furthermore be incorporated as a European company which is a new legal form under EU law. This new legal form allows companies carrying out business activities in more than one EU member state to be established as a single company and to operate throughout the EU with one set of rules and a unified management and reporting system. The SE offers the option to choose between a two-tier and a one-tier board system. The two-tier system features a management and a supervisory board and largely mirrors the structure of the stock corporation, which will be described below in more detail. In contrast, the one-tier system combines the functions of the management and the supervisory board into a single administrative board, as is common in many EU member states (cf. Gregory and Simmelkjaer, 2002). Since its introduction in 2004, this new legal form has been increasingly used by German firms. As of September 2009, there were 108 SE incorporated in Germany, of which 22 were shelf companies and 86 were active and carried out business operations (Habersack, 2009).

Since the stock corporation was originally the only legal form which allows the company to go public and to gain capital from the stock market, the stock corporation is the legal form chosen most frequently by large-scale companies. In 2008, 71 of the 100 largest German companies, based on value added, were organized as a stock corporation, whereas only 6 of these firms were limited liability companies (Monopolkommission, 2010). Four companies were organized as a European company. The number of European companies can be expected to increase as this legal form is particularly attractive for larger companies with international operations and subsidiaries abroad.

Structural characteristics of the German stock corporation
The Stock Corporation Act (*Aktiengesetz, AktG*) is characterized by the strictness of its norms. Deviations from the Act are only admissible in those cases to which reference is explicitly made in the Act (v. Werder and Talaulicar, 2011). Compared with the Anglo-American board model, the German stock corporation features three structural peculiarities. First, the stock corporation has a two-tier (or dual board) structure which strictly separates the roles of management and supervision. Whereas the management board is responsible for directing the enterprise, the supervisory board appoints, monitors and advises the members of the management board. In order to secure a balance of power and management's independence for running the day-to-day business of the firm, the supervisory board can remove a

management board member from office only for good reason. In any case, strict separation of management and supervision demands that the same person cannot be a member of both the management and the supervisory board of the company. In major companies, however, it was rather common that the former chair of the management board took over the chair of the supervisory board after his retirement from the management board. To strengthen the independence of monitoring, the Act on the Adequacy of Management Board Compensation (*Gesetz zur Angemessenheit der Vorstandsvergütung, VorstAG*) of July 31, 2009 meanwhile requires that management board members of listed firms may not become members of the supervisory board of the company within two years after the end of their appointment unless they are appointed upon a motion presented by shareholders holding more than 25 percent of the voting rights in the company.

Second, if the management board is comprised of several persons, as it is common and even mandatory in stock corporations having more than 2,000 employees, all board members have to participate in the management of the company on equal terms. They are jointly accountable for the management of the enterprise. No management board member (or CEO) is allowed to issue directions to the remainder of the board. The supervisory board, or in the absence of a decision concerning this matter, the management board on its own, can nominate one member as chair, or spokesperson, to coordinate the work of the management board. However, this chairperson is primus inter pares and not allowed to instruct his or her management board colleagues. Despite this legal requirement, it has repeatedly been lamented that the chair or spokesperson of the management board, particularly in some large stock corporations, de facto often takes the role of a strong CEO rather than just being first among equals (Grundei and Talaulicar, 2002).

Finally, the supervisory board can be and often is codetermined. Depending on the size of the company, not all members of the supervisory board are elected by the shareholders at the general meeting. Rather, up to one-half of the board members are elected by the domestic workforce of the company. These representatives of the employees are equally obliged to act in the enterprise's best interests as are the representatives elected by the shareholders. The supervisory board of stock corporations is generally composed of one-third employee representatives. In enterprises having more than 2,000 domestic employees, half of the board members are elected by the workforce. However, the chair of the supervisory board, who commonly is a representative of the shareholders, has the casting vote in the case of split resolutions (exceptions apply to just a few companies in the coal, iron and steel industries). Stock corporations having fewer than 500 domestic employees are not obliged to appoint employee representatives to their supervisory boards if, and only if, they are either family owned or founded after August 10, 1994. As might be expected, empirical evidence on the performance associations of codetermined boards is equivocal (e.g., Sadowski, Junkes and Lindenthal, 2000; Gorton and Schmid, 2004; Fauver and Fuerst, 2006).

The German Corporate Governance Code

Background of the Code

A code of corporate governance for German firms has long been regarded as unnecessary since essential governance aspects that are typically addressed by these codes like the separation of the roles of chairperson and CEO (see, for instance, Gregory and Simmelkjaer, 2002) are already mandatory under German law. In general, the legal system in Germany tends to be characterized by a rather high degree of regulation. Nonetheless, the Federal Ministry of Justice appointed a government commission to develop, under the given legal conditions, a uniform code for German listed corporations in order to further strengthen the governance quality and to make German corporate governance rules more transparent and better understandable.

This German Corporate Governance Code (GCGC) was introduced on February 26, 2002. The Code has a legal basis after Article 161 of the Stock Corporation Act was amended by the Act for the Further Reform of Corporation and Accounting Law, and of Transparency and Publicity (*Gesetz zur weiteren Reform des Aktien- und Bilanz-rechts, zu Transparenz und Publizität, TransPuG*), which was adopted on July 19, 2002. Accordingly, listed companies have to disclose a statement of conformity with the Code's recommendations every year. More specifically, the management board and supervisory board of listed companies have to declare once a year that the recommendations of the German Corporate Governance Code have been and are being complied with or which of the Code's recommendations are not being applied and why not. The requirement to explain why certain recommendations are not being applied ("and why not") has been added by the Act to Modernize Accounting Law (*Bilanzrechtsmodernisierungsgesetz, BilMoG*) of May 25, 2009. In the original version of 2002, listed companies were only obliged to disclose non-compliance without providing reasons for these deviations from the Code's recommendations. The declaration of conformity has to be made permanently accessible to stockholders.

Structure of the Code

With respect to their obligatory nature, three kinds of Code rules have to be distinguished. First, the GCGC reiterates provisions that firms are compelled to observe under applicable law ("must provisions"). The remaining categories ("shall recommendations" and "should or can suggestions") both consist of rules which go beyond prevailing law. As a consequence, companies can deviate from these rules. However, deviations from recommendations which are marked in the Code by use of the word "shall" have to be disclosed and explained in the aforementioned annual declaration of conformity ("comply or explain"). Third, the Code contains suggestions which are marked in the text by use of the words "should" or "can" and which can be deviated from without disclosure. These suggestions are intended to encourage progress without inhibitory requirements. In sum, the status of the Code rules which go beyond the applicable law enables companies to reflect sector- and enterprise-specific requirements. Thus, the GCGC contributes to more flexibility and more self-regulation in the corporate constitution.

The Code is structured in seven sections. In a foreword, some basics of German corporate governance and the GCGC are explained. The Code norms refer to shareholders and the general meeting (section 2), the cooperation between the management board and the supervisory board (3), the management board (4), the supervisory board (5), transparency (6) as well as the reporting and audit of the annual financial statements (7).

Acceptance of the Code

The acceptance of the GCGC is analyzed in annual studies by the Berlin Center of Corporate Governance. The most recent study was finalized in spring 2010 (v. Werder and Talaulicar, 2010). The then valid Code version of June 18, 2009 contained a total of 82 recommendations and 16 suggestions. The study's sample consisted of all 605 companies listed on the Frankfurt Stock Exchange. Some 175 useable questionnaires were returned.

The study shows that (1) overall the GCGC meets with great approval, (2) its acceptance tends to increase with the size of the companies and (3) the Code continues to initiate changes of the corporate governance of German listed firms. The average compliance rate with the recommendations is 85.8 percent. The companies that belong to the DAX, that is the blue chip index in Germany, which includes the thirty largest German securities in terms of market capitalization and order book turnover from classic and technology sectors, apply 96.3 percent of all recommendations. By the end of 2010 the compliance rate approached 87.8 percent (or for the DAX companies, 97.0 percent).

However, thirty-six recommendations (in the DAX: six recommendations) are applied by less than 90 percent of the companies and gain therefore somewhat lower acceptance rates. These provisions can be further grouped depending on whether they are at least being complied with by the majority (more than 50 percent) or being rejected by most of the companies. Two "shall" recommendations are rejected by the majority of all firms. The six recommendations that are obeyed by less than 90 percent of the DAX companies are the Code norms to agree a similar deductible (similar to the mandatory deductible for the management board) in any D&O policy for the supervisory board (DAX acceptance rate: 77.8 percent; total acceptance rate: 43.5 percent); to take care, in concluding management board contracts, to ensure that payments made to a management board member on premature termination of the contract without serious cause, including fringe benefits, do not exceed the value of two years' compensation (severance pay cap) and compensate no more than the remaining term of the contract (DAX acceptance rate: 84.6 percent; total acceptance rate: 58.1 percent); to calculate the severance payment cap on the basis of the total compensation for the past full financial year and if appropriate also the expected total compensation for the current financial year (DAX acceptance rate: 80.0 percent; total acceptance rate: 57.8 percent); to limit payments promised in the event of premature termination of a management board member's contract due to a change of control to 150 percent of the severance payment cap (DAX acceptance rate: 82.6 percent; total acceptance rate: 48.4 percent); to specify an age limit for members of the management board (DAX acceptance rate: 88.9 percent; total acceptance rate: 66.5 percent); as well as to provide fixed as well as performance-related compensation to the members of the supervisory board (DAX acceptance rate: 88.9 percent; total acceptance rate: 68.0 percent).

Compared with the Code recommendations, the "should" or "can" suggestions show a lower level of acceptance (amounting on average to 63.5 percent for all companies and to 85.4 percent for the DAX). This result is in accordance with expectations as the companies may ignore the suggestions without being compelled to disclose this deviation in their declaration of conformity. Therefore, there is less public pressure to implement the suggestions. By the end of 2010 the compliance rate of the suggestions approached 65.5 percent (or for the DAX companies, 85.6 percent).

The lower acceptance of the suggestions compared with the Code recommendations is also evident from the bigger portion of suggestions with acceptance rates below 90 percent. Thirteen of the sixteen suggestions were applied by less than 90 percent of the companies. Two of them are being complied with by less than 50 percent of the enterprises. Among the DAX companies, seven suggestions had acceptance rates below 90 percent. These are the suggestions that a representative to exercise shareholders' voting rights in accordance with instructions should also be reachable during the general meeting (DAX acceptance rate: 88.9 percent; total acceptance rate: 82.7 percent); that the company should make it possible for shareholders to follow the general meeting using modern communication media (DAX acceptance rate: 84.0 percent; total acceptance rate: 28.2 percent); that in supervisory boards with codetermination, representatives of the shareholders and of the employees should prepare the supervisory board meetings separately, possibly with members of the management board (DAX acceptance rate: 88.0 percent; total acceptance rate: 54.5 percent); that in their corporate governance report, the management board and supervisory board can also provide comments on the Code's suggestions (DAX acceptance rate: 73.1 percent; total acceptance rate: 51.8 percent); that for first-time appointments to the management board the maximum possible appointment period of five years should not be the rule (DAX acceptance rate: 87.5 percent; total acceptance rate: 61.8 percent); that the supervisory board can arrange for committees to prepare supervisory board meetings and to take decisions in place of the supervisory board (DAX acceptance rate: 88.9 percent; total acceptance rate: 67.3 percent); and that performance-related compensation of the members of the supervisory board should also contain components based on the long-term performance of the enterprise (DAX acceptance rate: 55.6 percent; total acceptance rate: 39.0 percent).

The German stock market

The German stock market has become more developed due to privatization activities (Bortolotti, Fantini and Siniscalco, 2003) and after the rise of pension funds and global investors (Becht, Bolton and Röell, 2003). The German stock market is structured into several segments depending on their regulation and listing requirements. Fully listed companies were to be traded either in the "official market" (*Amtlicher Markt*) or the "regulated market" (*Geregelter Markt*). In 2006, there were 308 domestic companies included in the official market and 348 companies listed at the regulated market of the Frankfurt Stock Exchange (*Frankfurter Wertpapierbörse, FWB*), which is by far the largest German stock exchange (Table 6.1). The taking effect of the Act Implementing the Markets in Financial Instruments Directive (*Finanzmarktrichtlinie-Umsetzungsgesetz, FRUG*) has led to operational changes of security paper permission for trading. This Act transposes MiFID (i.e., the EU Markets in

Table 6.1 *Number of listed domestic shares in Germany (as of December 31)*

	1990	1995	2000	2005	2006	2007	2008
Amtlicher Markt	497	522	365	294	308		
Geregelter Markt	163	173	95	354	348		
Regulierter Markt (Regulated Market)						658	638
Freiverkehr (Open Market)	116	117	160	187	322	387	416
Neuer Markt			283				
Sum of Frankfurt	776	812	903	835	978	1,045	1,054
Sum of all German stock exchanges	776	812	1,065	976	1,103	1,171	1,178

Source: Deutsches Aktieninstitut, 2009: 02–1–1–1 and 02–1–1–2

Financial Instruments Directive) into the German law. Consequently, the former division in Germany of the regulated markets into the listing segments "official market" (*Amtlicher Markt*) and "regulated market" (*Geregelter Markt*) has been removed. Since November 1, 2007, when the amendments to be brought in under the FRUG came into force, listing admission to the Frankfurt Stock Exchange is only to the so-called "Regulated Market" (*Regulierter Markt*), which consists of the General Standard and the Prime Standard. In 2008, 638 domestic firms were listed at the Regulated Market of the Frankfurt Stock Exchange (Table 6.1).

The General Standard is the EU-regulated segment of the Frankfurt Stock Exchange with the minimum legal requirements of the Regulated Market (Deutsche Börse AG, 2010b). This segment is deemed appropriate for companies which primarily target national investors and opt for a cost-effective listing. Admission of the securities only requires that the shares are listed in the Regulated Market. Main follow-up obligations demand, inter alia, to make ad hoc disclosures, to apply international accounting standards and to publish an interim report (Deutsche Börse AG, 2009b).

The Prime Standard constitutes the section of the Regulated Market with further follow-up mandatory reports. Admission to the Prime Standard is based on an application by the issuer, whose shares must be listed in the Regulated Market. The decision-making body is the Admissions Office of the Frankfurt Stock Exchange. Prime Standard is the EU-regulated segment of the Frankfurt Stock Exchange for companies also wishing to attract international investors. In addition to the requirements of the General Standard, Prime Standard companies have therefore to publish quarterly reports in German and English, to publish a financial calendar, to stage at least one analyst conference per year and to make ad hoc disclosures also in English (Deutsche Börse AG, 2009b). Admission to Prime Standard is a prerequisite for inclusion in the selection indices DAX, MDAX, TecDAX and SDAX (Deutsche Börse AG, 2010a).

The special market segment of "Neuer Markt", which was established during the dot.com euphoria as a new segment of the Frankfurt Stock Exchange in 1997 and modeled on the NASDAQ for young, innovative, fast growing companies in order to improve the supply of high-risk equity capital in Germany (Gerke and Fleischer, 2001; Martin, 2001; Vitols, 2001), has been integrated into the Prime

Standard. Neuer Markt was closed on June 5, 2003 after the integration of all essential private law elements from Neuer Markt in the Exchange Rules had rendered this segment redundant (for an economic analysis of this market consolidation, see Sell, 2006).

In addition to the above-mentioned access via markets regulated by the EU (EU-regulated markets), companies may access the capital market via markets that are regulated by the stock exchanges themselves (regulated unofficial markets). An initial listing in this so-called "Open Market" (*Freiverkehr*) can lead into the First Quotation Board or Entry Standard (Deutsche Börse AG, 2009a).

The Open Market is structured into First Quotation Board and Second Quotation Board. All companies with an initial listing in the Open Market are included in the First Quotation Board, which intends to attract domestic and international companies for a cost-efficient and fast admission of their shares to trading. All companies whose shares are already listed or included at another international or domestic trading venue and apply for admission to the Open Market are included in the Second Quotation Board.

Companies wishing to be positioned more visibly within the Open Market may choose to be admitted to the Entry Standard, which was launched on October 25, 2005 as a segment within the Open Market. The Entry Standard is a market segment organized under private law. Its legal framework stems from the General Terms and Conditions of Deutsche Börse AG for the Regulated Unofficial Market on the Frankfurt Stock Exchange (Deutsche Börse AG, 2009a).

While the Open Market and its segments offer an alternative way to access the capital market, companies traded in these segments are not listed companies in the strict legal sense. The admission of shares to trading is not equivalent to a stock exchange listing as defined in Article 3 para. 2 of the Stock Corporation Act. According to this legal definition, listed companies are (only) those companies whose shares are authorized to be traded at a market that is regulated and supervised by official authorities, that takes place regularly and that is publicly accessible. Consequently, only companies admitted to the "Regulated Market" (*Regulierter Markt*) are listed firms in this strict legal sense. In contrast, the Open Market and Entry Standard are not organized markets as defined in Article 2 para. 5 of the Securities Trading Act (*Wertpapierhandelsgesetz, WpHG*). These market segments are therefore excluded from certain regulations like the obligations to publish ad hoc announcements or to notify when threshold levels of share ownership are reached. The remainder of this chapter focuses on the group of listed companies and on initial public offerings in the corresponding market segments of the General Standard and Prime Standard.

IPO activity in Germany

Regulatory requirements

An initial public offering (IPO) in the EU-regulated Regulated Market of the Frankfurt Stock Exchange leads to the General Standard or the Prime Standard (Deutsche Börse AG, 2009b). The Regulated Market is an organized market according to Article 2 para. 5 of the Securities Trading Act. Prior to trading, the issuer of the securities has to file an application for admission to the Regulated Market to the Admissions Office of the Frankfurt Stock Exchange. The legal bases for admission are regulated in detail in the Stock Exchange Act (*Börsengesetz, BörsG*), the Stock Exchange Admission Regulation (*Verordnung über die Zulassung von Wertpapieren zum regulierten Markt einer Wertpapierbörse – Börsenzulassungs-Verordnung, BörsZulV*), the Securities Prospectus Act (*Gesetz über die Erstellung, Billigung und Veröffentlichung des Prospekts, der beim öffentlichen Angebot von Wertpapieren oder bei der Zulassung von Wertpapieren zum Handel an einem organisierten Markt zu veröffentlichen ist, Wertpapierprospektgesetz – WpPG*) and the Exchange Rules of the Frankfurt Stock Exchange.

The first admission of shares requires, inter alia, that the issuer must have existed as a company for at least three years; that the anticipated market value of the shares to be admitted or – if an estimate is not possible – the equity of the company amounts to at least EUR 1.25 million (USD 1.63 million); that the minimum number of shares is 10,000 for no-par value shares; and that the minimum free float is 25 percent, while exceptions are possible in accordance with Article 9 of the Stock Exchange Admission Regulation. The main admission document is a listing prospectus, which contains important information on the issuer and on the securities to be offered. This prospectus has to be approved by a governmental authority, that is, in Germany, the Federal Financial Supervisory Authority (*Bundesanstalt für Finanzdienstleistungsaufsicht, BaFin*).

The primary purpose of the prospectus is investor protection as this document enables potential investors to obtain an accurate picture of the offer and to substantiate their investment decision based on this information. At the same time, however, the prospectus is also a liability document: investors may under certain conditions claim damages from those responsible for the prospectus, if material information is represented incorrectly or incompletely (BaFin, 2010). The regulatory basis for the drawing up, approval and validity of securities prospectuses in Germany is the Securities Prospectus Act. This Act transposed EU Prospectus Directive 2003/71/EC into national law with effect from July 31, 2005 (BaFin, 2010).

The securities prospectus has to contain all information that a potential investor needs to make an investment decision regarding the issuer and the securities. On the issuer, a prospectus for shares must disclose general information on the company (e.g., legal form, date of incorporation, objects, shareholders, subsidiary undertakings, employees); general information on the management and supervisory boards (e.g., members of those boards, remuneration, conflicts of interest, corporate governance); the issuer's business; a description and discussion of historical financial information; past, current and future investments; material contracts; past, pending and threatened legal proceedings; working capital and business prospects; capitalization and indebtedness; audited historical financial information for the last three financial years; and, if available, interim financial information. On the securities, the prospectus has to include general information on the shares (e.g., ISIN/WKN, currency, restrictions on transferability, dividend rights); reasons for the offer; use of the IPO proceeds and expenses of the issue; terms and conditions of the offer; dilution; and lock-up agreements (BaFin, 2010).

The admission procedure can be initiated at the same time as the prospectus approval procedure by BaFin. Consequently, the admission resolution can be made on the same day on which the prospectus is approved and published on the Internet (Deutsche Börse AG, 2009b). Main follow-up obligations for the issuers of shares include to publish annual financial statements, an interim report for the first six months of the fiscal year, ad hoc disclosures in accordance with Article 15 and notifications in accordance with Article 21 of the Securities Trading Act.

Table 6.2 *IPO year and industry classification*

Industry	2006	2007	2008	Total
Basic materials	7	1	0	8
Consumer goods	1	0	0	1
Consumer services	1	0	0	1
Financials	4	4	0	8
Healthcare	1	1	0	2
Industrials	4	9	0	13
Information technology	4	0	0	4
Oil and gas	0	1	1	2
Technology	0	3	1	4
Total	22	19	2	43

IPOs between 2006 and 2008

Germany's equity markets remained rather small when compared to other economies of similar size and development due to the heavy reliance on bank financing (e.g., Sell, 2006). In line with this traditionally strong influence of banks (Franks and Mayer, 1998; Hackethal, Schmidt and Tyrell, 2005; Vitols, 2005) as well as the large degree of family ownership (Fiss and Zajac, 2004; Enriques and Volpin, 2007; Edwards, Eggert and Weichenrieder, 2009), leading to lower dependence on the equity market, IPO activities in Germany are rather limited – in particular in relation to the size and development of the economy. Moreover, as in other countries, the number of IPOs largely depends on the general market conditions (cf. Derrien, 2005; Freybote, Rottke and Schiereck, 2008; Klein and Li, 2009). Firms go public mostly during rather hot market periods (e.g., Goergen, Khurshed and Renneboog, 2009).

During the period 2006 to 2008, forty-three domestic companies were newly listed in the Regulated Market of the Frankfurt Stock Exchange. The majority of the IPOs took place in 2006 (twenty-two companies) and in 2007 (nineteen companies). In 2008, when the economy declined and the extent of the financial crisis became visible, only two companies did not withdraw their decision to go public (Table 6.2). The industries of the IPOs focused mainly on industrials (thirteen companies), basic materials (eight companies) and financials (eight companies).

The age, size and performance of the IPOs vary tremendously. IPO firms were originally founded between 1848 and 2007. The average founding year across the forty-three IPOs was 1987. Thus, the firms did, on average, go public twenty years after their foundation. However, the duration between foundation and IPO differs significantly across the studied firms. As can be seen in Table 6.3, IPOs have between 3 and 14,434 employees (mean: 1,695 employees) when they go public. Their sales range between USD 2 million and almost USD 7 billion (mean: USD 629 million); their assets vary between about USD 30 million and USD 4 billion (mean: USD 607 million). Performance indicators turn out to be rather low on average with a mean ROA amounting to 4.21 percent or even negative with mean ROE and ROS amounting to −61.34 percent or −17.12 percent, respectively. However, these low values are also related to few outliers with extremely negative performance data in the year of their IPO (Table 6.3).

Table 6.4 summarizes the ownership structures of the studied IPOs before and after their initial listing at the Frankfurt Stock Exchange. Several observations from this data are worth mentioning. First, the comparison of pre- and post-IPO data clearly indicates that, in line with expectations, ownership concentration decreases due to the going public. While the largest shareholder owns on average about 60 percent before the IPO, this stake falls to less than 40 percent after the going public. Eight of the 43 IPOs had one single owner prior to their going public. The maximum stake of the largest owner amounts to below 80 percent after the initial listing. With regard to the three largest shareholders, their aggregated ownership decreases from 85 percent to about 50 percent. In sum, these figures suggest that ownership concentration decreases due to the IPO but remains still rather high.

Second, the ownership role of banks, the government and business angels appears to have minor importance in German IPOs. While banks and the government traditionally had some influence on the German corporate landscape, there is evidence that this influence has in general been reduced (cf. v. Werder and Talaulicar, 2011). With regard to the studied IPOs, our data moreover suggests that there is a negligible governance role of these types of owners. The average ownership of banks and the government amounts to well below 3 percent prior to the IPO and to less than 2 percent after the going public (Table 6.4). A closer look at the data furthermore reveals that there are very few

Table 6.3 *IPO size and performance*

	Size			Performance		
	Employees	Sales (USD)	Assets (USD)	ROA	ROE	ROS
Minimum	3.00	2,095,130.52	29,052,400.00	−31.25%	−3,073.84%	−1,122.20%
1st quartile	64.00	24,343,200.00	75,234,600.00	2.66%	5.38%	3.22%
2nd quartile	234.00	90,209,700.00	154,820,689.74	4.97%	11.66%	7.22%
3rd quartile	1,342.00	741,759,100.00	780,023,200.00	9.24%	17.82%	11.67%
Maximum	14,434.00	6,970,932,360.00	4,105,332,000.00	25.45%	42.56%	105.95%
Mean	1,694.77	629,313,264.16	607,114,382.86	4.21%	−61.34%	−17.12%

Table 6.4 *IPO ownership structure, pre- and post-IPO (data in percent)*

	Family		Bank		Government		Venture capitalists		Business angels		Top 1		Top 3	
	pre	post	pre	post	pre	post	pre	post	pre	post	pre	post	pre	post
Minimum	.00	.00	.00	.00	.00	.00	.00	.00	.00	.00	20.00	10.30	49.00	31.45
1st quartile	.00	.00	.00	.00	.00	.00	.00	.00	.00	.00	32.90	23.43	73.87	45.39
2nd quartile	38.26	24.98	.00	.00	.00	.00	.00	.00	.00	.00	55.64	32.14	90.00	54.01
3rd quartile	90.65	55.64	.00	.00	.00	.00	9.69	5.07	.00	.00	94.00	55.31	100.00	60.84
Maximum	100.00	78.59	30.00	20.51	100.00	69.71	86.80	32.20	8.04	13.20	100.00	78.59	100.00	81.13
Mean	41.80	29.60	1.13	.76	2.33	1.62	9.44	4.94	.30	.54	60.63	38.01	85.16	53.81

companies that have banks or the government as owners. More specifically, only three companies disclosed having owners from the banking sector prior to the IPO, of which one firm indicates that the bank completely sold its stakes after the initial listing. The low ownership rates of banks may also be related to changes of their corporate strategy. Due to lower margins in their classical business domain of borrowing money, alternative businesses such as investment banking became more attractive and required divestitures in order to avoid conflicts of interest. Only one company had a governmental owner whose ownership was reduced from 100 percent to less than 70 percent after the going public. Similarly, business angels appear to play a minor role in the studied firms. There were only three firms that had ownership held by business angels prior to their IPO. This ownership ranged from 1.86 to 8.04 percent. Interestingly, the largest share of a business angel had been accrued after the IPO and amounted to 13.20 percent. The corresponding business angel was not engaged in the ownership of this firm prior to its IPO.

Third, compared with banks, the government and business angels, the ownership stake of venture capitalists (VC) turns out to be somewhat higher. Their mean ownership amounts to 9.44 percent prior to the IPO and decreases to 4.94 percent after the going public. These higher values are also related to the larger prevalence of VC ownership among the studied IPOs. More than one-quarter (twelve out of forty-three) of the included IPOs had VC owners before and after their IPO. There is no IPO where the VC utilized the initial listing to exit the investment completely by selling all previously held shares. Again, however, compared with other economies, there appears to be rather small use of venture capital financing in Germany, as has also been shown before for the German Neuer Markt (Elston and Yang, 2010).

Fourth, and somewhat relatedly, the family owners constitute the largest group of owners before and after the IPO. Their average ownership stake amounts to 41.80 percent before and to 29.60 percent after the going public. Five companies were solely family owned prior to their IPO. Even after the going public, in twenty-one companies the family owners continued to have more than 25 percent of the voting rights. In fifteen companies, they even continued to hold more than 50 percent of firm ownership. As a consequence, family ownership has naturally been reduced due to the going public but continued to be significant in a larger number of IPOs.

Table 6.5 *IPO management board structure and incentives*

	Size	Number of female members	Average remuneration (in 1,000 USD)	Average ownership, pre-IPO	Average ownership, post-IPO
Minimum	1.00	0.00	22.48	0.00%	0.00%
1st quartile	2.00	0.00	211.05	0.00%	0.00%
2nd quartile	3.00	0.00	387.71	4.25%	2.02%
3rd quartile	3.00	0.00	625.80	21.93%	14.20%
Maximum	5.00	1.00	2,085.93	85.55%	55.50%
Mean	2.88	0.09	541.67	11.33%	7.69%

With regard to the legal form and board structure, no company utilized the legal form of the European company and the corresponding option to establish a one-tier board structure with a single administrative board. Consequently, all forty-three IPOs feature a two-tier board system with a management board to run the day-to-day business of the enterprise and a supervisory board to appoint, monitor and advise the management board.

With one exception, all management boards consist of at least two persons. The size of the management board ranges from 1 to 5, with a mean of 2.88 members (Table 6.5). Only 4 out of altogether 124 management board members are female and no firm has appointed more than one woman to the management board. The average annual remuneration per management board member ranges from USD 22,500 up to well beyond USD 2 million, with a mean amounting to about USD 500,000. On average, firm ownership by management board members amounts to 11.33 percent prior to the IPO and decreases to 7.69 percent after the going public. Again, there is some variation across IPOs, as the corresponding values range from 0 percent to a maximum of 85.55 percent prior to the IPO or 55.50 percent after the going public, respectively (Table 6.5).

The size of the supervisory board varies between 3 and 16 members, with a mean of 5.35 members (Table 6.6). As was observed for the management board, there are only very few female supervisory board members. Nine out of altogether 230 supervisory board members are women. No supervisory board has more than one female director. The vast majority of the studied IPOs are released from supervisory board

Table 6.6 *IPO supervisory board structure and incentives*

	Size	Number of female members	Number of employee represen-tatives	Average remuneration (in 1,000 USD)	Average ownership, pre-IPO	Average ownership, post-IPO
Minimum	3.00	0.00	0.00	0.00	0.00%	0.00%
1st quartile	3.00	0.00	0.00	12.60	0.00%	0.00%
2nd quartile	3.00	0.00	0.00	22.20	0.00%	0.00%
3rd quartile	6.00	0.00	0.00	36.53	0.50%	0.43%
Maximum	16.00	1.00	8.00	66.62	18.67%	14.45%
Mean	5.35	0.21	0.98	25.09	1.47%	1.08%

codetermination because they have fewer than 500 domestic employees and were founded after August 10, 1994. These figures also substantiate the effectiveness of the Small Stock Corporations and Deregulating Stock Corporation Law Act, which has introduced this relaxation of codetermination rules for newly established small corporations, that apparently apply to a non-negligible portion of IPOs. The supervisory boards of the remaining eight companies were codetermined and consisted of one-third (two companies) or of one-half (six companies) employee representatives. The mean compensation of supervisory board members amounts to USD 25,000 per year. On average, aggregated firm ownership by the supervisory board members decreases from 1.47 percent prior to the IPO to 1.08 percent after the going public (Table 6.6).

Description of an IPO: Bauer Aktiengesellschaft

The firm before the IPO

The Bauer Group is an international construction and machinery manufacturing enterprise that is based in Schrobenhausen, Bavaria. The company views itself as a leader in the execution of complex excavation pits, foundations and vertical seals, as well as in the development and manufacture of related machinery for this market. In addition, the Bauer Group deploys its expertise in the exploration, mining and safeguarding of valuable natural resources (company information).

The Bauer Group has a long-standing family tradition. The roots of the company can be traced back to the eighteenth century when Sebastian Bauer acquired the right to set up a copper smithy in Schrobenhausen in 1790. In 1952, Dr.-Ing. Karlheinz Bauer (born 1928) joined the company. With his arrival started the move into specialist foundation construction and an upturn in the business of the company. Thirty years later, Prof. Dipl.-Kfm. Thomas Bauer (born 1955) joined the company and another four years later took over the management of the company. Thomas Bauer, who represents the seventh generation of the Bauer family to run the business, intensified the international expansion of the group's operations and made a number of major acquisitions. In 1994, Bauer Aktiengesellschaft was established in order to act as a holding company for all present and future Bauer subsidiaries. Two years later, Deutsche Beteiligungs AG became a shareholder of the firm.

Prior to the IPO of Bauer Aktiengesellschaft, there were 14,784,000 shares outstanding. The largest single shareholder was Deutsche Beteiligungs AG, which owned 41.15 percent of the shares. The remaining stakes were held, directly or indirectly, by members of the Bauer family. The largest family owner was Prof. Thomas Bauer (the chair of the management board) who owned 18.03 percent. A small portion of 3.04 percent was held by cross-holdings through Bauer Spezialtiefbau GmbH (1.63 percent) and Bauer Maschinen GmbH (1.41 percent).

The offer

The public offer was made solely by means, and on the basis, of the German securities prospectus that was approved by the Federal Financial Supervisory Authority on June 16, 2006, and immediately thereafter published on the corporate website. The initial listing was admitted to the Prime Standard of the Frankfurt Stock Exchange. The price range for bookbuilding was set between EUR 16.50 and EUR 21.50 per share. The consortium was led by Deutsche Bank AG as the sole global coordinator and sole bookrunner.

On July 3, 2006, the offer price was set at EUR 16.75 (USD 21.43) per share. This price was towards the lower end of the aforementioned price range. All shares, comprising approximately 2.35 million shares from a capital increase and approximately 0.45 million shares from subsidiaries of Bauer Aktiengesellschaft, as well as approximately

5.28 million shares from Deutsche Beteiligungs AG (excluding over-allotment), were allocated. The total placement volume, excluding the over-allotment, amounted to approximately EUR 135 million (USD 173 million). The company therefore expected to receive gross proceeds of EUR 47 million (USD 60 million). The proceeds were intended to be used to finance the organic growth of the company, particularly abroad, and to strengthen the equity base of the group which also allows investments in strategic acquisitions.

The firm after the IPO

Bauer Aktiengesellschaft went public on July 4, 2006. The opening price was EUR 16.60. The closing price at the end of the first trading day slightly increased to EUR 17.15. After the IPO, the ownership stakes of Deutsche Beteiligungs AG decreased to 1.16 percent (from 41.15 percent pre-IPO). The members of the Bauer family did not sell their shares. Due to dilution, however, the stakes slightly decreased, for instance from 18.03 percent pre-IPO to 15.56 percent for Prof. Thomas Bauer. Consequently, 50.67 percent of the company shares were free floated. On September 18, 2006, Bauer Aktiengesellschaft was admitted to the SDAX. Today, it is still the case that less than half of the altogether 17,131,000 shares outstanding are owned by the Bauer family, whereas the majority are widely held. The current free float amounts to 51.81 percent.

In 2009, the Bauer Group employed about 8,900 people and generated revenues of EUR 1.28 billion (USD 1.84 billion). The group activities are carried out in approximately 100 subsidiary companies in more than 60 countries. On September 22, 2008, Bauer Aktiengesellschaft was admitted to the MDAX. Today, the company activities are structured into three main segments, i.e., construction, equipment and resources. The IPO helped the firm to finance this trajectory of growth.

Conclusion

This chapter has provided an overview of corporate governance and IPO activities in Germany. The vast majority of German listed firms are organized as stock corporations. The alternative legal forms of the joint-stock corporation and the European company, which also allow issuing shares, are chosen much less frequently. The governance of the stock corporation is characterized by three structural peculiarities. First, the German stock corporation has a dual board structure with a management board that runs the day-to-day business of the corporation and a supervisory board that has the responsibilities to appoint, monitor and advise the management board. Second, the management board has to be organized as a collegial organ if it consists of several members. Finally, depending on the size of the stock corporation, its supervisory board is codetermined, i.e., up to one-half of the supervisory board members are elected by the domestic workforce rather than by the shareholders of the firm. These structural peculiarities are mandatory. The legal regime of the German stock corporation is, in general, characterized by the strictness of its norms as deviations are only admissible in those instances to which reference is explicitly made in the Act.

In 2002, Germany established an official code of good corporate governance. This German Corporate Governance Code marks a milestone in the further advancement of the German governance system because this instrument adds a new level to the regulatory framework. The Code cannot modify but only supplement extant legal norms. Since the Code norms are not legally binding, companies may diverge from the Code standards that go beyond the applicable law. However, listed companies have to disclose annually whether they have complied with the Code's recommendations or which recommendations have not been applied and why not ("comply or explain").

In addition to the general regulation of the German stock corporation, domestic companies that decide to go public have to observe further regulations that are associated with a listing at a German stock market. The highest requirements have to be met when the shares are admitted to the Prime Standard of the Deutsche Börse AG. Beneath the Prime Standard, the General Standard only applies the minimum requirements of EU-regulated markets. Both market segments, the General and the Prime Standard, add up to the Regulated Market of the Frankfurt Stock Exchange. If companies want to avoid the burdens associated with a listing in an EU-regulated market, they can choose to be traded at the Open Market or to be admitted to the Entry Standard. However, only admission to an EU-regulated market leads to a listing according to the Stock Corporation Act.

IPO activities of domestic firms appear to be rather limited in light of the size and the development of the German economy. In the period between 2006 and 2008, altogether forty-three domestic firms were initially listed in the Prime Standard or the General Standard of the Frankfurt Stock Exchange. Compared to other economies, these figures turn out to be rather low. Nonetheless, the German stock market has become much more developed during the recent past with regard to its volume and turnover (cf. Deutsches Aktieninstitut, 2009). The overall IPO activity is moreover very much related to the general market environment. Consequently, under the unfavorable market conditions of the year 2008, only two German companies realized their plans to go public.

References

BaFin. 2010. *The Securities Prospectus – Opening the Door to the German and European Capital Markets*, Bonn, Frankfurt am Main: Bundesanstalt für Finanzdienstleistungsaufsicht.

Becht, Marco, Patrick Bolton and Ailsa Röell. 2003. 'Corporate governance and control', in George M. Constantinides, Milton Harris and René M. Stulz (eds.), *Handbook of the Economics of Finance. Vol. 1B: Financial Markets and Asset Pricing*, Amsterdam: Elsevier, 1–109.

Bortolotti, Bernardo, Marcella Fantini and Domenico Siniscalco. 2003. 'Privatization around the world: evidence from panel data', *Journal of Public Economics*, 88, 305–32.

Derrien, Francois. 2005. 'IPO pricing in "hot" market conditions: who leaves money on the table?', *Journal of Finance*, 60, 487–521.

Deutsche Börse AG. 2009a. *Entry Standard: Tailor-Made Capital Market Access for Small and Medium-Sized Companies*, Frankfurt am Main: Deutsche Börse AG.

    2009b. *General Standard and Prime Standard: Access to European Capital Markets*, Frankfurt am Main: Deutsche Börse AG.

    2010a. *Guide to the Equity Indices of Deutsche Börse*, Frankfurt am Main: Deutsche Börse AG.

    2010b. *Taking Your Company Public – A Practical Guide*, Frankfurt am Main: Deutsche Börse AG.

Deutsche Bundesbank. 2010. *Kapitalmarktstatistik: Statistisches Beiheft zum Monatsbericht 2*, Frankfurt am Main: Deutsche Bundesbank.

Deutsches Aktieninstitut. 2009. *DAI-Factbook 2009: Statistiken, Analysen und Graphiken zu Aktionären, Aktiengesellschaften und Börsen*, Frankfurt am Main: Deutsches Aktieninstitut.

Edwards, Jeremy, Wolfgang Eggert and Alfons Weichenrieder. 2009. 'Corporate governance and pay for performance: evidence from Germany', *Economics of Governance*, 10, 1–26.

Elston, Julie Ann and J. Jimmy Yang. 2010. 'Venture capital, ownership structure, accounting standards and IPO underpricing: evidence from Germany', *Journal of Economics and Business*, 62, 517–36.

Enriques, Luca and Paolo F. Volpin. 2007. 'Corporate governance reforms in Continental Europe', *Journal of Economic Perspectives*, 21, 117–40.

Fauver, Larry and Michael E. Fuerst. 2006. 'Does good corporate governance include employee representation? Evidence from German corporate boards', *Journal of Financial Economics*, 82, 673–710.

Fiss, Peer C. and Edward J. Zajac. 2004. 'The diffusion of ideas over contested terrain: the (non)adoption of a shareholder value orientation among German firms', *Administrative Science Quarterly*, 49, 501–34.

Franks, Julian and Colin Mayer. 1998. 'Bank control, takeovers and corporate governance in Germany', *Journal of Banking and Finance*, 22, 1385–403.

Freybote, Theo, Nico Rottke and Dirk Schiereck. 2008. 'Underpricing of European property companies and the IPO cycle: a note', *Journal of Property Investment and Finance*, 26, 376–87.

Gerke, Wolfgang and Jörg Fleischer. 2001. 'Die Performance der Börsengänge am Neuen Markt', *Zeitschrift für betriebswirtschaftliche Forschung*, 53, 827–39.

Goergen, Marc, Arif Khurshed and Luc Renneboog. 2009. 'Why are the French so different from the Germans? Underpricing of IPOs on the Euro New Markets', *International Review of Law and Economics*, 29, 260–71.

Gorton, Gary and Frank A. Schmid. 2004. 'Capital, labor, and the firm: a study of German codetermination', *Journal of the European Economic Association*, 2, 863–905.

Gregory, Holly J. and Robert T. Simmelkjaer, II. 2002. *Comparative Study of Corporate Governance Codes Relevant to the European Union and Its Member States*, Brussels: Weil, Gotshal & Manges.

Grundei, Jens and Till Talaulicar. 2002. 'Company law and corporate governance of start-ups in Germany: legal stipulations, managerial requirements, and modification strategies', *Journal of Management and Governance*, 6, 1–27.

Habersack, Mathias. 2009. 'Reformbedarf im deutschen Mitbestimmungsrecht', *Zeitschrift für Wirtschaftsrecht*, 30 (48, Supplement), 1–5.

Hackethal, Andreas, Reinhard H. Schmidt and Marcel Tyrell. 2005. 'Banks and German corporate governance: on the way to a capital market-based system?', *Corporate Governance: An International Review*, 13, 397–407.

Klein, Dan and Mingsheng Li. 2009. 'Factors affecting secondary share offerings in the IPO process', *Quarterly Review of Economics and Finance*, 4, 1194–212.

Martin, Thomas A. 2001. 'The IPO of young, high growth SMEs on Neuer Markt', *Small Business Economics*, 16, 319–27.

Monopolkommission. 2010. *Achtzehntes Hauptgutachten der Monopolkommission 2008/2009*, Berlin: Deutscher Bundestag.

Sadowski, Dieter, Joachim Junkes and Sabine Lindenthal. 2000. 'The German model of corporate and labor governance', *Comparative Labor Law and Policy Journal*, 22, 33–66.

Sell, John W. 2006. 'The Neuer Markt is dead. Long live the Neuer Markt!', *International Advances in Economic Research*, 12, 191–202.

Vitols, Sigurt. 2001. 'Frankfurt's *Neuer Markt* and the IPO explosion: is Germany on the road to Silicon Valley?', *Economy and Society*, 30, 553–64.

2005. 'Changes in Germany's bank-based financial system: implications for corporate governance', *Corporate Governance: An International Review*, 13, 386–96.

v. Werder, Axel and Till Talaulicar. 2010. 'Kodex Report 2010: Die Akzeptanz der Empfehlungen und Anregungen des Deutschen Corporate Governance Kodex', *Der Betrieb*, 63, 853–61.

2011. 'Corporate governance in Germany: basic characteristics, recent developments and future perspectives', in Christine A. Mallin (ed.), *Handbook on International Corporate Governance. Country Analyses*, 2nd edn., Cheltenham, UK; Northampton, MA: Edward Elgar, 36–58.

7 | *Corporate governance and initial public offerings in India*

NISHA KOHLI

Corporate governance mechanisms

Indian society is diverse and multifaceted. Its social structure is quite complex because of ethnic, linguistic, religious and economic differences. Access to wealth and power also varies considerably. After a long period of British rule, India inherited a poor but democratic society with a well-functioning legal system. In addition, it benefited from a basic public stock market and a relatively well-developed equity culture. The Indian Companies Act of 1956 and other laws are all based on British traditions. Despite this influence, the evolution of shareholder capitalism and the market for corporate control was not very potent for many decades. Similar to other developing economies, the majority of firms in India were controlled by a dominant owner. However, concentration of ownership has led to lack of transparency and a great deal of clandestine control activities. Furthermore, business groups flourished in India's initial autonomous period after British rule ended.

As described above, corporate ownership in most of the firms in India is concentrated. Family owners are the most dominant category of shareholders, followed by institutional owners. Due to ownership concentration there is lack of transparency and exploitation of minority interests. There is a single-tier board structure with CEO duality whereby the CEO chairs the board. Corporate boards are a mix of executive and non-executive directors. In most firms, executive directors are from family and non-executive directors are independent. Non-egalitarian executive compensation prevails in most firms in India whereby the CEO and top management team, who are usually family owners, are often compensated with a heavy emphasis of variable compensation in the form of commission on profits or stock options.

Corporate law

All the companies in India, whether listed or unlisted, are governed by the provisions of the Companies Act, passed in 1956, and the Securities Exchange Board of India (SEBI) Act, passed in 1992. While the requirements in relation to corporate governance as set out in the Companies Act apply to all companies and are administered by the Department of Company Affairs, the listing agreement applies to listed companies and is administered by stock exchanges under the supervision of SEBI. Also, Indian companies are required to adhere to uniform and proper accounting standards, as the standards improve the utility of disclosure. Thus, corporate governance mechanisms in India are well supported by securities regulation, company law and accounting and auditing standards.

A fundamental concern of corporate governance is to ensure that directors act as careful representatives of shareholders. They are accountable for efficient utilization of assets of the business to shareholders who have provided capital to the company. Based on this concept, corporate governance guidelines and codes were developed in India over a period of five years from 1999 to 2004. Initiatives were taken and various federal committees were formed. Recommendations made in the reports of these committees led to the introduction of new regulations and amendments to the existing laws.

Out of all this regulatory activity, the introduction of "Clause 49" in the standard listing agreement was a notable achievement in the field of corporate governance. Clause 49 resulted from the recommendations made by the Kumar Mangalam Birla Committee. The recommendations pertained to the structure and composition of the board, the constitution of the audit committee and its processes, the remuneration and appointment of directors, that directors' reports should include management discussion and analysis, better transparency and disclosures through annual report, etc.

The Companies Act was also amended, first in 2000 and then in 2002, as a result of recommendations from various committees. Based on the recommendations of the Naresh Chandra Committee, the Companies (Amendment) Bill 2004 was introduced in Parliament to further amend the Companies Act.

As the main focus is directors' accountability, board composition is considered to be an important corporate governance mechanism.

Clause 49 of the listing agreement states that the board of directors should have at least 50 percent of the directors as non-executive directors. It also prescribes that at least one-third of the board should be comprised of independent directors in the case of a non-executive chairman and, in the case of an executive chairman, at least 50 percent of the board should be comprised of independent directors. An independent director is one who does not have any pecuniary relationship or transactions with the company or its senior management and its holding or subsidiary company. Also, there should not be any relation between an independent director and the promoters of the company who have substantial ownership and management control. The Companies Act does not provide a definition of promoters. However, according to Disclosure and Protection guidelines, promoters include person or persons: (1) who possess overall control of the company; (2) who are instrumental in the formulation of a plan pursuant to which securities are offered to the public; and (3) who are named in the prospectus as promoter(s).

With regard to size of the board, the Companies Act has fixed a limit on the maximum number of directors at twelve. Clause 49 specifies that board meetings shall be held at least four times a year, with a maximum gap of four months between any two meetings. It also limits the number of directorships that a director can hold. No director can be a member of more than ten committees or chairman of more than five committees across all companies in which he is a director (Clause 1C). A code of conduct is prescribed for the directors and senior management to tackle the issues related to insider trading (Clause 1D).

Section 292A (22) of the Companies Act obligates all the companies to have a paid-up capital of INR:[1] 5 crores[2] (equivalent to USD 1.1 million[3]) or more to have an audit committee. Section 292A (23) specifies that the committee shall consist of at least three directors; two-thirds of the total strength shall be directors other than managing or whole-time directors. The Annual Report of the company shall disclose the composition of the Audit Committee. If any default is made in complying with the said provision

---

[1] Indian Currency INR.   [2] One crore is equal to 10 million Indian rupees.
[3] USD 1 = INR 45.

of the Act, then the company and every officer in default shall be punishable with imprisonment for a term extending to a year or with a fine up to INR 50,000 (USD 1,100 approximately) or both. An amendment to the Companies Act was made through the Companies Bill 2004, which emphasizes audit processes and auditors' independence, and relationship with management. The bill specifies process of appointment and qualification of auditors and also certification of audited accounts by both the chief executive officer (CEO) and the chief financial officer (CFO). Clause 49 also stipulates that the audit committee should consist exclusively of independent directors. An audit committee charter should be prepared laying down the role and function of the audit committee (Clause II).

Section 211(23) specifies compliance with accounting standards in preparation and disclosure of the financial statements. It also prescribes the audit of such compliance. Non-compliance with this provision may result in punishment in the form of imprisonment for six months or a fine of up to INR 2,000 (USD 45 approximately) or both.

The Act stipulates that directors shall be elected and removed by shareholders and they shall also furnish a report to the shareholders annually. Section 309(1) of the Act requires that the remuneration payable to the executive as well as non-executive directors is required to be determined by the board according to the provisions of Section 198 and approved by shareholders in a general meeting. Further, Schedule VI to the Act requires disclosure of directors' remuneration and computation of net profits for that purpose. Every company is required to disclose the renumeration of directors as a whole, including salaries, commissions and directors' fees in the annual report. Renumeration of non-executive directors is to be approved by shareholders. There are other exhaustive requirements about disclosure of director information. Companies have to maintain registers under Section 301 of the Act disclosing all the material related to party transactions. According to Section 299 of the Act, every director is required to make a disclosure of his interest or the nature of his concern in a proposed contract or arrangement discussed at the board meeting.

In the interests of promoting corporate democracy and shareholder rights protection, Section 192A prescribes certain resolutions to be approved and passed through postal ballots by shareholders, and Clause 49 VII prescribes the formation of a shareholder grievance committee under the chairmanship of a non-executive director to specifically look into legally addressing the complaints of shareholders and investors. The law allows for one share, one vote and pre-emptive rights to purchase new shares. It also allows for cumulative voting or proportional representation to allow minority interests to gain representation on the board.

Code of good governance

Corporate governance initiatives in India began in 1998 with the Desirable Code of Corporate Governance – a voluntary code published by the CII, and the first formal regulatory framework for listed companies specifically for corporate governance, established by the SEBI. It was a result of recommendations of the Kumar Mangalam Birla Committee Report. The objective of this initiative was: to address concerns such as protection of investor interest, especially the minority shareholders; encourage transparency; to take a step towards international norms in terms of disclosures; and, through all of this, to develop a high level of public confidence in business and industry (CII Code, 1998). After the implementation of the CII Code, steps were taken to further refine the Code. Various other committees were formed and recommendations reported by these committees were used to amend the existing Code and regulations.

The main principles of the Desirable Code of Corporate Governance are listed in Table 7.1.

A recent report, the board index published by Spencer Stuart India in 2009, shows (see Table 7.2) that board sizes vary considerably in India. Over time, more and more Indian companies are moving towards separation of the CEO and the board chairmanship roles. There is a good mix of executive and non-executive directors and sufficient numbers of independent directors can also be seen on boards. Despite these developments, the availability of independent directors with appropriate skill sets and business knowledge is a pressing issue. Directors occupy positions on a large number of boards, giving them less time to effectively supervise the business of a company.

Table 7.1 *Main governance principles of the Indian code*

Board structure	Single-tier board structure
Number of non-executive directors	At least 50 percent of directors should be non-executive
Number of independent directors	At least two-thirds of directors should be independent in case of executive chairman and one-third in case of non-executive chairman
Number of board meetings	Board should meet at least four times a year with a maximum gap of four months
Attendance in meetings	Attendance record of directors should be made explicit at the time of reappointment. Those with less than 50% attendance should not be reappointed
Availability of information	Key and adequate information should be available to directors
Limit on number of directorships	No single person should hold directorships in more than ten listed companies
Remuneration of directors	Directors should be paid a commission not exceeding 1% (3%) of net profits for a company with(out) a managing director over and above sitting fees. Stock options may be considered too
Audit committee	Audit committee should have at least three members, all non-executive, competent and willing to work more than other non-executive directors, with clear terms of reference and access to all financial information in the company, and should periodically interact with statutory auditors and internal auditors and assist the board in corporate accounting and reporting
Disclosures and transparency	Companies should inform their shareholders about the high and low monthly averages of their share prices and about share, performance and prospects of major business segments (exceeding 10% of turnover). Stock exchanges should require compliance certificate from CEOs and CFOs on company Consolidation of group accounts should be optional

Source: Confederation of Indian Industry, 1998

Table 7.2 *The characteristics of the board of Indian listed companies*

Variables	Characteristics of Indian listed companies
Number of Bombay Stock Exchange listed sample companies	2,374 sample listed companies
Mix between executive and non-executive directors	11.86 members of the board: 3.48 executive directors and 8.38 non-executive directors. 6 non-executives are also independent directors
Percentage of executive/non-executive chairmen	54 percent of companies had non-executive chairmen
External directorships	40.9 percent of non-executive chairmen held external directorships in one to five companies, and 9 percent held no external directorships. 46.6 percent of executive chairmen held no external directorships
Nationality of members	29.7 percent of companies have at least one foreign director. They represent 0.89 percent of the non-executive directors in the sample
Gender of directors	29.7 percent of companies have at least one woman director, and they represent 3.9 percent of the directors in the sample
Number of meetings	Seven meetings
Audit committee	All companies had audit committees; 62 percent of audit committees comprised only independent directors with average of six meetings per year
Remuneration committee	86 percent have a remuneration committee with 40.6 percent comprised of only independent directors, and average number of meetings is three
Nomination committee	Very few
Board evaluation	30 percent of the boards have board evaluation process
Compensation of non-executive directors	Sitting fees varied widely from INR 2,500 (USD 55 approx.) to INR 20,000 (USD 445 approx.) per meeting, with an average fee of INR 13,000 (USD 290 approx.)

Source: Spencer Stuart Board Index, 2009

Stock exchange and listed companies

Public markets depend on a vibrant and transparent stock exchange in order to provide the capital to grow firms within a national economy. In addition to posing important governance challenges, they are central to the IPO market. This section provides an overview of the Indian exchanges.

Relevance of the Indian stock exchanges in the national economy

Capital markets in India play a vital role in its economic development. No financial news in India is complete without capital market news. The equity markets are currently the primary focus in India. The debt market, however, is almost non-existent (Gupta, 1998). There are twenty-three stock exchanges in India, major ones being Bombay Stock Exchange (BSE) and National Stock Exchange (NSE). BSE is the oldest stock exchange in India. The stock markets in India have grown over the past few years, both in terms of quality and quantity. The number of listed companies on BSE and NSE totaled 6,335 by the end of 2008 (Reserve Bank of India, 2009). This growth can be attributed to the modernization of stock exchanges through the implementation of advanced technology and online screen-based trading (Shah and Thomas, 1997).

Improvements in macroeconomic indicators and regulatory reforms, as well as governance frameworks, have also contributed to the growth of secondary markets through improved investor confidence (Chiang, Jeon and Li, 2007). The overall stock market in India is considered to be large in terms of the number of companies and the degree of market capitalization when compared with the country's current stage of economic development. This is supported by the fact that the stock market capitalization to gross domestic product (GDP) ratio has improved significantly in recent years from 27.2 percent in 2001 to 86.5 percent in 2007 (see Figure 7.1). A total of 412 initial public offers (IPOs) floated during 2000–1 to 2007–8 amounting to USD 23,151 million have added to stock market capitalization. Existing firms also raised additional capital amounting to USD 25,108 million during the same period (see Table 7.3). India has the third largest investor base in the world with over 20 million shareholders (Asian Development Bank,

Table 7.3 *The number of companies and shares listed on stock exchanges in India (data in USD million)*

	IPO		Listed	
	Number of companies	Amount issued	Number of companies	Amount issued
2000–2001	114	605	37	752
2001–2002	7	267	38	1,409
2002–2003	6	231	20	674
2003–2004	21	763	36	4,408
2004–2005	23	3,055	37	3,224
2005–2006	79	2,430	60	3,655
2006–2007	77	6,334	47	1,112
2007–2008	85	9,466	39	9,874
Total	412	23,151	314	25,108

Source: Securities and Exchange Board of India, 2009

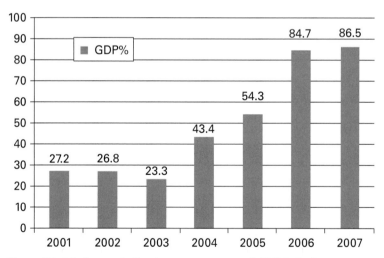

Figure 7.1 Market capitalization as percentage of GDP in India

2009). Financial institutional investors registered with SEBI have also increased from nil in 1992–3 to 803 in 2005–6 (Reserve Bank of India, 2007). This can be attributed to low transaction costs, shorter settlement cycle and consistent returns from the equities.

Table 7.4 *Shareholder-wise ownership structure of BSE-200 (March 31, percentage of outstanding shares owned)*

Category of shareholder	2001	2002	2003	2004	2005	2006
Indian promoters	30.27	31.43	33.24	31.2	30.71	30.69
Foreign promoters	11.76	11.73	12.13	12.15	12.45	12.86
Persons acting in concert	3.05	3.08	3.24	3.31	3.06	2.05
Promoters' holding	**45.08**	**46.24**	**48.61**	**46.66**	**46.22**	**45.6**
Institutions	21.1	20.21	19.43	23.51	24.99	27.78
Corporate bodies	8.48	8.28	6.86	7.08	7.01	6.4
Individuals (Indian public)	22.35	22.3	21.8	18.96	17.24	15.11
Others	2.99	2.97	3.3	3.79	4.54	5.11
Non-promoters' holding	**54.92**	**53.76**	**51.39**	**53.34**	**53.78**	**54.4**

Source: CMIE database, 2011

The ownership structure of Indian listed companies

The ownership structure of Indian listed companies is similar to the ownership structure in other Asian companies despite the differences in political, legal and economic conditions (Claessens, Djankov and Lang, 2000). Indian companies are marked with concentrated stock ownership with a dominance of family-controlled businesses and state-controlled enterprises that form an important section of the corporate sector in many of these countries.

As can be seen from Table 7.4, the average of promoters' holding from 2001 to 2006 is around 46 percent of the total shares outstanding. Thus, promoters have substantial control over ownership and management of the company. In the case of non-promoter holding, there has been an increase in the share of the institutions from 21 percent on March 31, 2001 to 28 percent on March 31, 2006, but a decrease in public shareholding and share of corporate bodies from 34 percent to 27 percent over the same time. The share of "others" (i.e., shares in transit with the National Securities Depository Limited (NSDL) and Central Depository Services Limited (CDSL), global depository receipts (GDR) etc.) has increased from 3 percent in 2001 to 5 percent in 2006. The share of institutional investors also has increased substantially by about 32 percent, indicating improved macroeconomic fundamentals, increasing returns and

Table 7.5 *Control structure of Indian companies listed in the BSE-200 (at March 31) (data available for 134 companies)*

Range of shareholding (%)	Indian promoters		Foreign promoters		Persons acting in concert	
	2001	2006	2001	2006	2001	2006
Less than 5	34	32	97	96	117	121
5–20	13	14	5	6	8	7
20–35	33	32	5	4	5	4
35–50	23	25	6	5	3	2
50 and above	31	31	21	23	1	0

Source: Kaur and Gill, 2007

greater international integration. Relatively, negligible changes can be seen in the shares of promoters and non-promoters, though there are changes in the distribution of shareholding amongst the categories.

In India, there is a traditional culture of wealthy family-controlled companies. For exercising control, a 35 percent ownership stake is considered significant in India (McGee, 2008). The voting rights are concentrated in the hands of family members and persons acting in concert. Persons acting in concert include individuals who are related to the promoter and companies in which the promoter and his family hold more than 26 percent equity shares. Thus, a family is able to dominate and influence the decision making in shareholders' meetings. After family owners, the second largest category of shareholders is institutional investors. Out of the sample, fifty-four companies had more than a 35 percent stake by Indian promoters in 2001, which marginally rose to about 56 companies in 2006 (see Table 7.5). However, in the recent past, trends towards increased shareholding by institutional shareholders have been seen. There is no evidence to show the significant shareholding of an individual in the sample companies.

High concentration of ownership protects companies against the likelihood of hostile takeovers. It also has the potential to reduce agency costs and problems of free riding as compared to dispersed ownership (Burkart et al., 1997; Burkart et al., 2003). On the other hand, this can lead to problems of liquidity because of lack of diversification in stock markets that may adversely affect the large shareholders through the company's idiosyncratic risk (Maug, 1998). Also, significant control and ability to influence decisions provides opportunities for these large shareholders to pursue their own interests by exploiting the minority group. Boards also become ineffective in such cases as the board members finally report to these large shareholders. All board decisions are approved by this majority class of shareholders. Thus, there is a challenge for the regulatory bodies to resolve the conflicts between minority and large and dominant shareholders.

IPO activity in India

We now turn our attention to a subset of the public equity markets, namely the IPO market in India. All of the data presented in this section is relevant to the 2006 to 2008 study period.

The regulation of IPOs

A new IPO is issued almost every day in the capital markets of India. The process of IPO in India goes through several different stages. It starts with the appointment of various entities such as book runners, issue managers and registrars to the issue. Then the company prepares a draft prospectus, also known as the draft red herring prospectus (DRHP) or offer prospectus, for submission to SEBI. The prospectus largely comments on the purpose of issue and provides details of how the proceeds of the issue will be utilized. It also contains detailed information about the promoters and directors of the company.

SEBI reviews the prospectus and suggests changes and additions to it. SEBI can also reject the DRHP. It is then submitted to the stock exchange for approval and verification of compliance with issuing requirements. When the date of issue and price is decided the offer document is called the final red herring prospectus. The price of shares can be decided either by the fixed price method or the book building method, or even a combination of both (see Table 7.6). Under the book building method, the company representatives must decide a price band and an electronic book is opened for at least five days. Online bidding takes place during this period and after that the bids are evaluated to determine a fixed price. The Bombay Stock Exchange (BSE) has the world's largest bidding platform, which spans over 350 Indian cities

Table 7.6 *Methods of IPO pricing in India*

Issue type	Offer price	Demand	Payment	Reservations
Fixed Price Issues	Price at which the securities are offered and would be allotted is made known in advance to the investors	Demand for the securities offered is known only after the closure of the issue	100 percent advance payment is required to be made by the investors at the time of application	50 percent of the shares offered are reserved for applications below Rs. 1 lakh and the balance for higher amount applications
Book Building Issues	A 20 percent price band is offered by the issuer within which investors are allowed to bid and the final price is determined by the issuer only after closure of the bidding	Demand for the securities offered, and at various prices, is available on a real time basis on the Bombay Stock Exchange website during the bidding period	10 percent advance payment is required to be made by the qualified institutional buyers along with the application, while other categories of investors have to pay 100 percent advance along with the application	50 percent of shares offered are reserved for qualified institutional buyers, 35 percent for small investors and the balance for all other investors

Source: Bombay Stock Exchange

through over 7,000 trader work stations. The platform is operated by syndicate members and book runners (BSE website).

After the book building process, shares are allotted and transferred to dematerialized accounts. Any excess money is refunded. Finally, the shares are listed on the stock exchange. Table 7.7 shows the listing requirements in India. Some of the requirements, such as the size of issue and minimum post-paid capital requirements, are different for large and small cap companies.

The IPOs between 2006 and 2008

During the period 2006–8, 150 Indian companies went public. In this section we have analyzed only 116 companies, a little more than 75 percent of the total companies that decided to go public in the BSE/NSE stock exchange and that have not been delisted since then. Most of the companies in the sample got listed on both BSE and NSE. A large number of companies went public in 2007, the number being forty-seven in the sample. In 2006, thirty-nine companies went public. And in 2008 only thirty companies came up with IPOs as the markets were hit by the financial crisis. The industrial sector had the largest number of IPOs, with the next being the basic materials sector. Very few IPOs were from the information technology and communication sector (see Table 7.8).

In India the average age of firms going public is about fifteen years. Most of the companies that raised IPOs were founded in the 1990s during the accelerated liberalization period. Companies that have an age of less than five years are promoted by the existing companies. Thus, none of the IPOs are promoted by new entrepreneurs.

The size of companies going public between 2006 and 2008 varied from very large to very small. The average number of employees of IPO companies is 937. Average revenue is USD 70 million and average assets are equal to USD 161 million (see Table 7.9). The smallest company, in terms of number of employees, is Shree Ashtavinayak with nineteen employees. It is an entertainment company founded in 2001. Orbit Corporation, a real estate company, is the smallest company in terms of revenue. On the other hand, Tech Mahindra has the highest number of employees (9,513). The largest company in terms of sales is Rural Electrification with a maximum turnover of USD 1,094 million, and Gwalior Chemicals is the largest in terms of assets, with assets of USD 7,478 million.

Table 7.7 *Listing requirements in India*

Large cap companies	
Minimum post-issue paid-up capital	INR 10 crore (USD 2.2 m)
Minimum issue size	INR 10 crore (USD 2.2 m)
Minimum market capitalization	INR 25 crore (USD 5.5 m)
Small cap companies	
Minimum post-issue paid-up capital	INR 3 crore (USD 0.6 m)
Minimum issue size	INR 3 crore (USD 0.6 m)
Minimum market capitalization	INR 5 crore (USD 1.1 m)
Minimum income/turnover	INR 3 crore (USD 0.6 m) in each of the preceding three 12-month periods
Minimum number of public shareholders	1,000
Due diligence	A due diligence study may be conducted by an independent team of chartered accountants or merchant bankers or appraisal of project by financial institution or a scheduled commercial bank
For all companies	
Age	3 years' tracking record normally required, at least 1 audited account
Promoter and promoters' holding	One or more persons with minimum 3 years of experience and at least 20 percent of the post-issue equity share capital individually or severally
Listing time	Within six months of IPO, otherwise norms of existing companies apply
Other information	Shareholding pattern, details of litigation and track record of directors
Free float	Free float worth at least INR 1 billion to have as little as 10 percent

Source: SEBI

Table 7.8 *IPO year and industry classification*

	2006	2007	2008	Total
Basic materials	7	9	4	20
Communication	3	0	0	3
Construction	2	2	0	4
Consumer goods	4	6	4	14
Consumer services	2	3	0	5
Financials	2	8	0	10
Healthcare	0	2	4	6
Industrials	9	10	11	30
Information technology	0	1	0	1
Manufacturing	1	1	1	3
Media	1	0	0	1
Oil and gas	2	0	0	2
Technology	4	2	2	8
Telecommunications	2	0	2	4
Utilities	0	3	2	5
Total	39	47	30	116

Table 7.9 *IPO size and performance*

	Size			Performance		
	Employees	Revenues	Assets	ROA	ROE	ROS
Min	19	179,556	17,400	0%	0%	1%
1st quartile	202	13,157,333	1,406,064	4%	13%	6%
2nd quartile	439	26,954,489	6,799,313	8%	22%	9%
3rd quartile	837	82,698,000	35,801,800	13%	34%	15%
Max	9,513	1,094,068,000	7,477,554,860	69%	124%	77%
Average	937	70,567,144	161,688,258	10%	26%	13%

IPO companies in India show favorable profitability ratios. Almost all the companies have positive net incomes. The most profitable company is V-Guard Industrials with maximum return on assets and return on equity. It manufactures electrical equipment and components for households and industry. This company was founded in 1996 with just two employees. Another company like Religare Enterprises, a financial service company, shows the highest return on sales of 77 percent. However, there are companies that show lower profitability as compared to others. An example of such a firm is Ammana Bio Pharma Limited from the healthcare sector.

A close look at the ownership structure of IPOs reveals that similar characteristics are shared by IPOs and existing listed companies. Average family shareholding is about 83 percent before the IPO and 61 percent after the IPO (see Table 7.10). The average ownership stake of the top shareholder is 46 percent pre-IPO, but that reduces to 34 percent post-IPO. Nonetheless, the ownership stake of the top three shareholders does not fall below 50 percent after IPO. This implies that, even after IPO, the major shareholders prefer to maintain their collective control. Control is concentrated in the hands of top share-holders who are mostly from the same family or their group of companies. Not a single company has ownership by banks, government or angels. Only 3 companies out of a sample of 116 have share ownership by venture capitalists, with an average of 25 percent pre-IPO and 15 percent post-IPO. In all the three cases, the venture capitalists are Indian. Thus, it is clear that in India IPOs are dominated by families and business groups. Another interesting feature noticed in the sample IPOs is that fourteen firms have a pyramidal ownership and control structure. In such a structure, promoters or true owners are located at the apex and below are the successive layers of firms (La Porta et al., 1999). This type of structure enables them to control the successive firms disproportionately to the amount of ownership they have in each of the successive firms (Bany et al., 2007). There is only one case where the control is bought by a syndicate agreement.

The average size of the boards of directors of IPO companies is 8 directors with equal number of executive and non-executive directors (see Table 7.11). There are in total 23 women directors on the boards of 116 companies constituting an average of 4 percent of the total directors present in each company. The average number of independent directors on the board is 4, which accounts for 50 percent of the average size of the board. This implies that even IPOs comply with the requirements of Clause 49. No employee directors are noticed in the sample companies. However, a number of family directors are seen to be holding executive directorships in these companies. A large number of directors have a background in throughput functions such as engineering, operations and research and development. There are some directors with a background in peripherals such as finance, accounting

Table 7.10 *IPO ownership structure (data in percent)*

	Family		Bank		Govt.		VC		Angels		Top 1		Top 3	
	pre	post	pre	post	pre	post	pre	post	pre	post	pre	post	pre	post
Min	30	23	–	–	–	–	14	10	–	–	7	4	4	2
1st quartile	72	51	–	–	–	–	43	19	–	–	27	19	56	37
2nd quartile	89	62	–	–	–	–	1	1	–	–	41	30	76	53
3rd quartile	100	71	–	–	–	–	2	1	–	–	61	47	97	69
Max	100	90	–	–	–	–	3	1	–	–	100	90	100	100
Average	83	61	–	–	–	–	25	15	–	–	46	34	71	52
No. of cases	116	116	0	0	0	0	3	3	0	0	116	116	116	116

Table 7.11 *IPO board of directors*

	Size	Executive directors	Non-executive directors	Engineering, operations, R&D	Marketing, sales	Finance, accounting, law
Min	4.00	0.00	0.00	0.00	0.00	0.00
1st quartile	6.00	3.00	2.62	2.62	0.00	1.28
2nd quartile	8.00	4.00	3.44	3.60	1.04	2.00
3rd quartile	9.25	5.00	5.00	4.80	2.01	3.97
Max	15.00	9.00	12.00	9.96	6.00	9.00
Average	7.99	4.13	3.86	3.75	1.33	2.63

and law and only one director with a background in output functions (e.g., marketing or sales).

In line with the regulatory requirements, all the IPOs have an audit committee. Except for ten companies in the sample, all others have a compensation committee. Only one company has a nominating committee. Almost all the companies have a shareholders' and grievance committee. The role of the shareholders' and grievance committee is to redress the complaints of shareholders. There were no company-created technology committees in our particular sample.

The description of an IPO: Educomp Solutions Ltd.

This concluding section focuses on one particular IPO firm in order to provide an in-depth perspective of the IPO process within India. The firm selected for review is Educomp Solutions Ltd.

The firm before the IPO

Educomp was incorporated by Shantanu Prakash and Anjali Prakash in the year 1994 as Educomp Datamatics Pvt. Ltd. It is the largest education company in India providing education solutions.[4] The company has products such as the "Smart Class" program aimed to improve teachers' effectiveness and Planetvidya.com which is an online learning portal.

---

[4] Educomp website, accessed on December 19, 2010.

In 2000, the Carlyle Group made strategic investment in the company amounting to USD 2.10 million for a 15 percent equity stake in the company. In the same year, the company converted into a public limited company. It set up its first fully-owned US subsidiary, Edumatics Corporation, in 2002. This was followed by the floating of another subsidiary known as Learning Mate Solutions Pvt. Ltd. in 2003. This subsidiary received additional capital from the Carlyle Group, which became the major shareholder in the same entity. However, the Carlyle Group exited from the company by selling its stake to the promoters in return for the promoters giving up their shares in Learning Mate Solutions Pvt. Ltd.

At the time of the IPO, the company had about 844 employees and was operating out of nine locations in India.[5] The company had a turnover of USD 7.13 million and a net income of USD 1.4 million in the IPO year. Its price-to-earnings ratio was 23. The company has a traditional ownership structure, which revolves around one family. At the time of IPO, Shantanu Prakash was the top shareholder holding 74 percent of shares, in addition to which Anjali Prakash held 12 percent, amounting to 86 percent of shareholding by family owners. Non-promoter owners held about 14 percent acquired through preferential allotment. At the time of the IPO, the board of directors of Educomp consisted of five directors. There was no separation in position of CEO and chairmanship. Two members from the family held executive director positions. Three directors are non-executive and, out of these, two were independent. The company created an audit, remuneration and shareholder grievance committee. The audit and remuneration committee had promoter directors as its members.

The offer

IPO occurred in December 2005 when the company submitted the prospectus (2005) to SEBI for approval and issued it to the public. The issue remained open for four days. The company offered 400,000 equity shares of INR 10, each with an issue price band of INR 110 to INR 125 per equity share. This led to an increase in the total number of shares from 11.95 million to 15.95 million. The ownership percentage of the promoter was targeted to be diluted from 86 percent to 65 percent. It was a 100 percent book building issue with discretion

---

[5] Final red herring prospectus, submitted to SEBI.

to issue 50 percent of the issue to qualified institutional buyers. The promoters have a lock-in period of three years. A price-to-earnings multiple of between 22 times and 25 times was used for calculating the price band. The issue was considered to be highly priced by the market. The cash from the offer varied between INR 44 and 50 million for a total market capitalization of the firm after the IPO varying between INR 1,754 and 1,994 million. Ultimately, 4 million shares were sold for overall proceeds of INR 50 million, equal to approximately USD 11 million.

The firm after the IPO

After the IPO, the share of promoters declined by about 21 percent and that of non-promoters declined by 4 percent, resulting in 25 percent dilution. However, like other Indian companies, the promoters still retained control by owning about 65 percent of the total shares in the company. The funds raised through IPO were invested in expansion activities. Educomp acquired a Singapore-based company called "Ask n Learn" to make its mark in South Asian markets. It also invested money in its Smartclass project, setting up pre-schools, online tutoring for US markets and other projects which involved government partnerships.

Post-IPO, the board consisted of six directors, four of whom were independent directors. The board decided to meet four times a year as prescribed by law. Also, the company decided to add an investors' relations section on the website to publish the financial statements, details of board committees and a code of conduct for its senior managers and directors. In the financial year 2006–7, the company paid approximately USD 140,000 to its CEO who is also chairman of the board. The company also offered stock options to its senior management and the directors in an endeavor to reward them for their performance.

Conclusion

Corporate governance norms and practices in India have evolved gradually. Development of formal codes and guidelines has been an important step in the field of corporate governance. The Code is based on recommendations by various committees and groups. These have positively affected shareholder activism, transparency, disclosure and board structure and composition. However, as the Code is based on an agency framework and is mandatory in nature, it is followed more in form than in substance. This is due to the fact that Indian companies are marked by high levels of concentrated ownership. In such situations, agency problems are almost non-existent as there is overlap of management, ownership and control. The boards also lose effectiveness in such situations as they draw powers from owners. Also, there are problems of the exploitation of interests of the minority and market for corporate control. These pose a great number of challenges for the corporate governance regime in India. However, recent trends in ownership structure show higher ownership of financial institutional investors and also dilution by family owners. Companies with higher participation of institutional ownership are considered to be better governed companies in India.

Phenomenal growth has been observed in market capitalization of the stock exchanges in India. Stock exchanges play a key role in the Indian economy and contribute significantly to the GDP. A large number of companies are listed on the stock exchanges such as BSE and NSE. Even in the period of 2006–8 more than 150 companies raised money through going public and getting listed. The number of companies that went public was high in 2006 and 2007 but low in 2008 due to the effects of the financial crisis. The features of these IPOs are similar to those of other listed companies. The average age of IPOs is about fifteen years. Largely, these companies are from the basic materials and industrials sectors. They have concentrated ownership by family. None of the companies have ownership by government, banks, angels or financial institutions. The average size of the board is eight with an equal number of executive and non-executive directors. There are sufficient numbers of independent directors and the majority of directors have experience in throughput functions.

References

Asian Develeopment Bank. 2009. 'Asia Capital Markets Monitor Report. 2009'.
Bany, Ariffin Amin Nordin, Fauzias, Mat Nor and Law, Siong Hook. 2007. 'Pyramidal Structure, Firm Investments and Ultimate Owners: Empire Building Motive', *Asia Pacific Journal of Economics and Business*, 11, 25–45.
Burkart, Mike, Gromb, Denis and Panunzi, Fausto. 1997. 'Large Shareholders, Monitoring, and Fiduciary Duty', *Quarterly Journal of Economics*, 112, 693–728.

Burkart, Mike, Panunzi, Fausto and Shleifer, Andrei. 2003. 'Family Firms', *Journal of Finance*, 58, 5, 2167–202.

Chiang, Thomas C., Jeon, Bang Nam and Li, Huimin. 2007. 'Dynamic Correlation Analysis of Financial Contagion: Evidence from the Asian Markets', *Journal of International Money and Finance*, 26, 1206–28.

Claessens, Stijn, Djankov, Simeon and Lang, Larry H.P. 2000. 'The Separation of Ownership and Control in East Asian Corporations', *Journal of Financial Economics*, Elsevier, 58, 1–2, 81–112.

Confederation of Indian Industry, 'Desirable Corporate Governance: A Code'. CII Code, 1998.

Educomp Solutions Limited, *Final Red Herring Prospectus, Educomp Solutions Limited*, December 2005. Available at: www.sebi.gov.in/, last accessed March 15, 2010.

Gupta, Laxmi C. 1998. 'What Ails the Indian Capital Market?', *Economic and Political Weekly*, 33, 29–30.

Kaur, Parmjit and Gill, Suveera. 2007. 'The Effects of Ownership Structure on Corporate Governance and Performance: An Empirical Assessment in India'. Available at: www.nfcgindia.org/pdf/UBS_for_website.pdf

La Porta, Rafael, Lopez-de-Silanes, Florencio and Shleifer, Andrei. 1999. 'Corporate Ownership Around the World', *Journal of Finance*, 54, 471–517.

Maug, Ernst G. 1998. 'Large Shareholders as Monitors: Is There a Trade-off between Liquidity and Control?', *Journal of Finance*, 53, 65–92.

McGee, Robert W. 2008. *Corporate Governance in Asia: Eight Case Studies*, Working Paper, Florida International University.

Reserve Bank of India. Report on Currency and Finance, various issues.

Securities and Exchange Board of India. 'Clause 49 of the Listing Agreement', SEBI Circular number – EBI/CFD/DIL/CG.2004.

Securities and Exchange Board of India, Handbook of Statistics on Indian Securities Markets, 2009.

Shah, Ajay and Thomas, Susan. 1997. 'Securities Markets – Towards Greater Efficiency', *India Development Report*, edited by K. Parikh. Oxford University Press.

Spencer Stuart Board Index – India 2009.

www.bseindia.com/bookbuilding, accessed on December 10, 2010.

www.educomp.com/MenuCompanyprofile.aspx, accessed on December 13, 2010.

www.nseindia.com/content/equities/eq_listeligibility.htm, accessed on December 10, 2010.

www.sebi.gov.in/cms/sebi_data/attachdocs/1287136670083.pdf, accessed on December 12, 2010.

8 | Corporate governance and initial public offerings in Israel

STAV FAINSHMIDT

Corporate governance mechanisms

Israel is a young country based on religion. The establishment of Israel rests upon the need for a country that serves as the home of, but not limited to, Jewish people. Consequently, it is a nation of immigrants with a very diverse population. Culturally, the most distinctive features are its high uncertainty avoidance and low power distance (Hofstede, 1983), together reflected in reliance on networks, connections, and ties in spite of the existence of robust regulatory systems (La Porta, Lopez-de-Silanes, Shleifer et al., 1998).

As a former colonial member of the British Empire, Israel's legal system is based mainly on common law which maximizes the role of the marketplace in sorting out economic affairs and constrains the role of the state. Nevertheless, being a young newly developed economy, Israel is still in the process of shaping an efficient market for corporate control (Ben-Zion, 2006). The specification of proper corporate behavior is quite formal and rule based, yet it was only in the second half of the last decade that these specifications were formalized and the adaptation of corporate entities still occurs. Borrowed from US-based governance mechanisms, information disclosure is highly specified and transparent. As might be expected, informal corporate governance codes are completely voluntary. Business groups are very dominant and are usually family controlled and highly diversified across different industries with a common pyramidal structure of ownership (Kosenko, 2007).

Corporate ownership in most firms is very concentrated (Blass, Yafeh, and Yosha, 1998). Around 85–90 percent of listed companies have a blockholder or a group of blockholders owning more than 50 percent of the shares. Family/entrepreneurial owners are generally the dominant ownership group, but in most IPOs as much as 80 percent of the offered shares are purchased by financial/institutional entities. Hence, institutional owners are also very dominant.

Minority ownership rights are well protected by law and shareholder activism for majority owners is highly constrained (La Porta, Lopez-de-Silanes, Shleifer et al., 1998). Corporate boards are always single-tier and it is very common to have CEO duality whereby the CEO chairs the board. In cases where there is no CEO duality, the CEO and the chairman are very likely to be somehow related. In general, both are usually related to, and appointed by, the major shareholder or controlling group.

Since most corporations do not go beyond the legal requirement of appointing two outside (independent) directors, boards of directors are mostly composed of non-independent directors, who are usually non-executive directors as well. Executive compensation is non-egalitarian in nature, and the CEO and top management team (TMT) are often compensated with a heavy emphasis of variable compensation that is usually tied to the financial performance of the firm (Amzaleg and Mehrez, 2004).

Corporate law

The Israeli Companies Law, which was enacted in 1999, underwent some significant upgrades and alterations in order to keep up with the development of proper corporate governance principles by the OECD. Traditionally, the corporate law required public companies to appoint two outside (external) directors, an audit committee, and an internal auditor. In Israel, the term "outside director" is synonymous with "independent director" in terms of independence requirements and qualifications.

Following the recommendations of the Goshen Committee in 2006, the Ministry of Justice published an amendment to the Israeli Companies Law in 2008. The amendment is relevant to all companies enacted under the Israeli Companies Law and contains both compulsory and voluntary sections. The amendment diverts the responsibility for the actions of the company towards the actual controlling entity of the company, including those that are not technically on the board of directors ("shadow directors"), and provides a limited framework for their authority. Additionally, the amendment suggested that: (1) companies include corporate governance principles in their articles of association in order to formalize the importance of proper governance practices, (2) half of the directors on the board should be independent in cases where none of the shareholders own more than 25 percent of the shares, and (3) one-third of the directors on the board should be independent in cases where at least one of the shareholders owns more than 25 percent of the shares. Other sections in the amendment emphasized the independence of the audit committee and expanded its authorities, created higher criteria for transactions with interested parties, and stricter enforcement (the ability to issue financial penalties) by external supervisory entities (Israeli Securities Authority (ISA) and Companies' Registrar) when a company does not comply with the law.

Also in 2008, an amendment to the Israeli Securities Law (1968) was published in order to improve corporate governance and to reinforce transparency in Israeli publicly traded companies. The amendment requires publicly traded companies to report immediately any compensation of a senior officer or any transaction involving an interested party or a controlling shareholder. Up until this point, corporations could offer high compensation packages to the executives of their subsidiaries and affiliated companies without having to disclose the transaction.

According to the "Doing Business 2011" report by the World Bank (2010), Israel ranks fifth in investor protection laws with a high score of 8.3 out of 10. This score is significantly higher than the average achieved by member states of the OECD. In January 2011 a new legislation process was initiated in Israel. In the past, if no women were on the board of directors, the law required the company to appoint a female outside director. In practice, most companies used to appoint a female family member or otherwise related female to avoid this requirement. The new bill proposes that in every case where there is only one woman on the board of directors, she must qualify as an outside director.

The board of directors is traditionally one tier and is appointed by the shareholders' general meeting, which is held at least once a calendar year. In general, Israel follows the "monistic" model, inspired by Anglo-American systems of corporate governance (Ventoruzzo, 2005). In the "monistic" system, the shareholders' meeting appoints only a board of directors (unitary board), but two of its members must possess independence requirements similar to the ones prescribed for the members of the board of auditors (*Collegio Sindacale*) in the Italian traditional model (Ghezzi and Malberti, 2008). In the traditional model, the board of auditors monitors the organization and management of the corporation and its members are to be free of any work/economic/first-degree family relationship with the directors of the company and its controlled entities (overall, any relationship that compromises or endangers the auditor's independence).

In general, outside directors serve for a three-year term with another optional three-year term under some conditions. Outside directors are to be included in the audit committee and to have at least one representative in all the other committees. The audit committee is also in charge of appointing an internal auditor, who may be an employee of the company but not an interested party or an office holder. Per the Israeli Companies Law, a person may not be appointed as an outside director if (1) the person's position or other activities create, or may create, a conflict of interest with the person's responsibilities; and/or (2) the person, or the person's relative, partner, employer, or an entity under that person's control, has or had during the two years preceding the date of appointment any affiliation with the company, or any entity controlling, controlled by, or under common control with the company. An interesting issue regarding director appointments in Israel is that if at the time an outside director is appointed all members of the board of directors are of the same gender, then that outside director must be of the other gender, which is in line with a growing trend of awareness of gender issues in the corporate world.

According to the Israeli Companies Law, the board of directors may exercise all powers and take all actions that are not specifically granted to shareholders. Additionally, there is a requirement from the board of directors of a public company to determine a minimum number of directors with "accounting and financial expertise", as such a term is defined in the regulations promulgated under the Israeli Companies Law, and to appoint at least one outside director with "accounting and financial expertise". Any other outside director must have "accounting and financial expertise" or "professional qualification".

Code of good governance

In the last decade the corporate governance of Israeli listed companies has been strongly influenced by the development of codes of best practices, especially in the US. Although codes of best practice do not contain compulsory rules, they describe a model of good governance that listed companies are encouraged to follow. In Israel, a formal code of good governance does not exist, although some main principles similar to a code of good governance were borrowed from the Sarbanes-Oxley Act 2002 and from common corporate governance practices in the OECD. The code is not compulsory, yet listed companies should comply with the code's recommendations or explain to the shareholders and to the Israeli stock exchange the reasons for the (total or partial) non-compliance (i.e., freedom with accountability).

The code's principles are embedded in, and were published as part of, the amendment to the Israeli Companies Law in 2008 (see above for more detail). The major suggestions of the code address issues such as the composition, scope of work, and authority of the board of directors (see suggested independence requirements above); the composition, scope of work, and authority of the audit committee; authorization procedures of transactions between the company and controlling groups; inclusion of a "management's affidavit" in quarterly and annual financial reports; and the suggestion to establish a special court of law that specializes in corporate law and securities. One example of a suggested principle is that the board of directors should conduct at least quarterly discussions of the CEO's and the TMT's performance, but not in their presence. Additionally, as institutional investors play a major role in the Israeli stock market, the code encourages them to be more active in voting and managing the corporations they invest in as well as issuing a descriptive quarterly report regarding their investments in these corporations.

Overall, the main governance suggestion of the code is that boards of directors (including audit committees) should be independent and have ultimate authority, accountability, and responsibility for the operations of the company. The code also suggested that the responsibilities of the board of directors and the CEO should be separated and that transactions with interested parties should be approved by the board of directors, the audit committee, and the majority of shareholders that have no financial interest in the transaction. Finally, the code suggested a full disclosure of all compensation details (e.g., plans and amounts) of directors and TMT members (the five biggest salary earning members).

The Israeli economy, stock exchange, and listed companies

In the last five years, including the global financial crisis in 2008, the Israeli currency (NIS – New Israeli Shekel) was among the few emerging currencies to stably strengthen against the US dollar, while European currencies experienced instability and decline. In the last decade Israel has engaged in two wars and nevertheless maintained a steadily growing economy, which enhanced the ingenuity of the Israeli business sector. Although its economy is relatively small, Israel is one of the biggest suppliers of foreign-listed stocks to US stock exchanges. Most of these cross-listers are listed solely on the US markets rather than dually listed, providing support for the "bonding" hypothesis (Coffee, 2002; Licht, 2003). Nevertheless, Licht (2003) contends that the opposite was the case in the early 2000s. He explains that "Israeli US-listed issuers staunchly resisted any increase in their corporate governance-related disclosure beyond the sub-optimal level they are subject to in the US. In a paraphrase of Brandeis' timeless maxim, listing in the US gave Israeli issuers an opportunity to avoid the disinfecting sunlight of their home country's securities laws – an opportunity they were unwilling to forego" (p. 162).

The capital market has a major role in the national economy. With the formation of the State of Israel in 1948, a pressing need arose to formalize trade in securities, which led to the establishment of the Tel Aviv Stock Exchange (TASE) in 1953 by several banks and other financial entities. The number of listed companies increased in the early 1990s together with the national GDP and the rise of stock prices (see Table 8.1). During 2003–5 a decrease in the number of listed companies occurred as a result of the financial crisis in 2001, yet the stock market regained its positive path in 2006. More than half of the biggest corporations in Israel are publicly traded, yet a lot of companies choose to remain private.

As mentioned before, Israel is known as one of the major suppliers of cross-listed companies on the NASDAQ (Licht, 2003). Consequently, dual listings are not rare in the TASE. Although not in large volume, almost every year some of the newly listed companies on the TASE were previously listed on foreign exchanges. For example, out of 108 newly listed companies between 2006 and 2008, 14 were new dual-listed companies. In 2010 the TASE witnessed its largest IPO when "Azrieli Group" raised approximately 521 million USD

Table 8.1 *The number of companies listed on the TASE 1992–2009 (data at year end)*

Year	Number of listed companies	New listed companies*	Year	Number of listed companies	New listed companies*
1992	378	95	2001	649	14
1993	558	186	2002	624	9
1994	638	82	2003	577	4
1995	654	19	2004	578	25
1996	655	7	2005	584	32
1997	659	12	2006	606	44
1998	662	14	2007	654	62
1999	654	13	2008	642	2
2000	665	37	2009	622	4

* Including new dual-listed companies.
Source: www.TASE.co.il

and entered the stock market with a market value of around 2.5 billion USD. The TASE is a private company owned by fifteen banks and fourteen non-banking financial corporations ("Members"). The TASE board of directors includes sixteen members, of which five are external (outside directors), one is a representative of the Bank of Israel, one is a representative of the Ministry of Finance, seven are representatives of TASE members, and two are the CEO and the chairman of the board, who both must also qualify as external directors.

As shown in Table 8.2, the ownership structure of Israeli listed companies is, similarly to other continental European countries, very concentrated (Ben-David, 2010; Blass, Yafeh, and Yosha, 1998). Approximately 90 percent of the publicly traded companies have a more than 50 percent shareholder. During the early 1990s the TASE expanded tremendously. Yet most new listers offered only up to 20 percent of equity to the public, which created a very concentrated holdings structure with banks and other financial institutions as the major players (Blass, Yafeh, and Yosha, 1998). Even the privatization processes of state-owned enterprises did not promote more dispersed ownership patterns since most of the privatized corporations were sold to large blockholders rather than to the public (Ben-Zion,

Table 8.2 *The public free float in the TASE 2006–8*

Free float	2006 Companies	2006 Market value	2007 Companies	2007 Market value	2008 Companies	2008 Market value
up to 20%	29%	5%	27%	7%	34%	8%
20%–50%	57%	54%	60%	56%	54%	40%
50%–75%	9%	19%	9%	14%	8%	13%
over 75%	4%	22%	4%	23%	4%	39%

Source: www.TASE.co.il

2006). This highly concentrated ownership structure centralizes the control of corporations in the hands of blockholders, which leaves less room for rule-based and other internal corporate control mechanisms.

Ben-Zion (2006) explains that the market for corporate control in Israel is still underdeveloped and plays a limited role. However, there is a movement towards more dispersed ownership structures. Blass, Yafeh, and Yosha (1998) indicate that there is only a very thin takeover market in Israel. Takeovers are rare events, and the blockholders' control is stable. The presence of an active and vigilant blockholder reduces the potential agency problem between shareholders and managers. However, it creates a second agency problem, i.e., one between controlling and minority shareholders. The problem is particularly relevant in the case of pyramidal groups where the separation between control and ownership rights determines a structural conflict of interest between the controlling shareholders of the holding company and the minority shareholders of the subsidiaries. In addition, the Israeli market is, similar to Italy, characterized by a high voting premium, resulting in potentially high agency costs (Levy, 1982; Shleifer and Vishny, 1997).

The dominant shareholders are traditionally banks, mutual funds, multinational companies, and, above all, wealthy entrepreneurial families. Although slightly increasing, the presence of companies with dispersed ownership structures or with large coalitions of subjects sharing the control of the firm is quite uncommon. The pressure of social democracies for developing social welfare increases agency costs between shareholders and managers. To reduce these costs shareholders should maintain a concentrated ownership structure that allows them to control corporate and company decisions.

Some characteristics of Israeli institutional investors indicate that they may play an active role in the corporate governance of listed companies: (1) they hold many important shareholdings; (2) their investment portfolios are sufficiently concentrated; and (3) coordination problems among them do not seem to be serious. However, Israeli institutional investors rarely play an active governance role. Some obstacles undermine their activism: (1) the presence of conflicts of interests due to the dominance of the market by banking groups, and (2) the concentrated ownership structure of listed companies.

The IPO market

The regulation of IPOs

The first step of an IPO process in Israel is the writing of a prospectus draft. In Israel the level of detail provided in the prospectus is very deep, compared to the US and the UK. An extreme example was in February 2007 when a company issued an IPO in the TASE with a prospectus of no less than 506 pages. Until recently, the draft was published to the institutional, strategic, and financial investors first and only afterwards to the public. Yet the new underwriting law requires the firm to publish the draft to the public together with the major investors. Following some rounds of alterations, the final draft is submitted to the ISA for approval. Underwriting is not required by law for Israeli IPOs, yet only a negligible percentage of IPOs is executed without at least one underwriter.

Following the submission to the ISA, the company goes on what is called the "road show" in which it tries to recruit large/institutional investors. The next step is by far the most important one in the IPO process. Only institutional investors, banks, and other major strategic investors are allowed to participate in the "institutional bidding" phase. During the bidding, up to 80 percent of the offered shares are allowed to be purchased. Failure to sell less than 80 percent in this step might result in the restructuring or cancellation of the IPO. Finally, a minimum of 20 percent of the offered shares is put on sale for the public and the rest is purchased by the underwriters.

The admission to listing on the TASE is subject to a process of business due diligence by the ISA and the underwriters to certify that the issuing firm complies with listing requirements. Companies must

Table 8.3 *Listing procedures and requirements (excluding R&D companies) (data in USD millions: 1 USD = 3.549 NIS as of 12/31/2010)*

Criteria	Procedure		
	1st	2nd	3rd
Shareholders' equity after listing*	7	9.9	–
Public-float value	5.6	8.5	22.5
Period of activity	12 months	12 months	–
Added value in the 12 months preceding listing**	1.1	–	–
The value of the public float which is derived from the shares issued to the public according to the offering prospectus on which the company's application for listing is based	5.6	5.6	22.5
Value of the company's shares	–	–	56.3

* Shareholders' equity before listing plus net offering funds from shares and warrants.
** Profit (loss) before taxes, plus payroll expenses, depreciation, and financing expenses, deducting financing income.
Criteria do not apply to companies for which the public float equals or exceeds 40 million NIS (app. 11.3 million USD).
Source: www.TASE.co.il

follow one of three listing alternatives and meet a minimum public-float value and rate, in addition to a minimum distribution of public holdings. These three alternative listing procedures are listed in Table 8.3. Having three different listing procedures offers a trade-off between equity, public free-float, period of activity, and company value requirements.

Table 8.4 presents float rate ratio requirements from listing companies. The required float rate ratio is a function of the value of the public float rate of the company and decreases as the value increases. In order to encourage R&D companies to list on the TASE, some lenient terms are offered to this type of IPO. An R&D company is one that invested at least 3 million NIS (approximately 750,000 USD) in research and development over the past three years.

Once a company is listed, it must follow the ongoing requirements of the TASE for public float rate, equity value, financial statements, and disclosure. A summary of these requirements is provided in Table 8.5.

Table 8.4 *Float rate requirements (excluding R&D companies)*
(data in USD millions: 1 USD = 3.549 NIS as of 12/31/2010)

Public float rate value	Required float rate ratio (%)
5.64	25
8.45	20
11.27	15
14.09	10
56.35	7.5

Source: www.TASE.co.il

Table 8.5 *Ongoing requirements for listed companies (data in USD millions: 1 USD = 3.549 NIS as of 12/31/2010)*

Minimum free float ratio	No less than 15 percent of the share capital (only if the public-float value is less than 4.2 USD million)
Minimum free float	No less than 1.4 USD million
Financial statements	Produce quarterly reports (within 2 months) and independently audited full-year financial reports (within 3 months from the end of the calendar year)
Transactions of significant persons and interested parties	To be communicated in the financial statements and reported immediately to the public
Minimum public holdings	At all times the minimum number of publicly held shares is 100 and the minimum value of holdings per holder is 4,500 USD
Equity	No less than 0.6 USD million, based on the released last four successive financial statements (only if the public-float value is less than 6.8 USD million)

Source: www.TASE.co.il

IPOs between 2006 and 2008

The Israeli IPO market in 2006 experienced a massive growth with thirty-seven newly listed companies, which resulted in approximately 803.5 million USD of proceeds from these offerings. The real-estate

Table 8.6 *IPO year and industry classification*

	2006	2007	2008
Total IPOs	37	56	1
Total value of IPOs (in USD millions)	803.5	2,688.1	9.2
Industry by companies:			
Commerce and services	24%	31%	0%
Real estate	30%	27%	100%
Manufacturing	30%	38%	0%
Investment and holdings	14%	4%	0%
Oil	3%	0%	0%
Industry by proceeds:			
Commerce and services	9%	13%	0%
Real estate	50%	12%	100%
Manufacturing	11%	74%	0%
Investment and holdings	29%	1%	0%
Oil	1%	0%	0%

Source: www.TASE.co.il

sector was the main actor in this process, accounting for as much as 50 percent of the proceeds (see Table 8.6). The growing shortage of land designated for construction in such a small country, together with the booming of the Eastern European real-estate market, turned a great deal of attention to Israeli real-estate companies, which exploited this attention to expand their activities both in Israel and Eastern Europe. The most interesting thing about the Israeli IPO activity in 2006 is the fact that in spite of the second Lebanon war and the deteriorating situation on the southern edge of the country (mainly the Gaza Strip), economic activity enjoyed massive growth and expansion.

This trend continued even more in 2007 with fifty-six IPOs and a proceeds value of around 2.7 billion US dollars, completing four years of prosperity in the Israeli stock market. During 2007, real-estate companies continued their vast expansion patterns, yet this year many R&D companies decided to issue an IPO as well. Also in 2007, the Israeli government decided to exploit the peak of the stock market and privatize its oil refineries, which was the biggest IPO seen in the TASE before the IPO of Azrieli Group in 2010. Additionally,

Table 8.7 *IPO size and performance (numbers in USD thousands)*

	Size			Performance		
	Employees	Revenues	Assets	ROA	ROE	ROS
Min	7	0	631	−201%	−145%	−32%
Max	3,488	1,298,666	1,165,504	10%	310%	9%
Average	414	175,174	168,740	−46%	25%	−3%

the positive trends of the TASE caught the attention of foreign investors who injected no less than 900 million USD into the stock exchange. The initial signs of the global financial crisis had only marginal effects on the stock prices of Israeli companies in 2007, yet in 2008 the IPO activity froze completely with only one IPO throughout the whole year.

Israeli companies going public may be either small or large companies. On average they have 414 employees, revenues of 175 million USD, and assets equal to 169 million USD (see Table 8.7). The size and profitability of the company going public are very much influenced by the industry it operates in. R&D companies are generally of smaller size and performance while industrial and real-estate companies are bigger, more stable, and have an established performance trend. Some of the R&D companies have as few as seven employees and no revenues at the time of the IPO and they rely on future potential and patents. Alternatively, real-estate companies rely on the value and future earnings of tangible assets.

As for performance, the case is similar to the size aspect mentioned above. Performance is mostly measured by the industry the company operates in as well as the company's age. BSP (Biological Signal Processing Ltd.), for example, is a medical biotechnology company founded in 1999 and focused on discovery, R&D, and clinical validation of non-invasive heart disease diagnosis. At the time of its IPO (May 2006) BSP had no revenues, ROA of −100 percent, and ROE of −129 percent. Nevertheless, they were able to raise 4.5 million USD. This is an example of a relatively young and small company raising funds in the TASE with poor performance indicators.

When it comes to ownership structure, IPOs present similar characteristics to Israeli listed companies. The largest shareholder of a

Table 8.8 *IPO ownership structure (data in percent)*

	Family		Bank		Govt.		VC		Angels		Top 1		Top 3	
	pre	post	pre	post	pre	post	pre	post	pre	post	pre	post	pre	post
Min	0	17	0	0	0	0	0	0	0	0	14	11	41	31
Max	84	65	10	36	1	1	52	44	0	0	100	73	100	74
Average	16	13	2	17	0	0	6	5	0	0	50	35	72	50
No. of cases	9	9	9	9	9	9	9	9	0	0	9	9	9	9

company that goes public is typically represented by either a family (entrepreneur or a group of entrepreneurs) or a family-held corporation. The government plays a very limited role in the IPO market, mainly because Israel went through an extensive privatization process prior to 2006. Even if companies going public show a decrease of the share capital owned by the first shareholder or the controlling group, these subjects prefer to retain the control of the company after the IPOs.

Banks and other financial institutional investors play a major role in Israeli IPOs. As much as 80 percent of every IPO is purchased by these parties, which creates 17 percent post-IPO average holdings. Table 8.8 also shows other interesting characteristics of Israeli IPOs. That is the absence of business angels in the share capital of companies before and after the IPO, and the relatively low involvement of venture capital and private equity funds. The data shows that venture capital and private equity funds do not play a large role in supporting Israeli IPOs. Finally, the ownership structure of Israeli companies that decided to go public in the period analyzed is, in terms of dual class shares, simpler than the one of listed companies, as none of them issued dual class shares. However, in terms of pyramidal structure, both are alike. About half of the IPO issuing companies were owned through a pyramidal group.

Boards of directors of IPO companies have on average five directors: one executive director and four non-executive directors. Only two companies had one outside director at the time of the IPO. The law requires only public companies to have outside directors on their board. Hence, outside directors are appointed only after the company is officially listed. The law requires every newly listed company to appoint two outside directors within three months from the closing of the IPO. In general, most changes in the governance practices and mechanisms, especially in the composition of the board, are executed during the first three months following the IPO.

Women and foreign directors are few, on average less than one for each board. There are no employees' representatives on the board as the law does not require them, while in family firms it is common to have a number of directors with family relationships. In terms of functional background, IPOs' boards have a majority of members with functional background in peripherals functions (such as finance, accounting, and law) and throughput functions (such as engineering, operations, and research and development), and less than one director with background in output functions (e.g., marketing or sales). Committees are not a common practice for Israeli listed firms and IPOs. The audit committee is usually assembled after the IPO, with the appointment of outside directors. Two companies in the sample had a compensation committee, yet none had remuneration, nomination, governance, or technology committees.

Description of an IPO: Babylon Ltd.

The firm before the IPO

Babylon Ltd. is a company founded in 1997 by Amnon Ovadia, who had the idea of creating an electronic dictionary that did not interrupt the reading and writing processes. In 1997, the company registered a patent for its innovative translation approach and has been developing and providing translation software and language learning solutions since. The software became popular very fast, with more than 4 million users by the year 2000. The company had also tried to enter the field of organizational information retrieval but decided to terminate this activity in 2006. At the time of the IPO, Babylon employed seventy-five workers, mainly in R&D and marketing departments. In the three years before the IPO, Babylon enjoyed a growth of approximately 20.5 percent in annual sales but presented net losses, mainly due to high salary-related costs. The IPO year ended with a negative ROA and ROE of around 48 and 145 percent, respectively.

The ownership structure of the company at the time of IPO sees the participation of a number of investors. There are no institutional investors, only private investors, the founder of the company, and other shareholders (including former employees and consultants).

The main shareholder of the company is Reed Elsevier Ventures 2004 Partnership, L.P. (a limited partnership incorporated under the law of the state of Delaware) with a direct shareholding of 27.19 percent. Then there are Formula Vision Portfolio Holdings, L.P. with 24.81 percent, Monitin Press Ltd. with 19.63 percent, Amnon and Bella Ovadia with 8.06 percent, and other small investors with varying shareholdings up to 5.27 percent.

The board of directors of Babylon includes five directors, of which one is the CEO, one is the chairman, one is the founder (Amnon Ovadia), and two are non-executive directors. Typically, the company has not created any committees and has not appointed outside directors. Only one of the board members is a shareholder of the company (Amnon Ovadia). The assembly meeting of the company deliberated before the IPO a stock option plan for about 15 percent of the share capital. The major beneficiary of the plan is Dov Peer (CEO). Other beneficiaries are Amnon Ovadia and current and former employees.

The offer

The IPO process happens in February 2007. The company targets the TASE as the local and global capital markets peak. The company offers up to 5.45 million new shares to be added to the existing 31.4 million shares prior to the IPO. As the offer involves newly issued shares, after the IPO the firm's shares will be 36.9 million. Along with every purchased share, two stock options (from two different series) are granted to the buyer without additional cost. The vast majority of the shares offered during the IPO (i.e., 73.1 percent) is allocated to institutional investors; the rest is offered to the public. The net cash from the offer is roughly 6 million USD for a total market capitalization of the firm after the IPO varying between 35 and 38 million USD. The offering price is 1.3 USD per share, yet the closing price of the first day of listing is 0.96 USD per share. The company designated the proceeds to be used in its regular line of business.

The firm after the IPO

After the IPO, the ownership structure of the firm sees an almost proportional decreasing (i.e., about 15 percent) of the shares owned by the shareholders. More precisely, Reed Elsevier Ventures 2004

Partnership, L.P.'s direct shareholding decreases to 23.17 percent, Formula Vision Portfolio Holdings, L.P.'s to 21.15 percent, Monitin Press Ltd.'s to 16.72 percent, Amnon and Bella Ovadia's to 6.8 percent, and other small investors with varying shareholdings, to 4.49 percent. In line with the Israeli tradition, after the IPO the firm's shareholding structure is still very concentrated. In order to be more in line with the Israeli listing and governance requirements, the board of Babylon decided: (1) to have at least four meetings per year, with a minimum frequency between them of three months, and (2) to appoint two outside directors and an audit committee.

The cash coming from the IPO will enhance Babylon's future investments. The firm aims, in fact, to pursue its development through internal investments, market expansion, and R&D. Following the IPO, Babylon expedites the development of a web 2.0 Internet portal for linguistic services and sources. Near the end of 2007 about 37 percent of the company's shares were sold to an investment company listed on the London Stock Exchange AIM division (AIM:LIV). During 2010 the Babylon software was categorized as malware for sixteen days by Microsoft, but the company repaired the software and regained its non-intrusive status. As of 2010, Babylon's user base contains more than 71 million desktop installations with a global distribution of no less than 200 countries.

Conclusion

Israeli corporate governance evolved radically in the last decades thanks to both the evolution of the corporate law, and the introduction of US and generally OECD-based principles of good governance. Today corporate governance of listed companies is characterized by a high protection of investors' rights, and board of directors' characteristics are – at least formally – very similar to the best practices at international level. Despite the evolution of corporate law and corporate governance, the ownership structure of Israeli listed companies is, similar to other continental European countries, very concentrated. Most new listers offer only up to 20 percent of equity to the public, which creates a very concentrated holdings structure with banks and other financial institutions as the major players (Blass, Yafeh, and Yosha, 1998). The high concentration of ownership structure, together with the lack of activism from the side of institutional shareholders, inhibits both the market for corporate control, and a real debate in the assembly meetings. However, there is a movement towards more dispersed ownership structures (Ben-Zion, 2006).

The capital market plays a major role in the Israeli economy. Companies follow the "monistic" model, inspired by Anglo-American systems of corporate governance. The largest shareholder of a company that goes public is typically represented by either a family (entrepreneur or a group of entrepreneurs) or a family-held corporation. The government plays a very limited role in the IPO market mainly because Israel went through an extensive privatization process prior to 2006. The presence of an active and vigilant blockholder reduces the potential agency problem between shareholders and managers. However, it creates a second agency problem, i.e., that one between controlling and minority shareholders.

In Israel the level of detail provided in the prospectus is very deep, compared to the US and the UK. Moreover, Israel has highly developed investor protection mechanisms and an effective judicial system (La Porta, Lopez-de-Silanes, Shleifer et al., 1998), both attracting the attention of local and foreign investors and creating a vivid IPO market. The size and profitability of the company going public are very much influenced by the industry it operates in. R&D companies are generally of smaller size and present weaker performance while industrial and real-estate companies are bigger, more stable, and have an established performance trend.

The characteristics of IPO issuing companies are very similar to those of listed ones: (1) their ownership structure, even after the IPO, is still relatively concentrated and often sees a family as major shareholder; (2) the involvement of venture capital and private equity is limited before and after the IPO, and business angels are absent; and (3) their board of directors has an average of five directors, one executive and four non-executives, the majority of whom have a background in peripherals and throughput functions (e.g., finance, accounting and law, R&D). The period after the three years examined here has been affected by a big financial crisis with very limited IPO activity. At the same time, some controlling shareholders decided to delist their companies in order to take profit of the low market prices. Nevertheless, even in the presence of financial distress, the TASE and the Israeli economy remain strong, growing, attractive markets.

References

Amzaleg, Yaron and Mehrez, Abraham. 2004. 'The one million club: Executive compensation and firm performance', *Israel Economic Review*, 2, 1, 107–47.

Ben-David, Nissim. 2010. 'Is the Israeli economy controlled by a tiny group of common interest members?', *International Journal of Social Economics*, 37, 7, 537–40.

Ben-Zion, T. Yael. 2006. 'The political dynamics of corporate legislation: Lessons from Israel', *Fordham Journal of Corporate & Financial Law*, 11, 185–339.

Blass, Asher, Yafeh, Yishay, and Yosha, Oved. 1998. 'Corporate governance in an emerging market: The case of Israel', *Journal of Applied Corporate Finance*, 10, 79–89.

Coffee, John C., Jr. 2002. 'Racing towards the top? The impact of cross-listings and stock market competition on international corporate governance', *Columbia Law Review*, 102, 1757–831.

Ghezzi, Frederico and Malberti, Corrado. 2008. 'The two-tier model and the one-tier model of corporate governance in the Italian reform of corporate law', *European Company and Financial Law Review*, 5, 1, 1–47.

Hofstede, Geert. 1983. 'The cultural relativity of organizational practices and theories', *Journal of International Business Studies*, 14, 2, Special Issue on Cross-Cultural Management, Autumn, 75–89.

Kosenko, Konstantin. 2007. 'Evolution of business groups in Israel: Their impact at the level of the firm and the economy', *Israel Economic Review*, 5, 2, 55–93.

La Porta, Rafael, Lopez-de-Silanes, Florencio, Shleifer, Andrei, and Vishny, Robert W. 1998. 'Law and finance', *Journal of Political Economy*, 106, 6, 1113–55.

Levy, Haim. 1982. 'Economic valuation of voting power of common stock', *Journal of Finance*, 38, 79–93.

Licht, Amir. 2003. 'Cross-listing and corporate governance: Bonding or avoiding?', *Chicago Journal of International Law*, 4, Spring, 141–63.

Shleifer, Andrei and Vishny, Robert W. 1997. 'A survey of corporate governance', *Journal of Finance*, 52, 737–83.

Tel-Aviv Stock Exchange, Israel, www.TASE.co.il and www.maya.TASE.co.il, last accessed December 31, 2010.

The Goshen Committee Report (Corporate governance in Israel), December 2006. www.ISA.gov.il/download/isafile_45.pdf, last accessed December 31, 2010.

Ventoruzzo, Marco. 2005. 'Experiments in comparative corporate law: The recent Italian reform and the dubious virtues of a market for rules in the absence of effective regulatory competition', *European Company and Financial Law Review*, 2, 207–69.

World Bank. 2010. *Doing Business 2011: Making a difference for entrepreneurs. Israel*, Washington: World Bank. Published on November 4, 2010. Retrieved on December 31, 2010.

9 Corporate governance and initial public offerings in Italy

ALESSANDRO ZATTONI AND
CHIARA MOSCA

Corporate governance mechanisms

The most distinctive cultural feature of Italy is a combination of large power distance, i.e., the acceptance of power inequality in organizations, and highly individualistic social culture (Hofstede, 1983). Coherently with this view, the economic system of the country is characterized by a large number of small entrepreneurial firms and business groups.

Italy is a Latin country characterized by a civil Romano-Germanic legal tradition that lately followed the French civil-law system where shareholders' rights are generally weak. Despite this tradition, things changed dramatically in the modern era, mainly under the pressure to adopt the European Directives that have largely increased the degree of protection granted to investors and minorities. Information disclosure has been subject to the same evolution and listed companies are today relatively transparent vis-à-vis investors. Many reforms also involved corporate governance rules; among them an important piece of regulation (even if not compulsory) is the code of corporate governance based on the "comply or explain" mechanism, that was first enacted in 1999 and updated twice until today.

Like small firms, listed companies present a concentrated ownership structure and very frequently one single shareholder holds more than 20 percent of the shares. Individual and family blockholders are the dominant ownership groups, whereas the state holds significant stakes in few large listed companies (mainly companies that have been privatized in the past) (Bianchi and Bianco, 2006). As a direct consequence of the high ownership concentration, changes of control are typically based on friendly agreements among buyers and sellers and the market for corporate control is not at all lively. At the same time, even if minority protection strongly increased over the years, shareholders' activism is low and institutional investors make a rare use of their voice.

The "traditional corporate governance model" – characterized by the presence of a board of directors and a board of statutory auditors – is the most widespread, and the two alternative models (one-tier and two-tier) are uncommon, both in private and listed companies. With regard to public companies, improvements can be noticed in the composition of the board of directors where non-executive directors are often present and CEO duality is quite rare. Traditionally, the CEO and the top management team are generally compensated with a fixed salary and with a short-term bonus; only recently has there been an increasing diffusion of long-term incentives tied to the financial performance of the firm (Zattoni and Minichilli, 2009).

Source of corporate law and governance structure

Italian jurisdiction deals with corporate governance mainly in the Civil Code, whose articles apply to companies limited by shares (*società per azioni*), both close and open corporations, and in the Financial Act of 1998 (Testo Unico della Finanza enacted by the legislative decree of February 24, 1998, n. 58) providing special regulation for listed or widely held companies (i.e., companies with more than 200 shareholders different from the controlling one and holding not less than 5 percent of the share capital).

From its enactment in 1998 the Financial Act has been amended several times. One of the most significant reviews dates back to 2005 as a reaction to some scandals in the Italian financial markets (e.g., Parmalat, Cirio and Giacomelli). This review is known as the "Investors' Protection Act" ("Legge per la Tutela del Risparmio", law December 28, 2005, n. 262), even if its rules have been transposed in the Financial Act which still represents the main legislation for listed companies.

As far as corporate governance rules are concerned, the Investors' Protection Act led to important innovations with regard to the appointment and composition of the board of directors. In particular, at least one member of the board should be chosen from a list of candidates submitted by the minority shareholders and one of them should be an independent director (or two of them when the board has more than seven members). Moreover, the articles of association should also impose good-standing requirements for the candidates for the board as provided by the Code of Corporate Governance and by the legislator.

In 2003 a radical review of the law regulating the *società per azioni* introduced three alternative governance systems, and provided that companies, in the articles of association, may adopt the system of corporate governance that best meets their needs (Ghezzi and Malberti, 2008). This important provision, which may be reversed (subject to the approval of the extraordinary shareholders' meeting), concerns the adoption of one of three systems of corporate governance: (1) the so-called traditional model, which is typical of the Italian jurisdiction and still represents the system of governance adopted by the great majority of companies; (2) the two-tier (or *dualistic*) system strongly inspired by the German tradition; and (3) the one-tier (or *monistic*) system whose structure comes from the Anglo-American experience.

In the Italian *traditional* system, the general meeting appoints the board of directors (*consiglio di amministrazione*) and the board of statutory auditors (*collegio sindacale*) which represents the peculiarity of this model. The main task of the board of auditors is to monitor the directors' activity, in terms of organization, information and lawfulness (Melis, 2004). Statutory auditors must possess professional qualifications and act with independence in respect of directors (i.e., no family relationships are allowed between directors and statutory auditors) and they should not have economic relationships with the company or its group (i.e., employees or consultants of the company or of subsidiaries cannot be appointed as statutory auditors). In listed companies, the chairman of the board of statutory auditors is elected among members designated by minorities. Moreover, the Financial Act limits the number of appointments as a statutory auditor or director that a single person should be in charge of in different companies.

It is worth noting that the task to monitor financial statements, with regard to the adherence to accounting evidence, as well as the correctness of evaluation criteria of assets and liabilities, is outside the scope of the board of auditors' duties. In this respect, Italian listed companies should appoint an external auditor, chosen from among the audit firms which act under the supervision of the Italian Authority (Consob). Even if the accounting task is assigned to the external auditor, the auditor board retains the duty to monitor the internal control system on aspects concerning the flow of information and the internal organization of the company.

In the traditional model, the general meeting of shareholders, in addition to the election of the board of directors and the board of auditors, should: (1) approve the financial statement; (2) fix the compensation for directors and auditors; and (3) promote liability suits against directors and auditors. In addition, the articles of association may provide for further decisions that directors should submit to shareholders' approval. However, directors' liability is never reduced by the authorization given by the shareholders' meeting.

In the two-tier or *dualistic* system, the shareholders' meeting appoints the supervisory board (*consiglio di sorveglianza*) that is in charge of the selection and appointment of the board of managing directors (*consiglio di gestione*). The supervisory board has a twofold nature. First, it has the duty to monitor directors with responsibilities similar to those of the *collegio sindacale* in the traditional model. Moreover, it has tasks that in the traditional model are accomplished by the shareholders' meeting: it approves the financial statement (unless the articles of association provide that one-third of the shareholders may ask the shareholders' meeting to approve the financial statement) and promotes the liability suits against the directors. The articles of association may also grant managing power to the supervisory board, providing that this board has the power to approve the strategic operations, as well as industrial and financial plans submitted by the managing board (Ventoruzzo, 2005).

In the one-tier or monistic system, no separate monitoring board is required, but the board of directors must nominate, within its members, the audit committee (*comitato per il controllo sulla gestione*). In the monistic model, one-third of the directors must possess independence requirements (the same prescribed for the members of the board of auditors in the traditional model), and among them the board appoints the members of the audit committee. The main task of the committee is to monitor managing activities, in organizational terms, with particular attention to the system of internal control. The members of the committee have a dual role within the board of directors since they contribute to the decisions of the board and, at the same time, they monitor and review the decisions taken, as well as the organizational structure of the company designed by the directors (Ghezzi and Malberti, 2008).

Powers granted to the members of the audit committee are different from those of the board of auditors in the traditional model. While auditors have the individual power to investigate within the structure of the company (they can also be supported by their staff, under the duty of confidentiality), the members of the audit committee in the monistic model do not have a similar power. They can, individually, request information from the directors or the directors of the subsidiaries, or they can ask for a meeting of the committee itself or of the board of directors. However, in their role of non-executive directors, members of the audit committee cannot, individually, do investigation; the committee as a whole has, instead, the power to demand an investigation within the company's structure (Mosca, 2006).

Despite the freedom offered by the reform, only few listed companies have adopted the new models. In 2007, only 13 out of more than 270 listed companies (less than 5 percent) adopted governance models different from the traditional one. In particular, nine companies adopted the dualistic model: four banks (Intesa Sanpaolo, Banco Popolare, UBI and Mediobanca; the latter has already overturned its decision once more to the traditional model), one public utilities company controlled by a coalition of shareholders (A2A), one family-controlled company (Monti Ascensori), two investment companies (Mid Industry Capital and Management & Capitali), and one soccer club (Lazio). Four companies adopted instead the monistic model: a digital entertainment company (Buongiorno), an e-commerce company (CHL), a consulting company in the ITC business (Engineering), and a company selling and promoting arts (FMR-Art'è) (Bellinazzo, 2007). The rate of adoption of the alternative systems of corporate governance is still relatively low also for close corporations since, in 2005, only 0.62 percent of them have adopted the one-tier or two-tier model (Notari, 2005).

Code of good governance

In the last decade the corporate governance of Italian listed companies has been strongly influenced by the development of codes of best practice. The committee for corporate governance introduced and updated the Italian code of good governance – first issued in 1999, and then revised in 2002 and in 2006 – with the aim of maximizing shareholders' value, as well as satisfying other stakeholders' interests. The code of best practice is not prescriptive; it rather describes a model of good governance that listed companies are encouraged to follow. Listed companies should comply with the code's recommendations or disclose to shareholders and the Italian Stock Exchange the reasons for (total or partial) non-compliance (i.e., freedom with accountability).

After the last revision (Committee for the Corporate Governance, 2006), the adoption of the code's recommendations is still voluntary; at the same time, the law provides that companies have to disclose, within the documents attached to the financial statements, which recommendations of the code they have implemented, and for the ones not implemented the reasons for the omitted or partial application. The Italian Stock Exchange constantly monitors the implementation of the code by listed companies and the development of the regulatory framework.

The code of corporate governance deals with many relevant aspects that may be grouped as follows: (1) role and composition of the board; (2) appointment and compensation of the directors; (3) directors' duty with regard to internal control system and related party transactions; (4) board relationships with auditors and shareholders.

(1) *Role and composition of the board.* The code recognizes that the board of directors plays a central role in the governance of a company, and should create value for shareholders. The board is responsible for performing a set of activities (including a formal self-evaluation – at least once a year). A director can accept the directorship when he or she is reasonably in the condition to devote the time necessary to the diligent performance of the duties. In vesting directors with specific powers it should be avoided to concentrate corporate offices in one single individual; in cases of identity of roles – in particular when the chairman is also the CEO or the controlling shareholder of the company – the board should designate a "lead independent director". In addition to the role of the board described above, it should promote the broadest possible participation of shareholders in the meetings, through the improvement of the dialogue with shareholders and the exercise of their rights.

(2) *Appointment and compensation of directors.* The code recommends transparent procedures with regard to the appointment of directors and emphasizes the opportunity to designate a "nomination committee", whose main functions should be to propose the

names of the candidates, and to advise about the size and composition of the board. The board should be composed by an adequate number of independent non-executive directors who, at least once a year, should meet themselves, without other directors. Because of the importance of the independence requirement, during their office the board is in charge of periodically evaluating directors' independence. The code also suggests to appoint a "remuneration committee", composed by non-executive directors (the majority of whom have to be independent), which should formulate proposals on the remuneration policy for managing directors and evaluate the criteria adopted for executives' remuneration. Moreover, the code provides for general guidelines for executive and non-executive directors' remuneration: it links the remuneration of the executive directors to the firm's long-term economic results, while it suggests the remuneration of non-executive directors should be proportional to their engagement, taking into consideration also if they are members of some board's internal committees.

(3) *Directors' duty with regard to internal control system and related party transactions.* According to the law the board is in charge of evaluating the internal control system in terms of adequacy to the nature, complexity and dimension of the company. Related to this important task, the board should define guidelines, such as the identification of an executive director for supervising the functionality of the internal control system, the creation of an "internal control committee" made up of non-executive directors (the majority of which are independent), and the evaluation of the correct use of accounting principles and of the accounting audit process. The code gives particular attention to transactions between directors and related parties which are subject to substantial and procedural fairness rules, e.g., reserving to the competence of the board the approval of the most important transactions, supported by the opinion of the internal control committee and, in some cases, of an independent external expert. Important to note that, in 2010, Consob enacted a very detailed regulation on related parties' transactions that mainly deals with procedural and fairness aspects. In addition, procedures adopted by the listed companies should be disclosed in the document (*relazione sulla gestione*) attached to the financial statements.

(4) *Board relationships with auditors and shareholders.* One chapter of the code is devoted to statutory auditors. It focuses on a transparent appointment procedure and provides for statutory auditors to be independent vis-à-vis shareholders that elected them. The statutory auditors should monitor the independence of the auditing firm and should execute their duty in close collaboration with the internal control committee.

The enactment of the code of good governance, as well as its frequent updates, enhanced the evolution and improvement of the quality of boards of directors in Italy. A recent report, the board index published by Spencer Stuart Italy (2010), shows (see Table 9.1): (1) a good mix between executive and non-executive directors; (2) a sufficient number of independent directors; (3) the high participation rate of board members at the meetings; (4) the large diffusion of internal control and remuneration committees.

Despite this encouraging picture, some open issues still exist, such as: (1) the low presence of foreign and women directors (a regulation on gender diversity has recently been approved); (2) the low number of meetings per year; (3) the high frequency of cases in which the same person is appointed in the governance bodies of several different companies; (4) the absence of nomination committees capable of protecting the board members from the influence of controlling shareholders; (5) the confusion between chairman and CEO roles, proven by the similar level of compensation.

Italian Stock Exchange and listed companies

The capital market has a limited role in the Italian economy: the domestic financial system has always been bank oriented rather than market oriented. The number of listed companies increased in the 1980s and 1990s (see Table 9.2). In the same period the market capitalization/GDP benefited from the privatization program. As of today, however, less than three hundred Italian companies are public; in addition, the number of foreign companies listed in Italy is negligible. The market capitalization of listed companies accounts for about 30 percent of national GDP (Consob, 2010).

In a 2003 study, the Italian Stock Exchange estimated that about 1,200 companies could go public. Among the many Italian companies

Table 9.1 *The characteristics of the board of Italian listed companies in 2009*

Variables	Characteristics of Italian listed companies
Sample	142 listed companies
Mix between executive and non-executive directors	11.5 members of the board: 3.1 executive directors and 8.5 non-executive directors. 4.9 non-executives are also independent directors
Number of positions in governance bodies	5.6 positions per director
Nationality of members	Foreign directors represent 7.3 percent of the directors in the sample
Gender of directors	Women directors represent 5.3 percent of the directors in the sample
Number of meetings	9.7 meetings
Length of meetings	134 minutes
Executive committee	33 companies have an executive committee with 5.7 members
Internal control committee	141 companies have an internal control committee with 3.2 members (o/w 2.6 independent)
Remuneration committee	137 companies have a remuneration committee with 3.3 members (o/w 2.5 independent)
Nomination committee	17 companies have a nomination committee
Board evaluation	103 companies
Lead independent director	65 companies
Compensation of board of directors	Chairman € 837,200 ($ 1,104,580), vice chairman € 561,900 ($ 741,354), Chief Executive Officer € 1,109,100 ($ 1,463,310), non-executive directors € 78,600 ($ 103,702)
Equity incentives	51 blue chip companies adopted long-term incentives plans
Compensation of board of statutory auditors	Chairman € 72,000 ($ 94,995), auditors € 56,700 ($ 74,808)

Source: Board Index 2010

that are still privately owned, there are also large multinational groups such as Barilla, with revenues of about $ 5.5 billion (2009), and Ferrero, with revenues of about $ 8.4 billion (2009). Among the reasons which contribute to explain the low attitude of Italian entrepreneurs to open the capital of their companies, there are: (1) the tax

Table 9.2 The number of companies and shares listed on the Milan Stock Exchange (1960–2010)

| | Regulated Markets | | | | Multilateral Trading Facilities | | | | | |
| | Main Mkt/MTA | | Others | | MAC | | AIM | | Total | |
Year	Companies	Shares	Companies	Shares	Companies	Shares	Companies	Shares	Companies	Shares
1960	140	145	0	0	0	0	0	0	140	145
1970	132	144	0	0	0	0	0	0	132	144
1980	141	170	28	29	0	0	0	0	169	199
1990	229	340	37	38	0	0	0	0	266	378
2000	242	305	55	56	0	0	0	0	297	361
2010	273	305	5	5	8	8	10	10	296	328

Source: Borsa Italiana

shield created by the possibility to deduct financial interests; (2) the attitude of companies not to disclose a substantial amount of corporate information to the financial market; (3) the unwillingness of majority shareholders – typically wealthy entrepreneurial families – to share the control of the company with minority shareholders; (4) the interest of the banking system to drive entrepreneurs toward banking debt as a way to establish long-term relationships; (5) the costs of going public and the complexity of the regulation of listed companies, perceived as overwhelming by small and medium companies.

The ownership structure of Italian listed companies

Similar to other continental European countries, the ownership structure of Italian listed companies is very concentrated (Barca and Becht, 2001). At the end of 2006, the first shareholder controls, on average, about 27.5 percent of capital of companies listed in the main market (MTA, Mercato Telematico Azionario) and about 32.2 percent of companies listed in the new market (Nuovo Mercato now merged in MTA). Other investors holding more than 2 percent of capital (the so-called relevant shareholders) own 15.2 percent of the shares of companies in the main market and 15.7 percent of shares of companies in the Nuovo Mercato. The market, i.e., shareholders with less than 2 percent of the capital, owns the majority of the shares: 57.3 percent in companies listed in the MTA and 52.1 percent in companies listed in the MTAX. The ownership concentration of Italian listed companies was even higher in the past. In the last decade the first shareholder reduced its shareholding by about 10 percent, while relevant and small investors increased gradually their shareholdings in listed companies (see Table 9.3).

In 2006, the vast majority of Italian listed companies (128 companies) are controlled by an entity owning the majority of share capital (i.e., higher than 50 percent). To a lesser extent Italian listed companies are controlled by an entity that – even if it does not own the majority of capital – is able to exert a dominant influence on shareholders' meetings (twenty-five companies). Then, a number of companies (twenty-six) are controlled through a shareholders' agreement that owns more than 50 percent of the share capital.

Table 9.3 *Ownership concentration of Italian listed companies (at 31 December)*

	MTA			MTAX (new market)		
	1st shareholder	Other relevant shareholders	Market	1st shareholder	Other relevant shareholders	Market
1997	38.7	8.4	52.9	0	0	0
1998	33.8	9.7	56.5	0	0	0
1999	44.2	8.2	47.6	0	0	0
2000	44.0	9.4	46.6	44.8	25.9	29.3
2001	42.2	9.2	48.6	41.8	23.7	34.5
2002	40.7	8.0	51.2	41.0	21.8	38.2
2003	33.5	11.6	54.9	36.2	19.4	44.4
2004	32.7	13.0	54.3	36.3	18.6	45.2
2005	28.6	15.5	55.9	33.2	15.4	51.5
2006	27.5	15.2	57.3	32.2	15.7	52.1

Source: Consob. MTAX/New Market has been merged in MTA, effective 2008

Shareholders' agreements are very widespread in Italian financial markets. They oblige members to vote likewise at the shareholders' meeting or they limit transferability since they forbid members to sell their shares to third parties for a certain period of time. They are called global agreements when they provide for both voting and selling constraints (Gianfrate, 2007). Shareholders' agreements have a deep impact on the ownership structure of Italian companies. Their duration cannot exceed three years, but they can be renewed at the end of this period.

Only few and very large companies (forty-four) do not have a controlling shareholder (see Table 9.4). However, also in these cases, the presence of important and very influential shareholders or coalitions of shareholders is very common.

With such a concentrated ownership structure, the market for corporate control plays a limited role. Takeovers in the form of hostile bids are rare events, and corporate control is in stable hands. When the concentration of the ownership structure derives from shareholders' agreements, control over the company is less stable because of the so-called breakthrough rule. This provision allows the parties to the agreement to withdraw from it without penalties if they accept a

Table 9.4 *Control structure of Italian companies listed in the MTA (at 31 December)*

	Controlled with more than 50% of shares		Controlled with less than 50% of shares		Controlled through a voting agreement		Not controlled	
	no. of companies	% on capitalization	no. of companies	% on capitalization	no. of companies	% on capitalization	no. of companies	% on capitalization
1997	122	48.1	28	12.4	27	6.3	28	33.2
1998	128	32.3	31	21.7	24	7.4	35	38.6
1999	148	55.0	31	16.7	29	10.8	32	17.5
2000	141	51.4	34	18.5	24	9.6	38	20.5
2001	135	49.7	37	22.5	21	11.4	39	16.4
2002	142	46.0	37	28.4	20	10.2	32	15.4
2003	130	40.2	25	25.5	28	15.3	36	19.0
2004	134	32.7	22	27.2	26	15.1	37	25.0
2005	124	22.8	28	30.6	24	16.5	44	30.1
2006	128	22.8	25	29.1	26	22.3	44	25.8

Source: Consob

public offer launched to acquire control over the company. However, the potential impact of this rule to dissolve the concentration of the ownership structure, making the company open to the market of corporate control, is mitigated by the threat of losing reputation, which discourages the participants from leaving the coalition (Mosca, 2010).

The presence of an active and vigilant block-holder reduces the potential agency problem between shareholders and managers. However, it creates a second agency problem, i.e., that one between controlling and minority shareholders. The problem is particularly relevant in the case of pyramidal groups where the separation between control and ownership determines a structural conflict of interest between the controlling shareholders of the holding company and the minority shareholders of the subsidiaries (Zattoni, 1999 and 2009).

Institutional investors traditionally play a marginal role, because of their limited shareholdings and a regulatory environment that does not facilitate their activism. The enactment in 1998 of the Financial Act was intended to strengthen minority shareholders' rights and had a significant effect on investor protection. Before this Act the anti-director rights index (La Porta, Lopez-de-Silanes and Shleifer, 1999) scored 1 out of 6 and Italy was considered among the countries with the lowest legal protection of shareholders' rights. After the Financial Act, the index dramatically improved, reaching 5 out of 6 (Aganin and Volpin, 2003). The rules of corporate governance introduced in 1998 – and improved by several amendments and reviewed over the years – were founded on the idea that active institutional investors would use, if necessary, their powers in the monitoring of listed companies (Bianchi and Enriques, 2005). In other words, the expectation was the institutional investors would make use of their *voice* (i.e., voting rights, derivative suits) instead of the *exit* strategy (selling their holding in the company) (Erede, 2009; Marchetti, 1998).

Three main features indicate that Italian institutional investors may play, in the future, a more active role in the corporate governance of listed companies. In particular: they manage investment portfolios that are relatively concentrated; they enjoy a certain degree of coordination through Assogestioni (the asset manager association); finally, in Italy the Shareholders' Rights Directive (Directive 36/2007) has been recently implemented, which facilitates participation in shareholders' meetings and the exercise of other rights. At the same time, among the obstacles that still undermine the activism of institutional investors, the absence of pension funds and the conflicts of interest arising from the control of the banking system over the industry of mutual funds should be underlined.

How to explain the ownership structure and the governance model of large Italian companies

As mentioned before, large Italian companies have a concentrated ownership structure, i.e., a shareholder or a coalition of shareholders is able to exercise control over the firm (Zattoni and Ravasi, 2000). Largest shareholders are traditionally wealthy entrepreneurial families and, in some situations, the state or foreign multinational companies.

What is quite uncommon, even if it is slightly increasing, is the presence of companies with dispersed ownership structures (e.g., public companies) or with large coalitions of subjects sharing the control of the firm. Moreover, there is not a diffuse presence of both the industrial and financial business groups characterizing the German-Japanese governance model, and the public companies that are peculiar of the Anglo-Saxon model (Zattoni, 2006).

In the country there are no strong relationships among industrial companies and financial intermediaries (e.g., banks, insurance companies, etc.) as in the German-Japanese model. The old banking law – issued in 1936 under a wave of banking scandals and under the influence of the Wall Street crisis – prohibited direct investments between commercial banks and industrial companies to avoid any propagation of industrial crises in the banking industry. Despite the fact that the more recent banking law issued in 1993 allows banks to own minority shareholdings in industrial companies, Italian banks did not modify their behavior and still recently they do not own relevant shareholdings in Italian industrial companies (Bianchi and Bianco, 2006).

The public companies are almost absent for a number of reasons. First, according to the so-called "law and finance" view, public companies are diffused only in countries with a common law legal tradition and strong investors' protection (La Porta, Lopez-de-Silanes and Shleifer, 1999; La Porta, Lopez-de-Silanes, Shleifer et al., 1997 and 1998). Second, the absence of public companies may also be caused by the lack of large and independent institutional investors and, in particular, of pension funds. Third, the Italian welfare state politics and the dominant role of state-owned enterprises in the national economy contribute to explain the lack of companies with a dispersed owner-ship. Social democracies push firms to stabilize employment, to expand their activities whether or not the growth creates value for shareholders, and to avoid changes that may disrupt the quality of the workplace (Roe, 2003). The pressure of social democracies for developing social welfare increases agency costs between shareholders and managers, and to reduce these costs shareholders should maintain a concentrated ownership structure that allows them to control com-panies' decisions. Finally, the large state intervention in the national economy may have hindered financial development, because the state acted as a substitute for financial markets (Aganin and Volpin, 2003).

IPO activity between 2006 and 2008

The regulation of IPOs

The key element in IPOs' process is the price setting as this has a fundamental impact on the result of the offer.

In Italy, as in many other European countries, the price setting is based on the so-called open price book-building method. Usually IPOs are performed with a two-tier offer, with an institutional tranche and a retail tranche. The former is managed by a limited group of financial institutions (i.e., the institutional consortium) while the latter is exe-cuted by a relatively large number of banks through their branch network (the retail consortium).

Retail investors are price takers that cannot participate in the pricing process. Institutional investors place orders with the institu-tional consortium indicating their individual curve of demand and elasticity toward the price. Based on such elements, book-runners (i.e., the leading participants in the institutional consortium) build an aggregate curve of demand, which is used to set the final price.

In case of oversubscription the book-runner can decide on a discre-tionary basis how to allot the orders. The target distribution of shares between institutional and retail offers is made public before the launch of the offer itself. However, a "clawback clause" is generally included in the offer's terms, allowing a reallocation of shares between the two tranches.

The offer to the retail investors is an offer to the public under the scope of the Prospectus Directive (71/2003), which implies strong information requirements, mainly fulfilled by the publication of the prospectus after the scrutiny of the Italian Supervisory Authority (Consob). The activity made by Consob on the prospectus is aimed at verifying the completeness, the consistency and the comprehensibility of the information included (Paleari, Pellizzoni and Vismara, 2005).

The prospectus, drawn according to the Prospectus Directive as transposed in the Financial Act, must provide detailed information on the firm, its subsidiaries and its controlling shareholders, as well as indications about the intended use of newly raised funds. Usually it does not provide any forward-looking statement. Italian law places a presumption of responsibility on the "placement agent" (i.e., the bank that leads the retail consortium) for the information given in the prospectus.

The listing of any financial instrument is a process that takes place under the supervision of Borsa Italiana. In the Italian context, after the adoption of the so-called Mifid Directive (39/2004) a distinction may be drawn between "admission to trading" and "admission to listing": while the first does not in itself require a prospectus to be published and involves the trading in multilateral trading facilities (different from the regulated market), the latter depends upon the judgment of Borsa Italiana and Consob which are in charge of the listing of securities in a regulated market.

Currently the main markets organized by Borsa Italiana are Regulated Markets under the definition given by the Mifid Directive, while the "junior" markets (AIM Italy, previously named Mercato Alternativo del Capitale or MAC) are Multilateral Trading Facilities. This distinction is of particular importance since the EU financial legislation (the Directives: Prospectus (71/2003), Market Abuse (6/2003), Transparency (109/2004), as well as the Takeover Directive (25/2004)) only apply to companies whose securities are listed in a Regulated Market, thus increasing the costs of being listed. For companies whose securities are traded in Multilateral Trading Facilities (without being listed at the same time) the application of the European legislation is not at all straightforward since it depends on the voluntary adoption of the regulation by the MTF (Moloney, 2008).

Several times during the last decade Borsa Italiana (which was privatized in 1998 and acquired in 2007 by the London Stock Exchange) has segmented its equity markets offer in an attempt to match investors' and issuers' expectations. The main market (MTA) has different segments: (1) Blue Chip, (2) STAR (segment with high requirements) and (3) Standard. Companies admitted to the STAR segment accept to maintain stricter corporate governance rules and a more pervasive disclosure regime.

Table 9.5 shows the main listing requirements for an IPO on the different markets organized by Borsa Italiana. The key requirements refer to: (1) a minimum free float (at least 25 percent) and a minimum market cap (40 million euro, i.e., about $ 52 million), (2) three years of tracking record (at least one audited), and (3) the ability to run an autonomous revenues generating business (this condition may undermine the listing of a controlled company) (Annunziata, 2010).

The main ongoing requirements concern: (1) the dissemination of price-sensitive information, (2) the release of quarterly, half year and annual accounting reports, and (3) the communication of internal dealings (i.e., transactions performed by directors and main shareholders).

The IPOs between 2006 and 2008

During the period 2006–8, fifty-one Italian companies went public in the Italian Stock Exchange. In this section, we analyze forty-six companies as we excluded two companies (Marazzi Group and Polynt) that were delisted after IPO, and three companies (Area Impianti, Raffaele Caruso, Tessitura Pontelambro) that had been admitted to trading on Multilateral Trading Facilities (MAC or AIM).

Most of the companies in the sample went public in 2006 (seventeen companies) and 2007 (twenty-five companies); only four went public in 2008 when the financial crisis hit the world economic system hard. Moreover, as Table 9.6 shows, IPOs are focused in some particular industries such as industrials (sixteen) and consumer goods (fourteen).

An interesting characteristic of Italian IPO regards the firm age. In fact, Italian companies going public are not only young entrepreneurial and high-growth companies, but include also companies with a long tradition. Almost half of the companies (twenty-two out of forty-six) were founded before 1980 and the average time to go public is higher than thirty-six years.

Italian companies going public were either small or large companies. On average they have 1,000 employees, revenues of $ 499 million and assets equal to $ 449 million (see Table 9.7). The smallest

Table 9.5 *Listing and ongoing requirements in Italy*

	Regulated markets		MTFs	
	MTA/MIV		AIM	MAC
Sponsor ("Nomad" for AIM)	Pre-admission assessments. Minimum 1 year appointment		Pre-admission assessment. Post-admission guidance and assistance	No pre-admission assessment. Minimum 3 year appointment
Track record	3 year track record		Track record as low as less than 12 months	1 year track record
Pre-admission documents	Prospectus and other documents		Admission document similar to the EU prospectus	Simplified informative report
Post-admission communications	Flow of information coming from multiple sources (law, regulations)		Sophisticated flow of information	Minimal flow of information
Corporate governance	Pre-vetted by Italian law		Nomad verifies and evaluates CG's adequacy and board's effectiveness	Board of directors/board of auditors must possess good-standing requirements
Accounting standard	Standard IAS		Standard IAS	National standards
Mandatory tender offer	Mandatory by law under EU Directive		Voluntary	Voluntary, but standard bylaw clause recommended
Retail investors	Admitted		Admitted	Not admitted (institutionals only)
Minimum free float	25%		10%	Not required
Trading mechanism	Continuous (presence of the specialist is mandatory on STAR)		Continuous (presence of the specialist is mandatory)	Daily auction with minimum lot (presence of the specialist is mandatory)

Source: Borsa Italiana

Table 9.6 *IPO year and industry classification*

	2006	2007	2008	Total
Consumer goods	5	7	2	14
Consumer services	0	2	0	2
Financials	1	4	0	5
Healthcare	1	2	1	4
Industrials	8	8	0	16
Information technology	1	0	0	1
Oil and gas	1	0	0	1
Technology	0	2	1	3
Total	17	25	4	46

Table 9.7 *IPO size and performance*

	Size			Performance		
	Employees	Revenues	Assets	ROA	ROE	ROS
Min	31	272,522	11,731,960	–59%	–115%	–333%
1st quartile	143	39,214,867	49,984,914	6%	8%	6%
2nd quartile	421	117,001,710	135,214,205	8%	17%	8%
3rd quartile	1,075	286,565,983	323,733,401	11%	29%	13%
Max	12,339	6,978,399,140	4,066,616,210	30%	80%	32%
Average	1,037	499,639,519	449,299,635	9%	20%	2%

company – in terms of employees and revenues – was Toscana Finanza, a company founded in 1987 and active in buying and managing risky credits. The largest company on all dimensions was Prysmian that in 2005 bought the divisions Cables and Energy Systems, and Cables and Telecom Systems, of Pirelli & C. S.p.A. Because of its dimension, the company was already considered a blue chip at the time of the IPO and it entered the S&P/MIB index briefly after.

In terms of performance, companies going public had high profitability ratios on assets, net capital and revenues (see Table 9.7). Only two companies in the sample were not profitable in the year preceding the IPO. They are two pharmaceutical companies such as Molmed and Pierrel. Molmed – the company with the worst economic performance in the sample – is a medical biotechnology company founded in 1996 and focused on discovery, R&D and clinical

Table 9.8 *IPO ownership structure (data in percent)*

	Family		Bank		Govt.		VC		Angels		Top 1		Top 3	
	pre	post	pre	post	pre	post	pre	post	pre	post	pre	post	pre	post
Min	5	4	3	0	53	42	3	3	0	0	21	17	47	38
1st quartile	80	52	7	6	65	44	6	4	0	0	66	39	83	52
2nd quartile	98	58	19	10	77	45	7	5	0	0	95	54	95	57
3rd quartile	100	64	72	54	88	46	17	5	0	0	100	63	100	64
Max	100	74	100	67	100	48	48	45	0	0	100	70	100	96
Average	86	56	39	26	77	45	16	12	0	0	82	49	89	58
No. of cases	34	34	11	11	3	3	6	6	0	0	46	46	46	46

validation of innovative therapies for the treatment of cancer. Pierrel is instead a global provider to the pharmaceutical and life science industries. The most profitable companies in the sample were Saras (ROA), Mutuionline (ROE) and Screen Service (ROS). Saras is one of the biggest refineries in the Mediterranean Sea, Mutuionline is a leading online retail credit broker and a major provider of credit-related outsourcing services to lenders in Italy, and Screen Service is active in the telecommunication sector and is now one of Italy's leading producers of television broadcasting equipment.

Considering the ownership structure, IPO companies present similar characteristics to Italian listed companies. Before going public, a family was the largest shareholder in thirty-three out of forty-six cases, with an average of 86 percent of share capital. Banks were the largest shareholder in three cases, with an average of 39 percent, and the Italian government in three cases, with an average of 77 percent. Moreover, even if companies going public show a decrease of the share capital owned by the first shareholder, the major shareholder prefers to retain the control of the company after the IPO. Families, banks and the government maintain, in fact, an average of respectively 56, 26 and 45 percent of the shares. In sum, the IPO leads to a decrease of the shares owned by both the first and the first three shareholders, but even after going public Italian companies tend to be dominated by the major shareholders.

Table 9.8 shows also other interesting characteristics of Italian IPOs. That is the absence of business angels in the share capital of companies before and after the IPO, and the relatively low involvement of venture capital and private equity funds. Beyond that, four

Table 9.9 *IPO board of directors*

	Size	Executive directors	Non-executive directors	Indepen-dent directors	Engineering, operations, R&D	Marketing, sales	Finance, accounting, law
Min	3	1	0	0	0	0	0
1st quartile	6	2	4	1.2	2	0	3
2nd quartile	7.5	3	5	2	3	0	4
3rd quartile	9	3	6	3	4	1	6
Max	16	7	15	6	9	2	12
Average	8.0	2.8	5.2	2.2	2.9	0.4	4.7

out of six venture capital and private equity funds supporting IPO companies were Italian.

Finally, the ownership structure of Italian companies that decided to go public in the period analyzed is less complex than the traditional ownership structure of Italian listed companies. In fact, there are no companies with dual class shares, and only four companies are owned through a pyramidal group. Shareholders' agreements are, however, still diffused. Our sample shows that they are the most significant device used to maintain the controlling power over a company.

Boards of directors of IPO companies have on average eight directors: three executive directors and five non-executive directors, of whom two are independent directors (see Table 9.9). Women and foreign directors are few, on average less than one for each board. There are no employees' representatives on the board as the law does not require them, while in family firms it is common to have a number of directors with family relationships.

In terms of functional background, IPOs' boards have a majority of members with a functional background in peripherals functions (such as finance, accounting and law), a limited number of directors with a background in throughput functions (such as engineering, operations and research and development), and less than one director with a background in output functions (e.g., marketing or sales).

In line with the traditional structure of Italian listed companies, a large number of IPOs have created an audit committee (twenty-nine) and a remuneration committee (thirty-two), but only three have created a nomination committee. No company created governance or technology committees.

Description of an IPO: Arkimedica

The firm before the IPO

Arkimedica is a company founded in 1996 by some of its current managers. In 1997 the company bought a 40 percent shareholding in another company (Cla) producing beds and furniture for hospitals. In 2005, Cape Natexis Private Equity Fund (CNPEF) entered into the share capital to support the growth of Arkimedica through the acquisition of a number of companies: Sogespa, managing medical and housing services for elderly people; Delta Med, producing items for hospitals; Icos, producing machines for sterilizing medical items; and later Dirra, producing medical products not reusable, and Aricar, designing and producing items for ambulances and special medical vehicles. After these acquisitions, Arkimedica became the holding company of a business group operating in the health services and medical products industries. The M&A activity of the group led to an increase in revenues from $ 62 million in 2004 to $ 96 million in 2005.

The ownership structure of the company at the time of IPO sees the participation of a number of investors. Beyond CNPEF, there are in fact institutional investors, private investors and managers, i.e., founders of the acquired companies that have become managers of one of the four divisions of the group (i.e., contract, care, medical devices and equipment). The main shareholder of the holding company is CNPEF with a direct shareholding of 29.09 percent and an indirect shareholding of 20.57 percent through Tech Med. Then there are Arkigest (controlled by Carlo and Antonino Iuculano) with 10.62 percent, Tamburi Investment Partners with 6.68 percent, and seventeen small investors with shareholdings varying between 0.56 and 3.34 percent. The shareholders have signed an agreement to block the control of the company for three years.

The board of directors of Arkimedica includes fourteen directors, and has a chairman, a vice chairman and two CEOs. The company created only one committee, i.e., the executive committee with three executive directors (i.e., the chairman and the two CEOs). Almost all the board members are shareholders of the company or have some relationship with major shareholders of the firm. Only two directors may be considered as independent.

The general meeting of the company deliberated before the IPO a stock option plan allowing a few managers to buy about 5 percent of the share capital. The beneficiaries of the plan are in equal parts three executive directors of the firm: Cinzio Barazzoni (CEO), Carlo Iuculano (CEO) and Paolo Prampolini (executive director).

The offer

The IPO process happened in July 2006. The company targeted the Expandi market as this was the most appropriate one for small and medium companies.

The company offered up to 22.4 million shares out of 64 million shares before the IPO. As the offer involved newly issued shares, after the IPO the firm's shares became 86.4 million. Almost all the shares offered during the IPO (i.e., 97 percent) were allocated to institutional investors; only a small fraction of shares went to friends and family, i.e., subjects identified by the board of directors. In case of over-allotment from institutional investors, the global coordinator could borrow and allocate to them up to 2.24 million shares (i.e., 10 percent of the shares offered in the IPO). The offer included also a greenshoe for the same amount of shares. Shareholders also signed a lock-up pact with the global coordinator according to which they could not sell their shares for 270 days after the IPO without a written approval from the global coordinator.

The cash from the offer varied between $ 33 and 37 million for a total market capitalization of the firm after the IPO varying between $ 126 and 143 million. The price range per share varied from a minimum of $ 1.47 to a maximum of $ 1.66. The price range has been defined using both the multiples (i.e., EV/EBITDA and EV/EBIT) of comparable companies in the medical and managed care industries, and the discounted cash flow analysis.

The firm after the IPO

After the IPO, the ownership structure of the firm saw an almost proportional decreasing (i.e., about 25 percent) of the shares owned by the shareholders. More precisely, CNPEF's direct shareholding decreased to 19.17 – as the greenshoe has been totally exercised – and the indirect shareholding to 15.24 percent, Arkigest's shareholding to 7.87 percent, and Tamburi Investment Partners' shareholding to 4.94 percent. In line with the Italian tradition, after the IPO the firm's shareholding structure was still very concentrated.

In order to be more in line with the requirements of the Italian code of good governance and the Financial Act, the board of Arkimedica decided: (1) to introduce a procedure for the internal dealing and for the related parties' transactions, (2) to have at least four meetings per year, with a minimum frequency of three months, (3) to create a section in the website devoted to disseminating useful information for shareholders and the financial market, (4) to nominate a person as responsible for the investors' relationship.

The cash coming from the IPO has been used to enhance Arkimedica's future investments. The firm aimed, in fact, to pursue its development both through internal investments and M&A activity. The financial crisis did not hit the growth of the company, whose revenues reached $ 231 million in 2009.

Conclusion

Italian corporate governance has evolved radically in the last decades thanks to both the evolution of the corporate law, the adoption of the European Directives and the introduction and revision of the code of good governance. Today corporate governance of listed companies is characterized by a relatively high protection of shareholders' rights, and board of directors' characteristics are – at least formally – very similar to the best practices at international level.

Despite the evolution of corporate law and corporate governance, the ownership structure of Italian listed companies is still very concentrated, in line with that of major continental European companies. The high concentration of ownership structure, together with the lack of active and independent institutional investors, inhibits both the market for corporate control, and a real debate in the general meetings. In order to contribute to solve this issue, Italian corporate law requires that listed companies allow minority shareholders to nominate some of the members of the board. Moreover, recent trends in ownership structures show a decline in the use of mechanisms aimed at separating ownership and control, so reducing the incentive to adopt an opportunistic behavior.

The Italian Stock Exchange does not play a relevant role in the national economy. To go public has not been, in fact, a very popular decision for Italian companies for a number of reasons, including a cultural resistance of national entrepreneurs, the large diffusion of family businesses, the small and medium size of companies, etc. Only a small number of companies go public despite the commitment of the national stock exchange to favor their access to the financial market. Even in the three years here investigated, only fifty-one companies decided to go public. Their characteristics are very similar to those of listed companies: (1) they operate in traditional industries (i.e., industrial and consumer products); (2) they are companies with a certain experience in the industry, i.e., their average age is high; (3) their ownership structure, even after the IPO, is still relatively concentrated and sees often a family as major shareholder; (4) the involvement of venture capital and private equity is limited before and after the IPO, and business angels are absent; (5) their board of directors has an average of eight directors, three executives and five non-executives, the majority of whom have a background in peripherals functions (e.g., finance, accounting and law).

References

Aganin, Alexander and Paolo F. Volpin. 2003. 'History of corporate ownership in Italy', *ECGI – Finance Working Paper No. 17*.

Annunziata, Filippo. 2010. *La disciplina del mercato mobiliare*. Torino: Giappichelli.

Barca, Fabrizio and Marco Becht (eds.). 2001. *The Control of Corporate Europe*. Oxford University Press.

Bellinazzo, Marco. 2007. 'Non piace la governance doppia', *Il Sole 24 Ore*, 10 December.

Bianchi, Marcello and Magda Bianco. 2006. *Italian corporate governance in the last 15 years: From pyramids to coalitions?*, working paper, ECGI.

Bianchi, Marcello and Luca Enriques. 2005. 'Corporate governance in Italy after the 1998 reform: What role for institutional investors?', *Corporate Ownership and Control*, 2(4), 11–31.

Committee for the Corporate Governance. 2006. *Corporate Governance Code*, Borsa Italiana.

Consob. Annual relation, various years.

Erede, Matteo. 2009. *Governing Corporations with Concentrated Ownership Structure: Can Hedge Funds Activism Play Any Role in Italy?*,

CLEA 2009 Annual Meeting Paper. Available at SSRN: http://ssrn.com/abstract=1397562.

Ghezzi, Federico and Corrado Malberti. 2008. 'The two-tier model and the one-tier model of corporate governance in the Italian reform of corporate law', *European Company and Financial Law Review*, 5, 1–47.

Gianfrate, Gianfranco. 2007. 'What do shareholders' coalitions really want? Evidence from Italian voting trust', *Corporate Governance: An International Review*, 15, 122–32.

Hofstede, Geert. 1983. 'The cultural relativity of organizational practices and theories', *Journal of International Business Studies*, 14(2), 75–89.

La Porta, Rafael, Florencio Lopez-de-Silanes and Andrei Shleifer. 1999. 'Corporate ownership around the world', *Journal of Finance*, 54, 471–517.

La Porta, Rafael, Florencio Lopez-de-Silanes, Andrei Shleifer and Robert W. Vishny. 1997. 'Legal determinants of external finance', *Journal of Finance*, 52, 1131–50.

1998. 'Law and finance', *Journal of Political Economy*, 106, 1113–55.

Marchetti, Piergaetano. 1998. 'Osservazioni sui profili societari sulla bozza di TU del mercati finanziari', *Rivista delle società*, 140–51.

Melis, Andrea. 2004. 'On the role of the board of statutory auditors in Italian listed companies', *Corporate Governance: An International Review*, 12(1), 74–84.

Moloney, Niamh. 2008. *EC Securities Regulation*. Oxford University Press.

Mosca, Chiara. 2006. 'I principi di funzionamento del sistema monistico. I poteri del comitato di controllo', *Il nuovo diritto delle società*, 2, 733–66.

2010. 'The Takeover Bids Directive: An opportunity for Europe or simply compromise?', *Yearbook of European Law 2009*, 28, 308–36.

Notari, Mario. 2005. 'Note a margine dei primi dati statistici sugli effetti della riforma delle società di capitali', *Rivista delle società*, 385–400.

Paleari, Stefano, Enrico Pellizzoni and Silvio Vismara. 2005. *A comparative study of initial public offerings in Italy and in the United Kingdom*, Bit Notes, December, n.15.

Roe, Mark. 2003. *Political Determinants of Corporate Governance. Political Context, Corporate Impact*. Oxford University Press.

Spencer Stuart. 2010. 'Board index – Italia 2010'.

Ventoruzzo, Marco. 2005. 'Experiments in comparative corporate law: The recent Italian reform and the dubious virtues of a market for rules in the absence of effective regulatory competition', *European Company and Financial Law Review*, 2, 207–69.

Zattoni, Alessandro. 1999. 'The structure of corporate groups: The Italian case', *Corporate Governance – An International Review*, 7(1), 38–48.

2006. *Assetti proprietari e corporate governance*. Milano: Egea.

2009. 'Corporate governance in Italy: The structural conflict of interests between majority and minority shareholders', in Felix J. Lopez Iturriaga (ed.), *Codes of Good Governance Around the World*. New York: Nova Science Publishers.

Zattoni, Alessandro and Alessandro Minichilli. 2009. 'The diffusion of equity incentive plans in Italian listed companies: What is the trigger?', *Corporate Governance: An International Review*, 17(2), 224–37.

Zattoni, Alessandro and Davide Ravasi. 2000. 'Grandi imprese e grandi gruppi in Italia. Assetto proprietario e performance', *Economia & Management*, 2, 55–72.

10 Corporate governance and initial public offerings in Japan

HIDEAKI SAKAWA AND NAOKI
WATANABEL

Corporate governance mechanisms

The Japanese corporate governance system is relationship oriented or bank centered. The Japanese legal tradition is civil law as the national legal system was developed in the nineteenth century based on the German Civil Law Code. Japanese public companies, like German companies, aim at satisfying the interests of shareholders, employees, and other stakeholders in general. The main bank system and Japanese business groups – called *financial keiretsu* – play an important role for both external and internal governance. The external corporate governance is centered on the president council of *financial keiretsu* and the concentrated ownership structure of *industrial keiretsu*. These inter-corporate shareholdings are a defensive response to hostile takeover threats. Japanese internal corporate governance is characterized by fewer outside directors and by the presence of bank-appointed directors. The main bank influence – i.e., the number of directors nominated by banks – tends to increase when the company suffers a loss or is facing a financial crisis.

Japanese corporate ownership is more concentrated than in the US or the UK. The major shareholders are the main banks and the *financial* and *industrial keiretsu*. Ownership structure is also characterized by a stable cross-shareholding. Japanese internal governance mechanisms evolved significantly in the last decade. The Japanese board was traditionally a two-tier system. After the amendment of the Commercial Law in 2002, the law allowed companies to create committees. After this legal change, an increasing number of companies introduced committees and followed the related provision to appoint more than 50 percent of outside directors. The amendment of the Commercial Law also pushed firms with a one-tier board structure to increase the number of outside directors. However, in traditional Japanese companies, almost all board members are still inside directors.

Corporate culture and law

Corporate governance mechanisms in Japan differ from "Anglo-Saxon" market-oriented corporate governance mechanisms (Aoki, 1990; Aoki, Patrick, and Sheard, 1994; Gerlach, 1992). The Japanese corporate governance system is defined as relationship oriented or bank centered (Aoki, 1990). The strong relationship between industrial companies and financial intermediaries is based on the main bank system. The salient feature of this system is the long-term relationship between the main bank, the borrowing companies and the other companies belonging to the business group. For a traditional industrial company, the main bank is one of the major shareholders, provides a large amount of financial resources, and is responsible for a close monitoring of the business.

The main bank both plays an advisory role and provides financial resources to industrial companies. The main bank has a large influence in the election of board members of industrial companies. This happens because the shareholder meetings of Japanese companies are similar to ceremonies and the voice of minority shareholders is generally neglected (Imamura, Sakawa, and Watanabel, 2007).

The Japanese corporate governance system is also characterized by the large diffusion of business groups, e.g., *financial keiretsu* and *industrial keiretsu* (Brown and Co. Ltd., 2001). The six major business groups (Mitsui, Sumitomo, Mitsubishi, Fuyo, Sanwa, and Daiichi Kangyo) and two small business groups (Tokai and IBJ) are *financial keiretsu*. They are organized around main banks and other large companies. Brown and Co. Ltd. (2001) classified thirty-five groups (such as Toyota Motor Corp. and Matsushita Electric Industrial Co.) as *industrial keiretsu*. Companies belonging to *financial* or *industrial keiretsu* are connected through presidential councils (*Shacho-kai*), mutually appointed directors, and cross-shareholdings (Berglof and Perotti, 1994; Hoshi and Kashyap, 2010).

The Japanese *financial keiretsu* differ from business groups of most Eastern Asian countries, such as Korean *Chaebol* (Claessens, Djankov, and Lang, 2000). They are not family controlled, but manager-dominated corporate groups. Morck and Nakamura (2005) find that managers of the most powerful firms within the *keiretsu* are in a position to transfer wealth from companies with weaker ties to the companies at the core of the group. Lincoln, Gerlach, and Ahmadjian

(1996) argue that this transfer of wealth is performed by managers of the core companies sitting as board members of peripheral firms.

The traditional Japanese corporate governance system was performing well before the asset bubble of the 1990s. After the 1990s, long recession periods – called the lost decades – began. This long period of recessions cast some doubts on the efficiency of the traditional Japanese corporate governance system. In 1997, the bankruptcy of Yamaichi Securities Co. Ltd., a large investment bank in Japan and a member of the *financial keiretsu* of Fuyo Group, occurred. Subsequently, many merger and acquisition activities of *financial keiretsu* groups occurred. In addition, the large city bank groups were merged into three megabanks during 2005. These mergers in Japanese companies inside *financial keiretsu* were organized to solve their difficult financial conditions. In fact, Dow and McGuire (2009) find that the ties of *financial keiretsu* groups were strengthened to overcome the tight financial conditions.

The M&A activities in the banking sector have dramatically changed Japanese *keiretsu*, especially *financial keiretsu*, and have led to the formation of four megabank groups in 2001. In 2005, the four banks merged into three megabanks: Mitsubishi-UFJ Financial Group, Mizuho Financial Group, and Sumitomo Mitsui Banking Corp. (Hoshi and Kashyap, 2010). These merger activities have probably weakened the main bank relationships. Moreover, some banks were saved by taxpayer funds and were therefore monitored by taxpayers. The traditional lending ties to the borrowing firms have also weakened. Consequently, the influence of banks in the election process of boards of borrowing companies has been reduced. Finally, the role of presidents' councils has also been weakened after the M&A of megabanks (Tanaka, 2004).

Amakudari or "descent from heaven" was regarded as the other most prominent peculiar feature of the Japanese corporate governance system during the 1990s. *Amakudari* are retired bureaucrats of Japanese government agencies that are appointed as board members of regulated companies. Many practitioners have reported that the force of regulators is traditionally strong in Japan and is still a Japanese corporate custom. This tradition can determine agency problems. Horiuchi and Shimizu (2001) point out that there are agency problems in the boards of directors, and argue that the *amakudari* relationship can produce a fragile banking system in Japan.

The recent reforms of the Koizumi Cabinet were intended to limit such appointments of *amakudari*. Although Aso's administration failed to eliminate *amakudari*, the Democratic-party-led government has discouraged and reduced recommendations of *amakudari* appointments of officials to agency-regulated businesses (Dickie, 2009).

Principles of good governance

After 2000, the Japanese corporate governance framework has largely changed. Governance scholars and practitioners still debate if the board of directors in Japan has effectively taken a role of monitoring. After the amendment of the Commercial Law in 2002, the legal framework for corporate governance allows companies to choose either a corporate auditor system, which requires no outside directors, or a committee system, which requires the appointment of outside directors. There has been no committee, such as an audit or a compensation committee, in Japanese listed companies since then.

Although the Japanese corporate governance system differs from the market-oriented "Anglo-Saxon" system, the recent corporate governance reforms in Japan aim at encouraging Japanese public companies to adopt good governance principles. Nakamoto (2009a) points out that the Asian Corporate Governance Association and the American Chamber of Commerce asked Japanese regulators to adopt some kind of regulation favoring the appointment of independent or outside directors. Nowadays, some corporate governance principles are established which are aimed at producing common understandings about what is good governance for Japanese public listed firms.

In March 2004, the Tokyo Stock Exchange (TSE) established the principles of corporate governance for listed firms. Then, in December 2009, the TSE revised the principles and presented a model of good governance that Japanese listed companies are encouraged to follow if they want to enhance the creation of shareholder value. The main principles of good governance issued in 2009 can be summarized in five points: (1) rights of shareholders, (2) equal treatment of shareholders, (3) relationship with stakeholders in corporate governance, (4) disclosure and transparency, and (5) responsibility of board of directors, auditors, and other relevant groups (see Table 10.1).

The update of the principles of good governance will favor the evolution of the characteristics of the boards of directors of

Table 10.1 *The summary of TSE (2009)*

Main governance principles	Content of good governance principles
(1) Rights of shareholders	Listed companies should protect the rights of shareholders. Listed companies should develop an environment in which shareholders are inclined to participate in general shareholders' meeting and exercise voting rights appropriately.
(2) Equal treatment of shareholders	To secure equal treatment, the listed companies should observe the following points: (1) the listed companies should prevent the abuse of positions such as those of directors or officers undertaken in the interests of controlling shareholders; (2) the listed companies should enhance the disclosure of information, especially in cases where companies are controlled by the specific concerned shareholders; (3) the offering of special benefits to shareholders with large holdings is prohibited.
(3) Relationship with stakeholders in corporate governance	Corporate governance of listed companies should help to create corporate value and jobs through the establishment of smooth relations between the company and its stakeholders, and further encourage sound management of the enterprise.
(4) Disclosure and transparency	Corporate governance of listed companies should ensure that timely and accurate disclosure is conducted on all matters including the financial condition, firm performance, and ownership structure. For this purpose, the development of internal systems to secure the accurate and timely disclosure and equal access rights to such information among shareholders are encouraged.
(5) Responsibility of board of directors, auditors, and other relevant groups	Three types of corporate governance models are proposed for listed companies. (1) Committee style (Western-style corporate governance): there are internal committees such as nomination committees, compensation committees, and audit committees under the board of directors. Through the decision making

Table 10.1 (*cont.*)

Main governance principles	Content of good governance principles
	undertaken by these committees, executive officers are monitored and supervised.
	(2) No committee and more than one-third of directors are outside directors. The company auditors are not permitted to act as board members. The internal auditing is augmented by corporate auditors and outside auditors.
	(3) No committee and at least one outside director on the board. The internal auditing is augmented by internal auditors on the board, and corporate auditors and outside auditors who are not on the board.

Source: "Report by the Financial System Council's Study Group on the Internationalization of Japanese Financial and Capital Markets"

Japanese listed companies. However, the process is slow as only fifty-six listed firms on the TSE and seventy-two firms listed in all Japanese financial markets have adopted the committee system in 2009 (Japan Association of Corporate Directors, 2010; Nakamoto, 2009a).

A code of good governance similar to that of Western market-oriented countries has not been developed yet. According to Nakamoto (2009a), more than half of the companies listed in TSE have no outside director. We cannot classify listed firms without outside directors as complying with the principles of good governance because even the third governance model (see (5) in Table 10.1) calls for at least one outside director. Therefore, the TSE announces guidelines calling for more independent directors to improve the quality of corporate governance. Nakamoto (2009b) states that there is a dialogue on these issues between the Keidanren, a powerful Japanese business lobby, and regulators. The opinions are still divergent as Mr. Fujio Mitarai, Chairman of Canon Inc. and a member of Keidanren, expresses a negative opinion about TSE listing requirements to appoint outside or independent directors (Nakamoto, 2009b).

Table 10.2 *Board characteristics of newly listed Japanese companies during 2008*

Variables	Characteristics of Japanese newly listed companies
Sample	42 listed companies in 2008
Mix between executive and non-executive directors	6.1 members of the board on average: 5.07 executive directors and 1.02 non-executive directors. 0.13 non-executives are independent directors
Nationality of members	No foreign directors are present in companies in the sample
Gender of directors	Women directors are present in 5 companies
CEO age	Average CEO age is 53
Board tenure	Average director tenure is 7.49 years
Members of top management team, designated as *Jomukai*	41 companies have a *Jomukai* as a meeting of top management team, with 231 members
Chairman of the board	Only 7 companies have a chairman of the board
Adoption of committee systems	No listed company in 2008 introduced a committee system
Compensation of all board members	Average compensation of board members is 148,000 USD per year
Stock options for executives	33 companies have stock option plans for executives

The boards of directors of forty-two companies that went public in 2008 show the following features (see Table 10.2): (1) the average CEO age is fifty-three, and is apparently young compared with large Japanese companies; (2) the board size is six members on average to prevent the drawbacks related to large boards that were a peculiar characteristic of Japanese traditional companies in the 1990s (Miwa and Ramseyer, 2005; Sakawa, Watanabel, and Ben-Zion, 2009); (3) executives of thirty-three firms receive stock option plans. Before 1997, Japanese commercial law banned the awarding of stock options to executives. In that period, Japanese executive compensation consisted only of cash salary and bonus, and the total amount was about 140,000 USD per executive. Executive compensation of Japanese IPO firms remains more or less at the same level. However, the award of stock options to executives in more than three-quarters of firms provided adequate incentives.

Despite this encouraging picture, some open issues remain, such as (1) an unfavorable mix of executive and non-executive directors; (2) the low presence of foreign and women directors; (3) a relatively high board tenure equal on average to 7.49 years, and the high stability of board members; (4) the diffusion of *Jomukai*, that is a kind of top management team, despite the confusion between chairman and CEO roles, as no chairman exists in more than 80 percent of the firms; and (5) all firms lack committee systems aimed at strengthening board members' monitoring functions.

Stock exchange and listed companies

Japan's capital market structure has unique features. Japan has three primary stock exchanges: the TSE, the Osaka Stock Exchange, and the Nagoya Stock Exchange. In this section, we introduce the Japanese IPO market and discuss the Japanese IPO ownership structure.

Japanese stock exchanges have been changing for the last two decades, especially during the "Big Bang deregulation" period of 1997–2001. As described previously, Japanese *keiretsu*, especially *financial keiretsu*, or the main bank system, were still existing during this period because four megabanks were formed and limitations of stock holding of commercial banks were lacking. In the process of market reform, new markets for small and medium-sized firms were established. The most representative IPO market in Japan is known as JASDAQ, which had been an over-the-counter market before 1998. In December 1998, JASDAQ became recognized as a market by amendment of the Financial Instruments and Exchange Act. The Mothers Section of TSE was opened in November 1999. In fact, the TSE, which is known as the largest stock exchange in Japan, also established a new market for small and medium-sized firms. In 2000, NASDAQ Japan was merged into the Osaka Stock Exchange, which had been cooperating with NASDAQ.

During the post "Big Bang deregulation" of 2001–9, the three new markets of JASDAQ, Hercules, and Mothers assumed a central role for IPO companies in Japan. Actually, NASDAQ Japan was abolished with the cooperation of NASDAQ in December 2002 and changed into the Hercules Section of the Osaka Stock Exchange. After 2004, the JASDAQ evolved into a stock exchange. In the Big Bang process, the ambitious section of the Sapporo Stock Exchange, the Centrex Section of the Nagoya Stock Exchange, and the Q-board Section of the Fukuoka Stock Exchange were also established, but the numbers of listings of these markets has remained lower.

Table 10.3 presents the numbers of listed companies during 1990–2008. The Japanese stock exchange in 1995 had 2,263 publicly traded companies; about 1,700 were listed in the first or second section of TSE, which is the largest stock exchange in Japan. This tendency implies that Japanese stock markets before 2000 mainly traded shares of large and mature firms; small and medium-sized firms have difficulty being listed on the stock exchange. During 2000, three representative Japanese stock markets for small and medium-sized firms were established: the Mothers Section of the TSE, JASDAQ, and the Hercules Section of the Osaka Stock Exchange. The purpose of these markets is to offer useful conditions for entrepreneurs intending to offer the stock of their new companies for sale to the public. After 2000, more than 1,000 companies were listed on the three new markets. Among the three markets, 979 firms were listed on JASDAQ in 2008. JASDAQ is the most representative market for IPO companies.

Table 10.4 presents the ownership structure of Japanese IPO companies during 2006–8. The ownership structure is highly concentrated. The first shareholder controls, on average, about 41.38 percent in the first and second sections of TSE and 44.72 percent in the three representative IPO markets at the end of 2006. The top three shareholders own about 60 percent of shares in the first and second section of TSE and more than two-thirds of shares in the three representative IPO markets. Family shareholdings account for more than 3 percent. The transition of ownership structure during 2006–8 shows that high and stable concentration ownership decreased during the last year. Claessens, Djankor, and Lang (2000) analyzed the family ownership structure of about 3,000 companies in Asian countries in 1996. Their survey shows that Japanese family ownership is about 9.7 percent. Compared with the IPO listed companies during 2006–8, family ownership is lower, which implies that Japanese IPO firms were not family controlled in the 2000s.

The control structure of Japanese IPO companies during 2006–8 is shown in Table 10.5. Dual classes shares are prohibited by the Japanese Commercial Law that underlines the principle of "Equality

Table 10.3 Numbers of companies and shares listed on Japanese stock exchanges (1990–2008)

| | Most representative markets in firms | | | Three representative markets for small and medium-sized firms | | | Excluding JASDAQ | All markets |
| | TSE | | | | Osaka Stock Exchange | JASDAQ | | |
Year	First section	Second section	Foreign companies	Mothers section	Hercules	All sections	All exchanges	Total
1990	1191	436	125	–	–	–	2071	2071
1995	1253	461	77	–	–	–	2263	2263
2000	1447	579	41	29	40	886	2595	3481
2005	1667	506	28	150	124	956	2853	3809
2006	1715	491	25	185	155	971	2958	3929
2007	1727	467	25	195	172	979	2976	3955
2008	1715	462	16	196	179	979	2951	3930

Source: Tokyo Stock Exchange website

Table 10.4 *Ownership concentration of Japanese IPO listed companies (31 December) during 2006–8*

	TSE first and second sections			Three representative IPO markets		
	First shareholder	Three major shareholders	Family share-holdings	First shareholder	Three major shareholders	Family share-holdings
2006	41.38	57.67	3.30	44.72	67.84	4.70
2007	49.87	66.59	7.96	43.29	67.11	4.62
2008	22.98	40.94	1.89	38.37	62.90	8.54

Table 10.5 *Control structure of Japanese companies listed during 2006–8 (31 December)*

	Controlled with more than 50% of shares	Controlled with more than 20% and less than 50% of shares	Not controlled
2006	62	92	22
2007	44	58	14
2008	10	31	1

of All Shareholders." A number of Japanese IPO companies (116 companies) are controlled by a subject owning the majority (i.e., higher than 50 percent) of voting rights in shareholders' meetings. In Japan, a controlling shareholder is defined according to TSE as a shareholder owning more than 20 percent of voting rights. A number of companies (181 companies) are controlled by a shareholder who owns more than 20 percent but less than 50 percent of shares.

Ownership and governance of large Japanese companies

Large listed firms such as Toyota and Matsushita have no concentrated ownership structure (La Porta, Lopez-de-Silanes, and Shleifer, 1999). They sometimes have a main bank among their major stockholders. Especially, the *financial keiretsu* are business groups whose shareholders are corporations, centered around the large commercial bank. In contrast, some listed firms such as Toyota Tsusho and

Matsushita Denko have parent companies. These firms have a concentrated ownership structure and are sometimes controlled by a parent company.

The main bank holds the equity of client firms, and this ownership mitigates agency costs that arise between creditors and shareholders (Prowse, 1990). In addition, when the client firm performance is negative, the main bank acts by appointing a new board of directors (Kang and Shivdasani, 1995; Kaplan and Minton, 1994; Morck and Nakamura, 1999). Especially in cases of financial distress, the main bank acts to safeguard all stakeholders' interests.

Cross shareholdings are common, i.e., company A holds shares of company B, and company B holds shares of company A. These cross shareholdings can be an entrenchment device for managers in both firms because the cross shareholdings can protect those managers from hostile takeovers and proxy contests (Hiraki, Inoue, Ito et al., 2003). Morck and Nakamura (1999) point out that the total amount of mutual shareholdings is high in large Japanese firms belonging to *keiretsu* groups. This evidence supports the view that these cross shareholdings of *keiretsu* are mechanisms to protect from the risk of a hostile takeover.

Non-financial firms tend to create business groups called *industrial keiretsu*. The TSE is willing to encourage listed subsidiary firms to have boards with independent directors (Financial Times, 2007). More than 300 Japanese listed companies have parent companies listed on the stock market.

IPO activity during 2006–2008

Regulation of IPOs

A decision that has a fundamental impact on the result of the offer is how to fix the IPO price. Two methods of offer have been used in JASDAQ, the largest IPO market in Japan since 1997: hybrid auction and book building. Under the hybrid auction method, the issuer designates a substantial portion of the issue to be offered directly via a discriminatory auction. A preliminary prospectus is made available ten days before the minimum price of the auction is determined. It contains no price information. Shares allocated to the auction are described in the "revised" prospectus; the minimum price of auction, which is normally 85 percent of fair value, is also public. Japanese regulation limits the maximum amounts of shares (5,000 shares). Under this regulation, institutional investors lose incentives for producing information related to fair value. A few days after the auction, the remaining stock is described in a second "revised" prospectus. The IPO prices are then set by the underwriter. The maximum price the underwriter can set is a weighted average price of the successful bid; the minimum one is not less than the minimum permissible bid price. Kerins, Kutsuna, and Smith (2007) empirically analyzed the price adjustment of IPO in the auction methods. Under book building, the underwriter seeks indications of interest from institutional investors. Institutional investors submit non-binding price and quantity indications. After gathering these indications, the underwriter offers a price reflecting due diligence and the estimated demand.

After 1997 in JASDAQ, book building methods were permitted for IPOs. Consequently, hybrid auction and book building methods have since coexisted for IPOs. In the Japanese hybrid auction system, almost half of the total offer is sold by discriminatory auction; the other half is sold in a public offer at a price below the weighted average successful bid from the auction. All issuers in Japan selected book building, although auctioning is still available as an alternative. Kutsuna and Smith (2004) reported that no IPO firms chose the hybrid auction system. Compared with the issuance cost weighting by issue size, the aggregate cost of book building and hybrid auction are almost equal. Their interpretation is that Japanese IPO firms prefer the book building method to a hybrid auction because it provides the advantage of more accurate pricing. The differences of long-term underperformance of IPO companies between both methods were analyzed by Kutsuna et al. (2009).

A unique rule exists in relation to trading systems in JASDAQ. The listed companies can choose the trading system used for their stock trades: an order driven system or a market maker system. In a usual stock exchange, the trading system of stocks is stable. For example, NASDAQ adopts a market maker system and the London Stock Exchange adopts an order driven system. In JASDAQ's criteria, a listed company which will not expect high liquidity in the market can choose the market maker system. In fact, many firms choose a market maker of their firms. Uno, Shimatani, Shimizu et al. (2002) point out that at end-September 2001, 314 issues listed on the

JASDAQ market were traded with designated market makers, more than one-third of the 902 issues listed on this market. These facts imply that many firms are small firms and cannot expect high liquidity in the market.

The Financial Instrument and Exchange Act defines the rules of regulated markets in Japan. All listed companies must produce a prospectus. Because all markets in Japan are regulated by the Financial Service Agency (FSA), all listed companies must produce a prospectus complying with the rules. The prospectus presents comments on the intended use of newly raised funds and provides detailed information related to the firm and its controlling shareholders.

The admission to listing is subject also to a process of due diligence approved by the FSA. A trust bank or clearing firm is selected as a transfer agency of the company. Its function is to produce documentation related to the issuing firm necessary to comply with the listing standards. Companies can apply for listing on any section of the stock exchange: the main market or a new market such as the Mothers Section of TSE, the JASDAQ, or the Hercules Section of the Osaka Stock Exchange.

Table 10.6 presents the listing requirement of the Mothers Section of TSE. The main listing requirements for an IPO company are to have a minimum free float (at least 25 percent) and a minimum market cap (at least 1 million USD), a two-year track record (at least one audited), and the ability to generate revenues in autonomy. As the listing requirements in the JASDAQ and Hercules Section of Osaka Stock Exchange are less stringent, the listed companies in the Mothers Section of TSE are fewer.

The ongoing requirements mostly relate to the information that listed companies must provide to their shareholders and the financial markets in terms of the times of dissemination of price-sensitive information (quarterly, half-year, and annual reports), and communications related to transactions made by significant persons.

IPOs during 2006–2008

During 2006–8, 334 Japanese companies went public in Japan. Most companies went public in 2006 (176 companies) and 2007 (116 companies). Only 42 companies went public in 2008, as in that year a deep financial crisis struck the world economic system.

Table 10.6 *Listing and ongoing requirements in the Mothers Section of TSE*

Admission requirements	
Free float	Minimum 25 percent
Market cap	At least 1 billion yen
Age	Two years track record normally required, at least one audited account
Autonomy	Ability to generate revenues in conditions of management autonomy
Transfer agent	Appointment of a sponsor who is permitted for the Japanese Commercial Law to assist the company in the listing process
Admission documents	Pre-vetted by the Stock Exchange
Prospectus	The company must publish a prospectus that complies with the requirement of the Financial Instruments and Exchange Act
Ongoing requirements	
Price-sensitive information	Timely dissemination to EDINET, which distributes to the public
Minimum free float	No minimum free float
Financial statements	Produce voluntary quarterly reports, half-year reports, and independently audited full-year financial reports
Transactions of significant persons	To be communicated

Note: Information gathered by Pronexus (2009)

Moreover, as Table 10.7 shows, IPOs were concentrated in some particular industries such as consumer goods (51), consumer services (60), telecommunications (48), and utilities (104). Japanese IPO booms have occurred in the 2000s. Technological innovation in the areas of IT and telecommunications were notable during this period. Therefore, many telecommunications companies decided to go public. Consumer goods and services companies using IT technology also chose to offer stock for sale to the public. In contrast, few other companies related to basic materials or industrial production went public during this period. In these industries, many Japanese companies are matured and have already gone public.

Table 10.7 *IPO year and industry classification*

	2006	2007	2008	Total
Basic materials	4	2	0	6
Consumer goods	25	21	5	51
Consumer services	38	14	8	60
Financials	16	12	5	33
Healthcare	5	4	4	13
Industrials	6	7	5	18
Technology	0	1	0	1
Telecommunications	26	16	6	48
Utilities	56	39	9	104
Total	**176**	**116**	**42**	**334**

An interesting characteristic of Japanese IPOs is related to the firm age. In fact, Japanese companies that go public are not only young entrepreneurial and high-growth companies as is common in other countries. They also include companies with a long and distinguished tradition. Almost one-third of the companies (108 of 334) were founded before 1980. The average time to go public was longer than twenty-two years. Most young companies chose to offer their stock for sale to the public in the three representative IPO markets, the Mothers Section of the TSE (72), JASDAQ (119), and the Hercules Section of the Osaka Stock Exchange (61), because the listing standards of these three markets are less stringent than others.

Japanese IPO companies include small and large companies. On average, they have 593 employees, revenues of 275,975,623 USD, and assets equal to about 524,072,413 USD (see Table 10.8). The smallest company in terms of employees was Ground Financial Advisory Company Ltd., a real estate service agent company founded in 2002. The largest one in terms of employees was Takata Corp., founded in 1956. Takata Corp. produces automobile parts and does not belong to an *industrial keiretsu*. This company has many foreign branches in the US, Singapore, Mexico, China, and so on. This company is so large that it has been listed on the First section of the TSE since its IPO.

Regarding performance, companies going public typically have high profitability ratios on sales. Only five companies in the sample reported negative profit. Two companies were listed on JASDAQ: Hibino Corp.

Table 10.8 *IPO size and performance for 334 firms in Japan during 2006–8*

	Size			Performance		
	Employees	Revenues	Assets	ROA	ROE	ROS
Min	6	874,513	1,345,801	–27.8%	–42.7%	–889.3%
1st quartile	63	20,969,257	10,637,761	3.5%	5.4%	2.9%
2nd quartile	141	45,517,104	25,109,284	6.3%	8.6%	4.9%
3rd quartile	362	140,639,224	94,582,301	10.0%	13.1%	9.4%
Max	36,051	28,279,814,720	40,466,930,137	43.0%	43.0%	72.7%
Average	593	275,975,623	524,072,413	7.3%	9.3%	27.6%

Table 10.9 *Pre-IPO ownership structure for 334 firms in Japan during 2006–8 (data in percent)*

	CEO	Family	Bank	Government	VC	Top 1	Top 3
Min	0.00	0.00	0.00	0.00	0.00	2.66	5.28
1st quartile	4.30	6.91	0.00	0.00	0.00	26.69	52.29
2nd quartile	24.57	30.87	0.00	0.00	2.55	41.25	67.33
3rd quartile	47.09	55.28	1.64	0.00	6.70	74.95	81.56
Max	95.88	98.97	25.16	0.00	74.71	100.00	100.00
Average	28.32	34.39	1.47	0.00	8.81	43.63	65.49

and ND Software Co. Ltd. The other three companies were listed in the Mothers, Second, and First sections of the TSE: Estic Corp., Iwai Securities Co. Ltd., and Fellisimo Corp. The most profitable companies in the sample were Mediscience Planning Inc. (ROA and ROE) and Hoshizaki Electric Co. Ltd. (ROS). Mediscience Planning Inc. is a biotechnology company that has had continuous operations for more than twenty years, whereas Hoshizaki Electric Co. Ltd. is an industrial machinery manufacturer that has a market share of commercial refrigerators and freezers greater than 50 percent. The company merged with a large vending machine company, the US Lancer Corp., in 2006.

Regarding the ownership structure, IPOs present similar characteristics to those of Japanese listed companies. The largest shareholder of a company that goes public is typically represented by a founder, although few companies are controlled by families, banks, and venture capitalists (see Table 10.9). Families, banks, and venture capitalists maintain, in fact, average shareholdings equal to respectively

Table 10.10 *IPO boards of directors during 2008*

	Size	Executive directors	Non-executive directors	Independent directors	Engineering, operations, R&D	Marketing, sales	Finance, accounting, law
Min	4	1	0	0	0	0	0
1st quartile	5	4	0	0	0	0	0
2nd quartile	6	5	1	0	0	0	0
3rd quartile	7	6	2	0	0	0	0
Max	12	11	4	1	1	1	1
Average	6.10	5.07	1.02	0.13	0.07	0.03	0.19

34.39 percent, 1.47 percent, and 8.81 percent. On average, the largest shareholder maintains 43.63 percent of shares and the top three shareholders maintain 65.49 percent.

Table 10.9 shows other interesting characteristics of Japanese IPOs: the absence of government ownership in the share capital of companies before the IPO. In addition, no companies have dual class shares in the sample because dual class ownership is prohibited. Our sample shows that family ownership and, to a lesser extent, venture capital are the most important shareholders of companies.

Boards of directors of IPO companies have, on average, 6.1 directors: 5.07 executive directors and 1.02 non-executive directors (see Table 10.10). Women and foreign directors are on average fewer than one on each board. No employees' representatives sit on the board because they are not required by law. Furthermore, the independent directors are less than one, on average.

In terms of the functional background, IPOs' boards have most members with no functional background regarding traditional Japanese companies; employees with general background are preferred. Such employees, designated as generalists, tend to be promoted on the board. Therefore, board members tend to have no specific functional background. In fact, few directors have backgrounds in peripheral functions such as finance, accounting, and law, throughput functions such as engineering, operations, and research and development, or output functions such as marketing or sales. Consistent with the traditional structure of Japanese listed companies, no company created committees on the board.

Description of an IPO: Gree Inc.

The firm before the IPO

Gree Inc. is an IT company founded in December 2004 by Yoshikazu Tanaka, who was an employee of Rakuten Inc. and a developer of unique Japanese social network systems (SNS). In 2004, SNS users exceeded 100,000. Mr. Tanaka decided to found new firms providing SNS services. In 2005, the equity fund of Apax Globis Japan bought shares to support the growth of Gree through the allocation of new shares. In 2006, the KDDI Corp. also bought shares of Gree through the allocation of new shares. Using the increased capital resources, Gree developed new mobile phone SNS services, which enhanced the availability of services to SNS users. The number of SNS users reached more than 8 million users in 2008. Mobile phone SNS services boosted ordinary income from −103 million yen (approximately −1 million USD) in 2007 to 1,051 million yen (or 9.9 million USD) in 2008.

The ownership structure of the company at the time of the IPO indicates the participation of a number of investors, such as institutional investors and managers (i.e., founders and board members of the company). The main shareholder is the founder of the company, Yoshikazu Tanaka, with a shareholding equal to 62.4 percent. Block shareholders holding more than 5 percent of shares are Apax Globis Japan with 9.82 percent, Recruit Co. Ltd. and KDDI Corp. with 6.89 percent, and Kotaro Yamagishi (who is a board member of Gree) with 6.75 percent. The ownership structure is concentrated in the hands of managers because Gree is a young company founded in 2004.

The Gree board of directors has six members. It has one CEO but no chairman. The company did not adopt a committee system prior to the IPO. Four board members are shareholders of the company. Only two directors might be considered as independent. The beneficiaries of the stock plan before IPO are three executive directors of the firm: Kotaro Yamagishi (executive director), Masaki Morimoto (executive director), and Naoki Aoyagi (executive director).

The offer

The IPO process took place in 2008. The company targeted the Mothers Section of the TSE, which is a representative IPO market for small and medium companies in Japan. The company offered up to 403 million shares out of 1,827 million shares before the IPO. Because the offer involves newly issued shares, after the IPO the firm's shares will be 2,230 million shares. In case of a greater allotment from executive directors, venture capital, and institutional investors, the company can borrow and allocate to them up to 400,000 shares (i.e., 0.1 percent of the shares offered in the IPO). Shareholders also signed a lock-up pact: they were not allowed to sell their shares for 180 days after the IPO. The IPO proceeds was about 37.36 million USD.

The firm after the IPO

After the IPO, the ownership structure of the firm underwent split decisions of major shareholders increasing or decreasing their shares. More precisely, Recruit Co. Ltd. shareholdings increased to 7.14 percent and KDDI Corp.'s shareholdings increased to 7.14 percent. Shareholders such as Recruit Co. Ltd. and KDDI Corp. expected that the cash coming from the IPO would enhance Gree's future investment and that the Gree investment plan would be profitable. Apax Globis Japan's shareholdings increased to 1.79 percent, and board member Kotaro Yamagishi's shareholdings increased to 3.98 percent. In contrast, CEO Yoshikazu Tanaka's shareholding decreased to 59.79 percent. An important aim of shareholders such as venture capitalists is apparent: Apax Globis Japan and managers cashed a large capital gain thanks to the high offering price of the IPO. The board size of Gree is six directors, which is the average board size of IPO firms in 2008. The Gree board includes two independent directors: one-third of the board, in compliance with the second model of company defined among the "Principles of Corporate Governance." The cash coming from the IPO will enhance Gree's future advertising and R&D activity. The firm aims to increase the number of customers using their SNS services. To pursue this objective, further investment opportunities will be considered. The IPO proceeds are mainly used to improve the investment in advertising and to fuel growth.

Conclusion

Japanese corporate governance is undergoing reform fueled by the debate between governance practitioners and scholars of the last decade. Especially after the Big Bang deregulation during the late 1990s, the offering of shares for sale to the public has been a popular decision for Japanese companies. Japanese traditional corporate governance features, such as *keiretsu* and main banks, did not perform well during the 2000s.

After amendment of the Commercial Law, the TSE published a revision of the "Principles of Corporate Governance." Corporate governance of listed companies in the TSE should comply with one of three alternative governance models (Table 10.1). Moreover, listed companies should respect minority shareholders' interests, and nominate at least one independent director to serve on the board. The appointment of independent directors is particularly important in *industrial keiretsu*, where a concentrated ownership structure creates excessive power of controlling shareholders.

Many companies went public in one of the three most representative IPO markets: JASDAQ, the Hercules Section of the Osaka Stock Exchange, and the Mothers Section of the TSE. Even during 2006–8, 334 companies chose to go public. Their characteristics can be summarized as follows: (1) they operate in some particular industries such as consumer goods, consumer services, telecommunications, and utilities; (2) they are companies with a long experience in the industry, i.e., their average age is greater than twenty-two years; (3) their ownership structure before the IPO is concentrated, often with a founder as the major shareholder; (4) the involvement of venture capital is limited; (5) the boards of directors have an average of 6.1 directors, 5.07 executives and 1.02 non-executives, most of whom have no specific background in peripheral, throughput, or output functions; (6) the number of IPOs in more recent years has been affected by the global financial crisis. In a regime of decreasing and volatile share prices, there has been very little IPO activity.

Japanese stock exchanges have many listed companies and play an important role in the national economy. New Japanese markets might be expected to converge mainly into two markets. In April 2010, JASDAQ, the largest IPO market, decided to merge with the Osaka Stock Exchange: a representative IPO market. This decision might be affected by the decrease in IPOs after 2008. Establishing the new IPO market might imply more reforms or convergence of markets for small and medium-sized companies in Japan. To increase the number and the relevance of nationally listed companies, Japanese stock exchanges should provide more favorable environments for potential listed firms and protect minority shareholders' interests for investors. To fulfill these objectives, the TSE principles of 2009 and the call for more independent directors on boards of listed firms can encourage the development of better corporate governance mechanisms.

References

Aoki, Masahiko. 1990. 'Toward an economic model of the Japanese firm', *Journal of Economic Literature*, 28, 1, 1–27.

Aoki, Masahiko, Hugh Patrick, and Paul Sheard. 1994. 'The Japanese main bank system: An introductory overview', in Masahiko Aoki and Hugh Patrick (eds.), *The Japanese Main Bank System – Its Relevance for Developing and Transforming Economies*. Oxford University Press, New York, 3–50.

Berglof, Erik and Enrico Perotti. 1994. 'The governance structure of the Japanese financial keiretsu', *Journal of Financial Economics*, 36, 2, 259–84.

Brown and Co. Ltd. 2001. *Industrial Groupings in Japan: The Changing Face of Keiretsu*. Brown and Company Limited, Tokyo.

Claessens, Stijn, Simeon Djankov, and Larry H. P. Lang. 2000. 'The separation of ownership and control in East Asian Corporations', *Journal of Financial Economics*, 58, 1–2, 81–112.

Dickie, Mure. 2009. 'War on the samurai', *Financial Times*, 30 June.

Dow, Sandra and Jean McGuire. 2009. 'Propping and tunneling: Empirical evidence from Japanese keiretsu', *Journal of Banking and Finance*, 33, 10, 1817–28.

Financial Times. 2007. 'Subsidiaries in Japan', 16 August.

Gerlach, Michael L. 1992. *Alliance Capitalism: The Social Organization of Japanese Business*. University of California Press, Berkeley, CA.

Hiraki, Takato, Hideaki Inoue, Akitoshi Ito, Fumiaki Kuroki, and Hiroyuki Masuda. 2003. 'Corporate governance and firm value in Japan: Evidence from 1985 to 1998', *Pacific Basin Finance Journal*, 11, 3, 239–65.

Horiuchi, Akiyoshi and Katsutoshi Shimizu. 2001. 'Did Amakudari undermine the effectiveness of regulator monitoring in Japan?', *Journal of Banking and Finance*, 25, 3, 573–96.

Hoshi, Takeo and Anil K. Kashyap. 2001. *Corporate Financing and Governance in Japan: The Road to the Future*. MIT Press, Cambridge, MA.

2010. 'Will the U.S. bank recapitalization succeed? Eight lessons from Japan', *Journal of Financial Economics*, 97, 3, 398–417.

Imamura, Mitsumasa, Hideaki Sakawa, and Naoki Watanabel. 2007. 'Does the amendment of Japanese commercial law increase the board's intensity? A legal and economic approach', *Osaka Economic Paper*, 56, 4, 65–76 (in Japanese).

Japan Association of Corporate Directors. 2010. List of companies with committees system (in Japanese), www.jacd.jp/news/manage/100728_01report.pdf.

Kang, Jun-Koo and Anil Shivdasani. 1995. 'Firm performance, corporate governance and top executive turnover in Japan', *Journal of Financial Economics*, 38, 1, 29–58.

Kaplan, Steven N. and Bernadette A. Minton. 1994. 'Appointments of outsiders to Japanese boards: Determinants and implications for managers', *Journal of Financial Economics*, 36, 2, 225–58.

Kerins, Frank, Kenji Kutsuna, and Richard Smith. 2007. 'Why are IPOs underpriced? Evidence from Japan's hybrid auction-method offerings', *Journal of Financial Economics*, 85, 3, 637–66.

Kutsuna, Kenji and Richard L. Smith. 2004. 'Why does book building drive out auction methods of IPO issuance? Evidence from Japan', *Review of Financial Studies*, 17, 4, 1129–66.

Kutsuna, Kenji, Janet K. Smith and Richard L. Smith. 2007. 'Banking relationships and access to equity capital markets: Evidence from Japan's main bank system', *Journal of Banking and Finance*, 31, 2, 335–60.

2009. 'Public information, IPO price formation, and long-run returns: Japanese evidence', *Journal of Finance*, 64, 1, 505–46.

La Porta, Rafael, Florencio Lopez-de-Silanes, and Andrei Shleifer. 1999. 'Corporate ownership around the world', *Journal of Finance*, 54, 2, 471–517.

Lincoln, James R., Michael L. Gerlach, and Christina L. Ahmadjian. 1996. 'Keiretsu networks and corporate performance in Japan', *American Sociological Review*, 61, 67–88.

Miwa, Yoshiro and Mark J. Ramseyer. 2005. 'Who appoints them, what do they do? Evidence on outside directors from Japan', *Journal of Economics and Management Strategy*, 14, 2, 299–337.

Morck, Randall and Masao Nakamura. 1999. 'Banks and corporate control in Japan', *Journal of Finance*, 54, 1, 319–39.

2005. 'A frog in a well knows nothing of the ocean: A history of corporate ownership in Japan', in Randall Morck (ed.), *A History of Corporate Governance Around the World: Family Business Groups to Professional Managers*. University of Chicago Press, 367–466.

Nakamoto, Michiyo. 2009a. 'Tokyo plans guidelines for independent directors', *Financial Times*, 26 May.

2009b. 'Corporate governance rules divide Japan', *Financial Times*, 28 May.

Pronexus. 2009. *Kabushiki Kokai Hakusho*. Pronexus Inc., Tokyo (in Japanese).

Prowse, Stephen D. 1990. 'Institutional investment patterns and corporate financial behavior in the United States and Japan', *Journal of Financial Economics*, 27, 1, 43–66.

Sakawa, Hideaki, Naoki Watanabel, and Uri Ben-Zion. 2009. 'Relation between board composition and firm performance in Japan', *Problems and Perspectives in Management*, 7, 3, 37–41.

Tanaka, Akira. 2004. 'Kigyou Syuudan to Sougousyousya no Sinkyoku-men', *Kagaku Keizai*, 51, 7, 86–94 (in Japanese).

Tokyo Stock Exchange. 2009. *Principles of Corporate Governance for Listed Companies*. Tokyo Stock Exchange Inc., Tokyo.

Uno, Jun, Takeshi Shimatani, Tokiko Shimizu, and Sachiko Mannen. 2002. 'Market microstructure and spread pattern in the JASDAQ market', *Financial Markets Department Working Paper*, 02-E-2, Bank of Japan.

11 | Corporate governance and initial public offerings in the Kingdom of Saudi Arabia

MAJDI QUTTAINAH AND WILLIAM PACZKOWSKI

Corporate governance mechanisms

The Kingdom of Saudi Arabia (KSA) is a complex country with several factors affecting policies, laws, and legislation. The fundamental source of law in the KSA is the Islamic law (Shari'ah). The Shari'ah is derived from the Holy Quran, the teachings of the Prophet Mohammed, and scholarly writings of the Islamic law. Shari'ah is the cornerstone for all legislation, policies, and laws throughout the KSA. However, Shari'ah is not the only source of legislation. Regional treaties shape policies in the Kingdom such as the Gulf Cooperation Council (GCC), the GCC Central Bank, and the GCC Patents Office that all maintain regional headquarters in the Kingdom. From a socioeconomic perspective, the Kingdom has a tradition of oil, petrochemical, and agricultural industries, despite the KSA having a desert climate. The government's participation in the economic development has been important to foster and improve these industries and perpetuate their development.

The Kingdom maintains an open economy with laws that protect newly formed companies as well as established national industries. The economy primarily depends on exports, investments, and sovereign wealth funds. The sovereign wealth fund is a state-owned investment that invests locally, regionally, and globally. It constitutes an important cornerstone for the socioeconomic development of the Kingdom. Most of the controlling shareholders (i.e., blockholders) of companies in the KSA are high net worth individuals who represent political figures or royal families who own dominant holding and investment companies (La Porta, Lopez-de-Silanes and Shleifer, 1999). Aside from blockholder ownership by KSA royalty or political figures, it is common for a family to have direct or indirect controlling stakes in many companies. This high degree of family ownership propagates strong incentives to monitor companies and their management.

The opaque nature of family ownership requires a highly reinforced need for corporate governance structure. This level of governance is required to address the principal–principal and principal–agent problems that can arise. The former is prevalent between the controlling shareholders and minority shareholders. In some instances, shareholders may use the voting power generated by their share ownership to manipulate companies' management decisions. The latter is prevalent in ownership structure known as "pyramid ownership" in which high net worth individuals or royal family members have stakes in various companies in multiple holding companies and company subsidiaries. This type of ownership structure is prevalent in all of the GCC countries. This control over companies that are listed on the Saudi Stock Exchange often generates leadership duality where the chairman also acts as the CEO of the company. However, the market for corporate control is virtually non-existent because institutional investors are not prevalent and shareholder activism is seldom observed.

Source of corporate law and governance

In the KSA, corporate governance has a significant impact on sustaining a professional, healthy, and safe environment for companies in the global arena. As such, the corporate governance methods imposed by public firms influence companies' share prices, liquidity status, and the ability to achieve financial goals efficiently. Accordingly, the Kingdom's corporate law is important to good stakeholder relations. Boards of directors have to possess and foster the corporate interest first, even when such interest might diverge from the (short-term) interest of shareholders.

Boards of Directors in the Kingdom of Saudi Arabia usually adopt a one-tier board, such that the board members hold both executive and supervisory responsibilities. The board's demographics depend on the ownership structure of the firm. If the firm is a fully owned subsidiary, or belongs to royalty, the board tends to be more of a mixture of both executive and independent directors. However, companies that are compliant with Islamic law are required to appoint another independent board known as the Shari'ah Supervisory Board (SSB). This board is appointed at the annual shareholders' general meeting. The SSB is responsible for examining and auditing the religious aspects of the products and services offered by Islamic institutions (Karim, 1990).

Firms that comply with Shari'ah are required to have an SSB to ensure compliance with Islamic law. Thus, the SSB provides higher moral and ethical conduct, constant and consistent monitoring, and controlling, advising, and counseling with ex-ante and ex-post auditing. The latter stems of the higher moral and ethical business conduct, transparency, and simultaneous ex-ante and ex-post Shari'ah auditing posit that SSBs correlate positively with investment banks' performance (Ghudda and Sattar, 2001).

It is important to note that the SSB is not equivalent to a two-tier board of directors (BOD) (Abu-Tapanjeh, 2009). For both board systems, there is a complete separation between the management and supervision functions of the board. However, in the two-tier system, the supervisory role is in relation to the competency of management. Further, the supervisory board appoints and dismisses management board members, instead of the shareholders (Weimer and Pape, 1999). Although the SSB may give advice, it does so in order to facilitate Islamic Law compliance rather than assessing the competency of the executives on the board.

While the Shari'ah is the overarching foundation of regulation in the Kingdom of Saudi Arabia, royal decrees are often issued by government agencies to institute detailed provisions and guidelines (Al Saati, 2003). The legal framework governing companies is the Corporate Law by Royal Decree Number M/6, the Capital Market Law by Royal Decree Number M/30, the Listing Rules of the Capital Market Authority by Decision No. 3–11–2004, and the Merger and Acquisition Regulations issued by the Board of the Capital Market Authority, Decision No. 1–50–2007. Furthermore, the Listing Rules, as well as Merger and Acquisition Regulations apply only to those companies listed on the Saudi Arabia Stock Exchange. The function of the Capital Market Authority (CMA) is to develop and regulate the Saudi Arabian Stock Exchange and market mechanisms by issuing compliance requirements, rules for transactions, and engaging all means necessary to implement the provisions of the Capital Market Law.

The CMA in the Kingdom unofficially started on February 20, 1950, and continued to operate successfully until the government set its basic regulations on September 3, 1988. It is an independent governmental organization with a separate budgetary authority over full financial, full legal, and full administrative independence, and has direct links with the Prime Minister. The US Department of Commerce's Country Commercial Guide defines the Kingdom's financial markets as generally open and free (US Department of Commerce, 2010).

The corporate governance provisions of the CMA were formed pursuant to Resolution Number 1/212/2006 dated November 12, 2006. These provisions are based on the Capital Market Law issued by Royal Decree Number M/30 for the same year. Control for market power and takeover provisions are stated in Royal Decree Number M/6 of 1965, which created the Companies' Law. This law, as amended from time to time, regulates and governs these takeover provisions for publicly listed companies. There are no specific takeover provisions regulating private companies in the Kingdom. The Ministry of Commerce and Industry has the power to regulate and issue any additional requirements as it determines to be necessary. The primary objectives are to create an appropriate investment environment, boost confidence, and reinforce transparency and disclosure standards in all listed companies, and to protect the investors and dealers from illegal acts in the market.

The CMA has investigative and enforcement action powers that it uses to regulate securities and the exchange as well as to monitor all parties that fall under its supervision. The CMA has also been improving its consultative process and has started more actively interacting with other relevant stakeholders in developing new regulations. The 2009 World Bank report on standards and codes documents a clear division of responsibility between the CMA and the Saudi Arabian Monetary Agency and specifically detected a "significant degree of cooperation between the various financial sector regulatory bodies" (World Bank, 2009). Both show competencies, possess adequate supervisory resources, and are economically independent.

It is the CMA's responsibility to monitor those companies listed in the Saudi Stock Exchange to ensure compliance with the appropriate corporate governance practices. In doing so, shareholders' and stakeholders' rights are protected. Consequently, the CMA continues to provide different options that enable the development of strategic goals that are implementable and viable for companies to pursue. The corporate governance codes help in protecting the interests of the minority shareholders, especially when a change in the corporate control is imminent. Revealing the rules and regulations governing any possible acquisition of companies, as well as unusual transactions such as mergers and sell-offs of a large section of a company, enables shareholders to understand the consequences and to protect their rights. Consequently, clarity of transactions protects the rights of all categories of shareholders.

The CMA amended its regulations in 2009 to include the requirement that firms establish internal control mechanisms that prohibit insider trading and self-dealing to protect the rights of minority shareholders. The defined roles and responsibilities of the board of directors must be unambiguous. Moreover, the CMA regulations mandate that each company must set forth a clear statement of its articles of association including the vision, mission, major business plans, and overall company strategy. Anticipated financial targets and annual budgets must also be addressed. Additionally, the board of directors' roles include monitoring and controlling the behaviors of management and the implementation of their business functions in order to ensure efficiency. Moreover, the board of directors must approve a written corporate governance policy for the company, oversee the policy's implementation, and monitor the level of compliance to the policy on at least an annual basis. Further, the BOD must draft a written code of business conduct, which states professional and business ethical standards that serve to regulate the relationship of the company with its stakeholders for protecting their respective rights.

Codes of good governance

Merger and acquisition regulations were issued by the Board of the Capital Market Authority pursuant to its Resolution Number 1–50–2007 dated October 31, 2007. The regulations apply to the restricted offer or purchase of shares, as well as traditional or reverse takeover offers. All regulations must be in conjunction with the Listing Rules issued by the Board of the CMA. For example, any merger and acquisition transaction involving an insurance company whose shares are listed on the Saudi Stock Exchange requires the approval of the Saudi Arabian Monetary Agency prior to any action being taken.

Under the established code of good governance, the board of directors must adhere to four primary functions. These functions are: (1) strategizing, advising, and monitoring the executive levels of authority of the firm, (2) introducing internal rules, regulations, and controlling systems to be utilized by the firm, (3) initiating conduct and compensation rules that are to be perpetuated by the BOD, and (4) complying with the guidelines set forth by the Shari'ah Supervisory Board.

(1) Strategizing, advising, and monitoring

The BOD must generate a formalized strategy that will be ingrained in all of the firm's business practices. This strategy must be in writing so that it is readily available for review by all shareholders, particularly those who have significant holdings (i.e., blockholders). In addition, the BOD is responsible for creating policies relating to risk management of the firm's activities. A continuing process of review, revision, improvement, and mandatory implementation is central to this function. Further, the BOD is required to appoint a compliance officer under the company's legal department to ensure that the policies are not circumvented.

These financial compliance and policy control mandates are reviewed on no less than an annual basis. It is important to note that the code of good governance generally requires the review by the BOD on a continuing basis to mitigate any drift from the core purposes of the firm strategy. Integration of the firm's capital structure with its strategic goals is of importance and a strict budgeting process is evaluated at least once per year.

Evaluation of the main capital expenditures, including those involving the acquisition or divesture of assets, is inherent in this budgeting process. The management team must implement these policies, and must regularly report the extent to which their activities are in conformance with the stated strategy of the firm. Finally, the BOD is tasked with the process of reviewing and approving the organizational and functional structures of the company. This is done on a periodic basis that is mandated by the policies that are to correspond with the firm's stated strategy.

The board of directors should be knowledgeable and possess relevant qualifications, experience, and skills. The majority of the members are to be independent members. In particular, the proportion of the independent directors should not be less than two individuals, or one-third of the members, whichever is greater. In addition, the company is responsible to determine the appropriate definition of an independent director. Furthermore, it is unlawful for a director to serve as a member in more than three companies at the same time. To ensure an appropriate balance of power, increased accountability, and greater capacity of the board for independent decision making, all companies must separate the position of the chairman from any other executive position in the company, such as the chief executive officer, the managing director, or the general manager.

(2) Introducing internal rules, regulations, and controlling systems to be utilized by the firm

A formal written policy is mandatory that regulates conflict of interest among BODs, executive management, and shareholders. In so doing, the agency considerations that are inherent in those companies that are listed on the Exchange are directly stated, and the means by which they will be mitigated. To this end, the BOD is tasked with ensuring and certifying the financial and accounting integrity, reliability, and procedures relating to financial reports, including control procedures for risks. In addition, the BOD will, on at least an annual basis, review and assess the effectiveness and viability of the internal control systems. Again, the code of good governance generally requires that the internal control systems be continuously evaluated.

(3) Initiating conduct and compensation rules that are to be perpetuated by the BOD

Performance objectives to be achieved by the firm under the auspices of the designated firm strategy are established by the BOD. The compensation and retention of the executives of the firm is contingent on their ability to perpetuate the overall performance of the company. The corporate governance code must not contradict provisions of the regulations imposed by the Exchange under KSA dictate, which are to include monitoring, controlling, advising, and counseling of company management. In addition, a critical function of the BOD is determining code effectiveness of the governance code and making amendments as may be required. Implementing specific and explicit policies that enhance all facets of the firm's governance mechanism is an overarching consideration for all BOD activities.

(4) Complying with the guidelines set forth by the Shari'ah Supervisory Board

At all times, the BOD must not diverge from the precepts of the Shari'ah as the supreme law of the KSA. The SSB is tasked with ensuring that the BOD maintains compliance with these rules, which are intrinsic to all functions of the company strategy. However, the goal of the BOD is not to seek to avoid these laws, with the SSB acting in an enforcement mechanism. Rather, the board must seek to constrain the company management activities so that compliance is maintained even if SSB action is not taken.

Despite the recommendations of the corporate governance codes of conduct, Table 11.1 depicts that not all listed companies comply with recommended corporate governance codes of conduct. In 2020, all codes become mandatory rather than voluntary, and failure to follow these codes can result in fines and/or delisting from the KSA exchange. The cultural norms of the KSA are such that women are not allowed to serve on the board of directors for any company. Furthermore, against the suggested codes of conduct, the independent directors do not meet the two-persons or one-third proportion of the board. Moreover, the code of conduct includes recommendations that at least three different committees are created: an audit committee, a compensation committee, and a nomination committee. Table 11.1 indicates that all companies comply with this requirement. The board of directors should further determine the advisability of adding other committees (such as risk management, investments, and corporate governance) with the conditions and necessities of the company.

According to the corporate governance codes of conduct, the chairman for each committee should be elected from among independent members of the board. Chairs of the board of directors may not chair any committee unless they are independent directors. In addition, the majority of the committee members should be of non-executive members. In accordance with the recommendation of the code of conduct, Table 11.1 illustrates this high level of interrelation of listed companies' executive committees, internal committees, and remuneration committees.

Stock exchange and listed companies

The Tadawul, which is the Saudi Stock Exchange, is the largest exchange in the Middle East in terms of market capitalization.

Table 11.1 *The characteristics of the board of Saudi listed companies*

Variables	Characteristics of Saudi listed companies
Sample	146 listed companies
Mix between executive and non-executive directors	14.2 members of the board: 6 executive directors and 8 non-executive directors. 2.6 non-executives are also independent directors
Number of positions in governance bodies	6.3 positions per director; 200 directors have 10 or more positions in other companies
Nationality of members	Foreign directors are present in 34 companies, and they represent 4.2 percent of the directors in the sample
Gender of directors	Women directors are not present in Saudi companies
Number of meetings	4 meetings
Presence at the meetings	An average of 57.3 percent of presence
Executive committee	99 companies have an executive committee with 3.8 members and 5.6 meetings
Internal control committee	101 companies have an internal control or an audit committee with 4 members and 2 meetings
Remuneration committee	103 companies have a remuneration committee with 5.5 members (3 are independent) and 1.2 meetings
Nomination committee	10 companies have a nomination committee with 5.2 members (2.2 are independent) and 3 meetings
Board evaluation	10 companies in 2006
Compensation of board of directors	Chairman $500,000, chief executive officer $290,000, non-executive directors $150,000

Source: CMA and KSA Stock Exchange (2009)

The Kingdom of Saudi Arabia Stock Exchange market capitalization reached $353.4 billion as of December 2010 (World Federation of Exchanges, 2010). Despite the fact that Saudi joint stock companies have existed since the mid 1930s with the establishment of the "Arab Automobile" company, there was not an exchange that regulated companies. In 1975, there were fourteen publicly owned firms in the

Table 11.2 *The number of companies listed on the Saudi Stock Exchange (1985–2010)*

Year	Companies
1985	*45*
1990	*65*
1995	*110*
2000	*115*
2010	*146*

Source: Saudi Stock Exchange (2011)

USA exchange. The rapid economic expansion, including the foreign banks' capital in the 1970s, subsequently led to the establishment of a number of large corporations and jointly owned banks. Nevertheless, the market remained informal until the early 1980s when the government formed regulated trading systems.

In 1984, a ministerial committee composed of the Ministry of Finance and National Economy, Ministry of Commerce, and Saudi Arabian Monetary Agency was formed to regulate and develop the market (Al-Twaijry, Briesly, Gwilliam et al., 2002). The Saudi Arabian Monetary Agency was the government's body charged with regulating and monitoring market activities until the formation of the CMA as the sole regulator and supervisor of the KSA capital market. The Saudi CMA has had an unlimited role in the national economy as of the crowning of the current King in 2005 (Capital Markets Authority, 2009). The King has since issued royal decrees reorganizing the economic and financial infrastructure. At first, there was investor resistance. However, by policing and reinforcing the royal decrees, the Kingdom managed to strengthen the CMA role. The market was liberalized in 2006, but foreign institutional and individual investors were unable to invest in the Saudi Stock Exchange. At that time, all other member countries of the GCC had provided foreign investors with the right to buy and sell shares in their respective national stock exchanges. It was not until August 2009 that the restrictions were lifted to allow foreign institutional and individual investors to participate in the Saudi Stock Exchange.

The Kingdom's capital market plays a pivotal role in its economy, and the attraction of the Stock Exchange has increased accordingly in the past few years. Table 11.2 depicts the number of publicly

Table 11.3 *Evolution of stock market capitalization as percentage of GDP (1985–2008)*

Tadawul	1985	1989	1990	1994	1998	2002	2006	2008
	75	88	92	98	99	111	132	150

Source: World Bank, yearly reports

listed companies in the Saudi Stock Exchange. The addition of companies that are included in the KSA Stock Exchange since its inception in 1985 has been a relatively slow process. As is set forth in Table 11.2, the number of listed firms has increased by almost 70 percent between 1985 and 1990. The increase in the number of firms was at an average pace of slightly less than 25 percent from 1990 to 2010.

The number of firms that have been listed on the KSA Stock Exchange since its formation in 1985 is not as indicative of the pace of growth as that of the overall market capitalization. Table 11.3 depicts the increase, which reflects the evolution of the stock market capitalization. In particular, from 1990 to the present, the Kingdom has gained an important part of its market capitalization due to the increased number of large capitalization companies. The latter increased the market capitalization and encouraged more mid- and larger-sized firms to undergo the initial public offerings (IPOs) process even if they were not highly capitalized. The average increase in market capitalization was approximately 10 percent for each reported time period, which is well below the increase of the number of firms added to the Exchange. It is apparent that the addition of new firms has not increased overall market capitalization in equivalent proportions.

The Kingdom's Stock Exchange, in contrast, has witnessed increased trading for most of the listed companies' stocks. The number of stocks traded refers to the total value of shares traded during the period. This indicator complements the market capitalization ratio by showing whether market size is matched by trading. Despite the healthy state of the Kingdom's fiscal policy, Table 11.4 indicates that the liquidity and velocity of the shares in the Saudi Stock Exchange have increased until the start of the recent financial crisis.

Table 11.4 *Evolution of stocks traded, total value as percentage of GDP (1990–2009)*

Tadawul	1990	1995	2000	2005	2007	2009
	7	8.8	19.2	25	38	20

Source: World Bank, yearly reports

The ownership structure of the Kingdom of Saudi Arabia listed companies

Listed companies in the GCC countries have high levels of ownership concentration due to the region's socio-economic, socio-political, and nomadic norms and traditions. This evidence also applies to the Kingdom of Saudi Arabia. With respect to the Saudi listed companies, the largest single shareholder possesses on average 65.5 percent of share capital. It is generally the case that a member of the royal family is the largest shareholder of these companies. The stake of the second largest shareholders is an average of 17.5 percent (Capital Market Authority, 2009).

Becht and Mayer (2001) studied the concentration of ownership from control perspectives using an analysis of power that they identified as "acting in concert." Their analysis explains how either a single shareholder or a group of shareholders control listed companies. Their measurement of control involves a legal standard that is a single shareholder controls a company when the shareholder holds at least 50 percent of the outstanding shares. They explain that a single shareholder may be able to control a company even with a stake that is less than 50 percent. This result may happen when there is a coalition through voting pacts and similar arrangements (Becht and Mayer, 2001). Understanding their study, we can investigate the components of the KSA market. Analyzing the listed companies in the Saudi Stock Exchange, we find that a single shareholder holding at least 50 percent of the shares controls 55 percent of Saudi companies. Moreover, a small number of listed companies (6 percent) have a dominant shareholder with a minimum stake of 75 percent. Furthermore, we find that 37 percent of listed companies are with a participation in share capital between 25 percent and 50 percent.

The characteristics of the Saudi capital market have important governance implications. First, the market for corporate control is less prominent in the Kingdom, since takeover mechanisms are widely used and have the capability to allow the transformation of control from inefficient to efficient management teams. Furthermore, these mechanisms encourage a convergence of interest between corporate management and shareholders.

Ownership by outside blockholders is not an unequivocally advantageous force from the perspective of the other shareholders. Holders of large blocks of shares are in a position to engage in activities that benefit themselves at the expense of minority shareholders (La Porta, Lopez-de-Silanes and Shleifer, 1999). The exploitation of the control position by a major shareholder to derive special benefits is referred to as "private benefits" (Berghe et al., 2002). While dispersed ownership creates weak shareholders and strong managers, ownership concentration creates strong majority shareholders, weak managers, and weak minority shareholders (Gugler, 2001). In both cases, there exists an unbalanced power position, providing the potential for misuse of corporate resources and the occurrence of conflicts of interest. In this perspective, boards of directors assume important monitoring governance devices. They are also instrumental in the function of protecting a company's interests as well as those of minority shareholders.

IPO activity between 2006 and 2008

The regulation of IPOs

Saudi Arabian initial public offering opportunities did not become readily available for private investors until 2003. The sole regulator of the IPOs is the Capital Market Authority of the Kingdom's official Stock Exchange (Capital Market Authority, 2009). The CMA maintains and enforces all rules and regulations relating to IPOs in order to generate efficiencies in the market. Since 2003, IPOs have gained traction in the Saudi Arabian market. Investigating IPO activity between 2006 and 2008 provides a useful exemplar of the types of firms that have expanded into the public market. As with the vast majority of IPOs, investment banks in the KSA are the propagators of the process of determining offering share price, the timing of the offer, and the number of shares to be sold. The potential buyers that are identified for an IPO are somewhat restricted in that these buyers must be legal residents of the KSA, members of the GCC, or legal residents of those countries comprising the GCC. Retail investors must also fall within the constraints of membership or residency in order to be able to participate in the IPO (CMA, 2000).

Regulators in the Kingdom approve the portion of the shares that will float in companies that intend to be listed on the Saudi exchange. The CMA issued Listing Rules in 2004 and significantly amended these in 2006. There are no different listing segments on the Stock Exchange, so all companies must meet the full listing requirements. Foreign companies are not allowed to list on the Stock Exchange. Companies that submit a request to be listed in the Saudi Stock Exchange should possess and fulfill certain criteria, and must sustain additional requirements to remain listed. Table 11.5 depicts the requirements that companies must fulfill for IPOs, admission to the Saudi Stock Exchange, and continued exchange listing.

The IPOs between 2006 and 2008

During the period of 2006–8, forty-one companies in Saudi Arabia were engaged in initial public offerings. Despite the market share that the Kingdom enjoys in worldwide petroleum production, only three companies are in the commodities or oil production industry. The number of IPOs was not predominant in any one year, so external market crises did not have the same influence as was endured by European markets.

The number of companies that went public in 2006 (fourteen companies) and 2007 (fifteen companies) was very similar to those that went public in 2008 (twelve companies) when the financial crisis negatively impacted the world economic system. As is set forth in Table 11.6, IPOs mainly involved consumer goods, financials, and industrials during this time period. The majority of the companies that underwent IPOs were originally family-owned companies, government-owned companies, or new ventures. The family-owned companies, including those owned by the KSA Royal Family, constituted approximately 43 percent of the total IPOs between the years 2006 and 2008. The government-owned companies constituted approximately 47 percent over these years. New startups fulfilled the difference, resulting in 10 percent of the total companies that went public. Thus, companies went public to expand their market shares locally, regionally,

Table 11.5 *Listing and ongoing requirements in the KSA*

Admission requirements

Classification	Saudi joint stock (public shareholding) companies
Duration of operations	(1) Carry independent business activities for at least 3 financial years under the same management
	(2) At least 2 years of tracking with an audited account
Senior management autonomy	(1) Must demonstrate to the Stock Exchange that senior management has the necessary expertise and experience
	(2) Ability to generate revenues to maintain business operations
Ownership	(1) Public ownership of at least 30 percent of the outstanding shares
	(2) At least 200 public shareholders (defined as all shareholders other than a director, senior executive, or substantial/significant shareholders with 5 percent or greater ownership)
Free float	Minimum 15 percent
Market cap	At least $30 million
Sponsor	Appointment of a sponsor to assist the company in the listing process
Admission documents	Pre-vetted by the Stock Exchange and the CMA
Prospectus	The company must publish a prospectus which complies with the requirements of the CMA

IPO requirements

Rules required by the CMA and the GCC	(1) Full compliance with Shari'ah
	(2) Preparation of a comprehensive prospectus
	(3) Rigorous determination of investment interest
	(4) CMA supervisory consent
	(5) Pre-IPO shareholder full consent

Ongoing requirements

Price-sensitive information	Timely dissemination to the CMA with the Stock Exchange that distributes to the public
Minimum free float	No minimum free float
Financial statements	(1) Produce quarterly reports (within 45 days)
	(2) Half-year reports (within four months)
	(3) Independently audited full-year financial reports (within 6 months from the end of the accounting period)
Transactions of significant persons	To be voluntarily communicated but not mandatory

Source: Kingdom of Saudi Arabia Capital Market Authority Law (2009)

Table 11.6 *IPO year and industry classification*

Industry	2006	2007	2008	Total
Commodities	1	0	0	1
Consumer goods	3	1	2	6
Consumer services	0	1	0	1
Financials	5	7	3	15
Healthcare	2	2	2	6
Industrials	2	2	4	8
Oil and gas	1	2	1	4
TOTAL	14	15	12	41

and globally. Others went public to capture a portion of profits. By so doing, the IPOs enabled the owners of the companies to expand regionally, especially because the GCC citizens and the Kingdom's citizens were the only ones allowed to subscribe to the IPOs.

Saudi companies that go public may be small, medium, or large companies. On average, they have 1,267 employees, revenues of $166,277,779, and assets equal to $265,110,100. The smallest company in terms of employees is AL Inma Bank and the smallest in terms of revenues is AL Babtain Company. The largest one on all dimensions is Saudi Arabian Oil, which is an exploration oil company. It is an important company not only to the Kingdom but also to the GCC countries. With its ownership structure, foreign owners boost the profitability of the companies that underwent IPOs. As Table 11.7 depicts, most of the companies that became public have high profitability ratios on assets, net capital, and revenues. The most profitable companies in the sample are Halwani Bros, Saudi Arabian Oil, AL Inma Bank, AL Ahli Takaful (ROA), Yanbu National, SABB Takaful, and United Cooperative Assurance Co. (ROE).

Table 11.8 depicts a change in the ownership structure before and after the IPOs initiated in the period 2006–8. There were thirty-six companies where there was family ownership both before and after the IPOs. While average ownership percentage decreased by more than 30 percent, the families retained some degree of ownership control. Banks did not have any stake in the sample companies prior to the IPOs in this time period, but gained 100 percent control of one company following an IPO. The Saudi Arabian government had total

Table 11.7 *IPO size and performance (USD)*

	Size			Performance	
	Employees	Revenues	Assets	ROA	ROE
Min	39	39,688	1,206,000	0.11	0.06
1st quartile	212	6,367,178	30,839,000	0.23	0.21
2nd quartile	730	23,666,130	85,183,500	0.34	0.30
3rd quartile	1,384	157,289,236	263,000,500	0.45	0.45
Max	7,430	1,233,334,875	1,621,537,000	0.57	0.65
Average	1,267	166,277,779	265,110,100	0.35	0.32

Table 11.8 *IPO ownership structure (data in percent)*

	Family		Bank		Government	
	pre	post	pre	post	pre	post
Min	0	0	0	0	0	0
1st quartile	30	20	0	0	0	0
2nd quartile	100	45	0	0	0	0
3rd quartile	100	60	0	0	0	0
Max	100	75	0	100	100	60
Average ownership	72	41	0	2	10	5
Number of cases	36	36	–	1	5	4

ownership of the five companies not held by families prior to the IPOs, but lost all ownership stakes in one of the companies following the IPO and had average ownership stake reduced to 5 percent. Accordingly, the concentration of the average ownership level of both family-owned and government-owned businesses decreased sharply following the IPOs initiated from 2006 to 2008.

Description of an IPO: Saudi British Bank (SABB) Takaful Company

The firm before the IPO

The stock market of the Kingdom of Saudi Arabia is complex in terms of allowing a non-Saudi entity to operate within its sovereignty. This holds true for all member countries in the GCC as well. Available alternatives for GCC conglomerates to enter the KSA market are in the form of joint stock companies. Hence, the SABB Takaful Company is a Shari'ah-compliant insurance company and is a Saudi joint stock company. It is an authorized insurance company by a Royal Decree Number M/60. The royal decree is dated October 9, 2006 and operates under Commercial Registration 1010234032, dated June 6, 2007. SABB Takaful Company is a Saudi joint stock company with a fully paid-up capital of $100,000,000. The Takaful Company was not in existence prior to the IPO.

The idea of establishing the SABB Takaful stemmed from the needs of the market and the desire of both the Saudi British Bank and the HSBC Bank to maintain a company that complies with Shari'ah. Thus, HSBC approached the Saudi British Bank, which is a Saudi joint stock bank that was established on January 21, 1978. The meeting had the result of creating a new company known as the SABB Takaful. The newly formed company is an associate company of both SABB and HSBC. The ownership structure of the Takaful Company at the time of IPO consisted of institutional shareholders, 32.5 percent owned by SABB, 32.5 percent owned by subsidiaries of the HSBC Group, and the balance owned by the public through an initial public offering. The company remains listed in the Saudi Stock Exchange. The SABB Takaful is an associate company of both the SABB and HSBC through HSBC Amanah, which is the global Islamic banking division of the HSBC Group. Accordingly, SABB Takaful Company is able to leverage HSBC Amanah's business experience. The expertise of HSBC Amanah in supporting banking ventures is greater than any other Islamic bank. HSBC Amanah engages in business relationships with a multitude of countries including Singapore, Malaysia, the UK, and the US. It helps provide high quality Shari'ah-compliant Takaful products and services in the KSA.

Board of directors

Two-thirds of the Takaful Company board of directors' members are non-executive positions. This is consistent with the CMA governance code of conduct relating to the board size and composition that requires that at least one-third of the board members should be independent. The SABB Takaful has a board size and composition that has fulfilled this code of requirement. The board of directors consists of eleven members, with one executive director (CEO) who serves as a board member on HSBC Amanah. In addition, the board of directors has eight non-executive directors, including two independent directors. The chairman of the board is also a board member for the Saudi British Bank. Two additional members of the board are members serving in the Saudi British Bank. Thus, three board members serve in both the SABB Takaful and the Saudi British Bank. The managing director of the SABB Takaful is an executive board member. The SABB Takaful is an associate company of both the Saudi British Bank and HSBC and both have four members serving on the SABB Takaful board. The board of directors has set up a nomination and remuneration committee, an audit committee, a technology committee, and a governance committee. Each committee is composed of three members who are exclusively non-executive directors; two of them are independent directors. Three directors, the CEO, the CFO, and the chief business officer, are members in the executive committee.

Shari'ah Supervisory Board

The Shari'ah Supervisory Board is responsible for implementing Shari'ah in all investment bank (IB) transactions. It plays a pivotal role in IBs' corporate governance. Shari'ah is "the ultimate goal and this entails the notion of protecting the interest and rights of all stakeholders within the Islamic Law (Shari'ah) rules"; this is of utmost importance (Hasan, 2008). The SSB is a strictly independent board that investigates, audits, and provides IBs with higher levels of corporate governance than those countries that do not have the requirement of a separate disinterested board that provides additional guidance and oversight. The higher religious corporate governance stems from the Shari'ah. Ex-ante and ex-post Shari'ah auditing in all IBs' financial transactions are a standard policy for all firms seeking to initiate the IPO process in the Kingdom (Shaffaii, 2008). Shari'ah law is integral to providing the religious guidelines to which IBs must adhere, and provides rules to circumscribe managing the allocation of resources, production, consumption, capital market activity, and the distribution of income and wealth.

The regulators' mandate is only a form of governance structure to ensure compliance with the teachings of Shari'ah, and not due to the direct relationship between the embeddedness of the SSBs with IBs'

Table 11.9 *SABB Takaful SSB members*

SSB member	Credentials
Sheikh Abdullah bin Sulaiman Al Manea	(1) Member of the Supreme Judiciary Committee of Saudi Arabia (2) Member of the Islamic Fiqh (Islamic Law) Academy in Jeddah, KSA (3) Former deputy president of Makkah Courts (4) Advisor to several Islamic financial institutions (5) Author of various books on Islamic banking
Sheikh Dr. Abdullah Mohammad Al Mutlaq	(1) Member of Supreme Judiciary Committee of Saudi Arabia (2) Former chairman of the Comparative Fiqh (Islamic Law) Department at Imam Mohammed bin Saud University (3) Advisor to several Islamic institutions (4) Author of various books on Islamic banking
Sheikh Dr. Mohammed A. ElGari Bin Eid	(1) Associate Professor and Former Director of the Center for Research in Islamic Economics at King Abdul Aziz University (2) Expert at the Islamic Fiqh Academy in Jeddah (3) Editor of the *Review of Islamic Economics* (4) Advisor to HSBC-Amanah Finance (5) Advisor to several Islamic institutions (6) Author of various books on Islamic banking

Source: www.sabb.com/1/2/sabb-en/about-us/profile/sahariah_advisory_commitee, last accessed January 2011

governance structure. Hence, SABB Takaful products are reviewed and approved by SABB Takaful's Shari'ah Supervisory Board comprising of reputable members that are known in the field of Shari'ah and Islamic law as well as contemporary finance. The Shari'ah Supervisory Board members serving on the SSB board in SABB Takaful are the same members serving on the Saudi British Bank Shari'ah Supervisory Board. The SABB Takaful Shari'ah Supervisory Board consists of renowned members with extremely diverse backgrounds, as set forth in Table 11.9.

The offer

The Capital Market Authority approved SABB Takaful's initial public offering in March 2007. SABB Takaful raised Saudi Riyal 350,000,000, which is equivalent to $100,000,000, through the public share offering. SABB's subscription manager was HSBC Saudi Arabia Limited, which is an associate company of HSBC. The IPO subscription opened to the public for nine business days and ended on March 26, 2007. The cash from the offer varied between $98,000,000 and $100,000,000 for a total market capitalization of the firm after the IPO varying between $120,000,000 and $250,000,000. The price per share ranged from a minimum of $8.50 to a maximum of $15.50. The Takaful Company successfully completed its IPO and was listed on the Saudi Stock Exchange in 2007 under the symbol "8080." Satisfying the conditions of the CMA expedited the officials to approve the initial public offering by offering 35 percent of the Saudi stock company to the public. The CMA, the Ministry of Finance, and the Ministry of Commerce perpetuated transparent and unambiguous laws of companies intending to go public and then to be listed. These laws expedited the process of maintaining approvals, and assisted in closing the IPO. SABB Takaful is a Saudi stock company and an associate company of the Saudi British Bank and the HSBC Bank. It is a raw model for transparency, and the process that governed the establishment of the Saudi joint stock company until it reached the initial public offering stage succeeded in creating a competitive environment that encouraged locals and foreign companies to have a lawful entity in the KSA and benefit from such a huge market.

The firm after the IPO

The ownership structure remained intact following the IPO. The proportional shares owned by the major shareholders was limited to 32.5 percent to avoid over-allotment of ownership. After the exercise of the IPO, the board of directors planned to use the cash proceeds to further develop the products and services in Islamic insurance. As was the case with most IPO introductions in this period, the Takaful Company maintained compliance with the Kingdom's code of corporate governance.

Conclusion

Corporate governance in the Kingdom of Saudi Arabia has considerably evolved in the last few years to include both new legislation and the introduction (and revision) of the corporate governance code for listed companies. The corporate governance requirements in the Kingdom of Saudi Arabia are comprised of two separate and highly distinctive parts. Boards of directors retain similar roles to those of many other countries that subscribe to the one-tier system of governance. However, the KSA and other countries (primarily those in the GCC) whose business entities adhere to the principles of Islamic law have an additional level of governance. The Shari'ah Supervisory Board provides an impartial supervisory role that is unencumbered by agency problems that otherwise may exist.

Despite the possibility of agency problems and the considerable evolution of the legislation relating to corporate governance, a higher proportion of listed companies has engaged in the process of adopting the recommendations of the corporate governance code. Due to the growing alignment between corporate governance codes, the characteristics of the Kingdom's boards of directors are increasingly similar to the best practices at the international level. However, the impact of insider shareholders on the board of directors remains a specific characteristic of many of the Kingdom's boards of listed companies. The ownership structure of the Kingdom's listed companies is still very concentrated. Combined with an absence of active and independent institutional investors, the board is selected by the major shareholder or the controlling shareholders.

The Saudi Stock Exchange plays a pivotal role in the KSA national economy. However, this role has been declining since the globalization of commerce. Socio-economic and socio-political pressures to retain laws to preserve and protect national and emergent industries are still prevalent in the KSA. However, family-owned businesses and other growing firms have commenced utilizing the Saudi Stock Market. This tendency has increased over recent years. As is the case with many GCC countries, the large diffusion of family businesses and smaller companies has led to the encouragement of national and GCC entrepreneurs to go public and to share control with third parties. Since bureaucracy is embedded within the socio-economic norms and traditions of the KSA, administrative costs of a public listing has affected the increasing number of recent listings on the Saudi Stock Exchange. Over the last few years, the Kingdom had approximately ninety companies that underwent IPOs, and the number increases significantly with the inclusion of IPOs of other GCC countries. More than three hundred companies underwent IPOs within the GCC countries from 2006 to 2008.

The present study has focused on those companies in the Kingdom that underwent IPOs between 2006 and 2008. They operate in a variety of sectors (i.e., industrial, consumer goods, and services). Despite the significant role that the KSA has in petroleum production, only four companies in the oil and petrochemical industries underwent IPOs. Venture capital divisions of banks and private equity have rarely played any significant role in most of the IPOs in the KSA. This phenomenon is partly due to the complex nature of the GCC countries, which plays an important role before, during, and after the IPO.

This study highlights the extent to which external and internal governance affects the IPO process. The unique influence of IPO rules and corporate governance resulting from the social complexity of the Shari'ah is also explored. The intertwining of all of these factors is grounded on the lasting nomadic customs, traditions, and norms of the region. Consequently, high net-worth individuals utilize their socio-economic and socio-political factors to obtain successful transactions in the Kingdom of Saudi Arabia. Most importantly, politically connected families and royalty manipulate the majority of companies that operate in the Saudi Stock Exchange.

References

Abu-Tapanjeh, Abdussalam Mahmoud. 2009. 'Corporate governance from the Islamic perspective: A comparative analysis with OECD principles', *Critical Perspectives on Accounting*, 20, 5, 556–67.

Al Saati, Abdul-Rahim. 2003. 'The permissible gharar (risk) in classical Islamic jurisprudence', *Islamic Economics*, 16, 2, 3–19.

Al-Twaijry, Abdulrahman A.M., Brierley, John A., and Gwilliam, David. 2002. 'An examination of the role of audit committees in the Saudi Arabian corporate sector', *Corporate Governance: An International Review*, 10, 4, 288–97.

Becht, Marco and Mayer, Colin. 2001. 'Introduction', in Frank Barca and Marco Becht (eds.), *The Control of Corporate Europe* (Oxford University Press), pp. 1–45.

Berghe, Lutgart, Van den Levrau, Abigail, Carchon, Steven, and Van der Elst, Christoph. 2002. *'Corporate Governance in a Globalising World: Convergence or Divergence?' A European Perspective* (Kluwer Academic Publishers, Boston).

Capital Market Authority. 2009. Downloaded from www.cma.org.sa/En/ Publicationsreports/Reports/CMA_finalENGLISH.pdf, November, 2011.

Ghudda, Abu and Sattar, Abdul. 2001. *The Foundation, Objectives, and Practices of Shari'ah Supervisory Board*, Paper presented at AAOIFI 1st Annual Conference of SSBs (in Arabic).

Gugler, Klaus. 2001. 'Corporate governance and performance: The research questions', in Klaus Gugler (ed.), *Corporate Governance and Economic Performance* (Oxford University Press), pp. 1–59.

Hasan, Zulkifli. 2008. *Corporate Governance from Western and Islamic Perspectives*, Paper presented at Annual London Conference on Money, Economy and Management, Imperial College, South Kensington, United Kingdom, July.

Karim, Rifaat. 1990. 'The independence of religious and external auditors: The case of Islamic banks', *Accounting, Auditing & Accountability Journal*, 3, 34–44.

La Porta, Rafael, Lopez-de-Silanes, Florencio, and Shleifer, Andrei. 1999. 'Corporate ownership around the world', *Journal of Finance*, 54, 2, 471–517.

Shaffaii, Suapi. 2008. 'How Shariah governance empowers Islamic finance', *Islamic Finance News*, 5, 36, 1–3.

US Department of Commerce. 2010. 'Doing business in Saudi Arabia: 2010 country commercial guide for U.S. companies'. Downloaded from http://trade.gov/td/standards/Markets/Africa,%20NearEast%20and%20 South%20Asia/Saudi%20Arabia/Doing%20Business%20in%20Saudi %20Arabia%202010%20Country%20Commercial%20Guide%20for %20U.S.%20Companies.pdf, November, 2011.

Weimer, Jeroen and Pape, Joost. 1999. 'A taxonomy of systems of corporate governance', *Corporate Governance*, 7, 152–66.

World Bank. 2009. 'Corporate governance country assessment: Kingdom of Saudi Arabia', report on the observance of standards and codes. Downloaded from www.worldbank.org/ifa/rosc_cg_saudia_arabia.pdf, November, 2011.

World Federation of Exchanges. 2011. Downloaded from www.world-exchange.org, November, 2011.

Supplementary sources

Capital Market Authority (CMA): www.cma.org.sa

Capital Market Authority Corporate Governance Regulations pursuant to Resolution No. 1/212/2006, 2006

Capital Market Authority Market Conduct Regulations, Resolution No. 1–11–2004, 2004
Capital Market Law, Royal Decree No. M/3, 2003
Companies Law, Royal Decree No. M/6, 1965
Cooperation Council for the Arab States of the Gulf: www.gcc-sg.org/eng/index.html
Foreign Investment Law No. M/1, 2000
Hawkamah Institute for Corporate Governance (Hawkamah): www.hawkamah.org
Kingdom of Saudi Arabia Ministry of Finance (MoF): http://old.mof.gov.sa/en/default.asp
Ministry of Commerce & Industry (MoCI): www.commerce.gov.sa
Saudi Arabian General Investment Authority (SAGIA): www.sagia.gov.sa
Saudi Arabian Monetary Agency (SAMA): www.sama.gov.sa
Saudi Organization for Certified Public Accountants (SOCPA): www.socpa.org.sa
Saudi Stock Exchange (Tadawul): www.tadawul.com

12 | Corporate governance and initial public offerings in Mexico

JOSE LUIS RIVAS

Corporate governance mechanisms

Mexico was a land inhabited by various indigenous civilizations (i.e., Mayas, Aztecs). It was conquered by the Spanish conquistador Hernan Cortes in 1521. The country today is a blend of its history: 80 percent of its population is a racial mix between the Spanish and the native cultures; the rest is divided among the mix between Spanish and black slaves from Africa, the indigenous inhabitants and European descendants. It is mostly a collectivist culture that is socially cohesive. It is, thus, a traditionalist society where family, religion and culture play a large role.

Power distance in Mexican culture is high. This means that power in society is accepted to be distributed unequally and, as a consequence of this, the country exhibits a relatively non-egalitarian executive compensation system where CEOs on average make between twenty-five and fifty times the average worker's salary. Variable compensation has grown in importance but it still comprises on average less than half of total compensation to CEOs and TMTs. Equity incentives are used by a small but growing proportion of firms.

The legal system is based in civil law as for most former colonial members of the Spanish empire. The role of the market place is constrained by the government and local interest groups such as unions, political parties, commerce chambers and private firms. As a result of this, the market for corporate control is weak and mostly inactive. Corporate governance codes are voluntary although they are being slowly incorporated into securities laws.

Corporate ownership in most firms is concentrated, and institutional investors – even though present – are still not major players in the market for corporate control. Minority ownership is protected for the standard of an emerging economy. Shareholder activism is uncommon. Corporate boards are single tier in nature and it is common to have CEO duality whereby the CEO is also chairman of the board. Corporate boards are made mostly of insiders and representatives of the controlling shareholders. Independent board members have grown in importance over the past decade but they still do not hold majority stakes in most firms.

Corporate law

Regarding equity investor rights, the "Law of Mercantile Societies", approved in 1934, is the main piece of legislation dealing with the creation of a limited liability firm (*sociedad anónima*). It establishes investors' property rights and the regulation of different monitoring/ counseling bodies of the firm, such as the board of directors, the stockholders' assembly and the commissioner. In the case of public corporations, there are special regulations established in the "Law of Securities Markets" from 1975, in the "Rules of the Law for Promoting and Regulating Foreign Investment" from 1989, and in memoranda issued by the Mexican Securities and Exchange Commission (CNBV). Mexico was basically regulated by the same piece of legislation for over thirty years and this fact probably inhibited the stock market's development. In 2005 the new "Law of Securities Markets" was approved. It had two basic objectives: one, to promote the introduction of new firms to public markets, simplifying regulations and making mid-size firms more attractive to venture capital; and two, to improve transparency, minority rights and the corporate structure of listed firms. The previous law was particularly vague when defining the roles of board and top management team (TMT) members. The new law emphasizes a proper identification of controversial matters and excess risks, compliance with norms related to audit matters and the vigilance of mechanisms that promote transparency. Of key importance here is the creation of the audit and corporate practice committees that must be formed entirely by outsiders (three members each). The corporate practice committee designates board candidates and reviews compensation and related transaction policies. It additionally convenes all shareholders' assemblies.

The external auditor figure now has to inform the CNBV of any issue that threatens corporate stability. External auditors must meet a specific set of personal and professional requirements and they are liable for any harm caused to firms by their misreporting. The chief executive officer (*Director General*) is now responsible for implementing all agreements reached in the shareholders' assembly and has to set guidelines for control and audit procedures. Moreover, it is now mandatory that the CEO rubricates financial statements as well as any relevant economic and legal information.

Top management and board members now have a duty of loyalty to the firm. Thus, its members must act in good faith, instituting shareholder value maximization policies. A breach of the duty of loyalty will occur if there is a conflict of interest whereby a group of executives or shareholders is benefited at the expense of others. Another possible breach of loyalty could occur if inadequate transactions are approved.

The board of directors in the new law is a one-tier board appointed by the shareholders with a maximum of twenty-one members. There is a possibility to designate proprietary and substitute board members. Proprietary members are the "owners" of the board seat irrespective of whether they have a share of the firm capital or not. It is then the proprietary members who designate their substitutes subject to board approval. Public boards should have as a minimum 25 percent of independent members. They require at least one audit and corporate practice committee made up entirely of independent board members. There should be at least four meetings per year. Minority shareholders representing 25 percent of capital can designate at least one board member if the board is made up of at least three members. If the firm is public the percentage is decreased to 10 percent. In its annual meeting, shareholders must define policies for the use of firm assets by executives or related board members, board member nominations and internal audit systems and procedures. Boards are in charge of setting strategy and internal control procedures, supervising top management, approving financial statements, setting top management compensation packages and authorizing relevant or related transactions.

At least half the board members should be present in each meeting to have a legal quorum which is usually not an issue. The majority of members should vote in order to have a quorum. Each board member has one vote. The law allows boards to take decisions without meeting, but this must be expressly allowed in a firm's statutes and there should be unanimous voting among board members on the issues.

The chairman of the board has a "quality" vote in case of a voting tie and does not represent the shareholders but the board itself.

Boards have the right and responsibility to oversee all firms' matters. Externally it is the body representing the firm in all operations inherently linked to achieving its objectives. The board should present at least one annual report that includes the prior year's financial statements.

One of the pending issues regarding regulations is the right to issue shares with restricted voting rights (maximum 25 percent of shares). Regulatory entities should understand that this right creates principal–agent problems where the principal (owner) is not able to exercise part of his rights and the agent (manager) can distinguish between a "first" and "second" class of firm owners. A one-share-one-vote policy has usually constituted a practice consistent with sound corporate governance practices.

One of the tragic episodes where the inadequacy of good corporate governance was evidenced was the Mexican financial crisis of 1994. A lack of adequate mechanisms to regulate firm indebtedness and the supervision of loan portfolios from financial institutions contributed to worsening a vicious circle created by excessive risk exposure to foreign currencies both by firms and banks.

Even with the 2005 law in place, corporate governance quality in Mexico can be described as "irregular"; there is a large variance in the adoption of best practices. In general, foreign firms have higher standards than domestic ones. And then, among local firms it is the public ones that have outpaced others because of their need to gain shareholder approval. The good news is that shareholders and regulatory entities are slowly but steadily taking measures to improve governance quality in the country. In the 2007 edition of "Doing Business", the World Bank named Mexico the leading country in shareholders' protection reforms during 2005–6. This report recognized that the new law of securities markets introduced specific duties for firm managers providing a legal framework for judges to punish firm managers for any malpractices against firm shareholders. Finally, the World Bank report also recognized a higher shareholder scrutiny of related transactions.

Code of good governance

The code of good governance was developed in 1999 by the Mexican Stock Exchange in collaboration with the International Institute of

Finance and the country's main business chambers. It was revised in 2006 with a special emphasis on board roles and a recommendation to issue ethics and social responsibility codes. In 2010 it was revised for a second time. Among its key recommendations are that board size should be from three to fifteen members with 25 percent of them being independent, the elimination of substitute board member figures, a reliance on outside support for audit, finance, planning and compensation practices and policies, and, finally, the supervision of the following tasks: (1) the firm's strategic vision, (2) CEO, TMT and board member performance reviews, (3) the protection of shareholder interests, (4) instituting information transparency and accuracy, (5) the existence of internal control mechanisms and the approval of relevant/related transactions, (6) establishing succession plans for CEO and TMT members, (7) the existence of contingency and information recovery plans, (8) assessing the compensation package of the CEO prior to his/her entry, (9) instituting a policy for CEO and TMT compensation and termination packages and, finally, (10) establishing an adequate framework to analyze and review firm risks.

Laws regulating financial entities have recently included some of the code of good governance recommendations, namely the size (three–fifteen members) and independent members (25 percent) plus other best practices such as (1) shareholders with 10 percent of capital have the right to designate at least one board member, (2) boards should meet at least every three months with the presence of at least one of the independent board members and finally (3) the existence of a board audit committee.

In their 2009 and 2010 studies of governance best practices among 144 Mexican private and public firms (Table 12.1), the consulting firm Deloitte concluded, among other findings, that board members stay for too long. Also, Mexican boards rely too much on audit committees, which can be a sign of a "compliance" culture. Governance best practices need then to be "internalized" by board members and special training programs might aid this purpose. Indeed, only 40 percent of firms have training programs for new board members. Thus, other committees should also play important roles – strategy, social responsibility, governance. A further weakness is the lack of CEO and TMT succession plans: 26 percent of board members are removed as a result of the chairman's recommendation; this practice should be substituted for others that could improve transparency and

Table 12.1 *Characteristics of Mexican boards*

Sample	186 firms
Industries	Financial services, manufacturing, consumer goods, services
Average board size	10
Average independents	3
Annual board sessions	6.5
CEO duality	42%
Ethics code	59%
CEO evaluation	69%

Source: Deloitte

accountability. Here, periodic performance reviews and specific policies might also help to solve this issue (most firms did not have performance reviews for its members or committees). Another interesting finding was that 49 percent of firms do not declare conflict of interest or related transaction conflicts in their annual reports. In fact, 6 percent of firms did not even know what these terms referred to.

A higher effort to increase regulation for public firms could also help to reduce the large variance observed among different kinds of firms operating in Mexico. But, because of the "compliance" culture perceived among Mexican boards, it could also be wise to associate future regulation efforts with marketing campaigns that could be co-sponsored by local universities and consulting firms. Another issue to address is CEO duality. It was present in 42 percent of firms. Both surveys also revealed a need to implement practices that continually improve treatment of minority shareholders since only 28 percent of board members agree that minority shareholder interests are adequately protected. Finally, more transparency on the nomination and compensation of board, CEO and TMT members was considered an area of future improvement since 79 percent of board members pay attention to shareholder or personal network suggestions when having to nominate board candidates.

Stock exchange and listed companies

The Mexican *Bolsa* (BMV) originally started in 1886 as the Bolsa Mercantil de Mexico (Mexican Mercantile Exchange). It changed its

Table 12.2 *Number of public firms in Mexico*

1966	1986	1996	2000	2010
64	152	129	179	137

Sources: Mexican Stock Exchange and Condusef

name in 1975 to its current name, Bolsa Mexicana de Valores, and acquired smaller exchanges in Monterrey and Guadalajara. For its first 114 years of existence BMV was owned privately, most recently by a group of Mexican banks and brokerages. Then, in Mexico's first public share offering (IPO) of 2008, BMV offered its shares to the public and became a listed company. More than 13,600 individual investors bought shares in the IPO to make it a widely held public company. Table 12.2 describes the number of firms in different time periods from 1966 to 2010.

According to the Bank of Mexico, at the end of 2010, foreign investment in the stock market amounted to 36 percent of its total value – 453 billion USD. Thus, the value of the stock market represented an estimated 44 percent of Mexico's gross domestic product (GDP) at the end of 2010. Institutional investor holdings (pension and mutual funds) in the stock market were valued at 38 billion USD also at the end of 2010. This amounts to 8.4 percent of the total stock market value. According to World Federation of Exchanges 2009 data, the Mexican stock market is fourth in capitalization value within the Americas (352 billion USD). First place would be the US, second Canada and third Brazil.

The Mexican Stock Exchange is a very concentrated market. Half of its market value is concentrated in three firms: America Movil (Telmex arm of mobile communication), Wal Mex (Wal-Mart's Mexican subsidiary) and México (a Mexican mining consortium). Over 40 percent of its market capitalization value is associated with one corporate group (Carlos Slim) and over 60 percent to its eight most important firms (America Movil, Wal Mex, México, Femsa, Telmex, Inbursa, Peñoles, Televisa). Concentration and low representativeness has not changed much over the years. However, the legal requirements and costs of doing an IPO have changed for good. Due to regulation changes there are now more institutional investors in the market.

A number of reasons contribute to the low propensity of Mexican firms to go public. Among them are: (1) the stock exchange is perceived as a club of "big" firms, (2) revealing firm information will alert competitors, (3) going public might mean losing control, (4) the required changes to internal control and governance mechanisms are complicated, (5) revealing identities of shareholders/TMT might be dangerous due to an insecurity climate in the country.

Ownership structure of Mexican listed companies

Mexican ownership structure is characterized by a predominant family participation and by a high concentration of property and control (Castañeda, 1999). In the representative index of Mexican firms, the IPC (*indice de precios y cotizaciones*), the average ownership for the top three shareholders is 44 percent as of 2010. Only 16 percent of firms do not have a family in its main controlling group.

In order to retain ownership control, owners issue shares without voting rights and develop pyramidal structures. By doing this, owners can gain access to capital without capital dispersion. According to Castañeda (1999), ownership in Mexican companies during the mid 1990s had a 66 percent concentration in its principal shareholder while voting rights concentration was 74 percent.

Castrillo and San Martín (2007) studied the relationship between ownership and board structure with managerial discretion in Mexican firms. They noted that monitoring mechanisms of family ownership, board characteristics and debt explained managerial discretion. Family ownership in Mexican firms works as an incentive alignment mechanism of the firm that benefits key owners to the detriment of minority shareholders.

Using a sample of ninety-nine public non-financial firms, Steinwascher (2007) concluded that Mexican firms with a higher ownership concentration have a governance structure that favors their main shareholder. Also, firms with a high family ownership concentration are characterized by implementing strategies with a small or non-existent diversification and a minimum level of risk. Large and independent boards have fewer committee members, a potential indicator of lower independence. These same boards are characterized by diversification strategies oriented towards export activities. Internal governance structure does not appear to be related to diversification strategies. Table 12.3 describes the ownership concentration in a sample of Mexican public firms in 2010.

Table 12.3 *Ownership concentration in a sample of public firms*

Company	Shareholder	Ownership %	Market cap (US$bn)	% total mkt
ALFA	Fam Garza	40.0%	6,293	1.4%
	Others	10.0%		
	Float	50.0%		
AMX	Fam Slim	30.0%	117,405	26.1%
	AT&T	19.0%		
	Float	51.0%		
ARA	German Ahumada	19.5%	845	0.2%
	Luis Felipe Ahumada	19.5%		
	Float	61.0%		
ARCA	Fam Barragan, Arizpe y Hernandez	33.0%	4,424	1.0%
	Banorte Trust	53.0%		
	Float	13.0%		
ASUR	Fernando Chico Pardo	33.0%	1,660	0.4%
	Float	67.0%		
AXTEL	Mexican Businessman	33.9%	640	0.1%
	CS & BBVA	9.5%		
	Private Equity	16.4%		
	Float	40.3%		
BIMBO	Fam Servitje, Jorba	80.0%	9,911	2.2%
	Float	20.0%		
BOLSA	Control Trust	47.0%	1,277	0.3%
	CME	1.9%		
	BME	1.0%		
	Float	50.1%		
CEMEX	Fam Zambrano & Control Group	4.0%	10,501	2.3%
	Float	96.0%		
CHDRAUI	Fam Chedraui	83.0%	2,989	0.7%
	Mgmt	1.0%		
	Float	16.0%		
COMPARC	Compartamos AC	31.8%	857	0.2%
	Accion	9.0%		
	IFC	7.9%		
	Other mgmt	21.2%		
	Float	30.1%		

Table 12.3 (*cont.*)

Company	Shareholder	Ownership %	Market cap (US$bn)	% total mkt
FEMSA	Cascade/Bill & Melinda Gates	6.5%	19,600	4.4%
	Family Trust	38.7%		
	Float	54.8%		
GAP	Grupo México	16.9%	2,231	0.5%
	AMP	15.0%		
	Float	68.1%		
GCARSO	Slim	70.0%	6,559	1.5%
	Otros	15.0%		
	Float	15.0%		
GEO	Control Group	15.6%	1,843	0.4%
	Float	84.4%		
GFINBUR	Slim	59.4%	14,448	3.2%
	La Caixa	20.0%		
	Float	20.6%		
GFNORTE	Gruma	8.6%	9,050	2.0%
	Other Banorte Board	6.2%		
	Fam Gonzalez Barrera	14.5%		
	JPM	3.7%		
	Other IXE	9.5%		
	Float	57.5%		
GMEXICO	Mr. Larrea	15.0%	29,748	6.6%
	Larrea Family Trust	35.5%		
	Others	9.5%		
	Float	40.0%		
GMODELO	AB Inbev	35.1%	19,946	4.4%
	Control Group	44.9%		
	Float	20.0%		
GRUMA	Fam Gonzalez Barrera	50.4%	1,229	0.3%
	Archer-Daniels-Midland	23.2%		
	Float	26.6%		
HOMEX	Fam de Nicolás	35.0%	1,821	0.4%
	Float	65.0%		
ICA	Fam Quintana & Employees Trust	9.0%	1,646	0.4%
	Float	91.0%		
ICH	Fam Vigil	64.6%	1,752	0.4%
	Float	35.4%		

Table 12.3 (*cont.*)

Company	Shareholder	Ownership %	Market cap (US$bn)	% total mkt
KIMBER	Kimber-Clark Corp	48.0%	6,438	1.4%
	Otros	16.0%		
	Float	36.0%		
LAB	Invex Trust	36.0%	2,774	0.6%
	Nexxus	8.0%		
	Float	56.0%		
MEXCHEM	Fam Del Valle	65.0%	6,450	1.4%
	Float	35.0%		
PEÑOLES	Grupo Bal	61.3%	12,634	2.8%
	Float	38.7%		
SORIANA	Fam Bringas & Soberon	86.0%	5,626	1.3%
	Float	14.0%		
TELEVISA	Azcarraga Trust	15.0%	11,838	2.6%
	Float	85.0%		
TELMEX	Carso Global Telecom	59.0%	15,673	3.5%
	AT&T	10.0%		
	Float	31.0%		
URBI	Fam Perez Roman	51.0%	2,322	0.5%
	Others	10.0%		
	Float	39.0%		
WALMEX	Wal-Mart	68.0%	50,853	11.3%
	Float	32.0%		
	TOTAL		381,283 USD	84.10%

Sources: Santander & BMV

IPO activity between 2006 and 2008

The regulation of IPOs

Firms wishing to list their shares must produce a prospectus complying with the rules of the Mexican Securities and Exchange Commission (i.e., *Comision Nacional Bancaria y de Valores* (CNBV)). The prospectus must largely comment on the intended use of newly raised funds and provide detailed information on the firm, its subsidiaries and its controlling shareholders. CNBV is in charge to verify the comprehensiveness of the prospectus, and the admission to trading

Table 12.4 *Listing and ongoing requirements in Mexico*

Operations history	Last 3 years
Stockholders' equity	$7,325,000 USD
Net earnings	Positive past 3 years
Securities subject to IPO	15% of common stock
Number of shares in IPO	10,000,000
Number of shareholders	200
Ongoing requirements	
Stockholders' equity	5,490,000
Minimum number of transactions	36 operations/semester
Average price/semester	Over 1 peso
Number of shareholders	100
Number of shares among investors	8,000,000
% common stock among investors	12%

Source: Mexican Stock Exchange (BMV)

of the company is subject to its approval of the document. Listed companies should comply both with listing and ongoing requirements (Table 12.4). The main listing requirements for an IPO company are: three years of operations history, a minimum stockholders' equity value of 7,325,000 USD (as of December 2010), positive net earnings for the past three years, a minimum free float of 15 percent of common stock, and to issue at least 10,000,000 shares with a minimum of 200 different shareholders. Ongoing requirements include: a minimum capital of 5,490,000 USD (as of December 2010), a minimum of thirty-six transactions per semester, average price above one peso, at least 100 shareholders, no less than 8,000,000 shares among investors and a minimum free float of 12 percent of capital.

IPOs between 2006 and 2008

During the period 2006–8, nine Mexican companies went public. In this section we analyze companies that decided to go public in the Mexican Stock Exchange and that have not been delisted since then.

The process of fixing the IPO price in Mexico is determined jointly by the IPO firm and the underwriter they choose for the offer. This number will be affected by the interest potential investors have in the firm and their outlook in its potential value. In Table 12.5 we can find the number and type of firms that did IPOs between 2006 and 2008.

Table 12.5 *IPO year and industry classification*

	2006	2007	2008	Total
Trade and transportation	2	0	0	2
Telecommunications	0	2	0	2
Financial services	1	2	1	4
Healthcare	0	0	1	1
Total	3	4	2	9

Four of these firms went public in 2007 (Megacable, Maxcom, Findep and Comparta). Two more also did so before the financial crisis hit the stock markets worldwide (Lab and Bolsa). Among these nine firms there is an interesting focus on certain industries. (1) Two firms are in the airport transportation business: OMA is the private operator of airports located in the central and northern part of Mexico and GAP operates the ones in the Pacific. (2) Another two firms are microcredit operations (Findep and Comparta) which is an industry that has blossomed in Mexico due to the low penetration of traditional banks. Finally, there are Megacable and Maxcom which are both cable TV, internet and fixed line service providers. The last three firms are Gfamsa, Lab and Bolsa. Gfamsa is a retailer of furniture, electronics and appliances that created its own bank to take advantage of its distribution network and client base. Lab is an OTC pharmaceutical and healthcare provider and Bolsa is the Mexican stock exchange organization. Only Gfamsa and Bolsa were founded before 1990. It is worth noting that both OMA and GAP were government privatizations from the late 1990s. Table 12.6 shows revenues, numbers of employees and assets of each of the newly listed firms.

Regarding ownership structure the largest shareholder of our sampled IPOs had 55 percent of the shares pre-IPO and that figure decreased to 35 percent after the IPO. Table 12.7 shows the type of pre- and post-ownership structure. Interestingly, players with more than 15 percent of capital were: venture capital firms (four) followed by banks (two) and families (two). Government did not participate in any of the sampled IPOs. It is interesting to note that families do not come out first even if they are still today the predominant shareholder among public firms. A potential reason for this might be that this is simply not a representative sample. Another possibility is that these

Table 12.6 *IPO size and assets*

	Revenues	Employees	Assets
LAB	189,615	NA	221,005
BOLSA	147,720	NA	1,640,879
MEGACABLE	382,052	4,343	931,726
MAXCOM	215,118	1,470	734,465
FINDEP	177,903	NA	342,242
COMPARTA	226,149	3,203	467,980
GAP	280,097	1,076	157,045
GFAMSA	1,182,404	NA	1,296,985
OMA	150,579	944	791,931

Table 12.7 *IPO ownership structure*

	VC		Banks		Family		Top 1		Top 3	
	Pre	Post	Pre	Post	Pre	Post	Pre	Post	Pre	Post
Average	34%	28%	48%	31%	15%	12%	55%	35%	85%	61%
Cases	5	4	2	2	4	4	7	7	7	7

Table 12.8 *IPO board of directors averages*

Independents	Women	Foreign	Family	Audit com.	Nomination com.
40.30%	6%	7%	44.40%	66.66%	22.22%

firms are evidence of how corporate structure is changing in the country. As mentioned before, institutional players (mutual and pension funds, banks and private/venture capital firms) have become increasingly important in the last few years. Evidence of our hypothesis might be the fact that six out of eight firms were founded after 1990.

There are no business angels in the share capital before and after IPOs in Mexico. Data shows that venture capital funds and banks play a relatively large role in supporting Mexican IPOs. Moreover, four of the VC funds supporting the IPO process are owned by foreigners and two by Mexicans. There were no dual class shares or pyramidal group structures in our sample.

Boards of directors of IPO firms have on average eleven members; 40 percent of them are independent, 6 percent are women and 7 percent foreigners. There are family-related board members in 44 percent of firms and the predominant functional background is peripheral (55 percent), which means that the majority of board members come from finance, accounting or law backgrounds. The majority of boards have an audit committee (66 percent) and only 22 percent of them have a nominations one. There are no other operating committees in our IPO sample.

The description of an IPO: Compartamos

Compartamos Banco was founded in 1990 as a non-governmental organization (NGO) with the purpose of offering small loans to entrepreneurial women. At the time the program was called "Generadoras de Ingresos" (Income Generators) and it was part of a strategy within the health and nutrition programs at Asociacion Compartamos Program, I.A.P.

From 1990 to 1993, Compartamos developed a methodology to grant small credits to low-income segments of the population – mostly women. At the end of 1993 the Inter-American Development Bank granted a 5,000,000 USD credit line to Compartamos, greatly contributing to its organic growth. By 1995 Compartamos already had 17,500 clients and had followed a policy of profit reinvestment. In 1996 Compartamos received support training and technical assistance from CGAP (Consultative Group to Assist the Poor). This further contributed to its growth and acquisition strategy of IT systems. In 1998 Compartamos was granted authorization to operate as a commercial financial institution and sold part of its capital to ACCION International in order to access urban markets.

It was 2002 when Compartamos first issued debt, becoming the first microcredit lender in the world to issue debt in capital markets. In 2006 the company started to operate with a banking license, strengthening its processes, systems, accountability and policies to comply with applicable regulations. Compartamos had by then 616,528 clients and 187 branches. As of December 31, 2006 Compartamos had a capital ratio of 40 percent.

Compartamos' equity was shared by several institutional investors, such as Compartamos A.C., an NGO based in Mexico with 39.20 percent,

Table 12.9 *Pre- and post-IPO capital structure: Compartamos*

Pre-IPO	
Compartamos A.C.	22.50%
ACCION Gateway Fund LLC	32.80%
International Finance Corporation (IFC)	10.10%
Individual shareholders	32.70%
Post-IPO	
Promotora Social México (formerly Compartamos A.C.)	31.80%
ACCION Gateway Fund LLC	5.40%
Floating capital	62.80%

Source: Compartamos

ACCION Gateway Fund LLC with 18.05 percent, the IFC (International Finance Corporation) with 10.57 percent and several individual investors. At the time of the offer Compartamos had 838,000 clients, 4,200 employees, 252 branches and an outstanding loan portfolio of 370 million USD.

The offer

The offering price per share was Ps. 40.00 (3.63 USD). A total of 111,572,532 shares were offered, representing 30 percent of ordinary capital stock. Eighteen percent of the offer was subscribed in Mexico and the rest in the US. The underwriters in Mexico were Accival (part of Citibank Mexico) and Banorte. In the US it was Credit Suisse.

The firm after the IPO

Compartamos' IPO did not have a direct impact on the capital structure of the company but allowed some of its shareholders to trade its shares publicly and legitimized the firm among its various stakeholders. Table 12.9 describes Compartamos' pre- and post-IPO capital structure. Even with the financial crisis in 2008–9 the firm has grown aggressively since the IPO; the number of clients increased 109 percent to 1,752,000 and the number of employees 113 percent to 9,127. There are also 40 percent more branches (352), their outstanding loan portfolio increased 110 percent to 710 million USD and, finally, their stock price increased 75 percent to 6.42 USD per share.

Their board structure did not change. There were still the same ten members as in 2006. Only the audit, compensation and evaluation

Table 12.10 *Compartamos growth 2007–10*

	2007	2010	Change
Number of clients	838	1,752	109%
Number of employees	4,277	9,127	113%
Branches	252	352	40%
Loan portfolio	4,186	8,784	110%

Source: Compartamos

Table 12.11 *Compartamos funding structure*

Debt issuances	39.50%
Interbank loans	47.80%
Other liabilities	12.70%

Source: Compartamos

committees absorbed the functions of the corporate governance committee required by securities legislation. An institutional investor relations office was created. In 2009 the board approved a structural change to the top management team structure; two of Compartamos' founders (Carlos Labarthe and Carlos Danel) who had been sharing the CEO role became chairman and vice chairman of the board respectively. Fernando Alvarez, who had been acting as CFO, became the new CEO and Jose Manuel Canal left the chairman role. Table 12.10 describes changes in key indicators of growth for Compartamos while Table 12.11 looks at their post-IPO funding structure.

In December of 2010 Compartamos Banco announced that Compartamos S.A.B de C.V., a holding publicly traded corporation, acquired 97 percent of Compartamos Banco's shares through a mandatory public tender and reciprocal subscription offer of shares in Mexico. This change will allow Compartamos more flexibility to expand internationally, since being a bank slows down new product authorization processes.

Conclusion

Mexican corporate governance has evolved rapidly in the past few decades. The evolution of corporate law (1975/2005), the introduction and revision of a code of good governance and the transition from being a commodities exporter in 1982 to a diversified economy with the most free trade agreements in the world are certainly signs of this. According to the World Bank in its "Doing Business 2008" report, protection of shareholder rights in Mexico equals that of OECD countries and is higher than the Latin American average.

Despite the evolution of corporate law and corporate governance, ownership of Mexican public firms is still concentrated. However, the increasing importance of venture capital firms and institutional investors should produce more debate, independence and diversity among Mexican public firms. The presence of women directors is remarkably low (6 percent) and, if Mexico aspires to be a truly global player, it should also strive to have more foreigners on its boards (only 7 percent today). Other areas to improve include: (1) the operation of a wider variety of board committees, (2) training board members, (3) serving time of board members which tends to be unusually high, (4) implementing board evaluations which are still a rarity, (5) implementing CEO and TMT succession plans, (6) increasing transparency of top-level compensation and nomination practices.

Corporate governance practices in Mexico compare to those of OECD countries but fare below its average. It is true, though, that within Latin America and in an emerging country context, they stand out. Thus, we can conclude that Mexico needs to improve its governance practices if it truly aspires to become a developed economy.

References

Castañeda, Gonzalo. 1999. *Governance of Large Corporations in México and Productivity Implications. International Conference 'Gobierno Corporativo: Desafíos para América Latina'.* Pontificia Universidad Católica de Chile Business School Santiago de Chile.

Castrillo, L.A. & San Martin, J.M. 2007. 'La propiedad familiar como mecanismo de gobierno disciplinador de la dirección en las empresas Mexicanas'. *Contaduría y Administración*, Mayo 2007, 59–82.

Deloitte. 2009. *Estudio de mejores prácticas en consejos de administración. Camino hacia un mejor desempeño.*

2010. *Estudio de mejores prácticas para la eficiencia y el crecimiento de los negocios. Hallazgos sobre la contribución de los órganos de gobierno y sus miembros.*

Steinwascher, William H. 2007. *Ownership, corporate governance and diversification strategies of Mexican firms: An exploratory study.* MPRA Paper, No. 11599.

World Bank and International Finance Corporation. 2008. 'Doing business 2008'.

13 Corporate governance and initial public offerings in the Netherlands*

HANS VAN EES AND TEYE MARRA

Corporate governance mechanisms

Historically, the Dutch are a population of traders and seafarers. During the golden age (16/17th century), the Dutch obtained a dominant position in world trade. From a cultural perspective, the Netherlands score relatively high on individualism and relatively low on uncertainty avoidance and masculinity. Together, these indicators represent combinations that characterize continental Northern-European countries. It reflects a society with relatively loose bonds with others, a reduced level of uncertainty within the population through regulation and policy and a more openly nurturing society. The Dutch society is characterized by a French civil law tradition, with a preference for co-operation and fine-grained arrangements between social partners (the famous *polder model*). Its economic order is characterized by a historically strong but fainting interference of the state into the private business domain, characteristic of a regulated market economy.

The history of corporate governance goes back as far as the Amsterdam Stock Exchange, founded in 1602 as the oldest exchange in the world. Fentrop (2002) describes that corporate governance issues already arose in the Dutch East India Company (*Vereenigde Oostindische Compagnie*). Historically investor protection is rather low and the market for corporate control is virtually absent. However, after the reform in the early 2000s, the Netherlands belong to the European frontrunners in terms of information disclosure and transparency. The comply-or-explain principle of corporate governance

---

* Parts of the discussion of corporate institutions and regulations in the Netherlands in this chapter are developed from D. Akkermans, H. van Ees, N. Hermes, R. Hooghiemstra, G. van der Laan, and T. Postma, 2009, 'The Dutch Experience with Corporate Governance Codes: A Ten Year Perspective', in F.J. Lopez Iturriaga (ed.), *Codes of Good Governance Around the World*, Nova Science Publishers, Inc.

codes is rooted in Dutch corporate law and business groups do not exist. Corporate ownership is relatively dispersed by European standards but concentrated from a US/UK perspective. Institutional owners are generally the dominant ownership group; private investors are more rare. Corporate boards are usually two-tier in nature and CEO duality does not exist. Dutch supervisory boards are completely composed of outside, non-executive directors. Executive compensation is becoming increasingly non-egalitarian in nature, without approaching the US standards in this respect. Finally, the median CEO is by and large rewarded through a fixed compensation *cum* annual bonus system, even though equity-based performance pay is standard among Dutch blue chip companies.

Corporate governance history

Since the Cadbury Report in 1992, corporate governance has proliferated around the globe. In the Netherlands, the first committee on corporate governance, the Peters Committee installed in 1996, formulated forty recommendations on corporate governance in the Netherlands. The lack of compliance with the recommendations led to a second corporate governance committee installed in March 2003, the Tabaksblat Committee. The Tabaksblat Committee was initiated by the Dutch government (Groenewald, 2005; Wymeersch, 2005). The Dutch corporate governance code, the so-called Tabaksblat Code, became effective as of December 2003. Rather than completely relying on self-regulation, from that date listed companies were legally required to report their compliance, on a comply-or-explain basis. In addition, adjustments in the legal regulation concerning corporate governance, focusing on transparent financial reporting and the enforcement of shareholder protection, were implemented in 2002 and 2004 respectively. And recently, in December 2008, the Dutch corporate governance code was amended and extended.

Legal regulation

Corporate law

Dutch firms are incorporated as private limited liability firms (*Besloten Vennootschap* or BV) or as public limited liability firms (*Naamloze*

Vennootschap or NV). An NV can issue shares either in tradable bearer form, or in registered form. A BV can only issue registered shares (Schuit and Bier, 2002). The NV status is a requirement for listing on Euronext Amsterdam (De Jong, De Jong, Mertens et al., 2001). Characteristic of Dutch corporate governance is the two-tier board structure, with a complete separation and independence of the management board (*raad van bestuur*) and the supervisory board (*raad van commissarissen*) (e.g., Cools and Van Praag, 2007; De Jong and Röell, 2005; Hooghiemstra and Van Manen, 2004; Van Ees, Postma and Sterken, 2003). As a consequence CEO duality does not exist. The management board is exclusively responsible for the company's strategy, as well as day-to-day operations (Schuit and Bier, 2002). In line with Fama and Jensen (1983), the supervisory board monitors management and provides advice. Dutch company law requires the management board to provide the supervisory board with all necessary information to perform its tasks. At least once a year, the management board has to report in writing to the supervisory board on the company's strategy, the strategic, legal, and financial risks, and the internal control system.

In performing their roles, both the management board and the supervisory board take into account the interests of the corporation. Article 140, Book 2 of the Dutch Civil Code prescribes that "[T]he duties of the supervisory board shall be the supervision of the policy of the management and the general course of affairs of the corporation and the enterprise connected therewith. It shall assist the management with advice. In the performance of their duties the members of the supervisory board shall be guided by the interests of the corporation and the enterprise connected therewith." There exists a *comminus opinio* in the Netherlands that supervisory board members take into account the interests of all stakeholders, including employees (Hooghiemstra and Van Manen, 2004).

According to corporate law, the decision rights of the supervisory board depend on the corporate regime (Maassen and van de Bosch, 1999; Moerland, 2002). In the so-called *Normale* regime, a management board is legally required and the formation of a supervisory board is voluntary (Maassen and van de Bosch, 1999). The distribution of decision rights between the supervisory board and the shareholders under the *Normale* regime favors shareholders. Shareholders appoint the members of the management and supervisory boards, approve annual accounts, and make major corporate decisions (Schuit and Bier, 2002). Furthermore, they ratify the employment contracts with top managers, unless the articles of association of the corporation specify otherwise. According to the reform act of 2004, in the so-called *Structuur* regime, the management board members are appointed by the supervisory board and shareholders appoint by a majority vote the members of the supervisory board.[1] Shareholders only appoint candidates nominated by the supervisory board but, during the nomination process, they are entitled to suggest candidates. Shareholders have the right to dismiss the entire supervisory board. This, however, requires a meeting in which the participating shareholders represent at least one-third of the issued share capital. Similar to the situation before the reform act, a number of important corporate decisions require the approval of the supervisory board. Examples include (de)listing decisions, decisions concerning major investments in other companies, those involving amounts equal to or exceeding one-quarter of the issued share capital and free reserves, and major corporate restructuring. With respect to these decisions, prior approval of shareholders is not required. However, regarding decisions related to the continuity of the company's business (e.g., the sale of a major subsidiary), the decision-making power is now vested with the shareholders. Finally, the Netherlands is one of the few countries where shareholders have a say on pay; both the remuneration policy and the annual accounts are under approval by the annual meeting of shareholders.

The *Structuur* regime legally applies to companies that have more than 100 employees, a legally required works council, and a book value of shareholders' equity of minimum €16 million. Companies that do not satisfy these criteria can voluntarily opt for the *Structuur* regime. In a study of Dutch listed companies, Van der Elst, de Jong and Raaijmakers (2007) reveal that in 2003 35 percent were legally required to apply the *Structuur* regime and an additional 13 percent voluntarily adopted the regime. Where the *Structuur* regime applies, a company is legally required to have a supervisory board of at least three members. In general, the corporate law does not make restrictions as to the eligibility of members. There are, however, two

---

[1] Before the reform act, however, supervisory board members were appointed through co-optation.

important exceptions. First, a person cannot sit both on the management board and the supervisory board. Second, neither employees nor labor union representatives are eligible for a position as a supervisory board member of a structured company. In the Netherlands, perhaps with the exception of the large blue chip companies, supervisory board members primarily comprise persons with prior management board experience and often include past members of management.

Anti-director rights

The Dutch law requires that at least one general meeting of shareholders is organized every year within six months after the end of the fiscal year. At the general meeting, "the board must give the shareholders all information they ask for [...], unless it is of vital importance to the company to withhold the information" (De Jong, Mertens and Roosenboom, 2006, p. 357). In general, resolutions require a simple majority, unless the articles of association stipulate differently. Schuit and Bier (2002, p. 97) conclude that shareholders have "a very limited role in the management and operations of the corporation." The most important rights of shareholders are to ask questions, raise issues, and vote at the annual general meeting of shareholders. Research by De Jong and Roëll (2005) indicates that on average 30 percent of the shares are present at the shareholders' meetings. In addition, their results suggest that, in the Netherlands, shareholder activism is limited despite recent incidental cases, e.g., ABN-AMRO, Stork, and Hagemeyer, in which company boards faced fierce opposition during the general meeting of shareholders.

Important explanations for shareholders' lack of influence are the many defensive mechanisms for which Dutch corporate governance is notorious (De Jong, Mertens and Roosenboom, 2006; Kabir, Cantrijn and Jeunink, 1997; Van Ees, Postma and Sterken, 2003). The defensive mechanisms "generally preclude that management is seriously disciplined by the stock market" (Van Ees et al., 2003, p. 45) and also explain why the Netherlands is considered a country with poor shareholder protection (La Porta, Lopez-de-Silanes, Shleifer et al., 1998). It is possible to distinguish legal, statutory, and non-statutory defensive mechanisms (Kabir et al., 1997). The *Structuur* regime is an example of a legal rule, which in reality serves as a defensive mechanism. Statutory measures include the issue of preferred defense or priority shares. Preferred defense shares are the most widely adopted defensive mechanism in the Netherlands (Kabir et al., 1997; Van Elst et al., 2007). In case of a takeover threat, the company can issue preferred shares to friendly parties, with only a statutory minimum of 25 percent of par value to be paid. Having full voting rights, substantial voting power is granted to holders of preferred defense shares (Kabir et al., 1997). Van der Elst et al. (2007) conclude that about 60 percent of the Dutch listed companies at least had the possibility to issue preferred shares in 2006. Their study also reveals that while about 40 percent of the listed companies had issued priority shares in 1992, this percentage dropped to 20 percent in 2006. Priority shares, typically owned by the founding family or a friendly foundation, carry special voting rights on matters of relevance, including the appointment of new management and/or supervisory board members, approval of share issues and mergers, and changing the company's articles of association. Obviously, priority shares result in a situation that deviates from the "one-share-one-vote" principle. A non-statutory way to effectively limit shareholders' influence is the certification of shares. Van Elst et al. (2007) estimate that still around 15 percent of the Dutch listed companies use this type of defense. In case the certification of shares is used, cash flow rights and voting rights are separated (De Jong et al., 2006; Kabir et al., 1997; Van Ees et al., 2003). The ordinary shares are placed at an administrative office, which issues depositary receipts to the investors. The owner of depositary receipts has the cash flow rights attached to shares, as well as the right to attend and speak at the general shareholders' meeting. However, the control rights remain at the administrative office, which in general comprises members from the company (i.e., the management or supervisory board) and outsiders. Furthermore, "while the chairman and majority of the [administrative] office must be outsiders, in practice, the [...] office is always friendly to existing management" (De Jong et al., 2006, p. 356).

Voluntary regulation, corporate governance codes

In 1996, the Peters Committee (named after the chairman of the committee) was the first corporate governance committee in the Netherlands. The forty recommendations issued in summer 1997 were aimed at listed companies. The recommendations relate to various governance issues, including the composition and independence of the supervisory board, transparency as to remuneration, the position of the auditor, and the right of shareholders to call a general meeting where they represent 1 percent or more of the company's share capital. A key element of the report of the Peters Committee is compliance through self-regulation (De Jong et al., 2005; Groenewald, 2005). However, several studies revealed disappointingly low compliance with the best practice recommendations (e.g., De Jong and Roosenboom, 2002; De Jong et al., 2005). In March 2003, the low compliance motivated the initiation of a new corporate governance committee, the Dutch corporate governance committee or the Tabaksblat Committee (named after its chairman, a former CEO of Unilever). The Tabaksblat Committee was established at the invitation of the Dutch government (Groenewald, 2005; Wymeersch, 2005). The committee represented the shareholder association, listed companies, the stock exchange (Euronext Amsterdam), and institutional investors. Its primary task was to develop a new corporate governance code. A draft of the Dutch corporate governance code was presented on July 1, 2003. After incorporating about 250 reactions the committee published the final version of the Dutch corporate governance code, the so-called Tabaksblat Code, in December 2003.

The Dutch corporate governance code

The Dutch corporate governance code contains twenty-one principles of good governance. These principles are decomposed into more than 120 specific best practice provisions, which make the Dutch code one of the most detailed in the world. "These provisions create a set of standards governing the conduct of management board and supervisory board members and shareholders" (Tabaksblat Committee, 2003, p. 4). The principles and best practice provisions cover five fields of corporate governance: (1) compliance with and enforcement of the code, (2) the management board, (3) the supervisory board, (4) the shareholders and general meeting of shareholders, and (5) the audit of the financial reporting and the position of the internal and external auditor function. In general, there is a close resemblance with, e.g., the British Combined Code and the German Corporate Governance Code (Hermes, Postma and Zivkov, 2006; Voogsgeerd, 2006).

The Tabaksblat Code applies to companies listed on the Dutch Stock Exchange and foreign listed companies with a statutory residence in the Netherlands. Similar to many other codes, the Dutch corporate governance code is based on the comply-or-explain principle. However, whereas in most European countries self-regulatory monitoring is the preferred mode of enforcement (Wymeersch, 2005), this is not the case in the Netherlands.[2] In accordance with the Fourth EU Directive, Dutch corporate law requires listed companies to include a statement in the annual report about their compliance with the provisions of the Dutch corporate governance code (Groenewald, 2005). In this statement, listed companies have to provide an explanation where they do not comply with the provisions of the code. By giving the comply-or-explain principle a legal status, management can be held liable where the annual report does not contain a compliance statement or the statement turns out to be incorrect (Groenewald, 2005).

Notwithstanding the legal requirement, case-based evidence illustrates that it is complicated to successfully file a complaint (Groenewald, 2005). To monitor compliance with the code the Dutch corporate governance code monitoring committee was installed by the Minister of Finance, the Minister of Justice, and the State Secretary of Economic Affairs in December 2004. The committee generally concludes that compliance is high, particularly for large blue chip companies. Despite high compliance, the committee has regularly introduced additional guidelines as to the interpretation of specific best practice provisions and amendments to the Tabaksblat Code. Moreover, as of December 2008 an amended Dutch corporate governance code has become effective. Generally, the amended code emphasizes the importance and relevance of the supervisory board as the most important institution of corporate governance, possibly at the expense of shareholder power. In that respect, the amended corporate

---

[2] In Germany, the law also refers to a corporate governance code. More specifically, the German Corporate Governance Code is incorporated into the *Aktiengesetz*. Similar to the situation in the Netherlands, German listed companies are required to annually publish a compliance statement in their annual reports (Goncharov, Werner and Zimmermann, 2006; Von Werder, Talaulicar and Kolat, 2005; Wymeersch, 2005). Unlike the Dutch-German way of enforcement, the British Combined Code is not part of the legal framework. Instead it is annexed to the Listing Rules (MacNeil and Li, 2006; Wymeersch, 2005). The consequence, however, is similar and requires listed companies to report on their compliance with the provisions of the Combined Code on the basis of comply or explain.

Table 13.1 *Characteristics of the supervisory boards of Dutch listed companies*

	AEX	AMX	AScX	Local	Total
Sample	21	23	20	35	99
Size (in numbers)	7.86	5.43	4.15	3.83	5.12
Average age (in years)	62	61	60	59	60
Gender diversity (Blau index)	0.47	0.24	0.19	0.09	0.23
Nationality diversity (Blau index)	0.52	0.34	0.17	0.20	0.30
Average tenure in years	5.3	5.5	6.0	4.9	5.3
Average number of supervisory board meetings per year	7.1	6.7	7.8	6.7	7
Number of committees	2.9	2.4	1.5	1.2	2

Sources: van der Laan et al. (2010) and Spencer Stuart Board Index (2008)

governance code can be regarded as an institutional response to the recent increase in shareholders' activism and the importance of private equity and hedge funds in global financial markets.

The issue and the update of the Dutch corporate governance code have contributed to enforcement of good governance in the Netherlands. Given the importance of (supervisory) boards in good governance, the Dutch corporate governance code has in particular affected the evolution of the characteristics of the board of directors of Dutch companies. Evidence shows that the average supervisory board in the Netherlands comprised five directors and held about seven meetings per year. In addition, 60 percent of the boards include at least one member who can be considered a financial expert and 87 percent of the boards consist of a majority of independent members. The degree of independence of supervisory board members is relatively high and constant over the years. On the other hand, the data also reveal a low representation of foreign and women directors, particularly in smaller companies. The representative board member is a Dutch male of about sixty years old, with previous experience in corporate management. Finally, the average number of directorships at listed companies per director at the board level is about two and about 24 percent of the supervisory boards in the Netherlands have a majority of board members who have more than 3 seats on supervisory boards (see Table 13.1).

In Table 13.2 median total compensation levels of Dutch listed firms are presented for the period 2002–6. In this period, the increase in

Table 13.2 *Median total compensation ($\times$ $1) of Dutch listed firms*

	2002		2003		2004		2005		2006	
	N	$	N	$	N	$	N	$	N	$
AEX funds										
CEO	25	1,347,636	28	1,959,956	28	2,600,929	23	3,857,462	22	4,327,136
Other execs.	92	884,477	90	1,380,119	88	1,730,600	78	2,360,034	87	2,221,829
Midcap funds										
CEO	30	563,301	29	823,361	29	1,093,632	30	1,126,894	31	1,027,233
Other execs.	63	431,668	61	663,079	65	685,337	60	807,142	70	793,790
Smallcap funds										
CEO	56	315,075	60	425,063	60	484,402	59	481,994	59	542,574
Other execs.	79	290,220	71	367,500	66	434,448	65	448,835	71	534,284

Source: Van Ees et al. (2007)

CEO pay is considerably larger than the increase in salary of the median employee. The median compensation of a CEO of a large AEX corporation is about twenty times as large as the salary of a median employee. The median Dutch corporation pays executives a fixed salary and a variable (cash) bonus. In the larger blue chip companies (AEX), the use of equity-based compensation is widespread. In the period 2002–6, on average, in large AEX companies CEO incentive-based compensation is 67 percent of total compensation and 36 percent is long term. For other executives, the incentive component is 40 percent and 32 percent of total compensation is long term. In small companies, these figures are lower. The variable CEO compensation is only 40 percent of total compensation and only 23 percent is paid out as long-term compensation. In smaller firms, other executives' variable compensation accounts for 26 percent of total compensation and 16 percent of total compensation is based on equity.

Ownership

De Jong et al. (2006) show that, between 1998 and 2002, the ownership structure in the Netherlands is characterized by relatively concentrated shareholdings with large stakes owned by institutional investors. Eumedion, an organization representing the interests of institutional investors, estimates that the share of the largest Dutch listed companies held by private investors dropped from 19 percent in 1995 to 5 percent in 2005. In the same period, the percentage of shares held by foreign investors increased to 75 percent. Under Dutch law, shareholders have to disclose ownership and trading date information when passing specific thresholds, starting at 5 percent. In Table 13.3, Panel A shows descriptive statistics of the stakes of all blockholders in a sample of 107 Dutch listed companies, owning a block of at least 5 percent of issued shares. Panel B presents descriptive statistics on blockholders per company. In Panel B, the average size of a company's blockholder, the largest known blockholder, the number of known blockholders per company, and the sum of the stakes of the known blockholders per company is depicted for the period 2002–6 (Ellis, 2008). Table 13.3 indicates the relevance of concentrated ownership in the Netherlands. It can be concluded that ownership concentration has been increasing in the Netherlands in the period

Table 13.3 *The ownership structure of Dutch listed companies*

	2002	2003	2004	2005	2006
(A) *Blockholder statistics*					
Number of blockholders	350	426	425	450	532
Blockholder size (percentage)					
Mean	11.37	11.49	11.26	11.00	11.21
Median	6.36	6.34	6.70	6.79	7.26
Maximum	75.20	77.40	95.60	87.50	100.00
Minimum	0.00	0.00	0.00	0.00	0.00
Std. Dev.	12.59	12.21	11.79	11.49	12.08
(B) *Company statistics*					
Number of firms	107	107	107	107	107
Average blockholder size (percentage)					
Mean	13.2	14.6	14.3	13.6	15.6
Median	8.2	9.7	8.9	8.9	9.2
Maximum	75.2	77.4	95.6	87.5	100.0
Minimum	0.00	0.00	0.00	0.00	0.00
Std. Dev.	13.05	13.15	14.55	14.07	18.30
Largest blockholder (in percentage)					
Mean	20.18	23.30	21.96	21.78	24.28
Median	12.10	15.90	15.20	15.00	15.40
Maximum	75.20	77.40	95.60	87.50	100.00
Minimum	0.00	0.00	0.00	0.00	0.00
Std. Dev.	19.35	18.91	18.76	18.82	21.16
Number of blockholders					
Mean	3.27	3.98	3.97	4.21	4.96
Median	2	3	4	4	5
Maximum	11	13	12	12	12
Minimum	0	0	0	0	0
Std. Dev.	2.39	2.73	2.63	2.71	2.81
Sum of blockholders' stake (percentage)					
Mean	37.21	45.76	44.72	46.24	55.76
Median	35.08	45.36	45.36	49.75	62.84
Maximum	98.10	98.30	98.30	98.30	100.00
Minimum	0.00	0.00	0.00	0.00	0.00
Std. Dev.	26.71	26.21	25.92	26.49	26.72

Source: Ellis (2008)

2002–6, while it should also be acknowledged that it was much higher in the 1990s. On the other hand, the median blockholder does not have a controlling share (>15 percent) in Dutch corporations even though largest blockholders generally have controlling blocks. De Jong et al. (2006) measure a significant positive price effect for block purchases directly around the transaction date, but not for block sales. Consequently, when a new blockholder enters the firm, the market reacts positively; this may indicate a governance premium. On the other hand, a significant price effect for the disclosures of block transactions could not be observed, which can be due to the fact that blockholders in Dutch companies, as mentioned before, face an array of anti-director rights frustrating their voting rights. Finally, levered controlling ownership is typically rare in the Netherlands. All in all, with respect to ownership concentration and control, the Netherlands takes something of an intermediate position between fairly concentrated ownership and dispersed ownership.

Going public in the Netherlands

Founded in 1611, the Amsterdam Stock Exchange is regarded as the oldest stock exchange in the world. Share trading developed in Amsterdam since the Dutch East India Company was in need of funds to finance the shipping of goods from Asia. The shares in this company were the first traded shares in the world. The Amsterdam Stock Exchange Association (*Vereniging voor de Effectenhandel*) was founded in 1851 to organize and regulate share trading in the Netherlands and a century later, in 1978, the Amsterdam Stock Exchange Association launched the European Options Exchange, the first options exchange in Europe and only the second in the world. In 2000, the Amsterdam Stock Exchange merged with the Brussels Stock Exchange and the Paris Stock Exchange to form Euronext and is now known as Euronext Amsterdam. In 2007 about 220 funds were listed on Euronext Amsterdam, with a total market capitalization of about $97 billion. In 2008, 211 funds were listed on Euronext Amsterdam, with a total market capitalization of about $374 billion (279 billion euro). The AEX index at Euronext Amsterdam represents the twenty-five largest blue chip funds; smaller corporations are listed on the AMS, AscX, and local index, respectively. Despite the long history and tradition of the Amsterdam Stock Exchange, equity funding is relatively unimportant in the Netherlands. The average Dutch firm finances its investments through internal funds and bank loans.

The Amsterdam Stock Exchange has two tiers, an "official" or regulated market and an "unofficial" or non-regulated market. The former is known as Euronext Amsterdam and the latter as Alternext. Alternext aims to attract smaller and younger firms that do not yet meet the entry requirements of an official listing and for which the cost of an official listing may be too high. Essentially, Alternext consists of several exchanges that are located at the main exchanges of the Euronext group, of which Alternext Amsterdam is one. Alternext Amsterdam was established in 2006, shortly after the establishment of the Alternext markets of Paris and Brussels.

Through the years the Amsterdam Stock Exchange has had several second-tier stock markets. In 1982, it established the *Parallelmarkt*. This market, however, was abolished in 1994 because of several scandals. In 1997, a second attempt was made to create a special market for younger and smaller firms. This market was first called NMAX (which stands for New Market Amsterdam Exchanges), and later Euro.NM Amsterdam. This market too was abolished, mainly because of some major bankruptcies as a result of the collapse of the internet bubble in 2000.

The primary market of the Amsterdam Stock Exchange, Euronext Amsterdam, is an EU-regulated market and is therefore subject to oversight by the Dutch Minister of Finance. The Dutch Minister of Finance has delegated the regulatory authority to the Dutch securities board (*Autoriteit Financiële Markten*, AFM) and the Dutch central bank (*De Nederlandsche Bank*, DNB). These authorities supervise both the primary and secondary market, but since the secondary market does not fall within the EU definition of regulated markets, it is subject only to the national laws and regulations.

As in most other countries nowadays, the Netherlands uses bookbuilding as the default method for conducting an IPO. Bookbuilding is an attractive method for conducting an IPO because the final issue price can be conditioned on the market demand. For more information about bookbuilding see, for example, the description of the IPO activity in Italy elsewhere in the book. All newly listed firms on Euronext Amsterdam must publish a prospectus approved by the local regulator. The prospectus should at least contain the following information: personal information on the members of the executive board and the supervisory board; information on affiliated companies; detailed segmented information; information on new products or services; information on research and development policies and processes; information on the dependence on patents or licenses, industrial, commercial, and financial agreements, or new production processes; the places of business that provide at least 10 percent of sales or production; staffing and development therein; important ongoing investments and investments over the last three years; and details of lawsuits or disputes that are expected to have an important effect on the firm's financial position. The authorities of the Amsterdam Exchange and AFM and DNB oversee to what extent issuing firms comply with the applicable rules and regulations.

The listing on the primary market of the Amsterdam Stock Exchange is subject to a due process and the requirement that a listing agent is involved. The listing agent shall guide and counsel the issuing firm with respect to listing issues for a period of at least six months following the listing. The formal listing requirements of the first-tier market of the Amsterdam Stock Exchange in 2010 are: (1) a minimum float of at least 25 percent, (2) a value of shareholders' equity in excess of approximately $6.7 million (€5 million, calculated on the basis of the offering price), and (3) a track record of at least three years. In case of a large number of securities the free float is allowed to be lower than 25 percent, with an absolute minimum of 5 percent. To adhere to requirement (3) the issuer has to have published audited annual statements for the three years preceding the year of admission to listing. For this requirement, however, dispensation may be granted if this is in the interest of the issuer. In that case, additional restrictive conditions, such as a higher minimum market capitalization and/or lock-up requirements, may apply.

The ongoing requirements of the first-tier market are mainly disclosure obligations. These include: (1) audited annual and (nonaudited) semi-annual and quarterly reports, (2) communications of significant changes in share ownership, and (3) timely dissemination of every fact or event that may have a significant effect on the share price.

The admission requirements for listing on the second-tier market of the Amsterdam Stock Exchange are, of course, set lower than those for the first tier. The main requirements are: (1) a value of shareholders' equity in excess of approximately $3.4 million (€2.5 million), and (2) a track record of at least two years. In addition, issuers on the second-tier market are obliged to hire a sponsor. The sponsor shall guide and counsel the issuer for a period no less than two years. It is also common for issuers on the second-tier market to be subject to stringent lock-up requirements. Since the second-tier market of the Amsterdam Stock Exchange is a non-regulated market according to EU definitions, the market is subject to less stringent requirements. As a result, financial statements need not necessarily follow IFRS, and issuers are neither subject to the Law on Disclosure of Major Holdings (*Wet Melding Zeggenschap*) nor the Dutch corporate governance code. Further, ongoing disclosure requirements are similar to those of the first-tier market. It is, however, explicitly stated in the formal listing rules that the issuer shall disclose transactions that lead to changes in the capital or voting rights whenever the threshold of 50 percent or 95 percent is passed (in both directions).

Dutch IPO activity between 2006 and 2008

In the period 2006–8 a total of only nineteen Dutch companies went public. Of these nineteen firms six chose to seek a listing on Euronext Amsterdam. The other firms were listed on the London Stock Exchange (seven on the AIM and two on the Official List), Warsaw Stock Exchange (two), NYSE (one), and NASDAQ (one). This section analyzes sixteen of the nineteen Dutch IPOs in the period 2006–8. We exclude three companies, in particular Plaza Centers, Polymer Logistics, and Pan European Hotel Acquisition Company, because we lack sufficient data for the first two companies and because the latter company is an investment fund. We also ignore listings on the secondary market of the Amsterdam Stock Exchange, Alternext, for lacking sufficient data. As of the start of Alternext Amsterdam in November 2006, only two companies have been listed on this market, The Member Company and Koninklijke Reesink.[3]

Table 13.4 shows that ten companies in the sample went public in 2006, five in 2007, and only one went public in 2008. The table distinguishes between Dutch firms that went public on the Amsterdam Stock Exchange (ASE) and Dutch firms that went public on other

[3] Koninklijke Reesink was first listed on Euronext Amsterdam.

Table 13.4 *IPO year and industry classification*

Industry	2006 ASE	2006 other	2007 ASE	2007 other	2008 ASE	2008 other	Total
Consumer goods	0	1	0	0	0	0	1
Consumer services	0	2	0	0	0	0	2
Financials	1	2	0	1	0	0	4
Healthcare	1	0	1	2	0	0	4
Industrials	1	1	1	0	0	0	3
Oil and gas	0	1	0	0	0	0	1
Basic materials	0	0	0	0	0	1	1
Total	3	7	2	3	0	1	16

markets. Strikingly, the Amsterdam Stock Exchange was not the main venue for Dutch IPOs, at least not in the period 2006–8. The decrease in the number of Dutch IPOs through the years 2006–8 coincided with the occurrence of the worldwide financial crisis. Table 13.4 further shows that of the relatively few Dutch IPOs in the period 2006–8, most were from the industries financials and healthcare (both four).

As is typical for the continental European public stock exchanges, the average age of IPOs is normally higher than that of the Anglo-Saxon countries. The average age of the IPOs in our sample is sixteen years, whereas the median is nine. The age of the IPOs ranges from one to eighty-seven. The age of the Dutch IPOs in the period 2006–8 was relatively low for a continental European stock market. Compare, for example, Italy where the average IPO-year was thirty-six years.

The average Dutch IPO between 2006 and 2008 had 2,872 employees, generated revenues of $544 million, and had total assets of $6.1 billion, as Table 13.5 shows. There were a few very large IPOs in the period that we analyze. For example, the largest IPO in terms of revenues and total assets was SNS Reaal, a large Dutch financial services group. The second largest IPO was New World Resources, a leading hard coal and coke producer, with revenues of $2.1 billion and total assets of $3.1 billion. The smallest company in the sample in terms of revenues was AMT Holding, a biotechnology firm. It had revenues of nearly $0.6 million, by far the lowest revenues of all IPOs

Table 13.5 *IPO size and performance*

	Size			Performance		
	Employees	Revenues ($)	Assets ($)	ROA	ROE	ROS
Min	2	572,821	4,955,326	−27%	−41%	−13,577%
1st quartile	92	11,450,127	61,557,636	1%	9%	3%
2nd quartile	486	53,219,630	155,935,000	5%	14%	9%
3rd quartile	3,792	264,940,844	1,042,818,920	9%	24%	20%
Max	18,360	4,468,668,000	87,431,800,800	16%	54%	376%
Average	2,872	544,474,726	6,134,671,561	2%	11%	−881%

in the sample. Accounting performance measures of the sample companies ranged from −27 percent to 16 percent for ROA and −41 percent to 54 percent for ROE, with averages of 2 percent for ROA and 11 percent for ROE. Sales margins (ROS) showed an extreme performance picture. The (extreme) minimum values for the three performance measures were for Octoplus (ROA and ROE) and AMT Holding (ROS), the only two biotechnology firms from the sample. The value for ROS was, of course, unrealistically low. Leaving out the performance measures for both Octoplus and AMT Holding the average performance measures become 6 percent, 18 percent, and 39 percent for ROA, ROE, and ROS, respectively. Together with Octoplus and AMT Holding, Eurand, a pharmaceutical company, also reports negative performances for all three measures. The other firms, thus, were all profitable according to the most common accounting performance measures, where New World Resources was the most profitable in terms of both ROA and ROE.

We lack the data to report meaningfully about the nature of largest shareholders before and after the IPO. Statistics of the data we have about ownership structure of the IPOs in our sample are reported in Table 13.6. We have data on the stake of venture capitalists and private equity funds. It is not surprising that venture capitalists held a minor stake in the IPO and that this stake did not change substantially directly after the IPO. Note that this information is derived from only a few cases. Further note that the majority of major shareholders of the IPOs in our sample held a majority stake in the company after the IPO. The median value of the stake of the major shareholder after the IPO exceeds 50 percent. The results show clearly that the

Table 13.6 *IPO ownership structure (data in percent)*

	Family		Bank		Govt.		VC		Angels		Top 1		Top 3	
	pre	post	pre	post	pre	post	pre	post	pre	post	pre	post	pre	post
Min	–	–	–	–	–	–	9	5	–	–	24	13	53	40
1st quartile	–	–	–	–	–	–	12	12	–	–	39	23	65	48
2nd quartile	–	–	–	–	–	–	19	15	–	–	86	54	86	52
3rd quartile	–	–	–	–	–	–	30	38	–	–	96	69	98	68
Max	–	–	–	–	–	–	46	39	–	–	100	77	100	84
Average	–	–	–	–	–	–	23	22	–	–	70	48	82	58
No. of cases	–	–	–	–	–	–	4	5	–	–	16	12	9	7

Table 13.7 *IPO board of directors*

	Size	Executive directors	Non-executive directors	Independent directors	Engineering, operations, R&D	Marketing, sales	Finance, accounting, law
Min	5	0	2	1	0	0	0
1st quartile	6	3	4	2	0	0	2
2nd quartile	9	4	5	3	0	0	3
3rd quartile	10	4	6	4	1	0	5
Max	20	11	9	8	3	2	7
Average	9.1	4.2	4.9	3.4	0.6	0.3	3.4

largest shareholders tend to retain control over the IPO companies in our sample. This ownership issue is supported by the fact that seven out of sixteen companies in our sample issued limited voting shares at the time of the IPO.

Table 13.7 shows that the boards of directors of the IPO companies in our sample had on average 9.1 directors, of which 4.2 are executive directors. On all boards 3.4 of the directors were independent on average. There were few female directors, only four in total, and nine of the boards have one or more foreigners on them. Only one of the companies has an employee representative on its board (SNS Reaal). The data on the functional background of the boards show that 3.4 directors on average had a background in support activities (finance, accounting, or law), and less than one director had a background in primary activities (engineering, operations, or research and development) or marketing or sales. Most of the corporations (fifteen) had an audit committee, of which the majority (twelve) also had a remuneration and a nomination committee. Only one company had created a governance committee (Eurand).

The description of an IPO: SNS Reaal

The firm before the IPO

SNS Reaal is a large Dutch financial services group. Its two main divisions are SNS Bank, primarily a retail bank, and Reaal Verzekeringen, an insurance company. It was founded in 1997 at the time of the merger between the SNS Groep and the Reaal Groep. In view of the relatively large financial services sector in the Netherlands, SNS Reaal can be considered a representative Dutch IPO. SNS Reaal obtained a listing on Euronext Amsterdam in 2006. In the year before the IPO it had revenues totaling €3,471 million ($4,656 million) and a net profit of €323 million ($433 million). Before July 27, 2005 all ordinary shares of SNS Reaal were owned by a foundation called *Stichting Administratiekantoor* SNS Reaal. This foundation issued non-voting shares (depositary receipts). In accordance with good governance practices in the Netherlands, this certification of the ordinary shares was abandoned after July 27, 2005.

The board of SNS Reaal consisted of eleven directors, of which four were executive directors (the management board), and three supervisory board members could be considered independent. The supervisory board created three separate committees: an audit, remuneration, and nomination committee. None of the directors held shares in the company.

The offer

The public offering of shares in SNS Reaal was executed in May 2006. It offered initially 70 million shares, of which 25.5 million were new shares, at a price range between €16 and €18.5. In the end, and after fully exercising the over-allotment option, SNS Reaal sold a total of 80.5 million shares at a price of €17, generating a total amount of €1.4 billion ($1.8 billion).

The firm after the IPO

As a result of the IPO the percentage of shares held by SNS Reaal declined from 100 percent to 65.5 percent. Hence, 34.5 percent of the shares float freely after the IPO. Nevertheless, SNS Reaal can still be classified as having a very concentrated ownership structure. By going public the company aimed at increasing awareness of its brands and the flexibility of its financing opportunities. According to the prospectus the proceeds of the IPO were used to fulfill the general goals of the corporation. Shortly after the IPO, SNS Reaal realized the takeover of two smaller financial institutions, Regio Bank and Bouwfonds Property Finance. After the IPO the board composition more or less stayed the same, and similar for executive compensation after the public offering.

Conclusion

Dutch corporate governance has undergone major changes in the last decade. The compliance with the Dutch governance code as well as the reform act in 2002 and 2004 have increased transparency in financial reporting, have eroded to some extent the so-called old boys network of Dutch supervisory board members, and shifted the power balance in favor of the shareholders. Nevertheless, partly due to weak investor protection, management control and in particular supervisory board control is still omnipresent in the Netherlands. The issue and the update of the Dutch corporate governance code have contributed to enforcement of good governance in the Netherlands. Given the importance of (supervisory) boards in good governance, the Dutch corporate governance code has in particular affected the evolution of the characteristics of the board of directors of Dutch companies. Dutch corporations are to a large extent owned by institutional investors; the blue chip companies are majority foreign owned. Despite increased transparency and accountability, anti-director rights still effectively limit control rights of Dutch shareholders. The presence of anti-director rights may to some extent explain the relatively low popularity of stock markets as a source of funding of Dutch corporations. Notwithstanding this, the corporate governance of the largest listed companies is characterized by a high protection of investors' rights, and board of directors' characteristics are – at least formally – very similar to the best practices at international level.

Apart from the ownership of the largest corporations, the ownership structure of the smaller Dutch listed companies is still rather concentrated, in line with major continental European corporations. It can be concluded that ownership concentration has been increasing in the Netherlands in the period 2002–6, while it should also be acknowledged that it was much higher in the 1990s. The median blockholder does not have a controlling share (>15 percent) in Dutch corporations even though the largest blockholders generally have controlling blocks. The Dutch stock exchange, Euronext Amsterdam, does not play a relevant role in the national economy as a source of funds. The median Dutch corporation is funded by internal funds and bank loans. To go public has not been, in fact, a very popular decision for Dutch companies. In the three years here investigated, only nineteen companies decided to go public, the majority of them not in Amsterdam but in London, on the London Stock Exchange – the Alternative Investment Market.

The characteristics of the IPO corporations are by and large similar to already listed companies: (1) they operate in industrial and consumer goods and financial sectors; (2) the ownership structure, after the IPO, is still relatively concentrated; (3) the involvement of venture capital and private equity is limited before and after the IPO, and business angels are absent; and (4) their boards of directors have an average of about nine directors, more or less evenly split between the executives and non-executives. The median age of the corporations is relatively low, i.e., nine years. Finally, the low IPO activity in the Netherlands may have been the effect of the recent financial crisis; nevertheless, the low number of IPOs in Amsterdam is also partly explained by the relatively low popularity of Euronext Amsterdam as the preferred exchange to go public.

References

Cools, Kees and Mirjam van Praag. 2007. 'The value of top executive departures: Evidence from the Netherlands', *Journal of Corporate Finance* 13, 721–42.

De Jong, Abe, Douglas V. DeJong, Gerard Mertens, and Charles E. Wasley. 2005. 'The role of self-regulation in corporate governance: Evidence and implications from the Netherlands', *Journal of Corporate Finance* 11, 473–503.

De Jong, Abe, Rezoul Kabir, Teye Marra, and Ailsa Röell. 2001. 'Ownership and control in the Netherlands', in F. Barca and M. Becht (eds.), *The Control of Corporate Europe*. Oxford University Press, 188–206.

De Jong, Abe, Gerard Mertens, and Peter Roosenboom. 2006. 'Shareholders' voting at general meetings: Evidence from the Netherlands', *Journal of Management and Governance* 10, 353–80.

De Jong, Abe, Gerard Mertens, Hans van Oosterhout, and Hélène M. Vletter-van Dort. 2007. *Substance or Symbolism? Corporate Governance of Institutional Investors*. Rotterdam: RSM/Erasmus University.

De Jong, Abe and Ailsa Roëll. 2005. 'Financing and control in the Netherlands: A historical perspective', in R.K. Morck (ed.), *A History of Corporate Governance Around the World*. University of Chicago Press, 467–506.

De Jong, Abe and Peter Roosenboom. 2002. 'De praktijk sinds 1997', in *Corporate Governance in Nederland 2002 – De Stand van Zaken*. Amsterdam: NCGS.

Ellis, Casper. 2008. *Do Shareholders Influence Executive Compensation?* Unpublished MSc thesis, University of Groningen.

Fama, Eugene F. and Michael Jensen. 1983. 'The separation of ownership and control', *Journal of Law and Economics* 26, 301–25.

Frentrop, Paul. 2002. *Ondernemingen en hun aandeelhouders sinds de VOC: Corporate governance 1602–2002*. Amsterdam: Prometheus.

Goncharov, Igor, Jörg R. Werner, and Jochen Zimmermann. 2006. 'Does compliance with the German Corporate Governance Code have an impact on stock valuation? An empirical analysis', *Corporate Governance: An International Review* 14, 432–45.

Groenewald, Edo. 2005. 'Corporate governance in the Netherlands: From the Verdam Report of 1964 to the Tabaksblat Code of 2003', *European Business Organization Law Review* 6, 291–311.

Hermes, Niels, Theo Postma, and Orestis Zivkov. 2006. 'Corporate governance codes in the European Union: Are they driven by external or domestic forces?', *International Journal of Managerial Finance* 2, 280–301.

Hooghiemstra, Reggy and Jaap Van Manen. 2004. 'Non-executive directors in the Netherlands: Another expectations gap?', *Accounting and Business Research* 34, 25–42.

Kabir, Rezaul, Dolf Cantrijn, and Andreas Jeunink. 1997. 'Takeover defenses, ownership structure and stock returns in the Netherlands: An empirical analysis', *Strategic Management Journal* 18, 97–109.

La Porta, Rafael, Florencio Lopez-de-Silanes, Andrei Shleifer, and Robert Vishny. 1998. 'Law and finance', *Journal of Political Economy* 106, 1113–55.

Maassen, Gregory F. and Frans A.J. van den Bosch. 1999. 'On the supposed independence of two-tier boards: Formal structure and reality in the Netherlands', *Corporate Governance: An International Review* 7, 31–7.

MacNeil, Iain and Xiao, Li. 2006. 'Comply or explain: Market discipline and non-compliance with the Combined Code', *Corporate Governance: An International Journal* 14, 486–96.

Moerland, Pieter W. 2002. 'Complete separation of ownership and control: The structure-regime and other defensive mechanisms in the Netherlands', in Joseph A. McCahery, Pieter W. Moerland, Theo Raaijmakers, and Luc Renneboog (eds.), *Corporate Governance Regimes: Convergence and Diversity.* Oxford University Press, 287–96.

Peters Committee. 1997. *Corporate Governance in the Netherlands: Forty Recommendations.* The Hague, available at www.ecgi.org.

Schuit, Steven R. and Barbara Bier. 2002. *Corporate Law and Practice of the Netherlands.* The Hague: Kluwer Law International.

Tabaksblat Committee. 2003. *The Dutch Corporate Governance Code. Principles of Good Corporate Governance and Best Practice Provisions.* The Hague, available at www.ecgi.org.

Van der Elst, Christof F., Abe de Jong, and Theo Raaijmakers. 2007. *Een overzicht van juridische en economische dimensies van de kwetsbaarheid van Nederlandse beursvennootschappen.* Onderzoeksrapport ten behoeve van de SER-commissie Evenwichtig Ondernemingsbestuur.

Van der Laan, Gerwin, Peter-Jan Engelen, and Annette Van Den Berg. 2010. *Samenstelling en functioneren van de raden van commissarissen van Nederlandse beursgenoteerde vennootschappen in 2009.* Onderzoeksrapport ten behoeve van de Monitoringscommissie Nederlandse corporate governance code.

Van Ees, Hans, Theo J.B.M. Postma, and Elmer Sterken. 2003. 'Board characteristics and corporate performance in the Netherlands', *Eastern Economic Journal* 29, 41–58.

Van Ees, Hans, Gerwin Van der Laan, Eric P. Engesaeth, and Camiel Selker. 2007. *De relatie tussen de bezoldiging van bestuurders van beursgenoteerde ondernemingen en de prestaties van deze ondernemingen.* Onderzoeksrapport ten behoeve van de Monitoringscommissie Nederlandse corporate governance code.

Von Werder, Axel, Till Talaulicar, and Georg L. Kolat. 2005. 'Compliance with the German corporate governance code: An empirical analysis of the compliance statements by German listed companies', *Corporate Governance: An International Review* 13, 178–87.

Voogsgeerd, Herman H. 2006. *Corporate Governance Codes: Markt- of Rechtsarrangement.* Deventer: Kluwer.

Wymeersch, Eddy. 2005. 'Implementation of corporate governance codes', in Klaus J. Hopt, Eddy Wymeersch, Hideka Kanda, and Harald Baum (eds.), *Corporate Governance in Context: Corporations, States and Markets in Europe, Japan, and the US.* Oxford University Press, 403–19.

14 | Corporate governance and initial public offerings in Nigeria

EMMANUEL AFOLABI ADEGBITE

Introduction

Corporate scandals around the world continue to reiterate the importance of sound corporate governance principles and practices for the health and vitality of the world economy. Consequently, corporate governance research has experienced a significant growth in the past two decades. However, in comparison with frequently studied countries such as the UK and the USA, less is known with regards to corporate governance developments in sub-Saharan Africa. Furthermore, whilst IPOs provide a unique context to study corporate governance and its development around the world as governance issues of IPOs are relatively unexamined compared to more established (larger) firms, the corporate governance of IPOs in sub-Saharan Africa (and Nigeria in particular) has received almost no scholarly attention. This chapter anticipates addressing these gaps, by contributing "a sub-Saharan African data-based perspective" to this book's overall attempt to better understand how corporate governance influences newly listed firms in a multinational context. This chapter's discussions are in the following order. First the national institutional environment is examined by analyzing the state of corporate governance in Nigeria and by providing an overview of the regulatory infrastructure, which includes relevant references to the system of corporate law and the code of corporate governance. Second the IPO environment in Nigeria is discussed with a particular focus on the IPO activity between 2006 and 2008. Here, discussions cover the regulatory environment for IPOs as well as the generic (e.g., size, industry, ownership) and governance characteristics of the IPO firms. Furthermore, a case study of Dangote Flour Plc, before and after the IPO, is inculcated to enrich discussions. Lastly, some conclusions are presented.

Corporate governance mechanisms

Nigeria received independence from Britain in 1960 and became a republic in 1963, comprising a British-defined democratic federal constitution that reflected three major geographical/tribal characters of the country which are the Northern Hausa, Western Yoruba and Eastern Igbo (Adegbite, 2010). Despite the colonial British influence, Nigeria characteristically has a rich cultural diversity, unified by a highly collectivistic social culture, as against individualistic Britain. Consequently, Nigeria is socially cohesive. The Nigerian law is based on a British-defined common law, precedents and local statute, where the laws in England further operate as a persuasive authority to complement the Nigerian law where there is a lacuna in the latter (Adegbite, 2010, 2012; Insol, 2008). Whilst the received common law legal system should maximize the role of the marketplace in sorting out economic affairs and constrain the role of the state, the Nigerian government has conventionally been prominent in the private sector, and the market for corporate control has traditionally been non-robust. However, following sustained democracy since 1999, viable corporate governance mechanisms have been developing in Nigeria. For example the recent resuscitation of the Nigerian Stock Exchange and the subsequent escalation in the volume of daily trading activities have further brought to the fore the need to ensure that mechanisms are in place to ensure honesty and transparency in the custody of investors' wealth (Adegbite, 2010). There has also been a renewed governmental desire to attract more domestic and foreign investments in order to strengthen the country's economy; thus major governmental policies and initiatives have since developed to promote transparency in corporate financial disclosure (which is considerably opaque), encourage boards' accountability and independence, and check managerial and board corruption (Adegbite, 2010, 2012).

A voluntary corporate governance code applies to all listed firms in Nigeria, while banks have to meet the extra requirements of a mandatory code. Business groups seem to be playing an increasing role in corporate governance. Corporate ownership in most firms is still relatively non-fragmented/concentrated. The foundation of most businesses in Nigeria is the family, and the overbearing influence of the family owner has been sustained in

Nigeria (Adegbite, 2010). Institutional shareholders are presently
playing limited roles in the ownership structure of Nigerian firms
when compared to individual and family blockholders. Although
minority ownership rights are well protected by law, majority shareholders have traditionally stifled firms in their interest (and at the
expense of minority shareholders); hence the recent increase in
shareholder activism for minority owners. Corporate boards are
always single tier in nature and it is becoming uncommon to have
the CEO chairing the board, especially in listed firms. Except in the
financial services industry, which has a non-egalitarian nature of
executive compensation, there is still not yet a strong performance-
related executive compensation culture in the country (Adegbite,
2010).

The state of corporate governance in Nigeria

Nigeria inherited the British corporate governance system, as issues
relating to the conduct and governance of Nigerian corporations,
which are contained within the provisions of the company legislation, have their roots in the country's colonial past (Adegbite and
Nakajima, 2011a, 2011b; Okike, 2007). Although there have been
several company law reforms over the years following independence
in 1960, the legal system of corporate governance in Nigeria has
remained fashioned along the Anglo-Saxon (UK) model (Adegbite,
2010). Whilst this may suggest that corporate governance practices
in Nigeria should bear some resemblance with those of the UK,
there is a growing doubt that this inherited corporate governance
system is complementary, reflective and tackles the challenges
peculiar to Nigeria's business climate (Adegbite, 2010). Indeed,
this system, operating in the context of weak market institutions
and corruption, has resulted in a bogus and uncompetitive corporate governance system with traditionally limited challenge to management's running of corporate enterprises and lax regulatory
enforcement in matters of corporate governance and accountability (Adegbite, 2010; Adegbite and Nakajima, 2011b; Ahunwan,
2002; Yakasai, 2001). The Nigerian governance environment
has thus been littered with several failures, including a considerable
number of high-profile and often inconceivable frauds which

have been perpetrated by managers and directors of listed corporations (Adegbite, 2010). For example, the 2008–10 banking crisis[1] in the country is an indication of the predominantly bogus state of governance and accountability across all sectors of corporate Nigeria. Recently passed examples of other corporate governance failures include the Cadbury Nigeria scandal of 2007, the Halliburton scandal of 2008, the Siemens scandal of 2009, and the 2009/2010 Nigerian banking industry scandal (Adegbite and Nakajima, 2011b).

Indeed corporate governance matters in sub-Saharan Africa are rarely discussed without reference to corruption, which has been a hindrance to socio-economic and political development in the region. Good corporate governance and accountability is thus gradually being seen by African corporate and capital markets regulators as one of the most effective tools to minimize corporate corruption (Mensah, Aboagye, Addo et al., 2003). However, whilst issues relating to corporate governance and investor protection are imperative to Nigeria's economic development and prosperity (Yakasai, 2001), the relevance of a corporate governance theory has traditionally been in doubt due to the traditionally undeveloped nature of the Nigerian economy as well as Nigeria's inheritance of an Anglo-Saxon defined framework of corporate governance (Adegbite, 2010; Adegbite and Nakajima, 2011b; Yakasai, 2001). Given that Nigeria's cultural setting/dominant ideology remains largely stakeholder oriented, there evolved a distorted theoretical frame for corporate governance in the country, with agency and stakeholder theories being prominent in shaping the Nigerian corporate governance system (Adegbite, 2010). In relation, despite globalization pressures, the development of corporate governance systems in sub-Saharan Africa is subject to both foreign influences and local underlying national conditions, such as the political, economic, legal and social environments as well as firm/industry values, culture, ethics and history (Adegbite and Nakajima, 2011a, 2011b).

---

[1] The 2008–10 banking crisis in the country has been largely attributed to significant corporate governance failures and corruption; indeed the Central Bank of Nigeria (CBN) under its new leadership has recently dismissed the chief executive officers and executive directors of eight major Nigerian banks for bad corporate governance and fraud (Adegbite, 2010).

The regulatory environment of corporate governance in Nigeria

The legal climate

The primary statute for corporate governance (and for shareholders to intervene in a company's affairs) in Nigeria is the Company and Allied Matters Act (CAMA) 1990 (as amended), which became law on January 2, 1990. The CAMA is an act which established the Corporate Affairs Commission (CAC), to provide for the incorporation of companies and incidental matters, as well as the registration of business names and the incorporation of trustees of certain communities, bodies and associations. The following paragraph presents some of the specific provisions in the CAMA which relate to corporate governance, including the laws that pertain to the directors' duties, disclosure requirements and executive compensation.

Every company shall have at least two directors. The members at the annual general meeting shall have power to re-elect or reject directors and appoint new ones. The board of directors shall have power to appoint new directors to fill any casual vacancy arising out of death, resignation, retirement or removal. The shareholding qualification for directors may be fixed by the articles of association of the company and unless and until so fixed no shareholding qualification shall be required. A company may by ordinary resolution remove a director before the expiration of his period of office, notwithstanding anything in its articles or in any agreement between it and him. The remuneration of the directors shall from time to time be determined by the company in a general meeting and such remuneration shall be deemed to accrue from day to day. A director shall act at all times in what he believes to be the best interests of the company as a whole so as to preserve its assets, further its business and promote the purposes for which it was formed, and in such manner as a faithful, diligent, careful and ordinarily skillful director would act in the circumstances. Accounting records shall be sufficient to show and explain the transactions of the company. Every officer of the company who is in default shall be guilty of an offense unless he shows that he acted honestly and that in the circumstances in which the business of the company was carried on, the default was excusable. A person guilty of an offense under this section shall be liable to imprisonment for a term not exceeding six months or to a fine of N500[2] ($3.3).

The aforementioned provisions further show that the Nigerian company law has historically been strongly influenced by the UK, where shareholders have, in principle, enjoyed similar legal rights as shareholders in the dominant Anglo-Saxon economies (Adegbite, 2010; Ahunwan, 2002). However, what is lacking in Nigeria is an effective judicial system to enforce these rights, which has traditionally increased the costs of contracting as well as making business activities much more risky ventures (Adegbite, 2010, 2012; Ahunwan, 2002; La Porta, 1998). Despite recent attempts to review CAMA, one of the caveats of the law has traditionally been its deterrent capacity, where penalties for offenders/law breakers have generally been between N25 ($0.17) to about N500 ($3.3) (Adegbite, 2012). As a result, a number of independent organizations have been mandated to pursue effective corporate governance regulation, with specific regulatory initiatives deployed in recent times to confront some of the impediments to good corporate governance in Nigeria (Adegbite, 2012). The following examines the roles of these key regulators.

The Corporate Affairs Commission

The Corporate Affairs Commission (CAC) was established by the Companies and Allied Matters Act (CAMA), which was promulgated in 1990, and works with the Securities and Exchange Commission (SEC) to regulate corporate governance. The chairs and chief executive officers of both commissions are appointed by the Nigerian president. The CAC is a governmental agency which regulates the formation, management and winding up of companies in Nigeria; it administers CAMA and has primary responsibilities for corporate governance (Adegbite, 2012). The ROSC noted that the CAC has neither an effective mechanism nor enough capacity to monitor and enforce requirements for accounting and financial reporting, and further highlighted the following shortcomings (ROSC, 2004: 8): (1) there is no rigorous enforcement of timely filing of the audited financial statements and directors' report with the CAC; (2) financial statements of non-listed public and private companies are not

---

[2] As at December 21, 2010, N1 is equivalent to $0.006585.

readily available; (3) most companies do not comply with the filing requirements, and sanctions are not applied; (4) there are significant weaknesses in the enforcement mechanism, worsened by endemic corruption and poor record-keeping by the CAC; (5) whilst CAMA requires that the audit committee review audit financial statements and report to the shareholders. However, authorities and others have not assessed the effectiveness of audit committees, making their capacity to monitor unknown.

The Securities and Exchange Commission

The SEC is the apex regulator of the Nigerian capital market and has the objective of developing and regulating a dynamic, fair, transparent and efficient capital market, in order to promote Nigeria's economic development (Adegbite, 2012). The Investments and Securities Act (ISA) of 1999 required the SEC to regulate the capital market with a view to protecting the interest of all investors in the market and to develop the capital market in order to enhance its efficiency. The SEC aims to be Africa's leading capital market regulator and has a board of eight members including the chairman, the director general, three executive commissioners and representatives from the Federal Ministry of Finance and Central Bank of Nigeria (Adegbite, 2010). The SEC regulates the following: the issuance of securities, capital market institutions, and the activities of capital market operators, through pre-registration requirements, rule making, inspection, surveillance, investigation and enforcement (Adegbite, 2010, 2012). Whilst the SEC acts as the guardian of the ordinary shareholder (Adegbite, 2012), the ROSC (2004: 8–9) report highlighted the following challenges that confront the SEC: (1) the SEC is not yet effective in monitoring compliance with financial reporting requirements and enforcing actions against violators; (2) its capacity to effectively monitor compliance with accounting standards is inadequate, but it is currently under reorganization; (3) its enforcement is weak, and administrative sanctions and civil penalties are not adequate to deter non-compliance.

The Nigerian Stock Exchange

One of the key reasons why the academic field of corporate governance in Nigeria is at a developmental stage is because the viable institutional machineries for effective corporate governance are still evolving (Adegbite, 2010). For example, whilst the stock exchange plays a crucial role in the mobilization of new capital in countries where it is established, the Nigerian Stock Exchange (NSE) has traditionally been a non-stock exchange-based financial system, such that Nigerian corporations have conventionally not seen the exchange as a means of raising new capital (Adegbite, 2010; Demirag, 1998; Okike, 2007). Indeed, whilst the NSE remains one of the biggest equities markets in Africa, it houses only around 300 companies (NSE, 2010). Habitually, this impeded the ability of the stock market to act as a market for corporate control and accountability (Adegbite, 2010).

The economic reform agenda embarked upon in 2004 by the Nigerian government led to the revival of the NSE; subsequently, the total market value of securities listed on the exchange has risen from N2.9 trillion ($19.25 billion) at year end 2005 to N9.56 trillion ($63.46 billion) at year end 2008 (NSE, 2006, 2009). The NSE is self-regulatory and supports the SEC in the supervision of securities market operations by exercising a certain degree of control through its financial reporting and disclosures rules, which apply to listed companies. Given that the roles of the NSE and the SEC are intertwined, the ROSC (2004) findings indicate that there are occasional conflicts of powers with respect to disciplining errant firms (Adegbite, 2010), which renders the disciplining capacity of the NSE ineffective. Okike (2007) further noted that whilst the NSE monitors compliance with the financial reporting requirements of listed companies on behalf of the SEC, the occasional conflicts between the SEC and the NSE require a revision of legislation to ensure clarity with regard to the roles and powers of these two institutions (Adegbite, 2012).

Code of Corporate Governance in Nigeria

The 2003 Code of Corporate Governance in Nigeria was developed with adequate input from relevant stakeholders, including members of professional organizations, the organized private sector and relevant regulatory agencies. The code was the first code of corporate governance in Nigeria and its development is connected to global inclinations towards corporate governance regulation, and in particular the need to prevent corporate scandals (Adegbite, 2012). Given that emerging markets are characteristic of very rapid and dynamic economic developments, corporate governance codes may require frequent revisions to reflect new economic conditions (Adegbite, 2010). As a result, on September 30, 2009, the SEC published a revised version of the code (draft copy), following consultations with key regulatory bodies, to further position itself to address the enforcement challenges contained in the 2003 Code (Adegbite, 2012). The revised code is due to be released on April 1, 2011 (Adegbite, 2012). Accordingly, unlike the previous code, the new code states that its provisions are intended to be fully enforceable by the SEC, in order to ensure the highest standards of transparency, accountability and good corporate governance in public companies, without unduly inhibiting enterprise and innovation (Adegbite, 2012).

According to the revised code, which is not intended as a rigid set of rules, the responsibility for ensuring compliance with or observance of the principles and provisions of the code is primarily with the board of directors. The code further states that whenever the SEC determines that a company or entity required to comply with or observe the principles or provisions of this code is in breach, the SEC shall notify the company or entity concerned specifying the areas of non-compliance or non-observance and the specific action or actions needed to remedy the non-compliance or non-observance. The code maintains that the principal objective of the board is to ensure that the company is properly managed, while it is the responsibility of the board to oversee the effective performance of the management in order to protect and enhance shareholder value and to meet the company's obligations to its employees and other stakeholders. According to the code, membership of the board should not be less than five and should not exceed fifteen persons, and the board should comprise a mix of executive and non-executive directors (headed by a chairman), where the majority of board members should be non-executive directors, with at least one that is an independent director. For all public companies with listed securities, the code maintains that positions of the chairman of the board and chief executive officer shall be separate and held by different individuals, and as far as practicable the chairman of the board should be a non-executive director.

The code prescribes that the remuneration of the CEO/MD should comprise a component that is long-term performance related and may include stock options and bonuses, which should be disclosed in the company's annual reports. Also, the code states that executive directors should not be involved in the determination of their remuneration, and companies should develop a comprehensive policy on remuneration which should be sufficient to attract, motivate and retain skilled and qualified persons needed to run the company successfully. In relation to board committees, the chairman of the board should not be a member of any committee, and only directors should be members of board committees; however, senior management may be in attendance. To effectively perform its oversight function and monitor management's performance, the code recommends that the board should meet at least once every quarter and that every director should be required to attend at least two-thirds of all board meetings. The code further requires the board to develop a written, clearly defined, formal and transparent procedure for appointment to the board of directors, and should also establish a system to undertake a formal and rigorous annual evaluation of its own performance, that of its committees, the chairman and individual directors; in doing this, the board may engage the services of external consultants.

Other relevant recommendations of the code include the following: the general meetings of the company should be the primary avenue for meetings and interaction between the shareholders, management and board; companies should pay adequate attention to the interests of its stakeholders such as its employees, host community, the consumers and the general public; public companies should demonstrate sensitivity to Nigeria's social and cultural diversity and should as much as possible promote strategic national interests as well as national ethos and values without compromising global aspirations where applicable; and companies should recognize corruption as a major threat to business and to national development and therefore as a sustainability issue for businesses in Nigeria. The code further recommends the following: the board should report annually on the nature and extent of its social, ethical, safety, health and environmental policies and practices; at least one board member of the audit committee should be financially literate; all companies should have an effective risk-based internal audit function and companies should have a whistle-blowing policy which should be known to employees, stakeholders such as contractors, shareholders, job applicants, and the general public; the CEO and the head of finance function of every public company should in a written statement to the board certify that the financial statements present a true and fair view of the affairs of the company; and the annual report should contain a statement from the board with regard to the company's degree of compliance with the provisions of this code.

Ownership characteristics of listed companies

Nigeria adopted a post-independent economic development strategy to limit foreign ownership and foster domestic ownership and control in principal areas of the country's economy, particularly the "oil and gas" and the "science and technology" sectors. As a result, the Foreign Exchange Control Act (FX Act) and the Nigerian Enterprises Promotion Decree (NEPD) were enacted in 1962 and 1972 respectively. Whilst government's intentions were not fully accomplished, as there were cases of Nigerians fronting for foreigners in order to satisfy the ownership requirements, the government's economic liberation strategy shaped the corporate ownership structure of modern Nigerian corporations (Achebe, 1989; Adegbite, 2010).

The following are groupings of the ownership structure of Nigerian corporations, as adapted from Ahunwan (2002: 271–2). Group A is composed of corporations wholly owned by government. Both the federal government and state governments operate wholly owned corporations, including major petroleum refineries and petrochemical plants. Group B comprises joint venture arrangements between the federal government and foreign crude oil producing corporations. A key indicator of the importance of this sector is the fact that the government of Nigeria derives about 97 percent of its total revenue from joint ventures in oil and gas. Group C consists of publicly listed corporations. Here foreign investors have traditionally operated with local investors in the industrial and commercial sector, where the foreign investors are mostly subsidiaries of multinational enterprises, and hold majority stakes. However, many public companies are now solely indigenously owned, across various sectors of the economy, including banking, insurance and manufacturing amongst others. This group constitutes the majority of public companies. Table 14.1 shows some Group B and C companies and their shareholding structure. Group D consists of privately owned corporations that are not listed on the stock market. Most of these are family owned and are small companies, owned and operated by families and friends and lacking

Table 14.1 *Some Group B and C companies and their shareholding structure*

Category	Name of company	Shareholding structure (%)	
		Foreign	Government
B	Shell Petroleum Nig Ltd	45	55
	Chevron Nigeria Ltd	40	60
	Mobil Producing Nig Ltd	40	60
	Nigeria Agip Oil Ltd	40	60
	Elf Nig Ltd	40	60
		Foreign	Others
C	Nigeria Breweries	41.67	58.33
	Guinness Nigeria Plc	42.21	57.77
	Nestle Foods Nigeria Plc	56.90	43
	Mobil Oil Nigeria Plc	60	40
	Total Nigeria Plc	60	40

Source: adapted from Ahunwan (2002: 272–3)

business sophistication. Some of these enterprises, however, are quite large, with a capital base comparable to many listed corporations.

Whilst corporate governance in the Anglo-Saxon context has generally been discussed in terms of aligning management's (agents') interests with that of shareholders (principals), the above classifications suggest that the principal–agent problem has traditionally been less pronounced in Nigeria, as often times many companies have their principal shareholders or their appointees involved in the daily running of the company (Adegbite, 2010). Historically the need to protect the "passive outsider owner" has thus been less important in the Nigerian context (Adegbite, 2010). Given that significant block ownership concentrates too much power on few individuals, corporate governance regulatory reforms, as well as the need to access capital in an increasingly competitive market, have led to some dilution of traditional block/family stocks (Adegbite, 2010). Nevertheless, a major agency conflict in Nigeria has largely been between majority and minority shareholders, where the former have one-stop access to relevant information with regard to the financial state of companies, and are thus able to drive firms in ways which

Table 14.2 *Statistical summary of market performance from 2005 to 2008*

	2005	2006	2007	2008
Market capitalization (billion)	$22.48	$40.32	$105.65	$80.6
The NSE all-share index	24,085.76	33,189.30	57,990.22	31,450.78
Total turnover volume (billion shares)	26.7	36.7	138.1	193.14
Total turnover value (billion)	$2.03	$3.7	$16.6	$20.1
Average daily volume (million units)	107.6	150.9	570.6	775.65
Average daily turnover (million)	$8.22	$15.24	$68.51	$80.5
Number of listed companies	214	202	212	213
Number of listed securities	288	288	309	301

Source: NSE (Nigerian Stock Exchange) 2005–8

promote their personal interests at the expense of information-deficient minority shareholders (Adegbite, 2010).

The nature of IPO in Nigeria: a look at the IPOs between 2006 and 2008

Capital market activity on the NSE between 2006 and 2008

There was significant activity in the capital market of the Nigerian Stock Exchange (NSE) from 2006 to 2008, principally due to the increased recourse to the stock market by companies. Table 14.2 shows a statistical summary of market performance from 2005 to 2008. Apart from the reduction in market capitalization and the NSE all-share index in 2008, which is attributable to the global economic crisis, there was a sustained market performance on the NSE. During this period, the NSE noted that growth was driven principally by the non-oil sectors, as the crisis in the oil-rich Niger Delta area constrained crude oil exploration and production, which continues to be the mainstay of the Nigerian economy.

IPO process

The regulatory approval process involved in completing an IPO in Nigeria has remained largely unchanged for many years and is considered dated, cumbersome and unduly lengthy: at about twenty-seven weeks, it is considerably longer than the issuance process in other emerging markets (SEC, 2009). Other procedural challenges include: the requirement for physical distribution of offer documents, especially given the challenges of the Nigerian postal system; the technical and logistical challenges faced by registrars when handling the increasing volume of applications and dispatching physical share certificates to subscribers; the prefunding requirement of IPOs; and the expensive cost of issuance (SEC, 2009).

IPO activity between 2006 and 2008: characteristics of IPO firms

Despite the challenges confronting the IPO process, the NSE stated that new issues approved in 2006 showed that the sum of N129.4 billion ($852.16 million) was raised through IPO (NSE, 2006). N719.93 billion ($4.7 billion) and N608 billion ($4 billion) were raised through IPO and supplementary issues in 2007 and 2008 respectively (NSE, 2007, 2008). This represents a significant proportion of the market value of the exchange, suggesting that the NSE is gradually being seen as a provider of capital by corporate Nigeria. Indeed, it must be noted that the total market value of 288 securities listed on the NSE was N5.12 trillion ($33.72 billion) by year end 2006; that of the 309 securities listed was N13.295 trillion ($87.55 billion) by year end 2007; whilst that of the 301 securities listed stood at N9.563 trillion ($62.98 billion) by year end 2008 (NSE, 2006, 2007, 2008). Based on limited available information, which was cross-checked across the NSE reports, companies' prospectuses and relevant public media outlets, thirteen IPO firms can be proved to have gone public on the NSE during the period 2006–8. The following paragraphs analyze all of these companies, as none of them has been delisted since their IPO. Whilst four companies each went public in both 2006 and 2007, it is important to note that five IPO firms were listed in 2008, particularly when the financial crisis affected the global capital market.

Indeed it must be noted that Nigeria's capital market managed to modestly withstand the turmoil of the global economic crisis (in comparison with the capital markets of developed countries) until the middle of 2008, before the country started to feel the impact more

Table 14.3 *IPO year and industry classification*

Industry classification	2006	2007	2008	Total
Consumer goods	1	1	1	3
Consumer services	1	0	1	2
Financials	1	2	3	6
Basic material	0	1	0	1
Industrials	1	0	0	1
Total	4	4	5	13

harshly through to 2009. Indeed African economies were previously considered to be relatively insulated from the global financial crisis, until the South African Stock Exchange lost 27 percent in 2008 and the rand slipped almost 30 percent, and the NSE all-share index dropped by 45.8 percent in Nigeria (NSE, 2008). Indeed

the Nigerian stock market felt the impact of the global meltdown from the second quarter with equity market capitalization dropping from a high of N12.64 trillion ($83.24 billion) on May 3, 2008 to a low of N6.21 trillion ($40.9 billion) on December 16, 2008 before finally closing at N9.56 trillion ($62.98 billion) on December 31, 2008. (NSE, 2008: 3)

Despite the declines in key market indicators, the NSE stated that the fundamentals of the capital market remained strong as indicated by strong corporate earnings and growth potentials; however, investors remained cautious while studying the effect of the global financial crisis on the domestic market (NSE, 2008).

In the light of this, the IPO activity during this period can be described as modestly impressive. Table 14.3 shows that the IPOs are focused in some particular industries such as financials (six) and consumer goods (three). It should be noted that three of the six IPOs in the financial sector are banks. This is partly an aftermath of a banking reform program embarked upon by the Central Bank of Nigeria (CBN) in 2004, which required all banks to raise their capital base to a minimum of N25 billion ($164.64 million). Whilst this consolidation exercise led to the injection of new capital by shareholders of some banks, and the merger of many other banks, it also required many banks to seek external funds on the stock market, which led to the reduction of majority stake ownership in the Nigerian banking sector (Adegbite, 2010).

Table 14.4 *IPO age and size*

IPO firm name	Year founded	IPO age	Employees	Revenue (US $)	Assets (US $)
Associated Bus Company	1993	13	998	990,194	18,965,729
Bank PHB	1989	18	1,814	58,964,784	2,645,168,796
Custodian and Allied Insurance	1991	17	100	3,989,248	27,467,113
Daar Communications	1988	20	500	1,549,466	81,597,892
Dangote Flour Mills	1999	8	600	14,616,252	377,000,063
Dangote Sugar Refinery	2000	6	672	64,945,022	207,399,294
Deap Capital Management and Trust	2002	5	32	686,932	9,594,032
First Inland Bank	2006	2	1,928	18,342,506	1,221,835,757
Honeywell Flour Mills	1985	23	500	5,653,113	102,440,310
Ikeja Hotel	1972	34	343	3,005,929	13,511,749
Nigerian Bag Manufacturing Company	1964	43	935	6,390,471	50,663,233
Skye Bank	2004	4	2,027	38,199,708	3,088,893,336
Transnational Corporation of Nigeria	2004	2	44	0	573,188,571

Another important characteristic of Nigerian IPO firms between 2006 and 2008 relates to their ages. Table 14.4 indicates that companies going public are not only young entrepreneurial and high-growth companies, but include also companies with a long tradition of private or family ownership. However, it must be noted that most of the IPO firms were older than ten years (seven out of thirteen), with four out of the remaining six firms five years or under before their IPO. The average time to go public is fifteen years. In terms of firm size, Table 14.4 further shows that Nigerian companies going public vary in terms of employee size, turnover and assets. On average they have 807 employees, with banks having the most employees prior to the IPO. The average employee number for the three banks is 1,923. On average, the IPO firms between 2006 and 2008 have an average revenue of $16.72 million before the IPO. In this regard, it is important to note that Transnational Corporation of Nigeria recorded nil revenue before the IPO as the company was only formed two years before the IPO and made no prior earnings but was in debt of $483.62 million. The average asset for the firms prior to the IPO is $603.43 million. The smallest company, in terms of employees, revenues and assets, is Deap Capital Management and Trust. Prior to the IPO, the company had thirty-two employees, revenue of around $687,000 and an assets figure of $9.6 million. Deap Capital Management and Trust provides funds/portfolio management and financial advisory services for high net worth individuals and institutions; it further performs the functions of an issuing house on the Nigerian capital market. The largest company in terms of employees and assets is Skye Bank. Skye Bank Plc is a commercial bank that has evolved into one of the top five financial institutions in Nigeria, following the CBN consolidation exercise. Skye Bank is the result of the following merged Nigerian banks: Prudent Bank, EIB International Bank, Reliance Bank, Cooperative Bank and Bond Bank.

In relation to firm performance, companies going public have high profitability ratios on assets, equity and revenues, as shown in Table 14.5. The companies have an average of 8.5 percent, 23.4 percent and 23 percent returns on assets, equity and revenue respectively. Ikeja Hotel, Dangote Sugar Refinery and Custodian and Allied Insurance exhibited the best performance before the IPO. Ikeja Hotel, formed in 1972, is a prestigious hotel in the capital of Lagos State, which is the second most populous state in Nigeria. Dangote Sugar Refinery Plc commenced business in March 2000 as the sugar division of Dangote Industries Limited, a leading manufacturer of consumer goods in sub-Saharan Africa. Custodian and Allied Insurance is a wholly owned Nigerian company, providing a wide array of insurance products. As previously suggested, only Transnational Corporation of Nigeria was not profitable in the year preceding the IPO.

In terms of the ownership structure, typical IPO firms are majorly owned by families, with the families still retaining sufficient shareholding post-IPO, as shown in Table 14.6. However, Bank PHB was

Table 14.5 *IPO performance*

IPO firm name	Performance before going public (percent)		
	ROA	ROE	ROS
Associated Bus Company	5	20	5
Bank PHB	2	24	24
Custodian and Allied Insurance	15	19	36
Daar Communications	2	2	21
Dangote Flour Mills	4	15	4
Dangote Sugar Refinery	31	49	16
Deap Capital Management and Trust	7	31	99
First Inland Bank	2	12	10
Honeywell Flour Mills	6	17	4
Ikeja Hotel	22	80	56
Nigerian Bag Manufacturing Company	13	16	10
Skye Bank	1	19	14
Transnational Corporation of Nigeria	0	0	0

15 percent owned by a bank prior to the IPO, and 8 percent bank-owned post-IPO. In First Inland Bank and Skye Bank, the Nigerian government held a 6 percent stake in both companies and 6.5 percent and 4.5 percent stakes post-IPO, respectively. This suggests that irrespective of the owners (i.e., whether banks, families or the government), there is a general retention of significant shareholding even after the IPO. This is also the case for the "majority ownership structure" of IPO firms. For example, even if companies going public show a decrease of the share capital owned by the top one and three shareholder(s), the major shareholder(s) still retains the control of the company after the IPO. This is in line with the previous discussion on the ownership structure of Nigerian corporations, which is still largely non-diversified, but one with significant majority ownership, by individuals, families, banks and the government. Table 14.6 also shows an interesting characteristic of Nigerian IPOs, which is the very strong presence of business angels in the share capital of companies as well as the high involvement of venture capital and private equity funds, before and after the IPO. For example, apart from Associated Bus Company, business angels, mostly Nigerians, retained a very

Table 14.6 IPO ownership structure (data in percent)

	Family		Bank		Govt.		VC		Angels		Top 1		Top 3	
	pre	post	pre	post	pre	post	pre	post	pre	post	pre	post	pre	post
Associated Bus Company Plc	68	38	0	0	0	0	0	12	30	5	67	37	98	56
Dangote Sugar Refinery Plc	100	83	0	0	0	0	0	0	0	0	97	79	100	83
Transnational Corporation of Nigeria Plc	0	0	0	0	0	0	5.4	0	0	0	5.4	0	16	0
Custodian and Allied Insurance Plc	19	9.7	0	0	0	0	11	8.9	5	4.4	19	9.7	45	26
Deap Capital Management and Trust Plc	0	0	0	0	0	0	18	17	58	45	18	15	28	26
Bank PHB	0	0	15	8	0	0	6.5	8.5	0	0	15	8.4	22	15
Ikeja Hotel Plc	0	0	0	0	0	0	15	14	8.1	7.2	15	13	38	30
Daar Communications Plc	100	65	0	0	0	0	0	0	0	0	100	65	100	65
Dangote Flour Mills Plc	100	83	0	0	0	0	0	0	0	0	91	67	100	83
Honeywell Flour Mills Limited	0	0	0	0	0	0	0	0	0	0	100	72	100	72
Nigerian Bag Manufacturing Company Plc	0	0	0	0	0	0	0	0	0	0	100	70	100	70
First Inland Bank Plc	0	0	0	0	6	6.5	0	0	2	2.5	10	9.1	16	17
Skye Bank Plc	0	0	0	0	6	4.5	5.8	4.5	0	0	5.8	4.5	11	13

Table 14.7 *IPO board of directors*

Board characteristics	Board size	Non-exec members (percent)	Female presence (percent)
Associated Bus Company	7	71	0
Bank PHB	9	75	6.25
Custodian and Allied Insurance	12	67	16.67
Daar Communications	6	62.5	12.5
Dangote Flour Mills	10	80	0
Dangote Sugar Refinery	16	77.78	11.11
Deap Capital Management and Trust	7	92.31	23.08
First Inland Bank	16	76.47	5.88
Honeywell Flour Mills	10	80	10
Ikeja Hotel	10	100	0
Nigerian Bag Manufacturing Company	10	50	0
Skye Bank	17	75	12.5
Transnational Corporation of Nigeria	16	75	8.33

significant amount of their shareholding post-IPO. It is also interesting to note that, in some situations, some venture capital firms increase their shareholding following the IPO. Also, there are no companies with dual class shares in the sample, and no companies are owned through a pyramidal group or a syndicate pact.

Board directors of Nigerian IPO companies are on average fifty-eight years of age. Table 14.7 shows that the average number of directors on the board of Nigerian IPOs is twelve. Here, most directors (75 percent on average) are non-executive. However, a very important governance characteristic to note is the absence of truly independent directors on the board of Nigerian IPO firms. In terms of gender composition on the board of Nigerian IPOs, women directors have an average of 8.2 percent representation. Although this is low, it is nevertheless impressive. Adegbite (2010) noted that board composition in Nigeria has traditionally been male dominated. He suggested that there are historical and cultural explanations for this; the female gender has traditionally been regarded as inequitable with the male, such that women have traditionally suffered societal discrimination, especially in terms of education (advanced education in particular). He further noted that this has resulted in a traditional education/professional gap between men and women, especially with regard to those who are capable of filling senior positions both in the public sector as well as in private organizations. However, this gap between male and female has reduced drastically in the past two decades.

IPO case study: Dangote Flour Mills

Before IPO

Dangote Flour Mills Plc commenced operations in 1999, as a division of Dangote Industries Limited – one of Nigeria's largest and fastest growing business conglomerates. Dangote Flour Mills Plc is in the business of flour milling as well as the processing and marketing of branded flour; its product portfolio comprises bread flour, pasta semolina and wheat offal. From an initial installed capacity of 500 Metric Tonnes (MT) per day in a single flour mill, Dangote Flour Mills has expanded rapidly by opening, in quick succession, three flour mills across different locations in Nigeria, resulting in a total installed capacity of 4,000 MT per day. These expansions were in response to a growing national demand for flour and flour-based products in addition to the company's drive for increased market share, which has made the company grow to become one of the industry leaders, with two wholly owned subsidiaries, namely Dangote Agro Sacks Limited and Dangote Pasta Limited.

The ownership structure of the company at the time of the IPO sees a strong participation by a prominent businessman who lives in Nigeria. The family of Mr. Aliko Dangote, Nigeria's first billionaire, who is number 334 on the Forbes world's billionaires list, fully owns the company directly or indirectly through Dangote Industries Limited. At the time of IPO, the board of directors of Dangote Flour Mills Plc includes nine directors, most of whom are shareholders of the company or have some relationships with major shareholders of the firm. Only two directors may be considered as independent, which are Mr. Asue Ighodalo and Mr. Samuel Teidi. Prior to the IPO, the company, with its 600 employees, had a net revenue of

$14,616,252.42, total assets of $377,000,063.80, earnings before interest of $333,892,693.90 and a total debt of $13,868,772,000. The company enjoyed a healthy growth of an average of 72.3 percent per year during the three years preceding the IPO. According to Dangote Flour Mills, some aspects of its corporate governance structure, at the IPO stage, are as follows: the position of the chairman is separate from the CEO; the board meets regularly and sufficient clear agenda/reports are given ahead of such meetings; all directors have access to the company secretary who can only be appointed or removed by the board; non-executive directors are not appointed for a fixed period, but shall instead remain in office until the company determines their tenure or by operation of law; the remuneration of the CEO is fixed by the board; full disclosure is provided for the highest paid director and remuneration of the chairman; the board audit committee, comprising executive and non-executive directors and representatives of shareholders, will be set up on completion of this offer; the audit committee will be chaired by a shareholder; and shareholders holding at least 10 percent of the new equity can be represented on the board.

Offer

The IPO process began with the application list opening on September 6, 2007. At the IPO stage, the company had an authorized shared capital comprising 6,000,000,000 ordinary shares, and issued/fully paid shares comprising 5,000,000,000 ordinary shares. The IPO was undertaken to give predominantly Nigerian investors an opportunity to become part owners of the company, and also for the company to meet the requirements for a listing on the NSE. The unit of sale was a minimum of 1,000 ordinary shares and multiples of 100 ordinary shares thereafter. Proceeds from the IPO were put at $118,419,281.70. During the IPO, 60 percent of the offer was preferentially allotted to investors. The IPO offer price was $0.1039 and, after the first year of trading, the share price closed at $0.1091 on the Nigerian Stock Exchange.

After IPO

Post-IPO, the family stake reduced to 83 percent. In this, Mr. Dangote's shareholding (the topmost shareholder) reduced from 91 percent to

67 percent after the IPO. Before and after the IPO, the company has no ownership stake retained by banks, business angels and venture capital firms or by the government. The company has remained successful post-IPO with its 2009 pre-tax profit jumping 70 percent compared to 2008. The company's corporate governance structure largely remains the same post-IPO.

Conclusion

Corporate governance in Nigeria has evolved in the last decade with an energetic momentum due to increased stakeholder advocacy for effective corporate governance to tackle corporate fraud and safe-guard against the loss of investors' money. Happenings on the global scene, including corporate scandals around the world, and the general emphasis on the need to promote good corporate governance, have led to the introduction in 2003 of the code of good governance and its revision in 2009. The corporate governance system, including corporate law, has ensured a degree of diversification in the ownership structure of Nigerian listed companies, and highlighted the roles and responsibilities of directors, managers and shareholders. The Nigerian Stock Exchange has traditionally not played a relevant role in the national economy, but the past five years has witnessed a significant activity on the stock market, with companies going public to seek funds to grow and remain competitive. However, only fifty-five companies, in the three years here investigated, decided to go public, and their characteristics are very similar to those of listed companies.

References

Achebe, Ifeanyi. 1989. 'The legal problems of indigenisation in Nigeria: A lesson for developing countries', *Hastings International & Comparative Law Review*, 663.

Adegbite, Emmanuel. 2010. *The Determinants of Good Corporate Governance: The Case of Nigeria*. Unpublished PhD thesis, City University, London.

    2012. 'Corporate governance regulation in Nigeria', *Corporate Governance*, in press.

Adegbite, Emmanuel and Chizu Nakajima. 2011a. 'Institutional determinants of good corporate governance: The case of Nigeria', in Elaine Hutson, Rudolf Sinkovics and Jenny Berrill (eds.), *Firm-Level Internationalization, Regionalism and Globalization*. Basingstoke: Palgrave Macmillan.

2011b. 'Corporate governance and responsibility in Nigeria', *International Journal of Disclosure and Governance*, 8, 3, 252–71.

Ahunwan, Boniface. 2002. 'Corporate governance in Nigeria', *Journal of Business Ethics*, 37(3), 269–87.

Demirag, Istemi (ed.). 1998. *Corporate Governance, Accountability, and Pressures for Reform: An International Study*. London: JAI Press Inc.

Insol. 2008. *Nigeria's Cross Border Insolvency*. Available at: www.insol.org/pdf/cross_pdfs/Nigeria.pdf (accessed on 8 August 2008).

La Porta, Rafael. 1998. 'Corporate ownership around the world' (NBER Working Paper 662).

Mensah, Sam, Kwame Aboagye, Elsie Addo and Seth Buatsi. 2003. 'Corporate governance and corruption in Ghana: Empirical findings and policy implications', *African Capital Markets Forum*, 7.

NSE (Nigerian Stock Exchange). 2006. Available at: www.nigerianstockexchange.com (accessed on 2 February 2008).

2007. Available at: www.nigerianstockexchange.com (accessed on 2 February 2008).

2008. Available at: www.nigerianstockexchange.com (accessed on 2 February 2008).

2009. Available at: www.nigerianstockexchange.com (accessed on 18 February 2009).

2010. Available at: www.nigerianstockexchange.com (accessed on 2 April 2010).

Okike, Elewechi N.M. 2007. 'Corporate governance in Nigeria: The status quo', *Corporate Governance: An International Review*, 15(2), 173–93.

ROSC (Report on the Observance of Standards and Codes). 2004. *Nigeria*. Available at: www.worldbank.org/ifa/rosc_aa.html (accessed on 7 December 2006).

SEC (Securities and Exchange Commission). 2009. *Nigeria's Capital Market: Making World-Class Potential a Reality*. Abuja, Nigeria: Securities and Exchange Commission.

Yakasai, Alhaji G.A. 2001. 'Corporate governance in a third world country with particular reference to Nigeria', *Corporate Governance: An International Review*, 9(3), 239–40.

15 Corporate governance and initial public offerings in Russia

SHEILA M. PUFFER AND DANIEL J. McCARTHY

Corporate governance mechanisms

Russia has a long history of tight, centralized government control over society during the tsarist and Soviet eras, accompanied by a highly collectivistic social culture. The country's transition beginning in the early 1990s from a centrally planned, communist system toward a market-oriented system has led to an increasing degree of individualism. The legal system is based in civil law, adopted from Western Europe by Peter the Great in the early eighteenth century, but is seen as largely ineffective in protecting individual rights, including those associated with business transactions, due to endemic corruption in the courts and law enforcement systems. As a result, the market for corporate controls is relatively inactive, but is more robust for public companies due to exchange listing requirements. The same can be said about information disclosure, which is generally opaque but more transparent for publicly listed companies. Those companies must comply with the country's 2002 Code of Corporate Conduct, or report deviations in their annual reports. Business groups such as Financial Industrial Groups (FIGs) comprise many of the largest Russian companies. However, while the majority of companies are unaffiliated with such groups, they often rely on informal networks to circumvent governmental bureaucracies to accomplish business goals.

Corporate ownership in most firms, including public companies, is highly concentrated, and single shareholders or small groups of block-holders usually have majority ownership positions. Minority ownership rights have not been well protected by law, and this situation has led to well-publicized lawsuits by investment companies such as Renaissance Capital and has limited the interest of international investors. Corporate boards are basically single tier in nature, although the Code of Corporate Conduct permits management boards as well. The code prohibits CEO duality, preventing that individual from also serving as the board chair. Corporate board composition varies in the percentage of outside versus executive directors, but publicly listed companies typically have some outside directors. The vast majority of boards have audit committees and compensation committees, but less than half have governance committees.

Boards of directors

The characteristics of boards of directors of large public Russian companies are described in the country's Code of Corporate Conduct of 2002 created by the Federal Commission for the Securities Markets. A Russian executive writing in 2004 explained that "long-term value creation, the ultimate goal of shareholders, depends to a large extent on the right balance between the rights and roles of shareholders, boards, and management, especially the professionalism and capacity of directors and executives to work together" (Shekshnia, 2004: 203–4). Similarly, the code notes that the primary functions of the board are the control over the executive management as well as determining the general strategy of the company. Russian law, in fact, requires that these issues are the function of the board of directors elected at the general shareholders' meeting. The law provides wide powers of supervision and control to the board, and holds it liable for failure to perform its duties. The board of directors is essentially a one-tier entity, although the code often refers to the managerial board, which is comprised of the company's senior management. Regarding the company's strategy, the board typically approves a financial and business plan recommended by the company's executive body each year, which should include a production plan, a marketing plan, and a business plan, as well as a budget for investment projects. Beyond the approval of the company's strategy, the board is expected to provide supervision over the implementation of both the financial and business operations of the company. The board is expected to establish risk management policies often embodied in the company's internal controls, and approve internal risk management procedures and compliance by management with such policies. The code is explicit in noting that the board of directors safeguards and protects the rights of shareholders by ensuring compliance of management with corporate procedures that provide the framework protecting shareholder rights. Although the code is essentially voluntary, Russian law requires that executive bodies are held accountable to shareholders and the company's board of directors. Yet, many in Russia are reluctant to take their case to court given the low level of confidence in the judicial system due to widespread corruption.

As well as controlling the operation of executive bodies, the board should suspend powers of directors general if such persons violate their duties. Companies should have a charter that states explicitly terms and conditions of employment contracts of senior managers, including their remuneration.

Members of the company's managerial board may serve as members of the board of directors, but must be wary of conflicts of interest that could be involved in voting on employment contracts and generally should refrain from doing so. Other members of the board should also be aware of such conflicts, and again, should refrain from voting if they deem a conflict to exist. The number of board members is not mandated, but should be sufficient to perform the necessary work of the board and its committees, and members should possess the skills to do so. Boards generally consist of three types of directors – executive, non-executive, and independent directors. The inclusion of independent directors is strongly encouraged to ensure that the board may receive objective opinions on company matters. Characteristics of independent directors are described in the code, but one clear criterion is that the person not be an affiliated person of the company's management or one associated with such a person, while another interesting criterion is that the person not be a representative of the government. An important but often violated recommendation is that the election of the board be conducted in a transparent manner that takes into account the diverse views and interests of shareholders, and is done so in compliance with statutory requirements. In electing the board, opinions of minority shareholders should be strongly considered and recognized by adopting cumulative voting to advance the protection of minority shareholder rights. Although Russian law allows executives to sit on boards of directors, but does restrict their participation, it does not provide procedures to enforce such restrictions. So a board's composition in actuality might not comply with the law or the Code of Corporate Conduct.

Similar to boards of directors' duties specified under agency theory, board members should act reasonably and in good faith in the interest of the company, discharging their duties under the law, the charter, and other internal company regulations, and should exercise the maximum amount of care and prudence. They should ensure that they have the most complete, timely, and quality information possible. Specifically, they should not accept gifts from anyone with a vested interest in company decisions. And if there is a conflict of interest, they should refrain from any actions in those situations. Although it might seem superfluous, board members are advised to participate actively in board and committee meetings, and interestingly, Russian law provides that any board member may demand a meeting of the directors. Regarding confidential information, directors should not disclose confidential or insider information, or use such information to their own interest or that of a third party. These and other more specific duties of board members are expected to be clearly defined and incorporated into a company's internal documents. The chairman of the board should ensure efficient organization and operations of the board, as well as its interaction with others in the company, particularly the management board. The chairman is responsible for developing meeting agendas, providing board members with opportunities to express their views, and organizing the work of board committees. In spite of the many duties specified in the code for directors, their main duty seems to be developing relationships with external parties, particularly among those in various levels of government (Melkumov, 2009).

Again, although it may seem superfluous, boards are recommended to conduct their meetings on a regular basis in accordance with a preapproved plan, and meetings every six weeks are advised. Provisions should be made for absentee votes by directors at most meetings, and should be so noted in the board's charter. Discussion at meetings should be in accordance with the importance of agenda items, and some items specified in the code should be voted on only by in-person votes, and include items such as election and re-election of the chair, convening the annual general shareholders' meetings, and suspension of the director general. Regarding committees, a number of standing committees are recommended that should be known to people familiar with boards operating under agency theory, such as company board committees in developed Western nations. The code places responsibility for committees with the board chair, and recommends that committee heads not be members of the management board. Specific committees recommended are consistent with the major functions and duties of the board and include the strategic planning committee, the audit committee, the human resources-remuneration committee, and the corporate conflicts resolution committee. The latter stems from traditions during Soviet times. A notable exception for Westerners would be the omission of a corporate governance committee, whose normal functions seem to be dispersed among the other committees, and an ethics committee is also recommended to ensure that a company complies with ethical standards and contributes to the creation of a climate of trust.

Related to the board of directors, the code recommends that the company's charter specify rights of shareholders to demand a meeting of the board of directors since that group represents the interests of shareholders. Consistent with that provision, the code recommends that detailed minutes be kept of board meetings. Regarding board remuneration, it is noted that remuneration for all board members should be the same whether they be executive, non-executive, or independent directors. Criteria for board as well as committee membership should be specified in board policies, as should a process for evaluating the board and its committees. Finally, as in developed Western countries, board members are liable for not discharging their duties in a proper manner. Criteria for holding a director liable are culpability or not acting reasonably and in good faith, and/or not exercising diligence and care in the performance of a director's function. Directors should be terminated if they are found liable for inflicting damages, and/or breaching their obligations to the company. As in Western countries, members are generally provided with liability insurance that allows the company to use civil law remedies for the company to defend them.

Code of Corporate Conduct

Corporate governance hardly seemed to exist in Russia after the collapse of the Soviet Union and the end of communism in late 1991. Privatization, which was supposed to distribute shares of privatized state-owned enterprises to management, workers, and the Russian public, was marred by the pillaging of the country's assets and trampling of shareholder rights (McCarthy and Puffer, 2002a). At least as egregious toward any civilized approach toward corporate governance was the blatant abuse of power by the oligarchs who

Table 15.1 *Code of Corporate Conduct contents*

Introduction
Chapter 1. Principles of Corporate Governance
Chapter 2. General Shareholders Meeting
Chapter 3. Board of Directors of the Company
Chapter 4. Executive Bodies of the Company
Chapter 5. Corporate Secretary of the Company
Chapter 6. Major Corporate Actions
Chapter 7. Disclosure of Information About a Company
Chapter 8. Supervision of Financial and Business Operations of the Company
Chapter 9. Dividends
Chapter 10. Resolution of Corporate Conflicts

gained control of the country's most valuable recently privatized assets (Hoffman, 2002). Such excesses were acknowledged early in President Putin's first administration (2000–4) as were their adverse effects on the country's risk profile for investment so badly needed to modernize companies' plant and equipment as well as the country's crumbling infrastructure.

In response, as noted above, the Russian Code of Corporate Conduct was promulgated by the Federal Commission for the Securities Markets (FCSM) in April 2002, with input from NGOs such as the Russian Institute of Directors, as part of a coordination council for corporate governance created by the FCSM. The code provided the foundation for corporate governance in large public Russian corporations with more than 1,000 shareholders. The code was a direct response to the numerous violations of minority shareholder rights that occurred during the privatization period of the 1990s (Puffer and McCarthy, 2003). It also provided for the activities of various stakeholders such as shareholders, managers, auditors, and others in an attempt to recognize the interests of stakeholders beyond that of the managers who controlled most large companies, an insight examined in a framework for analyzing corporate governance in Russia (McCarthy and Puffer, 2003). A comprehensive summary of the code and its implications was written by a US attorney who was involved in advising the Russian government on both corporate law and the code of corporate conduct (Perkins, 2002). The content of the code is contained in Table 15.1. An extensive review and analysis of the academic literature on corporate governance in Russia is provided in a recent journal article (Puffer and McCarthy, 2011). General principles of corporate governance are explained and detailed in the code's first chapter, "Principles of Corporate Governance." It notes in the preamble: "Corporate governance should be based on the respect for the rights and lawful interests of all participants and improve the quality of a company's operations ..." It emphasizes the importance of trust among everyone engaged in corporate governance, and that the principles are aimed at creating trust in the relations between the board and corporate management.

The code provides seven basic principles, each with a substantial number of specific recommendations, including the composition and structure of boards of directors. The seven principles stipulate that corporate governance practice should:

(1) provide shareholders with a real opportunity to exercise their rights in relation to the company; (2) provide for equal treatment of shareholders owning an equal number of shares of the same type – all shareholders should have access to effective protection in the event of a violation of their rights; (3) provide for the strategic management of the company's business by the board of directors, for effective control by the board over the executive bodies of the company, and for the accountability of the board of directors to shareholders; (4) provide executive bodies of the company with the ability to manage the day-to-day activities of the company reasonably, in good faith and solely in the interests of the company, and ensure that executive bodies report to the board of directors and the shareholders; (5) provide for timely disclosure of full and accurate information about the company, including information about its financial position, economic parameters, ownership and management structure, to enable shareholders and investors to make informed decisions; (6) take into account the statutory rights of interested persons including employees of the company, and encourage active cooperation between the company and interested persons with a view to increasing the assets of the company and the value of its shares and other securities, and to creating new jobs; (7) provide for the efficient control over the financial and business operations of the company in order to protect the rights and legal interests of shareholders.

It is clear that these principles are similar to those of corporate governance practices in Western economies that emphasize the importance of agency theory when considering the relationships among shareholders, directors, and management.

Russian law

The Russian law on joint stock companies of 1995, together with the Federal Law on the Securities Market of 1996, as well as the Russian Civil Code, constitute the fundamental legislation regulating the activities of joint stock companies in the country. The law on joint stock companies covers the requirements and obligations of an enterprise seeking to be classified as a joint stock company as opposed to a state-owned organization. Although the law covers both open and closed joint stock companies, IPOs apply only to open ones. The law specifies requirements for a written "founding contract" that covers the creation of the company, amount of the charter capital, categories and types of shares to be placed with the founders, the amount and procedure for their payment, and the rights and duties of the founders relating to the creation of the company. The law also specifies other requirements such as those to be included in a company's charter, for example the rights of shareholders of various classes of stock. The law has been updated a number of times, including a 2009 update recognizing the validity of shareholders' agreements. Although some aspects of corporate governance are embedded in the law, the Code of Corporate Conduct added far more specifics about corporate governance practices. And although the code is voluntary, an important feature is that the extent of companies' compliance with recommendations of the code must be included with their required fourth quarter financial reports. In fact, the voluntary nature of the code is consistent with that of a number of other countries for companies listing on their stock exchanges, such as London, Toronto, Hong Kong, Malaysia, and South Africa (Perkins, 2002).

The introduction to the code notes that attracting investment is a primary objective of a country's corporate governance, defined as a term "that encompasses a variety of activities connected with the management of companies. Corporate governance affects the performance of economic entities and their ability to attract the capital required for economic growth." It notes further that "improvement of corporate governance in the Russian Federation is vital for increasing investment in all sectors of the Russian economy from both domestic and foreign investors." It emphasizes that an objective of the code is providing that "one means to foster such improvement is to introduce standards that are based on an analysis of the best practices of corporate governance." The same conclusion was noted by various authors in their analyses relevant to Russian privatization and the cessation of government subsidies to enterprises (McCarthy and Puffer, 2002a; Shleifer and Vishny, 1997). The code emphasizes that such standards are most important for joint stock companies because that is where the separation between ownership and management is the greatest, and where conflicts in corporate governance are most likely to occur, a clear reference to the basic premise of agency theory.

The introduction notes that where shareholder protection is greatest, so will be investment capital available to Russian joint stock companies, and high ethical standards are most likely to exist. A substantial amount of research has studied the relationship between corporate governance and firm performance (Filatotchev, Wright, Uhlenbruck et al., 2003; Judge, Naoumova, and Koutzevol, 2003; Peng, Buck, and Filatotchev, 2003). Other research has shown that good company corporate governance was positively related to a firm's market valuation (Black, 2001; Black, Love, and Rachinsky, 2006).

The introduction to the code emphasizes that "Russian law already incorporates the majority of the fundamental principles of corporate governance, however, in practice, their use, especially in courts, and corporate governance traditions, are still in the formative stages." It emphasizes also that Russian legislation on such topics is relatively new, and that major problems in corporate governance arise from such newness rather than the quality of legislation. Regarding the law, it is noted that it establishes and properly so only general mandatory rules, accompanied by little detail, noting a second weakness in the law being that it is unable to react rapidly to changing corporate governance practices.

Additionally, the preamble emphasizes that many corporate governance issues lie outside the legal arena and are more ethical in nature than legal. For example, civil law regulations stipulate the possibility of applying requirements of good faith, prudence, and equity in the absence of applicable legislation, and thus moral and ethical standards of reasonableness, equity, and good faith are part and parcel of existing regulation. Still, the code recommends that companies act in accordance not only with statutory law, but also with ethical standards, which might be even more demanding. The potential conflict between Russian business ethics and those of developed countries in the West was analyzed and it was concluded that ethical standards of developed countries might be more difficult for Russian managers to embrace (McCarthy and Puffer, 2008). The code emphasizes that a company's corporate governance should be based on respect not only for the company's management but also its shareholders, and should help to strengthen the company and increase its profits.

The code goes on to note that its objectives are not only the development and improvement of Russian corporate governance practices, but also to promote the development of the Russian stock market, again a reference to the need for attracting investment. Referring again to Russian law, the introduction was developed within that context, as well as respect for existing Russian and foreign corporate governance practices, ethical standards, and the specific needs of Russian companies and capital markets at their present stage of development. Importantly, the code is based on internationally recognized corporate governance principles developed by the Organisation for Economic Co-operation and Development (OECD). Perhaps most importantly, and as noted earlier, the code is voluntary for companies, and companies may determine for themselves which rules and procedures they should follow. For those companies going public, it is critical for them to comply with the code in order to avoid having to report deviations from the code, and most seem to prefer compliance.

The role of NGOs in influencing corporate governance

With the 2008 global economic crisis, the quality of corporate governance and the related issue of attracting of investment became top priority in Russia. Non-governmental organizations (NGOs) had been given a voice in the formulation of the Code of Corporate Conduct in 2002 and were among the various groups that recognized continuing weaknesses in company corporate governance, and initiated efforts for improvement. For instance, in November 2010, the Russian Association of Managers along with KPMG Russia and the Commonwealth of Independent States (CIS), with the support of the Russian Institute of Directors, developed a project: Corporate Governance in Russia: In Search of a New Model (Russian Institute of Directors website: www.rid.ru). They were concerned with the inadequate introduction of corporate governance standards in Russia due to the peculiarities of the country's historical development, such as the concentration of management functions in one or a group of powerful shareholders, with nominal functions of the board of directors. This has led to difficulties in applying well-known international corporate governance models to Russia because of endemic problems of implementation that limit the effectiveness of the code of conduct as well as many areas of corporate law. Such difficulties were noted some years earlier in an article which explored different models for Russian corporate governance, including one more specific to Russia than that embodied in the 2002 Code of Corporate Conduct (McCarthy and Puffer, 2002b).

In the 2010 analysis referred to above, it was noted that a number of Russian companies are seeking strong, standardized corporate governance practices to successfully conduct business. Thus, the three organizations set the following objectives: to describe a model of corporate governance that balances stakeholder interests in various types of companies; to compare corporate governance in Russian firms in various sectors and ownership structures; to determine factors facilitating and inhibiting better corporate governance; and presenting recommendations to improve corporate governance. The initial attempt planned for 2011 to accomplish these objectives was to be surveys of 100 large and medium-sized Russian companies, as well as twenty interviews with Russian and international corporate governance experts. Such information would be used to address the group's corporate governance objectives.

Russian stock exchanges

There are two major exchanges in Russia: the Russian Trading System (RTS) and the Moscow Interbank Currency Exchange (MICEX), both regulated by the Federal Commission for the Securities Markets (FCSM). The latter body developed requirements for listing on the two exchanges. They designate different classes of securities and various criteria for each class such as: the common stock ratio held by an individual and affiliates, capitalization of shares, minimum length of the issuer's existence, and minimum monthly transaction volume for the last three months, as well as guidelines for maintaining listing and financial accounting standards (IAS/US, GAAP). Regarding corporate governance, listing shares requires disclosure of compliance or non-compliance with various criteria of the Code of Corporate Conduct, followed by quarterly reports. Important criteria include having independent director(s), audit committees, obligations of directors, committee members, and executives to disclose information about the issuer's holdings and security transactions; confirmation of internal documents stating rules and procedures for information disclosure; confirmation of documents regarding usage of relevant internal information and internal department oversight; and compliance with the legal statute regarding disclosure of the issuer's annual meeting. Most Russian companies seem to prefer listing on both exchanges, and sometimes on a foreign exchange such as the London Stock Exchange (LSE).

The Moscow Interbank Currency Exchange, founded in the early 1990s, is the largest of Russia's two domestic stock exchanges. With a reputed market share of 70 percent of on-exchange trading in Russian assets, it claims to be the main market for international investment in shares and bonds of Russian companies. In 2009, the total volume of trading was 41 trillion rubles ($1.304 trillion). The exchange organizes daily trading in 1,300 securities of about 700 Russian issuers, including shares in more than 230 companies such as Sberbank, Gazprom, Rostelcom, LUKoil, Rosneft, Norilsk Nickel, VTB Bank, Surgutneftegaz, Tatneft, and RusHydro, along with others, leading to a total capitalization of 20 trillion rubles ($750 billion). Trading participants include more than 650 professional participants with 700,000 investors as clients, while individual investors account for 53 percent of the total trading volume in shares. Regarding bonds, in 2009, 162 bond issues of 98 issuers were placed on the exchange, and the total volume of placements reached nearly 1 trillion rubles ($30 billion). In 2010, more than 700 issues of regional and corporate bonds and commercial paper from over 420 issuers were traded. The main indicator of daily stock values is the MICEX index, started in 1997, which is comprised of the thirty most liquid stocks of the largest, most rapidly developing Russian companies representing many economic sectors. Other indices are calculated for various sectors, some of which are oil and gas, power, telecom, financial, chemical, and consumer goods. There are also two bond indices, one for municipal bonds and the other for corporate bonds.

The Russian Trading System (RTS) is the oldest organized securities market in modern Russia, founded in 1995, relatively early in the country's privatization process, and presently trades the full range of financial instruments from equities to commodity futures, totaling over 500 different issues. The two main markets are the RTS Classica Market and the RTS Standard Market, while Futures and Options lists the widest range of financial instruments. The RTS exchange is a member of the RTS Group which has international investment banks as members, including Deutsche Bank, Credit Suisse First Boston, UBS, and Morgan Stanley. The RTS index has been recognized as the benchmark for the Russian securities industry and is composed of the exchange's fifty most liquid and highly capitalized shares. The RTS Standard Index is based on ruble-denominated prices where other indices, including sectoral ones, are calculated on dollar-denominated prices. The RTS Standard Index includes the fifteen most liquid stocks (blue chips), while the RTS-2 Index is based on mid- and small-cap shares. The seven sectoral funds are similar to those of the MICEX exchange, and the same large Russian companies noted above as MICEX listings are also listed on the RTS exchange.

IPO activity 2006–2008

A list of the companies that went public from 2006 to 2008 is presented in Table 15.2, along with their industries and IPO year. A summary of the industries represented by those companies is provided in Table 15.3. A total of twenty-six Russian companies went public, twelve in 2006 and twelve in 2007, reflecting the increasing company interest in raising capital for growth and partial liquidity for major owners in a relatively newly emerging IPO environment. However, the decline to only two in 2008 reflected the global financial turmoil which began in that year. The six real estate companies going public reflected the country's booming real estate market, particularly in the larger cities like Moscow and St. Petersburg. Not surprisingly, the five energy (oil and gas) company IPOs reflected the country's strong position in the world's oil and gas production and distribution. Both the metals and minerals sector and consumer goods/retail sector had three IPOs, with metals, like energy, exhibiting the attractiveness of the country's natural resource companies, while consumer goods and retail reflected the growing domestic demand for Russian goods and retail outlets. The chemicals and financial/banking sectors each spawned two IPOs. The remaining five IPOs were distributed among five different sectors – telecommunications, transportation, steel pipe production, media/IT, and a utility.

Table 15.2 *Companies with IPOs in 2006–8*

Company name	Industry	IPO year
Acron Group	Chemicals	2008
AFI Development	Real estate	2007
Amur Minerals Corp.	Metals & minerals	2006
Cherkizovo Group	Consumer goods	2006
Comstar-UTS	Integrated communications	2006
CTC Media	Financial	2006
Eurasia Drilling Co. Ltd.	Oil & gas	2007
Globaltrans	Transportation	2008
Integra Group	Oil & gas	2007
LSR Group	Real estate	2007
Magnit	Retail	2006
Mirland Development Corp.	Real estate	2006
MMK (Magnitogorsk)	Metals & minerals	2007
OGK-2	Utilities	2007
PetroNeft	Oil & gas	2006
Pharmstandart	Chemicals	2007
PIK Group	Real estate	2007
Polymetal	Metals & minerals	2007
RGI International Ltd.	Real estate	2006
Rosneft	Oil & gas	2006
SistemaHals	Real estate	2006
SITRONICS	Media/IT	2007
TMK	Steel pipe	2006
Trader Media East Ltd.	Consumer goods	2006
Volga Gas	Oil & gas	2007
VTB Bank	Banking	2007

Other important characteristics of the twenty-six companies are summarized in Table 15.4. The average company age at the time of their IPOs was eleven years, with a range of one to seventy-eight years. Seventeen companies had existed for less than ten years, and only two over twenty years. The rather young company age is indicative of the fact that private companies were not legalized until 1989 when President Gorbachev legalized cooperatives in some sectors. Two companies that dated back to that period, being seventeen years old at the time of their IPO, were the telecom company Comstar and CTC

Table 15.3 *IPO year and industry classification*

Industry	2006	2007	2008	Total
Chemicals	0	1	1	2
Consumer goods & retail	3	0	0	3
Financial & banking	1	1	0	2
Integrated communications	1	0	0	1
Media/IT	0	1	0	1
Metals & minerals	1	2	0	3
Oil & gas	2	3	0	5
Real estate	3	3	0	6
Steel pipe	1	0	0	1
Transportation	0	0	1	1
Utilities	0	1	0	1
Total	12	12	2	26

Media. Only two companies were over twenty years old, being privatized former state-owned companies, the chemical firm Acron, and MMK, a leading producer of steel piping primarily for energy companies. The average net proceeds from the twenty-six IPOs were $1.272 billion, an impressive number for a country where the stock exchanges had existed for little more than a decade. The average firm revenue at the time of the IPO was $782 million, with the highest being $4.3 billion, one of seven over $1 billion, and four companies being under $1 million. The average assets at the time of the IPO were $428 million, with only one company being under $1 million, while three had assets of over $1 billion. The average increase in stock price at the end of the IPO day was 9 percent or $1, from a beginning average price of $10.97 to an end of the day price of $11.97.

Regarding the board of directors, Table 15.4 shows that the average number of board members was nine, ranging from three to nineteen, while the average age was forty-six, ranging from thirty-seven to fifty-eight. 42 percent of firms had one woman director, with none having more than one. The post-IPO ownership for all board members averaged 10 percent, with a wide range among the twenty-six companies. The average ownership of the main shareholder post-IPO was 62 percent. The average annual number of board meetings was four, and 85 percent of those companies conducted evaluations of the board.

Table 15.4 *Summary of key characteristics of twenty-six companies with IPOs 2006–8*

Variables	Characteristics of Russian companies
Total company IPOs	26
Average company age at IPO	11
Average number of board members	9
Average age of board members	46
% of firms with women board members	42%
% of firms with an audit committee	80%
Average number of directors on audit committee	1.7
% of firms with a compensation committee	69%
Average number of directors on compensation committee	2.2
Average number of directors on governance committee	1.4
% of firms with governance committee	27%
% of firms with nominating committee	47%
Average number of directors on nominating committee	1.2
Main shareholder average ownership post-IPO	62%
% of total board member average ownership post-IPO	10%
% of companies with board evaluations	85%
Average yearly board meetings	4
Average net proceeds from IPO (USD, 000s)	$1.272 billion
Average stock price gain end of IPO day (%)	9%
Average firm revenue at IPO	$782 million
Average firm assets at IPO	$428 million
IPO in 2006	12
IPO in 2007	12
IPO in 2008	2

An important function of boards of directors is the creation and functioning of various committees. The most important in the eyes of many analysts is the audit committee, and 80 percent of the firms had such a committee, with 1.7 being the average number of directors serving on that committee. The fact that some firms did not have an audit committee, as well as the average number of directors serving being less than two, would likely raise a question among investors, since that committee is so critical to transparency and the quality of financial reporting. 69 percent of firms had compensation committees, with 2.2 being the average number of directors serving. Considering the importance of corporate governance to so many facets of company success, as noted earlier, it is regrettable that only 27 percent of firms had a governance committee, with an average of 1.4 members, although 47 percent had a nominating committee with an average number of members at 1.2. Nominating future directors is often a function of the corporate governance committee, and it might be expected that more companies would have such committees in the future and with more members involved in the nominating process.

Description of an IPO: Integra Group

The firm before the IPO

Integra Group was created in 2004 and was comprised of an integrated group of more than forty oilfield services and petroleum engineering companies. The company divided its business into two primary sectors: oilfield services and equipment manufacturing. The oilfield sector was comprised of three areas: drilling, workover, and integrated project management; technology services; and geophysics. The firm offered a highly diverse set of onshore oilfield services, operating at all stages of upstream oil and gas: exploration, development, and production. Additionally, the company was a leading Russian manufacturer of cementing equipment and various specialized equipment utilized in all of these upstream processes. The company also offered a variety of services, including drilling of vertical, deviated, and horizontal exploration and development wells, workover services, and project management. The customer list included virtually all major Russian and international oil and gas companies operating in Russia and the Commonwealth of Independent States (CIS). Among them were LUKoil and Rosneft, TNK-BP, Marathon Oil, and over thirty independent oil producers. The company had 20,000 employees based in the Urals, western Siberia, and Komi, as well as other countries in the CIS. Annual company net revenues at the time of the IPO were approximately $325 million, while assets totaled around $612 million. Total company debt was approximately $214 million.

Regarding corporate governance and board structure, the board had five members averaging forty-two years of age, and six meetings were held per year. The board also had audit, compensation, and governance committees, and the chairman was not the CEO. Also, like many other Russian public companies, the company conducted an annual evaluation of its board. Integra's IPO was intended to fund rapid growth both organically and through acquisitions. Its early February 2007 IPO might have seemed ill-timed since the company had a relatively poor year in 2006, with declining revenues and profitability. However, 2006 had been a strong year for Russian company IPOs, which provided some optimism for a receptive IPO market in 2007, so Integra evidently decided to test that receptivity.

The IPO offer

Integra Group's IPO occurred on February 22, 2007, approximately three years after the company's founding in 2004. The IPO was led by investment firm managers Morgan Stanley, Renaissance Capital, and Alfa Bank. Nearly 40 million GDRs were offered for public sale, with around 30 million offered by the company and 10 million by existing shareholders. Shares offered totaled around 2 million. The company intended to raise capital of $670 million, and in spite of Integra's weak 2006 financial results, the IPO was a great success. It was ten times oversubscribed and priced at the top of its range at $16.75 per share. The stock closed at $18.70 at the end of the first day, an 11.6 percent increase, bringing proceeds of nearly $700 million. The results made it clear that analysts and investors accepted well the company's forward-looking growth scenario as well as its forecast of a profitable 2007.

The firm after the IPO

Post-IPO, the ownership position of the board and top management team was 19.4 percent, after their having sold off 5.7 percent of their holdings. Non-executive directors continued to own 7.4 percent of shares after selling 2.2 percent, with the board chairman owning 7.5 percent post-IPO, after selling off 1.7 percent of his holdings. The ownership position of the top management team post-IPO was 11.9 percent, reflecting a sell-off of 3.5 percent of their shares. The three largest Integra shareholders continued to own 38.1 percent of the company after selling off 12.2 percent, while the largest shareholder owned 17.8 percent after selling off 4 percent.

Seeming to validate the optimistic view of investors, Integra contracted in May and July 2007 with Gazprom and Rosneft to produce eleven and four heavy drilling rigs respectively. Additionally, the company acquired Geotechsystem for $11 million in August and Obnefteremont for $80 million in October, as well as initiating a new coiled tubing business in September 2007. In short, the company seemed to be on its way to growing both organically and by acquisition. However, the world economic crisis took its toll on the Integra Group as it did on most major oil and gas companies as well as so many other companies around the world. The year 2009 followed 2008 as a relatively weak year for the company due to contraction of demand for oilfield services, largely as a result of the worldwide financial crisis. Sales in 2009 amounted to $836.2 million versus $1.45 billion in 2008, while the company's adjusted EBITDA decreased to $109 million versus $162 million the prior year. The company did, however, establish a major cost-cutting program which allowed the firm to use its free cashflow to decrease debt to $175 million in 2009 versus $335 million in 2008. Improvements seemed to be occurring in the first half (H1) of 2010 as revenue increased to $421 million versus $363 million for the same period in 2008, and EBITDA margin increased to 14.7 percent from 13.4 percent. Both measures help explain the company's return to a $4.4 million profit during that period versus a loss of $8.7 million in H1 2008. Antonio Campo, Integra Group's CEO, commented near the end of 2009 that the year had been one of transformation, and although the business was smaller in size, its capacity had been successfully aligned with current market demand, allowing improved EBITDA margins, increased cashflow, and a stronger balance sheet. As such, Integra was reasonably representative of companies that had weathered the financial crisis after going public, and restructured to meet the new realities of the post-crisis period.

Conclusion

The IPOs of the twenty-six Russian companies represent well a profile of the Russian economy during the years 2006 to 2008. The country was, and to a large extent still is, highly dependent on energy and other natural resources as well as heavy industry such as chemicals and steel pipe manufacturing. Yet, there has been some diversification toward consumer goods and retail businesses as well as financial services and banking. Additionally, the preponderance of real estate company IPOs is indicative of the increase in real estate values, especially in major cities like Moscow and St. Petersburg, which have become among the most expensive in the world in which to establish businesses, and for business travelers. The emergence of an IPO market in Russia is indicative of the development of the country's capital market institutions, which were non-existent until the early 1990s after more than seventy years under the Soviet centrally planned economy. The IPO market has allowed Russian companies to raise capital for growth, and has also provided an opportunity for many major stockholders to experience a liquidity event by issuing a relatively small percentage of their share ownership. The top shareholder maintained a post-IPO average position of 62 percent share ownership.

Our analysis of the twenty-six IPOs has provided a substantial view of the Russian IPO market and a conservative but incomplete picture of the country's total IPO environment. In addition to those twenty-six companies, we also uncovered fourteen additional IPO companies for which complete data were not available, increasing the number of actual IPOs by over 50 percent. There was sufficient data for these fourteen companies to indicate an even healthier IPO environment than would be reflected only by the twenty-six firms for which we were able to locate more complete data for this chapter. The industries represented by the additional fourteen firms were similar to the original twenty-six IPOs.

For additional perspective, not only in Russia but globally, 2008 was the year of a severe financial crisis and sharply restricted the opportunity for companies to launch an IPO. In Russia the numbers dropped from twelve in both 2006 and 2007, to only two in 2008. While we were able to identify one company, Transcontainer, that succeeded with an IPO in late 2010, a substantial pipeline of IPOs had been developing. Fifty-five companies were waiting in the wings to launch their IPOs, offering an average of 25 percent of their shares when the financial markets would become more receptive. As in the years 2006 to 2008, it is clear that an IPO does not result in widely held ownership, but that these companies remain closely held as has been the case since the privatization program of the early 1990s. And also in 2010, indications were that the Russian economy and its attractiveness to investment had been improving dramatically. Notably, PepsiCo Inc., in late 2010, purchased 66 percent of the Russian beverage and food company Wimm-Bill-Dann for \$3.8 billion, a 32 percent premium over its share price, with an agreement to purchase the remaining shares in the future as permitted by the Russian government (Lesova, 2010). Wimm-Bill-Dann, founded in 1992, was the third Russian company to list on the New York Stock Exchange, doing so in 2002, and has been notable for its exemplary corporate governance policies and practices. The year 2010 saw a substantial inflow of FDI including repatriated funds from Russians located overseas.

Additionally, one important source noted in late 2010 that there was renewed investor interest in Russia, signified by a return of foreign capital. Before the crash of 2008, the country was growing fast and furiously, and when the crash occurred, it happened violently. The report noted that "after bottoming spectacularly in early 2009, Russian equities rebounded sharply to double by the end of the year. The gains have continued in 2010, with the RTS index up around 20% so far this year" (Lagorce, 2010: 2). The same report noted that Russian companies were more welcoming of foreign investors and that it was much easier to get Russian managers to meet with foreign investors. If the positive investment trends of late 2010–11 continue, and with the myriad of Russian companies waiting to launch their IPOs, the country could become a leader in IPOs within the ensuing years. The major risk that such progress could be derailed is the country's endemic corruption, which the government has so far been unable to bring under control, even after some attempts over the past decade by both the Putin and Medvedev administrations to curb it. In this context, an additional motivation for an IPO by Russian companies has been seen by one researcher as providing "insurance" by discouraging attempts by government officials and others to expropriate, or in other ways threaten, the assets or ownership of companies with such public visibility (Markus, 2008).

As indicated by the data in Table 15.4, as well as our discussion of boards of directors and the Code of Corporate Conduct, Russian companies issuing IPOs have adopted corporate governance structures of boards and committees that reflect the Western-inspired agency theory basis of the country's Code of Corporate Conduct. Additionally, listing on either of the two major Russian stock exchanges requires that companies adhere to the requirements of the code, or report deviations in their policies and practices. Adherence to the code also facilitates Russian companies fulfilling the listing requirements of Western stock exchanges, particularly important since the London Stock Exchange is a favored listing destination for many Russian companies.

It is clear that Russia's code has had a strong and positive impact on the corporate governance of major Russian companies, particularly those that have had or planned to have an IPO. For this reason, our chapter explained the code in substantial detail, since it is the foundation of corporate governance for Russian companies. But it is also clear that there is still a need for substantial improvement on the part of numerous companies, especially those privately held firms that have not experienced the transparency requirements of an IPO and stock market listing. The need for such improvement is important not only for the development of the Russian economy, but specifically for the potential pipeline of IPOs to be well accepted by domestic and foreign investors.

References

Black, Bernard S. 2001. 'The corporate governance behavior and market value of Russian firms', *Emerging Markets Review*, 2, 89–108.

Black, Bernard S., Inessa Love, and Andrei Rachinsky. 2006. 'Corporate governance indices and firms' market values: Time series evidence from Russia', *Emerging Markets Review*, 7, 361–379.

Filatotchev, Igor, Mike Wright, Klaus Uhlenbruck, Lazlo Tihanyi, and Robert E. Hoskisson. 2003. 'Governance, organizational capabilities, and restructuring in transition economies', *Journal of World Business*, 38, 331–347.

Hoffman, David E. 2002. *The Oligarchs: Wealth and Power in the New Russia. Public Affairs*. Perseus Books: New York.

Judge, William Q., Irina Naoumova, and Nadejda Koutzevol. 2003. 'Corporate governance and firm performance in Russia: An empirical study', *Journal of World Business*, 38, 385–396.

Lagorce, Aude. 2010. 'From Russia with love: More open attitude to foreign investment encourages deals', *MarketWatch Emerging Markets Report*, December 2010. Downloaded from www.marketwatch.com/story/foreign-investors-wake-up-to-russias–recovery-2010-12-08, January 10, 2011.

Lesova, Polya. 2010. 'Deal boosts PepsiCo's presence in Russia: PepsiCo to buy 66% stake in Wimm-Bill-Dann Foods for $3.8 billion',

December 2010. Downloaded from www.marketwatch.com/story/ pepsico-to-buy-stake-in-russias-wimm-bill-dann-2010-12-02, January 10, 2011.

Markus, Stanislav. 2008. 'Corporate governance as political insurance: Firm-level institutional creation in emerging markets and beyond', *Socio-economic Review*, 6, 1, 69–98.

McCarthy, Daniel J. and Sheila M. Puffer. 2002a. 'Russia's corporate governance scorecard in the Enron era', *Organizational Dynamics*, 31, 1, 19–34.

2002b. 'Corporate governance in Russia: Towards a European, U.S. or Russian model?', *European Management Journal*, 20, 6, 630–640.

2003. 'Corporate governance in Russia: A framework for analysis', *Journal of World Business*, 38, 4, 397–415.

2008. 'Interpreting the ethicality of corporate governance decisions in Russia: Utilizing integrative social contracts theory to evaluate the relevance of agency theory norms', *Academy of Management Review*, 33, 1, 11–31.

Melkumov, Dmitri. 2009. 'Institutional background as a determinant of boards of directors' internal and external roles: The case of Russia', *Journal of World Business*, 44, 94–103.

Peng, Mike W., Trevor Buck, and Igor Filatotchev. 2003. 'Do outside directors and new managers help improve firm performance? An exploratory study in Russian privatization', *Journal of World Business*, 38, 348–360.

Perkins, Roswell B. 2002. 'The FCSM corporate governance code for Russian companies', *The Transnational Lawyer*, 16, 1, 75–110.

Puffer, Sheila M. and Daniel J. McCarthy. 2003. 'The emergence of corporate governance in Russia', *Journal of World Business*, 38, 4, 284–298.

2011. 'Two decades of Russian business and management research: An institutional theory perspective', *Academy of Management Perspectives*, 25, 2, 21–36.

'RID-sponsored project by AMR and KPMG (При поддержке РИД реализуется проект АМР и КПМГ – Исследование Корпоративное управление в России: поиск новой модели)', Russian Institute of Directors website. Available at www.rid.ru, November 9, 2010.

Shekshnia, Stanislav V. 2004. 'Roles, responsibilities, and independence of boards of directors', in Daniel J. McCarthy, Sheila M. Puffer, and Stanislav V. Shekshnia (eds.), *Corporate Governance in Russia*. Edward Elgar: Cheltenham, UK, and Northampton, US, 201–222.

Shleifer, Andrei and Robert W. Vishny. 1997. 'A survey of corporate governance', *Journal of Finance*, 52, 2, 737–783.

Additional sources

'IPO pioneers 4', 'IPO pioneers 3', and 'IPO pioneers 2'. The PBN Company: Washington, DC. Accessed at www.pbnco.com/eng/news/presentation. php, December 29, 2010.

'Joint stock companies'. Accessed at www.russianlawonline.com/content/ russia-joint-stock-company, December 29, 2010.

'Profile of the MICEX stock exchange'. Accessed at www.micex.com/group/ fbmmvb/profile, December 29, 2010.

'Russian Trading System Stock Exchange'. Accessed at www.rts.ru/s602, December 29, 2010.

Sources of IPO and company information for the Integra Group case study, in addition to company documents, were: www.Integra.ru/eng.

16 | *Corporate governance and initial public offerings in Singapore*[*]

M I C H A E L A . W I T T

Corporate governance mechanisms

Cultural factors, the multi-ethnic make-up of Singapore's population, and fairly high levels of immigration limit the extent of social cohesiveness in Singapore. As a former British colony, its legal system is based on common law. With the adoption of corporate governance codes over the past years, information disclosure of corporations has become fairly transparent, and deviations from the Code of Corporate Governance must be explained. At the same time, the market for corporate control remains mostly inactive. Prior research (Claessens, Djankov, and Lang, 2000) also suggested a relatively high level of cross-shareholdings, though it is not clear whether this pattern persists today.

Ownership concentration has historically been high (Claessens, Djankov, and Lang, 2000) and probably remains so, with families and the state representing major shareholders. Minority shareholder rights are well protected (World Bank and International Finance Corporation, 2010). Boards of directors are single tier, with independent directors on average accounting for a bit more than half of their composition. Executive compensation is non-egalitarian in nature.

Corporate law

The main provisions governing listed companies in Singapore include the Companies Act (1994 Revised Edition), the Securities and Futures Act (2002 Revised Edition), and the various listing requirements issued by the Singapore Exchange Ltd. In addition, a series of duties at common law apply.

[*] I would like to thank my colleagues Reto Callegari and Patrick Turner for their helpful input. I am further grateful to Clare Lee and Elaine Tan for providing outstanding research assistance, and to the Data Services Department of the Singapore Exchange for kindly providing historical data from their archives.

In line with Anglo-Saxon tradition, board structure in Singapore is single tier. While the Companies Act allows for private firms with single directors for listed firms, minimum board size is de facto three. For companies domiciled in Singapore, at least one director needs to be ordinarily resident in Singapore, and there need to be at least two independent directors on the board. Companies listed on the "mainboard" (main market) of the Singapore Exchange that are domiciled elsewhere must have at least two independent directors who are Singapore residents; for firms listed on the secondary board, Catalist, this number is reduced to one. For listed companies, directors are subject to an age limit of seventy years.

The Companies Act requires companies to hold an annual general meeting no later than fifteen months after the last such meeting. General meetings vote on directors' appointments, with each candidate being voted on separately unless a preceding unanimous resolution specifies otherwise. Such meetings may also remove directors by ordinary resolution.

The Companies Act further requires each listed firm to have an audit committee. This committee needs to consist of at least three directors, and the majority of these members must not be executive directors or related to executive directors, nor otherwise be "having a relationship which ... would interfere with the exercise of independent judgment" (Article 201B (2) (c)). The chairperson of the audit committee must be a non-executive, independent director.

Code of corporate governance

A government-appointed Corporate Governance Committee first put Singapore's Code of Corporate Governance forth on 21 March 2001. A revised code was issued on 14 July 2005 and came into effect for annual general meetings from 1 January 2007 onward. Since 1 September 2007, the Monetary Authority of Singapore and the Singapore Exchange Ltd. have overseen the implementation of the Code.

The Code of Corporate Governance follows the "comply or explain" approach. Specifically, the Singapore Stock Exchange requires listed firms to account for their corporate governance practices in their annual report and explain any divergences from the Code. The Code of Corporate Governance addresses four broad areas: "board matters" (principles 1–6); "remuneration matters" (7–9);

"accountability and audit" (10–13); and "communication with share-holders" (14–15). Table 16.1 summarizes the individual principles.

Regular surveys by the Singapore Exchange and the Singapore Institute of Directors suggest that these principles have influenced the corporate governance practices of Singapore-listed firms (Table 16.2). The most recent survey (2008/09) shows evidence of (1) a good mix between executive and non-executive directors; (2) a sufficient number of independent directors; (3) a decent educational background of the majority of directors; (4) relatively modest numbers of other board commitments; and (5) an almost universal adoption of audit, nominating, and remuneration committees. On the other hand, a number of issues require further attention, including (1) the role of the chairperson; (2) a low proportion of women on boards; (3) the presence especially of executive directors with long tenures on the board; and (4) further diffusion of board evaluation processes. However, with the exception of the last point, the trend has been going in the direction envisioned in the Code.

Stock exchange and listed companies

Development and relevance of the Singapore Exchange

The Singapore Stock Exchange has developed rapidly from the 1990s onward. In the past twenty years, the number of listings has more than quadrupled, and market capitalization has risen more than ten-fold (Table 16.3).

Singapore's stock market has attracted numerous listings from overseas (i.e., non-Singaporean) companies. According to Singapore Exchange Monthly Market Statistics for the end of 2010, out of 782 listed companies on both boards, 461 were Singapore companies, valued at about SGD 476 billion (USD 369 billion); 156 were China companies, valued at about SGD 56 billion (USD 43 billion); and 165 were overseas companies from countries other than China, valued at about SGD 372 billion (USD 288 billion). In other words, Singaporean companies accounted for about 59 percent of listings and 53 percent of market capitalization.

There are two boards, the mainboard and Catalist, which caters to smaller, fast-growing companies and has lighter listing and continuing requirements, as discussed below. Until December 2007, the junior board was known as Sesdaq.

Table 16.1 *Summary of corporate governance principles*

1. Every company needs an effective board. Task of the board is "to lead and control" the firm, working with management toward successful outcomes. Management is accountable to the board, whose members in turn share collective responsibility for company success.
2. Boards must be "strong and independent" in their ability to assess corporate matters. They are required to eschew undue influence from management and individual board members.
3. Firms should avoid a concentration of power by providing for a "clear division of responsibilities at the top of the company," that is, separate the work of the board and that of executives.
4. The process for appointing new directors should be "formal and transparent."
5. A process needs to be in place to effect a "formal assessment of the effectiveness" of both individual directors and the board as a whole.
6. Board members must receive "complete, adequate and timely information prior to board meetings and on an on-going basis."
7. Development of a remunerations policy and decisions on remunerations for individual directors must follow a "formal and transparent procedure." Directors must not have a say in the determination of their own pay.
8. Remunerations should be high enough to "attract, retain and motivate" good-quality directors; should not be excessive; and should link a significant portion of pay to company performance.
9. Annual reports must disclose "remuneration policy, level and mix of remuneration, and the procedure for setting remuneration" as well as explain the relationship between pay and corporate performance.
10. Assessments by the board on corporate performance, current conditions, and future prospects must be "balanced and understandable."
11. The board must create an Audit Committee and provide for its remit in writing.
12. The board is responsible for ensuring that management establishes a "sound system of internal controls."
13. Each company needs "an internal audit function that is independent of the activities it audits."
14. Communications with shareholders must be "regular, effective and fair."
15. Annual general meetings should "encourage greater shareholder participation," including opportunities to express views on company matters.

Source: Code of Corporate Governance, 2005

Table 16.2 *Board characteristics of firms listed in Singapore*

Variables	Characteristics
Average board size and composition	7.1 members: 2.2 executive directors, 1.2 non-independent non-executive directors, 3.6 independent non-executive directors
Average chairperson's shareholdings	controlling shareholder 45 percent, nominee of controlling shareholder 17 percent
Chairperson's status	27 percent independent, 26 percent non-independent non-executive, 26 percent chairperson and CEO, 20 percent executive
Sex of directors	about 93 percent male, 7 percent female
Average percentage of directors with university degree per board	85 percent (n=128)
Positions in other governance bodies	• 87 percent of executive directors (n=271) and 85 percent of non-executive directors (n=565) have directorships in at least one other listed firm, with the mode at 1 or 2 (77 percent for executive directors, 45 percent for non-executive directors) • 48 percent of executive directors and 64 percent of non-executive directors have directorships in at least one other non-listed firm, with the mode at 0 (52 percent for executive directors, 36 percent for non-executive directors)
Modal number of years on the board	executive directors >9 years (30 percent) (n=286), non-independent non-executive directors 1–3 years (34 percent) (n=151), independent directors 3 years (54 percent) (n=451)
Committee structure	Out of 97 firms:
Audit committee	97 have an audit committee with on average 3.3 members (0.1 executive, 0.4 non-independent non-executive, 2.8 independent) and 3.5 meetings in 2008
Executive committee	16 have an executive committee with on average 4.1 members (2.3 executive, 0.7 non-independent non-executive, 1.1 independent) and 3.6 meetings in 2008

Table 16.2 (*cont.*)

Variables	Characteristics
Nominating committee	91 have a nominating committee with on average 3.3 members (0.3 executive, 0.5 non-independent non-executive, 2.5 independent) and 1.5 meetings in 2008
Remuneration committee	95 have a remuneration committee with on average 3.3 members (0.1 executive, 0.5 non-independent non-executive, 2.6 independent) and 2.0 meetings in 2008
Firms with board evaluation process	72 percent, decreasing from 78 percent in 2005 and 85 percent in 2004
Modal compensation of board of directors	chief executive officer: SGD 250,000 to 499,999 (USD 193,710 to 387,420);[1] top 4 executive directors and/or senior executives: <SGD 250,000 (USD 193,710); non-executive directors: SGD 25,000 to 49,999 (USD 19,371 to 38,741)

Source: Singapore Board of Directors Survey 2008/09
Note: N=130 unless otherwise specified. Numbers may not sum to 100 percent or the equivalent value because of rounding. Compensation is only disclosed in brackets.
[1] SGD/USD exchange rates are as of 31 December of the respective year indicated, with the exception of the IPO data, which are converted using the exchange rate of the respective IPO dates.

The relevance of the stock market to the Singaporean economy is significant, but not as high at it appears at first glance. According to the World Development Indicators database, the 2009 ratio of market capitalization over GDP was 171 percent. This is among the highest in the world. However, since Singapore (like Hong Kong) lists a fairly large proportion of non-Singapore companies, these numbers over-state the significance of the stock market as a source of funds. At the end of November 2009, Singapore companies accounted for about 57 percent of market capitalization on the Singapore Exchange. This suggests a market capitalization to GDP ratio for Singapore firms of about 97 percent. This is still high, but lower than the (uncorrected) ratio for a number of other economies considered in this book, including Australia, the UK, Canada, Sweden, the United States, and China.

Table 16.3 *Number of listed companies and market capitalization, Singapore Exchange and its predecessors, 1980–2010*

	Mainboard		Sesdaq/Catalist		Total	
Year	Number of listed companies	Market capitalization, SGD/USD million	Number of listed companies	Market capitalization, SGD/USD million	Number of listed companies	Market capitalization, SGD/USD million
1980	261	51,119/n/a	–	–	261	51,119/n/a
1990	172	83,310/48,010	13	409/236	185	83,720/48,247
2000	388	389,516/224,764	92	3,986/2,300	480	393,502/227,064
2005	492	422,028/253,420	171	5,876/3,528	663	427,905/256,949
2010	651	895,469/693,845	131	6,462/5,007	782	901,931/698,852

Source: Singapore Exchange
Note: All data for end of respective year. 1980 exchange rates not available.

Table 16.4 *Percentages of shares held, directly or indirectly,*
by substantial shareholders

	Top substantial shareholder	All substantial shareholders
Minimum	0	0
Maximum	86.31	845.52
Average	35.7	132.4
Median	33.4	83.9

Source: Computation by the author using a random sample of 110 annual reports for 2009 of companies listed on the Singapore Exchange

Ownership structure of companies listed in Singapore

Ownership in Singapore is, on average, highly concentrated. Table 16.4 shows that on average for the given sample of 110 firms, the largest substantial shareholder has direct or indirect control of 35.7 percent of all outstanding shares of the respective company. If companies not reporting any substantial shareholders are omitted (N=92), the same average increases to 42.7 percent. In other words, to the extent firms have substantial shareholders, the respective top shareholder would effectively have control of the company.

Table 16.4 also shows the sums of the percentages held by all substantial shareholders taken together. These figures involve double counting because multiple individuals may be deemed to have the same indirect stake in a company, so they are not meaningful in and by themselves. However, the fact that these percentages are relatively high suggest close connections among several substantial shareholders, as would be typical, for instance, for family-dominated companies. Omitting companies with no substantial shareholders, the average increases to 158.3 percent.

Research in the late 1990s further suggested a role for cross-shareholdings and pyramidal control structures in the Singaporean economy as well as control of a quarter of the corporate sector by the ten largest families (Claessens, Djankov, and Lang, 2000). It is not clear to what extent these patterns still hold today.

An important enduring feature of the Singapore economic land-scape is the presence of "government-linked companies" (GLCs), that is, companies that are fully or partially state owned. Estimates suggest that these firms accounted for more than 60 percent of GDP in 2001

(Wilkin, 2004). Their present footprint is not precisely known but is still considered to be "dominant" (Miller and Holmes, 2010, p. 376). The primary vehicle for state ownership of these firms is Temasek Holdings. Temasek was established in 1974 to separate ownership of companies and investments from policy making and government administration. Temasek today is essentially a sovereign wealth fund, though it rejects being labeled as such because of its independence from government. Its sole shareholder is the Singapore Ministry of Finance.

Table 16.5 shows the major Singapore holdings of Temasek. Firms that are wholly owned by Temasek are, by definition, not listed on the Singapore Exchange and are included here for the sake of giving a comprehensive picture. Partially owned companies included in the table are all listed on the Singapore Exchange. As of the end of November 2010, the largest five firms in the table ranked among the top fifteen firms by market capitalization on the Singapore Exchange.

Unlike state-owned firms in many other countries, GLCs are run on a commercial and competitive basis. Prior research has found evidence that compared with non-GLCs: GLCs do not have easier access to credit (Ramírez and Tan, 2004); have equivalent returns (Feng, Sun, and Tong, 2004); have higher valuations (Ang and Ding, 2006; Ramírez and Tan, 2004); and have better corporate governance (Ang and Ding, 2006; Ramírez and Tan, 2004).

IPO activity between 2006 and 2008

Regulation of IPOs

IPO firms in Singapore usually determine the price of their offering in consultation with the underwriter (bookrunner) and placement agent, typically in conjunction with a book-building process. The output of this process is a single issue price for all new shares.

Companies can decide to list on one of two boards: the mainboard or Catalist, which is a secondary board with lower listing require-ments (Table 16.6). Companies wishing to list are required to produce an IPO prospectus. The prospectus contains information about the details of the offering, including the nature of the company's business; the number of shares on offer and the issue price; intended use of the

Table 16.5 *Major portfolio companies of Temasek Holdings, 2009*

Company	Industry	Market cap, SGD/USD million	Temasek stake
Singapore Telecommunications Ltd.	Telecommunications & media	40,295/28,678	54%
DBS Group Holdings Ltd.	Financial services	19,278/13,720	28%
Singapore Airlines Ltd.	Transport & logistics	11,826/8,416	55%
CapitaLand Ltd.	Real estate	9,889/7,038	40%
Keppel Corporation Ltd.	Infrastructure, industrial & engineering	7,982/5,681	21%
PSA International Pte. Ltd.	Transport & logistics	7,390/5,259	100%
Singapore Technologies Engineering Ltd.	Infrastructure, industrial & engineering	7,385/5,256	50%
Mapletree Investments Pte. Ltd.	Real estate	4,674/3,626	100%
Sembcorp Industries Ltd.	Infrastructure, industrial & engineering	4,179/2,974	49%
Singapore Power Ltd.	Energy & resources	4,052/2,884	100%
Fraser and Neave Ltd.	Consumer & lifestyle	3,516/2,502	15%
SMRT Corporation Ltd.	Transport & logistics	2,320/1,651	54%
Singapore Technologies Telemedia Pte. Ltd.	Telecommunications & media	2,232/1,589	100%
Neptune Orient Lines Ltd.	Transport & logistics	1,739/1,238	66%
MediaCorp Pte. Ltd.	Telecommunications & media	969/690	100%
STATS ChipPAC Ltd.	Technology	694/494	84%
Chartered Semiconductor Manufacturing Ltd.	Technology	343/244	59%

Source: Temasek Review, 2009

proceeds; current and expected post-IPO ownership and governance patterns; and financial information. For listings on the Singapore Exchange mainboard, the Singapore Exchange Ltd. will vet the contents of the prospectus. For listings on Catalist, the secondary board, an approved sponsor undertakes this task.

Table 16.6 *Listing and continuing obligations in Singapore*

Admission requirements

Free float	• mainboard: 12 percent–25 percent, depending on market capitalization • Catalist: 15 percent
Market capitalization	• mainboard: at least SGD 80 million (USD 62 million) for mainboard, except if the company fulfills certain pre-tax profit requirements in previous years • Catalist: no minimum
Operating track record	• mainboard: 3 years, with the same exceptions as under market capitalization • Catalist: no minimum
Sponsor	• mainboard: none • Catalist: approved sponsor required
Regulation and supervision	• mainboard: regulated and supervised by the Singapore Exchange • Catalist: regulated by the Singapore Exchange, supervised by approved sponsor
Prospectus	Required

Continuing obligations

Price-sensitive information	Timely dissemination via SGXNET
Minimum free float	10 percent for both boards
Financial statements	• listing or year-end market capitalization above SGD 75 million (USD 58.1 million): quarterly results within 45 days • below same market capitalization: semi-annual results within 45 days • regardless of market capitalization: annual results within 60 days
Transactions by interested persons	• at least 3 percent of latest audited net tangible assets: to be announced • at least 5 percent of latest audited net tangible assets: shareholder approval needed

Source: Singapore Exchange Ltd., 2010

Table 16.7 *IPO year and industry classification*

	2006	2007	2008	Total
Basic materials	0	11	1	12
Consumer goods	0	3	5	8
Consumer services	0	1	2	3
Financials	0	0	1	1
Healthcare	0	0	2	2
Industrials	0	10	11	21
Oil and gas	0	2	0	2
Technology	0	3	0	3
Total	**0**	**30**	**22**	**52**

IPO companies are subject to both listing requirements and continuing obligations (Table 16.6). In general, the main listing requirement is that between 12 percent and 25 percent of shares be in free float after the IPO, depending on the board on which the listing occurs and the market capitalization of the firm in question. Continuing obligations include the need to maintain a minimum level of free float and proper and prompt disclosure, including of transactions by interested persons. Firms that have reached a market capitalization above SGD 75 million (USD 58.1 million), either at the point of listing or at the end of any given year, are required to publish quarterly and annual financial statements even if their current market capitalization is below SGD 75 million (USD 58.1 million). Companies that have not crossed the threshold are required to publish semi-annual and annual financial statements.

IPOs between 2006 and 2008

From 2006 through 2008, a total of fifty-one firms went public on the Singapore Exchange, and one Singaporean firm went public on the London Stock Exchange. Most of these companies (thirty cases) went public in 2007, while not a single qualified listing occurred in 2006 (Table 16.7). The financial crisis is likely to have been a factor in the reduction in numbers in 2008 to twenty-two IPOs. As Table 16.7 illustrates, most of these IPOs were in the industrial sector (twenty-one cases), followed by basic materials (twelve cases).

Table 16.8 *IPO size and performance*

	Size			Performance		
	Employees	Revenues (USD)	Assets (USD)	ROA	ROE	ROS
Minimum	19	195,549	7,325,000	−95%	−259%	−1,304%
1st quartile	142	21,394,425	30,950,750	11%	31%	11%
2nd quartile	380	37,670,404	83,662,500	19%	50%	15%
3rd quartile	756	71,810,285	332,868,250	25%	89%	24%
Maximum	12,761	301,078,918	37,000,544,000	53%	1,072%	57%
Average	888	59,287,771	1,695,438,596	17%	76%	−7%

Most of the firms listed were nominally very young, with thirty-six (69.2 percent) of them founded in 2002 or later. A main reason for this phenomenon is that many of them represented pure listing vehicles, that is, they were founded specifically to enable pre-existing firms to list on the Singapore Exchange and thus acted as holding companies.

Firms going IPO ranged from very small to large (Table 16.8). On average, firms had 888 employees, revenues just shy of USD 60 million, and assets of about USD 1.7 billion. However, as the median numbers (2nd quartile) suggest, most firms were considerably smaller than the average, with some large cases pulling up the average considerably. The smallest IPO by employees and revenues was Artivision, a Singaporean technology company. Smallest by assets was Sinotel Technologies, a telecommunications company with main operations in China. Largest by number of employees was Samko Timber, a forestry firm active in Indonesia; by revenues, Yangzijiang, a shipbuilding firm with operations in China; and by assets, Sino Construction, a construction company active in China.

Profitability was usually good. Median return on assets was 19 percent; return on equity, 50 percent; and return on sales, 15 percent. Artivision was the only firm to turn a loss prior to IPO, a pattern that is consistent with that observed in startups elsewhere. Most profitable firms were Sinostar (ROA), a petrochemicals firm active in China; Dutech Holding (ROE), a technology firm from China; and Kencana Agri (ROS), a firm active in palm oil in Malaysia.

The majority of firms going public in Singapore are originally family-owned firms (Table 16.9). Forty out of fifty-two firms had at least some family ownership before the IPO, with an average stake of

Table 16.9 *IPO ownership structure (data in percent)*

	Family		Bank		Govt.		VC		Angels		Top 1		Top 3	
	pre	post	pre	post	pre	post	pre	post	pre	post	pre	post	pre	post
Minimum	0	0	0	0	0	0	0	0	0	0	19	16	40	30
1st quartile	5	4	0	0	0	0	0	0	0	0	49	38	78	57
2nd quartile	70	52	0	0	0	0	0	0	0	0	73	52	90	69
3rd quartile	89	66	0	0	0	0	0	0	6	4	85	63	99	73
Maximum	100	84	26	21	5	4	0	0	35	30	100	85	100	85
Average	54	41	1	1	0	0	0	0	5	3	67	51	85	64
No. of firms with this type of owner	40	40	9	10	1	1	1	1	25	25	52	52	52	52

54 percent and a median stake of 70 percent. Angel investors were the second most common owners of pre-IPO firms, though they held only 5 percent of shares on average and 0 percent in the median case. Banks follow in third position, with a negligible pre-IPO position of 1 percent on average and 0 percent in the median case. Venture capital firms and government were insignificant sources of capital, both before and after the IPO. The picture remains similar post-IPO. Noteworthy is that families retain on average 41 percent of shares, and thus a controlling stake. The median number is even higher at 52 percent.

This is related to a general pattern of ownership concentration among the IPO firms even after the IPO (Table 16.9). The leading shareholder retains on average 51 percent of shares after the IPO, with a median value of 52 percent. The three leading shareholders hold almost two-thirds (64 percent) of shares post-IPO, with a median value of 69 percent. Given these shareholding patterns, Singapore-listed firms apparently see little need to assert control through measures such as dual shares with different voting rights, pyramid structures, or voting syndicates. The former are absent from the sample. Two firms showed evidence of a pyramid structure, and one firm acknowledges the existence of a syndicate.

The average board of IPO firms has 6.4 members, of whom 1.1 are executive directors, 2.8 are non-executive directors, and 2.6 are independent directors (Table 16.10). Employees are not represented on boards as there is no legal requirement to that effect. By contrast, it is fairly common for there to be two or more family members on the

Table 16.10 *IPO board of directors*

	Size	Executive directors	Non-independent non-executive directors	Independent directors	Engineering, operations, R&D	Marketing, sales	Finance, accounting, law
Min	4	0	1	0	0	0	1
1st quartile	6	1	2	2	1	0	3
2nd quartile	6	1	3	3	2	0	4
3rd quartile	7	1	3	3	3	1	5
Max	11	3	6	4	6	3	9
Average	6.4	1.1	2.8	2.6	2.3	0.7	3.8

board of family-dominated firms. About 31 percent of firms have at least one woman on the board, a proportion that is considerably higher than the average for all listed firms in Singapore (Table 16.2).

In terms of functional expertise, the most common background of board members is in peripheral areas such as finance, accounting, and law. This kind of background is particularly common among independent directors, apparently in an attempt to complement operational experience inside the firm with financial and legal savvy from the outside. Throughput functions such as engineering, operations, and R&D are second, and output functions such as marketing and sales a distant third.

In accordance with legal requirements, all firms have audit committees. In addition, all firms have nomination and remuneration committees, as recommended by the Code of Corporate Governance. No company created a governance or technology committee.

Description of an IPO: Dutech Holdings Limited

Before the IPO

Dutech Holdings Limited was founded in Singapore on 1 June 2007 as an investment vehicle for two manufacturing companies located in the People's Republic of China (PRC), a construct that is typical for the overseas listings Singapore has been attracting in recent years. The firm grew out of a private limited company founded in Singapore in November 2006, which in turn was the result of a restructuring of the original lines of business in the PRC, founded in June 2000. Co-founders of the firm are Dr. Johnny Liu Jiayan and his brother

Liu Bin, both of whom were born in the PRC and are presumably still PRC citizens. Dr. Liu has extended work experience with a supplier of Ford and GM in the United States, and his Chinese business appears to have leveraged at least initially the knowledge and contacts he gained there.

Dutech Holdings Limited is an investment holding company. It owns 100 percent each in two other Singapore companies, Tri Star Security Singapore and Tri Star Semicon Singapore. These in turn own 100 percent each of Tri Star Inc. and Tri Star Semicon PRC, which are headquartered in Shanghai and manufacture in Nantong, China. Tri Star Inc. produces high-security safes for ATM and commercial uses. Tri Star Semicon PRC builds semiconductor testers and semiconductor and precision machining parts for use in the semiconductor and auto-motive industries.

About three-quarters of the group revenues come from the safe busi-ness. Geographically, about half of revenues are generated in the United States, and another third in Europe, especially Germany. Revenues in FY2006 were CNY 188.4 million (USD 24.9 million), with a CAGR over FY2004 of 160.3 percent. Profits for FY2006 reached CNY 47.9 million (USD 6.3 million), with a CAGR over FY2004 of 629.5 percent.

Using investment vehicles registered in the British Virgin Islands, Dr. Liu held 51.8 percent of the shares before the IPO. His brother controlled another 22.2 percent in the same manner. Advisors to the listing process received 5.4 percent of shares, which they held through another British Virgin Island company with the poetic name of "Flour-ishing Profits." OCBC Capital Investments held 9.3 percent, and the remaining 11.3 percent of shares were in the hands of various pre-IPO investors who had gained these shares through conversion of convert-ible loans, apparently at an average price of SGD 0.2359 (USD 0.155).

Dr. Liu occupied the dual role of chairman and CEO, while his brother was executive vice-chairman. The board further contained three independent directors, two from Singapore and one from China. Board composition was thus in alignment with Singaporean legal requirements of public firms.

The offer

Dutech Holdings Limited decided to obtain a listing on the Singapore Exchange mainboard. It extended its offer through a prospectus dated

24 July 2007, with applications due by 12 noon on 31 July 2007. The offer comprised a total of 85 million shares: 60 million in new shares and 25 million vendor shares. Of these, 82 million were intended for placement, and 3 million for public offer. The total number of outstanding shares after the offer would be 328 million shares. All existing shareholders agreed to a six-month moratorium on sales of the shares retained after the IPO.

OCBC Bank acted as manager, underwriter, and placement agent, and through a book-building process, the offer was priced at SGD 0.33 (USD 0.217) per share. IPO market capitalization was thus SGD 108.24 million (USD 71.2 million).

The new shares generated SGD 16.4 million (USD 10.8 million) in proceeds after expenses. Of this amount, SGD 6 million (USD 3.9 million) each was earmarked for investment in equipment and software in each line of business, safes and semiconductors. SGD 4.4 million (USD 2.9 million) was intended as general working capital.

As required by the Companies Act and the Code of Corporate Governance, the company established an accounting, nominating, and remuneration committee before the IPO.

After the IPO

The IPO was successful, with the first listing on 2 August 2007. Closing price on the first day was SGD 0.46 (USD 0.303), representing a 39.4 percent premium over the issue price and suggesting that the offering was substantially underpriced.

Post-IPO, Dutech's ownership structure looked as follows: Dr. Liu 40.28 percent, Mr. Liu 17.16 percent, OCBC Capital Investment 7.6 percent, Flourishing Profits 4.5 percent, other pre-IPO investors 4.6 percent. The remaining 25.86 percent of shares was in float. However, given their combined share of 57.44 percent, it is clear that the Liu brothers maintained control of the firm after the listing. In 2009, Dr. Liu received a remuneration between SGD 250,000 (USD 177,923) and SGD 500,000 (USD 355,847), with all other executives remaining below SGD 250,000 (USD 177,923).[1]

---

[1] In accordance with Singapore practice, the company discloses executive remuneration not in actual figures but in broad brackets.

The firm's strategy for the future was in essence to expand and upgrade its existing lines of business. Plans called for a new clean room, higher capacity, further R&D, CEN certification for high-end safes, and expansion to other geographic markets.

As of the time of this writing, Dutech Holding Limited shares traded around SGD 0.20 (USD 0.155).

Conclusion

The overall picture that emerges from this chapter is that Singapore has made considerable recent progress in growing its stock markets, not least through listings of foreign companies, and in putting corporate governance on solid foundations. However, ownership seems to remain fairly concentrated, and the state continues to play a substantial role in the stock market and the economy. IPO activity between 2006 and 2008 was fairly brisk, especially in 2007. Newly listed firms tend to be in the industrial sector, are fairly small on average, and retain a controlling stake in family hands after the listing, with the top shareholder in the average firm holding more than half of outstanding shares.

The literature has identified a number of areas of governance with potential for further development. In particular, it has been noted that corporate governance breaches, especially large-scale fraud such as the 2003 case of China Aviation Oil, should result in sterner criminal and civil action and the disqualification of directors (Mak, Lan, and Bin Buang, 2007). One of the challenges in this context is how to enforce standards provided for by Singapore law on the foreign listed companies in Singapore (Mak et al., 2007).

References

Ang, James S. and David D. Ding. 2006. 'Government ownership and the performance of government-linked companies: The case of Singapore', *Journal of Multinational Financial Management*, 16, 1, 64–88.

Claessens, Stijn, Simeon Djankov and Larry H.P. Lang. 2000. 'The separation of ownership and control in East Asian corporations', *Journal of Financial Economics*, 58, 81–112.

Feng, Fang, Qian Sun and Wilson H.S. Tong. 2004. 'Do government-linked companies underperform?', *Journal of Banking & Finance*, 28, 10, 2461–92.

Mak, Yuen Teen, Luh Luh Lan and Azrudi Bin Buang. 2007. 'Implementation and enforcement of rules in Singapore and the case of China Aviation Oil', in *Enforcement of Corporate Governance in Asia: The Unfinished Agenda*. Paris: OECD, 93–107.

Miller, Terry and Kim R. Holmes. 2010. *2010 Index of Economic Freedom*. Washington, DC: The Heritage Foundation.

Ramírez, Carlos D. and Ling Hui Tan. 2004. 'Singapore Inc. versus the private sector: Are government-linked companies different?', *IMF Staff Papers*, 51, 3, 510–28.

Wilkin, Sam. 2004. 'Maintaining Singapore's miracle'. Downloaded from www.countryrisk.com/editorials/archives/2004_08_17.html, 9 December 2010.

World Bank and International Finance Corporation. 2010. *Doing Business 2011: Making a Difference for Entrepreneurs*. Washington, DC: IFC and World Bank.

17 Corporate governance and initial public offerings in Spain*

FÉLIX J. LÓPEZ-ITURRIAGA
AND IGNACIO DANVILA DEL VALLE

Corporate governance mechanisms

Spain has a long historical inheritance that dates back to the Old Roman Empire. Its society is characterized by a high level of collectivism: citizens are integrated into cohesive groups and families play an important role. According to the country's civil law legal system (La Porta, Lopez-de-Silanes, Shleifer et al., 1997, 1998), laws are the key legal regulation tool. As a result of this history and other cultural dimensions (Hofstede, 1984), the market for corporate control has never fully developed. Although the corporate governance system has recently switched to a "comply-or-explain" approach, transparency and a smooth flow of information in capital markets continue to be undervalued. Consequently, the information disclosure is somehow biased towards opacity. In addition, cross-shareholdings and business groups are a common form of corporate governance.

Partially as a response to the lack of legal protection, corporate ownership is usually concentrated. That is, a certain shareholder or shareholders maintain majority control of the company. Family ownership plays an outstanding role in Spanish firms, and, as a result, families own dominant stakes in many firms, including some of the country's largest. Corporate boards are always single tier in nature, and the chief executive officer (CEO) commonly also chairs the board of directors. In recent years, the trend has been clearly toward non-executive directors. A significant variable component of the CEO's and top management team's compensation is usually tied to firm performance.

* The authors are grateful to Domingo J. García-Coto, Meritxell Pérez-de-Castro, Gonzalo Jolín, and managers and employees from *Clínica Baviera*, *Bolsas y Mercados Españoles*, and *Inmobiliaria San José* for providing insightful inputs. All the remaining errors are our sole responsibility.

Spanish corporate law

The lack of shareholder activism (Chung and Talaulicar, 2010), the negligible albeit growing importance of minority shareholders, and the dominant role played by banks and other blockholders have resulted in a transient corporate system with small reforms. Weak protection of minority stakeholder rights has allowed banks to dominate in the provision of large-scale funds and may have caused the relative underdevelopment of capital markets.

Spanish banks, like many others in Europe, have played an active role in the financial system as a whole, whereas the involvement of capital markets has been limited (Allen and Gale, 2001). From the beginning of industrialization, Spanish banks have followed the universal-relationship banking model, not only providing a full range of financing services but also keeping close ties with non-financial firms, both through credit and through the acquisition of shares. Conglomerates around banks gathered utilities and other strategic companies that held close financial ties with banks and, therefore, were able to remain unlisted. Additionally, during certain decades, the state played a central role in the Spanish corporate system. Therefore, the combination of state-owned firms and bank conglomerates has resulted in a commercial law at the core of which are large blockholders and lenders (Gonzalo, 2005).

Spain has added to the international mainstream of corporate governance reforms by attempting to strengthen its weak legal corporate system. The deep financial and economic global crisis of the 1970s ended in Spain in 1985 with fifty-eight banking failures, totaling more than 27 percent of the financial system assets. In addition to the external causes, brought on by the economic recession, a number of internal motives are commonly attributed to Spain's bank failures. Bank managers' lack of professionalism is among the most often cited ways in which Spain's banking system contributed to its own demise (López de Letona, 2005). These individual constructs were exacerbated by institutional weaknesses due to the absence of a legal framework that clearly allocated legal duties and responsibilities within firms and the lack of transparency of information in the capital markets. Unfortunately, Spanish economic authorities did not comprehend the need for a regulatory shift toward better supervision and increased investors' protection until the end of the 1980s.

The initiatives through which legal changes were made addressed three different areas of the statutory code: (1) the laws about the governing bodies of firms, (2) the legal framework of capital markets, and (3) the laws about auditing. First, regarding the regulation on governance of firms, the *Ley de Sociedades Anónimas* (Public Companies Act) was passed in 1989. This new law confirmed the shareholders' general meeting as the supreme governing body. According to the law, the meeting has the power to appoint the board of directors according to a monistic system, in which both executive and non-executive can sit. Second, the new legal framework of capital markets was developed under the *Ley del Mercado de Capitales* (Securities Markets Act) in 1988. The creation of the *Comisión Nacional del Mercado de Valores* (Spanish Stock Exchange Commission), an independent agency whose aim is to ensure stability and transparency in financial markets, protect investors, and make sure that brokers and intermediaries behave properly, is the cornerstone of this new system of governance. Finally, the *Ley de Auditoría* (Auditing Act) was passed in 1988 and required all listed and most of the unlisted firms to be audited.

Although some amendments to these laws were passed during the 1990s, the main legal changes were implemented more recently under the *Ley Financiera* (Amendment of Financial System Act), passed in 2002, and the *Ley de Transparencia de Sociedades Cotizadas* (Public Corporations Transparency Act), enacted in 2003. In general, this new legal framework improves the protection of shareholders and the information available in capital markets by constraining managers' discretion and increasing security and transparency in capital markets. More specifically, public firms now are obliged to disclose information about shareholder coalitions and ownership and governance structure. Both the board of directors and the shareholders' meeting are required to outline and operate under specific rules of procedure. The new laws made the corporate governance annual report mandatory and required its disclosure through the corporate website. An audit committee with a majority of independent directors is also mandatory. In addition, managers have imposed on them duties of diligence, faithfulness, and loyalty, together with their liability regime.

In addition to these domestic laws, the Spanish legal system has also been enriched in recent years with the implementation of a number of mandatory EU laws. They include recommendations on fostering an appropriate regime for the compensation of directors of listed companies (2004) and on the role of non-executive or supervisory directors of listed companies and on the committees of the board (2005) as well as the EU Takeover Bids Directive and the EU Transparency Directive on the harmonization of transparency requirements about public issuers.

In sum, although the Spanish commercial law system is not exactly a first comer to corporate governance, the Spanish government has recently moved decisively in this direction. In addition, the issuance of three recent codes of good governance, as outlined in the following discussion, complement and strengthen the legal system.

Spanish codes of good governance

The first official code of good governance was issued in Spain in 1998 and is commonly known as the Olivencia Report. Since then, two other official codes have been the Aldama Report in 2003, and the Spanish Unified Code of Best Practice in 2006. In addition, private institutions and foundations have also issued similar codes and initiatives including the Managers Circle of Madrid in 1996 (*Círculo de Empresarios de Madrid*), the Foundation of Financial Analysis (*Fundación de Estudios Financieros*), a foundation of the Spanish Association of Financial Analysts in 2002, and, more recently, the Institute of Directors (*Instituto de Consejeros*) and the Family Business Institute (*Instituto de la Empresa Familiar*).

The Olivencia Code recommendations are similar to those of the Cadbury Report (1992): the need for a non-executive majority on the board, the nomination of specialized committees made up exclusively of non-executive directors (i.e., the auditing, remuneration, and appointment committees), and the need to disclose managers' and directors' compensation schemes. Recommendations for a maximum and minimum board size and the setting of a retirement age for directors also appeared in the report. Given the high ownership concentration of Spanish firms, the report also established three types of directors: (a) non-executives who are, or who represent, large shareholders; (b) independent directors; and (c) executive directors.

The Olivencia Code was based on voluntary fulfillment and had limited success. As Gómez and Cabeza (2009) show, mean compliance with the code recommendations was around 56 percent, and only five out of sixty-seven questioned firms implemented all twenty-three recommendations. Fernández et al. (2004) report a weak positive market reaction to announcements of compliance, which cast doubts on the effectiveness of the code and suggested the need for additional rules.

The Aldama Report (2002) introduced the manager's duty of loyalty and diligence. The report, taking into account the ownership structure of Spanish firms, stated that the composition of the board of directors should reflect the firm's ownership structure. It also recommended the establishment of board committees and emphasized the importance of informational transparency. The core recommendation was that companies should be obliged to give fuller information about their systems of governance, which was an immediate echo in the Transparency Law, enacted a few months later (Gómez and Cabeza, 2009). This report followed the "comply or explain" principle and was thus more effectively implemented than previous codes.

The third code, the Unified Good Governance Code (also known as the Conthe Code after Manuel Conthe, the president of the committee), was passed in 2006. It applies only to quoted companies and to governance issues, not corporate social responsibility issues. This code is innovative in its use of binding definitions to refer to the different groups of directors. According to this stricter definition, a director can be considered independent only if he or she meets the minimum conditions that enable a person to perform his or her duties in a reasonable, objective, and independent manner. As such, no shareholders are allowed to appoint board members who cannot pass the independent consideration. This constraint approach also applies to the restriction of takeover defense and related party transactions. This code has brought new life to the Spanish corporate governance system (Gómez and Cabeza, 2009). That is, the code has intensified pressure on companies to improve the corporate governance practices. In addition, the principle of "comply or explain" is easier to apply within the scope of this new code.

Table 17.1 provides a summary of the main characteristics of the boards of Spanish companies. Similar to Italian boards (Zattoni, 2011), these data show (1) a good mix between executive and non-executive directors, (2) sufficient independent directors, (3) a strong attendance record of board members at meetings, (4) complete diffusion of internal control and remuneration committees, and (5) frequent board evaluation systems.

Table 17.1 *Characteristics of the board of Spanish listed companies, 2008*

Variables	Characteristics in 2008
Sample	130 listed companies
Average directors' ownership	23.6 percent (13.9 percent for individual directors and 9.7 for institutions)
Average mix between executive and non-executive directors	11.3 members of the board: 2.2 executive directors and 9.1 non-executive directors. 3.6 non-executives are also independent directors
Positions in other firms	25 percent of directors take part in the ownership and 18 percent of directors sit on the board of other companies
Duality of CEO and president of the board	39.7 percent (42.2 percent in 2007)
Gender of directors	Women directors are present in 57.7 percent of companies (51.1 percent in 2007), and they represent 7.6 percent of the directors (6.8 percent in 2007)
Number of meetings	10.1 meetings (9.8 in 2007)
Board size	11.3 directors (10.9 in 2007)
Presence at the meetings	71.75 percent (25.37 of free-float)
Average number of committees	2.7 committees (2.6 in 2007)
Executive committee	46 percent of companies have an executive committee with 5.9 members and 11.9 meetings
Strategy committee	15 percent of companies have a strategy committee
Internal control committee	100 percent of the companies have an internal control or an audit committee with 51.7 percent of independent directors
Remuneration committee	93 percent of companies have a remuneration committee
Nomination committee	96 percent of companies have a nomination committee with 93.8 percent of non-executive directors
Board evaluation	77.69 percent in 2008 (74.81 percent in 2007)
Committee evaluation	74.62 percent in 2008 (73.33 percent in 2007)
Average compensation of board of directors	€3,238,000 (55 percent fixed and 45 variable compensation)

Table 17.1 (*cont.*)

Variables	Characteristics in 2008
Average compensation of directors	€986,000 (executive), €84,250 (gray), and €89,500 (independent)
Relations with external auditors	72.2 percent of firms have other relations with external auditors

Source: Observatorio de Gobierno Corporativo. Fundación de Estudios Financieros. Observatory of Corporate Governance. Foundation for Financial Studies. 2009 and 2010

The Spanish Stock Exchange and listed companies

The Spanish Stock Exchange

Although capital markets have traditionally played a limited role in the Spanish economy relative to banks and other financial intermediaries, they have become more and more important in recent years. Figure 17.1 reports the proportion of stock market capitalization and market trading relative to gross domestic product. As shown, capital markets have grown considerably in recent years with two exceptions. The first exception is the 2000–02 dot-com crisis during which a number of technological firms became delisted or were underpriced. The second episode is the financial meltdown beginning in 2008, which has had a particularly important impact on the Spanish capital markets.

This increasing importance of capital markets has not, however, translated into an increase in listing activity. In fact, the number of quoted firms has slowly decreased since its peak in 1992. In April 2000, the *Nuevo Mercado* (New Market) was created for emerging and technologically intensive firms. Similarly to the experience of other countries (e.g., Germany's *Neuer Markt*, France's *Nouveau Marché*, Italy's *Nuovo Mercato*), this specialized market was closed in 2007 and these quoted companies were integrated into the general market.

Several factors can possibly explain why the number of quoted firms has not grown. First, Spanish firms have experienced a multinationalization process that has required them to increase in size. Part of this process has been fulfilled by merger and acquisition operations among listed firms. Second, legal prerequisites for becoming listed require a certain dispersion of firms' ownership. This requirement

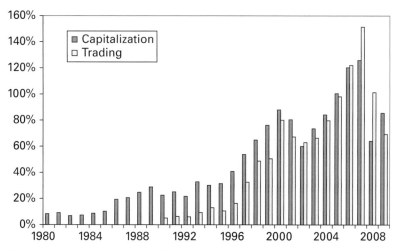

Figure 17.1 Capitalization and liquidity
Source: Studies Department. *Bolsas y Mercados Españoles* (Spanish Capital Markets)

disincentivizes family and other firms whose founders wish to keep control of the firm. Third, fixed costs of issuance are high, and are often prohibitive for small- and medium-sized firms. Finally, their close ties with banks allow firms to obtain funds for investments when necessary, thus negating their dependence on capital markets.

To some extent, the lack of proclivity of Spanish firms within the capital market system can be compared with *Latibex*, a branch of Spanish capital markets on which Latin American securities are traded. *Latibex* gives Latin American companies access to the European capital market. In turn, European investors can buy and sell shares and securities in Latin American companies through a single market using a single operating system for trading and settlement and a single currency, the euro. The number of Latin American firms has remained stable at around thirty firms since the market's creation in 1999.

The ownership structure of Spanish listed companies

The ownership structure of Spanish listed firms is quite concentrated. As shown in Table 17.2, this concentration of ownership has remained

Table 17.2 *Ownership concentration in Spanish listed companies*

	2004	2005	2006	2007
Largest shareholder	34.3	35.5	35.5	38.3
Three largest shareholders	47.1	48.3	48.3	52.3
Five largest shareholders	51.3	52.2	52.0	56.0

Source: Fundación de Estudios Financieros. Observatorio de Gobierno Corporativo.
Foundation for Financial Studies. Observatory of Corporate Governance. 2007–2010

largely unchanged in recent years. In fact, the proportion of shares held by the largest, three largest, and five largest shareholders has increased slightly. Specifically, in 2007, 33.1 percent of listed firms included a person with a majority of shares or with the ability to control the majority of votes, up from 32.4 percent in 2006.

At the end of 2007, directors held 27.5 percent of shares. Reference shareholders (i.e., blockholders who hold at least 5 percent of the shares) and other blockholders owned, on average, 33.7 percent, and minority shareholders owned 38.3 percent. The proportion of shares held by the firm itself was around 0.5 percent. Only 10 percent of firms do not have reference shareholders, and in 50 percent of quoted firms, the largest shareholder owns more than 30 percent of shares. Furthermore, in 25 percent of firms, the largest shareholder owns more than 55 percent of shares, and in 10 percent of firms, the largest shareholder owns more than 80 percent of shares.

In terms of kinds of shareholders, Table 17.3 shows the dominant position of non-financial companies, families, and foreign investors. First, using the methodology of control chains, Santana and Aguiar (2006) find that around one-half of Spain's listed firms have a family or individual investor as an ultimate shareholder. Although banks increased in importance through 2007, in 2008, banks liquidated a significant portion of their shares portfolio due to the financial crisis and the depreciation of their loans portfolio. Second, crossholding is a frequent practice among Spanish firms. Indeed, the stake of non-financial firms grew between 2000 and 2008 to the detriment of families and individual investors. Finally, foreign investors are the largest shareholder group in Spain and have increased their holdings in recent years. The country's low saving rates, the need to appeal to foreign investors, the multinationalization of Spanish companies,

Table 17.3 *Ownership distribution of Spanish listed companies*

	2000	2001	2002	2003	2004	2005	2006	2007	2008
Banks	7.3	7.9	7.1	7.7	8.7	8.6	9.3	9.4	7.6
Insurance companies	2.3	2.3	2.2	2.3	2.3	2.4	2.5	2.2	2.0
Mutual funds	4.8	4.9	5.2	5.6	6.3	6.2	7.2	6.0	5.4
State	0.2	0.2	0.4	0.3	0.3	0.3	0.3	0.2	0.3
Non-financial firms	20.3	21.7	22.0	23.0	23.1	24.7	24.4	25.4	26.0
Families	30.5	28.0	28.3	26.0	24.1	23.6	23.8	20.1	20.2
Non-residents	34.7	35.0	34.8	35.1	35.2	34.2	32.6	36.8	38.5

Source: Studies Department, *Bolsas y Mercados Españoles* (Spanish Capital Markets)

and the integration of Spain in the EU economic and monetary system explain this large proportion of shares held by non-residents.

These data point to the agency relation between large dominant shareholders and minority shareholders as a problem of collective decision making inside the firms. As a result, the most prominent conflict of interest inside Spanish firms is not likely to arise between managers and shareholders but rather between large dominant shareholders and minority shareholders (Becht and Röell, 1999; Cuervo, 2005; Faccio and Lang, 2002; Morck, Wolfenzon, and Yeung, 2005; Zattoni, 2009). Laeven and Levine (2008) and Maury and Pajuste (2005) both show that blockholders with too much power may expropriate benefits from minority shareholders. In the same vein, Santana (2010) shows that shareholders' coalitions are present in roughly one out of four listed companies; about 42 percent of the voting rights are linked to these coalitions. Moreover, a higher percentage of shareholders' coalitions are found in companies with large capitalizations, with high ownership concentration, without defensive measures, and within the pyramid structures.

As in other countries (Zattoni, 2011), to retain corporate control, firms with a concentrated ownership structure avoid an active role of the market. According to Santana and Aguiar (2007), 35 percent of firms maintain control-enhancing mechanisms to protect against takeovers. Among these control enhancing mechanisms, the requirement of qualified majorities in the shareholders' meetings along with vote caps are the most widely used. In fact, in 39 percent of the initial public offerings (IPOs), the company was controlled through a pyramid.

IPO activity between 2006 and 2008

The regulation of IPOs

In addition to specific legislation, IPOs must comply with Spanish regulation on primary markets. As required by the Capital Markets Act (1988), candidate firms must have a minimum equity of 1.2 million euro, and only the shares in the hands of shareholders who own less than 25 percent are taken into account. Firms must have at least 100 minority shareholders and be profitable enough to have paid out dividends of over 6 percent in two out of the latest three years. Additionally, firms must submit both periodical information (financial statements, profit and loss accounts, etc.) and non-periodical information (relevant facts potentially affecting the share price, significant participations in equity, managers' and directors' proportion of shares, etc.).

A key legal and informational tool in IPOs is the company prospectus. This prospectus, which must be approved by the Spanish Stock Exchange Commission, must provide all information relevant to the IPO, such as issuers, participating entities, dates, corporate governance bodies, main financial characteristics, and so on. Because IPOs usually precede a period of firm expansion, the prospectus must provide specific information regarding business risks, the issuer's financial risk, the IPO operation risks, and the proposed business plan.

IPOs are usually implemented in three brackets: employees, domestic investors, and international (qualified) institutional investors. The proportion of these brackets must be defined at the beginning of the IPO and reported in the informative prospectus. In case of demand excess, the allocation is prorated on the basis of first-come priority. Most commonly, a positive relation exists between the size of the minority shareholders bracket and the liquidity of the firm's stocks.

Spanish regulations governing IPOs require the participation of four kinds of entities. First, the global coordinating entities that are in charge of the whole IPO supervise the demand, bargain with the firm public-to-be over the final price, and, if necessary, make the distribution among the brackets. Global coordinating entities can hold the "green shoe" (i.e., a call option that must be exercised within thirty days after the IPO). Second, the assurance entities underwrite the economic performance of the operation, given the risk of collocation. To achieve the economic performance, global coordinating entities are allowed to act on the behalf of the assurance entities to stabilize the market price according to international regulations. Third, the director entities are accountable for the accuracy of the information reported in the prospectus and take part in the IPO preparation. In actuality, they oversee the operation more strictly than the assurance entities. Finally, the collocation entities serve as intermediaries between the firm and potential shareholders. They may also take on additional assurance responsibilities.

The price is fixed by agreement between the firm and the global coordinating entity during the subscription period. It can be set as a top price or as a price band, which may be either binding or non-binding. Spanish law allows for an independent expert to assess and fix both the top price and the price band. In a case in which the band is not binding and the final price is out of the band, a certain period is allotted to investors during which they have the right to revoke their demand. See Table 17.4 for a summary of listing and ongoing requirements.

IPOs between 2006 and 2008

Between 2006 and 2008, IPO activity in Spain was at its highest level since 1990 (García et al., 2010; Palacín Sánchez, 2004). The value of IPOs in 2007 was, by far, the highest in the history of Spanish capital markets. Between 2006 and 2008, twenty-three Spanish companies went public: ten were listed in 2006, and eleven were listed in 2007. During 2008, the financial crisis hit the world economic system, and, consequently, only two Spanish firms were listed. Four other companies also completed IPOs during 2008 (Arcelor Mittal, Reyal Urbis, Martinsa-Fadesa, and Vértice 360) but were subsequently involved in merger operations and were delisted prior to year's end.

As Table 17.5 shows, IPOs are particularly concentrated in the financial sector, with financial firms representing ten of the twenty-three IPOs. Five out of these ten companies belong to the real estate sector, and three are investment services companies. Consumer

Table 17.4 *Listing and ongoing requirements in Spain*

Requirement	Fulfillment
Admission requirements	
Free float	At least 100 shareholders
Market cap	At least €1.2 million
Age	Three years' tracking record required
Profitability	Enough to pay a 6% dividend in two out of the three latest years
Audit information	At least two audited years
Corporate governance information	Report on corporate governance required
Sponsors	Participation of a global coordinating entity, an assurance entity, a director entity, and a collocation entity
Admission documents	Previous acceptance by the Spanish Stock Exchange (CNMV)
Prospectus	The company must publish a prospectus with all the relevant information according to CNMV requirements
Ongoing requirements	
Price-sensitive information	Timely dissemination to CNMV
Kind of information to be issued	Periodical and non-periodical
Periodical information	Quarterly financial reports (financial statement and profit and loss account), half-year financial reports, and independently audited full-year financial reports
Non-periodical information	Ownership structure, insiders' transactions, and any other relevant information

Source: Madrid Stock Exchange (*Bolsa de Madrid*)

services firms had five IPOs, represented by vending machines, mass-media, and airline companies. The health care industry had four IPOs, represented by the three health care firms within the pharmaceutical industry and Clínica Baviera, S.A., which we address in more depth in the following discussion. Finally, the industrial sector also had four IPOs.

Table 17.5 *IPO year and industry classification*

	2006	2007	2008	Total
Financials	4	4	2	10
Consumer services	2	3	0	5
Health care	1	3	0	4
Industrials	3	1	0	4
Total	**10**	**11**	**2**	**23**

Table 17.6 *IPO size and performance*

	Size			Performance		
	Employees (*n*)	Revenues ($)	Assets ($)	ROA (%)	ROE (%)	ROS (%)
Min	93	70,149	63,744	–6.82	–7.52	–4.80
1st quartile	164	119,118	375,476	3.61	11.40	7.00
2nd quartile	518	389,892	933,209	5.72	16.75	14.29
3rd quartile	2,160	852,259	1,231,149	9.69	23.30	22.52
Max	8,076	4,002,081	43,055,151	26.93	61.55	69.44
Avg.	1,600	797,389	4,790,345	6.00	19.00	16.00

Firm age among Spanish IPOs, similar to Italian IPOs, ranges widely. Banco de Valencia is 108 years old, and Vueling Airlines is just 2 years old. Although the average age is 24.4 years, 55 percent of firms are less than 10 years old, 25 percent are 11 to 30 years old, and 20 percent are more than 50 years old. Therefore, companies that go public tend to be either young, high-growth firms or firms with a long tradition. Nearly every firm (22 out of 23) went public in the Spanish Mercado Continuo; 1 firm listed on the international Euronext.

Most IPO firms are medium-sized companies; as shown in Table 17.6, the average size is 1,600 employees. However, some exceptions apply: 3 firms had fewer than 100 employees, and 6 firms had more than 1,000 employees. For example, the real estate firm Astroc Mediterráneo had 93 employees, and the consumer services firm Codere had 8,076 employees. Average firm revenue is around $800,000, with one company clearly over the average. Specifically, Criteria Caixacorp, which is the result of transferring the industrial portfolio of La Caixa (one of the largest Spanish savings banks), has sales of just under $4 million. Due to the steady increase of the market value, Criteria Caixacorp has joined the ranks of blue chip stock indices both in Spain (IBEX-35) and Europe (FTSEurofirst 300, MSCI Europe, MSCI Pan Euro, and DJ Stoxx 300).

Interestingly, not all of the IPOs reported positive earnings at the time of their listing: Renta Corporación (a holding corporation), Solaria Energía y Medio Ambiente (a green and renewable energy firm), and Vueling Airlines all reported losses in the year of their IPOs. However, despite these few firms that showed a possible lack of initial profitability, most of the IPOs reported positive growth rates and a significant increase in performance, sales, and equity at the time of their listing. The most profitable companies in the sample were Clínica Baviera, S.A. (based on return on assets and return on earnings) and Criteria Caixacorp (return on sales).

The closing price was higher than the initial price in 64 percent of operations. In 27 percent of IPOs, the price went down, and in 9 percent of IPOs, the price remained stable. However, the total stock return (once the dividends are taken into account) during the year that the IPO took place is negative in around one-half of the operations. This evolution has been documented for other periods too (González and Álvarez, 2005) and is a counter-evidence of the efficient markets hypothesis (Álvarez, 2008).

The ownership structure of IPOs is quite similar to the structure of the other listed firms. As shown in Table 17.7, the largest shareholder of the companies that went public was typically represented by a family (thirteen out of nineteen cases), followed by banks (four cases) and venture capital (two cases). None of the IPOs were controlled by the government, and, in fact, the state had no stake in any of them. Following a wave of privatizations undertaken by the government at the end of the 1990s, the proportion of state-owned firms in Spain is currently very small.

Table 17.7 provides additional information regarding the IPO ownership structure. Families and venture capitalists maintain an average of 27.5 percent and 7 percent of the shares, respectively. These results confirm the outstanding role of individual and family stakes in Spanish corporations. Furthermore, IPOs in Spain do not result in a decrease of the shares owned by either the first and the three largest shareholders. Consequently, even after becoming public, Spanish

Table 17.7 IPO ownership structure (data in percent)

	Family		Bank		Government		VC		Angels		TOP 1		TOP 3	
	pre	post	pre	post	pre	post	pre	post	pre	post	pre	post	pre	post
Min	0.12	0	0	0	0	0	0.01	0	–	–	3.67	0.78	8.97	1.41
1st quartile	0.42	1.85	0.04	0	0	0	0.01	0.01	–	–	8.35	10.6	10.2	27.6
2nd quartile	15.9	17.3	1.04	0.21	0	0	10.3	0.06	–	–	10.3	26.8	28	43.9
3rd quartile	17.8	51.8	1.85	1.54	0	0	10.3	14.1	–	–	10.5	53.1	30.2	63.8
Max	52.1	65.8	8.35	80.2	0	0	20.9	20.9	–	–	51.8	79.9	62.8	80.8
Average	21.3	27.5	2.26	7.6	0	0	10.4	7.03	–	–	16.2	33.5	28.5	44.5
No. of cases	13	13	4	4	0	0	2	2	–	–	19	19	19	19

Table 17.8 *IPO board of directors*

	Size	Executive directors	Non-executive directors	Independent directors	Engineering, operations, R&D	Marketing, sales	Finance, accounting, law
Min	1	1	3	2	0	0	0
1st quartile	7	1	5	2	0	0	1
2nd quartile	10	2	7	3	0	1	2
3rd quartile	11	3	11	4	2	1	3
Max	16	5	15	8	3	3	5
Average	10	3.3	6.6	3.4	0.9	0.8	2.1

firms tend to be dominated by major shareholders. This post-IPO ownership concentration can be attributed to cross-shareholdings among firms as other individuals and non-financial firms take significant stakes in the new listed company. Table 17.7 shows also an absence of business angels in the share capital of companies before and after the IPO. In addition, venture capital has played a relatively minor role. Finally, out of the five private equity firms that completed IPOs, three of them were Spanish.

Boards of directors of IPO companies have, on average, ten directors; 75 percent of firms have between nine and sixteen directors, as shown in Table 17.8. More specifically, the boards of IPOs sit, on average, three executive directors and 6.6 non-executive directors, and one out of two non-executives is an independent director. As in other countries, women are solidly outnumbered by men: only one out of ten directors is a woman, and 44 percent of IPOs do not have any female directors. The frequency of foreign directors is also very low. Although 25 percent of IPOs sit a foreign director, foreign directors account for only 3 percent of total directorships. Employees' representatives are not seated on any boards as the law does not require them. Consistent with the typical ownership and governance structure of Spanish firms, 50 percent of directors have some kind of family tie. These directors are commonly associated with firms in which the founder is the CEO or director. This family link between founder–CEO/director occurs in 30 percent of IPOs.

83 percent of IPOs have formal annual board evaluation procedures (see Table 17.8). The Spanish codes of good governance have welcomed effective corporate governance through frequent board

meetings. Accordingly, the average number of meetings is 9.6 per year. With only one exception, all the IPO boards meet at least four times a year, and 44.5 percent meet at least once a month.

IPOs' boards have an important number of members with a functional background in peripheral functions (e.g., finance, accounting, law). The number of directors with backgrounds in throughput functions (e.g., engineering, operations, research and development) or output functions (e.g., marketing or sales) is limited. These data, provided in Table 17.8, refer primarily to independent directors. Therefore, independent directors seem to be hired on the basis of their expertise in finance, accounting, law, and other related disciplines. These figures can be attributed to the considerable proportion of financial firms that went public in 2006–8 and these firms' legal needs for audits or internal control committees. When we scale by the number of independent directors, we find that 62 percent of independent directors have expertise in finance, 26 percent in operations and research and development, and 24 percent in marketing.

All of the IPOs created an audit committee, and 85 percent formed a nominations committee. These data are consistent with recent trends in Spain for firms to maintain nominations and compensation committees. Indeed, only 5 percent of the IPOs created a compensation committee alone. 40 percent of firms developed a governance committee whereas no company formed a technology committee.

Description of an IPO: Clínica Baviera, S.A.

The firm before the IPO

Grupo Baviera is a Spanish multinational firm. It is currently made up by two divisions: the ophthalmological division (Clínica Baviera) and the aesthetical surgery division (Clínica Londres). The ophthalmological division accounts for around 84 percent of the firm's turnover. In 2010, the company had seventy clinics in Spain, Germany, the Netherlands, Austria, and Italy. Founded in 1992 in Valencia by the ophthalmologist Julio Baviera, most of the firm's dramatic expansion has occurred through internal growth. Specifically, in 1997, Clínica Baviera instituted an expansion plan across Spain, opening around four clinics each year. The aesthetical surgery/obesity division was created in 2004. In 2006, the company expanded internationally to

Milan (Italy). When the firm completed its IPO in 2007, it became the first listed European ophthalmological business group. Although continuing to primarily focus on internal growth, in 2008, Clínica Baviera acquired Care Vision, a medical firm with business centers in central Europe. This process of rapid expansion resulted in sales growth from $31.2 million in 2002 to $116.6 million in 2009. In 2008, the firm was awarded the quality certification ISO 9001:2008. Among its corporate social responsibility activities, Clínica Baviera is engaged in improving eye health care in a number of less developed countries and in promoting child health care campaigns.

Several shareholders participated in the ownership structure of the company at the time of its IPO. The largest shareholder was the Baviera family (the founder, Julio, and his brother, Eduardo), who controlled either directly or indirectly around 40 percent of shares. In addition, three significant institutional investors and a number of smaller shareholders were also involved. The health care industry was quite appealing to private fund investors at the beginning of the twenty-first century, leading some private equity funds to take a position in the sector (San Segundo, 2007). Accordingly, the 3i Group (a venture capitalist that had supported the firm's expansion process since 2005) owned 31.94 percent of shares. Other significant institutional shareholders were Inversiones Dario 3 (with 9.29 percent of shares) and Activos y Gestión Accionarial (with 5.39 percent of shares). This stable core of shareholders allowed the firm to pursue an internationalization process and diversification by investing in the aesthetical surgery industry. In addition, 6.32 percent of shares was held by a group of around fifty employees.

The board of directors of Clínica Baviera includes eight directors and a chairperson, who is simultaneously the chief executive officer of the firm. The board includes two inside directors, three gray directors appointed by significant institutional stakeholders,[1] and three independent directors. According to Spanish law, the firm created two committees: the audit committee and the compensation and nomination committee. Although not properly directors, the secretary and the vice-secretary take part in the board of directors.

---

[1] Gray directors are non-executive directors who are not completely independent because they represent blockholders' interests.

The offer

Clínica Baviera's IPO process occurred in March 2007. The initial offer was 5.8 million shares (with a possible extension of 0.9 million shares) out of 16.3 million shares. Besides the issuance of new shares, 3i Group decided to leave the company, so that the IPO also implied the sale of 3i's stake (2.4 million shares). The founding family also offered some shares (1.4 million shares). Most of the shares (85 percent) were allocated to institutional investors. In case of overallotment, the assurance entities were given the option to subscribe the additional 0.9 million shares. The offer also included a greenshoe for the same amount of shares.[2] Although not all, a number of shareholders signed a lock-up pact with the global coordinator according to which they could not sell their shares for 180 days after the IPO. The greenshoe option was exercised, and the global coordinator did not need to stabilize the operations.

The non-binding band for price was fixed between $21.07 and $24.52 per share, resulting in a market capitalization between $344 and $400 million. As explicitly stated in the prospectus, this price range was defined by the firm and the global coordinator without any independent expert on the basis of a number of multiples (price earnings ratio, equity value to earnings before taxes, depreciation and amortization, etc.) of comparable companies in the medical and health care industry. The final price was fixed at $23. The issuance was completely successful, and the price jumped 27.7 percent in the first day of trading (April 3) to reach $29.37. At the end of April the stock price was $30.5 per share. This increase is consistent with IPOs underpricing in Spanish capital markets (Álvarez, 2000, 2001; Álvarez and Fernández, 2003).

The global coordinator was UBS Limited, and some syndicates of assurance and collocation entities were created among Spanish banks (Banco Popular, Banco Español de Crédito, Banco de Castilla, etc.).

The firm after the IPO

Although institutional investors were initially the largest subscribers of the new shares, the sale of 3i's stake in the firm and some subsequent sales resulted in a decrease of the institutional ownership.

---

[2] A greenshoe option is a provision contained in an underwriting agreement (mainly IPOs) that gives the underwriter the right to sell investors more shares than originally planned by the issuer.

The fraction owned by the founding family also dropped from 40 percent to around 30 percent. At the same time, employees' stakes increased to around 11 percent. Even though the free float obviously increased too (to 43 percent of shares), the firm's shareholding structure after the IPO is still quite concentrated, which is consistent with the Spanish ownership pattern.

The IPO reinforced the firm's expansion process, especially in the international arena. Clínica Baviera will open its next clinics in Germany, and the firm has plans to expand to Italy.

Clínica Baviera has implemented the recommendations of the Spanish codes of good governance regarding the board of directors. The company also adopted a compensation policy of moderation. The total compensation of the board of directors was set at 7.3 percent of the firm's earnings, with most being paid out as fixed compensation. In recent years, the board has met nine times per year; the audit committee four times per year; and the compensation and nomination committee three times per year. The size of the board (eight directors) is between the highest and lowest limit suggested by the codes, and all of the directors have attended all of the meetings. Consistent with Spanish recommendations, independent directors have become more important, and the proportion has increased from 28 percent of directors to 37 percent since the IPO. To ensure independence, both the audit and the compensation committees are made up solely of outside directors, with a qualified majority of independent directors. The presidents of both committees are also independent directors.

The Clínica Baviera, S.A. case could be considered a representative case of recent Spanish IPOs. It evidences the important role that capital markets play in the process of international expansion of Spanish companies. In addition, firms that have become listed in recent years have had to implement the recommendations of the codes of good governance, which has reduced the range of heterogeneity among firms. Despite the IPO process, the ownership structure of quite a few firms remains concentrated with some majority shareholders that retain control of the company.

Conclusion

Spanish corporate governance has been improved in the latest decades insofar as the corporate law has evolved and three codes of good governance have been published (in 1998, 2003, and 2006). Due to the bank orientation of the Spanish financial system, capital markets have traditionally played a limited role relative to banks and other financial intermediaries. Therefore, the ownership structure of Spanish firms shows a high degree of concentration, in line with other major continental European companies. This high concentration of ownership has inhibited the market for corporate control.

Nevertheless, Spain has added to the international mainstream of corporate governance reforms with the aim of strengthening its legal corporate system. The legal changes have modified deeply both the governing bodies of firms and the legal framework of capital markets. This process has resulted in a more important role for capital markets.

The increasing importance of capital markets does not mean, however, that listing has become more popular. In fact, the number of quoted firms has slowly decreased since its peak in 1992. A number of reasons can explain why the number of quoted firms has not grown: the wave of mergers and acquisitions necessary to achieve a critical size for internationalization; the dispersion of ownership inherent in the IPOs, which runs contrary to the majority control of many firms; and the close ties between firms and banks, which provides firms with privileged funds and allows them to avoid becoming dependent on public capital markets.

In Spain, the period between 2006 and 2008 was the most active in terms of IPOs since 1990, with twenty-three companies going public. These IPOs were focused particularly on the financial industry, with ten financial firms going public. The firms tended to be either young, high-growth firms or firms with long traditions. Although most IPO firms are medium-sized companies, several large companies are included as well. Interestingly, not all the IPOs recorded positive earnings at the moment of becoming listed. Despite a few firms' possible lack of initial profitability, most IPOs showed positive growth rates and a significant increase in performance, sales, and equity. The ownership structure of IPOs is quite similar to the structure of the other listed firms. The largest shareholder of a company that goes public is typically a family; banks and other institutional investors also listed a few companies during the period.

Boards of directors in IPOs adhere to the prescriptions of codes of good governance: boards are medium in size, have a majority of non-executive directors, and meet nine to ten times a year. As in other countries, women and foreign directors are few. Consistent with the typical ownership and governance structure of Spanish firms, one-half of directors in IPOs have some kind of family tie.

A large financial meltdown has greatly impacted the period following the three years discussed here. Consequently, the number of IPOs subsequent to 2008 is dramatically lower as firms avoid the negative effects of the low market prices. Thus, the Spanish capital market will likely need to wait for more favorable economic conditions before revisiting the increasing trend in IPOs as was witnessed during previous years.

References

Aldama y Miñón, Enrique. 2003. *Informe de la Comisión Especial para el fomento de la transparencia y la seguridad en los mercados financieros y las sociedades cotizadas*. Madrid: Comisión Nacional del Mercado de Valores.

Allen, Franklin and Douglas Gale. 2001. *Comparing Financial Systems*. Cambridge, Mass.: MIT Press.

Álvarez Otero, Susana. 2000. "La infravaloración de las salidas a Bolsa (1985–1997)", *Bolsa de Madrid*, 87, 19–23.

2001. "Son las OPIs malas inversiones a largo plazo?", *Actualidad Financiera*, 6, 3, 21–35.

2008. "Análisis de la eficiencia en la valoración de las empresas que salen a Bolsa", *Revista Española de Financiación y Contabilidad*, 140, 691–722.

Álvarez Otero, Susana and Ana I. Fernández Álvarez. 2003. "La explicación de la infravaloración de las salidas a Bolsa", *Revista de Economía Aplicada*, 11, 33, 49–64.

Becht, Marco and Ailsa Röell. 1999. "Blockholdings in Europe. An international comparison", *European Economic Review*, 43, 4–6, 1049–56.

Cadbury, Sir Adrian. 1992. *Report of the Committee on the Financial Aspects of Corporate Governance*. London: Gee Publishing Ltd.

Chung, Huimin and Till Talaulicar. 2010. "Forms and effects of shareholder activism", *Corporate Governance: An International Review*, 18, 4, 253–57.

Comisión Nacional del Mercado de Valores. 2006. *Código Unificado de Buen Gobierno*. Madrid: Comisión Nacional del Mercado de Valores.

Cuervo García, Álvaro. 2005. "El gobierno de la empresa: Un problema de conflicto de intereses", in Eduardo Bueno Campos (ed.), *El gobierno de la empresa. En busca de la transparencia y la confianza*. Madrid: Pirámide, 115–35.

Faccio, Mara and Larry Lang. 2002. "The ultimate ownership of Western European corporations", *Journal of Financial Economics*, 65, 3, 365–95.

Fernández, Enrique, Silvia Gómez and Álvaro Cuervo. 2004. "Spanish firms' market reaction to the introduction of best practices codes", *Corporate Governance: An International Review*, 12, 1, 29–46.

Fundación de Estudios Financieros. 2007. *Observatorio de gobierno corporativo y transparencia informativa de las sociedades cotizadas en el mercado continuo español*. Madrid: Papeles de la Fundación, 19.

2008. *Observatorio de gobierno corporativo y transparencia informativa de las sociedades cotizadas en el mercado continuo español*. Madrid: Papeles de la Fundación, 22.

2009. *Observatorio de gobierno corporativo y transparencia informativa de las sociedades cotizadas en el mercado continuo español*. Madrid: Papeles de la Fundación, 29.

2010. *Observatorio de gobierno corporativo y transparencia informativa de las sociedades cotizadas en el mercado continuo español*. Madrid: Papeles de la Fundación, 32.

García Coto, Domingo J., Amelia Sánchez García and José Beiras Escudero. 2010. "Las salidas a Bolsa como eje de transformación económica y social", *Bolsa de Madrid*, 183, 2–15.

Gómez Ansón, Silvia and Laura Cabeza García. 2009. "Spanish codes of good governance: Lessons learned, present situation and future expectations", in Felix J. López Iturriaga (ed.), *Codes of Good Governance Around the World*. New York: Nova Publishers, 367–82.

González Méndez, Victor M. and Susana Álvarez Otero. 2005. "The long-run underperformance of initial public offerings: A methodological problem?", *Revista de Economía Aplicada*, 13, 37, 51–67.

Gonzalo Angulo, José A. 2005. "Influencias recíprocas entre información financiera y gobernanza empresarial", in Eduardo Bueno Campos (ed.), *El gobierno de la empresa. En busca de la transparencia y la confianza*. Madrid: Pirámide, 277–311.

Hofstede, Geert. 1984. *Culture's Consequences: International Differences in Work-related Values*. Beverly Hills: Sage.

La Porta, Rafael, Florencio López-de-Silanes, Andrei Shleifer and Robert Vishny. 1997. "Legal determinants of external finance", *Journal of Finance*, 52, 3, 1131–50.

1998. "Law and finance", *Journal of Political Economy*, 106, 1113–55.

Laeven, Luc and Ross Levine. 2008. "Complex ownership structures and corporate valuations", *Review of Financial Studies*, 21, 2, 579–604.

López de Letona, José M. 2005. "Luces y sombras en el gobierno de la empresa: El caso español", in Eduardo Bueno Campos (ed.), *El gobierno de la empresa. En busca de la transparencia y la confianza.* Madrid: Pirámide, 139–55.

Maury, Benjamin and Anete Pajuste. 2005. "Multiple large shareholders and firm value", *Journal of Banking and Finance*, 29, 7, 1813–34.

Morck, Randall, Daniel Wolfenzon and Bernard Yeung. 2005. "Corporate governance, economic entrenchment, and growth", *Journal of Economic Literature*, 43, 3, 655–720.

Olivencia Ruiz, Manuel. 1998. *El gobierno de las sociedades cotizadas.* Madrid: Comité especial para el estudio de un código ético de los consejos de administración de las sociedades.

Palacín Sánchez, María J. 2004. "Las ofertas públicas de adquisición en España (1991–2002)", *Bolsa de Madrid*, 128, 72–80.

San Segundo, Gonzalo. 2007. "El capital riesgo apuesta por el negocio sanitario", *Medical Economics*, 20–25.

Santana Martín, Domingo J. 2010. "Shareholders coalitions in Spain", *Universia Business Review*, 28, 46–61.

Santana Martín, Domingo J. and Inmaculada Aguiar Díaz. 2006. "El último propietario de las empresas cotizadas españolas (1996–2002)", *Cuadernos de Economía y Dirección de la Empresa*, 26, 47–72.

2007. *Una década de blindaje en España. 1996–2005.* Madrid: Comisión Nacional del Mercado de Valores.

Zattoni, Alessandro. 2009. "Corporate governance in Italy: The structural conflict of interests between majority and minority shareholders", in Felix J. López Iturriaga (ed.), *Codes of Good Governance Around the World.* New York: Nova Publishers, 281–316.

2011. "Corporate governance and initial public offerings in Italy", in William Judge and Alessandro Zattoni (eds.), *Handbook of Corporate Governance and Initial Public Offerings.* Cambridge, Mass.: Cambridge University Press.

18 | Corporate governance and initial public offerings in Sweden

JONAS GABRIELSSON

Introduction

Although corporate governance systems around the world may share a number of basic features, it also seems that every country has some specificity with respect to their external and internal corporate governance mechanisms (Judge, 2010). Sweden, for example, is a homogeneous society with strong social norms and a highly cohesive social culture. Its legal system can be classified as Scandinavian civil law, which is characterized by a somewhat higher investor protection compared to many other civil law countries, dual-class shares with differentiated voting rights and a system of employee co-determination. The market for corporate control is relatively active and there is a high incidence of public takeover bids on the stock market, although few of them can be characterized as hostile. The disclosure of information in annual reports among listed companies is specified and highly transparent, and Sweden has also implemented a national code of corporate governance which listed companies must follow on a "comply-or-explain" basis. Sweden also has a tradition of large business groups that control a substantial part of the Swedish stock market.

Although many Swedish listed companies have a relatively large number of owners, there is often one owner or a group of owners whose shareholdings and number of votes give them a controlling ownership position. There is, moreover, a significant degree of family ownership, and few listed companies lack a controlling owner. Another striking feature of the Swedish stock market is the presence of powerful investment companies with connections to wealthy owner families. Shareholder rights are quite advanced and minority owner-ship rights are protected by law. With respect to structure, boards of directors in Sweden can be placed somewhere in between the Anglo-Saxon one-tier model and the European two-tier model. Boards are, moreover, almost exclusively composed of non-executive directors,

422

and CEO duality is not allowed. Executive compensation is non-egalitarian in nature, and most listed companies have a system for variable compensation to the CEO.

In sum, Sweden provides an interesting and highly unique context for corporate governance. The rest of the chapter will have a closer look at issues related to the Swedish corporate governance system. In addition to a general overview of some main features of corporate governance in Sweden, there will be a special focus on how this relates to initial public offerings (IPOs), i.e., limited liability companies which are in the process of changing their ownership structure from privately-held to publicly-owned.

Corporate governance in Sweden

Main features of corporate governance in the Swedish context

When discussing the Swedish corporate governance system, there are some main features that should be emphasized. First of all, Sweden is a small and relatively homogeneous country with tightly knit personal networks among owners of firms, which allows a high level of social control and also enables information to travel quickly between economic actors (Stafsudd, 2009). Swedish culture is, moreover, characterized by the presence of strong social norms of honesty and high business standards, and the country scores very high on enforcement, such as efficiency of the judicial system and accounting standards (Thomsen, 2008). Informal governance mechanisms such as reputation and culture are thus generally regarded as more effective in Sweden than in larger countries.

Another characteristic feature of Sweden is its highly internationalized business society. This has deep historical roots and is related to Sweden being a vast but scarcely populated country with rich natural resources. The international character of Swedish businesses, in combination with an engineering culture, has favored technical inventions and the development of multinational companies such as ABB, Atlas Copco, Ericsson, Scania, SKF and Volvo (Carlsson, 2007). There is in this respect a tradition of doing business in highly export-oriented industries, often with significant support from the government (e.g., Glete, 1994; Högfeldt, 2005). This exposure to international markets means that international product market competition is a strong disciplining mechanism for many larger Swedish companies (Thomsen, 2008).

Corporate governance is also shaped by politics, and there is no doubt that Sweden has been influenced by its long periods of social democratic governments. This is shown, for example, in the system of mandatory co-determination, where employees or labor unions are granted the right to appoint board members in companies that have twenty-five or more employees. Before implementing certain types of major changes, the company must also consult the union, and there are disclosure requirements for providing union representatives with information about the economic status of the company. The overall experience of this system is positive among companies, board members and executives, and it is generally regarded as something that is well functioning and productive (Carlson, 2007).

The social democratic governments have also in the past, through compromises with the largest owners and the trade unions, historically favored large companies and concentrated ownership in their government policies (Högfeldt, 2005). This has, for example, been evident in tax policies, which have promoted retained equity as a primary source of capital. Another example is the use of control mechanisms, such as pyramiding and dual-class shares, which allow concentration of votes without corresponding ownership of cash flow rights. All this has led to a situation where Sweden has a high proportion of large listed companies controlled by a small number of controlling minority shareholders (Bebchuk, Kraakman and Triantis, 1999).

Another highly political issue that has been debated in Sweden is gender representation on the board of directors of public companies. The major debate relates to whether equal gender representation is something that should be supported by Swedish law, or whether it is up to owners to make such decisions. Although Sweden is well known for its long tradition of having a high share of women in the workforce, the country has a much lower proportion of women in higher corporate positions. However, there has been a notable change in the share of women in Swedish corporate boards in the past decade. The share of female directors in public companies, for example, has increased from about 4 percent at the end of the 1990s to 19 percent in 2008, a development which has been supported by the Swedish Code of Corporate Governance.

Another debated issue in Sweden is the compensation to executives. The general opinion is that CEOs are compensated too highly compared to the average worker, which largely reflects the egalitarian culture in Swedish society. Currently, CEOs are on average paid about fifteen times more than the average Swedish worker, while it can be up to forty times more in the largest listed companies. However, compensation to CEOs in Swedish listed companies is still far below the levels that are paid to their international competitors. The reason for this is often explained to be less use of variable compensation to Swedish executives. Although most listed companies have a system for variable compensation to the CEO, this usually accounts for only about 10 percent of total compensation.

An interesting feature in Swedish corporate governance is that the country is a somewhat unique case with respect to legal protection of shareholder rights and capital markets. La Porta, Lopez-de-Silanes, Shleifer et al. (1998) place Sweden as belonging to the special framework of Scandinavian civil law which is characterized by investor protection that is somewhat higher than in other civil law countries but lower than in common law countries. Sweden is in this respect argued to favor majority shareholders over minority shareholders in laws regarding shareholder protection, which is hardly surprising given Sweden's historical policies favoring both large companies and concentrated ownership. The simultaneous use of dual-class shares, pyramiding and cross-holdings in Swedish corporate governance has, for example, led to one of the highest vote-to-capital ratios in the world (Agnblad, Berglöf, Högfeldt et al., 2001; La Porta, Lopez-de-Silanes, Shleifer et al., 1998). This should theoretically lead to a situation where minority investors are expropriated, and result in a small and inactive stock market. However, the capital markets in Sweden are very active (Agnblad et al., 2001; Rajan and Zingales, 2003). Both market capitalization and turnover are almost as big as the combined stock markets of the other Scandinavian countries, thus being among the highest in Europe (Stafsudd, 2009). Sweden also has an active market for corporate control, and the incidence of public takeover bids on the stock market, for example, is more like the US and the UK than like continental Europe. The number of hostile takeovers is, however, low, partly due to concentrated ownership and the Swedish system of dual-class shares with differentiated voting power (Carlsson, 2007).

From an international perspective, Sweden also has very little minority shareholder expropriation (Gilson, 2006; Nenova, 2003) and there is thus no supporting evidence that controlling shareholders maximize their private benefits at the expense of other shareholders, something that is called *tunneling* (Agnblad et al., 2001; Holmén and Högfeldt, 2004). According to Stafsudd (2009), this anomaly can be explained by the fact that law enforcement and accounting standards in Sweden are of very high quality, coupled with strong social norms of honesty and high business standards in the networks of ownership (see also Collin, 1998). The quality of accounting rules is, moreover, high in Sweden, and the disclosure of information among Swedish listed companies is rather specified and highly transparent. Thus, taking these various governance mechanisms into account has led some authors to conclude that Sweden after all has a relatively high degree of investor protection (Agnblad et al., 2001).

Sweden also has a number of specific features when it comes to corporate ownership. For example, ownership of private shares, both directly and through mutual funds, is among the highest in the world. A vast majority of the Swedish population owns such shares, and total household direct holdings make up about 15 percent of total market capitalization (Carlsson, 2007). The ownership structure of Swedish listed companies is also markedly different from, for example, the UK and the US. Swedish listed companies are dominated by a few larger shareholders who are active owners with a long-term interest in the industrial development of the companies in which they are involved. Owners who are major shareholders are often present or directly represented in Swedish boards. These directors are moreover generally considered hierarchically superior by other board members (Kärreman, 1999) and they can thus in general be characterized as having a significant influence on board-level decisions.

Another significant feature when it comes to the ownership of Swedish listed companies is the presence of two very powerful business groups that have exerted substantial influence over corporate Sweden since the 1930s: Handelsbanken and the Wallenberg family. The two business groups consist of a collection of industrial and financial corporations, which is connected through relations of ownership, interlocking directorates and financial service (Collin, 1998). The business groups are centered on two large Swedish banks: SEB in the case of the Wallenberg group and Svenska Handelsbanken in the case of the Handelsbanken group. There are, moreover, strong ties with two industrial holding companies: Investor in the Wallenberg group and Industrivärden in the Handelsbanken group. Both business groups control multiple firms on the Stockholm Stock Exchange, primarily through the legal provisions used to concentrate voting power (Collin, 1998).

A further feature that should be mentioned is that there is a relatively high share of foreign ownership in Swedish listed companies. From a highly regulated capital market in the 1960s and 1970s, the 1980s saw the start of massive deregulation. The result was a significant increase in the amount of foreign ownership in Swedish public companies that were already much internationalized. Statistics Sweden has reported that foreign ownership changed from just above 7 percent in 1990 to 39 percent in 2000 and foreign ownership on the SSE is now about 30–35 percent (Statistics Sweden, 2009). Among foreign owners, UK and US institutional investors are in the majority (Sundin and Sundqvist, 2000). The increase in the amount of foreign ownership has not, however, changed the power and influence of the Handelsbanken and Wallenberg spheres. Rather, both players increased their control of the Swedish stock market from 1990 to 2000, mainly through investments in the oldest and largest stock companies by using high vote-to-capital ratios. Foreign investors, on the other hand, have a tendency not to invest in companies with dual share classes, which means that foreign ownership is not necessarily combined with large investments enough for foreign owners to constitute controlling minority owners (Stafsudd, 2009).

The Swedish Companies Act and the board of directors

The legal system surrounding corporate governance in limited liability companies in Sweden is described in the Swedish Companies Act (SFS 2005:551). The rules are based on codified civil law where limited liability companies (in Swedish: *Aktiebolag*) are extensively regulated. The law makes a formal distinction between private and public limited liability companies. A private limited liability company is not allowed to offer its shares to the public on the stock exchange or any other organized market. There must also be a minimum share capital of 50,000 SEK, which is equivalent to about 7,750 USD. A public limited liability company, on the other hand, is allowed to offer shares and other securities to the public. The minimum share capital is 500,000 SEK, which is equivalent to about 77,400 USD. There are also some other notable differences between private and public limited liability companies with respect to corporate governance, where private ones in many cases are given more flexibility to adjust according to the situation and the preferences of the owner(s). The change in governance needs when a company transitions from a private to a public limited liability company is consequently acknowledged and reflected in the Swedish Companies Act.

The essence of corporate governance, as expressed in the Swedish Companies Act, is that ultimate power should rest with the shareholders. Basically, the corporate governance system is legally built around three decision-making bodies: the annual general meeting of shareholders, the board of directors and the chief executive officer (CEO). In addition, there must be an independent statutory auditor appointed by the shareholders' meeting. The appointed auditor reviews annual accounts and accounting practices in the company as well as the performance of the CEO and the board of directors, all in the service of shareholders. Auditors are also obliged to report on the issue of discharge from liability and of any possible causes for liability of damages of directors and the CEO.

The relationship between the decision-making bodies is hierarchical, where higher-level decision-making bodies can give direction to and make decisions for lower-level decision-making bodies. The annual general meeting of shareholders is thus a sovereign decision-making body that can make decisions about all matters that concern the company. Its primary task is to formally establish the annual report, appoint the board of directors and the statutory auditors, and also eventually approve their discharge. If deemed necessary, the shareholder meeting can moreover give explicit instructions to the board and the CEO about the management of the company. It should, however, be noted that such direction is very unusual in Swedish listed companies.

All shareholders present at the annual general meeting of shareholders have the right to vote for all shares. There may be restrictions about the number of shares that can be used to vote, but these restrictions are not very common. The Swedish Companies Act, moreover, allows shares with different voting rights, with a maximum of 1:10. Shares with no voting rights at all are not allowed. About half of all Swedish listed companies have shares with differentiated voting rights.

The board nomination procedure in Sweden deviates from that in most other countries, and consists of a nomination committee which contains only representatives of the largest owner. This committee is accountable to the general assembly and reports directly back to it. Large shareholders consequently have a significant influence on the composition of the board. The board of directors, according to the Swedish Companies Act, is responsible for ensuring that financial reporting and control systems are functioning effectively and that the company complies with laws and regulations. Public companies must have at least three board members, and CEO duality is not allowed. They must also appoint a CEO. In private companies, it is up to the owner(s) to have more than one board member as long as they also have a deputy board member, and a CEO is not mandatory. Instead, the chairperson may also serve as the CEO.

The board follows the unitary board structure where both executive and non-executive directors are allowed to have seats. In practice, however, the board is more similar to the dual board structure. The tradition is to have only the CEO as a board member while the rest of the board members are non-executive, including the chairperson. Consequently, there is a clear-cut distribution of roles and responsibilities between the functions of supervision and management. In its basic structure, the Swedish model for corporate governance is thus somewhere in between the Anglo-American one-tier model and the two-tier model that is found in continental Europe.

Other compositional characteristics of Swedish boards are that at least half of the board members (including the CEO) must come from the European Economic Area (EEA), and that they must be over eighteen years old. Persons who have been declared personally bankrupt or been banned from carrying on a business are not allowed to be board members. Another compositional characteristic is the system of employee co-determination, where Swedish law allows employees to be represented on the board. These employees are regular board members with the same responsibilities and duties as other members of the board.

The role of the CEO is vaguely described in the Swedish Companies Act. In principle, it is the board of directors that defines the role of the CEO through its own work instruction (in Swedish: *arbetsordningen*), through the specific instruction to the CEO (in Swedish: *VD instruktionen*) and through the other documents that have been made to regulate the information to the board of directors. A main feature of the CEO is that she or he is not allowed to deal with issues that are of an unusual nature or significant importance. In these cases, the board of directors should be summoned to make the decision.

The Swedish Corporate Governance Code

A code of corporate governance is a set of codified guidelines and norms for what is perceived as good corporate governance. They provide specification at a higher level of ambition than statutory regulation, and typically contain rather specific recommendations about the composition and work of the board of directors, information disclosure, executive pay and investor relations (Thomsen, 2006). The overall aim of the Swedish Corporate Governance Code is to improve the corporate governance of companies listed on the Swedish securities market. It is an alternative to legislation and acts as a complement to the Swedish Companies Act and other regulations. The underlying principle of the Swedish Code, following the international tradition, is to "comply or explain", which means that companies should comply with the rules or explain why they choose not to comply. The Code thus represents a soft law approach where companies may deviate from individual rules as long as they report and explain each deviation together with a description of their own solution.

The first proposal of a Swedish national code of corporate governance was made in 2004 and it was then adopted in 2005. The Swedish Corporate Governance Code was later launched in 2008, and further revised in 2010. The private sector in Sweden was thus quite late in adopting a national code compared to other highly industrialized countries with an active stock market. The reason for the late adoption has among other things been related to the fact that Sweden implemented very good company and banking legislation as a foundation for good corporate governance practices already in the 1930s, in the aftermath of the so-called "Kreuger crash" (for a short but comprehensive overview of this, see Carlsson, 2007: 1046–47). This legislation was at the time relatively comprehensive and included the Swedish Companies Act, banking regulations, as well as accounting requirements and information disclosure in order to prevent future corporate breakdowns.

The Swedish Code emphasizes the importance of active ownership and stipulates that good corporate governance entails that companies are run in the best interests of their owners, which is largely in line with the spirit of the Swedish Companies Act. The Swedish Code, moreover, emphasizes the board of directors as central players in corporate governance, and the board's composition, tasks and responsibilities are given most space in its various recommendations. The following features related to the board of directors are emphasized in the Code.

Board tasks and responsibilities

The Swedish Code stipulates that the principal tasks of the board of directors include establishing overall operational goals and strategy, appointing, evaluating and dismissing the CEO, ensuring an effective system for follow-up and control of operations, ensuring compliance with laws and other regulations, defining guidelines for ethical conduct and ensuring open, accurate, reliable and relevant external communication. In addition, the board of directors should approve significant assignments of the CEO that are outside the company. The board of directors should also annually evaluate its own work as well as the work of the CEO, using a systematic and structured process. Furthermore, the board of directors should inform shareholders and the capital market regarding corporate governance and how it applies with the Swedish Code.

Board composition

The Swedish Code stipulates that the board of directors should have a composition that matches its operations, phase of development and other relevant circumstances. As a collective, board members should also exhibit diversity and breadth of qualifications, experience and backgrounds. To be somewhat more concrete, it is furthermore stated that the company should strive for equal gender distribution on the board. The board of directors must consist of three or more members and one of them must be appointed chair. This chairperson has particular responsibility for leading the work of the board and ensuring that it fulfills its legal obligations. Board members who are elected by the shareholders should be independent, which in the Swedish Code is defined in relation to both the company and its executive managers. At least two of the members of the board who are independent of the company and its executive management should also be independent in relation to the company's major shareholders. A major shareholder is defined as one that controls, directly or indirectly, at least 10 percent of the shares or votes in the company. No more than one of the directors elected by the shareholders' meeting may be on the executive management team of the company or one of its subsidiaries. Normally, this seat is taken by the CEO.

Organization of board committees

The Swedish Code stipulates that the company should have audit, nomination and remuneration committees. This is a difference from the Swedish Companies Act, which has no provisions governing such committees. Audit and remuneration committees are seen as subsets of the board of directors. The audit committee should comprise no fewer than three board members, while there is no such recommendation for remuneration committees. The audit and remuneration committees should, however, both be independent in relation to the company and its executive management. At least one of the committee members who is independent in relation to the company and its executive managers is also to be independent of the company's major shareholder. Noteworthy is that while the audit and remuneration committees are seen as subsets of the board, the nomination committee is not. Rather, the recommendations about a nomination committee follow the Swedish tradition of having an election committee (in Swedish: *valberedning*) where the major shareholders nominate board member candidates, and where the general assembly then decides on their appointment. The nomination committee should have at least three members and the majority should not be members of the board. Although not explicitly stipulated in the Swedish Code, it is fairly common for the nomination committee to consist of the chair of the board of directors and four or five representatives of the largest (or major) shareholders.

The Swedish stock exchanges and the market for IPOs

The Swedish stock market

The stock market is the very center of the financial system in Sweden. Its role and importance in the Swedish national economy have grown steadily during the past two decades, much in line with the increased mobility of international investment capital coupled with a significant increase in the amount of savings in shares, funds and insurances by Swedish households. Sweden has an estimated overall market capitalization of about 4,284 billion SEK, which is equivalent to about 617 billion USD. According to a global ranking made by Bespoke Investment Group in 2010, Sweden was ranked as number nineteen in the world, which makes it the biggest stock market in Scandinavia and number seven in Europe. To compare, the total market capitalization in the world was almost 47 trillion USD, of which the US stock market accounts for about one-third with 14.2 trillion USD. The US was followed by Japan with 3.7 trillion USD and China with 3.2 trillion USD. Among the top five were also the UK and Hong Kong.

The origin of the Swedish stock market dates back to the eighteenth century when merchants and bankers met to make business transactions and exchange goods, services and information. The first organized stock market in Sweden was later created in Stockholm in 1863. In 1918 when it introduced a new electrical marking system, the Stockholm Stock Exchange (SSE) became the most modern stock exchange in Europe at the time. Another milestone was in 1992 when the stock market monopoly was broken in Sweden. SSE was then turned into a limited liability company and became the first profit-oriented stock exchange in the world.

The Swedish stock market has experienced some major changes due to the wave of mergers among existing stock exchanges and the establishment of new marketplaces. In 1997, SSE was merged with OM, a company that has specialized in options and clearing and that had itself been listed on SSE since 1987. The aim with the merger was to strengthen the financial market in Stockholm and the other Nordic countries. OMX was created in 2003 as a result of a merger between SSE and HEX, the Finnish stock exchange company that had previously acquired the Latvian and Estonian stock exchanges. Between 2003 and 2006 OMX also acquired the Lithuanian, Danish and Icelandic stock exchanges. In 2008 OMX merged with NASDAQ, the second largest stock exchange in the US. The merger resulted in NASDAQ OMX which is a stock exchange group that covers markets in the US, the Nordic region and the Baltic region.

Swedish stock exchanges

A stock exchange is basically a company that is permitted to operate one or more regulated markets for shares and other securities. Other companies can then use the stock exchange to issue their own shares, and investors can subsequently buy and sell these shares. In Sweden it is the Swedish Financial Supervisory Authority (in Swedish: *Finansinspektionen*) which issues permits to operate a stock market and which also supervises and monitors companies operating in financial markets, for example to ensure that trade and pricing is functioning well. All approved securities exchanges and other marketplaces are subject to the Swedish Market Abuse Penalties Act (2005:377), which prohibits dealings on the basis of information which is not public knowledge. It also prohibits disclosure of information that is liable to materially influence the price of financial instruments, as well as measures designed to manipulate market prices. When listed on a regulated marketplace, companies must comply with the requirements placed both by Swedish legislation and by the specific marketplace. Listing requirements typically refer to company size, disclosure of information and corporate governance. The reason for the strict rules surrounding stock exchanges is basically to protect investors.

In Sweden there are three companies that are allowed to operate securities exchanges: OMX Nordic Exchange Stockholm, Nordic Growth Market NGM and Burgundy. The first company, OMX Nordic Exchange Stockholm, also referred to as the Stockholm Stock Exchange (SSE), is the provider of the primary securities exchange of the Nordic countries. All companies listed on SSE have to follow the Swedish Code of Corporate Governance. There were 320 companies listed on SSE at the beginning of 2011, divided into three lists based on the size of their stock of shares: Large Cap, which has 56 companies with market capitalizations of above 1 billion EUR; Mid Cap, which has 79 companies with market capitalizations between 150 million and 1 billion EUR; and Small Cap, which has 122 companies with market capitalizations under 150 million EUR. The total market capitalization of SSE at the beginning of 2011 was about 4,240 billion SEK, which is equivalent to about 611 billion USD. There is, however, a major bias in terms of the contribution to this amount. The lion's share comes from companies listed on the Large Cap list on SSE. Moreover, the ten biggest companies on the Large Cap list account for about 50 percent, or 2,000 billion SEK, of total market capitalization. Examples of such companies include Ericsson, H&M, Nordea and TeliaSonera.

The second company that is allowed to operate a stock exchange in Sweden is Nordic Growth Market (NGM). This company was the first organized marketplace for equities that broke the stock market monopoly of SSE. It has been an authorized market for shares since 1999 and it has been approved as a securities exchange by the Swedish Financial Supervisory Authority since 2003. The stock exchange is called NGM equity and it is primarily focused on small and medium-size growth companies. The formal listing requirements are the same as SSE, apart from less strict rules for the number of shareholders and the distribution of shares, and all companies listed on NGM equity have to follow the Swedish Code of Corporate Governance. There were at the beginning of 2011 twenty-four companies listed on NGM, with an estimated total market capitalization of about 2.7 billion SEK, which is equivalent to about 417.9 million USD.

The third company, Burgundy, was created in 2009 as a new Nordic marketplace for securities trading. In early 2011 it was approved by the Swedish Financial Supervisory Authority to operate a regulated market for warrants, certificates, structured products and fund units. They are also allowed to operate a Multilateral Trading Facility (see below) for trading with shares. It is not possible to list a company on Burgundy, but all shares that are traded on Burgundy are listed on NASDAQ OMX Nordic (Stockholm, Helsinki and Copenhagen) and the Oslo Stock Exchange. Burgundy is owned by the largest Nordic banks and brokerage firms, and they are also the trading partners of the market.

A simpler form of market for shares and other securities is called a Multilateral Trading Facility (MTF). A stock exchange or a securities institution can get a permit to run such a market. The MTF can include both companies already listed on an approved stock exchange and companies whose shares are traded exclusively on the MTF. The regulations surrounding MTFs are less detailed compared to a stock exchange, although they can adopt more stringent rules if they want. The simpler regulations mean less trouble when companies offer shares on this kind of marketplace, but also entail more risk for investors.

In Sweden there were at the beginning of 2011 four companies that are allowed to operate MTFs: NASDAQ OMX Stockholm (First North), Nordic Growth Market NGM (Nordic MTF), Aktietorget and Burgundy. First North is an alternative market for small growth companies. It is part of the OMX Nordic Stock Exchange and uses the same trading system. The rules for companies listed on First North are, however, less strict and they are formally not treated as publicly listed companies. At the beginning of 2011 there were ninety-nine companies listed on First North with an estimated total market capitalization of about 32.1 billion SEK, which is equivalent to about 4.6 million USD.

Nordic MTF is a platform for trading the shares of small and medium-size growth companies that are yet to become publicly listed. They are thus formally not treated as publicly listed companies. The trade is managed through Nordic Growth Market NGM. At the beginning of 2011 there were twenty companies listed on Nordic MTF with an estimated total market capitalization of about 727 million SEK, which is equivalent to about 105 million USD.

Aktietorget is a platform focused on trade with the shares of growing entrepreneur-led companies. The trade is managed through the trading system of OMX. At the beginning of 2011 there were 130 companies listed on Aktietorget with an estimated total market capitalization of about 8 billion SEK, which is equivalent to about 1.1 billion USD.

The IPO process

An initial public offering (IPO) refers to when a company issues shares to the public for the first time (Jenkins and Ljungqvist, 2001). The general perception is that IPOs are exclusively made by smaller, younger companies that seek capital to grow and expand their operations. However, IPOs can as well be made by large and mature, privately owned companies that want to go public, and they can also be the result of equity-carve-outs and spin-offs of certain business areas from existing public companies.

The IPO process is started by the decision to publicly offer the shares of the company – a decision that is formally made by the board of directors. At this stage, the company needs to make sure it has access to the knowledge and experience that are required for a listing.

These requirements in Sweden are both related to public regulations, such as the Securities Market Act (SFS 2007:528) and the Swedish Financial Supervisory Authority's regulations governing operations on trading venues (FFFS 2007:17), as well as the listing rules of the specific stock market. It is not unusual that Swedish companies that plan to go public change to an accountant who knows about such legislation and requirements and also has experience from working with public companies. The largest accounting firms in Sweden also offer the service to investigate whether a company meets listing requirements, and they can provide help in setting up and documenting necessary routines and procedures for accounting and the disclosure of information.

Based on the decision to go public, the company issuing shares enters into a contract with a lead underwriter (an investment bank) to sell the shares. Due to the wide array of legal requirements surrounding an IPO, the company often involves one or more law firms that typically specialize in securities law, and there may also be more underwriters involved in the IPO process. The Swedish Financial Instruments Trading Act (LHF 1991:980) requires a prospectus to be published when a company issues shares to the public, unless particular exemptions apply such as in the case of a secondary listing.[1] The prospectus should contain all information necessary for an investor to make qualified evaluations of the performance, status and future prospects for the issuing company and the shares. A few years ago it was common to have a financial advisor as a support in the writing of the prospectus. However, today it is more common to have a lawyer doing this work. Since 2006 it is the Swedish Financial Authority that approves and registers all prospectuses in Sweden.

It is the lead underwriter that approaches investors with offers to sell the shares of the issuing company. The share price is set through the underwriter's effort in gathering indications of interest among potential investors, a method generally referred to as *book building*. Success in this part of the IPO process is related both to attracting capital and to getting a good mix of investors with varying degrees of investment horizons. According to Sherman (2005), the role of the

---

[1] For a detailed overview of rules about prospectuses, see the Swedish Prospectus Directive and the recommendations from the Committee of European Securities Regulators (CESR).

underwriters is crucial in the IPO process since they manage access to shares for potential investors, allowing them to reduce the risk for both the issuing company and future investors and also to control spending on information acquisition, thereby limiting either under-pricing or aftermarket volatility. For a further, detailed description of the IPO process in Sweden, see Örtengren (2008, in Swedish). For an overview of the IPO process in an international perspective, see Jenkins and Ljungqvist (2001).

IPO activity in Sweden 2006 to 2008

This section will take a closer look at Swedish IPOs between 2006 and 2008. The sample is based on IPOs identified in the *EURIPO Fact-book* for each respective year (Paleari, Redondi, Piazzalunga et al., 2006; Paleari, Piazzalunga, Redondi et al., 2007; Paleari, Trabucchi, Redondi et al., 2008). The initial screening identified eighty-seven IPOs in the period. After a closer review of the companies, we removed one utility firm, ten spin-offs, seven secondary listings, three companies not registered in Sweden, and one company which went public on the London Stock Exchange (LSE), which resulted in a final sample of sixty-five Swedish IPOs. All identified companies issued their shares on First North or OMX Nordic.

The distribution of IPOs per year was twenty-eight in 2006, thirty-one in 2007 and six in 2008. Obviously, there was a downward trend in the number of IPOs in Sweden during 2008. This trend reflects the economic recession and financial uncertainty that were experienced in the world economy this year, which heavily influenced stock markets over the world. For example, about 30 percent of total market capitalization was erased on SSE in October 2008 after an 8 percent dip in share prices.

Detailed information about the companies was collected from pro-spectuses, annual reports and, in some cases, also IR departments. A closer look at the companies reveals that they consist of a rather heterogeneous sample of companies. The Industry Classification Benchmark (ICB) system[2] shows that most companies in the sample belong to industrials, followed by consumer services and financials. Together, these three account for over half of the sample. However, there is no single industry that dominates Swedish IPOs and,

---

[2] www.icbenchmark.com

Table 18.1 *Industry belongingness according to ICB*

Industry	2006	2007	2008	Total
Industrials	4	8	2	14
Consumer services	7	3	2	12
Financials	7	3	0	10
Technology	0	5	2	7
Consumer goods	2	4	0	6
Healthcare	2	3	0	5
Industrials	2	2	0	4
Information technology	4	0	0	4
Oil and gas	0	2	0	2
Telecommunications	0	1	0	1
Sum	28	31	6	65

moreover, there is no consistent dominant pattern to be found over the three years. The distribution of IPOs classified according to ICB can be seen in Table 18.1.

The heterogeneity among Swedish IPOs is further underlined when looking closer at the characteristics and performance of the companies in the sample. The companies have a mean age of 11.7 years and with an average of 267.4 employees. However, the descriptive statistics show that the distribution of data is skewed. The median (Q2) age is 8 years and the third quartile (Q3) is 14.25, while the maximum value is 63. Likewise, the median number of employees is 31 and the third quartile is 134.8, while the maximum value is 4,240. This means that almost 75 percent of the sample consists of small and medium-sized companies[3] that are less than fifteen years old. Hence, while most companies are relatively young and small, there are some larger companies that have gone public in the observation period that influence the central tendency in the sample with respect to company age and size. Company age and size were correlated, at $p > .01$. The average sales growth[4] of the companies is 11.1 but, here too, we can note a

---

[3] According to the EU definition, an SME is a company with fewer than 250 employees.

[4] Sales growth over the past three years was calculated as: (sales IPO year – sales 3 years earlier)/(sales 3 years earlier). This was intended to capture the average growth for the 3-year period leading up to the IPO. In cases when the company did not have 3 full years of sales history, the previous year total was used.

Table 18.2 *Company characteristics and performance at IPO*

Company characteristics	Mean	S.D.	Min	Q1	Q2	Q3	Max
Age	11.7	13.6	0	2.75	8	14.25	63
Employees	267.4	746.7	0	14	31	134.8	4,240
Sales growth	11.0	65.1	−0.62	0.12	0.59	2.63	452.3
ROA	−0.12	0.50	−1.75	−0.18	0.04	0.10	0.64
ROE	−0.40	2.86	−13.2	−0.22	0.12	0.45	9.92
ROS	−26.13	151.6	−1,101.0	−0.57	0.02	0.09	1.85

skewed distribution in the data. The median sales growth is 0.59 and the third quartile is 2.63, while the maximum value is 452.3. This pattern of skewness is evident also when looking at various profitability ratios, such as return on assets (ROA), return on equity (ROE) and return on sales (ROS), where some companies report rather extreme values. In all, the data show that the IPOs vary a lot with respect to performance as well. There were no significant correlations between company age and size and the various performance measures in the sample. Descriptive statistics for the IPOs can be seen in Table 18.2.

Entrepreneurs, together with their family members, are the single biggest source of ownership among the transitioning companies. The data in the prospectuses show that this owner category on average has almost one-quarter of the stock in the company before the IPO. Their influence in the companies remains after the IPO, even if their total share of stocks decreases. The prospectuses moreover indicate that about 44 percent of the companies are controlled by pyramid ownership and 18 percent of the companies have dual-class shares with differentiated voting rights. Ownership for various categories for the IPOs can be seen in Table 18.3.

The prospectuses also reveal information about the board of directors in the companies. The companies have on average 5.82 board members at the time of the IPO. Most of them consist of non-executive directors, while there are few that can be classified as independent according to the definition in the Swedish Code of Corporate Governance. The number of directors and the share of NEDs are more or less equal to what has been found in studies of privately held companies in Sweden (Gabrielsson, 2007).

There are few women directors on the board – over half of the sample has no women at all on the boards. No industry bias could be

Table 18.3 *Ownership characteristics before and after IPO*

Ownership characteristics	Mean	S.D.	Min	Q1	Q2	Q3	Max
Family ownership – pre-IPO	0.24	0.30	0	0	0.09	0.43	1.0
Family ownership – post-IPO	0.12	0.19	0	0	0	0.21	0.71
Bank ownership – pre-IPO	0.13	0.26	0	0	0	0.17	1.0
Bank ownership – post-IPO	0.08	0.18	0	0	0	0.07	0.86
VC ownership – pre-IPO	0.07	0.19	0	0	0	0	1.0
VC ownership – post-IPO	0.05	0.15	0	0	0	0	1.0
Business angel ownership – pre-IPO	0.05	0.08	0	0	0	0.05	0.30
Business angel ownership – post-IPO	0.03	0.60	0	0	0	0.02	0.21

detected with respect to women's involvement on the board of directors. However, the number of women on the board was correlated with company size, at $p > .01$. In total, the average share of women directors in the sample is 12.3 percent, which is considerably below the reported average for all Swedish publicly listed companies of 19 percent. There are only a few founder directors on the boards. There are also relatively few employee directors on the boards, which probably merely reflects the fact that many of the companies are relatively small and young. The number of employee directors is correlated with company age and size, both at $p > .01$.

The frequency of board meetings (nine meetings per year) is relatively high compared to both previous empirical studies of boards of directors (Gabrielsson, 2007) and general best-practice recommendations, which probably reflects the higher work load in the board prior to listing. Moreover, about one-fifth of the companies have organized their work in audit and remuneration committees, which is prescribed in the Swedish Code of Corporate Governance. The presences of audit and remuneration committees are correlated with each other, at $p > .01$. They are also correlated with company size, at $p > .05$ and $p > .01$ respectively. Furthermore, 15 percent of the companies have board members as part of the nomination committee. There is, however, no significant correlation between having board members as part of the nomination committee and having audit and remuneration committees. Data

Table 18.4 *Board governance at IPO*

Board governance	Mean	S.D.	Min	Q1	Q2	Q3	Max
Board members	5.82	1.4	3	5	5	6	10
Non-executive directors (NEDs)	3.40	1.9	0	3	3	5	9
Independent directors	1.41	2.1	0	0	0	3	7
Female directors	0.68	0.9	0	0	0	1	4
Founder directors	0.80	0.9	0	0	1	1	4
Employee directors	0.70	0.7	0	0	0	0	3
Board meeting frequency	9.23	4.4	3	5	9	12	23
Audit committee	0.20	0.4	0	0	0	0	1
Remuneration committee	0.22	0.41	0	0	0	0	1
Nomination committee	0.15	0.36	0	0	0	0	1

Table 18.5 *Type of board members*

Type of directors	None	1–2	3+
Female directors	53.8%	43.1%	3.1%
Non-executive directors (NEDs)	10.8%	12.4%	76.8%
Independent directors	63.1%	9.2%	27.7%
Founder directors	44.6%	52.3%	3.1%
Employee directors	84.6%	13.8%	1.6%

on board governance and type of board members in the companies are reported in Table 18.4 and Table 18.5.

The IPO process: a case description of HMS Industrial Networks

HMS Industrial Networks AB (HMS) is a company that develops, produces and markets intelligent communication technology for automation equipment. It was founded in 1988 by Nicolas Hassbjer and Staffan Dahlström based on an exam project in computer engineering. At the time, both founders were graduate students at Halmstad University, a regional university college on the west coast of Sweden. The company is still located in the city of Halmstad, close to the university.

The company was focused from the start on products for industrial network communication, based on proprietary technological solutions. Since then the company has developed into a fast-growing and profitable company with world-leading technology. The company has two main product groups. The first is "Embedded products," consisting of network cards that make it possible to monitor and communicate with production units, such as robots, engines and control systems, in a network, and it accounts for about 75 percent of total sales. The second is "Gateways," consisting of communication devices that connect networks with incompatible protocols, and it accounts for the remaining 25 percent of sales. HMS aims to be a technology leader and continually develops new products and services to strengthen its position as the leading supplier of communication solutions and industrial applications.

In the past decade, HMS has enjoyed an average growth of 30 percent per year. This has placed the company on the list of Swedish high-growth firms (also known as "Gazelles", after Birch, 1987). The company has also won various awards, for example Sweden's best electronics company in 2003 and Sweden's best export company in 2008. The company has grown from 77 employees in 2005 to 114 employees in 2007 when it went public. During this period there was an average organic growth rate of about 26 percent.

In 2009, HMS reported 201.6 million SEK in total sales, which is equivalent to about 31.4 million USD. More than 70 percent of total sales come from international markets. The products are manufactured in Sweden and sold to three different areas: Europe, Asia and the US. HMS sells its own products to customers in fifty countries, and the company has its own selling companies in the US, Germany, Italy, France, Japan and China. Customers include large Swedish companies such as ABB and Atlas Copco, and foreign companies such as Toshiba, Hitachi, Panasonic and Rockwell Automation.

The main owner before the IPO in 2007 was Segulah AB, a private equity company based in Stockholm which specializes in owning and developing mid-market companies. Segulah acquired about 60 percent of the shares in HMS in 2004 from the previous owners, IDI and SEB Företagsinvest. The previous owners that sold their shares had been involved in the company since the late 1990s, when they were invited by the founders to finance a planned expansion.

The board of directors prior to the IPO consisted of five board members. Four of them were NEDs, including the chairperson.

Two of the NEDs were representatives of the main owner Segulah. The fifth board member was a founder and part of the management team. In addition, the CEO (the other founder) and the CFO were present at board meetings. With respect to committees, the board of directors had a remuneration committee which consisted of the board chairperson together with one NED and the CEO as an adjunct committee member. Following Swedish tradition, the nomination committee consisted of three representatives from the three largest owners and was chaired by the board chairperson. The board did not have any audit committee before the IPO.

The offer

On October 19, 2007, HMS targeted the Small Cap list of the OMX Nordic market, which is an official Swedish regulated market for shares for companies with an estimated stock market value under 150 million EUR. The company had not offered its shares to a wider public before this occasion. The offer was made by Segulah and the other two main owners to the general public and institutional investors to buy 6,491,050 existing shares in the company, which was equivalent to 61.4 percent of the shares and votes in the company. In addition, Segulah offered to sell an extra 649,105 shares to cover a potential over-allotment. As the offer only included sales of existing shares, the company was thus not receiving new capital. The price was set to 74 SEK per share, which at the time was equivalent to 4.7 EUR or 6.7 USD. There was great interest in HMS among investors, and at first it seemed that the share was to be over-allotted three times over. However, the share price fell shortly after the IPO, partly due to the growing uneasiness on the Swedish stock market in fall 2007, and Segulah thus remained in the company after the IPO.

The company after IPO

After the IPO the ownership structure of HMS changed significantly. The two founders, Nicolas Hassbjer and Staffan Dahlström, were now main owners with 15 percent of the shares respectively. In addition there were also two institutional investors which had received significant shares in the company: Lannebo Fonder with 9.9 percent, and SEB Fonder with 7.6 percent. For reasons explained above, Segulah remained involved in the company in a period after the IPO with an ownership share of 6.1 percent. The rest of the ownership was divided among various smaller shareholders. At the end of 2007, HMS had about 3,000 shareholders, and board members and executives together controlled about 31 percent of the votes and the capital stock in the company.

The composition of the board of directors remained much the same after the IPO. However, in line with the Swedish Code, an audit committee was created and implemented, consisting of all board members. At the 2008 annual meeting one of the owner representatives from Segulah left his board position and was replaced by a non-executive director (NED), reflecting the reduced ownership stake by the private equity company. In May 2008, Segulah sold the remaining shares in HMS to Investment AB Latour, a Swedish investment company, which then controlled about 10 percent of the capital and votes in the company. The affair was initiated by Latour, who contacted Segulah about their offer to buy the remaining shares. The shift in ownership resulted in another board membership change in the 2009 annual meeting, when the last owner representative of Segulah was replaced by a board member representing Latour who now had increased their share of ownership in HMS to 14 percent. In 2009 co-founder Nicolas Hassbjer also left the position as company CEO, and he was replaced by the other founder, Staffan Dahlström. At this time, Hassbjer also took Dahlström's seat on the board. This resulted in a board composed of three NEDs, one board member representing Latour and one board member representing the two founders who still were significant owners. At the end of 2009, HMS had about 2,800 shareholders, and board members and executives together controlled about 30 percent of the votes and the capital stock in the company.

Conclusion

In this chapter, literature and empirical evidence related to the corporate governance context for IPOs in Sweden have been reviewed and presented. The review has emphasized that its special features with respect to ownership and control of listed companies make it an interesting case for corporate governance. Swedish company law, for example, is based on the idea that the ultimate power of the company should rest with shareholders, and Sweden has a tradition of controlling owners that take an active part in the development of the companies in which they are involved. However, Sweden has also a system of co-determination where employees have the right to appoint regular board members, and this arrangement is typically satisfactory for both labor and management. The corporate governance structure in Sweden also differs from both the Anglo-Saxon one-tier model and the European two-tier model, placing itself somewhere in between. A Swedish Code of Corporate Governance has been in effect since 2005, and its content is very much similar to what can be found in other countries, such as the UK Code. A special feature in the Swedish Code, however, includes a double kind of board independence, defined in relation to both executive managers and controlling owners.

Sweden has, in addition to several MTFs, three companies that have been officially approved to operate regulated markets for securities. The Swedish stock market can be characterized as active and it has been ranked as number five in Europe in terms of its total market capitalization. An examination of Swedish IPOs in the period 2006 to 2008 shows a largely heterogeneous sample of companies. However, most of the companies are relatively young and small. The most common ownership category before the IPO is the entrepreneur and his or her family, and the board of directors is composed of about five directors where NEDs are in the majority. In all, the chapter provides unique insight into the Swedish governance context and characteristics of Swedish IPOs.

References

Agnblad, Jonas, Erik Berglöf, Peter Högfeldt and Helena Svancar. 2001. 'Ownership and control in Sweden – strong owners, weak minorities, and social control', in Fabrizio Barca and Marco Becht (eds.), *The Control of Corporate Europe*, Oxford University Press, 228–58.

Bebchuk, Lucian A., Reinier Kraakman and George G. Triantis. 1999. *Stock pyramids, cross-ownership, and dual class equity: The creation and agency costs of separating control from cash flow rights*, NBER Working paper series No. 6951, National Bureau of Economic Research, Cambridge, MA.

Birch, D. 1987. *Job Creation in America: How Our Smallest Companies Put the Most People to Work*, New York: The Free Press.

Carlsson, Rolf H. 2007. 'Swedish corporate governance and value creation owners still in the driver's seat', *Corporate Governance: An International Review*, 15, 6, 1038–55.

Collin, Sven-Olof. 1998. 'Why are these islands of conscious power found in the ocean of ownership? Institutional and governance hypotheses explaining the existence of business groups in Sweden', *Journal of Management Studies*, 35, 719–46.

Gabrielsson, Jonas. 2007. 'Boards of directors and entrepreneurial posture in medium-size companies: Putting the board demography approach to a test', *International Small Business Journal*, 25, 5, 511–37.

Gilson, Ronald J.R. 2006. 'Controlling shareholders and corporate governance: Complicating the comparative taxonomy', *Harvard Law Review*, 119, 1642–80.

Glete, Jan. 1994. *Nätverk i näringslivet: ägande och industriell omvandling i det mogna industrisamhället 1920–1990*, Stockholm: SNS.

Högfeldt, Peter. 2005. 'The history and politics of corporate ownership in Sweden', in Randall K. Morck (ed.), *A History of Corporate Governance around the World*, Chicago University Press.

Holmén, Martin and Peter Högfeldt. 2004. 'A law and finance analysis of initial public offerings', *Journal of Financial Intermediation*, 13, 324–58.

Jenkinson, Tim and Alexander Ljungquist. 2001. *Going Public: The Theory and Evidence of How Companies Raise Equity Finance*, 2nd edn., Oxford University Press.

Judge, William. 2010. 'Corporate governance mechanisms throughout the world', *Corporate Governance: An International Review*, 18, 3, 159–60.

Kärreman, Matts. 1999. *Styrelseledarmöters mandat – ansats till en teori om styrelsearbete i börsnoterade företag*, Lund: Lund Business Press.

La Porta, Rafael, Florencio Lopez-de-Silanes, Andrei Shleifer and Robert W. Vishny. 1998. 'Law and finance', *Journal of Political Economy*, 106, 1113–55.

Nenova, T. 2003. 'The value of corporate voting rights and control: A cross-country analysis', *Journal of Financial Economics*, 68, 325–51.

Örtengren, Torsten. 2008. 'Börsintroduktion på OMX Nordiska börs i Stockholm', in Catarina Sandeberg and Robert Sevenius (eds.), *Börsrätt*, Lund: Studentlitteratur.

Paleari, Stefano, Renato Redondi, Daniele Piazzalunga and Silvio Vismara. 2006. *Academic EurIPO Fact Book 2006*, New York: BookSurge Publishing.

Paleari, Stefano, Daniele Piazzalunga, Renato Redondi, Fabio Trabucchi and Silvio Vismara. 2007. *Academic EurIPO Fact Book 2007*, New York: BookSurge Publishing.

Paleari, Stefano, Fabio Trabucchi, Renato Redondi, Daniele Piazzalunga and Silvio Vismara. 2008. *Academic EurIPO Fact Book 2008*, New York: BookSurge Publishing.

Rajan, Raghuram G. and Luigi Zingales. 2003. 'The great reversals: The politics of financial development in the twentieth century', *Journal of Financial Economics*, 69, 5–50.

Sherman, A.E. 2005. 'Global trends in IPO methods: Book building versus auctions with endogenous entry', *Journal of Financial Economics*, 78, 3, 615–49.

Stafsudd, Anna. 2009. 'Corporate networks as informal governance mechanisms: A small worlds approach to Sweden', *Corporate Governance: An International Review*, 17, 1, 62–76.

Statistics Sweden. 2009. *Ägandet av aktier i bolag noterade på svensk marknadsplats*, www.scb.se/ (web page last accessed January 20, 2011).

Sundin, Sven-Ivan and Ann-Mari Sundqvist. 2000. *Ägarna och makten* (Owners and power in Sweden's listed companies), Ägarservice, Halmstad, Sweden.

Thomsen, Steen. 2006. 'The hidden meaning of codes: Corporate governance and investor rent seeking', *European Business Organization Law Review*, 7, 4, 845–61.

2008. *An Introduction to Corporate Governance: Mechanism and Systems*, Copenhagen: DJOF Publishing.

19 | Corporate governance and initial public offerings in Switzerland

WINFRIED RUIGROK AND DIMITRIOS
G. GEORGAKAKIS

Introduction

Switzerland is an interesting country to study the dynamics of initial public offerings (IPOs) because it offers two paradoxes. Understanding the backgrounds of these paradoxes helps to appreciate the nature of the Swiss corporate governance system, and the direction that this system may take as a result of recent IPO activity. First, Switzerland has recently been ranked as the most competitive country in the world (World Economic Forum, 2010: 14). Specifically, its position as second in the world in terms of "innovation and sophistication factors" suggests that Switzerland may be the home of a large number of IPOs. However, over the period 2006–8, only sixteen IPOs were registered in Switzerland that met the IPO definition that is used in this volume.

Second, located in the heart of Europe with a population of 7.6 million people, Switzerland is the home of many leading multinational corporations (MNCs) such as Nestlé, Novartis, Roche, Zurich Financial Services, UBS and Credit Suisse. Indeed, with almost 2 Fortune Global 500 firms per 1 million Swiss citizens, Switzerland has the highest density of Fortune Global 500 firms in the world. Furthermore, Switzerland has also been the object of large-scale foreign direct investments by non-Swiss MNCs keen to relocate headquarter-type activities to Switzerland. However, efforts to raise the attractiveness of Switzerland to foreign institutional investors have been less than successful and foreign investors have thus far played a modest role in the Swiss corporate governance scene.

Similar to countries like Austria, Germany and Japan, Swiss listed companies operate under Germanic civil law. The Swiss governance system is often categorized as belonging to the continental European model of corporate governance. Indeed, Swiss listed firms have traditionally been characterized by comparatively high rates of ownership concentration. Today, major blockholders tend to be large corporations and family owners rather than banks. Bank ownership in Swiss listed firms has been significantly reduced during the last few years.

However, the Swiss corporate governance scene differs from other Germanic civil law economies in two key respects. First, Swiss listed firms are free to adopt a board structure that best fits their business requirements, i.e., they can establish either a one-tier or a two-tier board. The only category of Swiss listed firms that have no choice in terms of board structure are banks which are required by law to set up a two-tier board. Second, most corporate governance regulations of the Swiss code are based on the "comply or explain" principle. However, the Swiss Stock Exchange (SIX) has drafted additional requirements stipulating that all listed firms have to publish specific corporate governance details (such as total executive remuneration, board composition, share ownership and financial performance information) in their annual reports.

In the past, Switzerland has occasionally been criticized for inadequate investor protection standards (World Bank, 2010), high ownership concentration (OECD, 2006) and a lack of response to international pressures for a more shareholder-oriented model of governance (US Commercial Service, 2009). In response to such criticism, Switzerland has over the years introduced a series of corporate governance reforms aiming to enhance convergence with international governance standards (Ruigrok and Canepa, 2005; Schleiffer and von Planta, 2009; Schweizer, 2006). For Switzerland, it is essential to adopt governance guidelines that correspond with what are perceived as international best practices and to transform the governance system in a way that is in line with more dispersed ownership, in order to be an attractive investment location for foreign investors.

The importance of attracting institutional investors from both inside and outside the country is particularly crucial for newly listed IPO firms. The risk of investing in IPO firms is higher than it is in large, already listed companies, since IPOs are usually young firms that lack a long operating history and publicly available performance information (Certo, 2003). IPO firms that manage to attract foreign investors may broaden their investment base and have a higher likelihood to attract specialized investors that understand the IPO firm's business. Thus, adopting efficient corporate governance principles that meet foreign investors' preferences and promote ownership dispersion is crucial for (Swiss) IPO success.

The present chapter describes the current state of corporate governance in Switzerland following the most recent governance reforms introduced in 2007. Subsequently, it explains the Swiss IPO process and, by using a sample of all Swiss IPOs between 2006 and 2008, it investigates whether newly listed firms tend to follow the recommended corporate governance principles and whether ownership concentration in these firms continues to be high. Descriptive statistics show that IPO firms in Switzerland tend to adopt the established corporate governance guidelines. This suggests that Swiss IPO firms and, in extension, the Swiss governance system are increasingly falling in line with international governance standards. Despite this positive picture, however, ownership concentration in Swiss IPOs still remains high.

Corporate governance mechanisms

The Swiss code of best practice

The first Swiss corporate law, also known as "Code of Obligations" (CO), came into effect in July 1992 with the purpose to maximize shareholders' value, to serve stakeholders' interests and to attract foreign and domestic investors. The year 2002 signaled radical reforms for the Swiss governance system; the Swiss Business Federation (Economiesuisse) presented the Swiss Code of Best Practice for Corporate Governance (Swiss Code) with guidelines applicable to all companies listed on the Swiss Exchange (SWX; today SIX). This code was established on a voluntary basis with the aim of protecting minority shareholders' rights and clarifying the responsibilities of the board of directors (Economiesuisse, 2007). In parallel, the Swiss Exchange introduced a Directive on Information Relating to Corporate Governance (DCG) by providing mandatory principles for companies listed at the SWX with the purpose to increase transparency and accountability of issuers.

The most recent updates to the Swiss Code were made in 2005 and 2007. Emphasis was given to further enhance convergence between the Swiss system and the international corporate governance principles. According to Schweizer's report (2006: 57): "the Swiss reforms enacted in 2005 demonstrate an increasing global convergence of some basic corporate governance standards, such as external audit and auditor supervision, internal control, risk management, as well as transparency requirements for companies". The reforms were greatly influenced by the development of the Sarbanes-Oxley Act in the USA. In 2007, however, the International Monetary Fund (IMF) claimed that Swiss regulatory bodies should "further strengthen the comparability of financial information disclosed to investors, and introduce proper supervision and sanctioning of auditors and listed companies" (IMF, 2007: 13). As a quick response to that, Economiesuisse introduced some further reforms to the Swiss Code during the same year. Changes mainly referred to the remuneration of directors and senior managers, the reinforcement of shareholder rights, as well as other internal control issues (Economiesuisse, 2007). To shed more detailed light on the Swiss governance system, the following paragraphs present the major characteristics of the Swiss Code with regard to the rights of shareholders and the responsibilities and composition of the board of directors based on the most recent reforms introduced in 2007.

Shareholder rights

The most important process of corporate governance is the general shareholders' meeting which is compulsory for all listed companies at least once a year. During the meeting, shareholders can make suggestions on the items given in the meeting's agenda and ask the board of directors to provide detailed information concerning company matters. Shareholders can make decisions regarding personnel issues at the top level of the organization, such as appointing auditors and electing new board members (Economiesuisse, 2007). To put an additional subject on the meeting's agenda, a shareholder must own shares with a nominal value of at least 1.06 million[1] USD (CO, art. 699). Furthermore, shareholders with more than 10 percent of registered shares have the right to call for additional general meetings (CO, art. 699). Such shareholder powers have led some scholars to characterize the Swiss system as the most shareholder-oriented system of the "European continental governance block" (Pedrazzini, 1998). However, other studies argue that further reforms with regard to the protection of minority shareholders are required in order to enhance convergence with the international governance standards (Mach, Schynder, Lupold et al., 2007).

---

[1] Amounts converted from CHF to USD as of 31/12/2010.

Board structure and composition

According to the Swiss Code, listed firms are required to have a board of directors responsible for the executive control and management of the organization. All firms, apart from banks, have the flexibility to structure their boards based on their business requirements. There are three board structures that Swiss listed firms can have: (1) *the unitary board structure* (the board of directors has the responsibility for both control and management of the organization), (2) *the dual board structure* (two-tier boards) and (3) *the mixed board structure* (boards that consist of both executive and non-executive members). Banks, however, must consist of two-tier boards: the supervisory board that is responsible for monitoring executive behaviors and actions, and the executive board responsible for the adequate management of the organization (Economiesuisse, 2007).

In case of a mixed board structure, the Swiss Code recommends that the majority of board members should be non-executive independent directors. In Switzerland, the definition of directors' independence differs from most countries. According to the Swiss Code, directors are characterized as independent if they have no personal and/or professional relationship with the focal firm for three years before their appointment. This differs from the more widely accepted five-year period. Furthermore, Swiss listed firms are free to determine whether the roles of the CEO and chairperson should be separate or combined (duality). Finally, another recommendation concerning the composition of Swiss boards is about the nationality of directors. The Swiss Code recommends that boards of Swiss firms that operate abroad should consist of members who have "long-standing international experience" and/or who are foreign nationals (not Swiss). The purpose of this recommendation is to enhance the attractiveness of Swiss companies to foreign institutional investors (Economiesuisse, 2007). No gender quota stipulations exist, despite the, even by international standards, very low female board participation ratio (Ruigrok, Peck and Tacheva, 2007).

Board responsibilities and committees

The Swiss Code implies that the main responsibilities of boards of directors in Swiss listed firms are: (1) defining the strategic goals and the means to achieve them, (2) supervising and monitoring the executive management, (3) preparing the annual report as well as the agenda of the general shareholders' meeting, (4) appointing and/or removing executive members and (5) actively representing the company inside and outside the organizational context (CO, art. 716a). To fulfill these responsibilities effectively, boards should meet at least four times a year in order to discuss important company matters and to evaluate the performance of executive members. Additionally, the compensation of all members of the supervisory and executive board, as well as the characteristics of shareholders with more than 5 percent of shares, should be reported in the firm's annual report. Finally, the Swiss Code recommends that boards of directors should set up audit, nomination and compensation committees. These committees should consist of a majority of independent directors who have a relationship of no more than three years with the company and who have no family ties with any member of the executive management (Economiesuisse, 2007).

Swiss exchange and ownership concentration

The Swiss exchange (SIX) was established in 1995 after the merger of Switzerland's three stock exchanges (stock exchanges of Geneva, Basle and Zurich). The number of companies listed in the SIX decreased from 263 in 2007 to 229 in 2009. This decrease in the number of Swiss listed companies between 2007 and 2009 may be a reflection of the global financial crisis that has occurred since 2008. According to Deloitte's Swiss Stock Exchange Analysis report (2009), the Swiss Performance Index (SPI) declined by a total of 45 percent between June 2007 and March 2009. This decline in the SPI index is relatively low compared to the Dow Jones Industrial Average (DJIA) index which dropped 53 percent during the same period. In addition, other key economic indicators show that the Swiss economy experienced only a 1.5 percent GDP decrease at the year end 2009, which is also low compared with other economies like the European (EU) economy (−4.1 percent), the Japanese economy (−5 percent) and the US economy (−2.4 percent) (Deloitte, 2010). The SPI declined due to the weight of the Swiss financial services industry. Yet, while the Swiss financial services industry suffered from the financial crisis, a healthy and export-oriented manufacturing sector at the same time benefited from robust demand in emerging markets even despite a strong Swiss franc (CHF).

Concerning corporate governance in Swiss listed companies, recent studies have shown that average board size is seven board members.

Table 19.1 *Share ownership in Swiss listed firms*

	One shareholder with over 50% of stake	At least one shareholder with stake between 25% and 50%	No shareholder with over 25% of stake
Belgium	59.46	21.62	18.92
Switzerland	47.37	17.54	35.09
France	41.10	32.19	26.71
Germany	41.11	27.78	31.11
Denmark	29.69	34.38	35.94
Netherlands	17.86	20.24	61.90
Norway	15.79	47.37	36.84
Sweden	11.11	37.78	51.11
United Kingdom	5.84	12.34	81.82

Source: OECD (2006)

The majority of directors in Swiss listed firms are outside directors (89 percent) while only a smaller proportion of them can be regarded as independent (58 percent) based on the Swiss definition of board independence. Furthermore, the presence of female directors in Swiss listed firms has been relatively low (average 0.37 directors) while the majority of listed firms (57 percent) have established the three recommended board committees (Hu, 2009; Keller, 2003; Ruigrok, Peck and Keller, 2006). In 2003 Switzerland had the second highest ownership concentration rate among nine Western European countries (Table 19.1). Specifically, 47 percent of Swiss listed firms had one blockholder possessing more than 50 percent of shares (OECD, 2006). This high ownership concentration undermines the attractiveness for foreign (institutional) investors to invest in Swiss companies. However, efforts have been made to increase transparency about ownership dispersion rates. Based on the 2007 corporate governance reform, Swiss listed firms must name the shareholders who hold more than 5 percent of shares in their annual reports (Economiesuisse, 2007).

IPO activity in Switzerland (2006–2008)

The IPO process in Switzerland

At the very beginning of the IPO process, the issuer should find a "recognized sponsor" (i.e., listing agent) that will act as representative

Table 19.2 *Listing requirements in Switzerland*

	Main standard	Domestic standard
Financial track record	At least 3 years track record	At least 2 years track record
Minimum capital	At least 26.5 million USD	At least 2.6 million USD
Free float	Minimum 25%	Minimum 20%
Market capitalization	At least 26.5 million USD	At least 5.3 million USD
Accounting Standards	IFRS/US GAAP	Swiss GAAP ARR/IFR/SUS GAAP

Source: SIX (2010)

of the IPO firm. Once the listing agent has been identified, the next step of the IPO is to fix the offering price which is determined by "book-building". During the book-building procedure the IPO firm offers a price at which investors can bid. At the same time, investment banks are getting information about the firm and trying to find potential institutional investors. This helps the underwriter to fix the final offer price and to create a list of potential investors (Ernst & Young, 2008; SIX Listing Rules, 2006). Once the final price has been determined, Swiss IPOs should publicly provide an offering prospectus that includes the following information: (1) the number of shares offered and the price for each share, (2) the amount of expected proceeds during the first year of listing, (3) information about the prior financial record of the firm, (4) major shareholders and their stakes prior to and after the offering and (5) detailed information regarding the composition of the board of directors and executive team. The IPO prospectus should be reviewed by the respective listing agent and receive a formal approval from the Swiss Exchange (SIX, 2010).

To receive the final listing admission, IPO firms need to fulfill specific standards depending on the segment in which they intend to be listed. As Table 19.2 shows, there are two alternative segments; the first (i.e., main standard) refers to firms that want to have access to foreign markets and satisfy the needs of foreign institutional investors, while the second segment (i.e., domestic standard) refers to firms that are only interested to attract domestic investors and/or do not yet fulfill the requirements of getting listed under the main standards. Firms going public under the main standards must have a minimum capital of 26.5 million USD and a free float (the number of freely tradable shares in circulation) of at least 25 percent. On the other hand, the minimum standards for the domestic track are substantially lower, with a minimum capital of 2.6 million USD and 20 percent minimum free float.[2] After the admission, firms have to follow the recommended corporate governance practices and to publicly report their performance at least twice a year.

IPO activity between 2006 and 2008

During the period 2006 to 2008, a total number of twenty-eight firms went public on the Swiss stock exchange (SIX). In line with EurIPO (2006), a Swiss IPO was defined as: (1) a firm that made a new issue of a common stock (not a new issue of a debt instrument), and (2) a firm that was not listed in any other stock exchange before its public offering at SIX. From the total number of twenty-eight newly listed firms indicated at the SIX website, the study excluded those that did not fulfill the above criteria. In addition, all firms that went public after spin-off activities were kept out of the sample since such firms cannot be regarded as "truly new" public offerings (Carpenter, Pollock and Leary, 2003). This resulted in a final sample of sixteen Swiss IPOs (Table 19.3) belonging to five different industrial sectors based on the ICB classification. The three industrial sectors with the highest number of IPOs between 2006 and 2008 were: financials (35 percent), industrials (29 percent) and technology (18 percent). The dominant listing agent was Credit Suisse (24 percent of IPOs) followed by Zurich Cantonal Bank and UBS (18 percent and 12 percent of IPOs respectively). These three agents handled 54 percent of IPOs between 2006 and 2008. The year 2007 was the "hottest IPO year" of the study period with eight IPOs, followed by 2006 with six IPOs and lastly 2008 with only two IPOs. The low number of IPOs in 2008 compared with the other years may be a reflection of the global financial crisis that started in 2008.

Fifteen out of sixteen IPOs went public under the main standards, while only one firm (Meyer Burger Technologies Ltd.) went public

---

[2] Amounts converted from CHF to USD as of 31/12/2010.

Table 19.3 IPO activity in Switzerland 2006–8

	IPO year	Open price[1]	Close price[1]	Price 1 year[1]	New shares	Duality	Board compensation (cash)[1]	Board committees	Foreign investors
Addex	2007	59.40	55.33	33.87	1,875,000	No	–	2	10
BFW	2007	25.05	26.51	23.39	1,351,810	No	166,785	0	2
Burckhardt Compression	2006	68.06	74.44	235.42	735,935	No	222,120	2	10
Burkhalter	2008	115.42	112.54	88.57	540,000	No	1,314,853	0	3
Goldbach Media	2007	33.74	45.79	41.09	2,163,170	No	–	2	6
Gottex	2007	65.06	65.06	67.75	8,355,029	Yes	–	3	12
Meyer Burger	2006	–	–	–	–	–	–	–	–
Newave Energy	2007	33.72	44.00	47.16	625,000	No	634,209	0	7
Orascom Development	2008	126.64	135.81	36.33	1,254,000	Yes	1,097,594	3	13
Partners Group	2006	48.15	64.20	115.89	801,000	Yes	1,414,570	3	28
Petroplus	2006	52.25	58.02	–	18,000,000	Yes	1,335,094	4	33
SAF	2006	21.10	21.47	38.01	1,278,150	Yes	–	1	13
Santhera	2006	72.35	72.87	104.50	983,859	No	487,432	3	7
U-Blox	2007	46.61	52.16	23.50	1,250,000	No	148,031	3	11
Uster Technologies	2007	44.28	44.79	14.97	2,000,000	No	–	3	7
VZ	2007	59.47	78.23	74.67	–	Yes	–	1	0

[1] Values are expressed in USD

under the domestic standards. This shows that most newly listed firms are interested in fulfilling the SIX standards for attracting not only domestic but also foreign investors. Additionally, seven out of fifteen Swiss IPO firms with available data (47 percent) had established the three recommended committees, while five companies (33 percent) had one or two board committees. Only three (20 percent) IPO firms had no established board committees at all (Table 19.3). This shows that newly listed companies generally tend to follow the recommendations of the Swiss Code with regard to the establishment of board committees. Furthermore, 40 percent of Swiss IPOs adopted a dual leadership structure and, with just one exception, all Swiss IPOs managed to attract foreign investors.[3]

The majority of IPO firms experienced a reduction in their share price one year after their initial public offering (Table 19.3). Specifically, eight out of fourteen companies (57 percent) with available share price information had a decrease in their share price after one year of trading. However, IPO share prices did not perform significantly worse (or better) than the Swiss Market Index, which, like other stock exchanges, experienced the effects of the global financial crisis which started in 2008. IPO firms with the highest reduction in their share price are Orascom Development, Addex Pharmaceuticals and Uster Technologies. On the other hand, six out of fourteen firms experienced an increase in their share prices after the IPO event. Of particular interest are the cases of Burckhardt Compression, Santhera Pharmaceuticals and Partners Group, firms that managed to double their share price within the first year of listing (Table 19.3). All these three firms went public in 2006, a year that was financially favorable for new listings in Switzerland (SIX, 2010).

Moreover, IPO firms had on average 1,089 employees, 686 million USD revenues and 390 million USD total assets at the time of their initial public offering (Table 19.4). The smallest firm in the Swiss IPO sample in terms of number of employees and total assets is SAF, while the largest one is Petroplus, an oil and gas company, with 7.8 billion USD revenues and 3.5 billion USD total assets. Petroplus has assets and revenues that are far higher even than the second largest Swiss IPO in this period, and raises the IPO averages illustrated in

[3] Data about investing firms were collected from the Thomson one banker-ownership database.

Table 19.4 *Firm characteristics and performance of Swiss IPOs*

Firm characteristics				Prior IPO performance	
	Assets*	Revenues*	Employees	ROA	ROE
Min	8,614,282	3,893,219	47	−0.54	−0.71
1st quartile	58,600,000	12,600,070	70	0.02	0.08
2nd quartile	101,000,000	98,800,070	156	0.17	0.33
3rd quartile	236,000,000	106,400,008	638	0.32	0.50
Max	3,464,800,000	7,819,700,000	9,500	0.52	1.50
Average	390,000,000	686,000,008	1,089	0.13	0.25
N	15	15	14	15	14

* Numbers are expressed in USD

Table 19.4. In addition, firm performance one year prior to the offering for all IPOs was relatively high with an average ROA of 0.13 and an average ROE of 0.25. Only three IPOs in the sample show negative profitability prior to the offering, with lowest ROA being −0.54 and lowest ROE being −0.71.

As noted earlier, another feature of the Swiss governance system is the high concentration of ownership in the hands of blockholders. Recent corporate governance reforms have attempted to reduce ownership concentration and to encourage more dispersed ownership structures based on the Anglo-Saxon standards. An interesting point in the Swiss IPO sample is that ownership concentration of the Top-1 shareholder is significantly reduced from the year prior to the offering to the year after the offering. More specifically, in eleven IPOs the Top-1 shareholder owned less than 25 percent of the firm's share capital (Table 19.5). On the other hand, however, in 62 percent of all IPOs with available ownership information, the Top-3 shareholders owned between 25 percent and 50 percent of total shares after the first day of trading. Although this shows a slight improvement compared with ownership concentration in Table 19.1, further efforts to reduce the ownership concentration in Switzerland are required in order to reach the Anglo-Saxon standards. Additionally, venture capital firms and entrepreneurial families own less than 25 percent of shares after the IPO.

Table 19.5 *Ownership in Swiss IPOs 2006–8 (data in percent)*

	Top 1		Top 3		Venture capital		Family	
	pre	post	pre	post	pre	post	pre	post
Less than 25% ownership	27	60	0	15	78	100	55	73
25% to 50% ownership	33	20	15	62	11	0	27	9
51% to 75% ownership	20	20	46	15	11	0	9	18
Over 75% ownership	20	0	39	8	0	0	9	0
N	15	15	13	13	9	9	11	11

Table 19.6 *Board characteristics of Swiss IPOs*

	Non-executive directors	Female directors	Board average age	Board size	Highest degree PhD	Highest degree MBA	Highest degree Masters	Highest degree Bachelor
Min	20%	0%	45	4	0%	0%	5%	15%
Max	100%	20%	60	10	60%	50%	67%	62%
Average	63%	5%	52	7	27%	13%	26%	26%
N	15	15	15	15	15	15	15	15

Board composition in Swiss IPOs

As shown in Table 19.6, boards of directors in Swiss IPOs have on average seven members; the smallest board consists of four members while the largest one consists of ten members. The majority of directors are non-executives (63 percent) with a minimum proportion of 20 percent and a maximum of 100 percent (companies with boards consisting of only non-executive directors have adopted two-tier board structures[4]). Furthermore, in line with Swiss corporate governance patterns, female directors are relatively few (average female participation is 5 percent), while the average age of board members is fifty-two years. Another interesting characteristic of Swiss IPO

---

[4] A two-tier board of directors in the Swiss context is more comparable to a board of directors in the Anglo-American context than a supervisory board in the German context. In Switzerland the term "supervisory board" is not typically used but rather considered as a German institution. The executive board is considered as the top management team.

boards is the educational qualification level of directors. As Table 19.6 shows, the average proportion of directors with a PhD degree is high (27 percent), while many others hold at least an MBA or Master of Science (MSc) degree (13 percent and 26 percent respectively). The educational level of directors has been characterized as a signal of a firm's reputation (Certo, 2003) and, faced with uncertainty, Swiss IPOs appear to communicate the competence level of the people involved in the company to potential investors.

Demographic diversity in Swiss IPO boards and TMTs

Researchers have argued that diversity in the boardroom brings more information processing abilities (Richard and Shelor, 2002) and higher quality of executive monitoring (Hillman and Dalziel, 2003). Investors may consider board and top management team (TMT) diversity as a positive signal for IPOs' likelihood of success (Certo, 2003). Nationality and educational level diversity was measured using Blau's (1977) index, calculated as $1 - \Sigma pi^2$, where p represents the proportion of board members in the ith nationality/educational category (Elron, 1997; Harrison and Klein, 2007; Tihanyi, Ellstrand, Daily et al., 2000). Since age is an interval variable, age diversity was calculated by dividing the standard deviation by the mean of age for each board and TMT (Tihanyi, Ellstrand, Daily et al., 2000; Zimmerman, 2008). High scores indicate high age, educational level and nationality diversity.

As mentioned earlier, the Swiss Code recommends that boards of directors and management teams of Swiss companies listed under the main standards should consist of members who have extended international experience and/or who are foreign nationals. As Table 19.7 illustrates, the average nationality diversity in Swiss IPOs is relatively high with a mean score of 0.41 diversity index. This indicates that newly listed firms tend to follow this recommendation. Moreover, educational level diversity of IPO boards is also high with an average diversity index of 0.59, while age diversity is lower. Similar to boards, TMT nationality and educational diversity of Swiss IPOs is relatively high (0.31 and 0.55 respectively) while age TMT diversity remains lower. In general, TMTs of Swiss IPOs tend to be less diverse in the three demographic attributes than boards of directors.

Table 19.7 *Board and top management team diversity in Swiss IPOs*

	Board nationality diversity	Board age diversity	Board educational diversity	TMT nationality diversity	TMT age diversity	TMT educational diversity
Min	0	0.20	0.38	0	0.03	0.32
1st percentile	0	0.12	0.53	0	0.08	0.38
2nd percentile	0.50	0.14	0.61	0.28	0.11	0.55
3rd percentile	0.76	0.16	0.66	0.56	0.17	0.65
Max	0.82	0.24	0.80	0.78	0.19	0.85
Average	0.41	0.14	0.59	0.31	0.12	0.55
N	15	14	15	10	14	15

Description of a Swiss IPO: Burkhalter Group

The firm before the IPO

Burkhalter Group, formerly Ernst-Burkhalter AG, is an electrical installation company founded in 1959 in Zurich. The company provides electrical installation services to residential, industrial and commercial buildings. The initially small and locally active electrical installation business grew in the next three decades as an active group of companies across the four language regions of Switzerland. In 1987, the company was sold to Zellweger Luwa AG, an electrical equipment company, while in 1997 Burkhalter Holding AG became independent again. Until the year end 2000, almost 40 percent of the company's capital was owned by employees and initial owners, while one year later the company's capital and the number of owners increased. In the year before the IPO (year end 2007) the company generated 363 million USD revenues, had 252 million USD assets and 2,520 full-time employees, and operated in eighty-four locations throughout Switzerland. Three major shareholders were holding 43 percent of the total capital. The company's share capital before the offering was 573,942 shares, and three major shareholders were holding 43 percent of this capital. Six months prior to the offering, Burkhalter's former CEO Tarzisius Caviezel resigned and was replaced by Marco Syfrig who became the new CEO and a member of the board of directors. At the end of IPO year Marco Syfrig received an annual cash remuneration of 403,550 USD. In addition, two board members stepped down during the same year, resulting in a total board size of five directors. At the year end 2007, the directors owned 36 percent of the firm's capital and received 1.31 million USD total annual compensation.

The offer

Burkhalter Group went public in June 2008 under the main SIX standards. Zurich Cantonal Bank was the responsible agent of Burkhalter Group's IPO. During the offer, the company doubled its share capital from 9,463,287 to 18,366,807 USD through the issue of 540,000 registered shares with a nominal value of 16 USD and an opening price of 115 USD for each offered share. The total number of shares after the offering was 1,113,942, while 42,073 of them were held by the company and its subsidiaries. The majority of shares were allocated to domestic institutional investors, while the board possessed 247,151 shares. Concerning ownership concentration, the Top-1 shareholder had 10 percent and the Top-3 shareholders had 21.5 percent of the share capital. Burkhalter's initial public offering was not supported by any venture capital firm or business angel. The first opening price slightly dropped at the first day of trading (115 USD and 112 USD first opening and first closing price respectively). At the time of the offering, the firm was expecting to compensate its investors with a total amount of 60,000,000 IPO proceeds USD.

The firm after the offering

One year after the offering, Burkhalter's share price dropped from 112 (first closing price) to 89 USD. An important factor of the drop in Burkhalter's share price is the total drop of the SIX market index due to the financial crisis in 2008. However, two years after the IPO (June 2010), Burkhalter's share price increased to 136 USD, a price that is even higher than its first opening price. During the first year of listing the board consisted of five members where two of them were non-executives (mixed board structure) and one was an independent director. In addition, the top management team consisted of three members holding the positions of CEO, COO and CFO.

Despite the Swiss Code recommendations for establishing board committees, the firm had no established board committees in 2008. For the adequate internal control of the company the board used some monitoring tools such as: (1) monthly reporting of management performance, (2) quarterly statements, and (3) approval of annual budget and group's strategy twice a year. In addition, the proportion of share ownership of the Top-3 shareholders increased from 21.5 percent at the time of the offering to 30.8 percent one year after and reached the proportion of 30.1 percent at the year end 2009. This shows that although Burkhalter Group had a lower rate of ownership concentration than the average in Swiss IPOs at the time of its initial listing, it reached the average ownership concentration within the first year after the offering.

Finally, all members of both board and executive management were Swiss nationals, a feature that fits well with the firm's domestic strategy. However, the company became listed under the main standards with the intention to attract foreign institutional investors. The number of foreign investors during the first quarter after the offering was particularly low compared with other firms in the Swiss IPO sample (only three investors). This small number of foreign investors can be a reflection of Burkhalter's high degree of TMT and board nationality homogeneity. In 2008 Burkhalter Group acquired Electra Buin SA and two other smaller companies in Switzerland. Burkhalter Group aims to further expand its operations through M&A activities within the country. As Burkhalter's CEO, Marco Syfrig, claimed: "By continuing our acquisition strategy and constantly strengthening our risk management procedures we will be able to more than compensate for any organic sales decline at Group level" (Burkhalter Group, 2008).

Conclusion

The aim of this study was to describe the current state of corporate governance in Switzerland and to consider whether newly listed firms tend to comply with the recent corporate governance reforms. Descriptive statistics of all Swiss IPOs between 2006 and 2008 show that a high proportion of firm shares in most IPOs are owned by three major shareholders immediately after the initial public offering. Despite recent efforts to encourage more dispersed ownership, the ownership structure of IPO firms still remains concentrated. This is clear in the described IPO sample where, in most cases, the top three shareholders possessed a high percentage of the total shares (above 25 percent). On the other hand, Swiss IPOs have tended to follow the recommendations of the Swiss Code concerning the composition of the board of directors and the establishment of board committees. More specifically, most Swiss IPO boards consist of a majority of non-executive directors, have on average seven members, the majority of whom are highly educated, and have established the three recommended board committees. However, there are some other governance features that need to be considered, such as the low representation of female directors and the dualistic leadership structure that some IPOs tend to adopt.

The paradoxes identified at the beginning of this chapter will probably live on in the near future. First, high share ownership concentration in Switzerland may have served as a reason for the comparatively low number of Swiss IPOs: Swiss entrepreneurial ventures have other means to attract investors than via IPOs only. Indeed, Swiss IPOs do not appear to significantly contribute to a reduction of ownership concentration ratios. Second, although nationality diversity levels in Swiss IPO TMTs and boards are exceptionally high, the presence of foreign investors seems modest. It is possible that foreign IPO TMT or board members have studied or lived in Switzerland for some time, and do not act as a force of change in the Swiss corporate governance system. In short, there are tendencies of the Swiss corporate governance system to converge to more Anglo-American or global standards. However, findings presented in this chapter suggest that Swiss IPOs, as nascent corporate governance arrangements, do not serve as a force of such convergence. The convergence process may take longer than some think.

References

Blau, Peter M. 1977. *Inequality and Heterogeneity*, Glencoe, IL: Free Press.

Burkhalter Group. 2008. *Annual Report*. Available from: www.burkhalter. ch/upload/public/0/24/BURKH39863E_Portraet_GzD_def.pdf. Accessed on: 20/12/2010.

Carpenter, Mason, Pollock, Timothy and Leary, Myleen. 2003. 'Testing a model of reasoned risk taking: Governance, the experience of principal and agents, and global strategy in high-technology IPO firms', *Strategic Management Journal*, 24, 9, 802–20.

Certo, Trevis S. 2003. 'Influencing initial public offering investors with prestige: Signaling with board structures', *Academy of Management Review*, 28, 3, 432–47.

Code of Obligations. Available from: www.admin.ch/ch/d/sr/2/220.de.pdf. Accessed on: 26/12/2010.

Deloitte. 2009. *Swiss Stock Exchange Analysis*. Available from: www. deloitte.com/view/en_CH/ch/services/corporatefinance/bb08fd8cbd4f2 210VgnVCM200000bb42f00aRCRD.htm. Accessed on: 26/12/2010.

2010. *Swiss Stock Exchange Analysis*. Available from: www.economiesuisse. ch/de/PDF%20Download%20Files/pospap_swiss-code_corp-govern_ 20080221_de.pdf. Accessed on: 26/12/2010.

Economiesuisse. 2007. *Swiss Code of Best Practice for Corporate Govern-ance*. Available from: www.economiesuisse.ch/web/de/pdf%20Download %20files/pospap_swiss-code_corp-govern_20080221_en.pdf. Accessed on: 26/12/2010.

Elron, Efrat. 1997. 'Top management teams within multinational corpor-ations: Effects of cultural heterogeneity', *Leadership Quarterly*, 8, 4, 393–412.

Ernst & Young, 2008. *IPO insights: SWX Swiss exchange*. Available from: www2.eycom.ch/publications/items/2008_ipo_insights/2008_ey_ipo_ insights_swx.pdf. Accessed on: 20/12/2010.

EurIPO. 2006. *Academic EurIPO Factbook*, Bergamo-Italy: Universoft.

Harrison, David A. and Klein, Katherine J. 2007. 'What's the difference? Diversity constructs as separation, variety or disparity in organiza-tions', *Academy of Management Review*, 32, 4, 1199–228.

Hillman, Amy J. and Dalziel, Thomas. 2003. 'Boards of directors and firm performance: Integrating agency and resource dependence perspec-tives', *Academy of Management Review*, 28, 3, 383–96.

Hu, Yan. 2009. *The adoption of board committees in Swiss listed firms*. PhD thesis, Research Institute for International Management, St. Gallen, Switzerland.

International Monetary Fund (IMF). 2007. *Switzerland financial sector assessment program*. Available from: www.imf.org/external/pubs/ft/ scr/2007/cr07202.pdf. Accessed on: 20/12/2010.

Keller, Hans Ulrich. 2003. *The determinants and effects of interlocking directorships and board composition: An empirical analysis of corpor-ate governance in Switzerland*. PhD thesis, Research Institute for Inter-national Management, St. Gallen, Switzerland.

Mach, Andre G., Schnyder, Gerhard, Lupold, Martin and David, Thomas. 2007. 'Transformation of self regulation and new public regulations in the field of Swiss corporate governance (1985–2002)', *World Political Science Review*, 3, 2, 1–30.

OECD. 2006. *Corporate governance of non-listed companies in emerging markets*. Available from: www.oecd.org/dataoecd/48/11/37190767.pdf. Accessed on: 20/12/2010.

Orlando, Richard and Shelor, Roger M. 2002. 'Linking top management team age heterogeneity to firm performance: Juxtaposing two mid-range theories', *International Journal of Human Resource Management*, 13, 6, 11–23.

Pedrazzini, Mario. 1998. *Gesellschaftsrechtliche Entscheide, eine Sammlung für das Studium*, Bern: Stampfli Verlag.

Ruigrok, Winfried and Canepa, Ancillo. 2005. *The Impact of Audit Committees on Swiss Companies*, Ernst & Young/University of St. Gallen. Available from: www.fim.unisg.ch/org/fim/web.nsf/SysWebRessources/The+Audit+Committee+Impact+on+Swiss+Companies/$FILE/ The+Audit+Committee+Impact+on+Swiss+Companies.pdf. Accessed on: 26/12/2010.

Ruigrok, Winfried, Peck, Simon and Keller, Hans Ulrich. 2006. 'Board characteristics and involvement in strategic decision making: Evidence from Swiss companies', *Journal of Management Studies*, 45, 5, 1201–26.

Ruigrok, Winfried, Peck, Simon and Tacheva, Sabina. 2007. 'Nationality and gender diversity on Swiss corporate boards', *Corporate Governance: An International Review*, 15, 4, 546–57.

Schleiffer, Patrick and von Planta, Andreas. 2009. 'Switzerland' in *The International Comparative Legal Guide to Corporate Governance 2009*, London: Global Legal Group. Available from: www.iclg.co.uk/ khadmin/Publications/pdf/2958.pdf. Accessed on: 20/12/2010.

Schweizer, Markus. 2006. *Recent Corporate Governance Reforms in Switzerland*, Switzerland: Economiesuisse. Available from: www.eycom.ch/ library/items/200603_cogo/en.pdf. Accessed on: 26/12/2010.

SIX. 2010. Available from: www.six-swiss-exchange.com/index.html. Accessed on: 20/12/2010.

SIX Listing Rules. 2006. Available from: www.six-swissexchange.com/ news/new_admissions_en.html. Accessed on: 20/12/2010.

Tihanyi, Lazlo, Ellstrand, Alan E., Daily, Catherine M. and Dalton, Dan R. 2000. 'Composition of the top management team and firm international diversification', *Journal of Management*, 26, 6, 1157–77.

US Commercial Service. 2009. *Doing Business in Switzerland 2009*. Available from: www.buyusainfo.net/docs/x_5002686.pdf. Accessed on: 20/12/2010.

World Bank. 2010. *Doing Business in Switzerland 2011*. Available from: www. fim.unisg.ch/org/fim/web.nsf/SysWebRessources/The+Audit+Committee+ Impact+on+Swiss+Companies/$FILE/The+Audit+Committee+Impact+ on+Swiss+Companies.pdf. Accessed on: 20/12/2010.

World Economic Forum. 2010. *The Global Competitiveness Report*. Available from: www3.weforum.org/docs/WEF_GlobalCompetitivenessReport_2010-11.pdf. Accessed on: 24/12/2010.

Zimmerman, Monica A. 2008. 'The influence of top management team heterogeneity on the capital raised through an initial public offering', *Entrepreneurship Theory and Practice*, 32, 3, 391–414.

20 | Corporate governance and initial public offerings in Turkey

SIBEL YAMAK AND BENGI ERTUNA*

Corporate governance mechanisms

Turkey has a collectivistic culture and in spite of the presence of different social groups or minorities it is relatively socially cohesive. It is a civil law country and its legal system contributes to the central role of the state in the Turkish business system. The market for corporate control is inactive. Family business groups are the dominant actors in corporate control. Firms are expected to comply with corporate governance codes. Where they do not comply, they are required to explain the reasons for non-compliance. Information disclosure is rather opaque.

Corporate ownership is often very concentrated where one or two families hold more than 50 percent of the firm's shares. Therefore, they usually dominate the board. Institutional owners are not among the major ownership groups. The protection of the minority ownership rights is limited but improving. Corporate boards are single tier and CEO duality is observed in only a very limited number of companies on the Istanbul Stock Exchange. Corporate boards are composed of mostly insider directors. Executive compensation is non-egalitarian.

Company law

The current Turkish Commercial Code (TCC), which has been in use since 1957, is the main source of Turkish company law (Nilsson, 2007). The company law provisions on joint stock companies and on limited liability companies are basically adapted from Swiss company law (Nilsson, 2007). La Porta, Lopez-de-Silanes and Shleifer (2008) maintain that culture and ideologies become integrated in legal

* The authors are grateful to Galatasaray University Research Fund for the support provided to this study.

and political infrastructure by affecting the choice of the method of social control. In Turkey's case, this choice consisted of adopting French civil law in the nineteenth century, as a part of the modernization efforts of the Ottoman Empire (La Porta et al., 2008). So, Turkey is among the countries with French civil law origin which leads to weaker shareholder rights (La Porta, Lopez-de-Silanes, Shleifer et al., 1998).

Legislation such as the Turkish Commercial Code, the Capital Market Law and the regulations by the Capital Markets Board (CMB) of Turkey, as well as specific sets of laws for the banking and telecommunications sectors, frame corporate governance in Turkey (Atakan, Özsoy and Oba, 2008). The Capital Market Law (CML) of 1981 authorizes the CMB to regulate the capital markets, to control compliance with the legislation, to take necessary measures to prevent breaches and finally to apply sanctions in case breach occurs (Nilsson, 2007).

The ongoing process of adaptation to the EU law as a result of Turkey's EU candidacy introduces substantial revisions into the codes including the Turkish Commercial Code (Altay and Amasya, 2007). In fact, the Turkish Corporate Code has been revised, and the draft which was submitted to the Parliament in 2005 (Nilsson, 2007) has recently been approved as of January 13, 2011 by the Parliament. However, it will become effective on July 1, 2012, while some of its parts are planned to be implemented in 2013. The new code includes, among other things, issues such as the definition of qualifications for becoming a board member, minority rights protection, establishment of proxy voting and electronic voting principles, permission for on-line general meetings via websites, specification of the minimum informational content required in annual reports and company websites and the prerequisite regarding the auditors to be independent audit firms or certified public accountants (Atakan et al., 2008). Another novelty introduced by the new code is the possibility of forming a corporation with a sole shareholder and eventually a board with a sole director. The new code also introduces a comprehensive system for groups of companies and suggests a special liability regime for parent companies (Altay and Amasya, 2007).

According to the current Turkish code, the board of directors is composed of at least three members who are elected by simple majority at the shareholders' meeting (Kort, 2008). In companies with a controlling block of shareholders, the simple majority rule may lead to the fact that all the members of the board can be elected by the majority shareholder (Nilsson, 2007). The current TCC and the CML do not impose any independence requirements. Most of the directors in Turkish firms have some kind of relationship with the company, either directly or as shareholders (IIF EAG, 2005). However, the new code requires independent directors.

It also eliminates the restriction that board members should be shareholders. There is no provision for employee representation at the board (Nilsson, 2007). The current TCC does not require any expertise or particular education for becoming a board member (Kort, 2008). However, the new code requires that at least half of the directors or the sole director (in the case of one-man company boards) should be a university graduate. There is also a requisite of expertise and education for banks' directors and executives in the banking law (Banking Law No. 5411, Arts. 23–25) and also in CMB's recent amendments (Atakan et al., 2008).

According to the current TCC, all shares principally bear equal voting rights. However, special voting rights or other privileges are granted to certain classes of shares (Yurtoğlu, 2000). The current TCC has no restrictions on the granting of special class rights. Nilsson (2007) claims that the right to nominate directors to the board appears to be one of the most frequently used special class rights. The extensive exercise of multiple voting rights for founders and privileged shares is one of the major devices for securing and maintaining family control (IIF EAG, 2005). In 2004, about 42 percent of the companies quoted on the Istanbul Stock Exchange had provisions in their articles of association that enabled the use of class rights to nominate board members (Nilsson, 2007). Orbay and Yurtoğlu (2006) also report that 43 percent of the companies exhibit deviations from the one-share-one-vote rule by using pyramidal ownership structures and dual-class shares.

The current TCC defines shareholders holding a minimum of 10 percent of the shares as minority shareholders (Nilsson, 2007). This has been reduced to 5 percent for publicly held companies by the Securities Law (Art. 11/8 CML). The current TCC grants the following rights to such "minority" groups: the right to ask statutory auditors to investigate allegations, the right to have special auditors appointed, the right to call a shareholders' meeting or to insert items on the agenda, the right to veto the release of directors' liabilities due to their transactions during the incorporation of the company and the right to ask the company to sue the directors for their liability (Anlam and Amasya, 2007). However, only shareholders holding a minimum of 10 percent of the shares (the minority) are entitled to propose items to be included in the agenda (Nilsson, 2007). The presence of a controlling family in the majority of the companies (Yurtoğlu, 2000) makes many measures of minority shareholders' protection ineffective (IIF EAG, 2005). Concerning the measures on how strongly the legal system supports minority shareholders against dominant shareholders, a score of 2.0 is reported for Turkey, which is lower than the French origin civil-law average of 2.33 (La Porta et al., 1998). The new code includes new articles to improve the protection of minority shareholders, but the earliest implementation is scheduled for the second half of 2012.

In 2002, the CMB made it obligatory for listed companies to have an audit committee composed mainly of non-executive directors. According to capital market legislation, listed companies must also have an internal control system (Nilsson, 2007).

Briefly, boards in Turkish companies appear to act as a rubber stamp for the controlling shareholders' decisions (Kort, 2008). The Turkish corporate governance system can typically be categorized as insider-controlled (Yurtoğlu, 2003).

Code of good governance

The Corporate Governance Principles (CGP) have become the cornerstone of the corporate governance framework (OECD, 2006), as the existing laws and regulations do not adequately address corporate governance issues. The Capital Markets Board (CMB), the regulatory authority of capital markets in Turkey, published the CGP initially in 2003. These principles, which are mainly based on the OECD Corporate Governance Principles, were reviewed and finalized in 2005, following the revision of the OECD Principles in 2004. Improving the corporate governance environment and integrating the Turkish capital markets with global financial markets are denoted by CMB as the major aims in the preparation of the principles. The CGP have also been operational in the partial fulfillment of one of the conditions of the stabilization package, relating to the stand-by credit from the IMF

in 2001, which imposed that Turkey should introduce "good governance" to both private and public sectors (Ertürk, 2003). Consequently,
international investors and access to international funds appear as the
sole motivator behind the development of the CGP.

Similar to corporate governance codes of most of the countries, the
Turkish principles apply only to listed companies. In the implementation of the principles, the CMB has adopted the "comply or
explain" approach and required listed companies either to comply
with these principles or to disclose their compliance status together
with their reasons for non-compliance in a report. This compliance
report is an integral component of their annual reports which are
required to be disclosed according to the existing law. Although the
CGP are voluntary in nature, some of its principles are mandatory
since they are requirements of the Capital Market Law and/or the
communiqués of the CMB (OECD, 2006). Furthermore, an important number of provisions of the CGP are also included in the new
Commercial Code and will become mandatory when it becomes
effective. Thus, the CGP represent a blend of voluntary and mandatory provisions, without mentioning which ones are required by the
existing laws and communiqués. This characteristic is cited among
the factors inhibiting the effectiveness of the CGP as a guidance tool
in the corporate governance assessment report of Turkey by the
OECD (2006).

According to the OECD, another factor limiting the effectiveness
of the CGP relates to its content. The OECD (2006: 16) states the
CGP "consolidate some but not all of the relevant corporate governance standards", but admits that they provide a detailed framework for companies in improving their practices. The guidance that
CGP provide is basically in line with the internationally accepted
good governance principles. As a consequence, the principles do not
specifically address the most relevant governance issues of the
Turkish context. Kort (2008) states that the Turkish principles stress
mainly the role of international investors and capital markets as he
compares the CGP with the German Code. The CGP emphasize the
importance of equal treatment of shareholders and concentrate
mainly on shareholder rights. The principles also mention the equal
treatment of all stakeholders, but with much less emphasis as compared to shareholders. This emphasis is consistent with the source
and the aims of the CGP.

The main principles of the CGP are presented in four sections, namely: shareholders; public disclosure and transparency; stakeholders; and board of directors. Although the CGP provide an extensive framework for corporate governance practices, companies seem to have difficulty in implementing the principles. According to the OECD (2006), detailed guidance on implementation by related authorities is not sufficient. The entire corporate governance process is a relatively recent concept for Turkish companies and they are making efforts to understand and interpret its implications. The OECD's (2006: 17) assessment states that "it can be challenging even for motivated companies to determine how to implement some of the standards".

The CMB conducts and publishes annual surveys on ISE listed companies' implementation of the CGP. These reports do not describe the recommended practices or common misconceptions in detail (OECD, 2006), thus failing to provide sufficient guidance to companies on how to implement the principles. Furthermore, not all the CMB annual survey results are published publicly. The most recent report dates back to 2007. The results of this report indicate better implementation in the ISE30 companies as compared to all listed companies (CMB, 2007).

In order to encourage companies to adopt the CGP, the ISE has developed a corporate governance index that includes listed companies which have a corporate governance rating score of six out of ten. The index became operational in 2007, when the number of companies with a rating score exceeded five (Atakan et al., 2008). The index includes twenty-nine companies as of December 2010.

A qualitative assessment study on the CG practices reports that the ISE50 companies have mostly implemented the easy-to-do changes, but the principles addressing the relevant conflicts of interests remain largely untouched (Ertuna and Tükel, 2007). Additionally, studies on transparency and the disclosure practices of companies report that the scores of companies are low as compared to developed countries (Aksu and Kösedağ, 2006) and that the level of voluntary disclosure is very low (Ağca and Önder, 2007). Oba, Ozsoy and Atakan (2010) attribute the reluctance of companies in implementing the CGP to the Turkish management culture. The Turkish context is characterized by high power distance, low individualism and high uncertainty avoidance (Hofstede, 1980; Kabasakal and Bodur, 2007). Oba et al. (2010) attribute, for example, the incidence of hierarchical systems such as stock pyramids to the high power distance score in Turkey. They also relate low individualism (thus, high collectivism) to the principal–steward relationship in the Turkish boards. Finally, they claim that a high score on the uncertainty avoidance index is associated with the opaque disclosure through which conflict and competition is avoided.

Stock exchange and listed companies in Turkey

Consistent with the predictions of the Legal Origins theory (La Porta et al., 2008), the economy is mostly guided by state-desired allocations rather than market-based outcomes. The economy is bank-based (Ertürk, 2003); thus the role of the capital market in the national economy is limited. Free market discourse and the market mechanism were introduced to the economy with the macroeconomic stabilization and financial liberalization program of January 1980 and it was in the 1990s that the market mechanism gained in importance (Keyman and Koyuncu, 2005). The Istanbul Stock Exchange (ISE) was established in 1986 within the framework of the Capital Market Law, which was enacted in 1981 as a part of the financial liberalization program. At its establishment, there were only forty-two companies listed in the ISE. In its first year of operations, the annual volume of trade was 13 million USD and total market capitalization of companies was 938 million USD as of the end of 1986 (Ertuna, Ercan and Akgiray, 2003). Similar to other emerging markets, the development of the ISE exhibited a rapid but volatile growth both in terms of number of companies, total market capitalization, trading volume and the returns on the market index. Table 20.1 displays the developments in these indicators for the period 1990–2009. As of 2009, total market capitalization of the stock market corresponds to 27 percent of GNP (DPT, 2009), while total bank assets to GNP is 87 percent (BDDK, 2010). In spite of its fluctuating and rapid growth, the role of the stock market remains relatively modest in the national economy.

The number of listed companies is relatively limited. Even large companies are reluctant to issue their shares to the public. Only 90 companies, out of the largest 500 industrial companies, are listed in the ISE in 2009 (ISO, 2010). There are several reasons for not going public. Both the current legislative and regulatory environment and the control characteristics of the companies may explain this

Table 20.1 *Market indicators of the ISE*

Year	Listed co. number	Market cap.	Trading vol.	Index	Number of IPOs	IPO proceeds
		Mil USD	Mil USD	ISE-100		Mil USD
1990	110	19,065	5,870	33	34	1,308.5
1991	134	15,508	8,277	44	21	343.9
1992	145	9,756	8,346	40	13	93.1
1993	160	36,613	21,126	206	16	152.4
1994	176	21,605	21,667	273	25	270.5
1995	205	20,772	50,889	400	28	24.5
1996	228	30,312	36,233	976	27	167.9
1997	259	61,095	56,088	3,451	29	418.4
1998	278	33,646	68,485	2,575	20	263.0
1999	286	112,716	81,099	15,208	10	11.0
2000	316	69,659	178,998	9,437	35	2,805.7
2001	311	47,150	74,530	13,783	1	0.2
2002	289	34,217	69,937	10,370	4	37.7
2003	285	68,379	98,160	18,625	2	11.2
2004	297	98,299	146,605	24,972	12	457.5
2005	304	161,538	200,858	39,778	9	1,532.7
2006	316	162,399	222,724	39,117	16	919.4
2007	319	286,572	294,295	55,538	9	2,897.7
2008	317	118,329	247,893	26,864	2	1,876.9
2009	315	233,997	301,127	52,825	1	6.8

Sources: World Federation of Exchanges members, CMB and ISE

reluctance. In the current legislative environment, controlling owners do not want to lose their control over the company. Furthermore, costs of compliance with transparency and corporate governance requirements also seem to restrain companies from going public.

Since the inception of the ISE in 1986, both the number of companies going public and the amount of IPO proceeds have exhibited an irregular pattern (see Table 20.1). There has been an upsurge of IPOs in certain years, such as the years 1990 and 2000, together with years in which there was very little IPO activity (Ertuna et al., 2003). In the years following the financial crisis of 2001, only a few companies offered their shares to the public. In spite of this fact, the proceeds have been relatively high in certain years, such as 2005, 2006 and

2008. These years include the IPOs of privatization of two large state banks and Turkish Telekom, the leading telecommunications company in Turkey. Following the stagnant years of the IPO market, the ISE and the CMB signed a protocol with the Union of Chambers of Commerce in 2008 in order to encourage companies to offer their shares to the public. As a result, the IPO market has started to revitalize in 2010, with nineteen companies going public and generating a total proceeds of 1,218 billion USD from IPOs.

The ownership structure of Turkish listed companies

The ownership structure of Turkish listed companies is rather concentrated (Demirağ and Serter, 2003; Mandacı and Gümüs, 2010; Orbay and Yurtoğlu, 2006). Large blockholders dominate the ownership structures of firms as in the case of most countries outside of the US (Claessens, Djankov and Lang, 2000; La Porta, Lopez-de-Silanes and Shleifer, 1999). In the ISE, families own more than 75 percent of all companies and they also retain majority control (Yurtoğlu, 2000). This leads to agency problems, not in the form of managers expropriating shareholders, but of controlling families expropriating the minority shareholders. Three major ways are used to retain control in the ISE: companies may issue shares with different voting rights, organize the ownership structure in a pyramid or use cross-shareholdings (Yurtoğlu, 2000).

In our setting, families retain control over companies not only with a majority of voting rights, but also with a majority of cash flow rights. The wedge between the cash flow and control rights is relatively low (Demirağ and Serter, 2003; Gugler, Mueller and Yurtoğlu, 2008; Orbay and Yurtoğlu, 2006). Examining the hundred largest ISE companies in 1999, Demirağ and Serter (2003) report that sixty-eight companies are controlled by families, with average voting rights of 65.75 percent, obtained with average ultimate ownership (or cash flow rights) of 52 percent. By dividing voting rights by ultimate ownership, they calculate an average control leverage ratio, similar to the "wedge" in La Porta, Lopez-de-Silanes, Shleifer et al. (2002), of 1.26 for family-controlled companies, and conclude that cash flow and control rights in Turkey are more aligned as compared to other family-dominated insider systems such as Italy and various East Asian countries (Demirağ and Serter, 2003).

Table 20.2 *Ownership concentration of Turkish listed companies*

	Controlled with more than 50% of shares	Largest shareholder	Other shareholders (shareholders other than largest owner and market)	Market (dispersed shares)
	No. of firms	%	%	%
1999	116	43.76	22.53	33.71
2009	139	46.22	14.64	39.14

Source: Yamak and Ertuna, 2010

Table 20.2 displays the change of the ownership structure in the last decade. The first shareholder appears to control on average 43.76 and 46.22 percent of cash flow rights in 1999 and 2009, respectively. The relative increase in the shares of the first shareholder during the last decade is worth noting. At the same time, free float, indicating the shareholdings of small investors, also seems to have increased during the same period. While free float was around 34 percent in 1999, it reached approximately 39 percent in 2009. On the other hand, the shareholdings of the other relevant investors are reduced to about 15 percent in 2009 from an initial 23 percent in 1999. The increase in concentration is also observed in the number of investors holding 50 percent or more of the shareholdings. While in 1999 there were 116 such companies, this number reached 139 in 2009. Average shareholdings of business groups increased from 53 percent in 1999 to 54.59 in 2009. Family-controlled business groups (FBGs) constitute the overwhelming majority among the business groups.

Although there are a number of companies where free float shares exceed 95 percent, it is not possible to claim that these are companies without a controlling shareholder. Even in that case it is possible to see that the company is affiliated with a business group or a coalition of shareholders who are able to control the firm.

This concentrated ownership structure eliminates takeover risks. It is usually not possible to acquire a firm without the consent of the controlling shareholder. Given the limited openness and the concentrated ownership of the firms, there is not an active market for corporate control; thus the market does not have a disciplining effect on poor performance (Yurtoğlu, 2000).

There is also very limited presence of domestic institutional investors among the shareholders, which is located at less than 1 percent in the case of listed manufacturing companies (Yamak, Ertuna and Bolak, 2006). Foreign institutional investors are generally in the free float. According to data published by the Central Registry Agency of Turkey, the share of foreign institutional investors in total free float on the ISE was 27.4 percent as of year end 2006.

It seems that there is an overall increase in all types of foreign investors in the ISE. Both number of foreign investors and their average shareholdings seem to have increased during the last decade. While there were only fourteen companies where more than 50 percent of the shares were held by foreign investors in 1999, there were thirty-eight such companies in 2009. In companies with at least one foreign shareholder, average foreign shareholding reached about 53 percent in 2009 from an initial 35 percent in 1999.

The ownership and governance model of large Turkish companies

Similar to their counterparts in other emerging countries (Claessens et al., 2000), Turkish companies are also subject to highly concentrated ownership structures, which are often controlled by families. Turkey has long been identified by various sources as a large emerging market, and as having a state-dependent business system according to Whitley's (1994) typology (Ertuna and Yamak, 2011). State-dependent business systems are characterized by family dominance at the managerial level. In fact, the Turkish business context is typically characterized by family business groups (Guillén, 2001) which were encouraged by the Turkish state. The state formed partnerships with these businesses, provided credits from state banks and low cost inputs, and protected them from foreign competition (Buğra, 1994). The intricate nature of the relationship between the state and the business firms necessitates a careful handling of this link and enforces owning families to take part in the management of their companies (Buğra, 1994).

The Turkish FBGs are formed by the investments of a single family or a small number of allied families (Ararat and Yurtoğlu, 2006). In the Turkish business groups the control is retained by a central management unit where key management positions are held by the founder of the company and his descendants even in the case of large listed companies (Yurtoğlu, 2000). Interlocking directorates across the companies of the FBG (Yildirim and Üsdiken, 2007), low representation of outsiders (Göksen and Üsdiken, 2001; Selekler-Göksen and Karatas, 2008), qualification of the retired employees as outsiders (Üsdiken and Yildirim-Öktem, 2008) and cross-shareholdings (Yurtoğlu, 2003) are other tools used by the family to control the firm. The boards are typically insider dominated (Selekler-Göksen and Karatas, 2008). In the largest Turkish FBGs, the percentage of the family members in the board room of the holding may attain as much as 40 percent (Göksen and Üsdiken, 2001).

Although chairmen of both the holding company and the affiliated companies are often family members (Yurtoğlu, 2000), duality is rarely observed (Yamak et al., 2006). The chairman and the CEO are usually two different persons in listed companies. The CEOs do not seem to be as powerful as their counterparts in Anglo-Saxon countries; some of them are not even board members. However, their remuneration is not egalitarian in comparison to other employees in the company. The salary they receive is more than ten times the average worker salary (EkonomiBorsa, 2011).

There are signs of professionalization of management in Turkey, although its level is low. It has been observed recently that the number of insider professionals is increasing to the detriment of the family members in the boards (Selekler-Göksen and Karatas, 2008). Similarly, in family business group affiliated companies, the direct shareholdings of family members are also decreasing (Yurtoğlu, 2000). In fact, a comparison of the percentage of shares held by individual family members among ISE companies in 1999 and 2009 indicates that there is a decrease of 2.4 percent (Yamak and Ertuna, 2010). The averages for 1999 and 2009 are 12 percent and 9.6 percent respectively. Family members usually hold the shares of the holding company, which in turn owns the shares of the affiliated companies.

The holding company which has a central role in Turkish corporate governance is legally a stock corporation which aims to hold the stock of other companies and to manage them (Yurtoğlu, 2000). Financial reasons such as tax benefits stand for the adoption of this form as a way of managing the BGs in Turkey (Yurtoğlu, 2000). Most of the major holding companies, such as Koç Holding, Sabancı Holding, Doğan Holding and Eczacıbaşı Holding, are traded in the ISE.

In the ISE, along with the family business groups, there are also non-family business groups. The major ones in this category are the Türkiye İş Bankası and OYAK groups. Türkiye İş Bankası controls directly or indirectly about fifteen firms in the ISE as of 2009. It is a quasi-private bank with an unusual ownership structure and managerial control (Yurtoğlu, 2000). 42 percent of its shares belong to the retirement fund of the bank's employees and about 28 percent of the shares are held by a political party. It has investments in the financial sector and glass industry. OYAK, the second business group without a family affiliation, was incorporated in 1961 by a special law with the purpose of providing to the Turkish army members a variety of social services such as loans and retirement income. The company identifies itself as an assistance and pension fund committed to achieve the highest returns for its members. The group is managed by professional managers and has investments in financial services, food and cement industries among others. As of 2009 the group has eight listed companies.

In Turkey there is no domination of banks in the ownership structure of the companies (Nilsson, 2007). Banks have a major role in the financial intermediation and they act as the major source of credit for industrial firms, but do not generally participate in the ownership of companies. Hence, Turkish banks do not fulfill the same governance task as their Japanese counterparts, which are subject to special obligations such as offering or coordinating support for the company in times of crisis, nor like their German counterparts, which assist effective mobilization of dispersed shareholdings through deposited share voting rights (Yurtoğlu, 2000). Many banks in Turkey are rather dominated by large business groups (Nilsson, 2007). For example, the largest Turkish FBG, Koç Holding, controls Yapı ve Kredi Bankası. Other groups such as Doğuş, Fiba and Sabancı control alone or with their partners respectively Garanti Bankası, Millennium Bank-Turkey and Akbank. However, the number of FBGs possessing a bank decreased following the banking crisis in 2001.

There are also large multinational foreign companies among listed firms. Their number and investment amount have considerably increased after the 2001 Turkish banking crisis when foreign investors bought financially distressed Turkish companies. There are also large multinational companies such as Ford Company or Fiat who formed joint ventures with large Turkish FBGs on an equal share basis.

Due to the ongoing privatization efforts, the shareholdings of the state institutions in ISE companies are decreasing. As of 2009, ten companies are controlled by the different state-related institutions in the ISE.

IPO activity between 2006 and 2008

The regulation of IPOs

The CMB sets the rules for the IPO process. After preparing the required documents and making the necessary changes in their articles of association, companies apply to the CMB for registration and to the ISE for being traded in the market. After on-site company visits and examination of the documents by the experts of the CMB and the ISE, the CMB evaluates the application to see whether the information presented in the prospectus and the circular fulfills the public disclosure requirements. The CMB registers the prospective issue by ascertaining that all the documents required by the related legislation are fully disclosed in a fair manner. Registration is followed by the public announcement of the prospectus.

The issuer and the underwriters determine the price and the methods of sales and distribution, which are also disclosed in the prospectus. The companies can decide either to offer their shares directly in the stock market or to use the book-building method. In the book-building method, demand is collected from investors either at a fixed price, by price offers or in a given price range. Price is determined and the shares are distributed to investors based on demand. Under this method, shares can also be allocated to different groups of investors, such as domestic individual investors, domestic institutional investors, foreign institutional investors and company employees, provided that percentage allocation is presented in the prospectus. In the case of excess demand, the issue can include the sale of additional shares, which is also disclosed in the prospectus. The underwriters publicly declare the results of sales to the CMB and the ISE after the completion of the sales transaction. Upon the decision of the Executive Council of the ISE, the shares of the company start trading in the market, after the public offering results, the prospectus and other required information are announced to the public through the Daily Bulletin and/or the Public Disclosure Platform of the ISE.

Companies can apply for listing on the National Market, the Corporate Products Market and the Second National Market (for the companies which are not able to meet listing requirements). The Corporate Products Market is for mutual funds, real-estate investment trust and warrants and it has recently been organized. Listing requirements of the ISE Listing Regulation apply for the National Market and the Corporate Products Market, while the ISE National Market Circular is used as the regulation for the Second National Market. The Second National Market offers a more flexible way for small companies to go public. Additionally, the ISE has organized a new market, called the Emerging Companies Market. Although this market is not active yet, it will be a market where small and medium-sized companies can go public by selling their shares of capital increases only.

The companies in the National Market and the Corporate Products Market comply both with the listing and ongoing requirements of the ISE. Listing requirements are mainly based on the share of the free float and the size of the company. In this respect, free float requirements are formulated in relation to firm size under three different groups. Companies in Group 1, with a minimum market cap of 100,000,000 TRL (62,500,000 USD) and a minimum shareholders' equity of 25,000,000 TRL (15,625,000 USD), do not have a minimum free float requirement. Group 2 includes companies with a minimum market cap of 50,000,000 TRL (31,250,000 USD) and a minimum shareholders' equity of 16,000,000 TRL (10,000,000 USD) which are required to have a free float ratio of at least 5 percent. The minimum free float ratio is 25 percent for companies in Group 3, with a minimum market cap of 25,000,000 TRL (15,625,000 USD) and a shareholders' equity of 10,000,000 TRL (6,250,000 USD). Presence of a pre-tax profit is required in at least one of the two years prior to the IPO for companies in Groups 1 and 2, while companies in Group 3 are required to have a pre-tax profit in both of the two years. For all companies in the National Market, three years should pass since the establishment of the company for being listed. Furthermore, the listing requirements include items on information disclosure, legal structure and examination of financial results by the ISE management. The ongoing requirements concentrate on the timely disclosure of information, namely the quarterly financial statements, transactions of the significant persons and price-sensitive information. There is a free float requirement for continuing to be listed. The listing and ongoing requirements of the ISE are presented in Table 20.3.

Table 20.3 *Listing and ongoing requirements in Turkey*

Admission requirements	
Free float	Group 1 – 0%; Group 2 – 5%; Group 3 – 25%
Market cap	Group 1 – TRL100,000,000; Group 2 – TRL50,000,000; Group 3 – TRL25,000,000
Shareholders' equity	Group 1 – TRL25,000,000; Group 2 – TRL16,000,000; Group 3 – TRL10,000,000
Profits before tax	Group 1 – in at least one of the last two years; Group 2 – in at least one of the last two years; Group 3 – the last 2 years
Age	For companies in the National Market, at least three calendar years must have elapsed since the establishment of the corporation, and financial statements of the last three years must have been publicly disclosed For companies in the Corporate Products Market, companies go public in the same year of the establishment
Admission documents	Pre-vetted by the ISE
Prospectus	The company must publish a prospectus which complies with the requirement of the Capital Market Board
Legal structure	The corporation's articles of association must not include any provisions restricting the transfer and circulation of the securities to be traded on the Exchange or preventing the shareholders from exercising their rights Significant legal disputes which might affect the corporation's production or activities must not exist The corporation's legal situation in terms of its establishment and activities as well as the legal situation of its shares must be documented to verify their compliance with the respective legislation The companies must have an independent lawyer prepare a legal report which confirms the legal structure of the company and its shares
Financial situation	The Exchange management must examine the corporation's financial structure and confirm its ability to continue as an ongoing concern
Ongoing requirements	
Price-sensitive information	The company must disclose all the price-sensitive information via PDP (Public Disclosure Platform) until the next day's opening of the transaction session
Minimum free float	No minimum free float requirement

Table 20.3 (*cont.*)

Financial statements	Produce quarterly reports (for unconsolidated statements within 4 weeks, for consolidated statements within 6 weeks), limitedly audited half-year reports (for unconsolidated statements within 6 weeks, for consolidated statements within 8 weeks), and independently audited full-year financial reports (for unconsolidated statements within 10 weeks, for consolidated statements within 14 weeks)
Transactions of significant persons	Must be distributed to public via PDP according to rules of the CMB's communiqués of Vol. VIII, No. 54

Source: Compiled from the Istanbul Stock Exchange Listing Regulation of the CMB issued in Official Journal dated 24.6.2004, No. 25502 and the "Regulation Amending Istanbul Stock Exchange Listing Requirements" published in the Official Journal dated 8.8.2007, No. 26607

The IPOs between 2006 and 2008

The period 2006–8 represents a weak IPO market in the ISE. In this period, there are twenty-seven companies that have gone public. Out of these twenty-seven IPOs, sixteen took place in 2006, nine in 2007 and only two in 2008. In this section, we analyze the sixteen IPOs which satisfy all of the criteria to be included in this study. Due to the lack of sound information about many of the necessary criteria, we have excluded eleven IPOs. The resulting data includes nine IPOs in 2006 and seven IPOs in 2007.

Breakdown of issuing companies with respect to industry displays a concentration in financials. Out of sixteen IPOs, eleven belong to companies that are operating in the financials industry. These include seven mutual funds and investment companies, two banks, one real estate fund and one holding company. Table 20.4 displays the breakdown of IPOs with respect to years and industry.

The sample includes the IPOs of newly formed companies as well as the IPOs of old, established companies. According to the regulations, mutual funds and investment companies offer their shares to the public in the year they are established. During the period analyzed, these companies offered their shares to the public in the National

Table 20.4 *IPO year and industry classification*

	2006	2007	2008	Total
Consumer goods	1	0	0	1
Consumer services	1	0	0	1
Financials	5	6	0	11
Industrials	0	1	0	1
Technology	2	0	0	2
Total	9	7	0	16

Market, while they have been organized as Corporate Products Markets at the end of 2010. Since there are seven mutual funds and investment companies in the sample, the minimum firm age, as well as the first quartile average, is zero. The average firm age of IPOs is about fifteen years while the maximum is sixty-nine years. Firm age statistics of the issuing companies in the 2006–8 period is consistent with those of the 1996–2000 period (Gürünlü, 2009), with a minimum of one, a maximum of forty-six and an average of seventeen years.

Companies display a wide variety on all the three measures of firm size. Mutual funds and investment companies issuing their shares to the public have one to three employees and relatively smaller revenues and total assets. In terms of number of employees, Tekfen Holding is the largest company with 11,791 employees, followed closely by Halk Bankası, which has 10,500 employees. Halk Bankası is the largest company in terms of both revenues and total assets. It is a large state bank that has a nationwide network of branches.

In the year before their IPO, issuing companies perform well on profitability ratios, namely on return on assets (ROA), return on equity (ROE) and return on sales (ROS). There are two companies, a mutual fund and a real estate investment company, that generated a loss in the year prior to their IPO. Companies that exhibit highest profitability are Karel Elektronik Sanayi (ROA), TAV Havalimanları Holding (ROE) and Tacirler Yatırım Ortaklığı (ROS). Karel Elektronik is a manufacturer and supplier of telecommunications equipment and TAV Havalimanları Holding is a group of companies that operate in the business of construction of airport buildings and management of airports. Tacirler Yatırım Ortaklığı is a mutual fund. Descriptive statistics on size and performance are presented in Table 20.5.

Table 20.5 *Firm size and performance of companies going public*

	Size			Performance		
	Employees	Revenues (USD)	Assets (USD)	ROA	ROE	ROS
Min	1	0	2,235,213	−3.1%	−3.9%	−2.2%
1st quartile	2	754,354	2,859,187	1.0%	0.09%	0.2%
2nd quartile	82	26,497,188	26,097,336	2.5%	3.6%	6.1%
3rd quartile	3,881	310,514,744	1,276,993,186	4.1%	54.1%	18.8%
Max	11,791	3,222,414,567	24,191,673,567	15.70%	114.5%	56.3%
Average	2,131	456,849,016	1,916,445,708	3.4%	25.3%	13.0%

In the sample, thirteen companies have individual entrepreneurs and family members, two companies have bank ownership and one company has state ownership. Besides the ownership of entrepreneurs and individual family members, families have significant ownership positions through family-owned companies. The average ownership stake of individual family members is 76.6 percent prior to the IPO. Following the IPO, average family share declines significantly to 30 percent. After the IPO, bank ownership declines from 53.8 percent to 45.4 percent and government ownership of the state bank decreases from 100 percent to 75 percent. The ownership structure of IPO companies is highly concentrated. Before the IPO, average share of the largest owner is 65 percent, while the first three shareholders own on average about 90 percent of shares. After the IPO, there is a substantial decline in both the share of the largest shareholder and of the first three shareholders, where the average ownership stakes decrease to 25 percent and 35 percent, respectively. It is worth noting that the stake of the largest shareholder of all the listed companies is 46.3 percent, which is almost the double of the IPO companies in the sample. The difference can be attributed to the relatively high number of mutual funds and investment funds going public in this period. We observe that funds display different ownership patterns, especially on family ownership and ownership concentrations. While the average ownership stakes of families are similar for funds and other companies before the IPO, they significantly diverge from each other in the post-IPO period. The post-IPO average stakes of families is 10.9 percent for mutual funds and 52.4 percent for other companies. The ownership structure of companies other than mutual funds resembles those of the listed companies. Table 20.6 displays the notable

Table 20.6 IPO ownership structure (data in percent)

	Family		Bank		Govt.		VC		Angels		Top 1		Top 3	
	pre	post	pre	post	pre	post	pre	post	pre	post	pre	post	pre	post
Min	23.0	0.0	30.0	28.8	100.0	75.0	–	–	–	–	25.8	0.1	59.5	0.1
1st quartile	70.3	4.5	41.9	37.1	100.0	75.0	–	–	–	–	36.4	8.0	79.5	1.1
2nd quartile	99.2	18.5	53.8	45.4	100.0	75.0	–	–	–	–	58.9	20.2	98.8	40.1
3rd quartile	100.0	57.3	65.7	53.6	100.0	75.0	–	–	–	–	97.5	33.6	99.8	61.6
Max	100.0	79.0	77.6	61.9	100.0	75.0	–	–	–	–	100.0	77.3	100.0	79.9
Average	76.6	30.0	53.8	45.4	100.0	75.0	–	–	–	–	64.9	25.0	90.3	35.0
No. of cases	13	13	2	2	1	1	0	0	0	0	16	16	16	16

Table 20.7 *Board of directors of companies going public*

	Size	Executive directors	Non-executive directors	Indepen-dent directors	Engineering, operations, R&D	Marketing, sales	Finance, accounting, law
Min	3	0	0	0	0	0	1
1st quartile	4.75	1.75	0	0	0	0	2
2nd quartile	5	3	2.5	0	1	0	3.5
3rd quartile	6.25	5	4	0.25	2.25	1	5
Max	15	6	10	3	5	3	10
Average	5.93	3.25	2.68	0.5	1.5	0.5	3.87

absence of venture capital and private equity funds in the ownership structure of companies.

The average board size is six. The average board is composed of three executive directors and three non-executive directors and less than one independent director. Consistent with previous evidence (Yildirim-Öktem and Üsdiken, 2007) most of the companies do not have any independent directors. On the other hand, incidence of women directors is relatively high; seven companies have women directors. Family involvement in boards is common practice. In fact, thirteen companies have their founders on the board at the time of going public.

The most commonly observed functional background of directors is in the peripheral functions such as finance, accounting and law. On average, there are four directors with backgrounds in peripheral functions. Directors with backgrounds in throughput functions, such as engineering, operations and research and development, are less commonly observed, while directors with backgrounds in output functions, such as marketing or sales, are a rarity. Descriptive statistics on board size and structure are presented in Table 20.7.

All companies, except two, have formed their audit committees. However, most of these audit committees do not include independent directors, as required by the regulations. Boards seem reluctant in forming the committees which are recently introduced by the CGP. The recent introduction of these structures into the context and the resulting unfamiliarity of the Turkish businesses with them are the main reasons for the observed reluctance. Boards have not yet set up their nomination, compensation and technology committees. There is only one company with a nomination committee. Corporate governance committees are more common. Three companies have boards which have created corporate governance committees.

Description of an IPO: Tekfen Holding

The firm before the IPO

Tekfen was founded in 1956 by three young engineers, Feyyaz Berker, Nihat Gökyiğit and Necati Akçağlılar, who used to work at the Ministry of Public Works. The company started as an engineering and consultancy firm, operating basically in construction, and soon extended its activities into the field of pipelines and oil-gas facilities as a subcontractor of foreign companies. In 1971 the company became a holding company. Its first international contract was signed in 1978, which was followed by new projects and investments, first in the Middle East and Russia, then in China, North Africa and other countries. Finally, Tekfen Holding turned into a multi-business holding active in various domains ranging from construction, banking and retailing to airplane services. Around 85 percent of the construction projects were realized out of Turkey. Tekfen's construction company ranked among the largest 100 construction companies in the world. The other leading company of the group is Toros Gübre, which is the largest player in the Turkish fertilizer market. The company underwent reorganization in 2000 and reduced its range of activities into construction, agriculture, finance, real estate development, textiles and international trade. The ownership structure was also simplified. Owners held shares only in the holding company, which in turn retained the shares of the affiliated companies. Share ownership of the affiliated companies and that of owners in other affiliated companies were eliminated.

Rotation of the chairmanship is adopted in the boardroom. Each of the three founders chairs the board for one year, at the end of which he passes the baton to the other. Right before the IPO, significant changes took place in the board, management structure and voting rights. While the previous board was composed of the founders and their family members, three independent directors were added before going public. The board comprised nine members, namely two founders, four relatives of the founders (one of them being the replacement of the third founder due to his poor health) and three independent directors. Two founders and the spouse of the third founder act as managing directors in the board. Furthermore, a vice president in charge of corporate governance was appointed in 2006. He was also in charge of planning the IPO process. Similarly, dual-class shares were also eliminated. Total shares held by the founders and their families were located at around 78 percent before the IPO.

The CEO of the group is Erhan Öner, who started his career in the company about forty years ago. Long tenures of top executives are typical in the Turkish business system (Yamak and Üsdiken, 2006). Only a trusted few can make it to the top positions in the company (Yildirim-Öktem and Üsdiken, 2007). The CEO of Tekfen is not a member of Tekfen Holding's board, which is another characteristic of the upper echelons in this context. In almost half of the ISE manufacturing companies, the CEO does not sit on the board of the company he manages (Yamak et al., 2006).

The offer

The IPO process for Tekfen Holding took place in 2007. The shares were sold to the public on November 23, 2007 after a period of book building at the maximum level of the price range per share between 4.70 and 5.80 TRL. The offer is a hybrid offer which includes both the sales of existing shares, as well as the newly issued shares. The initial offer included the sale of 22,557,000 existing shares and 66,775,000 newly issued shares by restricting the pre-emptive rights of the existing shareholders. Additionally, the issue included the right to sell an additional number of shares (15 percent of total shares offered) and this right was exercised as the demand for the issue was strong. As a result, a total of 102,386,800 shares, which corresponds to 34.5 percent of the total, were offered to the public in the IPO. The shares offered to the public were allocated to different groups on the following basis: 30 percent was allocated to domestic individual investors, 0.5 percent was allocated to domestic institutional investors and the remaining 69.5 percent was allocated to foreign institutional investors. The shares were sold to the public at 5.7 TRL per share, leading to total proceeds of 583.6 million TRL (490.8 million USD) for the issue, out of which 380.6 million TRL (320.1 million USD) was raised as cash for the company and the remaining for the existing shareholders. The cash generated by the company is planned to be used for investments according to the prospectus. A total of 341.1 million USD shares were sold to foreign investors, corresponding to 69.5 percent of the issue. After the offer, the return on the first day of trading was 6 percent, while the one-year buy-and-hold return for the issue has been −56 percent due to the impact of the global financial crisis in 2008.

The firm after the IPO

The year following the IPO coincided with the global economic crisis. The first three-quarters of 2008 were financially successful but in the last quarter the company's profitability reduced significantly. The company used IPO proceeds to support investments especially on real estate development, which continued in spite of the crisis.

Since the major changes in governance were accomplished before going public there are just a few slight changes to mention concerning the post-IPO period. After the IPO the shares of the founders and their families were reduced to 57.9 percent. The board still comprises nine members with the same positions: three managing directors, three independent directors and three representatives of the founders. However, one of the founders, Feyyaz Berker, has appointed an outsider instead of a family member to represent his shares along with himself. Managing directors and the CEO as well as most members of the board and the management team remained the same. The company is still controlled by the family. The total of the shares of the entrepreneurs exceeds 50 percent. About 35 percent of the shares of the company are traded in the ISE.

Conclusion

The legal infrastructure in relation to corporate governance is subject to changes in Turkish context. Although some changes occur in the CML, and in company law, the fact that the new law will be put into effect in 2012 (and some of its parts even later) puts doubts about the decisiveness of the government about the regulations concerning companies. Minority shareholder protection, qualifications and functions of boards, compliance and accurate reporting are some of the issues that are covered by the new law. In Turkey, attracting foreign investors appears as the main motivation in adopting the CGP. Rules which satisfy the specific conditions of the Turkish context need to be elaborated.

Although the stock market is growing and new laws have been introduced, there is limited change in the basic characteristics of the companies. The companies are highly concentrated. Family business groups, as the major actors of this context, dominate ownership and control. This high concentration limits the disciplining effect of the market. It also leads to a specific agency problem between majority and minority shareholders. This concentration seems to have further increased in the last decade. This high concentration, accompanied by low minority rights, ensure that the dominant shareholder assumes the control of the company. Family blockholders are typical of the ISE. Family members usually assume the chair role and select the potential board members. High ownership concentration and control is also an issue in other (non-family) business groups.

In spite of the recent developments, the ISE has a limited role in the Turkish economy. Although going public may be a good opportunity to raise capital and to make the transition from a family company to a professional one, even the large firms are reluctant to issue their shares to the public for fear of losing control. During the period 2006–8 only twenty-seven companies went public. The fact that the last year under consideration was a global crisis year might have contributed to this limited score in the ISE. IPO firms in our sample, consistently with other studies, are relatively younger firms with an average age of fifteen years. Their pre-IPO ownership structure is quite concentrated. The concentration decreases following the IPO in our sample. Family domination is also seen in the case of IPOs. Venture capital, private equity and angels are not familiar tools. Average board size is six. They are usually composed of three executive and three non-executive directors. Independent directors exist in only four companies. Furthermore, the incidence of women board members is high. The most commonly observed functional background in the board room of the IPO firm is the peripheral functions such as finance, accounting and law.

The Turkish stock market makes progress but there is still much to accomplish. The new company law may contribute to the development of the companies when it comes into force in July 2012.

References

Ağca, Ahmet and Önder, Serife. 2007. 'Voluntary disclosure in Turkey: A study on firms listed in Istanbul Stock Exchange', *Problems and Perspectives in Management*, 5, 241–51.

Aksu, Mine and Kösedağ, Arman. 2006. 'Transparency and disclosure scores and their determinants in the Istanbul Stock Exchange', *Corporate Governance: An International Review*, 14, 277–96.

Altay, Anlam S. and Amasya, Serap. 2007. *Draft of the New Turkish Code of Commerce: New Challenges for Turkish Commercial Law*, Istanbul.

Ararat, Melsa and Yurtoğlu, Burcin B. 2006. 'Yönetişim ve küresel rekabet', *Yönetim Araştırmaları Dergisi*, 6, 5–44.

Atakan, Serap, Özsoy, Zeynep and Oba, Beyza. 2008. 'Implementation of good corporate governance in Turkey: The case of Dogan Yayın Holding', *Human Systems Management*, 27, 201–16.

BDDK (Banking Regulation and Supervision Agency). 2010. 'Türk Bankacılık Sektörü Genel Görünümü – Eylül 2010'. Downloaded from www.bddk.org.tr/WebSitesi/turkce/Raporlar/Diger_Raporlar/8664tbs_genel_gorunum_eylul_2010.pdf, December 24, 2010.

Buğra, Ayşe. 1994. *State and Business in Modern Turkey: A Comparative Study*. State University of New York Press, Albany.

Claessens, Stijin, Djankov, Simeon and Lang, Larry H.P. 2000. 'The separation of ownership and control in East Asian corporations', *Journal of Financial Economics*, 52, 81–112.

CMB (Capital Market Board). 2007. 'Paylari IMKB'de islem gören ve Ulusal 100 endeksine dahil olan sirketlerin kurumsal yönetim uygulamalarina iliskin degerlendirme'. Downloaded from www.spk.gov.tr/displayfile.aspx?action=displayfile&pageid=461&fn=461.pdf&submenuheader=null, December 24, 2010.

Demirağ, Istemi and Serter, Mehmet. 2003. 'Ownership patterns and control in Turkish listed companies', *Corporate Governance: An International Review*, 11, 40–51.

DPT (State Planning Organization). 2009. 'Mali piyasalarda gelişmeler'. Downloaded from www.dpt.gov.tr/DocObjects/View/7742/mpg-1209.pdf, December 24, 2010.

EkonomiBorsa. 2011. 'CEO'lar farkı açıyor'. Downloaded from www.ekonomiborsa.com/039ceo039lar-farki-aciyor.html.

Ertuna, Bengi, Ercan, Metin and Akgiray, Vedat. 2003. 'The effect of the issuer–underwriter relationship on IPOs: The case of an emerging market', *The Journal of Entrepreneurial Finance and Business Ventures*, 8, 3, 43–55.

Ertuna, Bengi and Tükel, Ali. 2007. 'Board composition and control mechanisms in ISE50: Form outscores substance'. Paper presented at the proceedings of ECGI Corporate Governance in Emerging Markets, Sabancı University.

Ertuna, Bengi and Yamak, Sibel. 2011. 'Foreign equity configurations in an emerging country: Implications for performance', *European Management Journal*, 29, 2, 117–28.

Ertürk, Ismail. 2003. 'Governance or financialisation: The Turkish case', *Competition & Change*, 7, 185–204.

Göksen, Nisan S. and Üsdiken, Behlül. 2001. 'Uniformity and diversity in Turkish Business Groups: Effects of scale and time of founding', *British Journal of Management*, 12, 325–40.

Gugler, Klaus, Mueller, Dennis C. and Yurtoğlu, Burcin B. 2008. 'Insider ownership, ownership concentration and investment performance: An international comparison', *Journal of Corporate Finance*, 14, 688–705.

Guillén, Mauro F. 2001. *The Limits of Convergence: Globalization and Organizational Change in Argentina, South Korea, and Spain*. Princeton University Press.

Gürünlü, Meltem. 2009. 'The evolution of corporate governance mechanisms after going public: Evidence from Turkish panel data', *International Journal of Economic Perspectives*, 3, 59–82.

Hofstede, Geert. 1980. *Culture Consequences: International Differences in Work-related Values*. Beverly Hills, CA: Sage.

IIF EAG (International Institute of Finance Equity Advisory Group Task Force). 2005. 'Corporate governance in Turkey: An investor perspective'. Downloaded from www.iif.com/gcm/corpgovern/reports/article+81.php, December 24, 2010.

ISO (Istanbul Chamber of Industry). 2010. *Türkiye'nin 500 büyük sanayi kuruluşu 2009*, Istanbul.

Kabasakal, Hayat and Bodur, Muzaffer. 2007. 'Leadership and culture in Turkey: A multifaceted phenomenon', in J.S. Chokkar, F.C. Brodbeck and R.J. House (eds.), *Across the World: The GLOBE Book of In-depth Studies of 25 Societies*. Mahwah, NJ: Lawrence Erlbaum Associates, pp. 835–74.

Keyman, E. Fuat and Koyuncu, Berrin. 2005. 'Globalization, alternative modernities and the political economy of Turkey', *Review of International Political Economy*, 12, 1, 105–28.

Kort, Michael. 2008. 'Standardization of company law in Germany, other EU member states and Turkey by corporate governance rules', *European Company and Financial Law Review*, 5, 4, 379–421.

La Porta, Rafael, Lopez-de-Silanes, Florencio, Shleifer, Andrea and Vishny, Robert W. 1998. 'Law and finance', *Journal of Political Economy*, 106, 1113–55.

La Porta, Rafael, Lopez-de-Silanes, Florencio and Shleifer, Andrea. 1999. 'Corporate ownership around the world', *Journal of Finance*, 54, 2, 471–517.

La Porta, Rafael, Lopez-de-Silanes, Florencio, Shleifer, Andrea and Vishny, Robert W. 2002. 'Investor protection and corporate valuation', *Journal of Finance*, 57, 1147–70.

La Porta, Rafael, Lopez-de-Silanes, Florencio and Shleifer, Andrea. 2008. 'The economic consequences of legal origin', *Journal of Economic Literature*, 46, 2, 285–332.

Mandacı, Pınar E. and Gümüs, Guluzar K. 2010. 'Ownership concentration, managerial ownership and firm performance: Evidence from Turkey', *South East European Journal of Economics and Business*, 57–66.

Nilsson, Gül O. 2007. 'Corporate governance in Turkey', *European Business Organization Law Review*, 8, 195–236.

Oba, Beyza, Ozsoy, Z. and Atakan, Serap. 2010. 'Power in the boardroom: A study on Turkish family-owned and listed companies', *Corporate Governance*, 10, 603–16.

OECD. 2006. *Corporate Governance in Turkey: A Pilot Study*. Paris: OECD Publishing.

Orbay, Hakan and Yurtoğlu, Burcin B. 2006. 'The impact of corporate governance structures on the corporate investment performance in Turkey', *Corporate Governance: An International Review*, 14, 4, 349–63.

Selekler-Göksen, N. and Karatas, A. 2008. 'Board structure and performance in an emerging economy: Turkey', *International Journal of Business Governance and Ethics*, 4, 132–47.

Selekler-Göksen, N. and Özlem Yildirim Öktem. 2009. 'Countervailing institutional forces: Corporate governance in Turkish family business groups', *Journal of Management and Governance*, 13, 193–213.

Üsdiken, Behlül and Yildirim-Öktem, Özlem. 2008. 'Kurumsal ortamda degisim ve buyuk aile holdingleri bunyesindeki sirketlerin yonetim kurullarinda "icrada gorevli olmayan" ve "bagimsiz" uyeler', *Amme idarbsi Dergisi*, 41, 1, 43–71.

Whitley, Richard. 1994. 'Dominant forms of economic organization in market economies', *Organisation Studies*, 15, 153–82.

Yamak, Sibel, Ertuna, Bengi and Bolak, Mehmet. 2006. 'Sahiplik dagılımının birlesik liderlik yapısı üzerine etkileri', *Yönetim Arastırmaları Dergisi*, 85–107.

Yamak, S. and Ertuna, B. 2010. *Ownership Characteristics of Turkish Companies: Changes from 1999 to 2009*. Unpublished manuscript.

Yamak, Sibel and Üsdiken, Behlül. 2006. 'Economic liberalization and the antecedents of top management teams: Evidence from Turkish "big" business', *British Journal of Management*, 17, 177–94.

Yildirim-Öktem, Özlem and Üsdiken, Behlül. 2007. 'Reconciling family-centric and professionalized governance: Boards of firms within family business groups'. Paper presented at the Academy of Management Best Papers Proceedings, Philadelphia, USA.

Yurtoğlu, Burcin B. 2000. 'Ownership, control and performance of Turkish listed firms', *Empirica*, 27, 193–222.

2003. 'Corporate governance and implications for minority shareholders in Turkey', *Journal of Corporate Ownership & Control*, 1, 1, 72–86.

21 | Corporate governance and initial public offerings in the United Kingdom

R. GREG BELL

Corporate governance mechanisms

The United Kingdom (U.K.) is a nation of cultural and ethnic diversity consisting of four countries, each with a clear identity: England, Scotland, Wales, and Northern Ireland. Since World War II the U.K. has accommodated large immigrant populations. This cultural and ethnic diversity helps promotes individuality and constrain social cohesion. The legal system is common law and is the basis of common law legal systems across most Commonwealth countries. The market for corporate control is quite active in the U.K. because there are few institutional or legal barriers to takeover. Indeed, threat of takeover is considered a disciplinary mechanism on management, helping to ensure that underperforming managers are replaced by more effective ones. The U.K. is among the world leaders in promoting a transparent corporate information environment supporting the disclosure of ownership and financial information. Listed firms in the U.K. are guided by a set of good governance principles set forth in the U.K. Corporate Governance Code 2010. Listed firms are required to disclose how they have complied with the Code, and explain where they have not applied the Code. This is what the Code refers to as "comply or explain". There is no requirement for disclosure of compliance among private companies; however, even these entities are also encouraged to conform to the Code. Finally, business groups were fairly common governance mechanisms at the middle of the twentieth century. However, their prevalence declined as a result of continual pressure from institutional investors on boards.

Most major U.K. companies are listed on the stock market and voting control is typically not concentrated in the hands of families, banks, or other firms. In fact, fewer than three out of ten of the country's publicly listed companies have a shareholder that retains more than one-fifth of the shares. Hence, ownership of U.K. firms is quite dispersed and fragmented. The dominant shareholders in the U.K. are institutional investors with occupational pension funds accounting for the largest proportion of these shareholders. Given the level of ownership dispersion, and the strength of the regulatory framework, minority ownership rights are considered well protected in the U.K. The U.K. has a single board system. All board members, both executive and non-executive directors, are normally elected by the shareholders. The U.K. Corporate Governance Code (2010) recommends that all listed companies have at least half the board comprised of non-executive directors and have at least two independent non-executive directors. In addition, CEO duality is not common in the U.K. Finally, the compensation of top executives in the U.K. is non-egalitarian in nature and often includes a significant variable compensation component that is tied to the financial performance of the firm.

Corporate law

Companies incorporated within the U.K. are subject to the Companies Act 2006 which enables companies to be formed by registration, and sets out the responsibilities of companies, their directors, and secretaries. In providing a comprehensive code of company law for the U.K., the Companies Act 2006 amends or restates almost all of the Companies Act 1985. In particular, the Companies Act 2006 codifies certain existing common law principles, such as those relating to directors' duties. Non-compliance is a criminal offense for both executive directors and non-executive directors.

The Financial Services Authority (FSA) is an independent non-governmental body that is given statutory powers by the Financial Services and Markets Act 2000. The FSA is accountable through Treasury Ministers to Parliament. In May 2000 the FSA took over the role of UK Listing Authority from the London Stock Exchange and today operates independent of government and is funded entirely by the firms it regulates. Its objectives are to help maintain market confidence in the financial system, promote public understanding of the financial system, protect consumers, and help reduce financial crime. The FSA is referred to as the UK Listing Authority or UKLA when it serves as securities regulator and focuses on the companies which issue the securities traded in financial markets. The UKLA sets the requirements for listing and the rules for procedures and documents related to listing.

Companies that are publicly traded on the official list of the London Stock Exchange (LSE) are also subject to the U.K. Listing Authority's Listing Rules (2008), Prospectus Rules (2008), and Disclosure and Transparency Rules (2008). Appended to the Listing Rules is the Combined Code (1999, 2003, 2006, 2010) with which companies that are U.K. incorporated are obliged to comply or explain their non-compliance. The Disclosure and Transparency Rules and Listing Principles provide a fundamental protection for investors by requiring full disclosure to the market of all relevant information on a timely basis. This aims to ensure that all users of the market get the same information at the same time. By making and enforcing the Disclosure and Transparency Rules, the Listing Rules, and the Prospectus Rules, the FSA aims to protect investors and foster appropriate standards of transparency, conduct, shareholder rights, and due diligence.

Code of good governance

The U.K. Combined Code of Corporate Governance ("the Code") is widely regarded as an international benchmark for good corporate governance practice. This system established corporate governance guidelines, yet compliance with the U.K. "Code of Best Practice" is not mandatory. Indeed, the Code offers companies a choice between complying with its principles or explaining why they do not. Hence, the Code stands in sharp contrast to mandatory systems, such as those in the U.S., which mandate corporate governance provisions through the Sarbanes-Oxley Act. Indeed, firms are free to not comply as long as an explanation is provided for any deviation from the Code. Supporters of "comply or explain" systems contend they are built upon the concept of principles, rather than strict regulation (Hubbard and Thornton, 2006), which allow firms the ability to modify and adapt their corporate governance policies to their particular needs. This flexibility is thought to encourage companies to adopt the spirit of the Code, rather than the letter, because a more statutory regime would presumably lead to a "box-ticking" approach that would fail to allow for sound deviations from the rule and would not foster investors' trust.

The development of corporate governance in the U.K. has its roots in a series of corporate collapses and scandals in the late 1980s and early 1990s, most notably the collapse of the BCCI bank and the Robert Maxwell pension funds scandal, both in 1991. In response, the "comply or explain" approach was introduced for the first time in 1992 by the Cadbury Report. This report produced a set of recommendations (provisions) listed in a Code (the Cadbury Code) of commonly recognized principles of best practice on various corporate governance aspects (e.g., board structure, committee composition, and independence). The premise behind this approach was that raising standards of corporate governance cannot be achieved by mandating structures and rules alone. Because all firms are different, each should have the ability to choose the structure that best suits them. The Cadbury Report's recommendations were for firms to appoint non-executive directors and an audit committee to oversee greater control of financial reporting and the separation of the role of the chair and chief executive.

Since 1992, the Cadbury Code has been modified several times, but has continued to retain the original principle of "comply or explain". Three years later, the Greenbury Report recommended that firms appoint a remuneration committee to determine directors' remuneration, and a nomination committee to oversee new appointments to the board. In 1998, the Turnbull Report recommended that boards make an annual statement on the effectiveness of internal controls, and that it was the responsibility of boards, not operational managers, for risk management and internal control. In 2002, the Directors' Remuneration Report introduced a requirement that directors of listed companies produce an annual report containing extensive disclosures about directors' remuneration. The Higgs Report (2003) described the role of non-executive directors, provided a new definition of "independent" directors, and recommended that board chairs and chief executives be separate individuals. Other recommendations were that non-executive directors be assessed annually and not serve more than two three-year terms on the board. In 2003, the Smith Review recommended that audit committees be comprised of at least three members, all independent non-executive directors, and that one audit committee member have significant, recent, and relevant financial experience.

The main principles of the Code (updated in 2010) relate to company leadership, board effectiveness, accountability, remuneration, and stakeholder management.

- Leadership: the Code suggests there be a clear division of responsibilities at the head of the company between the running of the board and the executive responsibility for the running of the company's business and that no one individual should have unfettered powers of decision. Some additional guiding principles are that the roles of chairman and chief executive should not be exercised by the same individual and that non-executive directors should constructively challenge and help develop proposals on strategy. The Code recommends that at least half the board, excluding the chairman, should comprise non-executive directors determined by the board to be independent. However, smaller companies should have at least two independent non-executive directors.
- Effectiveness: boards should have the appropriate balance of skills, experience, independence, and knowledge of the company to enable them to discharge their respective duties and responsibilities effectively. Boards should undertake a formal and rigorous annual evaluation of their own performance and that of their committees and individual directors. All directors should be submitted for re-election at regular intervals, subject to continued satisfactory performance. The Code calls for firms to have a nomination committee to lead the process for board appointments and make recommendations to the board. The Code recommends that members of the nomination committee be independent non-executive directors.
- Accountability: the Code recommends that boards present a balanced and understandable assessment of the company's position and prospects, maintain sound risk management and internal control systems, and establish formal and transparent arrangements for corporate reporting and risk management. A key mechanism to help accomplish this is for firms to establish an audit committee of at least three, or in the case of smaller companies two, independent non-executive directors.
- Remuneration: the Code suggests that a significant proportion of executive directors' remuneration should be structured so as to link rewards to corporate and individual performance. In addition, the

Code recommends that firms establish a remuneration committee of at least three or, in the case of smaller companies, two independent non-executive directors.

- Shareholder relations: the Code advises that it is the responsibility of the entire board to ensure that a satisfactory dialogue with shareholders takes place.

While the principles contained in the Code have become increasingly specific since the original Cadbury Report, the Code is not impervious to criticism. For instance, the Code makes clear that governance is not primarily concerned with the relationship between managers and regulators. Rather, governance is about the relationship between company managers and shareholders, and the objective is to improve the quality of this relationship. Unfortunately, however, there is no formal authority established to monitor the veracity of both the compliance statement and the explanation provided, which are left to shareholder monitoring. The Code is also criticized for not contributing to the stakeholder debate, i.e., the notion that managers should take into account employer, investor, and supplier interests (among others) rather than those of only shareholders (Parkinson and Kelly, 1999). Finally, and perhaps most importantly, the Code is only a guide in general terms to corporate governance principles, structure, and processes. The Code does not guarantee effective board behavior simply because compliance with the Code is, in effect, voluntary.

Given the considerable room within the framework of the Code in which firms can structure themselves, it is worthwhile to consider the extent in which U.K. public firms align with the Code's governance recommendations. The Spencer Stuart executive search and consulting firm provide an annual review on the characteristics of boards of directors of publicly traded financial and non-financial companies across many developed countries. The annual survey helps provide a comprehensive review of practice in the largest companies at a given point, to compare it with previous years, and to identify major trends. Results of the 2009 survey are provided in Table 21.1. Of the U.K. firms surveyed, boards averaged ten members and were balanced between insiders and non-executives. The survey found that increasing numbers of firms are identifying whether non-executives are independent. In keeping with the Code's recommendations, the number

Table 21.1 *Board characteristics of listed U.K. firms*

Variables	Characteristics of London listed companies
Sample	150 listed companies
Size	Average board size is 10.3. Most U.K. firms have 9 board members
Mix between executive and non-executive directors	Boards contain on average 67 percent non-executives; 93 percent of non-executives are considered independent
Duality	3 percent (5 companies) are led by chairman-CEOs
Number of positions in governance bodies	83 percent of board chairs hold other quoted directorships, 36 percent have one other, and 19 percent two. 47 percent of CEOs serving on external quoted company boards
Nationality of members	Foreign directors are present in 30 percent of the sample
Gender of directors	Women directors are present in 9.9 percent of companies
Number of meetings	74 percent of companies now hold between six and ten meetings and 57 percent hold eight meetings or fewer
Executive committee	No companies have an executive committee
Internal control committee	100 percent of companies have an audit committee and meet on average 5 times per year
Remuneration committee	100 percent of companies have a remuneration committee with fees paid to members ranging from $8,000 to $130,000
Nomination committee	100 percent of companies have a nomination committee
Additional committees	Corporate/social responsibility 19 percent; health, safety, environment 9 percent; risk/compliance 6.7 percent
Board evaluation	81 percent of companies report their boards are evaluated annually
Compensation of board of directors	Chairman $496,000; CEO $2,350,000; senior independent directors $23,800; non-executive directors $79,000

Source: Spencer Stuart 2009 U.K. Board Index

of companies with a combined chairman and chief executive is quite low (3 percent). Also, every company has an audit committee, and remuneration and nomination committees, in compliance with the Code's recommendations, and increasingly companies are adopting formal board committees that deal with responsibility and ethics. Finally, the proportion of foreign directors (both executive and non-executive) is 30 percent, and women constitute roughly 10 percent of U.K. boards.

Stock exchange and listed companies: the LSE and AIM exchanges

The London Stock Exchange (LSE) is one of the world's largest and most international stock exchanges and plays a pivotal role in the development of global capital markets. Established in 1698, the LSE's Main Market is home to some of the world's largest and best-known companies. Today there are over one thousand companies on the Main Market with a combined market capitalization of £1.7 trillion ($2.76 trillion). Along with the Main Market, the AIM market has emerged as the most successful growth market of its kind in the world. Table 21.2 demonstrates the growth in popularity of both of these stock exchanges.

Since its launch in 1995, the AIM has developed rapidly both in terms of the number and diversity of companies admitted to the market, and the range of institutional and retail investors involved. The AIM market's success is built on a simplified regulatory environment designed specifically for the needs of small and emerging companies. Domestic and international firms choose to join either the Main Market or the AIM because they provide access to capital for growth, and because they enable companies to raise finance for further development, both at the time of admission (through an IPO) and through further capital raisings (through seasoned equity offerings (SEOs)). Joining a London exchange creates a market for the company's shares, helps to broaden the shareholder base, and places an objective market value on the company's business. Finally, firms list on the LSE to help incentivize the long-term motivation and performance of employees by making share schemes more attractive and by increasing the company's ability to make acquisitions by using quoted shares as currency.

Table 21.2 *Listed firms on the LSE and AIM exchanges*

Exchange	Main Market (U.K. and Intl.)		AIM (U.K. and Intl.)	
Year	Number of companies	Equity market value ($m)	Number of companies	Equity market value ($m)
1998	1,890	2,413,260	312	7,479
1999	1,747	2,923,410	347	21,632
2000	1,678	2,644,630	524	21,982
2001	1,563	2,205,300	611	16,167
2002	1,522	1,824,930	704	16,299
2003	1,393	2,299,230	754	32,036
2004	1,304	2,816,970	1,021	61,235
2005	1,214	3,157,160	1,399	100,345
2006	1,146	3,796,560	1,634	178,177
2007	1,129	3,929,260	1,694	198,370
2008	1,080	1,920,780	1,546	56,214
2009	1,026	2,813,780	1,293	93,818

Source: London Stock Exchange

The ownership structure of U.K. listed companies

Institutional investors have been the dominant investors in the U.K. for many years, and owned a greater proportion of corporate equities than in any other of the market-based systems (Pendleton, 2005). The ownership of U.K. firms is summarized in Table 21.3. Institutional investors (insurance companies, pension funds, unit trusts, investment trusts, and other non-bank financial institutions) have historically owned just below 50 percent of equities. During the 1980s and 1990s, the proportion of U.K. company shares owned by rest of the world investors increased substantially from 3.6 percent in 1981 to around 13 percent during the period 1989–92 and rose again to 16.3 percent in 1993 and 1994.

In 2008 investors from outside the U.K. owned 41.5 percent of U.K. shares listed on the U.K. Stock Exchange. Within the foreign investor category, 34 percent had their beneficial owner in Europe, with North American beneficial holdings at 30 percent. The proportion of shares held by individuals has been on a downward trend since 1963 when individuals owned 54 percent of quoted shares. Although the trend was flat at around 20 percent between 1989 and 1994, the proportion of holdings has continued to fall to 10.2 percent today.

Table 21.3 *Ownership structure of London firms 1990–2008*

	1990	1995	2000	2002	2004	2006	2008
Total foreign investors	11.8	16.3	35.7	35.9	36.3	40	41.5
Total domestic investors	88.2	83.7	64.3	64.1	63.6	60	58.5
Private financial enterprises	61.2	60.2	45.4	47.8	47.7	44.4	43.4
Collective investment	60.5	59.8	44	45.7	45	41	39.9
Insurance & pension funds	52.1	49.7	38.8	35.5	32.9	27.4	26.2
Investment companies	2.3	3.3	4.1	9	10.7	12	11.9
Mutual funds	6.1	6.8	1.1	1.2	1.4	1.6	1.8
Banks & savings banks	0.7	0.4	1.4	2.1	2.7	3.4	3.5
Private non-financial companies	4.7	2.4	2.9	1.9	1.7	2.7	3
Individual investors/ households	20.3	20.3	16	14.3	14.1	12.8	11
Public sector	2	0.8	0	0.1	0.1	0.1	1.1
Total	100%	100%	100%	100%	99.9%	100%	100%

Source: United Kingdom Office for National Statistics

Table 21.4 provides a breakdown of ownership by industry and helps to underscore how the financial crisis of 2008 led to unprecedented government intervention and public sector ownership in the U.K. financial industry. The initial recapitalization of the Royal Bank of Scotland Group plc (RBS) in November 2008 included an injection of £15 billion ($24.3 billion) in return for acquiring an approximate 58 percent ownership stake in the company. The dispersion of ownership in the U.K. has also been demonstrated in a number of studies. For example, Franks and Mayer (1997) found that just 16 percent of U.K. firms had a single shareholder owning 25 percent or more of the equity, compared with 79 percent in France and 95 percent in Germany. Using 20 percent ownership as a cut-off point, La Porta, Lopez-de-Silanes and Shleifer (1999) found that 100 percent of the largest twenty U.K. corporations based on market capitalization are widely held. Likewise, Faccio and Lang (2002) found that in 63 percent of U.K. firms there were no controlling owners with 20 percent ownership equity.

Table 21.4 *Beneficial ownership of companies by industry: 2008*

	Financial companies	Non-manufacturing companies	Manufacturing companies	Total
Insurance companies	21.9	49.7	28.3	100
Pension funds	24.1	44.2	31.7	100
Individuals	25	61.9	13.1	100
Unit trusts	24.9	37.6	37.6	100
Investment trusts	29.9	29.9	40.3	100
Other financial institutions	29.1	38	32.8	100
Charities, churches	19.5	63.2	17.2	100
Private non-financial companies	1.7	70.6	27.7	100
Public sector	93.1	5.4	1.5	100
Banks	20.7	53.2	26.1	100

Source: United Kingdom Office for National Statistics

IPO activity between 2006 and 2008

The regulation of IPOs

IPO firms in the U.K. can choose to list on the Main Market as ordinary common share issues, or as a Depositary Receipt (DR). There are different requirements for each listing type (see Table 21.5 for an overview). Firms that choose to list ordinary common shares must first be admitted to the U.K. Listing Authority (UKLA), an arm of the Financial Services Authority (FSA), and then be admitted to trading by the LSE. The main requirement for firms with ordinary common share issues on the Main Market is to file financial information prepared in accordance with U.K. or U.S. GAAP or International Accounting Standards (IAS).

Interestingly, the provisions of the UKLA's listing rules that seek to protect minority investors do not apply to foreign firms raising capital in the U.K. (Coffee, 2007). The Code applies only to companies incorporated in the U.K., meaning that firms incorporated outside of the U.K. are not required to comply nor are these firms required to explain why they have chosen not to comply. The listing requirements

Table 21.5 *Listing criteria for AIM and Main Market*

	Main Market	AIM
General listing requirements	• Minimum market capitalization • Normally three-year trading record required • Minimum 25% shares in public hands • Prior shareholder approval for substantial acquisitions and disposals • Pre-vetting of prospectus by the UKLA	• No minimum market capitalization • No trading record requirement • No prescribed level of shares to be in public hands • No prior shareholder approval for most transactions • Nominated adviser required at all times • Admission documents not pre-vetted by the UKLA
Corporate governance	• Combined Code – "comply or explain" principle • Combined Code recommends a majority of independent non-executive directors • Independent non-executive chairman • Separate audit, nomination, and remuneration committees	• Combined Code does not apply; however, firms are recommended to at least shadow requirements • 70% of AIM companies comply with Code
Tax benefits	• No tax benefits	• AIM investors are exempt from capital gains tax
Ongoing requirements	• Information on annual accounts and any price-sensitive news • Financial statements must be prepared in accordance with the applicant's national law • IAS Accounting Standards	• Information on annual accounts and any price-sensitive news • Financial statements must be prepared in accordance with the applicant's national law or IAS Accounting Standards

Source: London Stock Exchange

for firms raising capital via DRs are less demanding than those for ordinary listings in that financial information need not be prepared in accordance with IAS or U.K. or U.S. GAAP.

Firms listing in London can also choose to list on the AIM exchange and take advantage of the minimal listing requirements. For instance, admission documents are not pre-vetted by the UKLA, there is no minimum market capitalization, and there is no minimum public float requirement. AIM rules impose a "general duty of disclosure requiring information which it (the issuer) reasonably considers necessary to enable investors to form a full understanding of the financial position of the applicant". Importantly, a substantive component of an AIM listing is that firms secure a nominated adviser ("Nomad"). Nomads, which are normally lower and medium-tier investment banks, serve as gatekeepers, advisers, and regulators of AIM-listed companies. Nomads serve a gatekeeper role in that they are responsible to AIM to decide whether an issuer is suitable for admission. Alternatively, Nomads act as an adviser providing assistance and guidance to the issuer through the flotation process, as well as after flotation, to ensure that it complies with AIM rules. Because Nomads play such a critical role in the AIM regulatory framework, the LSE monitors their performance. The LSE does take disciplinary action against a Nomad when it breaches its responsibilities under the eligibility criteria, fails to act with due care and skill, or has impaired the reputation and integrity of AIM. For example, the Nomad Blue Oar was recently subject to disciplinary action for failing to act with due care and skill and for impairing the reputation and integrity of AIM through its conduct or judgment (London Stock Exchange AIM Disciplinary Notice, June 2009).

The IPOs between 2006 and 2009

Table 21.6 provides a breakdown of a sample of U.K. firms that made their capital market debut on either the Main Market or the AIM exchanges between 2006 and 2009. For comparison purposes we include only new issues of common shares and exclude issues of Depositary Receipts. Overall, the most active U.K. industries for new issues are the financial industry, industrials, and consumer services. Origo Sino-India, Cenkos Securities, B.P.Marsh and Partners, and Clarkson Hill Group are just a few U.K. financial firms that made

Table 21.6 *IPO year and industry classification*

Industry	2006	2007	2008	Total
Basic materials	20	11	4	35
Consumer goods	3	3	0	6
Consumer services	22	15	1	38
Financials	50	28	2	80
Healthcare	7	3	0	10
Industrials	20	20	1	41
Information technology	10	0	0	10
Oil and gas	7	8	3	18
Technology	0	3	0	3
Telecommunication	2	0	0	2
Total	141	91	11	243

Source: London Stock Exchange

IPOs in 2006. Likewise West China Cement, Northern Bear, and May Gurney Integrated Services are IPOs in the industrials industry. Finally, Debenhams, UTV Motion Pictures, DQ Entertainment, and Boomerang Plus are consumer firms that went public between 2006 and 2009. As Table 21.6 reveals, however, there has been a significant reduction in 2008 in domestic IPOs in London. Most were oil and gas firms such as Cadogan Pet and EnegiOil.

IPO size and performance between 2006 and 2009

Between 2006 and 2009 there was also considerable variance in the size and performance of IPOs (see Table 21.7). In terms of employee numbers, the largest firms were Eurasian Natural Resources Corp., Qinetiq Group, and Ferrexpo. Similarly, Eurasian Natural Resources Corp. (ENRC) led in terms of revenue size prior to IPO. ENRC is a U.K. incorporated natural resources firm with integrated mining, processing, energy, logistical, and marketing operations. The majority of the Group's assets were acquired in the privatization process undertaken in Kazakhstan in the mid 1990s. Another large firm in terms of assets was Japan Leisure Hotels, a Japanese leisure hotel chain incorporated in the U.K. Interestingly, over thirty firms went public during this period without any assets on their balance sheet. The previously identified firms, along with Fresnillo, were the most profitable firms in

Table 21.7 *IPO issuer size and performance ($000)*

		Company size and performance				
	Employees	Revenues	Assets	Debt	Earnings before taxes	Net profit
Min	1	$0	$6	−$714	−$6,934	−$30,398
1st quartile	15	$0	$1,930	$137	−$44	−$258
2nd quartile	46	$1,286	$8,692	$2,266	$0	$0
3rd quartile	159	$17,849	$35,988	$14,277	$2,429	$1,345
Max	11,400	$3,256,000	$7,644,000	$7,044,000	$997,000	$686,000
Average	439.2	$77,907	$169,126	$87,080	$12,617	$9,435

Table 21.8 *IPO prices and performance*

	Offer price	Closing price	Shares issued	Underpricing	Proceeds (in $000s)
Min	0.02	0.02	520,000	−57.4	231
1st quartile	0.48	0.60	7,667,056	2.9	7,061
2nd quartile	1.64	1.78	20,219,400	9.2	21,089
3rd quartile	2.41	2.78	58,754,407	17.1	93,936
Max	14.36	14.69	1,068,421,053	400.0	3,022,425
Average	1.95	2.12	55,134,301	16.6	111,298

the period leading up to their IPO. There are also considerable differences in U.K. IPOs in terms of the prices and proceeds of U.K. IPOs (see Table 21.8). Offer prices of U.K. IPOs averaged $1.95. Firms with the highest offer price per share were China Real Estate Opportunities ($14.36), Valiant Petroleum ($14.25), and R.G.I. Intl ($11.40). IPO share offer size averaged 55 million shares. Firms that issued the most number of shares, and had the highest proceeds from their IPO, were Experian Group, Fresnillo, and Debenhams. Among those with the highest underpricing levels was Oxeco, a firm formed exclusively to invest in or acquire assets in technology and science sector firms. Underpricing levels (the percentage difference between the IPO offer price and first day closing price) for U.K. IPOs averaged approximately 16 percent.

Table 21.9 *IPO ownership structure (data in percent)*

	Top 1 shareholder ownership		Top 3 shareholder ownership		Board ownership	
	pre	post	pre	post	pre	post
Min	0	0	0	0	0	0
1st quartile	19	11	43	22	0	3
2nd quartile	35	20	68	38	22	14
3rd quartile	64	36	94	57	62	36
Max	100	90	100	99	100	90
Average	42	26	64	40	34	22

Table 21.9 outlines a number of interesting ownership characteristics of U.K. IPOs. First, the largest owners of IPO firms owned on average a 42 percent stake prior to IPO, and on average 26 percent after IPO. On average the top three shareholders owned on average 64 percent of the firm prior to issue and on average 40 percent of the firm once the firm went public. The board of Plant Offshore, an energy holding company, retained 90 percent of the firm immediately after issue. There are other ownership characteristics of U.K. IPOs. For instance, the retained ownership of founders of the software firm Imaginatik is 70 percent, yet founder ownership levels average 8 percent across U.K. IPOs. Likewise, angel-retained ownership levels range as high as 79 percent (Tawa plc), yet average 4 percent. Independent directors retain quite low ownership levels (0.01 percent), while non-executive directors retain on average 4 percent. Finally, the average retained ownership level of board chairmen is 6.03 percent and company insiders retain on average 17.19 percent of outstanding shares following their IPO.

Table 21.10 reveals a number of characteristics of IPO boards. First, boards average 5.56 members. Eurasian went public with thirteen board members. While the average age of boards is fifty, they can average as high as sixty-two. On average firms go public with three non-executive directors; however, Eurasian went public with eleven non-executive directors. Interestingly, at the time of IPO, most U.K. firms do not specify whether their non-executive directors are in fact independent. Other firms are like Clarkson Hill by being transparent with prospective investors and acknowledging in their prospectus that they do not have

Table 21.10 *IPO board of directors*

	Size	Age	Exec.	Non-exec.	Indep.	Eng. & Ops.	Mark. & Sales	Fin. & Acct.
Min	1	38	0	0	0	0	0	0
1st quartile	4	48	1.9	2	0	1	0	2
2nd quartile	5	51	2	3	0	2.01	1	3
3rd quartile	7	54	3	4	1	3.99	2	4.02
Max	13	62	8	11	8	10.01	7.02	9
Average	5.56	50.93	2.43	3.07 (55%)	0.7 (11%)	2.43	1.22	3.34

an independent director and do not comply with the Combined Code at the time of admission. However, they specify that their intention is to appoint independent director(s) within the twelve months following admission. Other firms have a rather high number of independent directors on their board. For example, Eurasian went public with eight of their eleven non-executive directors identified as independent.

In terms of their expertise, most U.K. IPO boards are filled with members who have experience in finance, accounting, or law, followed by IPOs with engineering backgrounds. Also, despite the Code advising firms to separate the chair and CEO roles and designations across multiple individuals, approximately 28 percent of U.K. firms go public with one person serving as CEO and also chair (duality). A closer examination reveals that duality is most prevalent among financial and consumer services firms, and lowest among oil and gas firms. Finally, most firms go public with the governance committees the Code recommends. On average, 86 percent of firms go public with an audit firm, followed by 78 percent of firms with compensation committees. However, at the time of their IPO only 36 percent of firms have a nominating committee established.

Description of an IPO: DQ Entertainment

The firm before the IPO

DQ Entertainment was established by Tapaas Chakravarti initially as a financial and management consultancy firm before moving into animation production in 2001. In 2007, the firm began to leverage its strength in 3D animation to engage in game asset development. In December 2007 the firm went public on the AIM exchange. While incorporated in the Isle of Man, DQ Entertainment's production facilities are in Hyderabad, India. Today DQ Entertainment Ltd is a leading animation production company, with over 2,200 full-time employees. The company produces animation for films, television series, and console-based games for a number of international production houses. While animation series have historically been aimed at children, the target audiences for animation have been broadened to include teenagers and adults alike. The firm saw revenues reach $15.2 million in 2007 immediately prior to IPO.

DQ identified a number of strategic reasons for raising equity capital. First, DQ intended to expand its production facilities and workforce. Also, the firm planned investment into global intellectual property partnerships. The Group proposed to invest in the co-production of feature films, DVD productions, and television productions with European and US-based production houses to obtain larger percentages of the global, cross-platform intellectual property and distribution rights in its productions. Finally, the company planned acquisitions, strategic investments, and joint ventures with the IPO proceeds.

There were a number of interesting features associated with DQ's board. Tapaas Chakravarti founded DQ Entertainment Ltd in 2001 and served as both chairman and CEO in the period leading up to IPO. His service in both of these positions is despite Code recommendations that the roles of CEO and chair be separated. Chakravarti's experience is in sales and he has a number of ties to international educational and charitable organizations. His education is in science; however, he completed a Masters in Business Administration from BHU University. The rest of DQ's board includes four non-executive directors. However, each of these non-executives was identified as being independent. Finally, the firm has an audit, nomination, and compensation committee. Hence, DQ's governance includes aspects that are in compliance with the Code (board independence and committee structure) along with features that are not (chairman/CEO filled by the same individual).

Prior to the IPO, the ownership of DQ Entertainment was led by the chairman/CEO Tapaas Chakravarti with 28 percent while non-executive director Rusi Brij owned 4 percent. There were three others who held voting rights representing 3 percent or more of the issued share capital of the company. International Finance Corporation owned 25.7 percent and Florida Properties Limited retained 25.5 percent. Along with these owners, one angel investor owned 10.4 percent of the firm following admission.

The IPO offer

DQ Entertainment's IPO was on the AIM stock exchange and involved the placing of 19,727,961 ordinary shares of 0.1p each at 136p per share. The firm's nominated adviser and broker was Evolution Securities Limited and joint broker was E*TRADE Securities Limited. DQ paid Evolution Securities and E*TRADE a commission of approximately 3.64 percent and paid Evolution Securities a corporate finance fee of £350,000 ($568,000). The significant shareholders of the firm signed a lock-in agreement not to dispose of any ordinary shares held at admission for twelve months following the IPO.

The firm after the IPO

Following the IPO, the ownership of DQ Entertainment was led by the chairman/CEO Tapaas Chakravarti with 12.7 percent. Another director, Rusi Brij, retained 1.8 percent. Besides Chakravarti, there were three others who would hold, directly or indirectly, voting rights representing 3 percent or more of the issued share capital of the company. International Finance Corporation retained 11.6 percent ownership and Florida Properties Limited retained 11.5 percent. The firm's angel investor retained 4.7 percent of the firm following admission.

Since IPO, Tapaas Chakravarti has continued to serve as both chairman/CEO. However, the structure of the firm's board has changed and now three of the non-executive directors are identified as independent, in accordance with the Code recommendations. In addition, none of the firm's directors are members of more than ten committees or identified as chairman of more than five committees across all the companies in which they are serving as directors. In addition, the frequency of board meetings increased to nineteen following IPO. Following IPO, the size of DQ's audit committee increased from three board members to four. There were no changes in the size of the firm's nomination (2) or compensation (2) committees following IPO.

Today the company has entered its tenth year since its inception. DQ has successfully established a diverse client-partner base consisting of over 100 major producers, licensees, and distributors from Europe, the U.S., the U.K., and Asian countries, namely Walt Disney Animation Group, Nickelodeon Animation Studio Inc. USA, Electronic Arts – USA, Marvel Comics, American Greetings, NBC Universal, and BBC Group UK.

Conclusion

The U.K. "comply or explain" approach to governance allows firms the freedom to choose governance structures appropriate to their circumstances. Our review identified the numbers of non-executive directors and independent non-executive directors to be in line with Code recommendations among large, established U.K. firms. However, the number of non-executive and independent non-executive directors is quite low among firms leading up to their IPO. In addition, a review of over 240 U.K. IPOs between 2006 and 2009 identified as many as 28 percent of U.K. firms going public, with one individual serving in both the CEO and chair roles despite Code recommendations against such practice.

The divergence from Code recommendations among firms leading up to their IPO may be due in large part to the costs and benefits of governance. As firms become larger and more complex there may be a prevailing belief in the U.K. capital market context that board independence is less critical. Studies have shown that the number of non-executive directors on the board has been found to be correlated with company size, and the presence of independent non-executive directors often depends on the monitoring and advising needs of the companies (Boone, Field, Karpoff, et al., 2007). Certainly the Code allows firms the flexibility to add independent directors as they become larger, or even choose to keep the chairman/CEO roles aligned with one individual. This flexibility may help smaller firms deflect governance costs in the periods prior to IPO. However, in the absence of a formal authority that actively monitors firms who choose to diverge from Code recommendations, shareholders are left to discern for themselves whether the lack of board independence or the consolidated control of chairman/CEO is best for the IPO firm and minority shareholder interests. Indeed, this flexibility may reveal the potential dark side to "comply or explain" governance models. Their effectiveness resides in shareholders having the requisite expertise and ability to actively monitor the adequacy or appropriateness of firms explaining their deviations from Code recommendations.

References

Boone, Audra, Laura Casares Field, Jonathan Karpoff, and Charu Raheja. 2007. 'The determinants of corporate board size and composition: An empirical analysis', *Journal of Financial Economics*, 85, 1, 66–110.

Coffee, John C. 2007. 'Law and the market: The impact of enforcement', *University of Pennsylvania Law Review*, 156, 229–311.

Faccio, Mara and Larry Lang. 2002. 'The ultimate ownership of Western European corporations', *Journal of Financial Economics*, 65, 365–95.

Franks, Julian and Colin Mayer. 1997. 'Corporate ownership and control in the UK, Germany and France', in D. Chew (ed.) *Studies in International Corporate Finance and Governance Systems*. New York, Oxford University Press.

Hubbard, Glenn and John Thornton. 2006. 'Action plan for capital markets', *Wall Street Journal*, November 30, A16.

La Porta, Rafael, Florencio Lopez-de-Silanes, and Andrei Shleifer. 1999. 'Corporate ownership around the world', *Journal of Finance*, 54, 2, 471–517.

Parkinson, John and Gavin Kelly. 1999. 'The combined code on corporate governance', *Political Quarterly*, 70, 1, 101–7.

Pendleton, Andrew. 2005. 'How far does the United Kingdom have a market-based system of corporate governance? A review and evaluation of recent developments in the United Kingdom', *Competition and Change*, 9, 107–26.

22 Corporate governance and initial public offerings in the United States

KRISTA LEWELLYN AND WILLIAM JUDGE

Corporate governance mechanisms

The United States is a nation of immigrants whose most distinctive cultural feature is its highly individualistic social culture. Consequently, it is not very socially cohesive. As a former colonial member of the British Empire, the U.S. has a common law legal system which maximizes the role of the marketplace in sorting out economic affairs and constrains the role of the state. As a result of this history and collective values, the market for corporate control is relatively robust for firms that underperform their industry, and the specification of proper corporate behavior is quite formal and rule based. Information disclosure is highly specified and relatively transparent compared to other nations. As might be expected, informal corporate governance codes are completely voluntary and business groups are not a common form of corporate governance.

Corporate ownership in most firms is fragmented as it is relatively rare for any one owner to hold more than 10 percent of the firm's shares. Institutional owners are generally the dominant ownership group, but there are individual and family blockholders of some firms. Minority ownership rights are well protected by law, but shareholder activism for majority owners is highly constrained. Corporate boards are always single tier in nature and it is very common to have CEO duality whereby the CEO chairs the board. Corporate boards are composed of mostly outside, non-executive directors. Executive compensation is non-egalitarian in nature, and the CEO and top management team are often compensated with a heavy emphasis on variable compensation that is usually tied to the financial performance of the firm.

Corporate law

In the U.S. market-oriented system, which is characterized by well-developed stock markets, dispersed shareholders, and an active market for corporate control, the prevention of misconduct and abuse of investors' rights are largely constrained by a combination of economic incentives, societal norms, markets, and laws (Moerland, 1995; Thompson and Sale, 2003). The governing structure of U.S. public companies is typically made up of shareholders who own equity in the company, and a unitary or single-tier board of directors who are elected, sometimes with differing term lengths, at annual meetings required by state laws. Directors have fiduciary responsibilities, i.e., a relationship imposed by law where they have voluntarily agreed to be custodians of the shareholders' investment (Charkman and Ploix, 2005).

In common law legal systems, such as in the United States, the judiciary apply constitutional and precedent rules to cases, which subsequently influence corporate governance practices (Jacobs, 2009). Each state has its own law-creating legislative body and court system, and most regulations concerning public companies have been developed and enacted at the state level. The regulations of the state of incorporation are typically those influencing the way the company is managed and controlled. Since the early 1900s most public companies have been incorporated in the state of Delaware, with slightly more than half of the Fortune 500 companies having been incorporated there (Black, 2007). Unlike other states in the U.S., Delaware has a specialized Chancery Court which deals with corporate law cases and is seen to have corporate laws that are clear, more fully defined, and business friendly (Waisman, Wang, and Wuebker, 2009). Delaware also has relatively less restrictive anti-takeover laws compared to other states, indicating a greater likelihood for firms to be takeover targets, increasing the disciplinary effect of the market for corporate control and the possibility of positive valuation effects (Daines, 2001).

The Securities and Exchange Commission (SEC) was established in 1934 as a means of restoring confidence in the capital markets following the U.S. stock market crash of 1929, by protecting private investors and the public interests against misconduct, such as insider trading, as well as for assuring adequate disclosure of information to the investing public (Benston, 1973). The SEC explicitly states on its website that the basis for the creation of the commission is that "Companies publicly offering securities for investment dollars must tell the public the truth about their businesses, the securities they are selling, and the risks involved in investing" and "people who sell and trade securities – brokers, dealers, and exchanges – must treat investors fairly and honestly, putting investors' interests first" (U.S. Securities and Exchange Commission, 2010).

State laws tend to give corporate managers broad and flexible power to manage the internal affairs of the company and do not generally mandate board composition nor activities, while federal regulations and laws see these as key provisions for protecting investors' rights (Thompson and Sale, 2003). Historically, state corporate laws play a key role in how companies are managed and controlled and federal securities law fulfills a supporting role, as demonstrated by the U.S. Congress establishing the Private Securities Litigation Reform Act, which was designed to limit the use of federal securities laws to prevent "frivolous" class action fraud lawsuits (Thompson and Sale, 2003). However, in the past decade, federal securities law and enforcement through securities fraud class actions have become much more common as a means of regulating corporate governance along with the incidence of increasing regulation of the capital markets (Thompson and Sale, 2003). One such SEC lawsuit, asserting a company's investors were misled about the risks associated with subprime mortgage products, was recently settled in July of 2010, with Goldman Sachs agreeing to pay $550 million (New York Times, 2010).

Traditionally corporate governance has been concerned with mismanagement and the pursuit of managerial self-interests, but recent corporate scandals have placed additional focus on financial reporting, risk management, and executive compensation (Thompson and Sale, 2003). The most prominent example of recent regulations is the Sarbanes-Oxley Act (SOX) which became law in July 2002 in emergency legislation processes as a direct response to high-profile corporate scandals (Linck, Netter, and Yang, 2009). The SEC chairman at the time, William Donaldson, in a statement to the U.S. Congress, said, "the Act represents the most important securities legislation since the original federal securities laws of the 1930s" (Donaldson, 2003). More recently, in July 2010, following the global financial crisis, resulting in the most acute and longest economic downturn since the Great Depression, the U.S. President Barack Obama signed the Dodd-Frank Wall Street Reform and Consumer Protection Act. It is intended to help deal with the "too big to fail" banks, by improving transparency and accountability in the financial system, specifically by requiring that certain financial derivatives be traded in markets that come under government regulations and oversight, and with provisions designed to further increase disclosure and protect shareholders (U.S. Central Intelligence Agency, 2010).

Code of good governance

The United States was the first country to issue a code of good governance, when in 1978, following a substantial amount of merger and hostile take-over activity, the U.S. Business Roundtable published *The Role and Composition of the Board of Directors of the Large Publicly Owned Corporation*, designed to make explicit the responsibilities of directors with the goal of upgrading the quality of corporate governance in U.S. public companies (Aguilera and Cuervo-Cazurra, 2004). The SEC and both the NASDAQ and New York Stock Exchange (NYSE) along with other business associations have issued various codes since 1978. Some scholars (e.g., Aguilera and Cuervo-Cazurra, 2009) have argued that codes of good governance represent "soft regulations" as opposed to mandatory "hard laws" such as the Sarbanes-Oxley Act of 2002. However, since the intentions of codes of good governance are to provide "best practices" with respect to the structure and activities of a company's board of directors so that governance and accountability to shareholders are enhanced (Aguilera and Cuervo-Cazurra, 2004) and the Sarbanes-Oxley legislation is the primary vehicle dictating such company governance elements, it is considered in the discussion.

The SEC states the Act is intended to enhance corporate responsibility, enhance financial disclosures and combat corporate and accounting fraud (U.S. Securities and Exchange Commission, 2010). Specifically, the NYSE and NASDAQ, in accordance with the SEC regulations, stipulate that boards of directors must be comprised of a majority of independent directors, compensation and nominating/governance committees must consist entirely of independent directors, the audit committee must have a minimum of three members and, again, be entirely made up of independent directors, and each audit committee member must be financially literate, with one member being deemed an "audit committee financial expert." If the company does not have such an expert, it must explain why (Linck et al., 2009). At the same time that the Sarbanes-Oxley Act was put into effect, the NYSE and NASDAQ also adopted new listing standards not only mandating changes in governance practices but signaling that the expected behavior of boards was in need of change (Linck et al., 2009). Adherence to the code is clearly evident in the information provided in Table 22.1.

More recently in 2009, in response to the global financial crisis, the NYSE created the Commission on Corporate Governance, made up of representatives from a wide variety of companies and other institutions. Members of the Commission reviewed governance changes that have been enacted over the past ten years and concluded that "the current governance system generally works well" (NYSE, 2010a: 2), but issued a report presenting a number of guiding principles for the governance of companies. The first guiding principle deals directly with the role of the board and states: "The board's fundamental objective should be to build longterm sustainable growth in shareholder value for the corporation, and the board is accountable to shareholders for its performance in achieving this objective" (NYSE, 2010a: 3). The Commission explicitly highlighted the importance of (1) eliminating and preventing corporate policies that encourage excessive risk-taking in pursuit of short-term increases in stock price performance, (2) aligning compensation plans with long-term value creation, (3) establishing relationships with long-term oriented investors who have an understanding that long-term decisions take time to produce results, (4) increasing the diversity of boards, and (5) specifying qualifications for directors and boards, including such issues as term limits, mandatory retirement, and other personal factors relating to individual director ability (NYSE, 2010a).

As can be seen in Table 22.1, an annual review on the characteristics of boards of directors of the Standard & Poor's 500 Index companies indicates not only adherence to the Sarbanes-Oxley provisions with regard to independence requirements of boards and board committees but also some other interesting characteristics of large U.S. publicly traded firms. 65 percent of the companies had a dual leadership structure where the CEO also serves as the board chairperson, often suggested in codes of good governance to be an undesirable attribute

Table 22.1 *Board characteristics of listed U.S. companies*

Variables	Characteristics of U.S. listed companies
Sample	500 listed companies (S&P 500)
Mix between executive and non-executive directors	On average 81% of the directors are considered to be independent
Duality	65% are led by chairmen-CEOs; 13% have chairmen considered to be independent
Number of positions in governance bodies	CEOs serve on 0.8 outside boards
Nationality of members	Non-U.S. directors make up slightly less than 7% of all directors
Gender of directors	Women directors are present in 91% of companies; 16% of all directors are women
Number of meetings	8.3 meetings (8.4 in 2006); 15% of boards met 12 or more times
Executive committee	39% of companies have an executive committee and only 4% are composed entirely of independent directors
Internal control committee	100% of companies have an audit committee composed entirely of independent directors, meeting an average of 9.5 times per year; 52% of all audit committee members are identified as "financial experts"
Remuneration committee	100% of companies have a compensation committee composed entirely of independent directors, meeting an average of 6 times per year
Nomination committee	100% of companies have a nomination committee composed entirely of independent directors, meeting an average of 5 times per year
Additional committees	Finance 33%; public policy 11%; social & corporate responsibility 5%; legal/compliance 5%; science & technology 5%; environment, health & safety 5%; investment/pension 4%; risk 3%; acquisitions/corporate development 3%; strategy & planning 3%
Board evaluation	100% of the companies review the performance of the entire board annually; annual evaluation of individual directors is done by 34% of the companies

Table 22.1 (*cont.*)

Variables	Characteristics of U.S. listed companies
Compensation of board of directors	$211,179 is the all-inclusive average total compensation for non-employee directors, with equity accounting for 57%, cash fees 35%, and all other compensation at 8%

Source: Board Index 2007

(e.g., the U.K. Combined Code of Corporate Governance). Non-U.S. directors make up approximately 7 percent of all directors on the boards, and women constitute 16 percent of the directors on boards, with 91 percent of the companies having at least one woman director, supporting the calls from the 2009 NYSE Commission on Corporate Governance for the need to increase the diversity of corporate boards. All of the companies surveyed indicated the performance of the entire board is evaluated annually, though only 34 percent conduct evaluation of individual directors.

With the passage of the Dodd-Frank Wall Street Reform and Consumer Protection Act in 2010, companies will be subject to several new disclosure and communication requirements once the specific regulations are written. Some of the requirements highlighted by Mary Shapiro, the U.S. SEC Chairwoman, in an address at the National Association of Corporate Directors' Annual Corporate Governance Conference in October 2010, include the requirement for advisory say-on-pay votes at all companies at least once every three years starting at meetings on or after January 21, 2011. Shareholders will have a similar "say" on the practice of golden parachutes. Companies will be required to disclose why they choose to have a particular board leadership structure, such as combining the CEO and chair. The SEC has also been tasked with writing new regulations entailing more detailed descriptions about compensation and consultants' fees and activities, as well as requiring companies to describe in much greater detail why board candidates have been selected, i.e., what in his or her experience and skills suggests he or she will be a valuable contribution to a company's board (Shapiro, 2010).

Stock exchange and listed companies

There are approximately 16,000 publicly listed companies in the United States, trading on one of the fourteen national securities exchanges that are registered with the SEC under section 6(a) of the Securities Exchange Act of 1934. At the end of 2008, the market value of U.S. publicly traded firms was $11.7 trillion, down from $19.9 trillion in 2007 (U.S. Central Intelligence Agency, 2010).

The NASDAQ and NYSE account for the majority of equity trading occurring in the United States (Terrell, 2010). NASDAQ, founded by the National Association of Securities Dealers in 1971, was the first electronic stock market, and in 2000, NASDAQ was restructured and became a public for-profit company (Terrell, 2010). In May 2007, NASDAQ joined with OMX, the Swedish exchange operator, and in November 2007, NASDAQ OMX announced that it was acquiring the Philadelphia Stock Exchange, the oldest stock exchange in the U.S. founded in 1790 (Terrell, 2010). The NYSE was founded by twenty-four New York City stockbrokers in 1792, outside at 68 Wall Street, initially trading five securities, with the first listed company being the Bank of New York (NYSE, 2010). In April 2007, the NYSE Group, Inc. combined with Euronext N.V. to create the holding company NYSE Euronext.

The NASDAQ and NYSE have different structural elements as well as rules and listing requirements. The NASDAQ is a dealer's market, where transactions occur through a dealer, known as a market maker (Bennett and Wei, 2006). Traditionally, the NASDAQ has lower listing fees and has been perceived as the most appropriate market for high-tech and/or growth-oriented companies, whereas the NYSE is considered to be an auction market and is seen to be where more established and blue chip companies are listed, with more firms moving from the NASDAQ to the NYSE over time (Rao, Davis, and Ward, 2000). Throughout the past two decades the number of listed companies has fluctuated between the two exchanges, as seen in Table 22.2. The market capitalization of the listed firms has also fluctuated during the 2006–9 period (Table 22.3) as the U.S. economy went into and out of recession. At the end of 2010, there were 2,778 companies, 10.7 percent foreign owned, listed on the NASDAQ, with the total listings having a market capitalization of $3.9 trillion (World Federation of Exchanges, 2011). The NYSE had 2,317 listed

Table 22.2 *Number of listed companies and market value of all sales of equities on U.S. stock exchanges, 1990–2010*

	Number of companies listed			Market value
Year	American SE	NASDAQ OMX	NYSE Euronext (US)	Equities sold, all US exchanges ($B USD)
1990	859	4,132	1,774	2,154
1991	860	4,094	1,989	2,590
1992	843	4,113	1,750	3,078
1993	889	4,611	1,945	4,180
1994	824	4,902	2,128	4,502
1995	791	5,127	2,242	6,208
1996	751	5,556	2,476	8,124
1997	710	5,487	2,626	11,488
1998	711	5,068	2,670	14,903
1999	650	4,829	3,025	22,813
2000	649	4,734	2,468	35,557
2001	606	4,063	2,400	25,636
2002	571	3,649	2,366	22,658
2003	557	3,294	2,308	22,292
2004	575	3,229	2,293	27,158
2005	595	3,164	2,270	33,222
2006	592	3,133	2,280	41,796
2007	599	3,069	2,297	63,064
2008	486	3,023	1,963	78,653
2009	–	2,852	2,327	57,566
2010	–	2,778	2,317	Not available

Source: U.S. SEC, "Select SEC and Market Data," www.sec.gov

Table 22.3 *Market capitalization of U.S. stock exchanges 2006–10*

	Market capitalization (December 31st)				
Exchange	2006	2007	2008	2009	2010
American SE	283	258	–	–	–
NASDAQ	3,865	4,014	2,249	3,239	3,889
NYSE	15,421	15,651	9,209	11,838	13,394

Source: World Federation of Exchanges Annual Statistics, www.world-exchanges.org

companies, 22.4 percent foreign owned, with the market capitalization of all companies over $13.4 trillion (World Federation of
Exchanges, 2011).

These large numbers of publicly traded companies significantly
affect the U.S. economy, as taxpaying entities, employers of a large
proportion of the working population, and as a major vehicle for the
savings and pensions of citizens. The large number of publicly listed
companies along with a large number of shareholders gives rise to
extensive trading of shares on the major stock markets as evident in
Table 22.2, showing the overall market value of all sales of equities
reaching over $57 trillion at the end of 2009.

Ownership structure of listed companies

Close to half of all U.S. households, over 52 million, own equity in
public companies. There has been a steady increase during the past
twenty years, from 39 percent in 1989 to approximately 45 percent in
2009, driven in large part by the substantial growth (from 36 million
to 65 million between 1989 and 2004) of defined contribution retirement savings plans, such as 401(k) plans (Investment Company Institute, 2010). There has been a decrease from a high of 53 percent in
2001 to the current level, which has been attributed to increasing
market volatility, which has reduced many domestic investors' toler-
ance for risk (Wall Street Journal, 2009). Table 22.4 depicts the
volatility seen in U.S. stock exchanges, indicating the average annual
percent change in total stock returns, including capital gains and
dividend payments, based on the Standard & Poor's 500 index.

The ownership of U.S. public firms, based on monetary value, is
summarized in Table 22.5. Individual investors account for the largest
percentage, with the level fairly stable since 2005 despite the economic
downturn which saw U.S. stock markets drop 55 percent between
October 2007 and March 2009 (Wall Street Journal, 2009). Ownership by institutional investors (life insurance companies, pension
funds, mutual funds, and ETFs) has also remained fairly stable,
ranging from owning 35 percent in 2000 to 38.8 percent in 2009,
with the highest level occurring in 2007 at 40.6 percent. Likewise,
state and local government pension funds have also shown stability
over the past decade in their level of ownership. The percentage of
U.S. listed firms owned by foreign investors has grown steadily since

Table 22.4 *Total returns of U.S. stocks 1980–2009 (average annual percent change based on Standard & Poor's 500 index)*

Period	Capital gains	Dividends and reinvestment	Total return after inflation
1980–1989	12.59	4.40	11.85
1990–1999	15.31	2.51	14.85
2000–2006	−0.49	1.63	−1.10
2000–2008	−5.40	1.58	−6.68
2002	−23.37	1.65	−23.91
2003	26.38	1.82	26.31
2004	8.99	1.73	7.38
2005	3.00	1.85	1.45
2006	13.62	1.91	11.97
2007	3.53	1.89	1.35
2008	−38.49	1.88	−37.10
2009	23.45	2.44	23.11

Source: U.S. Census Bureau, Statistical Abstract of the United States: 2011

2000, to 12 percent at the end of 2009. At the end of 2009, Europeans made up the greatest proportion, accounting for just over half. Investors from the United Kingdom, Cayman Islands, and Canada accounted for 40 percent of all foreign holdings.

The financial crisis of 2008 led to unprecedented federal government intervention, with the enactment of the Troubled Asset Relief Program (TARP) in October 2008, designed to help stabilize financial markets with the government using part of the funds to buy equity in several U.S. banks and in General Motors. The U.S. Treasury, in May 2010, reported to the U.S. Congress that $383.52 billion had been paid out to specific institutions and $194 billion had been paid back (Hughes, 2010).

Corporate governance and IPOs

The regulation of IPOs

Making the transition from a private to a public company in the United States requires meeting both SEC rules and a variety of requirements put forth by the stock exchange where the securities will be traded. Table 22.6 provides an overview of the standards that must

Table 22.5 *Equity ownership structure of U.S. publicly listed firms 2000–9 (in billions of U.S. dollars as of December 31; minus sign indicates net sales)*

Type of investor	Holdings										Net purchases				
	2000		2005		2007		2008		2009		2000	2005	2007	2008	2009
Individual investors/households	8,205	46.7%	7,993	38.7%	9,465	37.0%	5,881	37.3%	7,698	37.6%	−637.5	−409.9	−795.1	28.2	126.9
Life insurance companies	892	5.1%	1,162	5.6%	1,465	5.7%	1,002	6.3%	1,142	5.6%	111.3	65.9	84.1	81.8	21.1
Private pension funds	1,971	11.2%	2,542	12.3%	2,863	11.2%	1,665	10.5%	1,946	9.5%	62.8	−4.6	−217.0	−256.7	−159.0
State and local govt. retirement funds	1,299	7.4%	1,716	8.3%	1,986	7.8%	1,212	7.7%	1,526	7.5%	11.6	−5.6	−35.3	−6.7	−8.2
Mutual funds	3,227	18.4%	4,176	20.2%	5,477	21.4%	3,014	19.1%	4,172	20.4%	193.1	129.6	91.3	−38.1	85.5
Exchange-traded funds	66	0.4%	286	1.4%	574	2.2%	474	2.2%	670	3.3%	42.4	50.0	137.2	154.2	70.5
Foreign investors	1,422	8.1%	2,039	9.9%	2,812	11.0%	1,776	11.3%	2,455	12.0%	199.7	56.9	218.5	91.2	122.8
Total*	17,571		20,636		25,577		15,785		20,451		5.6	−76.6	−460.5	308.9	327.0

Source: U.S. Census Bureau, Statistical Abstract of the United States: 2011
*Total includes other types not shown separately.

Table 22.6 *Listing and ongoing requirements in the U.S.*

Initial Listing Criteria for NASDAQ Global, Global Select, and NYSE stock exchanges

	NASDAQ Global	NASDAQ Global Select	NYSE
Financial and Qualitative	$4 stock price & 1,100,000 publicly held AND one of the following: (a) income from continuing operations = $1 million in latest fiscal year, shareholders equity = $15 million, market value of publicly held shares = $8 million OR (b) shareholders equity = $30 million, market value of publicly held shares = $18 million, 2 year operating history OR (c) market value of listed securities = $75 million, market value of publicly held shares = $20 million OR	$4 stock price, 1,250,000 publicly held shares & market value of shares of at least $45 million AND one of the following: (a) pre-tax earnings > $11 million total for past 3 years along with each of the two most recent fiscal years > $2.2 million and each of the prior three fiscal years > $0 OR (b) total cash flow in prior three fiscal years > $27.5 million and each of the prior three fiscal years > $0 and revenues in previous fiscal year > $110 million and previous year's average market capitalization > $550 million OR	$4 stock price, 1,100,000 publicly held shares and outstanding market value of public shares = $40 million AND one of the following: (a) total pre-tax income the last 3 years = $10 million with a minimum of $2 million in the two most recent years OR (b) total pre-tax income for last 3 years = $12 million with minimum in the most recent year = $5 million and minimum in the next most recent year = $2 million OR (c) market capitalization = $500 million, revenues (most recent 12-month period) = $100 million, total adjusted cash flow for past 3 years = $25 million OR (d) market capitalization = $750 million, revenues (most recent fiscal year) = $75 million

	(d) Total assets and revenues each = $75 million, market value of publicly held shares = $20 million	(c) revenues in previous fiscal year > $90 million and previous year's average market capitalization > $850 million OR (d) market capitalization = $160 million and total assets of $80 million in the past fiscal year and stockholders equity = $55 million	OR market capitalization = $150 million, total assets = $75 million, stockholders' equity = $50 million
Corporate Governance	Companies listed on and seeking to list on NASDAQ must meet the requirements outlined in the Rule 5600 Series. These include: A majority of the board of directors must be comprised of independent directors. An audit committee of at least three members, each of whom must be independent. At least one member of the audit committee who has past employment experience in finance or accounting, requisite professional certification in accounting, or any other comparable experience or background which results in the individual's financial sophistication.		Companies listed on and seeking to list on the NYSE must comply with code 303A. These include: A majority of the board of directors must be comprised of independent directors. A nominating/corporate governance committee composed entirely of independent directors. Listed companies must adopt and disclose corporate governance guidelines that address: director qualification and responsibility standards, director compensation, director orientation and continuing education,

Table 22.6 (*cont.*)

Initial Listing Criteria for NASDAQ Global, Global Select, and NYSE stock exchanges

NASDAQ Global	NASDAQ Global Select	NYSE
	Director nominees must either be selected, or recommended for selection, either by: (A) independent directors constituting a majority of the board's independent directors or (B) a nomination committee comprised solely of independent directors. Compensation of the CEO must be determined, or recommended to the board for determination, either by: (A) independent directors constituting a majority of the board's independent directors or (B) a compensation committee comprised solely of independent directors. IPO companies are allowed to phase in independence requirements according to a specified schedule within the first year of listing. Each company shall adopt a code of conduct applicable to all directors, officers, and employees, which shall be publicly available. A code of conduct satisfying this rule must comply with the definition of a "code of ethics" set out in Section 406(c) of the Sarbanes-Oxley Act of 2002. Additionally there are rules concerning shareholder meetings, including proxy solicitation and quorum; review of related party transactions; and shareholder approval, including voting rights.	succession planning, annual performance evaluation of the board, website posting of corporate governance guidelines, and disclosure in annual proxy statement or in Form 10-K that corporate governance guidelines are available on the company website.

Sources: NASDAQ Listing Criteria, 2010a, NYSE Listing Criteria, 2010b, NASDAQ Series 5600 Rules, 2010b, and NYSE Corporate Governance Code, 2010c, section 303A

be met in order to list on the two largest primary stock markets in the United States, the NASDAQ and the NYSE.

The IPO process in the United States is complex and governed by the 1933 Securities Act, which divides the process into three periods, the *pre-filing period*, the *waiting period*, and the *post-effective period* (Jenkinson, Morrison, and Wilhelm, 2006). The pre-filing period, while not specifically defined in the regulation, is subject to important legal considerations that must be adhered to, specifically avoidance of "gun-jumping," which has been broadly interpreted by the SEC as not only expressing offers to sell securities but also any publicity (e.g., press releases, analyst reports, corporate communiqués) that may arouse public interest in a proposed offering (Jenkinson et al., 2006). The period is generally considered to occur once the services of an underwriter are secured (Jenkinson et al., 2006). The process of hiring a lead underwriter typically begins with what is often referred to as a "beauty contest" whereby the company that wishes to go public meets with investment banks that are interested in coordinating the offering to discuss price ranges for the stock as well as future market-making (Barondes, Nyce, and Sanger, 2007).

These meetings will lead to selecting one or more investment banks to serve as the lead underwriter(s) of the IPO. The lead underwriter will manage and coordinate the IPO process for the company. Following selection, the lead underwriter prepares a letter of intent, which is a document outlining the underwriters' compensation schedule, referred to as the gross spread or underwriting discount, arrangement of the 15 percent over-allotment option (i.e., additional shares to be sold to the public at the request of the investment bank), and an agreement to cooperate in due diligence efforts (Dalton, Certo, and Daily, 2003).

The initial service the underwriters provide during the IPO process is to draft the SEC-required S-1 registration statement, which serves as a preliminary or provisional prospectus, also referred to as the "Red Herring" (Dalton et al., 2003). Development of the prospectus involves not only the underwriters but also company accountants and lawyers, all of whom conduct a due diligence review of the IPO company in order to provide accurate and reliable information to potential investors about the company. The prospectus provides historical financial data, information about the company's board of directors and executives, as well as descriptions of markets, competitors, and strategy. The preliminary prospectus usually includes an estimate of the stock's selling price, often given as a range, but as the underwriters acquire additional information, the estimate may change (Barondes et al., 2007).

Once the registration statement has been filed with the SEC, the second stage of the IPO process, the *waiting period*, commences. It is governed by the 1971 SEC regulation 5180, enacted to prevent the issuing of forecasts, or predictions related to revenues and earnings per share, or publication of "opinions concerning values" (Bradley, Jordan, and Ritter, 2003, p. 5). According to Bradley et al. (2003), this quiet period is intended to give investors time to evaluate the fair value of a company's underlying assets without being unduly influenced by insiders. Also, during this time, the SEC, the National Association of Securities Dealers (NASD), and other relevant state securities organizations review the document for any omissions or issues. If the agencies do find problems with the prospectus, the company and the underwriting team will have to make corrections with amended filings (Baronades et al., 2007).

Twenty days after the filing of the preliminary prospectus, it becomes the official prospectus and the SEC has another twenty days to review the official prospectus (Ellis, Michaely, and O'Hara, 1999). Once the prospectus is official, the marketing and bookbuilding takes place, in what is referred to as the *road show* (Dalton et al., 2003). The road show, typically lasting three to four weeks, consists of the IPO company managers making presentations around the country to potential investors to solicit and gauge interest in the shares of the offering (Ellis et al., 1999).

Once the prospectus is effective, approved, and issued to potential investors, the offering is said to be in the post-effective period, with the underwriter and the IPO finalizing the offer price and number of shares to be sold (Jenkinson et al., 2006). The formal underwriting agreement and final prospectus are prepared and the actual selling of the IPO company's shares begins (Dalton et al., 2003).

The underwriter and the IPO firm normally agree on a lockup period, stipulating that any shares held by executive officers, directors, employees, and affiliated parties after the offering will not be sold until 180 days after the registration statement becomes effective. Similar to that of the quiet period, the rationale for the lockup period is that it allows market forces to determine the appropriate value for the security without interference from market analysts or corporate insiders (Ellis et al., 1999).

IPO market between 2006 and 2008

During the period 2006–8, the number of offerings on U.S. exchanges by domestic issuers totaled 340 (Wilmer Cutler Pickering Hale and

Table 22.7 *IPO year and industry classification in the U.S.*

Industry	2006	2007	2008	Total
Basic materials	4	2	2	8
Consumer goods	4	2	0	6
Consumer services	15	8	2	25
Financials	14	4	1	19
Healthcare	26	30	4	60
Industrials	17	12	5	34
Oil and gas	6	9	2	17
Technology	21	32	3	56
Telecommunications	2	1	0	3
Total	109	100	19	228

Dorr, 2008), with most of the companies going public in 2006 (163 companies) and 2007 (149 companies), with a dramatic decrease in 2008 (28 companies) when the financial crisis hit the global economy.

Table 22.7 categorizes by industry the sample of U.S. firms used in this study that had an offering on the NASDAQ or NYSE during the 2006–8 time period. From 2006 to 2008, the most active industries for IPOs were healthcare, technology, and industrials. Healthcare and technology companies that went public had a median age of seven years, compared to thirteen years for industrial companies. For the overall sample, the median time for a company to go public was eight years.

The companies going public between 2006 and 2008 varied considerably in size and operating performance. The smallest company in the sample, in terms of employees, is Catalyst Pharmaceuticals Partners, a specialty pharmaceutical company developing prescription drugs to treat a variety of addictive disorders. At the time of the IPO (November 8, 2006), the company had five employees, zero revenues, and an accumulated deficit of $1.8 million. At the other end of the spectrum is Science Applications International Corporation (SAIC), a provider of scientific, engineering, and technical services to the U.S. military and government agencies, with 43,100 employees on its IPO date (October 13, 2006). It represented one of the largest IPOs of 2006, raising $1.2 billion after selling 75 million shares of common stock, which represented about a 19 percent stake in the company.

Table 22.8 *IPO size and performance in the U.S. market*

	Size			Performance		
	Employees	Revenues	Assets	ROA	ROE	ROS
Minimum	5	0	789,000	−365%	−758%	−359%
1st quartile	105	25,136,000	30,039,000	−24.0%	−9.46%	−10.0%
2nd quartile	277	66,748,000	81,755,000	−0.20%	8.14%	0.50%
3rd quartile	816	243,597,000	337,640,000	6.90%	34.9%	7.75%
Maximum	57,000	10,146,000,000	27,069,266,000	77.60%	727%	213%
Average	1,720	338,020,000	515,131,000	17.31%	0.49%	11.4%

SAIC reported prior year revenues of $7.8 billion and earnings before interest and taxes of $497 million in its filed IPO prospectus. In terms of assets, VISA, going public in 2008, reported the greatest total assets at just over $27 billion.

As shown in Table 22.8, on average the companies in the sample had 1,720 employees and reported return-on-assets of 17.3 percent in the year prior to going public. Median values are lower at 277 employees and −0.2 percent return-on-assets. Seventeen companies reported zero revenues in the year prior to the IPO offering, with thirteen of those being pharmaceutical or bio-tech companies.

With respect to ownership structure of the 2006–8 IPO companies, 104 (46 percent) had some level of family ownership prior to and following the IPO. On average, family ownership was 11.6 percent prior to the offering and 8.6 percent following. Eight of the companies had bank ownership prior to and following the offerings. None of the companies in the sample had government ownership before or after the IPO. Venture capital firms are the category with the greatest ownership pre- and post-IPO, with ownership stakes in 187 (82 percent) of the companies prior to the IPO and in 185 (81 percent) following the offering. Their average pre-IPO ownership was 29.7 percent and post-IPO ownership was 20.6 percent. Business angels were shareholders of record in only five of the companies, pre- and post-IPO.

As shown in Table 22.9, on average, the largest shareholder of a company that goes public owns 42.1 percent prior to the offering and 29 percent following. The top three shareholders on average own 67 percent of the shares pre-IPO and 47.4 percent post-IPO.

As shown in Table 22.10, boards of directors of IPO companies have on average 7.4 directors: 1.5 executive directors and 5.9 non-executive

Table 22.9 *IPO ownership structure in the U.S. market (data in percent)*

	Family		Bank		Government		Venture capital		Angels		Top 1 shareholder		Top 3 shareholders	
	pre	post	pre	post	pre	post	pre	post	pre	post	pre	post	pre	post
Minimum	0	0	0	0	0	0	0	0	0	0	4.2	0	11.8	0
1st quartile	0	0	0	0	0	0	11.6	8.6	0	0	22.6	16.5	51.3	36.48
2nd quartile	0	0	0	0	0	0	23.8	17.5	0	0	32.7	24.1	64.2	46.5
3rd quartile	13.4	9.5	0	0	0.0	0.0	39.5	28.6	0	0	55.7	36.7	90.0	57.3
Maximum	100	90	50.4	34.9	0.0	0.0	100	79.9	11.6	8.3	100	96.5	100	96.5
Average	11.6	8.4	0.97	0.5	0.0	0.0	29.7	20.6	0.19	0.14	42.1	29.0	67.0	47.4

Table 22.10 *IPO board of directors in the U.S. market*

	Board size	Executive directors	Non-executive directors	Indepen-dent directors	Engineering, operations, R&D	Marketing, sales	Finance, accounting, law
Minimum	4.0	0	1.0	0	0	0	0
1st quartile	6.0	1.0	5.0	0.8	1.7	0	2.7
2nd quartile	7.0	1.0	6.0	3.5	3.0	0	4.0
3rd quartile	8.0	2.0	7.0	5.2	4.0	1	5.0
Maximum	18.0	8.0	16.0	12.7	12.7	5.6	12.9
Average	7.4	1.5	5.9	3.4	3.1	0.5	3.9

directors, with 3.4 of those meeting the standards for being independent. As discussed in Table 22.6, IPO companies are allowed to phase in director independence requirements according to a specified schedule within the first year of listing. The directors of the IPO companies were on average 52.8 years of age and had served on the boards for an average of 3.8 years.

Thirty-one percent of the IPO companies have at least one woman director. Just about half of the companies (49.6 percent) have CEOs who also serve as chairs of the board of directors. In terms of functional background, most (on average 3.9) IPO directors have functional backgrounds in peripheral areas, such as finance, accounting, and law, closely followed by those (on average 3.1) with a background in throughput functions, such as engineering, operations, and research and development. Less than one director with a background in output functions (e.g., marketing or sales) are present on the IPO boards in this study. In line with the listing requirements of the NASDAQ and NYSE exchanges, all of the IPOs have audit committees and almost all have remuneration committees (97 percent) and nomination committees (89 percent). Companies without remuneration and/or nomination committees do state in their SEC filing documents their intention of establishing such committees following the offering of their shares to the public.

Description of an IPO: TomoTherapy Inc.

The firm before the IPO

TomoTherapy Incorporated is a medical instrument company that develops, markets, and sells advanced radiation therapy systems that are used to treat various forms of cancer. The company was founded by Dr. Thomas Rockwell Mackie and Paul J. Reckwerdt, who, along with a research team at the University of Wisconsin, funded by the Wisconsin Alumni Research Foundation (WARF), had been working throughout the 1990s on conceptual research and development of helical tomotherapy (Mackie, 2006). Helical tomotherapy was designed to kill cancer cells by precisely delivering radiation with sub-millimeter accuracy while reducing radiation exposure to surrounding healthy tissue (Mackie, 2006).

Additional funding, both federal and industrial, was challenging early on, but research support was obtained from General Electric Medical Systems (GEMS) in 1994 and continued until 1997, at which time GEMS sold its radiotherapy business, leaving a major funding gap for the tomotherapy project. The previous year (1996), Mackie and Reckwerdt had merged their treatment planning company, Geometrics, with ADAC and had capital ($150,000) available to start a company that could continue development of the clinical prototype as well as begin the process of commercialization. In the late fall of 1997, after successfully negotiating with the WARF to obtain exclusive rights to the technology, TomoTherapy Inc. was incorporated in the state of Wisconsin (Mackie, 2006; WisBusiness, 2008). TomoTherapy was one of only 6 percent of the 2007 IPO companies that were incorporated outside the state of Delaware (Wilmer Cutler Pickering Hale and Dorr, 2008).

Developmental work during the eighteen months from the end of 1997 to the summer of 1999 was funded primarily by the University of Wisconsin Comprehensive Cancer Center and the Departments of Medical Physics and Human Oncology, as finding capital for the company, during this "dot com bubble" period, was proving difficult. In 1999 two venture capital firms (Venture Investors of Wisconsin and Avalon Technology in California) came on board and, with their investment, TomoTherapy Inc. began the transition from a research-based group to a business-like company, with Mackie becoming the chairman of the board and Reckwerdt serving as chief executive officer (CEO) (Mackie, 2006). Reckwerdt would continue in this capacity until September 2000, when John Barni, a former CT executive from Marconi Medical, was hired to lead the company, followed by Frederick Robertson in 2005.

The prototype was completed in 2000 and the first tomotherapy patient, a dog, was treated in late 2001 (Mackie, 2006). The U.S. Food and Drug Administration (FDA) approved marketing of the helical tomotherapy system on January 29, 2002, and the first human patient was treated in the summer of 2002 with the first sales to major cancer centers in the U.S. and Canada (Mackie, 2006). By the end of 2006, the year prior to the IPO, seventy-five helical tomotherapy systems were in clinical use in North America, Europe, and Asia and revenues had grown to $156.1 million, representing growth of 106 percent from the previous year (TomoTherapy SEC Prospectus, 2007).

The principal shareholders of the company at the time of the IPO were the same entities that had provided funding for expanding manufacturing, customer service capabilities, and support infrastructure since the founding of the company and through five rounds of venture capital, culminating in a total of $79 million: Venture Investors (17.3 percent), Avalon Technology (12.9 percent), the Endeavors Group (12.6 percent), Open Prairie Ventures (6.1 percent), Ascension Health Ventures (5.5 percent), and WARF (5.2 percent) (Hamilton, 2007; TomoTherapy SEC Prospectus, 2007). All seven of the non-employee directors were initially appointed to the board of directors according to an investment agreement, which terminated upon the closing of the offering. Of the three remaining directors, co-founders Mackie (also the board chairman) and Reckwerdt (the company president) each owned 6.4 percent of the shares and the CEO, Robertson, owned 2.2 percent. Under the NASDAQ Global Market rules, all of the directors except for the chairman (Mackie), president (Reckwerdt), and CEO (Robertson) were considered to be independent. The board had three committees: the audit committee, the compensation committee, and the nominating and corporate governance committee.

According to the prospectus (form 424B4) filed with the SEC on May 5, 2007, the intended use of the net proceeds from the IPO would be to finance expansion of marketing and selling efforts, to increase research and development programs, to expand international service, for working capital, and for possible acquisitions or investments in complementary businesses, products, or technologies.

The offer for this IPO

Approximately a month before the IPO, in April 2007, TomoTherapy Inc. set its planned offering on the NASDAQ National Market at

10.9 million shares with an estimated $15 to $17 selling price per share (Reuters, 2007). On May 8, 2007, the day before the IPO, the underwriters (Merrill Lynch & Co., Piper Jaffray, Thomas Weisel Partners LLC, Robert W. Baird & Co., and William Blair & Co.) announced the IPO size was increased to 11.7 million shares and that shares were priced at $19 per share in filings with the U.S. Securities and Exchange Commission (Reuters, 2007). In a press release that same day, the company announced it expected to receive net proceeds from the offering of approximately $185 million.

The opening day price of TomoTherapy was $24 a share, with an early high of $24.73. The first day closing price was $22.67. The gross proceeds to the company were $201.5 million. The underwriters were paid a commission of $14.1 million and incurred additional offering expenses of approximately $2.7 million. After deducting the underwriters' commission and the offering expenses, the net proceeds were approximately $184.7 million. In addition, 2,901,973 shares were sold by selling shareholders, 1,761,513 of which were purchased by the underwriters' exercise of their over-allotment option.

The firm after the IPO

Through December 31, 2009, $82.9 million of the net proceeds from the IPO had been used for working capital ($59.4), to purchase property and equipment ($16.0), to purchase test systems ($5.7), to acquire Chengdu Twin Peak Accelerator Technology Inc., a Chinese firm supplying a critical component ($1.5), and repayment of debt ($0.3) (TomoTherapy Inc., 10K form).

Following the IPO, the three non-independent directors owned approximately one-fifth less of the firm, going from a total of 15 percent to 12 percent ownership. The most recently filed proxy statement (March 22, 2010) indicates the largest shareholder is Janus Capital Management LLC at 6.0 percent, with Frederick Robertson (CEO) the next largest shareholder at 3.6 percent, followed by chairman T. Rockwell Mackie at 3.3 percent. This proxy statement also indicates that seven of the pre-IPO directors remain on the board.

TomoTherapy's 2007 revenues grew 37 percent over 2006 to reach $214 million, but dropped 18 percent and 31 percent the next two years to $120 million for 2009. The stock price three years after the IPO had dropped 84 percent to $3.69 per share compared to a 17 percent decrease for the S&P Healthcare index over the same period (May 9, 2007 to May 10, 2010). Since the IPO, approximately 200 additional helical tomotherapy systems have been purchased and installed around the world.

Conclusion

In the U.S. over 600 billion public company shares are voted at more than 13,000 annual shareholder meetings (Shapiro, 2010). The crucial role public companies play in the U.S. economy, as employers, as taxpayers, and as vehicles for savings and investments, underscores the attention paid by the public and government to matters of corporate governance. While IPO activity dramatically decreased during the global financial crisis, 2010 saw approximately 160 IPOs on the NASDAQ and NYSE. Due to the listing requirements of both exchanges, in general the IPO companies have similar corporate governance practices to well-established publicly listed companies, having boards with a majority of independent directors and independent board committees. The IPO firms did have lower incidences of dual leadership structures and in general exhibited much less diversity in their board members. With the passage of the Dodd-Frank legislation in 2010, which further increased disclosure requirements for publicly listed companies, the structuring and administering of corporate governance continues to be a dynamic and important part of engaging in public enterprise, whether as a long-established company or as one that is offering public investors the opportunity to buy equity for the first time. The U.S. stock exchanges will continue to be a top choice for companies wishing to go public and raise capital for growing their businesses, providing a driving force of innovation in the broader economy (Schaefer, 2009).

References

Aguilera, Ruth and Alvaro Cuervo-Cazurra. 2004. 'Codes of good governance worldwide: What is the trigger?', *Studies in Organizational Management*, 25, 3, 415–43.

2009. 'Codes of good governance', *Corporate Governance: An International Review*, 17, 3, 376–87.

Barondes, Royce, Charles Nyce, and Gary Sanger. 2007. 'Underwriters' counsel as gatekeeper or turnstile: An empirical analysis of law firm prestige and performance in IPOs', *Capital Markets Law Journal*, 2, 2, 164–90.

Bennett, Paul and Li Wei. 2006. 'Market structure, fragmentation, and market quality', *Journal of Financial Markets*, 9, 1, 49–78.

Benston, George. 1973. 'Required disclosure and the stock market: An evaluation of the Securities Exchange Act of 1934', *The American Economic Review*, 63, 1, 132–55.

Black, Lewis. 2007. 'Why corporations choose Delaware', *Delaware Department of State Division of Corporations*. Downloaded from www.corp. delaware.gov/whycorporations_web.pdf, January 14, 2011.

Bradley, Daniel, Bradford Jordan, and Jay Ritter. 2003. 'The quiet period goes out with a bang', *The Journal of Finance*, 58, 1, 1–36.

Charkman, Jonathan and Helene Ploix. 2005. *Keeping Better Company: Corporate Governance Ten Years On*. Oxford University Press.

Daines, Robert. 2001. 'Does Delaware law improve firm value?', *Journal of Financial Economics*, 62, 3, 525–58.

Dalton, Dan, S. Trevis Certo, and Catherine Daily. 2003. 'Initial public offerings as a web of conflicts of interests: An empirical assessment', *Business Ethics Quarterly*, 13, 3, 289–314.

Donaldson, William. 2003. Testimony concerning implementation of the Sarbanes-Oxley Act of 2002 before the Senate Committee on Banking, Housing, and Urban Affairs, September 9, 2003. Downloaded from www.sec.gov/news/testimony/090903tswhd.htm, January 13, 2011.

Ellis, Katrina, Roni Michaely, and Maureen O'Hara. 1999. 'A guide to the initial public offering process', *Corporate Finance Review*, 3, 5, 14–18.

Hamilton, David. 2007. 'TomoTherapy, cancer-treatment system maker, gets enthusiastic IPO reception'. Downloaded from www.venturebeat. com/2007/05/09/tomotherapy-cancer-treatment-system-maker-gets-enthusiastic-ipo-reception/, January 13, 2011.

Hughes, Darrell. 2010. 'TARP repayment surpasses loans', *Wall Street Journal*, June 11, 2010 edition. Downloaded from http://online.wsj. com/article/SB10001424052748703509404575300502253092016.html, January 13, 2011.

Investment Company Institute. 2010. *Factbook*. Downloaded from www. ici.org/pdf/2010_factbook.pdf, January 13, 2011.

Jacobs, Jack. 2009. 'The reach of state corporate law beyond state borders: Reflections upon federalism', Brennan Lecture, *New York University Law Review*, 84, 1149–68.

Jenkinson, Tim, Alan Morrison, and William Wilhelm. 2006. 'Why are European IPOs so rarely priced outside the indicative price range?', *Journal of Financial Economics*, 80, 1, 185–209.

Linck, James, Jeffry Netter, and Tina Yang. 2009. 'The effects and unintended consequences of the Sarbanes-Oxley Act on the supply and demand for directors', *Review of Financial Studies*, 22, 8, 3287–328.

Mackie, Thomas Rockwell. 2006. 'History of tomotherapy', *Physics in Medicine & Biology*, 51, 13, R427–R453.

Moerland, Pieter. 1995. Alternative disciplinary mechanisms in different corporate systems. *Journal of Economic Behavior and Organization*, 26, 1, 17–34.

NASDAQ. 2010a. NASDAQ Listing criteria. Downloaded from https://listingcenter.nasdaqomx.com/assets/nasdaq_listing_req_fees.pdf, December 21, 2010.

2010b. Series 5600 rules. Downloaded from http://nasdaq.cchwallstreet.com/NASDAQTools/PlatformViewer.asp?selectednode=chp_1_1_4_2_8&manual=%2Fnasdaq%2Fmain%2Fnasdaq-equityrules%2F, December 21, 2010.

New York Times. 2010. 'Securities and Exchange Commission', July 16, 2010 edition. Downloaded from http://topics.nytimes.com/top/reference/timestopics/organizations/s/securities_and_exchange_commission/index.html, January 13, 2011.

NYSE. 2010a. Report of the New York Stock Exchange Commission on Corporate Governance. Downloaded from www.ecgi.org/codes/documents/nyse_cgreport_23sep2010_en.pdf, December 21, 2010.

2010b. Listing Criteria. Downloaded from www.nyse.com/regulation/nyse/1147474807344.html, December 21, 2010.

2010c. Corporate Governance Code, section 303A. Downloaded from http://nysemanual.nyse.com/LCMTools/PlatformViewer.asp?searched=1&selectednode=chp_1_4_3_1&CiRestriction=303A&manual=%2Flcm%2Fsections%2Flcm-sections%2F, December 21, 2010.

Rao, Hayagreeva, Gerald Davis, and Andrew Ward. 2000. 'Embeddedness, social identity and mobility: Why firms leave the NASDAQ and join the New York Stock Exchange', *Administrative Science Quarterly*, 45, 2, 268–92.

Reuters. 2007. 'TomoTherapy IPO priced at $19', *Reuters*, May 8, 2007 edition. Downloaded from www.reuters.com/article/idUSN0820288320070508, December 26, 2010.

Schaefer, Steve. 2009. 'IPO class of 2010', *Forbes*, September 1, 2009. Downloaded from www.forbes.com/2009/09/01/ipo-market-rebound-markets-equities-public-offerings.html, December 26, 2010.

Shapiro, Mary. 2010. Speech by SEC Chairman: Remarks at the NACD Annual Corporate Governance Conference, October 19, 2010.

Downloaded from www.sec.gov/news/speech/2010/spch101910mls. htm, January 13, 2011.

Terrell, Ellen. 2010. 'History of the American and NASDAQ stock exchanges', *Library of Congress – Business Reference Services*. Downloaded from www.loc.gov/rr/business/amex/amex.html, January 14, 2011.

Thompson, Robert and Hillary Sale. 2003. 'Securities fraud as corporate governance: Reflections on federalism', *Vanderbilt Law Review*, 56, 859–910.

TomoTherapy. 2007. May 5. SEC 424-B prospectus.

U.S. Census Bureau. 2011. Statistical Abstract of the United States: 2011. Downloaded from www.census.gov/compendia/statab/, January 13, 2011.

U.S. Central Intelligence Agency. 2010. 'United States economy', *The World Factbook*. Downloaded from https://www.cia.gov/library/publications/ the-world-factbook/geos/us.html, January 13, 2011.

U.S. Securities and Exchange Commission. 2010. 'The investor's advocate: How the SEC protects investors, maintains market integrity, and facilitates capital formation', *U.S. Securities and Exchange Commission*. Downloaded from www.sec.gov/about/whatwedo.shtml#create, January 14, 2011.

Waisman, Maya, Haizhi Wang, and Robert Wuebker. 2009. 'Delaware incorporation matters for new ventures: Evidence from venture capital investment and the going public process', *Venture Capital*, 11, 3, 213–27.

Wall Street Journal. 2009. 'Why do investors sit tight in 401(k)s?', *Wall Street Journal*, September 9, 2009 edition. Downloaded from http://online. wsj.com/article/SB125209938267387389.html, January 14, 2011.

Wilmer Cutler Pickering Hale and Dorr. 2008. 'IPO report', *IPO Guidebook*. Downloaded from www.ipoguidebook.com/files/upload/2008_ IPO_Report.pdf, December 23, 2010.

Wisbusiness. 2008. 'Mackie: TomoTherapy CEO offers tips for business success', *Wisbusiness*, November 20, 2008. Downloaded from www. wisbusiness.com/index.iml/?Article=142175, December 26, 2010.

World Federation of Exchanges. 2011. Downloaded from www.world-exchanges.org/statistics, January 13, 2011.

Index

Index of names